FIELDING'S
HAWAII
1991

Current Fielding Titles

FIELDING'S BERMUDA AND THE BAHAMAS 1991
FIELDING'S BUDGET EUROPE 1991
FIELDING'S CARIBBEAN 1991
FIELDING'S EUROPE 1991
FIELDING'S HAWAII 1991
FIELDING'S ITALY 1991
FIELDING'S MEXICO 1991
FIELDING'S PEOPLE'S REPUBLIC OF CHINA 1991
FIELDING'S SELECTIVE SHOPPING GUIDE TO EUROPE 1991

FIELDING'S ALASKA AND THE YUKON
FIELDING'S BUDGET ASIA and Southeast Asia and the Far East
FIELDING'S CALIFORNIA
FIELDING'S FAMILY VACATIONS USA
FIELDING'S FAR EAST 2nd revised edition
FIELDING'S HAVENS AND HIDEAWAYS USA
FIELDING'S LEWIS AND CLARK TRAIL
FIELDING'S LITERARY AFRICA
FIELIDNG'S TRAVELER'S MEDICAL COMPANION
FIELDING'S WORLDWIDE CRUISES 5th revised edition

FIELDING'S
HAWAII
1991

BY

RACHEL JACKSON CHRISTMAS

FIELDING TRAVEL BOOKS
℅ WILLIAM MORROW & COMPANY, INC.
105 Madison Avenue, New York, NY 10016

ISBN: 0-688-07364-6
ISBN: 0-340-53978-X (Hodder & Stoughton)

Printed in the United States of America
First Edition
2 3 4 5 6 7 8 9 10

Text design by Marsha Cohen/Parallelogram

All maps by Mark Stein Studios

ABOUT THE AUTHOR

Rachel Jackson Christmas is a freelance writer whose work has taken her from Hawaii, French Polynesia, and Australia to England, Brazil, and throughout the Caribbean. Her articles have appeared in publications including the *New York Times,* the *Washington Post, Travel & Leisure, Travel-Holiday, Essence, Ms.,* and *Woman's Day.* She has lived in both Mexico and Spain. Her first book, *Fielding's Bermuda and the Bahamas,* which she wrote with her father, is in its eighth edition.

ACKNOWLEDGMENTS

A multitude of thanks goes to my research assistants, especially Mary Anne Howland, whose thorough and enthusiastic work helped me cover a great deal of territory.

Among the scores of other people who made invaluable contributions to this book are Phyllis Kanekuni, Susan Sunderland, Joyce K. Matsumoto, Patti Cook, Donna Jung, Kepa Maly, Connie Wright, Manu Boyd, Lindy Boyes, Noni Landen, Noelani Whittington, Julie L. King, George Applegate, Sheila Donnelly, Diana Reutter, Ruth Limtiaco, Cathy Pescaia, Pamela Gentry, Mary Gresham, and Bryan C. Klum.

Randy Ladenheim-Gil and Curtis March, my editors, deserve awards for their encouragement, patience, and understanding. Finally, I'd like to express my deepest appreciation for my first editor, the late Eunice Riedel, who, in many ways, has remained with me from the start.

WHAT'S INSIDE

There is no doubt that Hawaii is a place of overwhelming beauty, exciting outdoor activities, good restaurants, countless stores and boutiques, and fabulous resorts. However, it is not simply a place to be consumed. Instead, it is appreciated most when it is also examined beneath the surface, with more than a few glimpses of life beyond the tourist industry. In the pages that follow, the emphasis is on the Hawaiiana that remains or has been revived, not on the things travelers could find in other American states. Island chapters contain sections called **Hawaiian Roots** (in the introductory segment), **Hawaiiana** (in *Sights*), and **Hawaiian Style** (in *Night Life*). These entries spotlight cultural and social issues, sights, and activities concerning the islands' original inhabitants (such as traditional games, competitions, and the Hawaiian rights movement). Folklore, legends, and historical anecdotes are sprinkled liberally throughout the book. I steer readers away from the more commercial attractions and toward places where they can uncover aspects of the indigenous culture. For example, as far as luaus are concerned, it's best to check local newspapers for the more authentic, more intimate luaus hosted by civic groups and hula schools to raise money for various causes. I introduce readers to life away from the resorts, including Hawaiian, Japanese, Chinese, and Filipino cultural festivals and practices.

In addition to evaluations of sights, hotels, restaurants, shops, beaches, and sports, you'll find plenty of details about hiking, camping, and other activities and out-of-the-way places that put vacationers in touch with Hawaii at its most unspoiled. This book is not an encyclopedia of everything one could possibly say about Hawaii. Instead, I've chosen the best of the most popular and the least known places and activities. I include unusual tidbits, such as how to mail unboxed coconuts to the mainland, which seats not to take during a helicopter ride, how to arrange to go on a Maui Art Tour, where to find redwood forests and volcanic swimming holes, when to pick various wild fruits, where to spot whales from shore. Readers are told which sightseeing tours to avoid, and which roads and routes to steer clear of at certain hours or times of year.

Nowadays, most vacationers who visit Hawaii are going to one or two islands instead of taking the if-it's-Tuesday-this-must-be-Kauai tours of the past. The **Island Snapshots** section in **Why Hawaii?** will allow you to quickly compare the islands without having to read through each island chapter first. I've designed **The Best Places for . . .** so that you can zero in on exactly which island or islands will suit your desire for atmosphere, action, or relaxation. Entries include Adventure, Escape, Art, Budget Conscious Travel, Luxury, Families with Children, Getting Married, Hawaiian Culture and History, Murderous Fun (murder mystery weekends), Singles, Unusual Sports, and Whale Watching.

In **Nuts and Bolts,** I give information on handling jet lag, festivals and special events, safety when swimming and in the sun, travel for the disabled, and decoding the Hawaiian versions of East, West, North, and South. **The People of Hawaii** focuses on the backgrounds of the various ethnic groups that make up the state's population. **The Hawaiian Tongue** chapter, with its extensive list of Hawaiian words, will help you pronounce the language—essential since it is found in so many place names throughout the state. The order of island chapters is from the busiest and most developed (Oahu) to the quietest and most natural (Lanai). Each of these chapters begins with a general, lay-of-the-land section that will give you an idea of where sights and attractions are in relation to each other. Further details about the most intriguing sights are found in **What to See and Do.** Attractions that are **off the beaten path** are highlighted by asterisks (*). **Personal Favorites** will help you sort through and narrow down the many choices.

Night Life includes places frequented by residents, such as local theater and outdoor concerts. From plain to fancy, all levels of **restaurants** are covered, not just those in hotels. I concentrate on eateries patronized by residents—including fruit stands, mom-and-pop bakeries, even greasy spoons. In **Where to Sleep,** I warn vacationers about less than desirable hotels and condominiums that travel agents might try to book them in, such as those with brochures that make them appear to be on the beach when they are actually across the street. I also make it clear when the location of an accommodation is far more appealing than its rooms and facilities. Information about bed & breakfasts, private cottages, and housekeeping cabins is found in this section as well. **Details,** at the end of each island chapter, covers such subjects as transportation between airports and accommodations, getting around, how to have emergency cash wired to Hawaii, where to go for medical attention, where to rent video cameras, how to participate in local Alcoholics Anonymous or Weight Watchers meetings, and numbers to call about volcano action, surfing conditions, weather, and the local time. In the **Accommodations Charts,** you'll find addresses, phone numbers, and approximate prices of rooms.

Accommodation Ratings

I have used a star rating system to give you more information about hotels, condominiums, bed & breakfasts, and cottages. These ratings are based on my own opinion as well as the views of my researchers, island guests, and residents of Hawaii. Note that some condominiums and smaller accommodations may not have air conditioning, but ceiling fans and tradewinds usually do the trick. Not all places to stay have telephones or televisions in rooms.

☆ Hollow stars indicate the number of quality of facilities, along with the location and overall comfort of the accommodation.

★ In addition to all of the above, filled stars denote charm, atmosphere, impressive or unusual decor, and/or exceptional service.

★★★★★ Top of the line
★★★★ Excellent
★★★ Very good
★★ Good
★ Plain or modest

No Stars

Accommodations undergoing major renovations or other changes, or those not yet open at press time; low-budget hotels with very limited facilities and/or services; camping shelters.

Accommodation Prices

On islands other than Maui, the daily prices of standard double rooms (not including tax or service charge) are categorized as follows:

Very Expensive: more than $140
Expensive: $110 to $140
Moderate: $80 to $110
Inexpensive: less than $80

On Maui, prices are

Expensive to Very Expensive: more than $140
Moderate: $80 to $140
Inexpensive: less than $80

Note that I've quoted these rates only to give you an idea of comparative costs. Most people pay less by booking package deals (including flights, accommodation, and rental car) through airlines, travel agents, and tour companies (see Costs in **Nuts and Bolts,** and the **Details** sections at the end of island chapters). Another good way to cut down on expenses is to share a room or condo with more than one person.

Restaurant Prices

The prices below are based on the approximate cost, per person, of a full dinner, not including drinks, tax, or tip.

Very Expensive: more than $65
Expensive: $40 to $65
Moderate: $20 to $40
Inexpensive: less than $20

Symbols, Abbreviations, and Telephone Numbers

In the What to See and Do sections, asterisks (*) point out attractions, places, and activities that are **off the beaten path.** No asterisks are given for Molokai or Lanai, since all of each island is away from the masses.

In the restaurant sections, credit card acceptance is indicated as follows: American Express—A, MasterCard—M, Vis—V, Carte Blanche—C, and Diners Club—D.

When no area code is given, this indicates that a phone number is local and uses the state-wide 808 area code.

Updates

During our frequent wanderings around the Hawaiian islands, my researchers and I gather the most accurate and up-to-date information possible. However, hotels, restaurant decor and menus, sights, and airlines do not remain static during the course of the year. I welcome any comments or suggestions about things that may have changed since the book went to press or about the guide in general. (Note that all prices quoted should be considered approximate.) Write to me % Fielding Travel Books, William Morrow & Co., Inc. 105 Madison Avenue, New York, NY 10016.

—Rachel Jackson Christmas

CONTENTS

Maps

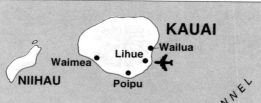

KAUAI

Wailua

Lihue

Waimea

NIIHAU

Poipu

KAUAI CHANNEL

OAHU

Kahuk

Makaha

Kaneohe

Honolulu

Waiki

KAIW

THE HAWAIIAN ISLANDS

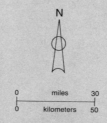

N

| 0 | miles | 30 |
| 0 | kilometers | 50 |

PACIFIC OCEAN

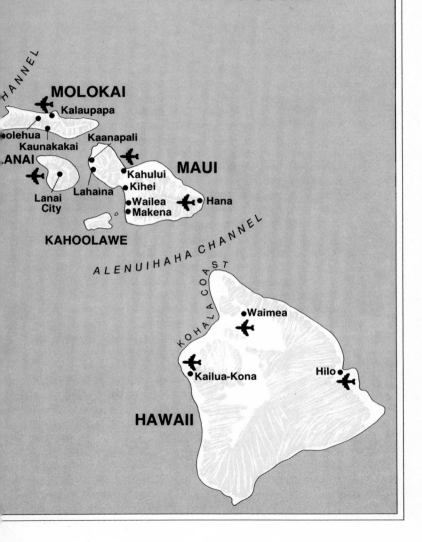

PACIFIC OCEAN

MOLOKAI

Kalaupapa

olehua
Kaunakakai

ANAI

Kaanapali

Kahului
Kihei
MAUI

Lanai
City
Lahaina

Wailea
Makena
Hana

KAHOOLAWE

ALENUIHAHA CHANNEL

KOHALA COAST

Waimea

Kailua-Kona
Hilo

HAWAII

WHY HAWAII?

The umbrellalike monkeypod trees, tubular African tulips, and splashes of magenta bougainvillea enchanted my friend and me as we drove along one of Hawaii's winding roads. Just as our stomachs began to grumble, we came to a fruit stand piled high with papayas and bananas. But no vendor was in sight. Then, to our surprise, we noticed the sign that invited us simply to take some fruit and leave our money in a box.

This honor system was one of my earliest encounters with the trusting *aloha* spirit that the ancient Polynesians brought to this Pacific archipelago more than a millenium ago. Often replacing the words "hello" and "good-bye," *aloha* has come to mean many different things—from tolerance, graciousness, and understanding to friendliness, caring, and love. Above all, it encompasses the ideal of healthy interaction among human beings and between people and their environment. Now existing in varying degrees, aloha has certainly faded in and out over the centuries. The selling of artificial leis and "handmade" plastic "wood carvings" speaks to the unfortunate commercialization of aloha here and there. But it has never disappeared completely, nor has it ever been distorted beyond recognition.

Having survived encounters with exploitative European explorers, self-righteous, disapproving American missionaries, and, in some areas, overzealous real estate developers, this spirit is clearly apparent in the welcoming faces of Hawaii's residents today. The cushiony aroma of fresh flowers hugs visitors the moment they step off the plane. Laden with fragrant leis, locals wait at airports to greet arriving travelers the traditional way: They brush visitors' cheeks with kisses and place the thick floral garlands around their necks. Few other places rival the mostly harmonious racial and cultural blending that characterizes the diverse population of this fiftieth American state. This is one of the reasons that, in a world with countless other gorgeous, beach-fringed islands to choose from, more than 6 million vacationers find their way to Hawaii each year.

Some 130 islands, sandbars, and exposed reefs make up this Pacific state. The seven inhabited islands are certainly not devoid of problems—racial, economic, or otherwise. Yet somehow, the awe inspired

1

by the drama of their stunning landscapes seems to spill over into a deep respect and appreciation for people's differences—and commonalities. Negative thoughts about anything seem ridiculous once you've viewed the massive cliffs of Kauai's Na Pali Coast from a dwarfed rubber raft, watched the sun rise over the crater of Maui's Haleakala volcano, or stretched out under a palm tree on the coal-black sand of a beach on the Big Island of Hawaii. Throughout the islands, rich pumpkin-colored earth peeks through the flourishing greenery while waterfalls carve ridges into mountainsides.

With its closest neighbor the diminutive Christmas Island chain, about 2000 miles to the south, Hawaii is the most isolated group of islands on earth. Some 2400 miles of ocean lie between this U.S. state and North America, the nearest continent. The islands of Hawaii began forming 25 to 40 million years ago when volcanoes gurgled, spouted, and belched their way up through cracks in the ocean floor. In a few short centuries, the spirit of aloha may spread to a new member of the archipelago, about 30 miles off the coast of the Big Island, another island, Loihi, is in gestation. Erupting as recently as 1980, this underwater volcanic cone is already nearly 16,000 feet tall, with only about 3000 feet to go before it breaks the ocean's surface.

A vacation in Hawaii can mean very different things to very different people. Travelers with opposing tastes can easily find what they want here, often even within a single island. From quiet Molokai, which some claim is the most Hawaiian of the main islands, to action-oriented Oahu with its many T-shirt shops and fast-food restaurants, each island has an atmosphere all its own. If mobs of camera-toting visitors happily herded onto tour buses isn't the kind of scenery you have in mind, head for one of the quieter areas or one of the more tranquil islands. Those who turn up their noses at commercial luaus, crowded shopping malls, and high-rise resorts can camp out in a beachfront park or book a room in a bed-and-breakfast or a former plantation cottage. Independent travelers can check into a condominum. For a break from the tropical heat, rustic wooded cabins complete with well-used fireplaces are nestled high in the cool mountains. Serving a variety of cuisines (including continental, regional American, Japanese, Italian, Chinese, Thai, Mexican, and Korean), restaurants range from candlelit to homestyle.

There are so many choices of settings in Hawaii that it doesn't matter that, for instance, what is elegant to one person may be overkill to another. I heard a couple talking at one of several megaresorts that began cropping up in the late 1980s. The pair had just finished wandering around the grounds, past horse-drawn carriages, life-size Far Eastern statues, marble columns almost as wide as Redwood trees, canals with Venetian gondolas, and waterfall-fed swimming pools. Shaking his head, the man said to his companion, "After all this, the ocean seems superfluous, huh?" She replied with a frown, "After all this, *Hawaii* seems superfluous!'' Mind you, this couple was surrounded by scores of other open-mouthed guests who were totally thrilled with the hotel.

While the mere mention of Hawaii conjures up visions of a tropical paradise in many people's heads, the state is also full of surprises. As you might expect, Hawaii is just the place for surfing, snorkeling, scuba diving, deep-sea fishing, hiking, riding outrigger canoes or catamarans, watching volcanoes erupt or whales bound through the waves. It's the place for sightseeing from helicopters, sipping mai tais or Kona coffee, and munching macadamia nuts or fresh, juicy pineapple. But you may not be aware that it's also a place where cowboys show their stuff in rodeos. On the Big Island, it's not unheard of to go water skiing one day and snow skiing the next. And beaches come with white, black, and even green sand. If you know which nooks and crannies deserve a peek, you can uncover hidden volcanic swimming pools or ancient *heiau* (stone temples) and rock carvings. You can explore deep, jungled valleys on horseback or on foot. On some islands, you can arrange to be picked up from the airport in a limousine complete with champagne or let a helicopter whisk you off to a secluded spot for an intimate picnic lunch.

Several of the things that have come to be associated with life in Hawaii actually originated elsewhere. For instance, the ukulele, which no luau worth its kalua pig is without, was first brought from Portugal. The requisite mound of rice in fast-food ''plate lunches'' might not have become ever-present if the Chinese and Japanese had never arrived. And cockfighting, which goes on behind many a bush in residential areas, came from the Philippines.

Some people proudly announce their multi-cultural heritage. Your chatty tour bus driver might mention that he's Hawaiian-Chinese-Portuguese or if you get into a conversation with your waitress, she might talk about her Filipino-Puerto Rican-Korean ancestry. There is a greater concentration of Asians in Hawaii than anywhere else in the country. This is the only U.S. state where Caucasians are not the majority.

Many residents are quick to make the distinction between being Hawaiian (a descendant of the original brown-skinned inhabitants of the islands) and being *from* Hawaii (anyone who was born here or has lived here a long time). Since 1778, when the first known Europeans set foot on these shores, the Hawaiian race has shrunk dramatically in number and much of its culture has disappeared or been diluted. According to recent estimates, Hawaiians now comprise only between 10 and 20% of the state's one million residents. Particularly since the early 1970s, Hawaiians have been pushing for reform of the social and economic system that has left them a disadvantaged minority in their own islands. They have also been attempting to revive pride in and respect for Hawaiian culture. Indeed, visitors will certainly find plenty of elaborate luaus and sensuous hula performances. Some people still leave offerings of shells, rocks, and leaves at *heiau*. Celebrating "Aloha Friday" is a popular custom among locals. On the last day of the work week, many residents deck themselves out in colorful, floral prints. People are simply saying "TGIF" by wearing sweet-smelling leis, muumuus, and aloha shirts to work that day, even to offices where the dress code generally dictates stockings and heels or business suits. For the most part, however, Western and Asian influences have replaced the Hawaiian way of life.

With few exceptions, the Hawaiian language is alive only on street signs, in place and hotel names, and in a sprinkling of words that pepper English and "pidgin," the local dialect. You'll hear common terms such as *kamaaina* (longtime island resident), *malihini* (visitor, newcomer, stranger), and *haole* (Caucasian and/or mainlander). As exotic as these islands may seem, resist the urge to refer to the rest of the country as "the United States" or "America." If you say "the mainland" or "the continental U.S.," you'll avoid annoyed corrections.

Generally speaking, weather in Hawaii can be divided into two seasons: summer and winter. Summer, which lasts from about May through mid-October, brings daytime temperatures in the 80s. This is the drier time of year; when it does rain, showers are usually brief. In the winter season, lasting from about mid-October through April, daytime temperatures hover in the mid-70s to low 80s. High season, when some hotel prices are steeper and reservations are more difficult to come by, runs from about late December to mid-April.

As you flip through the pages of this book, you'll find practical information about the most popular places, times, and ways to play, relax, and absorb nature's handiwork in Hawaii. You'll also learn about the islands' little-known treasures, the pulse of the people, and life beyond the resorts. Both despite and because of its geographic isolation, Hawaii has long been a powerful magnet for peoples from across the globe. Once you get a firsthand taste of the Islands' physical beauty and the pervasive aloha spirit, you'll understand why.

ISLAND SNAPSHOTS

Hawaii's seven inhabited islands are at the southeastern end of the Hawaiian chain, along with Kahoolawe, which is unpopulated (unless you count the wild goats that roam its semiarid landscape). Oahu, Maui, Kauai, and Hawaii draw many more visitors and are much more developed than Molokai, Lanai, and Niihau. Islands other than Oahu are jointly referred to as the "Neighbor Islands."

Many first-time visitors choose to sample two or three islands during their stay. Two are usually enough for people who truly want to get a feel for each place they visit. You may want to arrange your island hopping before you embark, but it's also possible to take advantage of package deals to other islands after you arrive in Hawaii. While there are flight-seeing tours that will take you to all the major islands in a single day, I don't recommend them since you get only a brief, superficial look at each destination. For aerial views, a helicopter tour of a single island is more rewarding.

To give you a glimpse of the distinct personalities of the main Islands, some highlights follow. As with the chapters later in the book, the order of the islands is from the most developed to the least developed. Where more than one pronunciation of a name is given, the first is the most common and the last, with an abrupt pause before the final syllable, is the more correct.

Oahu (oh-*wah*-hoo):   The home of Honolulu, the capital of the state, Oahu is Hawaii's best-known island. It is only the third largest, after Hawaii and Maui, yet almost four-fifths of the state's total population resides here. Along with Waikiki Beach, Pearl Harbor and the U.S.S. *Arizona* Memorial are the most popular tourist attractions in the state. Two other stops that are high on most lists are the Polynesian Cultural Center (where you'll learn about ancient Hawaiians and others in the Pacific region) and Sea Life Park (where whales, dolphins, and other aquatic entertainers put on great shows). The North Shore, across the island from Honolulu, is a world away from the high-rises, shopping malls, and crowds of Waikiki. On this pastoral northern coast, waves curl at 30 feet during winter months. To the surprise of many who picture only Honolulu and Waikiki when they think of this island, most of mountainous Oahu is carpeted with countryside.

Maui (*mow*-ee):   The second most popular island among visitors, Maui is sometimes referred to as "Southern California" because of all of the Golden State residents transplanted from the mainland. Looking down on it from the air, you'll see what appears to be two islands joined by a valley. The West Maui Mountains dominate the smaller northern segment, while towering Haleakala volcano rises in the southeastern region. Quiet towns, eucalyptus forests, and wild rodeos are found along the cool "upcountry" slopes of Haleakala. Watching the sun rise over its crater, then horseback riding or hiking into it, or riding a mountain bike down the volcano are favorite activities among visitors. Some see Kaanapali Beach, a long, gentle crescent backed by high-rise hotels and condominiums, as a younger, more low-key version of Waikiki. Other smaller resort areas offer less congested choices. Historic Lahaina, the old whaling port, was once the capital of the whole Hawaiian kingdom. During the winter, Maui is Hawaii's whale-watching mecca. One of Maui's most spectacular drives is along the winding coastal "highway" that leads to isolated Hana, a lush, drowsy town tucked away in the southeast.

Kauai (cow-*why*, *cow*-why, or cow-*wah*^ᶜ ee): By many accounts the most beautiful Hawaiian island, Kauai is a relative newcomer to tourism. Tiny rural towns are flanked by miles of sugarcane fields and flourishing foliage. The island's jagged mountains, plunging waterfalls, and isolated beaches have played supporting roles in films such as *Raiders of the Lost Ark, Body Heat,* and *The Thorn Birds* television mini-series. Although Kauai receives more rain than other Hawaiian islands, a visit here is well worth risking a few soggy days. Besides, the lush landscape is almost as stunning when wet. The driest part of the island is around Poipu in the south, where sandy crescents scallop the shore. Probably Kauai's most impressive natural attractions are massive, dry Waimea Canyon and the awesome cliffs of Na Pali coast.

Hawaii (hah-*why*-ee, hah-*why*^ᶜ ee, or hah-*vye*^ᶜ ee): Commonly referred to as the Big Island, Hawaii is so much larger than its siblings that the rest of the chain could fit inside it—with room to spare. Hawaii is the only island where you can see active volcanoes, which spout fireworks from time to time. With stark, ebony lava flows stretching for miles, it is also the most unusual-looking member of the family. The sand of beaches comes in white, black, salt and pepper, and even green! In sharp contrast to its volcanic moonscape, the island boasts rain forests, flower nurseries, and lush valleys. Rodeos are held on one of the largest privately owned cattle ranches in the U.S. The beach-rimmed Kohala Coast, in the west, is treated to the least amount of rainfall in all of inhabited Hawaii. When conditions are right, you can actually ski down the slopes of snowcapped Mauna Kea.

Molokai (*mole*-oh-kye or mole-oh-*kah*^ᶜ ee): Mention Molokai to mainlanders, and the first thing many say is, "Oh, you mean where the leper colony is?" Molokai is certainly famous for the victims of Hansen's Disease whose tragic story you can learn all about. But it is also known for its unspoiled landscape, slow pace, and delightfully small number of tourists. One of Molokai's most exciting activities is a ride down a 2000-foot cliff on the back of a mule. In the verdant eastern region, the road winds heavenward to striking cliff-edge views. In the parched west, photo safaris are conducted through a sprawling wildlife preserve inhabited by all kinds of animals from East Africa and Asia. In January, hundreds of locals pack Kaunakakai Park for the annual

Makahiki Festival, a revival of an old Hawaiian peacetime celebration marked with food, music, and competitions in Hawaiian games.

Lanai (lahn-*eye* or lah-*nah*ᶜ ee):   In 1922, Jim Dole bought most of Lanai to start the pineapple fields that still stretch across so much of the island. After slumbering happily with a single 10-room hotel since the 1940s, Lanai has just been transformed in a major way by the birth of two Rockresorts. Before now, most visitors were friends of residents, hunters, or hardy travelers looking for unadulterated peace and quiet *way* off the beaten path. True, the number of hotels has tripled. But since the grand total is only three, the island remains almost as undeveloped as before. Searching for ancient petroglyphs (rock carvings) and eerie rock formations continues to be a favorite pastime. Locals are still quick to strike up conversations with visitors over drinks on the creaky wooden porch of the island's original accommodation, Hotel Lanai. Many residents of Lanai "City," the quiet inland plantation town nestled amid spikey Norfolk pines, welcome the advent of all the non-plantation jobs that larger-scale tourism has brought.

Niihau (*nee*-ee-how):   Known as "The Forbidden Island," Niihau has no tourist accommodations—or plumbing, electricity, telephones, cigarettes, alcohol, or guns, for that matter. Only about 250 people live here, virtually all of them pure Hawaiians. While the rest of Hawaii has galloped into the 20th century, the daily lives of residents of Niihau differ little from those of their ancestors. This is the only island in the state where Hawaiian remains the dominant language. Most residents work on the cattle and sheep ranch run by the Robinsons, the haole family that has owned the island since 1864. Some outsiders applaud the Robinsons' success in preserving a culture that has nearly disappeared elsewhere in the state. Others call this family paternalistic and complain that they are simply maintaining indentured servitude.

With rare exceptions, until 1988, the island owners allowed only native Hawaiians to set foot on Niihau soil. Now helicopter flights from neighboring Kauai introduce outsiders to this mystery island. However, some people who have taken the flights characterize the trips as "too much money to see too little." The whirlybirds land in dry, barren areas far from where people live. If you've got (very) deep pockets, shop on other islands for the delicate necklaces made of minuscule Niihau shells. (See "Kauai" for more information about this island.)

Kahoolawe (kah-ho-oh-*lah*-vay):   The smallest of the main islands, semiarid Kahoolawe is controlled by the U.S. Navy, which has used it for target practice since 1941. The idea of bombs missing their mark has never set well with residents of Maui, only six miles away. Peppered with sites of ancient Hawaiian settlements and *heiau* (temples),

Kahoolawe became a focal point for Hawaiian activists during the 1970s. In a series of demonstrations against the status quo, whereby most Hawaiians are at the bottom of the social and economic totem pole, they protested the island's military use. They felt that the return of Kahoolawe to state government jurisdiction and allowing the public to have access to it could help spark a newfound respect for and pride in Hawaiian culture and land.

DAYS GONE BY

In the Beginning

According to ancient legend, Hawaii might never have existed had it not been for the chemistry between Papa, the earth mother, and Wakea, the father of the sky and the heavens. Their first offspring was the Big Island of Hawaii and their second, Maui. Worn out by the vigors of childbearing, Papa went to Tahiti to recuperate. While she was away, Wakea began an incestuous relationship with one of their daughters, producing Molokai and Lanai. Papa got wind of this affair and returned to Hawaii in a jealous rage. Wakea soon soothed away her fury, and they went on to produce Oahu, Kauai, and Niihau. With their energy nearly spent, Kahoolawe was the last island they could manage.

Geologists, who beg to differ, say that Hawaii's true genesis lies in a hot spot deep inside the earth. Somewhere between 25 and 40 million years ago, a long cleft opened up in the ocean floor. Molten lava pulsed through, forming water-covered craters. Inch by inch and over millions of years, the part of the earth's crust called the Pacific Plate slowly shifted above the hot spot, resulting in a chain of undersea mountains. They grew taller with each eruption, but it wasn't until a few million years ago that, one by one, they finally broke the ocean's surface in their trek toward the sky.

The first of these mountain peaks to hit the air were the smallest islands, those at the northwestern end of the Hawaiian chain. Of these, the ones that survived the severe battering by natural elements remain deserted and mostly barren. Far to the southeast, the volcanic peaks that last appeared above the Pacific's surface became the inhabited group best known today. Wind, rain, and pounding waves carved jagged cliffs and scooped out wide valleys in the young islands. Plants began to sprout from spores that had traveled on the ocean breezes, and later from seeds brought by the tides and migrating birds.

Compared to most of the world's land masses, which came into their own about 300 million years ago, the Hawaiian Islands are geologic infants. Kauai is the oldest inhabited island in the chain, and the Big Island of Hawaii is the youngest. As you read these words, not only is a new island forming (the submerged Loihi, near the Big Island), but the Big Island itself is still growing. Here, the Kilauea and Mauna Loa volcanoes continue to put on periodic fiery displays that add land mass to the island. Although these are the state's only two active volcanoes, Hawaii also has a trio of dormant volcanoes: the Big Island's Mauna Kea and Hualalai, and Maui's Haleakala. Mauna Kea is now Hawaii's giant at nearly 14,000 feet above sea level. If measured from the ocean floor to their summits, Mauna Kea and Mauna Loa are the world's two highest mountains. Rising 30,000 feet from their aquatic bases, they beat Mt. Everest by a few hundred feet.

Strangers in a Strange Land (300 A.D.–1778)

Hawaii-loa, the Polynesian sailor who legend says discovered these Pacific islands, gave them his name. The most recent archaeological research indicates that Hawaii's first inhabitants, thought to be from the Marquesas Islands (now part of French Polynesia), probably arrived around 750 A.D. (or as early as 300 A.D., according to some historians). About 3000 years earlier, their ancestors had begun making their way west from Asia, traveling through Indonesia and other groups of islands. Following the stars, watching the paths of migrating birds, and interpreting the wind and the ocean currents, these early Polynesians were master navigators.

Landing first at Ka Lae on the Big Island (now the southernmost tip of the U.S.), they traveled the 2500 miles in double-hulled canoes connected by wide platforms on which they built shelters. Carrying whole families along with dogs, pigs, and fowl, some of these masted vessels were nearly 100 feet long. They also brought plants that would become staples in Hawaii, among them taro, breadfruit, yams, sugar cane, coconuts, and bananas. Around the year 1300, the first settlers were joined by Tahitians, most likely from the island of Raiatea (whose ancient name was Haiviki). Historians still puzzle over why, after sailing back and forth between Tahiti and its neighbor Raiatea for more than a century, these early settlers abruptly stopped leaving Hawaii somewhere in the 1500s.

In addition to plants and animals, the cargo transported by these hardy travelers included the intangible forces that were the glue of their lives. They not only brought *aloha,* but they also imported *mana,* the spiritual power that could give people unparalleled strength, skill, or courage. Mana, said to be found in varying degrees in human beings as well as in objects and in the land, was passed down from the gods. Contact between two people who had different amounts of this force could be gravely dangerous for the less powerful person.

To guard against such a situation and, above all, to follow the will of the gods, a system of strict *kapus* (taboos) evolved. Adhering to kapus was considered crucial to the well-being of individuals and of the group. Some of these restrictions were dietary. For instance, women were not allowed to prepare or cook food, nor were they permitted to eat bananas, coconuts, or pork. Men were prohibited from eating dog-meat. Violating these or any other kapus, even unknowingly, would result in severe punishment, often swift death. The gods were also appeased with human sacrifices. When a *heiau* (temple) was being built, for instance, members of the enslaved class would be buried at each of the foundation's corners.

The caste system that controlled ancient Hawaiian society was extremely rigid. Each island had its own king. The *alii* (ah-*lee*-ee)—aristocracy or chiefs—were next in line, followed by the *kahuna* (high priests) and the *makaainana* (mah-kah-eye-*nah*-nah) or commoners. The *kauwa* (*cow*-wah) were the enslaved people in the lowest class. The more directly a person was believed to be descended from the gods, the higher his or her rank. Marriages between brothers and sisters were celebrated, especially if the amorous siblings were of high-born bloodlines. On the other hand, if a kauwa and a member of the alii had the misfortune of producing a child, that infant was immediately killed. Polygamy, for both men and women, was also an accepted way of life. It was not uncommon for a couple with several children to give one to a childless couple to care for as their own. After all, since raising children was a group effort in many ways, the biological parents could still be involved in their children's lives.

Each island was divided into pie-slice sections; thus each wedge included inland and waterfront regions. The alii owned and governed these segments. For the privilege of farming the land, the makaainana paid them taxes, in a semi-feudal setup. Despite the spirit of aloha, ancient Hawaiians seemed to thrive on warfare. Chiefs continually battled each other for land and power.

However, while they may have shed a lot of blood, one thing Hawaiians painstakingly preserved was their environment. Conserving their natural resources, these early ecologists were careful not to exploit their plants or animals. They faithfully followed rules restricting the catching of certain kinds of fish during particular seasons. Not only was this balance with nature essential to their physical health, but they believed that it also maintained an important spiritual connection with their ancestors.

Hawaiians approached daily life with an artistic flourish. Their basketry and woven sleeping mats were intricately patterned. Kapa cloth (made from pounded bark) was not only decorated, but the dye used for the designs was often scented with flowers. Hangers for water containers looked as if they had been crocheted. Capes and helmets worn by chiefs were covered with a velvety layer of closely sewn feathers. When it was time to party, food and music were accompanied by foot races, wrestling matches, spear-hurling contests, surfing and diving competitions, and other games. Children flew kites, threw square balls, swung from vines, and slid down hillsides on a cushion of leaves.

Without a written language, Hawaiians preserved much of their history as we know it today in their lyrical legends, soothing songs, expressive hula dances, and detailed oral genealogies.

Captain Cook and his Floating Islands (1778–1779)

Since warfare was so common, every year during the winter months, a "cease fire" festival called *makahiki* was held. Honoring the god Lono, this peaceful and sacred season was celebrated with unbridled feasting and dancing, wrestling and boxing matches, and other frivolity. It was at this time of year, in 1778, when British captain James Cook and his men landed in Hawaii. Over the decades, occasional white foreigners had accidentally found their way to these shores, probably including the Spanish explorer Juan Gaetano in the mid-16th century. Thus the term *haole* was already part of the vocabulary.

On the night when Cook's two ships, the *Resolution* and the *Discovery*, reached the coast of Kauai, several Hawaiian men were fishing from their canoes in Waimea Bay. Suddenly, to their amazement, two hulking masses eased out of the darkness. Seeing the flickering lights on board, they decided that these must be floating islands, and they knew just who must be on one of them. The god Lono, whose festival was in full swing, had promised to arrive someday on moving islands. The tall masts must be the islands' bare trees. After all, weren't the sails just like the white kapa cloth banners that fluttered from the canoes of the chiefs who honored Lono at this time of year?

The awestruck fishermen rushed ashore to report the news, which washed over the island like a tidal wave. By the time the sun's first rays lightened the sky, the shore was jammed with people eager for a glimpse of Lono and his attendants. Torn between fear and wonder, some went out in their canoes to get a closer look. A priest and a chief even paddled out to the ships to present Lono with a red kapa cloth and to perform the sacred welcoming ceremony. Few paid any attention to the skeptics who, having heard stories of white-skinned strangers arriving in the past, said that these were nothing more than haoles.

Only one violent incident marred Cook's otherwise harmonious reception. Metal was extremely rare in the islands, found every once in a while in driftwood. A man who tried to take a piece of iron from one of the ships was fatally shot. Hawaiians were used to severe punishment for offending the gods and they had never seen a stick spout fire before. So they were more convinced than ever that this must be Lono himself.

Throngs of women swam out to the ships, scrambling onto the decks to offer their bodies to please Lono and his sacred attendants. In an attempt to prevent the spread of venereal disease from his men to Hawaiians, Cook had given strict orders against sexual relations. But after such a long time at sea, his crew members did not even attempt to resist the eager women. Thus began the decimation of the Hawaiian population.

Until the arrival of Captain Cook, Hawaii had been free from communicable diseases. Hawaiians' immune systems were therefore not equipped to combat them. The spread of gonorrhea and syphilis from Cook's crew to Hawaiian women, and from the women to Hawaiian men, had far-reaching effects. Not only did large segments of the population die from venereal disease, but sterility became a widespread problem, even for future generations. Measles and other Western ailments also began wiping out chunks of the population.

During the few days that Cook and his men spent anchored off Kauai, they traded iron and other popular items for fresh water and food. After leaving gifts of pigs, goats, and seeds for onions, melons, and pumpkins, they sailed away from Hawaii, journeying north, only to return during the following makahiki season. This time, when Cook and his crew reached Kealakekua Bay on the Big Island, they were welcomed in even greater numbers. The water around the boats churned with hundreds of people swimming or bobbing in canoes. When Cook came ashore, people gave him the highest respect by falling to the ground and covering their faces until he had passed.

A good-natured cultural exchange took place. Cook and his men were escorted into the mountains and thick forests, where they watched craftsmen making canoes and artisans collecting brightly colored feathers to be fashioned into elaborate cloaks and helmets for chiefs. In turn, the British entertained with a flute and violin concert and invited Hawaiians to tour the ships and see blacksmiths at work.

During the weeks that followed, Cook and his men began to strain the hospitality of the islanders by demanding large numbers of provisions, including the fence of a *heiau* (a temple)—to be used for less-than-sacred purposes—as firewood. Cook's men seemed to have an insatiable (and ungodlike) appetite for sex. When Hawaiian chief Kalaniopuu put a kapu on women visiting the ships, Cook's men simply mobbed the villages.

After virtually exhausting the resources of the Kona district, Cook and his crew finally left the Big Island. Then, to the distress of the residents, they returned a week later. A storm had damaged the ships and they had decided to come back to make repairs. Particularly since they had reappeared once the makahiki festival had ended, people began to share their doubts as to whether Cook and his crew were truly divine beings. Thefts of the ships' metal began to occur. Finally, after a long-boat was stolen, a livid Cook went ashore with some of his men, determined to take Chief Kalaniopuu hostage until the boat was returned.

A scuffle broke out and one of the chief's protectors struck Cook. As the British captain screamed in pain, the Hawaiians realized that if he could be hurt, surely he must not be a god. Showered with more blows, he fell dead in the water at the rocky shore. Despite Cook's unmasking as the mortal he was, his body was given the sacred honors of an alii (a chief closely related to the gods), in a ceremony in which his bones were removed. His dismembered remains were turned over to his horrified and uncomprehending crew. They responded by burning a village, decapitating two Hawaiians, and, with the heads displayed on poles at the prows of their longboats, they returned to their ships. Surprisingly enough, by the time the British sailed away from Hawaii several weeks later, tensions had eased.

Kamehameha the Great (1779–1819)

Kamehameha, the nephew of Chief Kalaniopuu, whom Captain Cook met his end trying to capture, was said to have been a towering six foot, six inches tall. Halley's Comet had marked the year of his birth, 1758, perhaps foreshadowing the unusual man he would become. According to some stories, as a teenager he moved the mammoth Naha Stone in Hilo, on the island of Hawaii. This awesome act not only exhibited superhuman strength but also heralded the fulfillment of the prophecy that the man who could do so would someday unify the Hawaiian Islands.

Cook's "discovery" of the Sandwich Islands, which he christened after his sponsor the fourth Earl of Sandwich, sparked a great deal of interaction with foreign seamen. Hawaii became a regular port of call for reprovisioning of trade ships. The late 18th century brought more British sailors, as well as French and American ships. Others came from China and Spain. Some sailors jumped ship and made new lives for themselves in Hawaii. Wanting to explore the world beyond their islands, some Hawaiians joined the crews of foreign vessels. Rapidly multiplying sheep, goats, cattle, and horses had been introduced. Hawaiians discovered that hooves could get them around faster than feet.

When Cook arrived, Kamehameha was an extremely curious young man in his early 20s. After meeting the British captain, he was invited to spend the night on the *Resolution,* where he became fascinated by the Western weaponry that in later years would play a major role in his consolidation of power. Making sure that foreigners dealt with him as an equal, Kamehameha learned as much as he could about Western technology. Once he became a chief, he began a large collection of muskets, cannons, and swords acquired from traders. To teach him how to use these weapons, he enlisted John Young, an Englishman who arrived on an American ship, and Isaac Davis, a Welsh seaman. In exchange, he gave these two haole men the status of chiefs. Settling in

Hawaii, they acquired lands and married Hawaiian women. John Young's granddaughter, Emma Rooke, would wed Kamehameha IV in 1856.

Trade flourished as Chief Kamehameha exchanged land and export rights to natural resources for foreignmade goods. Unable to resist such a lucrative market, he began the sandalwood trade that would eventually nearly deplete Hawaii's forests of the trees. To satisfy the voracious appetite for the beautiful wood in China, the strict adherence to conservation that had sustained Hawaiians for centuries was forgotten. More and more of Kamehameha's subjects were forced into this arduous work, which required their going increasingly deeper into the forests and higher into the mountains.

Legend has it that the demigod Maui tried to pull all the Hawaiian islands together by snaring them with a huge fishhook broken from a tremendous coral reef. When he failed, he decided that it simply couldn't be done. Nevertheless, Kamehameha decided to give it a shot. Using many of the weapons that had so intrigued him on Cook's ship, the ruthless chief had won the rule of Oahu, Maui, Lanai, Molokai, and Hawaii, his island of birth, by 1796. Kauai and Niihau were the only islands that remained beyond his grasp.

With a fleet of more than 600 war canoes, he set out from Oahu to capture Kauai, 90 miles across a treacherous channel. But he was forced to turn back after a vicious storm capsized the boats, killing many of his warriors. A few years later, he prepared to depart once again, this time with a fleet consisting of 800 canoes and 20 Western-style ships. The gods were still not with him. His men were hit with a plague that wiped out nearly half of them. Then finally, in 1810, by promising the chief of Kauai and Niihau nominal power, a tireless Kamehameha finally tricked him into agreeing to place these two islands under his domain.

In 1795, Chief Kamehameha had married high-born Keopuolani. Her royal breeding meant he could now father children of the supreme alii rank. Unfortunately, only three of his eleven children survived to maturity. However, both of his surviving sons lived to succeed him on the throne: Prince Liholiho became Kamehameha II and Prince Kauikeaouli, Kamehameha III.

For all her high status, Keopuolani was not Kamehameha's favorite wife. His heart belonged to six foot tall, two hundred pound, strikingly beautiful Kaahumanu. Even though she was never able to bear him any children, he cherished this feisty and independent woman, whom he had married in 1785.

Kaahumanu was alone at her husband's bedside when he died in May of 1819. She claimed that with his last breath, he had named her *kuhina nui,* the person who would run his kingdom and take care of his heir, 20-year-old Liholiho. Although her words filled people with shock and disbelief, no one dared question the veracity of the imposing, intimidating favorite wife of Kamehameha the Great. So that the power that had driven the beloved king would never find its way into the wrong hands, Kamehameha's bones were hidden somewhere near Kailua-Kona on the Big Island.

Breaking Bread—and Tradition (1819)

By the time King Kamehameha died, the Hawaiian islands were much more than a stopover for vessels sailing across the Pacific. Choosing to seek their fortunes in this tropical paradise, many foreigners never reboarded their ships. A new community was rapidly growing, including Britons, Scots, Spaniards, French, Portuguese, Italians, European-Americans, and at least one African-American, a freedman from New York. Alcohol, tobacco, and the sight of boisterous whalers and merchant sailors were now commonplace. These foreigners behaved with far fewer restraints than the kapu system allowed Hawaiians. Yet no gods flew down from the heavens to punish these disrespectful haoles. Many Hawaiians began to grumble about the choke hold their stifling kapus had on their lives.

Kaahumanu counseled Liholiho, who had become Kamehameha II. One of society's most vocal critics, she relentlessly prodded the young king to do away with the kapu system. Liholiho wavered, unable to turn his back on the ways of his ancestors, yet tempted by the idea of a less constricted life. One day Kaahumanu decided to force the issue by breaking two kapus at once: she boldly ate a banana (taboo for women) and she did so in the King's presence (men and women were not allowed to see each other dine). She went unpunished, but still Liholiho could not bring himself to make a decisive move.

Then came the night in late 1819 when Kaahumanu held an extravagant feast. The influences of foreign lands were clearly apparent in the absence of a screen to separate the men's and women's tables and in the clothes the guests wore. Sitting at the head of the men's table, Liholiho had donned at British naval uniform, while several of the wives and mothers at the women's table were decked out in Chinese silks. On each table, Kaahumanu had placed both men's and women's foods.

Finally, Liholiho stood, walked to the women's table, and took a seat. As if this were not audacious enough, he then proceded to eat dogmeat, along with other foods that were kapu to men. Everyone waited for the world to come to a cataclysmic end. When nothing happened, they realized the king's symbolic actions must have done away with the supreme power of their gods forever. Most chiefs and commoners were ecstatic, gleefully smashing temple walls and setting fire to once sacred images.

Bibles and Muumuus (1819–1824)

Perhaps the Hawaiian gods remained silent throughout the desecration of their temples because they knew this new-found freedom would be short-lived. Another brand of religious restraint was on its way to Hawaii. The first group of American missionaries—who would soon succeed in imposing their own strict code of behavior on Hawaiians—had already departed from Boston aboard the *Thaddeus*. Henry Obookaiah, one of the Hawaiians who had traveled overseas, had found his way to New England and had converted to Christianity. In many a sermon, he had requested that American missionaries go to the Sandwich Islands to spread the message that had brought him so much joy and peace of mind. His death from pneumonia had spurred the group of Protestant missionaries, led by the Reverend Hiram Bingham, to grant him his wish.

Along with three Hawaiian assistants, who had been in school with Obookaiah in Connecticut, the first company had set out on the six-month voyage to the Pacific. During their many weeks at sea, the 14 Americans diligently studied the Hawaiian language under the tutelage of the Hawaiian mission assistants. In April 1820 the *Thaddeus* finally arrived at Kealakekua Bay on the Big Island, where Captain Cook had met his end in early 1779.

Scandalized by all the bare-breasted women they found, and the practices of premarital sex, polygamy, and incest, the missionaries had their work cut out for them.

Clad in long-sleeved, dark-colored, scratchy woolens in the tropical heat, they seemed to believe the more uncomfortable they were, the more noble their challenge. First they set about convincing the women to cover up with the ankle-length, free-flowing dresses that would become today's muumuus. Then they began their campaign against such sinful pursuits as flying kites (long a beloved diversion), dancing the hula, and wearing flower leis. Boxing, wrestling, and starting fires on Sundays also had to go, along with the newly adopted vices of drinking alcohol and smoking.

With morals so alien to the people of the islands, the missionaries had no easy time foisting their religion on Hawaiians. However, having just lost their faith in their own gods, the highly spiritual Hawaiians were far more susceptible to the teachings of the missionaries than they might have been otherwise. Just as the break with the kapu system had come from the top down, so did the massive conversion of Hawaiians to Western religion.

Once Keopuolani, the mother of the king, was converted, others began following suit. But the greatest number of Hawaiians owed their conversion to the persuasive Kaahumanu, the kuhina nui. Before becoming gravely ill in 1823, she could hardly have been less interested in the message of the gospel. Then, as this powerful woman lay in an unaccustomed weakened state, she was cared for by Sybil Bingham, the wife of the mission leader. By the time of her miraculous recovery, Kaahumanu had become thoroughly convinced that her restored health was due to nothing other than Mrs. Bingham's prayers. Afterward, this born again woman dedicated herself to converting as many other Hawaiians as she possibly could.

The American missionaries also prided themselves in presenting Hawaiians with the first written version of their language. The alphabet they developed would have been many times longer than its twelve letters if the Westerners had included all of the different sounds Hawaiian contained. But by using one letter to cover more than one sound, they felt they were simpfliying the process of learning to read for Hawaiians. Having altered the pronunciation of the language considerably, they printed scores of primers and Bibles. By 1846, Hawaiians would become among the most literate people in the world.

Today, a common saying in Hawaii is, "The missionaries came to do good and they did very well indeed." Actually, for the most part, economic prosperity was reaped not so much by the first missionaries as it was by their descendents, whose wealth, concentrated in sugar plantations, created the famous Big Five family businesses. For the early New Englanders, life was pretty rough.

Just as the missionaries appeared to believe that the righteousness of their task was in direct proportion to their personal discomfort, they seemed to think that the greater the self-loathing of Hawaiians, the more deeply religious and virtuous they could become. Hawaiians were taught they were inferior to white people, that their culture and past were degenerate. Adopting Western religion could make them less inferior, but nothing could ever make them the equals of whites.

The more Protestantism spread through the islands, the more demoralized Hawaiians became. By 1823 epidemics of foreign diseases and widespread sterility resulting from imported venereal disease had taken a huge bite out of the Hawaiian population. It was in these troubled times that Liholiho, Kamehameha II, decided to take a trip to England to meet with King George IV. He planned to ask for advice on better ruling his islands and on improving his control of commerce and other interactions with foreigners in Hawaii. Accompanied by Queen Kamamalu, his sister and the favorite of his five wives, he set out on the seven-month voyage in November 1823. The merchant ship they traveled on carried $25,000 in gold coins for spending money and a cargo of sperm oil. In 1824, less than two months after arrival, Kamehameha II and the queen both caught measles and died. The king was only 28 years old.

The Other Kamehamehas (1824–1872)

When Liholiho's brother, Kauikeaouli, became Kamehameha III at the age of nine, Kaahumanu remained in power as kuhina nui and regent. In the care of Reverend Hiram Bingham, the child received a Christian education. However, although Bingham attempted to instill in him an unquestioning love for Western values, Kamehameha III would grow up to be steadfastly pro-Hawaiian in culture and beliefs. Locking horns with Bingham, the king would not agree to make the Ten Commandments the official law of his land.

Kaahumanu died in 1832 and was succeeded by the king's half sister, Kinau, who seemed to share more of Bingham's views than her brother's. In 1833, after an argument, Kamehameha III angrily stripped Kinau of her title. To further spite her, he declared all Western-influenced rules and regulations null and void.

For a brief period, Hawaiians happily reverted to their old customs and pastimes, enjoying a more guilt-free existence. Then in 1835, Kamehameha III had a change of heart and returned Kinau to power. To make sure that he was back in her good graces, he promised to declare her youngest son, Alexander Liholiho, his successor. With Kinau once again at the helm, Bingham's influence crept back in as well.

Together Bingham and Kinau established two exile colonies to keep the people in line. To Kahoolawe, they sent men convicted of theft, adultery, or murder. To Lanai, they banished women found guilty of these crimes. However, they underestimated both the strength and the sex drive of their captives: The men swam the six miles from Kahoolawe to Maui, liberated canoes and food, paddled to Lanai, freed the women, and took them back to Kahoolawe. When Kinau died in 1839, Bingham's political power was buried with her. Deciding there was another way to leave his mark on Hawaii, Bingham built Kawaiahao, the massive stone church that still stands today, in Honolulu.

The love affair between Kamehameha III and his sister, Nahienaena, had the highest approval of traditional Hawaiians. They were thrilled at the meshing of the sacred mana of the last two living children of Kamehameha the Great and the high-born Queen Keopuolani. In 1836, Nahienaena died, at barely 20 years of age, not long after giving birth to a still-born baby. Even though both she and her brother had other lovers by this time, many people believed that the infant was his. A grief-stricken Kamehameha III moved the kingdom's capital from Honolulu to Lahaina, Maui, so that he could be close to the mausoleum of his beloved sister.

During the 1840s, the mortality rate among Hawaiians rose sharply, due only in part to foreign diseases. Hundreds of people weakened and wasted away, stricken with severe depression after having been told for so long by white people that their brown skin and their culture made them inferior human beings. A common saying at the time described the emotional malaise: *"Na kanaka okuu wale aku no i kau uhane"* ("The people simply dismissed their souls and died").

This decade was also a period when the independence of the Hawaiian kingdom was being threatened. France, a Catholic country, was convinced that its trade options in exporting wine and brandy were being limited. Liquor was not looked upon very kindly in these Protestant-controlled islands. France grumbled that it would annex Hawaii if its trade conditions did not improve. However, it was Britain, not France, that took over Hawaii for a few tense months in 1843. The British government charged that the property rights of Britons in Hawaii were not being honored. Kamehameha III regained power during a period when the whaling trade was about to peak, then slowly decline. It would finally fizzle out completely with the discovery of oil in the U.S. in 1859.

Maintaining autonomy for his kingdom was extremely important to Kamehameha III, so he attempted to surround himself with influential people he believed had Hawaii's best interests at heart. But it was the Scottish man who became his minister of foreign affairs, Robert Crichton Wyllie, who helped clear the way for the eventual downfall of the monarchy. Wyllie convinced the king to officially give all the rights of native-born Hawaiians to all foreigners who decided to reside in Hawaii. This meant that these "honorary Hawaiians" could serve in the highest governmental posts. When the king convened the first legislature in Honolulu in 1845, he had filled four out of five cabinet posts with foreigners, much to the displeasure of many Hawaiians.

As Hawaii's economy changed, Kamehameha III felt the need for foreign advisers. Land that had once been used for subsistence farming, during the heyday of the kingdom's semifeudal period, now sprouted crops for export. With the Great Mahele of 1848, a major reform ordered by King Kamehameha III, land once owned exclusively by chiefs and worked by commoners was turned into real estate to be bought and sold. The increase in export farming and the decrease in the Hawaiian population meant that foreign labor had to be recruited.

The first groups of indentured laborers arrived in Hawaii in 1852 and 1853 from China. While most came to work on sugar plantations, some were brought to serve as domestics for wealthy haole families. In a sense, this move signaled a return to the semifeudalism of the past. It was also the beginning of the major change in Hawaii's population that would alter the racial makeup of the islands forever.

The kingdom's economy, government, and religious leanings were pulled in various directions by the often conflicting interests of foreign powers. Although the Protestants in Hawaii tried to prevent them from doing so, Catholics and Mormons established missions in the islands.

When Kamehameha III died in 1854, he was content that the joint treaty that had just been signed by France, Britain, and the United States would continue to insure Hawaii's independence. But as the deceased monarch's nephew, Alexander Liholiho, became Kamehameha IV, the possibility of annexation by the U.S. to secure American interests remained in the air.

Kamehameha IV had already had a first-hand taste of American hypocrisy and was adamantly opposed to U.S. annexation. While riding a train during a visit to the U.S. some five years earlier, he had been mistaken for an African-American by a Pullman conductor and ordered to leave the car. He had never faced racism in France, England, or anywhere else in his travels. Insulted and infuriated, he found it ironic that a country that took such pride in its liberty could treat people with such a lack of respect.

Kamehameha IV married Emma Rooke, the granddaughter of the haole chief John Young whose advice on Western weapons had helped Kamehameha the Great unite the islands into a single kingdom. The king and queen were deeply disturbed by the decline in the native population and feared that Hawaiians might eventually die out altogether. In an attempt to stave off the highly contagious, imported diseases that Hawaiian immune systems could not handle, they built Queen's Hospital in Honolulu, named in honor of Queen Emma. (Today called Queen's Medical Center, it is Hawaii's largest hospital and has received international recognition for its cardiovascular department.) Unfortunately, the efforts of the royal couple did little to improve the situation. Hawaiians continued to succumb to illnesses in large numbers. By the early 1860s, leprosy would pose a new problem, and victims of the disease would ultimately be shunted off to a remote peninsula on the island of Molokai.

In 1858, the good news was that the queen had given birth to a prince, the first heir to the throne born to a reigning monarch since the time of Hawaii's first king. Then four years later, the child died. Kamehameha IV was overwhelmed by guilt, since the little boy had fallen ill soon after he had held him under cold water to punish him for having a tantrum. Kamehameha IV carried another heavy burden as well. Two years earlier, he had shot a close American friend, in a jealous rage over murmurings that the man had eyes for Queen Emma. When the rumors were later proven false, a remorseful king spared no expense in caring for his wounded friend. But just before the death of the king's son, the man had finally expired from his wounds. In 1863, a 29-year-old Kamehameha IV, run down by grief, guilt, alcohol, and asthma, followed them to the grave.

By this time, missionaries and their families had begun to go into the sugarcane business. Two former spreaders of the gospel, Samuel Northrup Castle and Amos Starr Cooke, founded what is now the multinational Castle & Cooke corporation, which owns the island of Lanai. Haoles were becoming increasingly entrenched in Hawaii's economy and politics. Hawaiian commoners, and other landless citizens, were restricted from voting or holding elective office. Alexander Liholiho's brother Lot, who became Kamehameha V in 1863, pressed for a greater degree of self-determination and a resurgence of the indigenous culture. Strengthening the power of the monarchy, he drafted a new constitution in 1864.

He built the luxurious Hawaiian Hotel, in Honolulu, in an attempt to expand tourism as an alternative to the sugar-based, foreign-controlled agricultural economy. But agriculture continued to be the dominant business. At the end of their terms, Chinese contract laborers, free at last, could not leave the plantations fast enough. New Chinese workers were brought to Hawaii to replace them, as well as thousands of indentured laborers from other countries including Portugal, Norway, and Germany.

In 1872, Lot, the last of the Kamehamehas, died without having chosen a successor. For the first time in the history of the kingdom, a monarch would be elected.

The Twilight of the Hawaiian Monarchy (1872–1893)

Fondly known as Prince Bill, William Charles Lunalilo had a reputation for heavy-duty drinking, womanizing, and spending. His father had to persuade him to appoint financial guardians so that he wouldn't squander his inheritance. Nevertheless, as the great-grandnephew of Kamehameha I, Lunalilo was the highest-ranking alii of his time and the legitimate heir to the throne.

Despite his royal blood, Lunalilo decided to prove his worth and popularity to anyone who thought him too irresponsible to be king. He would run in an electioin. His opponent, David Kalakaua, was outspoken in his pro-Hawaiian sentiments and did not take kindly to the trend of foreigners gaining increasing power and land in Hawaii. Lunalilo was more moderate in his expression of pro-Hawaiianism and more sympathetic to the interests of haole politicians and businessmen. In addition to being supported by foreigners, Lunalilo was also backed by the alii, who were making good money by leasing their lands to haole planters. In 1873, Lunalilo became Hawaii's first elected king.

To demonstrate his solidarity with his people, he walked barefoot to Kawaiahao Church to take the oath of office. During his brief reign, he restored the vote for Hawaiian commoners as well as their right to hold elective office. Run down from years of fast living and overindulgence in alcohol, Lunalilo caught tuberculosis and died in 1874. He had ruled for little more than a year. Again to illustrate his camaraderie with his subjects, he had asked to be buried at Kawaiahao Church, among commoners, instead of with the other kings and chiefs, who were traditionally laid to rest at the Royal Mausoleum in Oahu's Nuuanu Valley.

David Kalakaua decided to give the throne another shot, this time running against Queen Emma, the widow of Kamehameha IV. Despite her American grandfather, Emma Rooke was thoroughly anti-American, antimissionary, and completely confident she would win. If Hawaii should be forced to lose its independence, she hoped it would be the British who took over. When Kalakaua won the election in 1874, Queen Emma and her supporters were both flabbergasted and furious. Her followers rushed wildly into the courthouse, where the legislators had cast their ballots. The melee had to be quelled by British and American marines whose ships happened to be in Honolulu harbor.

Reviving and maintaining the Hawaiian heritage was a high priority for Kalakaua. He resuscitated the hula, which had been banned by missionaries for many years, even contributing his own new dances. By playing his ukulele and composing songs, he ushered in a renewed appreciation for Hawaiian music. He wrote the words to "Hawaii Pono'i," the national anthem of the kingdom, which has since become Hawaii's state song.

Haoles complained he was trying to return Hawaii to its heathen past. They dubbed him "The Merrie Monarch" because of his jolly style and his love of the performing arts. They were no less displeased when he built the new, opulent Iolani Palace in 1882 and held a lavish coronation ceremony for himself on the grounds. His supporters saw this as a welcome way to bolster national pride, but others said that the hefty expenditure would have been better spent elsewhere.

While Kalakaua viewed a strong cultural identity as essential to the well being of Hawaiians, he realized the importance of ensuring friendly relations with foreign powers as well. In 1881, he had left for an around-the-world tour to find new sources for immigrant labor and to ensure that Hawaii's independence was recognized and respected across the globe. He became the world's first reigning monarch to make such a trip and to visit the U.S., where he met with Ulysses S. Grant. During his rule, Pearl Harbor was granted to the U.S. for use as a naval base and the Reciprocity Treaty was passed, doing away with the tariff barrier, thereby giving a major boost to the American-controlled sugar industry.

Although the 1870s had brought more contract laborers from China and the Portuguese islands of the Azores and Madeira, there were still not enough workers for the ever-expanding sugarcane plantations. Kalakaua initiated a large-scale Japanese immigration, the first group of which came in 1885. His greatest hope was that the Japanese would intermarry with Hawaiians and help "repopulate" the race. By 1886, with people from so many different nations having settled in the islands, Hawaiians had become a minority.

Haoles did not appreciate all the competition from the many Chinese businesses that were cropping up as these immigrants left the plantations. They blamed Kalakaua for allowing the Chinese so much economic freedom. Finally, in 1887, the king was pressured into giving in to the demands of the Hawaiian League, a group of influential haoles. Believing this was the only way to maintain peace in Hawaii, even though it meant that his power would now be nominal, he fired his cabinet and signed what came to be known as the "Bayonet Constitution." The new laws of the land stripped the Chinese of the vote and limited Hawaiian political power, basically turning the islands over to American and British residents.

In 1889, a coup attempt led by Robert Wilcox, a Hawaiian educated in Italy, was quickly squelched by the haoles and in 1891, having lost what he had worked so hard to build, Kalakaua, the last of Hawaii's kings, died in San Francisco, California. Upon his death, his sister Liliuokalani became the queen of an American-controlled nation. In 1893 she announced that she would draw up a new constitution, one that would return the rule of the country to the monarchy and restore the right to vote and to run for office to all citizens of Hawaii. Declaring her intended actions revolutionary, a small, independent group of Americans (most of whom were Hawaiian-born sons of missionaries) promptly deposed her.

U.S. Annexation (1893–1941)

Hawaii's life as an autonomous kingdom had come to an end. For the next five years, the newly christened "Republic of Hawaii" would be ruled by a provisional government with Sandford Ballard Dole as president. In vain, nearly 40,000 people—practically every Hawaiian in the islands—signed a petition of protest sent to the President of the United States. They wrote that they deeply resented the gall of the members of the provisional government, who had no right, legal or otherwise, to take control of them as if they were "a flock of sheep" or "a horde of savages." How dare this foreign minority presume to rule them? they asked. Not only had these independent Americans acted without the approval of the U.S. government, but they could not even claim "conquest by fair-handed warfare."

In 1895, after a failed coup attempt was carried out by her supporters, Liliuokalani was taken from her Washington Place mansion and held captive in Iolani Palace. She spent the next eight months locked in a spartan room, permitted few comforts and allowed no visitors. The lonely queen passed her time by composing music and writing lyrics, including the words to the well-known "Aloha Oe." She was told that if she did not sign the abdication papers presented to her, the 200 people who had been imprisoned for their loyalty to her would be killed. Believing she had no choice, she gave them her signature. Still bitter over her kingdom's loss of independence, Liliuokalani, Hawaii's last monarch, died in 1916.

With the onset of the Spanish-American War, which fumed in the Philippines, the U.S. Navy needed more control than it already had over Oahu's Pearl Harbor. In addition, the U.S. wanted a larger chunk of the profits from Hawaii's thriving sugar business. President William McKinley gave annexation the green light.

The changing of the flags ceremony took place on August 12, 1898, at Iolani Palace in Honolulu. After the lowering of the Hawaiian flag, accompanied by a 21-gun salute from the American naval vessels in the harbor, the spectators heard a loud, grief-laden moan seeping out of Kawaiahoa church, a block away. While most of the people on the palace grounds were haoles, many Hawaiians had gathered in mourning at the nearby church. The doleful sound was soon replaced by cheers from the grounds of the palace as a specially designed version of the American flag was raised.

Although Prince Kuhio had been imprisoned as one of Liliuokalani's loyalists, he was chosen by the Republican-dominated Hawaiian government to be their Congressional delegate. His support by residents of the islands would come in handy. He would be instrumental in the design of the Hawaiian Homes Act, passed in 1919, which set aside 200,000 acres of land for farms or residential lots for people whose ancestry was at least half Hawaiian.

During the early years as an American territory, the population became more multiethnic than ever. A rainbow of foreign field laborers poured in at the turn of the century, including thousands of Puerto Ricans, Koreans, Russians, Spanish, Filipinos, Okinawans, and African-Americans. The Big Five companies—Castle & Cooke, Alexander & Baldwin, C. Brewer & Co., AmFac (American Factors), and Theo. H. Davies—continued to flourish, and they remain strong today. Tourism picked up on Oahu. Guests still check into both the elegant Moana Hotel, built in 1901, and the lavish Royal Hawaiian, finished in 1927.

Hawaii could have done without the attention it received in 1931 when a highly controversial crime hit mainland headlines. Thalia Massie, the young white wife of a U.S. Navy lieutenant, left a party alone late one night and went walking in Honolulu. When she was found, she was bruised and nearly incoherent, her jaw broken, her clothes ripped and bloodstained. Five Hawaiians and a Japanese-American were quickly arrested after she claimed she had been beaten and raped by a group of dark-skinned men. The public was never told that a drunken white naval lieutenant commander, with fingernail scratches on his face and a torn uniform, had been picked up that same night in the same area. As the hysteria over the case rose, haoles howled that white women were no longer safe in Hawaii. When the defendants were acquitted due to lack of evidence, Thalia Massie's husband and mother were beside themselves with rage. They kidnapped one of the accused men and murdered him. Although Lieutenant Massie and his mother-in-law were found guilty, the sympathetic territorial governor commuted their sentence to one hour. They served out their 60-minute punishment sitting comfortably in the governor's office in Iolani Palace. Ironically, this office was right across the hall from the room that had held Queen Liliuokalani prisoner for eight long months.

Pearl Harbor (1941–1954)

Thousands of U.S. servicemen and many civilians died when the Japanese attacked Pearl Harbor on December 7, 1941. Along with many German, Austrian, and Italian aliens, scores of Japanese-Americans were rounded up and sent to internment camps on the mainland. But only on the island of Niihau was there a problem with patriotism, and it was an isolated incident at that.

Mr. Harada, a shopkeeper, was one of just two Japanese who lived among the 300 Hawaiians on haole-owned Niihau. A Japanese plane leaving Oahu after the attack was forced to land on Niihau. The desperate pilot convinced Harada to help him. They took Mr. and Mrs. Benjamin Kanahele hostage, to prevent them from alerting others that the enemy plane had landed. Hours later, tormented by guilt, Harada killed himself. The pilot was so unnerved by this that he shot Benjamin Kanahele. Enraged, the large Hawaiian man snatched the pilot into the air and ended his life by dashing him against a wall. Viewed as a local hero, Kanahele recovered from his wound.

The armed forces finally decided to accept *nisei* (American-born children of Japanese immigrants) volunteers in 1943, after realizing that Americans of Japanese descent could prove just as loyal as other citizens. Perhaps because they had so much at stake, the Japanese-American men of the 100th Batallion and the 442nd Regiment won the highest honors of any American army unit in combat.

The years following the war saw the spread of unionization. Laborers throughout the islands were attempting to improve the conditions imposed on them by large corporations. Because of the virus of McCarthyism, sweeping across the U.S., many people began to believe that union activity was backed by Communists. Turning to the Democratic party, the labor movement fought against the interests of Big Business, historically the Republican domain. Led by World War II veteran and future Senator Daniel K. Inouye, pro-union Japanese-Americans were largely responsible for the 1954 shift of the territorial legislature from Republican to Democratic control.

The Fiftieth State (1959–Present)

On August 21, 1959, Hawaii officially became the 50th state of the Union. Wild celebrations broke out on all the islands. Statehood brought a surge in development, with the greatest thrust on Oahu and then Maui. Hotels and condominiums sprouted up everywhere and new freeways cut across the countryside. As jets began to swoop down on Oahu, tourism became the major economic base. Many visiting mainlanders even turned themselves into residents. In 1972, Hawaii became the first state to ratify the Equal Rights Amendment. This was not surprising, since, at the time, Hawaii had the country's largest number of working mothers.

The 1970s were also a period of rebirth for Hawaiian cultural pride. Some say the Hawaiian Renaissance began with the 1975 launching of the *Hokulea*, a modern-day replica of a 60-foot Polynesian sailing canoe. Many haole historians believed that the Hawaiian Islands had been settled accidentally, after Polynesians lost in the stormy seas had stumbled upon them. The idea that ancient non-Europeans could have been expert navigators who knew exactly what they were doing and where they were going did not sit well with Westerners. Non-Hawaiian Americans were particularly uncomfortable with the notion that these Polynesian journeys of thousands of miles over open ocean could have taken place some 2000 years before the Vikings did their thing.

The *Hokulea* was built to prove that the ancient Polynesians had indeed sailed from Tahiti to Hawaii in order to settle it. Hawaiian legends and petroglyphs (rock drawings) served as blue prints for the canoe. People from other, remote Polynesian islands who had preserved old traditions were brought in on the act. The vessel would be sailed using only ancient navigational techniques and equipment, so people familiar with these techniques had to be found. Women from other islands taught the people building the canoe the art of weaving sails from pandanus fronds and making rope from braided sennit. However, some adjustments had to be made. Trees in 20th-century Hawaii did not grow as massive as they once had, so the hull could not be cut from a single log. Instead, the canoe was constructed of fiberglass.

The year following a 1975 voyage around the Hawaiian Islands, The *Hokulea* set sail from Maui for a month-long voyage to Tahiti. The 17-man crew was welcomed by a crowd of 15,000 Tahitians. When they sailed back to Hawaii, they were met with another uproarious greeting. During the 1980s, the *Hokulea* (now on display in Oahu) sailed throughout the Pacific, stopping at many islands, following the path of the ancestors of present-day Hawaiians. In 1987, when the canoe returned to Hawaii after its two-year "Voyage of Discovery," distant cousins—including Tahitians, Samoan chiefs, Maoris from New Zealands—had come from all over the Pacific to join the celebration.

With the boom in tourism, Hawaii's economy continued to flourish, if not always in expected or respected ways. Nudging sugarcane and pineapple aside, marijuana had become the most profitable (though, of course, illegal) crop by 1979. In 1986, John D. Waihee III was elected Hawaii's first governor of Hawaiian descent. This made him the first Hawaiian to lead the Islands since the overthrow of the Hawaiian monarchy nearly a century earlier.

Today the cost of living in Hawaii is higher than that of almost any other state. However, residents also enjoy a high standard of living. Besides, how many other states can boast such a seductive blend of exotic surroundings, sophisticated creature comforts, and a warm, multiracial population?

(Also see ''The People of Hawaii.'')

THE PEOPLE OF HAWAII

"Where are all the Asians?" a Japanese-American friend of mine from Hawaii asked during her first trip to the mainland. This is a question that occurs to many residents of the 50th state when they first visit the continental U.S.

Of Hawaii's 1 million Hawaiians, European-Americans, Chinese, Japanese, Portuguese, Koreans, Filipinos, Puerto Ricans, Samoans, and others, no single ethnic group is larger than the rest of the collective population. At about 30% each, Caucasians and Japanese make up the two biggest groups. Between only 10% and 20% of Island residents are Hawaiian or part-Hawaiian. Many people are products of a varied heritage. Nearly half of Hawaii's marriages each year are between people of different races and/or ethnic backgrounds.

Hawaii's economy has everything to do with its cultural diversity. Beginning in the mid-19th century, thousands of immigrants from many different countries were recruited to work in the Islands' sugarcane and pineapple fields. While Hawaii is certainly something of a cultural melting pot, many ethnic distinctions have remained sharp over the decades. This is in part due to the way the residential camps on the plantations were set up. Each housing area was reserved for a particular ethnic group. One village would be inhabited only by Hawaiians, another strictly by Japanese, another limited to Filipinos.

Living with people who shared a language, diet, and culture certainly made the transition to a foreign land a bit easier; in this way, immigrants maintained many aspects of their old religions, festivals, and culinary traditions and passed them on to their Hawaii-born children. However, the reason ethnic groups were separated was to discourage them from joining forces en masse against the haole plantation owners. In most cases, living and working conditions were horrific. *Lunas* (akin to overseers) would sometimes whip or beat workers who did not move fast enough. It was common practice to pay Asians less money than Caucasian laborers doing the same work. Picking pineapples was especially arduous. Even in the sweltering heat, workers were forced to wear hats, scarves over their faces, and other heavy clothing to protect themselves from bugs and dust, and gloves to avoid cutting their hands on the serrated leaves.

For those lucky enough to escape the plantations, harsh treatment of Asians and other non-Caucasians did not end. Threatened by the success of many Chinese businesses, the haole-controlled Hawaiian government began to throw roadblocks at Asians who tried to open stores and restaurants. Laws were also passed that prevented people born in Japan or China from ever becoming Hawaiian citizens, a privilege that was available to other foreign residents.

After the arrival of the first Europeans in 1778, the Hawaiian population dwindled steadily. Many were killed or made sterile by newly encountered Western diseases that their immune systems were not equipped to handle. Those Hawaiians who survived disease and cultural genocide (which included the overthrow of their last monarch by a group of American businessmen) found themselves at the bottom level of society.

Today, racial tensions, though certainly not pervasive, do exist in Hawaii. Public schools have not been able to end the tradition known as "Kill a Haole Day," an excuse for tearing up and causing trouble. After suffering misdirected discrimination following the Japanese attack on Pearl Harbor in World War II, Japanese-Americans in Hawaii now face being painted with another broad stroke. Resentment is high against businessmen from Japan who are buying up real estate in Hawaii with a vengeance.

However, despite its problems, Hawaii remains one of the most intriguing cultural potpourris in the world. Here's a closer look at the main ethnic groups:

The Hawaiians

When Polynesians first arrived in the uninhabited Hawaiian Islands, somewhere between 300 and 750 A.D., they brought *aloha aina*. Inherent in this profound love for the land and the sea was a reverence for all life that the earth and ocean made possible. Therefore, preservation of the environment was of the utmost importance to ancient Hawaiians. Although in some parts of the state aloha aina has been overshadowed by real estate development, there are many places for visitors to see a Hawaii that has changed little since the early days.

Some modern families settle arguments with the *hooponopono* ritual, as ancient Hawaiians did: after everyone has gotten their concerns off their chests, they all eat the tender leaves of *limu kala,* a variety of seaweed (*kala* means to "forgive"). Some Hawaiians still leave offerings at *heiau,* the crumbling stone temples found around the Islands. Many, even those who practice Christianity, still worship old Hawaiian gods such as Pele, the powerful volcano goddess, who resides on the Big Island. To this day, people claim from time to time that they have seen Pele, with her fiery tresses, wandering about.

In the past, loved ones who had died were buried around their houses so that their *aumakua* (positive spirits) wouldn't have far to go when they returned to help living relatives. *Lapu* were the tormented spirits of the deceased who were unable to get out of the limbo between the worlds of the living and the dead. As late as the end of the 19th century, cases were reported in which people swore they had seen groups of lapu socializing on the corner of King and Nuuanu streets in Oahu's Chinatown. *Kupua* were the spirits that inhabited inanimate objects. Today, people tell stories of rocks at construction sites that could not be moved until after a Hawaiian *kahuna* (priest) arrived and had a tete-a-tete with the spirits inside the stones.

Most present-day Hawaiians are not racially pure, so they are not nearly as brown-skinned as their ancestors. However, they still tend to be large—in both height and weight. In Hawaiian culture, size was once equated with power, wealth, and social status—in other words, the bigger, the better. Rotund Kaahumanu, the favorite wife of King Kamehameha I, was said to be at least six feet tall and the monarch to have towered over her. A local joke about Hawaiian women in those loose-fitting dresses asks, "How is a Hawaiian woman in a muumuu like a bank?" Answer: "You know it's in there. You just don't know how much."

In the early 1970s, Hawaiian activists began fighting for the interests of the indigenous population. They pushed for land rights for Hawaiians and for restoration and preservation of ancient historic and religious sites. More people began taking Hawaiian language classes and joining *hula halau* (hula groups).

Activists have been vocal on the issue of digging up ancient Hawaiian burial sites. In the 1980s, they were successful in forcing the builders of the Ritz Carlton Hotel on Maui to move the resort inland, away from a sacred spot containing hundreds of antique skeletons. Periodically, battles erupt among archaeologists, developers, and Hawaiians. They argue over whether the knowledge gained from dating and studying the bones or the economic surge that comes from building yet another hotel or shopping mall should outweigh the rights of present-day Hawaiians to respect their ancestors the way they see fit.

Some Hawaiians are succeeding very well in business, politics, and other areas today. Established in Honolulu for children of Hawaiian descent, the Kamehameha schools are a renowned academy. (In 1986, John D. Waihee III became the state's first Hawaiian governor.) However, too many Hawaiians are still struggling to gain a foothold, some even giving in to hopelessness or apathy. A disproportionate number of inmates in state and county jails are of Hawaiian descent. A large segment of the Hawaiian community receives state or federal welfare. Many young people drop out of school or become teenage and/or unmarried parents.

To help combat these problems, the Office of Hawaiian Affairs works with service organizations in the areas of health, economic development, education, legal services, and the promotion of an understanding of indigenous culture. Thanks to Prince Kuhio, the 1919 Hawaiian Homes Act set aside thousands of acres of land for farms and home lots for people who are at least half Hawaiian. Unfortunately, as well intentioned as this Congressional act was, most of the land is of poor quality. The cost of developing it has sometimes been astronomical, sending many Hawaiian families deeply into debt. Even so, the waiting list is decades long for these $1 a year, 99-year leases.

(Also see Strangers in a Strange Land and The Fiftieth State in "Days Gone By.")

The Caucasians

No, *haole* ("*how*-lee") is not in itself a derogatory term (although it can be used as such). Most Caucasians in Hawaii refer to themselves that way. The word simply means foreigner, but has come to be synonymous with white people and/or mainlanders.

British Captain James Cook was the first known Westerner to arrive in Hawaii, in 1778. Many *kamaaina* (longtime Island resident) *haoles* are descendants of the New England missionaries who began showing up in 1820. These religious enthusiasts are credited with introducing Hawaiians to Bibles, muumuus, and quilts and with transforming the Islands into a literate society, among other achievements. They turned Hawaiian into a written language and taught the native population to read it. Descendants of missionaries moved on to agriculture and many were highly successful planters whose wealth became the foundation of present-day Hawaii. The Big Five, a powerful group of businesses, has its roots in missionary families.

Often called "Portagee" or "guavas" by locals, a few hundred Portuguese had settled in Hawaii before the arrival of Americans. They had reached these shores as sailors on whalers and had decided to jump ship. But it wasn't until 1878, during the reign of King Kalakaua, that people from Portugal's Azores and Madeira islands began coming in large numbers. Unlike Asian immigrants, who had to start at the bottom, many Portuguese men found jobs as plantation *lunas* (foremen). Once out of the sugarcane and pineapple fields, some climbed the socioeconomic ladder to high-level government or clerical positions.

The Portuguese are best known today for their sausage, red bean soup, *malasadas* (doughnuts without the holes), and the guitarlike instrument that came to be called the *ukulele*. Held in Hawaii during the spring, the Seven Domingas are weekly religious festivals and feasts that date back to 13th-century Portugal.

(Also see "Days Gone By.")

The Chinese

The first known Chinese to set foot in Hawaii came as crew members on two ships sailing from South China and western Canada in 1789. But they didn't stay. In the 1790s, foreign traders started buying aromatic sandalwood from Hawaiian chiefs to be sold in China. The Chinese used this prized wood to make elaborate carvings and incense. The traders became wealthy and within four decades Hawaii's sandalwood forests had been completely denuded.

Groups of Chinese immigrants were first brought to Hawaii in 1852. They intermarried with Hawaiians and people of other races more readily than most other ethnic groups did. Many converted to Christianity. At the ends of their terms, Chinese contract laborers, free at last, could not leave the plantations fast enough. Japanese immigrants had to be brought in to pick up the slack.

Contrary to popular belief, however, not all Chinese came as plantation laborers. Hundreds also migrated to these islands to work in restaurants and other businesses owned by relatives and friends or to serve as domestics for wealthy haoles. Many settled in Honolulu, creating the Chinatown that exists today.

Hawaii had a great deal to do with the early shaping of present-day China. In the late 19th century, Sun Yat-sen became one of the best-known members of Hawaii's Chinese community. He did so well at the school he attended in Honolulu from 1879 to 1883 that King David Kalakaua honored him for his accomplishments in English. After attending medical school in China, he returned to Hawaii where he formed a political organization that would eventually lead to the overthrow of China's Manchu Regime. In 1912, Sun Yat-sen became the first provisional president of the new Republic of China.

No matter how successful they became, Chinese residents of Hawaii had to contend with many obstacles, such as the U.S. Chinese Exclusion Acts of 1882–1884 that prevented them from becoming citizens. In 1892, another act was passed (and not repealed by Congress until 1943), this time to restrict Chinese immigration. Then the U.S.-controlled provisional government proposed prohibitions on any expansion or increase in Chinese businesses. The great number and prosperity of Chinese restaurants and stores threatened the economic monopoly that haoles wished to maintain in Hawaii.

In vain, the Chinese protested by the thousands, complaining that the government was all too happy to collect taxes from them, but when it came to treating them as the law-abiding, industrious people they were, that seemed to be another matter.

Today few travelers visit Honolulu without strolling through the picturesque streets of Chinatown. Celebrated here in full force with lion dances, long dragon costumes, and fireworks, the Chinese New Year is a major event on Oahu. The Chinese community also observes Buddhist, Confucian, and Taoist holidays.

Among the best known Hawaiian residents of Chinese descent are Republican Hiram L. Fong, the first Asian-American to be elected to the U.S. Senate, in 1959; and nightclub entertainer Don Ho. When many people think of the Islands, Earl Derr Biggers' sterotypic Charlie Chan mysteries come to mind. These stories were based on the well-known Hawaiian-Chinese detective Chang Apana, who left the Honolulu Police Department in the 1930s.

The Japanese

From the ashes of indentured labor, racial discrimination, Pearl Harbor, and World War II internment camps, Japanese-Americans have risen to become probably the most politically and economically powerful ethnic group in Hawaii. They first came to Hawaii in significant numbers in 1868, followed by a second wave of immigration under King David Kalakaua in the 1880s. The king hoped that the Japanese would intermarry with Hawaiians, creating a new race that would repopulate the Islands. When the first group stepped ashore in 1885, they were overwhelmed by masses of Hawaiians who welcomed them with gifts of fish, poi, and vegetables. By the time the Hawaiian Kingdom drew to a close in 1895, nearly 30,000 Japanese had migrated to Hawaii.

Unfortunately, however, Kalakaua's plan was a flop. The Japanese tended to stick to themselves. Not only did they rarely marry Hawaiians or members of other ethnic groups, they failed to embrace Christianity, instead holding hast to their Buddhist beliefs. They set up Japanese Language Schools to teach their children how to become proper citizens of Japan and started Japanese-language newspapers.

During the 1880s, Japanese plantation workers began protesting the harsh conditions under which they toiled. Their marches, strikes, and walkouts inspired other ethnic groups to follow suit. During World War II, Japanese-Americans who attempted to prove their patriotism by volunteering for the army were rejected at first. Ever persistent, they kept trying to join the war effort. When they finally did, the 442nd Regiment and the 100th Batallion (made up of *nisei*, American-born children of Japanese immigrants) became the war's most successful and highly honored American military combat unit. Daniel K. Inouye (pronounced "in-*no*-way"), a veteran of the 442nd, led a labor movement that resulted in the demise of Hawaii's traditional Republican political control. In 1954, the labor-backed Democrats took over the territorial legislature. Inouye went on to become the first Japanese-American congressman, and later a U.S. senator who gained national prominence as a member of the Senate Watergate Committee in the 1970s. In the 1980s, he served as chair of the Iran-Contra Hearings.

Eating *soba* (buckwheat noodles) and *mochi* (rice soup) for good luck on New Year's Eve is a Japanese tradition shared by many non-Japanese residents of Hawaii. The springtime Cherry Blossom Festival is another way Hawaii honors Japanese culture.

In Hawaii, it is not uncommon to see a Japanese-American screw up his face with disgust when talking about "the *Japanese*." For some, Pearl Harbor has never been forgiven. A recent version of this negative attitude was born when droves of investors from Japan began swooping down on Hawaii in the 1980s, buying up luxury homes and resorts as if they were paying for T-shirts. Most of Hawaii's major resorts and many of its commercial buildings are now Japanese-owned. While some people welcome the boost to Hawaii's economy, others complain that housing prices have soared. Locals wonder if their children will be able to afford to own property in Hawaii.

The Koreans

Koreans, many of whom intermarried with people from other backgrounds, have succeeded in reaching a very high educational and economic level in Hawaii. There is a higher proportion of professionals among Koreans than in any other ethnic group. This is quite an accomplishment, considering their early years in the Islands.

The sugar plantation laborers who begin arriving in 1903 came without wives or girlfriends. In later years, the Korean men began sending for "picture brides" from home. Some Korean women worked as waitresses in a few of Honolulu's earliest and most popular "hostess bars," which were owned by Korean businessmen. Today, the term "Korean bar" is used to refer to any of the sex clubs scattered throughout Honolulu and parts of other Islands, even though the owners and hostesses are now of many different races.

Kim chee, vegetables pickled with garlic and chili peppers, is probably Korea's best-known culinary contribution in Hawaii.

The Filipinos

As field laborers began standing up for their rights, plantation owners decided to bring in Filipinos. Many were illiterate, and owners believed (in some cases, rightly so) that education meant activism. Filipinos, eager to get away from U.S. colonial rule in their own country, fled to

Hawaii. Those who were educated pretended that they couldn't read or write and that they were too stupid to even consider joining a union. Plantation owners fell for it, and recruited thousands of workers from the Philippines, beginning in 1906. Much to their bosses' surprise, Filipinos pulled together some of Hawaii's earliest labor unions.

The first Filipinos to live in Hawaii arrived in 1888. They were musicians and acrobats who were members of an entertainment troupe on their way to San Francisco after performing in Japan and China. Four of the men who stayed ended up joining King Kalakaua's Royal Hawaiian Band.

In June, Fiesta Filipina erupts on Oahu and other islands. Though illegal, cockfighting matches (begun by Filipino plantation workers) draw smokey crowds. Men often bring their wives and children, making a family outing of this bloody sport. Heavy-duty betting is part of the action. On quiet country roads, you might see front yards studded with the raised, open-air, triangular shelters where fighting cocks reside.

Others in the Melting Pot

At the turn of the century, large numbers of Puerto Ricans (a mixture of American Indian, Spanish, and African races) came to Hawaii from the Caribbean. A Puerto Rican civic group occasionally holds salsa dances in Honolulu, but for the most part, these Latinos have been absorbed into the broader Hawaiian culture.

Mexican cowboys went to the Big Island in the 1830s to teach Hawaiians about cattle ranching. The Hawaiian pronunciation of the word *Espanol* (Spanish for *Spanish*) resulted in *paniolo,* the term still used for ''Hawaiian cowboy'' today.

Other groups of immigrants brought to work on Hawaiian plantations were Germans, Norwegians, Russians, Spanish, and African-Americans from Tennessee.

Hawaii's newest immigrants are Samoans, mostly from American Samoa. Many of them first arrived in 1952, the year after the control of their islands changed from the U.S. Navy to the U.S. Department of Interior. Samoan men, some of whom have drawn national attention as football players, are renowned for their accomplishments in sports. Many have also excelled in soccer, rugby, and cricket. Samoan parties and political meetings often feature traditional sarongs, chants, dances, songs, and the drinking of potent *kava* juice, made from the kava root. Many Samoans have settled in the Mormon community of Laie on Oahu, where the Polynesian Cultural Center is located.

NATURAL HAWAII

Even on Oahu, home of the skyscraper-studded capital of Honolulu, the wonders of nature are the main attraction. Vivid color is everywhere, from the neon blue of the ocean, the vibrant green of sugarcane fields and palm fronds, and the burnt-orange soil to the kaleidoscope of flowers, trees, birds, and fish.

If you've ever wondered why leaves are flat, a Hawaiian legend explains: In the old days, the sky weighed heavily upon the earth, barely leaving breathing room between the ground and the heavens. Plants, with their bulbous leaves, were forced to push the clouds and the sky up into the stratosphere, inch by inch. The more they shoved, the flatter their leaves became. Eventually, the sky was raised far enough to allow human beings to crawl around from place to place. Then for the price of a drink from a woman's gourd, Maui, the demigod, hoisted the skies up even farther, past the tops of trees, beyond the summits of mountains. Thus, men could finally walk upright on earth.

Because of the direction in which the wind blows the clouds and air mass across the Pacific, the northeast sides of all of Hawaii's islands are wet and the southwest sides dry. As the clouds bump up against the mountains, they drop rainfall on one side, leaving the other side dry.

The seeds of Hawaii's first plants floated ashore or were carried by the wind and migrating birds. One new species appeared on Hawaii about every 40,000 years! When the ancient Polynesians began to settle the Islands, they brought a variety of fruits and vegetables, including bananas, coconuts, breadfruit, taro, and yams. At first ancient Hawaiians lived in a world free from biting and stinging insects and poisonous snakes. They also had no communicable diseases. The arrival of European explorers in 1788 changed all that. Within a century after the first appearance of white people, the Hawaiian population had been devastated by new diseases they had no immunities to combat.

While Hawaii is certainly flourishing with all kinds of plant life, many of its more delicate native species have been crowded out by the more aggressive newcomers brought to Hawaii by outsiders. The introduction of cattle (for ranching) and other grazing animals has also killed off many of the Islands' original plants. For millions of years, these plants had lived in a world with no natural enemies; there had been no need to grow hardy. Thus, when a leaf or a branch was bitten off or trampled, the whole plant withered away.

Land and Sea Animals

Hawaii's only native land animal is a small brown **bat. Dolphins** are often spotted jumping playfully out of the water in pairs, and impressive **humpback whales** migrate to Hawaii during the winter. The early Polynesians, traders, and European explorers imported the small selection of animals that roam wild in Hawaii today: **pigs, cattle** (wild and domestic), **deer, antelope, bighorn sheep, goats, jungle fowl, mice, rats**— even a small group of **wallabies** (like small kangaroos) on Oahu. The long, low **mongooses** that often dart across roads in front of cars were brought to kill off the rats that wreaked havoc on sugarcane plantations. Unfortunately, people realized too late that rats are nocturnal while mongooses like to party during the day. Needless to say, their paths rarely crossed and both rats and mongooses were fruitful and multiplied.

Fish

Snorkeling and diving are wonderful in Hawaii. Darting in jerky unison around coral heads and sea plants, schools of fish surround human visitors to this underworld. Perhaps my favorite are the **parrotfish,** with their bright, iridescent colors. **Angelfish** could teach humans a thing or two about monogamy: They choose mates for life and forever swim in pairs. **Blowfish** are fun to watch when they feel threatened: They puff themselves up to more than twice their normal size; the thorns on their skin protrude, making predators think twice about attempting to swallow them.

Some of the other fish swimmers can see are **stripeys, Moorish idols,** and **triggerfish** such as the **humuhumunukunukuapuaa,** Hawaii's tiny state fish. Also moving through the ocean are awesome but gentle **manta rays,** whose wingspan can be as great as 20 feet; **brown stingrays,** which can grow as long as four feet; and **eagle rays.** Big-game fishing enthusiasts find plenty of **sailfish, Pacific blue marlin, striped marlin,** and **broadbill swordfish.** (Also see "Food and Drink" for information on edible fish.)

Although there are **sharks** in some of Hawaii's waters, as there are in all oceans, they tend to leave humans alone. Watch out for the elaborate jellyfish called the **Portuguese man-of-war,** whose hump protrudes above the water like a fin while its stinging tentacles dangle below.

Birds

Frigate birds, called *iwa* ("thief") in Hawaiian, could hardly be less neighborly. Instead of finding their own food, these seabirds glide through the air looking for other birds with fish clutched in their talons. They then attack these meal-carrying birds, forcing them to let go of the wriggling fish, which the frigate promptly snatches out of the sky. Other seabirds include the clumsy **Laysan gooney birds** and **tropic birds,** with their red or white tails.

Polynesian jungle fowl, which strut around Oahu's north shore, the path to Kauai's Fern Grotto, and other areas, are said to be descended from the chickens that arrived aboard canoes with Hawaii's Polynesian settlers. Their long, bright feathers resemble tresses of straight human hair.

The **nene goose,** Hawaii's state bird, lives at high altitudes on mountainsides on the Big Island and Maui. Also rarely seen is the **Hawaiian stilt,** which thrives in remote bodies of fresh water, mostly on the Big Island and Kauai. Hawaii is also home to a colorful variety of **cardinals, doves,** and **egrets** (some of which park themselves on the backs of cattle to enjoy a meal of insects).

Trees

The **koa,** Hawaii's tallest native tree, can pierce the air 60 to 80 feet above its base. It is also among the oldest species of trees in Hawaii. Its prized reddish wood and striking grain, once cut into 15-foot royal surfboards and 70-foot royal canoes, is still used to make handsome bowls, furniture, wall paneling, ukuleles, necklaces, and earrings. Complex religious rites were performed whenever a koa tree was felled to be transformed into a canoe. Unfortunately, these trees are no longer as abundant as they once were.

Koa forests throve long before human beings came to Hawaii. Botanists are stymied over how the koa originally reached Hawaiian shores, since its heavy seeds don't float. It seems to have come from Australia or Mauritius, off the coast of Africa, so it clearly had to travel across thousands of ocean miles.

Sacred to the Chinese, the **sandalwood** tree was probably brought to Hawaii by human beings. Like those of the koa, its seeds are too large to be eaten and excreted by birds, and too heavy to float on the ocean. But unlike more durable koa seeds, sandalwood seeds aren't viable for very long. Within several decades after Westerners and Hawaiian chiefs began getting rich by selling fragrant sandalwood to China to be made into incense or carvings, sandalwood forests had been almost completely decimated.

Ohia trees are noted for their fluffy blood-red blossoms, which are considered sacred to Pele, the volcano goddess. According to ancient Hawaiians, Madame Pele would send rain storms, claps of thunder, or volcanic eruptions if mortals were fool enough to pick one of her flowers. This is Hawaii's most common native tree.

The **kukui** (or candlenut) is Hawaii's state tree. Roasted and shelled kukui nuts became candles for ancient Hawaiians. Strings of these lamp-nuts were tended by children, whose job it was to keep them burning. Lamp oil was made by grinding the meat of the nuts. But their useful-ness did not end here. Dyes for kapa cloth were made from their husks, their oil became skin lotion (especially soothing after too much sun), and the nuts themselves were polished and made into gleaming neck-laces. You can find kukui nut necklaces for sale in stores today.

Two of my favorite trees in Hawaii are the **African tulip,** with its blazing crimson flowers; and the striking, smooth-barked **rainbow eu-calyptus tree,** its trunk decorated with bright red, yellow, and brown vertical stripes, as if someone had spilled paint down its torso. Also called the gum tree, the eucalyptus gives off a wonderful aroma. The **jacaranda,** with its pear-shaped mauve flowers, and the **monkeypod,** with its dangling, globular clusters of blossoms, are other beauties.

The **hapuu tree fern** of the Hawaiian rain forest always amazes me. As it grows up from the ground, the end of each branch is tightly coiled, like the top of a cello's neck. This plant takes more than half a century to reach its full height.

The yellow, buttercuplike blossoms of **hau** trees open yellow in the morning and turn red as the day goes by. The long, thin branches of this low-growing tree are like a mass of tangled, bony arms. Leaves of the **pandanus** are used for *lauhala* weaving ("lau" means leaves and "hala" is the Hawaiian name for the tree). Towering in rain forests and other areas, stands of **bamboo** serve as a musical instrument for the blowing wind. **Banyans,** with those tentacles dripping from their branches, can sprawl as wide as a house. One of the most impressive is in Lahaina on Maui. Don't be put off by the dark fruit of the **baobab;** it only *looks* like rats dangling by their tails. **Norfolks** and **ironwoods** (also called casuarinas) are two distinctly different types of evergreens. The first is a perfectly triangular pine, while the second is a wispy, windswept, somewhat asymmetrical affair. The wood of **kiawes,** also known as mesquite, is used for cooking, to add a scrumptious flavor to grilled food.

Flowers and Plants

With thousands of varieties, the **hibiscus** is Hawaii's state flower. Each bright blossom can be anywhere from an inch and a half to ten inches across and have single, double, or ruffled petals. Some flowers are one color, while others are two- or three-tone. The most common, however, are a bright, solid red.

Tiny-petaled **bougainvillea** bushes sprinkle pink, yellow, orange, white, purple, and red throughout Hawaii. These flowers are especially dramatic on the Big Island, where they often grow in stark contrast to desolate charcoal lava flows.

As soon as most visitors step off the plane, they are surrounded by the mesmerizing fragrance of **plumeria** (known as frangipani elsewhere). These petals from flowering trees are most commonly strung into the leis that many travelers find placed around their necks as part of the traditional Hawaiian lei greeting. Parks and other open areas fortunate enough to have these trees are enveloped by their wonderful perfume.

Ginger plants come in many shapes, colors, and sizes, from a few inches tall to 15 or more feet high. Visitors can wander through one of the largest ginger gardens in the world at Waimea Falls Park on Oahu. Another extensive ginger garden is Nani Mau Gardens in Hilo on the Big Island. The edible type of ginger root is widely used to flavor Asian and Polynesian cooking. Small, aromatic ginger petals were once more widely fashioned into leis than the larger plumeria. But since ginger only blossoms from June to December (unlike plumeria, which blooms year-round), and since it took far more ginger petals to create a decent lei, plumeria eventually won out. Until the 1960s, many young girls would hang ginger leis in their bedrooms, leaving them there to scent the air for months after they dried.

While white and yellow ginger were brought from the Himalayas, India, and the Caribbean in the 1880s, **shampoo ginger** probably came hundreds of years before, with the early Polynesian immigrants. It produces a bright-red, three-inch bulb. The thick juice of the ripe plant quenched thirst on long journeys. The clear no-suds liquid was, and still is, also used to wash hair, leaving it soft and silky. The Paul Mitchell hair care company has even turned it into a commercial product.

One of Hawaii's rarest plants is the **silversword.** Growing on the lunarlike heights of Maui's Haleakala volcano, it resembles a cone-shaped, gray sea anemone. This delicate-to-the-human-touch-yet-hardy-to-the-elements plant thrives where few others can. There are extreme temperature fluctuations at these heights; after a 90-degree day, there might be a snowfall at night. It is against the law to remove or even touch a silversword plant.

Here are some more of Hawaii's impressive blossoms:

Pikake ("peacock"), a sweet-smelling white jasmine that was named for Princess Kaiulani. Before her untimely death, she was known for her love of both peacocks and this flower.

Stiff, waxy **anthurium** has a pencil-like staff that sticks up in the center of the usually red (but sometimes green, white, pink, or orange) spade-shaped flower.

The most common type of **heliconia** is orangy-red and looks like a group of lobster claws stacked on top of each other.

The tall gold or orange **bird of paradise** looks like an abstract sculptor's version of its name. **Gardenias** emit a soft aroma and **oleander** come in red, pink, or white.

I often wear leis when in Hawaii, but until the day a friend put a deep purple **orchid** lei around my neck, I had never received such a barrage of compliments. Everywhere I went, people fingered the moist, fleshy blossoms with admiration. The flowers come in many other colors as well.

Another plant to keep an eye out for is the **ti plant.** Hawaiians still use it for wrapping and cooking food. Since it is flame retardant, it also serves as the lining for *imu* (earthen ovens dug into the ground). Unlike grass skirts, which originated on other islands, ti-leaf hula skirts are authentically Hawaiian. You may come across hikers with these leaves tied around their ankles or waists. Old-time Hawaiians will explain that a mischievous spirit hides behind bushes and rocks, waiting to trip up innocent passersby. However, since the ti plant is sacred to the god Lono, the spirit will not grab an ankle tied with its leaves.

Fruit

Not only can you enjoy fresh, juicy fruit in restaurants or roadside stands, but, especially while hiking, you can also pick quite a bit of it yourself. Coconuts, bananas, and pineapple are delicious in the 50th State. Here's a rundown on some of the other popular natural snacks:

Guavas are best for picking between June and October, when they are softest to the touch and unmarred. They contain five times more Vitamin C than oranges. The most common type of this thin-skinned fruit is the yellow, lemon-sized variety. Another, smaller kind is called the strawberry guava, because of its taste and red color.

The yellow, oval **lilikoi** (passion fruit) is ripe during the summer and fall. It grows on vines that drape themselves on bushes and over tree limbs. The vines of the small, round purple passion fruit burst into color with their white and lavender flowers. The vines of the yellow, banana-shaped banana passion fruit bloom with pink blossoms. Lilikoi makes a wonderfully refreshing beverage.

Growing on bushy, towering trees, **mangoes** are a favorite tropical fruit. They are extremely juicy and their meat is slippery when ripe (during the spring and summer). Part of the fun—especially for children—is making a mess while eating them.

Summer is the best time to pluck **papayas** off their skinny trees. They are best when they are just starting to turn yellow.

High up in lush, shady regions of Hawaii, **mountain apples** are waiting to be sampled. The trees bloom with fluffy red flowers. The small, pear-shaped fruit is red on the outside, with white meat inside. Mountain apples ripen between July and December.

Usually ripe in late May or early June, **Methley plums** (also called Kokee plums) are found throughout Kokee State Park on Kauai.

Be sure to try soft, sweet **lychee** and **poha** (Cape gooseberries). Peel the skin off the **red berries** that grow on coffee trees around November and suck on the two beans in each. The coating has a candylike flavor (but don't try to eat the beans!). **Avocados,** very popular in salads or pseudo-Japanese **sushi,** ripen from June to November in their towering trees.

THE HAWAIIAN ARTS AND OTHER PASTIMES

In the old days, the Hawaiian Islands themselves served as both a canvas for artistic expression and a playground for happy abandon. Stick-figure drawings were carved into the petrified lava flows that still blanket vast areas. Many of these petroglyph fields remain today, especially on the Big Island of Hawaii. Trees were whittled into totem pole–like *tikis*. The breasts of brightly plumed birds were plucked clean so that their feathers could be used to decorate cloaks and helmets worn by the *alii* (chiefs or aristocracy). Bowls and water containers made from gourds were often etched or painted with elaborate designs.

In the high art of **lauhala,** pandanus leaves were woven into baskets and sleeping mats. Roots, vines, and other fronds used for weaving were frequently dyed black, red, and white to create intricate patterns when braided. Especially among the alii, **surfing** was a favorite sport. People also amused themselves with foot and canoe races, wrestling matches, sliding down hillsides on sleds, and many other games. Singing, dancing the hula, and strumming the **ukeke** (a Hawaiian stringed instrument not to be confused with the ukulele, a Portuguese import) were also popular pastimes.

When American missionaries began arriving in 1820, they swiftly put an end to all this frivolity. As far as they seemed to be concerned, Hawaiians were simply having too much fun. Where once there had been pride and enjoyment, the missionaries instilled guilt and a sense of shame—for the scanty way Hawaiians dressed, their sexual freedom, their sensual dances, their music (which sounded atonal to Western ears).

Hawaiians had always been a spiritual people, with a strong and extremely strict religion. They prayed to and obeyed a variety of gods. However, as increasing numbers of foreigners had begun to pass through the Islands, Hawaiians began to question their confining *kapus* (taboos). Their gods, whom they had believed controlled the lives of all people, didn't seem to mind when foreigners broke divine rules. By chance, it was just before the arrival of the missionaries that Hawaiians decided that they had had enough and did away with their old gods, trashing ancient *heiau* (temples) and celebrating their newfound freedom. Western religion arrived just in time to fill the void left by the abandonment of Hawaiian beliefs.

The Arts

After decades of suppression by missionaries, the arts were briefly brought back to life in the late 1800s by King David Kalakaua, who earned himself the nickname "The Merrie Monarch" in the process. Then the overthrow of the monarchy and U.S. annexation of the Islands sent this side of Hawaiian culture back underground. It was not until the 1970s that Hawaiian arts began to experience the renaissance that is still apparent today.

Some say that this renewed pride in things Hawaiian was sparked by the 1974 voyage of the *Hokulea,* a 60-foot reconstruction of an ancient Polynesian sailing canoe. With several voyages back and forth to Tahiti and throughout the Pacific, this vessel proved once and for all that the stories told in ancient Hawaiian chants and dances had been historically correct: The ancient Hawaiians had indeed been master mariners who had set out for and arrived at the Hawaiian Islands on purpose, not by accident.

Ancient traditions that had been forbidden by the missionaries were once again embraced. Today, many hotels give free classes in *lei*-making, *lauhala* weaving, and *hula* dancing. Some hotels, especially those along the Kohala Coast on the Big Island, are virtual museums, packed with Hawaiian and other Pacific art and artifacts. A few Big Island hotels conduct tours of their art collections or *petroglyph* fields.

One contemporary artist who has dedicated himself to preserving ancient events and traditions is noted Hawaiian-Irish sculptor Rocky Kaiouliokahikoloehu Jensen. Through his work at **Hale Naua III, the Society of Hawaiian Artists,** Jensen and other members use art to foster an understanding of and appreciation for Hawaiian culture. They research artistic techniques and details of Hawaiian history by digging through dusty archives and family records, by visiting Oahu's renowned Bishop Museum, and by talking to old-timers. With chants, songs, featherwork, watercolors, oil paintings, photographs, sculpture, and other mediums, they pull the past into the present.

Jensen uses a variety of Island woods for his powerful sculpture, including kiawe, hau, koa, and mango. His work has been sold for thousands of dollars, such as the giant tiki purchased for $20,000 and on display at the McDonald's in Waimanalo, Oahu. Artwork done by

Hale Naua members has been shown all over Hawaii, including the State Capitol and Honolulu's City Hall.

Also working to keep old art forms alive is Kanae Keawe, a craftsman based in Hilo on the Big Island. In addition to featherwork, lauhala weaving, lei-making, and woodcarving, he has tried to recapture the lost skill of making *kapa*. Ancient Hawaiians created this cloth by pounding water-soaked bark. Unfortunately, few records remain of the specifics of this intricate, time-consuming process, so Keawe has had to teach himself by trial and error. He holds kapa-making seminars (sponsored by the Bishop Museum, the Honolulu Academy of Arts, Hawaiian civic groups, the University of Hawaii, and other institutions) throughout the state.

For the most part, what is sold in Hawaii today (such as that at Oahu's Polynesian Cultural Center) is the kind of bark cloth called *tapa* that is still produced in Fiji and other Pacific Islands. (It makes gorgeous wall hangings, by the way.) Unlike bark cloth from elsewhere, Hawaiian *kapa* is often imprinted with a watermark design (the kind you see when you hold a sheet of bond paper up to the light).

In the old days, kapa was decorated with a wide variety of patterns and colors, from black, brown, and red to lavender, blue, and yellow. Men wore *kapa malo* (loin cloths) and women dressed in *kapa pa'u* (long skirts). Capes were used by both sexes, and sandals, blankets, house partitions, even wicks for stone lamps were also made from kapa. Beating out a length of the cloth could take anywhere from several hours to a full day.

Women were responsible for creating this cloth—no simple feat. First they had to soak the bark of mulberry trees in the sea for a week. Then they pounded it and soaked it for another seven days. After beating it again until it was thin enough, and allowing it to be dried and bleached by the sun, they painted or stamped designs onto it using woodcuts, ferns, or bamboo to apply dyes made from fruit, roots, leaves, or minerals. As if this weren't enough, they often scented the kapa by blending fragrances into the dyes.

Having the right anvil for pounding the kapa was very important. Women often judged the quality of their implements by the sound they made when struck, since different wood made different music. Women living a distance apart in the same village would sometimes communicate with each other through their percussive thumping.

When ancient Hawaiians looked up into the sky and saw fluffy clouds, they knew that what they were really seeing was kapa spread out to dry by the goddess Hina, a renowned kapa maker. To hold the cloth down, she put large stones at the corners. When Hawaiians heard thunder, they were convinced that the weighty stones were being blown away by strong winds. When they saw lightning, they understood that

Hina was rolling up her kapa and sunlight was glinting off the moving cloth.

Beginning in the late 18th century, when Westerners introduced Hawaiians to their own more durable woven fabric, the painstaking production of delicate kapa eventually came to an end.

Featherwork was another prized art in old Hawaii. Deep in the forests, birds were caught with poles or nets smeared with a gluelike paste. While their breast feathers may have been snatched off, the birds were not necessarily killed. Their brilliantly colored plumes, sewn so close together that they looked and felt like smooth velvet, were fashioned into royal leis, capes, and helmets. Helmets were often topped off with clumps of human hair from unfortunate enemies.

If ancient Hawaiians wanted to know what they looked like in all their feathered finery, they simply gazed into a mirror. They found their reflections in the smooth, flat slabs of lava rock they put in water or shined with oil. Combs carved from tortoise shell or bone were worn as decoration in women's hair. Necklaces were set off with pendants of whale's teeth, kukui nuts, shells, or wood strung on human hair. Bracelets were often made from the tusks of boars. During dance performances or other entertainment, some men wore necklaces and anklets made from row upon row of dogs' teeth.

With the demise of kapa, **quilts,** introduced by missionary women, began to replace Hawaiian blankets. These New England women stitched pieces of cloth together in geometric patterns. But since woven cloth was new in Hawaii and scraps were scarce, whole lengths of material were used instead. Known as *puiki* in Hawaiian, Island quilts developed their own distinctive style.

Remember those snowflakes you used to cut from folded paper as a child? Well, similar cutout patterns form the basis of designs for Hawaiian quilts. Nature is strongly reflected in Island patterns. Some say that the first Hawaiian-style quilt was inspired when a woman saw the shadow of the branches of a tree splashed across a sheet she had laid out to bleach in the sun. Hawaiian quilts are generally two colors: a bold, bright fabric appliqued onto a white background. Designs suggesting birds, fruit, flowers, and trees are common.

Considered real treasures, these comforters are very expensive today, whether new or antique. Since stitches are so intricate, they can take anywhere from several months to two years to produce. Finishing a quilt is such a major accomplishment that, in the old days, everyone honored the occasion by drinking *koele palau* (sweet potato wine) for a week. If you can't afford the few thousand dollars it could cost you to commission a quilt of your own, at least take a look at those on display in places such as the corridors of the Mauna Kea Beach Hotel on the Big Island.

Nineteenth-century whalers also made a major contribution to art in Hawaii, in the form of **scrimshaw.** Now Maui is one of the best places in the world to buy these bones, teeth, and tusks etched with nautical and other designs. The centuries-old Japanese art of **raku pottery** is another foreign form of creative expression that has found a place in Hawaii. Red-hot ceramics are removed from the kiln and put in a covered container filled with straw, dried leaves, paper, and other flamable materials that create irregular patterns on the surface of the pottery when they suddenly catch fire. This pottery is characterized by its cracked glaze, darkened non-glazed areas, and textured, matte finish. You can learn about this process at the **Hui Noeau,** an art institute in upcountry Maui.

With the beating of **ipu drums** in ancient evenings, everyone knew it was time for **hula** dances to begin. Surprisingly enough, hula was first performed exclusively by men. It was part of a religious ritual and was considered outside the realm of proper female activity. Much of Hawaii's history was passed on through the hand and hip movements of the meaning-laden dances and through the accompanying chants. In the more fanciful dances, performers would tell humorous tales of the soap-opera love lives of the alii.

Modern hula, now danced almost exclusively by women, tends to be more graceful and sensual than the ancient style of dance. The bright green ti-leaf skirts worn by dancers are authentically Hawaiian (if not somewhat skimpier than in the past), but the grass skirts you'll also see actually originated elsewhere in the Pacific.

Whether or not people have visited Hawaii, most are familiar with its trademark (if sometimes sentimental) **music.** From 1935, when it was first broadcast from the Moana Hotel in Waikiki, until the 1970s, the popular "Hawaii Calls" radio program introduced many main-landers to these Pacific sounds.

Contemporary Island music has been influenced by everything from ancient Hawaiian chants, Christian hymns, and European classical pieces to Portuguese **ukuleles** and Mexican cowboys playing Spanish guitars. *Ukulele,* by the way, is a Hawaiian word meaning "jumping flea." Hawaiians thought the fast-moving hands of Portuguese immigrants on this, four-stringed instrument looked like they were busy scratching fleas. This is not to be confused with the three-stringed **ukeke,** a Hawaiian instrument that was around before Europeans arrived. Other early instruments were the shell trumpet, the nose flute, and gourd and ti leaf whistles.

"Aloha Oe," probably the best-known Hawaiian melody, was written as a love song in 1878 by Liliuokalani, Hawaii's last queen. Also during the 1870s, King Kamehameha V hired a German composer to teach music to the royal family. The king wrote the words to "Hawaii Pono'i" (set to music by this composer), once Hawaii's national anthem and now the state song.

Its dulcet tones long associated with Hawaii, the steel guitar (*kila kila*) was developed by 15-year-old Joseph Kekuku in 1889. Also called slack key guitar, it is played by sliding a steel bar against its loosened steel strings. With the renaissance of Hawaiian music in the 1970s, slack key guitar playing was revived. However, it remains music with a very local appeal. It is generally played at family gatherings or while sitting around talking story (shooting the breeze) with friends.

Fun and Games

The best-known and most popular ancient sport, **surfing** was once called "the sport of kings." This was because certain beaches and kinds of boards could only be used by the alii. Boards were once cut from koa or breadfruit trees, then lovingly carved, stained, and preserved with a rubbing down of glistening kukui oil. After missionaries succeeded in suppressing surfing—they were aghast that it was done in such scanty clothing, and sometimes even naked!—the sport made its comeback in the early 1900s. Travelers from all over would come to learn at the expert hands of the "beachboys" who helped make Waikiki famous.

Canoes were often used for races, sometimes involving bets that caused the defeated to lose land or even wives. **Konane,** similar to checkers, was played with black and white stones. Children amused themselves by flying kites made from kapa or pandanus leaves, walking on stilts, swinging from vines, or throwing square balls made from woven pandanus leaves.

During the annual **Makahiki Festival,** bellicose pursuits were pushed aside in favor of pleasant diversions. This season of peace, lasting from October to February, was celebrated with wild feasting and heavy-duty competitions in games. Today, travelers can take part in annual revivals of this ancient event at Waimea Falls Park on Oahu in October or at the very local, very popular Makahiki festival on Molokai in January. The games include *ulu maika* (lawn bowling), *'o'o ihe* (spear hurling), *kukini* (foot races), *pohaku ho 'oikaika* (throwing a weighty rock or shotputting), *hukihuki* (tug of war), *uma* (handwrestling), *haka moa* (arm wrestling in a circle while standing on one leg), and *moa pahe'e* (sliding a wooden dart across the grass through two sticks).

Hawaiians didn't need snow to go sledding (although they could certainly find the white stuff at the summit of Mauna Kea on the Big Island). Children slid down hillsides on clusters of ti leaves. Adults had the sport called *holua,* the highlight of the Makahiki festival. Competitors lay on narrow wooden sleds, called *papa,* and whizzed headfirst (sometimes faster than 40 miles an hour) down a runway made from piled, packed lava rocks cushioned with grass and doused with hundreds of gallons of water. You can see a remnant of one of these impressive runways on the Big Island.

(Also see Festivals and Special Events in ''Nuts and Bolts.'')

FOOD AND DRINK

The old saying "You are what you eat" couldn't be more true than in Hawaii. The food here is a melange of American, Hawaiian, Japanese, Chinese, Portuguese, Korean, Filipino, European—and so are the people. Some ancient Hawaiian culinary traditions have survived, but many have been lost, a few happily so. No one today seems to miss the old practices of eating dogmeat, having separate dining quarters for men and women, and banning women from consuming pork, bananas, coconuts, and other "manly" foods.

Using planting, gathering, digging, and cooking utensils made of wood, ancient Hawaiians lived off such staples as breadfruit, sweet potatoes, taro, bananas, and coconuts. They used shells to remove skins from cooked taro and breadfruit and fashioned knives from bamboo, rocks, and sharks' teeth. Gourds, sometimes painted with intricate geometric designs, were transformed into bowls and drinking cups. Wooden plates were reserved for high-ranking individuals. These *alii* also used special bowls to dispose of their leftovers and bones. It was the job of their servants to hide this uneaten food so that no one could use it to cast evil spells on the alii.

As in the old days, locals today have luaus to celebrate births, birthdays, weddings, and simply being alive. These are quite different from the commercial affairs most tourists are herded off to. At these gatherings of family and friends, someone might spontaneously begin to sing, or play the slack key guitar. Nothing feels packaged or rigidly programmed. If you scour local newspapers and listen to radio stations, you might be lucky enough to find out about a luau sponsored by a civic organization or other group to raise money for one cause or another.

You'll have plenty of chances to sample **pupus** (appetizers), usually a variety of tidbits served on a platter during happy hours. Also be sure to try the trademark dish of modern Hawaii: a **plate lunch** (also called **mixed plate,** a **Bento lunch,** or a **box lunch**). This blend of Japanese, Hawaiian, and Chinese food comes in the form of a meat or fish entree served with two scoops of white rice (which isn't considered rice unless it's moist and sticky), and a scoop of macaroni salad. It's often eaten with chopsticks and is sold in many Mom-and-Pop fast-food joints. Also look out for **Hawaiian-style curry,** which is green and not very hot.

Here are some more of Hawaii's most popular foods:

From the Sea

Ahi: Hawaiian big-game yellowfin tuna that often turns up grilled, ground into burgers, baked inside ti leaves, or served raw as sashimi or in sushi
   Aku: Skipjack tuna
   A⟨u: Marlin or broadbill swordfish
   Hapu: Hawaiian sea bass
   Lehi: Orange snapper
   Limu: One of the few ancient Hawaiian culinary traditions that thrives today is the preparation and consumption of *limu,* commonly known as seaweed. This vegetable is extremely rich in vitamins and minerals. It is served with raw fish as part of sashimi and sushi or cooked in soups and stews. Today, some Hawaiians still collect edible seaweed that has washed ashore, just as their ancestors did. Many varieties of this sea plant are also an important part of the diet in Asian cultures, such as Japan's. The Japanese presence in Hawaii has added to the wealth of traditional Hawaiian seaweed dishes. Most of the seaweed used for sushi in the state is imported from Japan.
   Lomi lomi: Salmon diced with green leaf onions and tomatoes, served cold; Hawaiians created this dish with the salted and smoked salmon introduced by 19th-century whalers.
   Lomi o⟨io: With its bones soft enough to chew, raw bonefish is mashed and mixed with limu.
   Mahi-mahi: A dolphin fish—not a mammal, so it's no relation to Flipper; the texture has been compared to moist pork chops. Perhaps Hawaii's best-known fish, it is especially delicious grilled.
   Onaga: Red snapper
   Ono: A game fish also called wahoo. The very appropriate name is the Hawaiian word for "delicious."
   Opakapaka: Pink snapper; popular for the first meal of the day.
   Poke: Cubed or sliced raw ahi, mixed with pounded limu, tomatoes, onions, and kukui nuts
   Sashimi: A Japanese favorite; paper-thin slices of raw fish
   Sushi: Becoming almost as common as tacos in some mainland cities, this dish is made by rolling rice, vegetables, and/or raw fish in seaweed. It is even served in some McDonald's in Hawaii.
   Uku: Gray snapper
   Ulua: Deep-sea pompano

From the Land

Breadfruit: This large, round, starchy vegetable was brought to Hawaii by the early Polynesians. It is served baked, fried, roasted, or boiled. Its mild flavor makes it a good side dish with highly seasoned food.

Chicken luau: Cooked with coconut milk and taro leaves

Kalua pig: The centerpiece of any luau; the entire (often deboned) porker is cooked in an *imu* (an earthen oven). The pig is stuffed with fiery hot lava rocks, wrapped in moistened burlap bags and ti leaves, surrounded by more hot rocks, and roasted in the pit for several hours, along with breadfruit, yams, fish, and other goodies. The crispy skin is considered the best part by many. At some luaus, guests are invited to observe the ceremony involving the removal of the pig from the ground.

Kim chee: Korean pickled and spiced cabbage or other vegetables

Kula or Maui onions: Some of the sweetest onions around. You may be lucky enough to find them made into breaded rings and served with spicy mustard.

Lau lau: Ground pork and/or fish wrapped in taro or ti leaves and then steamed or baked

Macadamia nuts: Perhaps macadamia nuts taste so good because they are so long in the making: It takes about seven years for a tree to grow its first nuts, then about eight more years before it is producing to capacity. They're also hard to get to: 300 pounds of pressure per square inch is needed to crack their shells. However, you won't have to worry about cracking them. They are sold in endless varieties, but shell-covered isn't one of them. You'll find them plain, salted, dipped in chocolate, or dressed in caramel or coconut glaze. You can also sample them in cookies, ice cream, pies, and on and on. They are rich and creamy in texture, and far from low in calories. Although they contain no cholesterol, they are usually roasted in coconut oil, a saturated fat.

Manapua: This steamed dough stuffed with pork or black beans originated in China.

Poi: pounded, fermented taro root, cooked and mashed into a sticky paste. Sort of brownish-purple-gray in color, this side dish, served with meat or fish, has a mild, slightly sour or tangy taste. When mainlanders say poi tastes like wallpaper paste, Hawaiians remark that they don't know what that means since wallpaper paste isn't eaten in Hawaii. "You keep your sauerkraut and cottage cheese and we'll keep our poi," they joke. This dish is eaten with the fingers. Two-finger poi is thicker than the three-finger variety, because it takes fewer fingers to spoon up.

Portuguese sausage: Spicy, popular, often eaten with rice for breakfast or used in Portuguese bean soup to add flavor

Saimin: Noodle soup with dumplings and vegetables topped with sliced pork and/or seafood. Some say it originated in Japan while others maintain it was inspired by a Chinese dish called *sae mein*.

SPAM: Remember that canned meat you haven't gone near since the days when your mother used to stick it in your lunch box? Well, in Hawaii everybody eats SPAM with a vengeance. This chopped pork shoulder and ham, in its blue Hormel tin, was introduced to Hawaii during the 1940s, mainly for use by the military. It thus has come to be referred to as *S*outh *P*acific *A*rmy *M*eat, but its name is actually a contraction of "spiced ham." People in Hawaii eat it like a delicacy, putting it in soups, stews, on the side for breakfast, and as the main event for lunch and dinner. As a matter of fact, since 1987, Maui has hosted an annual summer SPAM cookoff where both professional and novice chefs compete for prizes for the tastiest, most creative recipes using the meat.

Teriyaki beef: A spicy Japanese dish made with soy sauce, sugar, vegetables, and strips of meat; can also be made with chicken or fish

Taro: Starchy root from which poi is made; also served baked or roasted. When cooked, it looks and tastes something like a potato. Be sure to try highly addictive taro chips, sold in grocery stores like potato chips. Taro leaves are used to wrap meat or seafood for steaming or boiling.

Ti leaves: Ancient Hawaiians believed that the ti plant held a godly power that warded off evil spirits. Food is often wrapped in these leaves for cooking or storage. The genuinely Hawaiian hula skirts are made from ti leaves (as opposed to the grass skirts you'll see a lot, which actually originated elsewhere in the Pacific).

Sweets

To satisfy a sweet tooth in Hawaii, you can start with all kinds of juicy, fresh fruit, including papayas, guavas, mangos, bananas, pineapple, coconuts, mountain apples, plums, and poha berries. Here are some other local favorites:

Haupia: Jiggly coconut pudding cut into squares. People often bring it to luaus the way mainlanders might carry a bottle of wine to a friend's house for dinner.

Lilikoi: Also known as passion fruit; makes a tart pie or is sweetened and turned into a beverage, often mixed with other fruit juices

Malasadas: From Portugal; sugary balls of fried dough often called "holeless doughnuts"

Manju: Sweet Japanese pastry with black bean paste inside

Molokai sweet bread: Reflecting the "chop suey" heritage of many locals, this bread, based on a Portuguese recipe, is created in a Japanese bakery on Molokai.

Shave ice: Called a snow cone in some parts of the mainland, this refreshing cup of crushed ice is flavored with syrup made from lilikoi, pineapple, coconut, or other fruit.

Other Snacks

The Original Maui Kitch'n Cook'd Potato Chips, those thick and crunchy wonders, have played a large part in changing the face of potato chips across the mainland. There are other chips with "Maui" in their names, but this brand is the best. If you're on the Big Island, Hilo also produces a version.

Looking like potato chips with purple threads running through them, **taro chips** are also delicious. Other nibblets eaten straight from the bag are dried shrimp, which can be very salty. They are also used in cooking.

Beverages

Sure, you'll find plenty of rum-based **Mai Tais** and **Blue Hawaiis,** but for my money, nothing is more enjoyable than Hawaii's wonderful fruit juices, especially **guava nectar** (a pink beverage that has a thick, grainy texture something like pear nectar) and **lilikoi.**

If you want a potent kick, try some **okolehao,** a Hawaiian whiskey made from the root of the ti plant.

THE HAWAIIAN TONGUE

Once, as I was passing through a parking lot outside a hotel in Kauai, I overheard a mainlander struggling to extract a piece of information from a tour bus driver. "Is this the bus to Wammy?" she asked. When he replied, "Where?" and she repeated her question, his face remained perplexed. Finally she snapped in indignant annoyance, "Wammy Canyon, I said!" She seemed to think that the driver should have known immediately that what she meant was "Waimea (why-*may*-ah) Canyon." This woman was like the proverbial Ugly American who visits Italy and raises her voice—in English—when an Italian does not understand her. If she had paid any attention to the spelling of the word and taken a few moments to bone up on the pronunciation of Hawaiian, she would have been showing respect and staving off hassles at the same time. A local joke tells of a tourist on his way to a *luau* (feast) who ends up at a *lua* (toilet).

The credit for first putting Hawaiian on paper goes to the New England missionaries, who arrived in the islands in 1820. As they created an alphabet, their Western ears had a tough time sorting through the language's dozens of different sounds. Unable to hear the distinction between *t* and *k*, or *l* and *r*, or *b* and *p*, for instance, the missionaries whittled the language down to a mere 12 letters. *Honoruru* turned into *Honolulu*; *Ranai* became *Lanai*; *Mauna Roa* was transformed into *Mauna Loa*; and *taboo* into *kapu*. Although missionaries forever altered the way island tongues would move, Hawaiians learned to read with voracious speed. Within a little more than two decades, they were among the most literate people in the world. Today, one of the few arenas where the legacy of Hawaii's ancient Polynesians lives on in full force is in the state's street signs and place names, the vast majority of which are Hawaiian. Familiarizing yourself with the pronunciation of the language will make it easier for you to ask directions, get around, and remember where you've been (or even the name of your hotel).

Since it's phonetic, Hawaiian is not nearly as difficult to pronounce as it appears to the uninitiated. It consists of only seven consonants (*h*, *k*, *l*, *m*, *n*, *p*, *w*) and five vowels (*a*, *e*, *i*, *o*, *u*), and no letter is silent. Each syllable ends with a vowel. The accent is usually on the next to last syllable of a word.

Consonants sound just as they do in English, with th exception of *w*. This letter is pronounced like a *v* when it precedes the last vowel of a word (such as *ewa* or *Kahoolawe*). Vowels sound like those in Spanish: *a* as in *around; e* like the *a* in *day; i* like the *ee* in *see; o* as in *so;* and *u* as in *sue*. When two or three vowels are together, they each get their own syllable (unless they are part of a diphthong). The double *o* in *Kahoolawe* sounds like "oh-oh" and the double *a* in *Kapaa* sounds like "ah-ah." The four diphthongs are *au*, pronounced *ow; ae* and *ai,* both pronounced like the *y* in *sky;* and *ei*, which rhymes with *hay*.

A mark like a backwards apostrophe was once commonly used in many words to signal a sharp pause between syllables. This punctuation is rarely seen in writing anymore and pronunciations have changed accordingly. To purists, however, Hawaii (Hawaiʻi) will always be "Hah-vyʻee." You'll also hear some people correctly pronounce the names of Neighbor Islands: "cow-*wah*ʻee" (Kauaʻi), "*mole*-oh-*kah*ʻee" (Molokaʻi), and "lah-*nah*ʻee" (Lanaʻi) instead of "cow-*why*," "*mole*-oh-kye," and "lah-*nye*." In this book, I've used this mark only when two letters might otherwise appear to be a diphthong, to indicate the difference between *pau* ("pow"—finished) and *paʻu* ("*pah*-oo"—a long skirt), for instance.

You'll notice that even though quite a few names are long, in many cases syllables are simply repeated. Take, for example, one of the rainiest places in the world, *Mt. Waialeale* (why *ah*-lay *ah*-lay) on Kauai, or the historic valley on the Big Island of Hawaii called *Pohakuhaku* (poh *hah*-koo *hah*-koo). Wrapping your tongue around *humuhumunukunukuapuaa* (a small trigger fish with a shark-sized name) may appear an impossible feat at first. But if you look closely, you'll see that the trick is to sound redundant: *hoo*-moo *hoo*-moo *noo*-koo *noo*-koo *ah*-poo *ah*-ah.

Most residents today will greet you with "aloha" and say "mahalo" instead of "thank you." Knowing other common Hawaiian words can prevent you from going places you shouldn't, such as into a men's room (many of which are marked *kane*) if you're a *wahine* (woman). When you don't understand what people are saying, the Hawaiian language will rarely be the reason. Japanese, Korean, Tagalog, Cantonese, and Pidgin, the local dialect, are far more widely spoken. Sometimes referred to as "lazy English," Pidgin is used with a real flourish among young Hawaiians and other locals. Originating with the laborers who came to work on Hawaii's plantations, it is a colorful blend of Hawaiian, English, Cantonese, Portuguese, and a chop suey of other tongues.

Its vocabulary and pronunciation can vary from island to island and even region to region.

When Hawaiian residents speak English, their accent tends to be sing-songy, elevating in pitch at the end of a sentence. Someone who answers your telephone call might ask you to "Hold on, yeh?" A person who gives you directions might end with, "Simple, yeh?" Be sure to spend some time "talking story" (chatting or gossiping) with locals.

Not all communication in Hawaii is either oral or written. When someone raises his hand with the three middle fingers down and the thumb and pinky extended and gives it a couple of quick shakes, this is a greeting or a good-natured signal to "hang loose" ("relax" or "cool out").

Here are some common Hawaiian and Pidgin words and expressions:

aa (*ah*-ah): the rough kind of lava

ae (eye): yes

ahi (*ah*-hee): yellowfin tuna; or sometimes albacore or big-eye tuna

aikane (eye-*kah*-nay): friend

alii (ah-*lee*-ee): Hawaiian chief, royalty, person or people of high rank

aloha (ah-*low*-ha): welcome, hello, good-bye, love, friendship, . . .

aole (ah-*oh*-lay): no

brah (bra): bro' (brother), friend

cockaroach: to steal something or take something in an underhanded manner

da kine (dah kyne): thingamajig, whatchamacallit

diamondhead: east (toward Diamond Head on Oahu)

ewa (*ay*-vah—as in Eva Gabor): west (toward Oahu's Ewa Plantation)

hale (*hah*-lay): house

haole (*how*-lee): Caucasian, mainlander, foreigner

hapa (*hah*-pah): half

hapa-haole (*hah*-pah *how*-lee): part Caucasian and part Hawaiian; not authentically Hawaiian

hauoli la hanau (how-*oh*-lee lah hah-*now*): Happy Birthday

hauoli makahiki hou (how-*oh*-lee mah-kah-*hee*-key *ho*-oo): Happy New Year

heiau (hey-ee-*ow*): ancient Hawaiian temple

holo holo (*hoe*-low *hoe*-low): to cruise, bar hop, go from place to place, visit

hono (*hoe*-know): bay

hoolaulea (ho-oh-lau-*lay*-ah): gathering, celebration

Howzit? How goes it? What's happening?

hula (*who*-lah): traditional Hawaiian dance

imu (*ee*-moo): underground oven still used in luaus

kahuna (kah-*who*-nah): Hawaiian priest

kai (kye): ocean

kamaaina (kah-mah-*eye*-nah): longtime resident

kane (*kah*-nay): man

kapu (kah-*poo*): taboo, forbidden, off limits, keep out

kau kau (cow cow): food

keiki (*kay*-kee): child

kiawe (key-*ah*-vay): mesquite tree or wood

koa (*ko*-ah): an increasingly scarce tree prized for its wood

kokua (ko-*koo*-ah): help

lanai (lah-*nye*): terrace, balcony, patio, porch

lauhala (low-*hah*-lah): pandanus leaves (used for weaving)

lei (lay): long necklace made of flowers

li' dat (lie dat): like that

li' dis (lie dis): like this

lilikoi (*lee*-lee-koy): passion fruit

lua (*loo*-ah): toilet

luau (*loo*-ow): feast, celebration

mahalo (mah-*hah*-low): thank you

mahi mahi (*mah*-hee *mah*-hee): dolphin fish (not the mammal)

makai (mah-*kye*): in the direction of the sea

malihini (*mah*-lee-*hee*-nee): visitor, newcomer

malo (*mah*-low): loin cloth once worn by Hawaiian men

mauka (*mow*-kah): toward the mountains, inland

mauna (*mow*-nah): mountain

mele kalikimaka (*may*-lay keh-*lee*-key-mah-kah): Merry Christmas

muumuu (moo-moo or moo-oo-moo-oo): roomy, full-length dress

ohana (oh-*hah*-nah): clan, family

okole (oh-*ko*-lay): buttocks

onago (oh-*nah*-go): snapper

ono (*oh*-no): a fish similar to mackeral; also meaning that something tastes delicious

opakapaka (oh-*pah*-kah-*pah*-kah): pink snapper

pahoehoe (pah-*hoy*-hoy): smooth or ropy lava

pakalolo (pah-kah-*low*-low): marijuana

pali (*pah*-lee): cliff

paniolo (pah-nee-*oh*-low): cowboy in Hawaii

pau (pow): finished

pau hana time (pow *hah*-nah time): when the work day is over

pa'u (*pah*-oo): a long skirt once worn by Hawaiian women

poi (poy): gooey, porridgelike food made from cooked and pounded taro root

puka (*poo*-kah): hole

pupu (*poo*-poo): hors d'oeuvres

shaka! (*shah*-kah): All right! Great! Excellent!

suck 'em up: go drinking

talk story: chew the cud, chat, gossip

tutu (too-too) or **tutu wahine** (too-too wah-*hee*-nay): grandmother

ukulele (oo-koo-*lay*-lay): small, guitarlike instrument with four strings; literally ''leaping flea''

wahine (wah-*hee*-nay): woman

wikiwiki (*wee*-kee-*wee*-kee): fast, quick

THE BEST PLACES FOR...

To help you decide which island or islands to visit, here is a rundown of the best places in Hawaii for various pursuits. I compiled this section with the following question in mind: "What would I be sure to tell a friend who had all the time in the world to explore, play, and relax in Hawaii?" Individual island chapters have additional details.

ADVENTURE: In a 23-foot-long rubber raft, you can cruise **Kauai's** northern shore, where the dramatic cliffs of the Na Pali Coast rise from the electric-blue water. The raft is small enough to zip past waterfalls and into craggy caves at the bottom of the cliffs. This area is frequented by sea turtles and dolphins jump out of the water as if their moves had been choreographed. Excursions run during the spring and summer when the rough water is at its calmest.

On **Maui,** the 38-mile bike ride down Haleakala volcano is spectacular. The road winds through magnificent scenery with frequent changes in sights and aroma. You can take the late-morning ride, but I highly recommend the sunrise excursion, even though you'll have to leave at around 3 a.m. to get to the summit on time. You'll ride down after watching the sun come up over the crater. If you'd like to become better acquainted with the stark crater, which is about the size of Manhattan Island, arrange to go horseback riding or hiking in it.

Another summit worth seeing is that of snow-capped Mauna Kea on **the Big Island,** where immense telescopes gaze at the heavens. Also visit the moonscape of Hawaii Volcanoes National Park on this island. Waipio Valley, a deep dip along the northern coast, hasn't changed a whole lot since the time of ancient Hawaiians. Take a shuttle tour in a four-wheel-drive jeep or go horseback riding here. The narrow "roads" are actually rocky riverbeds, and flowers and thick vegetation are everywhere. The black-sand beach is a great locale for a picnic, but swimming is best in the river that cuts across the sand, leading to the ocean.

On **Molokai,** a 3.2-mile trail snakes down a 1600-foot-tall cliff on the north shore overlooking a huge peninsula that protrudes into the Pacific like the tongue of a giant. Hiking the trail is certainly possible, but most people go on the backs of sure-footed mules. Once below, they are given a tour of the area made famous by the victims of Hansen's Disease who were once forced to live here. At Molokai Ranch Wildlife Park, take a safari through land that closely resembles the East African and Asian habitats of the exotic animals that now roam freely here in the Pacific.

Helicopter rides are especially exciting on **the Big Island,** particularly when a volcano is erupting, and on **Kauai,** with its sprawling Waimea Canyon and Na Pali Coast.

Biking is a good way to tour the islands. Among the companies that arrange two-wheel excursions are: On the Loose Bicycle Vacations, 1030 Merced Street, Berkeley, CA 94707, (415) 527–4005; and Vermont Bicycle Touring, Box 711, Bristol, VT 05443-0711, (802) 453–4811.

(Also see Roughing It and Unusual Sports in this chapter.)

ART: Hawaii probably isn't the first place you think of going when you're in the market for quality paintings, sculpture, and ceramics. However, Oahu, Maui, Kauai, and the Big Island are peppered with thriving, tasteful galleries. **Maui** weighs in with nearly 50 art showplaces, some featuring the work of locally known artists while others emphasize those with international reputations. You can arrange to take a Maui Art Tour, complete with a gourmet picnic: You'll be driven to the studios of a couple of artists to discuss their work with them. Art expos and festivals are sprinkled throughout the year. A few Kaanapali Beach hotels, such as the Westin Maui and the Hyatt Regency Maui, are virtual museums of enormous sculptures, basketball player–sized vases, and weathered artifacts from the Pacific, Asia, and Europe.

If hotels that look like spectacular museums are your thing, you'll get your fill along the **the Big Island**'s Kohala Coast. Art tours are conducted regularly at the Mauna Kea Beach Hotel. The Hyatt Regency Waikoloa is another art-lover's dream. On **Kauai,** the Westin Kauai also has a fabulous collection.

(Also see Shopping in this chapter.)

BEACHES: As far as beaches in breathtaking settings are concerned, Hawaii has an abundance of riches. However, because the Pacific can be quite rough, some are better suited to sunbathing and photographing than to swimming.

On **Oahu,** there is no question that with hulking Diamond Head in the background, **Waikiki Beach** is a striking setting. However, especially during the winter months, people are packed body to body on the sand. This is a good place to learn to surf or to take an outrigger canoe ride. Most of Oahu's hotels are clustered in this area. Kite flying is all the rage at **Ala Moana Park,** where the waters are protected by a reef. **Hanauma Bay Beach Park** is a mecca for snorklers and divers. This palm-shaded crescent is backed by mountains. Only expert surfers can negotiate the crashing waves at **Sunset Beach.** Waves can rise to 30 feet during the winter.

On **Maui, Kapalua Bay,** in the tranquil north, is shaded by coconut palms and has an exceptional view of Molokai. Despite the hotels and condos that line **Kaanapali,** this gentle curve is the kind of beach many people fantasize about. When locals want to get away from the crowds, they head for quiet **Big Beach** in the south. The beaches in **Wailea** are much less developed than Kaanapali, but anyone who chooses to stay in this area will have many of the same conveniences in the hotels and condos here.

On **Kauai,** it will seem as if the winding dirt road goes on forever, but when you finally reach **Polihale State Park,** you'll forget about the hassles of getting there. This is one of Hawaii's longest, widest beaches, with some of the deepest sand. The dunes, towering cliffs, and its isolation make it an extra-special locale. Up north, **Lumahai** was made famous by Mitzi Gaynor in *South Pacific.* This tucked-away cove is a good place to escape the rest of the world. Although the Poipu area in the south is probably the island's most popular region, you won't find many other folks here on **Mahaulepu.**

While **The Big Island** doesn't have as many beaches as the rest of Hawaii, it can certainly claim some of the most dramatic. At **Panaluu Beach Park,** palm trees rustle above coal-black sand that must be seen to be believed. To wiggle your toes in the green sand on the coast at **Ka Lae,** you'll need a four-wheel drive. Soft, white sand blankets the twin crescents of **Hapuna Beach. Anaehoomalu** is adjacent to ancient fishponds. **Old Airport,** teeming with marine life, is excellent for snorkeling.

On **Molokai,** long, broad **Papohaku,** backed by sand dunes, can be dangerous for swimming, but there aren't many settings as picturesque as this one. At secluded **Moomomi,** you might stumble upon freshwater pools in some of the dunes. This is a great spot for snorkeling.

On **Lanai,** wide **Hulapoe Beach** has changed dramatically since the arrival of the deluxe Manele Bay Hotel. However, the hotel sits on a hillside overlooking the sand, so the beach itself remains just as gorgeous. The most "crowded" times used to be on weekends, when a sprinkling of local families gathered for picnics.

(Also see Swimming and Sun in "Nuts and Bolts.")

BUDGET-CONSCIOUS TRAVEL: Since competition for your presence is so stiff among accommodations in Hawaii, there are many moderately priced, comfortable hotels, condominiums, and inns to choose from. My personal favorite is the Plantation Inn in Lahaina, **Maui.** Built in Victorian style during the 1980s, its appointments include individually decorated rooms, stained glass, canopied beds, floral wallpaper, and period telephones. This cozy hotel comes complete with one of Maui's best French restaurants, Gerard's.

Rustic Hotel Lanai on the island of **Lanai** used to be the only game in town before it was joined by two Rockresorts. Despite the island's newer, more upscale accommodations, this one continues to draw independent travelers who enjoy mixing with the locals who hang out on the front porch every evening. In **Molokai,** try Paniolo Hale (near the Kaluakoi golf course) or the Polynesian-style Hotel Molokai. Plantation Cottages on **Kauai** is a good choice. On **the Big Island,** busy Hotel King Kamehameha puts you smack in the middle of the restaurant- and store-filled town of Kailua-Kona.

In **Oahu,** I've gotten good reports about the Breakers Hotel and the family-run Royal Grove Hotel, both right in Waikiki. The Outrigger chain has nearly two dozen hotels, most in Waikiki and most of which appeal to the not-so-fat wallet. Also worth checking into is Oahu's Manoa Valley Inn. Since they are generally in residential areas, bed & breakfasts throughout the island will put you in close touch with everyday Hawaii.

(Also see Roughing It and Escape in this chapter.)

ESCAPE: The islands of Lanai and Molokai are famous for being far off the beaten path. But while other islands are more developed, there are regions on each where you can escape the crowds and surround yourself with Hawaii at its most naturally beautiful. On **Kauai,** try rustic Waimea and Kokee or pastoral, upscale Princeville. Despite the bustle of Waikiki, most of **Oahu** is open countryside. The north shore remains undeveloped, even though surfers flock there, and the Kahala region is another good choice. Once you've traveled down the nearly vertical road to Waipio Valley on **the Big Island,** you know you're truly getting away from the world. Makena is one of **Maui**'s quietest, least developed resort areas. Lush, isolated Hana, tucked away on the eastern coast of Maui, is extremely quiet between visits from day-trippers. This is a good place to spend a few (very) low-key nights.

(Also see Budget-Conscious Travel and Roughing It in this chapter and Camping and Hiking in "Nuts and Bolts.")

FAMILIES WITH CHILDREN: As far as activities go for *keikis* (children) beyond the beach and pool, **Oahu** entertains with the greatest number of choices: Sea Life Park, the Honolulu Zoo, the Waikiki Aquarium, Paradise Park (where trained birds do tricks), the Polynesian Cultural Center (where some of the exhibits and demonstrations will leave kids wide-eyed), the Children's Touch and Feel Museum, Castle Park (a small amusement park), and kite flying in Kapiolani Park.

The main islands have glass-bottom boat trips and other cruises that appeal to families (try **Maui** for winter whale-watching excursions). Botanical gardens, especially those on **Kauai** and **Maui,** make good destinations for family outings. On **Maui,** kids get a kick out of the 1890s-style Lahaina-Kaanapali & Pacific Railroad, also known as the Sugarcane Train.

During the annual Makahiki Festival on **Molokai** in January, visiting children will enjoy watching their Island peers compete in ancient Hawaiian games. Also consider the Molokai Wagon Ride, which ends up with a beachfront party including arts and crafts and Hawaiian-fishing-net-throwing demonstrations.

Condominiums, with separate bedrooms and kitchens, can be convenient for families. Many are on the beach and most have swimming pools. You might also consider renting a private home. Babysitting can be arranged through most condominiums and hotels, and cribs are also widely available.

Especially during the summer and Christmas and Easter vacations, some of the larger resorts sponsor supervised children's programs that leave parents free to do their own thing. Some programs are free, while others cost about $35 to $45 per child, per day. Activities include lei-making classes, basket-weaving workshops, sightseeing excursions, athletic competitions, and sand castle–building contests. Some resorts also offer movies and other entertainment at night. Among the resorts that have children's programs are Kona Village and the Mauna Lani Bay Hotel on **the Big Island;** the Stouffer Waiohai and the Aston Kauai Resort on **Kauai;** the Kahala Hilton on **Oahu;** and Sheraton and Hyatt hotels on **Maui, Oahu** and **the Big Island.** Whether or not they have programs specifically designed for kids, the vast majority of accommodations happily accept children.

No matter where you're coming from, flight time is long, especially for children. So when you're making flight reservations, request seats in the bulkhead of the plane, since this area is more spacious. Infants less than two years of age fly free on most airlines, as long as they are held in someone's lap. The cost for children ages 2 through 11 is usually 75% of the adult fare.

FISHING: Because of its calm waters and abundance of blue and striped marlin, sailfish, swordfish, and tuna, and Kona coast on **the Big Island** is a favorite for deep sea fishing. The annual Hawaiian International Billfish Tournament is held here each August. Other good fishing locations are **Oahu'**s Waianae coast; **Maui'**s southwest coast; and the northern coasts of **Kauai** and **Molokai.** Kauai has an exceptional variety of fish and the bonefish are extra large and plentiful here.

If you follow the lead of locals, you'll find good fishing off beaches and rocky overlooks throughout the islands, such as at Hulopoe Beach on **Lanai.** It's not unusual to see residents fishing from outrigger canoes or even from surfboards in calm lagoons or near reefs.

(Also see Fishing in "Nuts and Bolts.")

GETTING MARRIED: There is no question that Hawaii is the stuff countless romantic dreams are made of. Not only do newlyweds from the mainland and Japan come to Hawaii by the planeload, but many couples kick off their honeymoons with a wedding here as well. Among favorite places for tying the knot are the thatched-roof chapel built by Columbia Pictures for Rita Hayworth for her Sadie Thompson role, at the Coco Palms Resort on **Kauai;** the columned waterfront gazebo at the **Westin Kauai;** the torchlit lagoon at Polynesian-style Kona Village Resort on **the Big Island;** and the lush, waterfall- and bird-filled grounds of the Hyatt Regency **Maui.** One of the most popular spots is Fern Grotto on **Kauai,** which the bride and groom cruise to in a special wedding riverboat. At the mouth of this cave that is dripping with ferns, the acoustics for "The Hawaiian Wedding Song" could hardly be better. Beaches at sunset, botanical gardens, waterfalls, and boats also make wonderful wedding settings.

Quite a few of the larger hotels and condominiums offer honeymoon and wedding packages including pampering such as airport pickup in a limousine, a bottle of champagne upon arrival, a honeymoon suite, a moonlight cruise, and a helicopter ride. Some resorts have wedding coordinators who will help you find the most appealing locale to say "I do." They also make arrangements for flowers (such as bridal strands of *pikake*—fragrant Chinese jasmine—a sign of love), *maile* leis (which symbolize long life and prosperity), the cake, champagne, and a video or still photographer. They'll let the bride know that she should tuck a ti leaf inside one of her garters for good luck. Independent companies can handle all these details for you as well. Try Greeters of Hawaii, P.O. Box 29638, Honolulu, HI 96820, (800) 367–2669.

You'll need to obtain a marriage license from the State Department of Health in Honolulu or through agents on other islands. There is no waiting period, and the license, which costs about $17, is good for 30 days in Hawaii. Women are required to show a certificate confirming premarital screening for rubella. For a marriage information packet, contact the State Department of Health, P.O. Box 3378, Honolulu, HI 96801, (808) 548–5862.

GOLF: Even nongolfers are drawn to Hawaii's golf courses, if only to absorb the striking colors: smooth greens contrasted with dark lava outcroppings, shimmering moss-colored ponds, and the vivid blue Pacific.

According to *Golf Digest,* **Maui** has some of the best courses in the state. The sixth tee at **The Village Course** at Kapalua Bay Hotel affords a fabulous view. From this hilltop perch, you'll take in mountains that dip into pineapple fields, with the ocean in the distance. It will be difficult to resist feeding the ducks at the glistening lake here. **The Bay Course,** also at Maui's Kapalua Bay Hotel, hosts the annual Isuzu Kapalua International tournament each November. If you're lucky, you'll catch a glimpse of humpback whales off the coast near the tee on the fifth hole. Ancient lava rock walls have been incorporated into the **Wailea Orange Course.** Other good choices in Maui are the **Royal Kaanapali North Course,** designed by Robert Trent Jones, Sr., and backed by the West Maui Mountains; and **the Blue Course** at the Wailea Golf Club.

At the **Frances Ii Brown Golf Course,** Mauna Lani Bay Resort, **the Big Island,** the rough, chocolate-colored lava sets off the electric green swards. Like everything else on the Big Island, **Mauna Kea**'s course is in a very dramatic setting. One of the state's most difficult courses, it was designed by Robert Trent Jones, Sr. Its greens wind through desolate-looking lava flows. The **Makai Golf Course,** Princeville Resort, **Kauai,** was designed by Robert Trent Jones, Jr. The 27 holes are surrounded by lush greenery. Even though this part of the island receives a lot of rain, golfers still flock to this course. The **Kiele Course** at the Westin Kauai is the island's newest and it was designed by Jack Nicklaus.

HAWAIIAN CULTURE AND HISTORY: Many of the larger hotels have periodic demonstrations or classes in lei making, hula dancing, and lauhala weaving. Some also have experts on hand to tell you all about poi making, canoe making, playing konane games, lomi lomi massage, making feather cloaks, and other old-time activities.

For a more in-depth look at Hawaiiana, **Oahu**'s Polynesian Cultural Center is a good place to start. The historical exhibits and the authentic, recreated villages are fascinating, but the best part is lingering after the demonstrations to chat with the enthusiastic performers from Hawaii and other Pacific Islands. In beautiful Waimea Falls Park you'll see old-fashioned hula demonstrations (a far cry from today's variety). You can also watch divers plunge into a pool from the top of a crashing waterfall. Honolulu's Bishop Museum houses a fascinating display of Hawaiiana, from koa wood bowls and royal crowns to an authentic grass hut. Take an outrigger canoe ride at Waikiki Beach. Larger versions of this kind of boat carried the ancient Polynesians to Hawaii from Tahiti. Opulent, European-inspired Iolani Palace is the only former royal palace on American soil. Less elegant but just as intriguing is Queen Emma's Summer Palace.

On **Kauai,** see how poi was once pounded and baskets once woven at Kamokila, a recreated village on the banks of the Wailua River. Nearby, stop for a drink during the torch-lighting ceremony at Coco Palms Resort, nestled amid an ancient royal Hawaiian palm grove. While the torch-lighting ceremony may not be historically authentic, it was inspired by ancient custom and is certainly captivating to watch. Hiking along Kauau's Na Pali Coast, you may encounter ruins of agricultural terraces, *heiau* (temples), and other remnants of ancient Hawaiian communities that once thrived in the valleys here. According to many historians, this was the first region settled on the island.

For more history, explore the petroglyph fields on **the Big Island, Lanai,** or **Molokai.** These ancient rock carvings provide insight into early Hawaiian art. Half the adventure is finding the petroglyphs, many of which are hidden in remote areas. Some Big Island hotels offer guided walks to and through the petroglyph fields. Start with Anaehoomalu, on the grounds of the Waikoloa Beach Resort. In addition to petroglyphs, the Big Island's Kohala Coast has many other remnants of Hawaiian history: ancient royal fishponds, heiau, burial sites, canoe sheds, fishing shrines, and an old trail to the beach worn by royal feet. The tastefully upscale hotels along this coast are packed with intriguing Pacific art.

South of here, totem pole–like *tikis* guard the waterfront at the Place of Refuge. This was where ancient Hawaiians went to avoid the severe punishment (often death) that resulted from breaking a kapu. In the Big Island's town of Kailua-Kona, oceanfront Hulihee Palace was a vacation retreat for *alii* (chiefs and kings). Puukohola Heiau and Mookini Heiau are two of the best preserved of the many ancient Hawaiian temples that once scattered the islands.

The picturesque town of Lahaina, on **Maui,** has been the capital of the Hawaiian kingdom and a whaling village. It's now a National Historic Landmark. Most of the people who live in remote Hana, a quiet town on Maui's east coast, are part Hawaiian. Hana is a good place to mingle and "talk story" with residents.

Skip the commercialized luaus (most of those that take place at hotels or that you'll hear about through hotels) and check local newspapers for those sponsored by civic groups and other organizations. Fundraising luaus are sometimes hosted by *halau* (hula groups) preparing to participate in the annual Merrie Monarch Festival (held on the Big Island) to cover the cost of costumes, airfare or ground transportation, and accommodations during this major hula event.

(Also see Festivals and Special Events in "Nuts and Bolts.")

HELICOPTER TOURS: As far as I'm concerned, birds gaze down on the most awesome scenery from the skies above **Kauai** (with Waimea Canyon, waterfall-bedecked Mount Waialeale, jagged Na Pali Coast, and hidden sandy coves). Helicopter rides are also impressive on the alternately flourishing and desolate **Big Island,** especially if Kilauea volcano is erupting; and **Maui,** with its stark Haleakala crater and verdant Hana. While a helicopter tour of **Oahu** can have its thrilling moments, I recommend taking a whirl here only if you're not visiting any of the other islands.

Try to find a company whose helicopters have no middle seats (note that some ads say, "Every seat is a window seat"). Some copters are 4-seaters while others seat 6. By all means, take your camera and plenty of film, but don't spend so much time clicking the shutter that you miss the scope of your surroundings. Some people have a tendency to glue their eye to their camera's viewfinder instead of enjoying the breadth of the scenery. No photo can capture the panoramic scope of what whirlybirds lay out before you, nor the feeling of the land suddenly dropping out from beneath you like a trap door as you fly over the edge of a cliff.

LUXURY: Hawaii has some of the world's plushest and splashiest beach hotels. Each of the resorts that cropped up in the late 1980s seemed to be striving mightily to outdo the last. Four of Hawaii's most spectacular are along the Kohala Coast of the Big Island: the Hyatt Regency Waikoloa, Kona Village, Mauna Lani Bay Resort, and Mauna Kea. Two of the state's most dignified are Oahu's Halekulani (which feels isolated even though it's smack in the middle of Waikiki) and the Kahala Hilton (which really is away from it all, on the tranquil side of Diamond Head).

Here are the top hotels for unadulterated pampering in luscious surroundings:

Oahu

- Halekulani
- Hilton Hawaiian Village
- Kahala Hilton
- Royal Hawaiian
- Sheraton-Makaha
- Sheraton Moana Surfrider
- Turtle Bay Hilton & Country Club

Maui

- Hotel Hana-Maui
- Hyatt Regency Maui
- Kapalua Bay
- Kapalua Villas
- Makena Surf
- Maui Inter-Continental Wailea

- The Four Seasons Resort
- The Grand Hyatt Wailea (due to open by early '91)
- Maui Prince
- Stouffer Wailea Beach Resort
- The Westin Maui

Kauai

- Kiahuna Plantation
- Puu Poa Condominiums
- Sheraton Princeville
- Stouffer Waiohai
- The Westin Kauai
- The Hyatt Regency Kauai (due to open by early '91)

The Big Island

- Hyatt Regency Waikoloa
- Kona Village
- Mauna Kea Beach Resort
- Mauna Lani Bay
- The Ritz Carlton Mauna Lani

Lanai

- Manele Bay Hotel (due to open by early '91)
- Koele Lodge

MURDEROUS FUN: You're at a cocktail party at a Waikiki hotel and suddenly the person next to you gags on her wine and collapses dead on the carpet. No need for alarm. Just take notes. It's only a Murder Mystery Weekend (or Evening). Over *pupus* (hors d'oeuvres) and during gourmet meals, you'll be collecting clues in an attempt to figure out whodunit. As you meet the other guests (some of whom are actors pretending to be guests), you might witness another murder or two. Prizes are given for the most unforgettable, the most absurd, and the most hilarious solutions to the crimes. Plots continually change, so guests may become embroiled in a different murder mystery during another visit.

For details about hotel package deals, contact Murder Mystery Weekend, 1750 Kalakaua Ave., Suite 3-443, Honolulu, Hawaii 96826, (808) 538–0272.

NIGHT LIFE AND DINING: For sheer variety, Waikiki on **Oahu** is the place to be. However, other islands also have a healthy choice of quality restaurants and after-dark action. Kaanapali and Lahaina on **Maui** have many restaurants and night spots. To a lesser degree, Kailua-Kona and Keauhou on **the Big Island** offer a good selection of restaurants and a sprinkling of evening hangouts. The resorts along the Big Island's Kohala Coast are also worth checking out.

Most hotels either host their own *luaus* (elaborate banquets of Hawaiian specialties, accompanied by performances of hula and Hawaiian music) or they can make arrangements for guests to attend one elsewhere. Many visitors enjoy these commercial affairs, but I prefer the more authentic, down-to-earth luaus hosted by civic groups and other local organizations. Keep an eye out for these in local newspapers or listen for radio announcements.

ROUGHING IT: Whether you want to **hike** through dense wilderness or across stark volcanic craters and lava flows, you'll have plenty of choices of trails in the Hawaiian Islands. Treks can be either guided or independent. On **Kauai,** the rugged trail along the cliffs of the Na Pali Coast leads to wonderfully isolated beaches. Hiking the rim of Kauai's Waimea Canyon or the Kalalau Trail to Kalalau Valley could hardly be more exhilarating. Iao Valley, a thick rain forest on West **Maui,** is another good place to wander. Like a giant finger, 2250-foot Iao Needle pierces the clouds. Maui's remote Hana, an area known for its profusion of flowers and series of volcanic pools, also draws many amblers. In the moonscape of Volcanoes National Park on **the Big Island,** you'll feel as though you're on another planet. Up north, you can hike through stunning Waipio Valley, and even follow the trail that connects it with the neighboring valley. In the eastern part of **Molokai,** an exceptionally scenic trail leads from Halawa Valley to 250-foot Moaula Falls. Reward yourself with a swim in the bracing mountain pool at the bottom of the cascade.

Campgrounds are just as varied, from mountainous settings where the air is thin and cool to sun-splashed beachfronts. Spartan, but comfortable cabins in state and national parks are available on **Maui, Kauai,** and **the Big Island** for about $5 to $10 per person, per night. In many cases, beds and linens are provided, and some cabins contain hot showers, kitchens, and cooking utensils.

Hapuna Beach State Park, with one of **the Big Island**'s prettiest sandy shores, has A-frame shelters for rent. You might consider booking a room in Tom Araki's tiny "hotel" (which has no electricity, mind you) in Waipio Valley. Cabins are available in **Kauai**'s elevated Kokee State Park. Pitch a tent in Palaau State Park in a thick forest in **Molokai**'s mountains near the cliffside trail down to Kalaupapa peninsula. If you can brave the cold, try camping out in Haleakala crater on **Maui.**

Wilderness Travel leads hiking and camping expeditions on Kauai, the Big Island, Maui, and Molokai. The one- to two-week trips include hiking, camping, mule rides, sailing, snorkeling, and sightseeing. Travelers might be accommodated anywhere from an inn or private home to a Buddhist temple. (Wilderness Travel, 801 Allston Way, Berkeley, CA 94710, (415) 548–0420; outside California (800) 247–6700.)

Wilderness Hawaii sponsors 4- or 15-day trips that include destinations such as Maui's Haleakala National Park and the Big Island's Volcanoes National Park. In addition to hiking and camping, you'll swim at isolated beaches, fish, and relax. (Wilderness Hawaii, P.O. Box 61692, Honolulu, HI 96839, (808) 737–4697.)

If you'd rather spend some time at sea, **American Wilderness Experience** offers a six-day sail on a 35-foot sloop, departing from Oaha. You'll cruise along the coasts of Maui and Molokai, with plenty of time for fishing, swimming, pigging out on fresh seafood, and hiking to ancient petroglyphs. These intimate groups consist of a mere five passengers. Fourteen-day, four-island hiking and camping trips are also available. (American Wilderness Experience, P.O. Box 1486, Boulder, CO 80306, (303) 444–2632) or (800) 444-0099.

(Also see Camping and Hiking in ''Nuts and Bolts.'')

SCUBA DIVING AND SNORKELING: Dramatic dropoffs, caves, hapless coral-encrusted ships, airplane wrecks, and, of course, a profusion of marine life—it's all wet in Hawaii. To participate in group dive excursions, rent gear, or fill tanks in Hawaii, divers must have taken a local resort course or be certified. Half-day resort courses are widely available through hotels or independent dive operators for those who don't have the time or money to take the five-day certification course. Most islands offer dive packages and guided dives. If you are considering diving on your own, note that scuba can be dangerous along unprotected coasts during winter months. At this time of year, the water is much rougher, with strong rip tides and undertows.

If you've never snorkeled before, don't worry—it's simple. Ask anyone who's done it to teach you tricks such as how to make sure your mask fits properly (without using the strap, place the mask against your face, breathe in, and bend your head down. If the mask doesn't fall off, the fit is fine, and no water should seep in while you're swimming); how to prevent the mask from fogging up (spit on the inside of the glass, rub your saliva around, then quickly dip the mask in the ocean—the secret ingredient is the enzymes in saliva); to be sure not to look back at your feet while swimming, lest you inhale a snorkel-full of salty water; and how to blow out any water that does get into your snorkel. You'll make fast aquatic friends if you bring along a bag of frozen peas to feed the fish.

Oahu has the greatest number of dive facilities in Hawaii. Scuba is year-round on the protected leeward coast, where Waikiki is located. During the summer when the water is ''flat,'' the diving is excellent along the beach-rimmed north shore. This is a good place for inexperienced divers. Hanauma Bay tops many lists for both snorkeling and scuba. Scores of far-from-timid fish are used to receiving edible goodies from human fingers, and the curving, palm-shaded beach is backed by mountains. The only problem with the beauty of the setting and the kaleidoscope of fish is that you'll probably be appreciating this spot with a slew of other people.

With Molokini and Lanai nearby, **Maui** is a great homebase for diving and is especially good for snorkeling. Playful dolphins often join snorkelers in Honolua Bay, north of Lahaina. Molokini, a partially submerged volcanic crater off Maui's southwestern coast, draws both snorkelers and divers. The waters around isolated Hana are also excellent for diving and snorkeling.

The Big Island's Kona Coast may have fewer sites, but some people say that this island has the best diving in the state, in part because of the clarity of the water. There is wonderful snorkeling in Kealakekua Bay, near the Captain Cook Monument, even though it can be crowded. Snorkeling is also great in Honaunau Bay near the Place of Refuge, an ancient religious site.

Although **Kauai** has a wider selection of exciting dive sites than snorkeling locales, it is a good location for both activities. Sea turtles and dolphins are often around the reef off the site of Nualolo Kai, an old fishing village in the north. The little-visited dive sites along the northern shore of the neighboring island of **Niihau** feature caves, walls, and arches.

For more specific underwater details, obtain a copy of a booklet containing the state's top 40 dive sites, by contacting Dive Hawaii, P.O. Box 90295, Honolulu, HI 96835,

---

SHOPPING: Even on some of the Neighbor Islands, Hawaii is a Nirvana for shopping mall addicts. **Oahu,** of course, is where you'll find the widest selection of stores, in and outside of malls. Chic boutiques and T-shirt shops line Kalakaua Avenue and other streets in Waikiki. The convenient Royal Hawaiian Shopping Mall is centrally located in Waikiki. ABC discount stores, one of which seems to be on every corner, sell Kona coffee and macadamia nuts, usually at very appealing prices. Off the main tourist strip, the Ala Moana Shopping Center is among the world's largest malls. If you can't find it here, it probably doesn't exist. Also in Honolulu, the Ward Center is an attractive, upscale shopping and dining complex. The walkways and the fine selection of boutiques and eateries are decked out with gleaming brass railings and glossy wooden trim. Nearby is the older Ward Warehouse, with more stores to browse through.

For atmosphere, it is difficult to beat **Kauai**'s Kilohana Plantation. Bedrooms, hallways, and even bathrooms in this handsome mansion and outbuildings have been converted into eye-pleasing (if not always wallet-friendly) boutiques. Pottery, jewelry, antiques, and paintings by local artists are plentiful. Other good areas for spending money are Lahaina and Kaanapali (Whaler's Village) on **Maui** and Kailua-Kona on **the Big Island.** Many hotels, especially the larger ones, have shops, but you generally pay more for the convenience.

Now that I've dealt with where to buy it, here's what to buy:

If you absolutely *must* have an **aloha shirt,** I'd steer clear of the modern, most common (polyester) variety. Stop at thrift shops and other boutiques to sift through vintage shirts. Most are made of rayon (a natural fiber) or silk. They often have coconut shell buttons. Many of the best in quality date back to the 1930s and '40s and are silk-screened or stenciled with more subdued floral prints than the somewhat garish contemporary shirts. The only problem is, these older shirts run anywhere from $60 to well over $100. For **muumuus,** I would also suggest staying away from the more commercial outlets.

In shopping areas and malls as well as hotels throughout the main islands, you'll find a wide variety of **sportswear.** Whenever I'm in Hawaii, it seems as if I see more **bathing suits** or **T-shirts** in any single store than I've seen my entire life. With branches on the major islands, Crazy Shirts is one of the best places to go for quality T-shirts. **Pareaus** (also called **sarongs**) imported from Tahiti and other islands make wonderful beach cover-ups for women.

If you want something truly Hawaiian and are willing to dig deep into your pockets, consider a delicate **Niihau necklace.** Tiny, rare shells from the island of Niihau (where only Hawaiians are allowed to live) are painstakingly fashioned into intricate designs. Each a work of art in itself, these garlands can run hundreds of dollars. Another worthwhile investment is a **Hawaiian quilt,** especially an antique one. Easily recognizable, these attractive comforters usually have a bold, one-color cut-out design appliqued onto a white background. A new quilt can run well over a thousand dollars, and if it is commissioned, it can take up to two years to complete. However, your patience and money would be well spent, since you would then have an extremely durable heirloom to pass down in your family.

Many travelers return home laden with bowls, jewelry, and tikis (totem pole–like Hawaiian carvings) carved from glossy **Island wood,** such as koa or monkeypod. Necklaces of chestnutlike **kukui nuts** (candlenuts), Maui's **scrimshaw** (intricate designs etched onto whale bone or teeth), and locally made **paintings** and **ceramics** are also popular. Imports from other Pacific island groups are plentiful, including **tapa** (or **kapa**) **cloth** (made from pounded bark), which can make striking wall hangings. There is also no scarcity of Asian imports, such as **Chinese jade** and **Japanese vases.**

At flower nurseries (especially on the Big Island) you can buy **ex-**

otic blooming plants, either seedlings or mature, to be shipped (after being inspected) to the mainland. In downtown areas on the main islands, **lei** stands are everywhere. Interested in taking one of these fresh floral garlands home? You can pick one up at most airports. Planning to keep a lei around your house as decoration after it dries? Orchids are among the blossoms that age nicely.

A burst of flavor has often transported me back to the place where I first experienced the taste. Hawaii certainly makes it easy to return over and over again, without having to get back onto a plane. Few people leave the Islands without **Kona coffee** (fresh beans, ground, or instant). The rich volcanic soil of the Big Island, where it is grown, has a great deal to do with its trademark flavor. **Macadamia nuts**—plain, chocolate-covered, in cookies, or in many other incarnations—are another hot item. You can arrange to have juicy, fresh **pineapples** inspected, boxed, and sent to your departure gate at the airport. **Jams and jellies** made from lilikoi (passion fruit), guava, papaya, and mangoes can be found in many stores. Once you taste thick, crunchy **Maui potato chips,** you'll probably want to take home a few bags. For your liquor cabinet, consider a bottle of Okolehao (**Hawaiian whiskey,** flavored with the native ti plant) or **wine from Maui's vineyard,** such as a sparking white or a light pineapple wine.

(Also see Art in this chapter and Sending Hawaii Home in "Nuts and Bolts.")

SINGLES: Since "Hawaii" and "honeymoon" are practically synonymous, you'll see plenty of goo-goo-eyed couples everywhere. But travelers can certainly enjoy the Islands just as much alone. Many young singles head to Waikiki Beach and the North Shore on **Oahu;** Kaanapali, Lahaina, and Kihei on **Maui;** Poipu and Kapaa on **Kauai;** and Kailua-Kona on **the Big Island.** You may want to avoid the larger, more luxurious resorts, which tend to be honeymoon havens. Midsize hotels that sponsor group activities, small hotels, inns, and bed and breakfasts are probably most conducive to meeting people. Joining sightseeing tours and group sports (taking a snorkeling excursion or playing volleyball, for instance) is a good way to mingle. It's not uncommon to run into solitary visitors who are hiking and camping their way through Hawaii, making new friends at every stop. Whenever I travel alone in Hawaii, I find that residents and other visitors are much quicker to draw me into their social circles than when I'm with someone.

(Also see Safety and Traveling Solo in "Nuts and Bolts.")

SURFING AND WINDSURFING: Winter is serious surfing season in Hawaii and the state's premier surfing area is **Oahu's** North Shore. The waves here don't stop gathering steam until they reach heights of 30 feet or so. The relatively calm waters and the choice of good instructors draw many novice surfers to Waikiki. Quiet as it's kept, **Kauai** is also an excellent island for surfing. Here Poipu and Kapaa are the two leading surfing meccas. Even when waves are at their most enticing, beaches in these areas are far less crowded than on Oahu and Maui. During the winter, **Maui**'s Honolua Bay and Hookipa Beach Park are where most people ride the waves. In the summer, surfers head for Kaanapali beach, Maalaea Bay, and Lahaina. On **the Big Island,** surfing conditions are often excellent near Hilo Bay and at south shore beaches. A major competition is held at Banyans Drive on Kailua Bay during the winter. Magic Sands Beach Park is popular with body surfers and boogie boarders.

While windsurfing is possible on all the major islands, **Maui** is heaven for this sport. **Oahu** also has some good spots for it.

TENNIS: Most of the larger hotels and condominiums have tennis courts. Since **Maui** has so many—in Wailea, Kapalua, Kaanapali, and Makena—you are likely to have a good deal of flexibility, playing when and where you want. If you'd like to hit those balls on clay courts, head for the Coco Palms Hotel on **Kauai,** which has Hawaii's first.

UNUSUAL SIGHTS: For my money, **the Big Island** wins hands down in this category for its contrasting vistas. This island looks like few other places on earth. Not only does it have a pair of active volcanoes, but it also sports coal-black sand beaches, as well as a shore with green (yes, green) sand (olivine crystals). Smooth ebony lava flows form an eerie wasteland in sharp contrast to the lusher parts of the island. Waipio Valley, with its own black sand beach, is a flourishing hideaway that is not to be missed. Black sand and an impressive volcano can also be found on **Maui,** and other islands are certainly not lacking in magnificent scenery.

UNUSUAL SPORTS: From December to April, **skiers** can tackle the slopes of **the Big Island**'s 13,796-foot Mauna Kea volcano—that is, if Mother Nature is cooperating. Unfortunately, it's not every winter she blesses the mountaintop with the necessary minimum of two feet of snow. The panoramic views from the summit can be fabulous when the weather is clear. The first people to glide down these slopes did so in 1937. But before they could go down, they had to climb the mountain with their wooden skis tied to their shoulders. Today, four-wheel-drive vehicles transport skiers to the top. Some people may suffer from altitude sickness; warning signals are fatigue, headache, and nausea.

If you're daring enough, try **hang gliding** on Oahu or Maui. Introductory lessons and certification courses are available with certified instructors. On Maui, advanced hang gliders can soar over Haleakala crater. **Sailplane** rides can be arranged on Oahu's North Shore.

For the less adventuresome, **parasailing** is also wonderfully exhilarating. Try it on Oahu, Lahaina in Maui, and Kailua-Kona on the Big Island. On Waikiki Beach and a couple of the Neighbor Islands, visitors can ride the waves as the ancient Hawaiians did—in **outrigger canoes.** On Kauai and Oahu, go **kayaking** past beautiful scenery.

If you'd rather be on the sidelines, the **Hawaii Polo Club** battles it out on Sundays during the summer on Oahu.

WHALE WATCHING: From about November through March or April, 40- to 50-foot long humpback whales migrate from Alaska to Hawaii. **Maui** is the best vantage point for getting close-up views of these majestic, graceful giants. Several whale-watching cruises depart from Lahaina and Maalaea harbors. But you don't have to leave the shore to get an eyeful (just remember: the higher your perch, the better). Actually, naturalists would prefer that whale-watching by boat be kept to a minimum or eliminated altogether. The noise from the motors interferes with mating. Spots on **the Big Island, Molokai,** and **Lanai** are also good for watching these giant mammals. You might want to bring a pair of binoculars, but they aren't essential. Early morning and late afternoon are the best times for spotting Moby Dick's brethren.

NUTS AND BOLTS

ACCOMMODATIONS: There is a wonderfully varied array of places to stay in Hawaii, from Tom Araki's tiny, electricity-less "hotel" deep in a Big Island valley to the opulent Westin Kauai, where guests cruise through canals in sleek boats and ride around the manicured grounds in horse-drawn carriages. Choices in between these extremes are plentiful.

Top Hotels • Several of the most luxurious of these are referred to as "megaresorts" or "Hawaiian Disneyland," since there is so much to do and see on the premises that guests need never leave the property. (I can't imagine, though, why anyone would want to come all the way to Hawaii and remain on the grounds of a hotel.) Especially outside of Oahu (where Waikiki hotels are close together), most top hotels are in sprawling, beautifully landscaped, oceanfront settings. Particularly on the Neighbor Islands, many have open-air lobbies with ponds and flourishing foliage. Some have extensive collections of Hawaiian, Polynesian, and Asian art.

While those in Waikiki may not be as spacious, all top hotels have features including swimming pools; air-conditioned rooms with remote-controlled color TV, stocked minibars, one or more telephones, clock-radios, and *lanais* (balconies or patios); several restaurants (of far higher quality than you would expect to find in most mainland hotels); room service; daily and nightly entertainment; luaus; Hawaiian crafts demonstrations; a full menu of sports; a tour-booking desk; and a highly professional, attentive staff. Extras often come in the form of fresh flowers; bathrobes and slippers (for use during your stay); double sinks and an array of toiletries; in-room safes; coffee-makers; refrigerators; and nightly turn-down service with chocolates on your pillows. FAX machines and other business-related services are often available.

Even if you can't afford to spend your whole vacation in a top hotel, consider booking a room in one for a night or two just for the fun of it.

Mid-range Hotels • Often on or near beaches, many of these have a wide array of facilities, activities, and services, including swimming pools, tennis courts, a choice of restaurants, and nightly entertainment. Quite a few of these hotels are frequently packed with tour groups.

Budget Hotels • Some are near beaches and many have swimming pools. Rooms tend to be basic, but comfortable. The decor throughout may be nondescript or unappealing. Fans often cool rooms instead of air conditioners. Some of the better budget hotels attract tour groups.

Condominiums • These are a pleasant alternative to luxury or midlevel hotels. Some are nearly indistinguishable from top hotels, except that each unit has a kitchen and most have one or more separate bedrooms. Condos tend to be quieter, offering more independence and privacy. Many are on or near beaches. Most have swimming pools, TVs, and laundry facilities. Some have tennis courts.

While you may receive more personal attention from staff, services are likely to be fewer. The front office may not be open at night and it may be closed or have limited hours on weekends. There may not be an Activities Desk to help you arrange tours or helicopter rides. Although there are no restaurants in most condos, kitchens come complete with cooking and dining utensils. You probably won't be able to have meals brought to your room or your bags carried by porters. Maid service is generally available, but it is not always daily, and it sometimes requires a surcharge. Some condominiums don't accept credit cards. Especially on the Neighbor Islands, ceiling fans are often in place instead of air conditioning. Some units have no telephones. During the most popular times of year, a minimum stay of several nights may be required.

United Airlines arranges Condominium Vacation packages that include flights, condo stay, and a rental car. Many hotels and condos offer economical packages focused on golf, honeymoon activities, scuba diving, or other specialized interests. See Costs in this chapter for more information about package deals.

Private Homes • Renting a home will afford you even more independence and privacy than a condominium. Many rental homes are very upscale and therefore expensive. They tend to be in quiet, nontouristy areas.

Bed and Breakfasts and Inns • B&B rates include a bedroom and breakfast (often continental, often to be prepared by you) in a private home. Your hosts may be living on the premises, or you may be put up in a separate cottage or apartment. While small, inns usually have more guest rooms than B&Bs. Guests are usually invited to use a common living room, often with a television. Both inns and B&Bs are generally in residential areas.

Housekeeping Cabins • Rustic, spartan cabins in state and national parks are an inexpensive way to go. Basic kitchen facilities are on hand, and linens are provided.

When it's time to pay your hotel bill, you'll find that a 5% hotel tax and a 4% sales tax have been added.

For addresses and phone numbers of hotels and condos see the ''Accommodation Quick Reference Charts'' at the back of this book. Approximate daily rates are also included in the charts.

(Also see Costs and Camping and Hiking in this chapter.)

AIRLINES: Hawaii is served by a wide selection of major airlines, so you'll have a lot of flexibility in booking a flight. United offers the greatest number, with more than a hundred nonstop weekly flights from the mainland to Hawaii. Heavy competition for your business means that while traveling to Hawaii is certainly not cheap, each airline has periodic economical deals and packages to convince you to fly with them instead of with another carrier.

The best time to select your seat is when you make your reservation. You can also reserve special meals at this time, such as vegetarian, kosher, low-salt, seafood, or fruit.

Many tour group– or package deal–travelers are met at the airport with the traditional **lei greeting.** This translates into a kiss on the cheek and a wreath of aromatic fresh flowers around the neck—pure heaven after all those hours in the air! Independent travelers arriving on any Island can get in on the act by arranging their own lei greeting through companies such as Honolulu-based **Greeters of Hawaii** ((800) 367–2669) or **Aloha Lei Greeters** ((800) 367–5255).

National Airlines

America West • Nonstop service to *Honolulu* from Phoenix and Las Vegas.

American • Daily flights to *Honolulu* from San Francisco, Los Angeles, Chicago, and Dallas/Ft. Worth. Flights from New York stop in California. Connecting service available from many mainland cities to Honolulu, and to *Maui* via Honolulu.

Canadian Air • Weekly flights from Vancouver or Toronto to *Honolulu*.

Continental • Weekly service to *Honolulu* from Los Angeles, San Francisco, and Vancouver. Nonstop weekly flights from Denver and Newark.

Delta • Many nonstop weekly flights between *Honolulu* and Los Angeles, San Francisco, San Diego, Dallas, or Atlanta. Connecting service from most large mainland cities, as well as from Toronto, Montreal, and Vancouver. Nonstop flights from Los Angeles to Kahului, *Maui.*

Hawaiian • Daily flights to *Honolulu* from San Francisco, Los Angeles, Seattle, and Portland. Weekly flights from Las Vegas and Anchorage.

Northwest • Daily service to *Honolulu* from San Francisco, Los Angeles, Minneapolis, Seattle, and Portland.

Pan Am • Weekly nonstop flights to *Honolulu* from New York. Daily New York/Los Angeles/San Diego service to Honolulu. Direct flights from Boston, Philadelphia, Baltimore, and Washington, D.C.

TWA • Daily service to *Honolulu* from Los Angeles and St. Louis. Connecting flights from most major East Coast cities available.

United • Many nonstop weekly flights to *Honolulu* from San Francisco, Los Angeles, Denver, Seattle, and Chicago. Nonstop service to Kahului, *Maui,* from San Francisco and Los Angeles. Direct service to Kona, *the Big Island of Hawaii,* and Lihue, *Kauai,* from San Francisco, Los Angeles, and Chicago.

Interisland Airlines

Aloha Airlines • (Not to be confused with Aloha IslandAir, a commuter airline.) Daily interisland service to *Honolulu;* Kahului, Kapalua-West Maui, and Hana on *Maui;* Kona and Hilo on *the Big Island;* and Lihue on *Kauai.* Call (800) 367–5250 from the U.S. mainland or (800) 663–9471 from Canada.

Hawaiian Airlines • Daily interisland flights to *Honolulu;* Kahului, Kapalua-West Maui, and Hana on *Maui;* Lihue on *Kauai;* Kona and Hilo on *the Big Island;* Hoolehua on *Molokai;* and *Lanai.* Call (800) 367–5320 from the U.S. mainland; (800) 663–3389 from Eastern Provinces, Canada; (800) 663–6296 from Alberta; (800) 663–2074 from British Columbia; (808) 537–5100 in Oahu; 244–9111 in Maui; 245–3671 in Kauai; 935–0811 in the Big Island of Hawaii; 553–5321 in Molokai; and 565–6429 in Lanai.

Aloha IslandAir • This commuter airline, formerly Princeville Airways, is not to be confused with its larger sister carrier, Aloha Airlines. Aloha IslandAir absorbed Air Molokai in 1989. Daily flights to and from *Honolulu;* Kahului, Kapalua-West Maui, and Hana on *Maui;* Princeville on *Kauai;* Kamuela on *the Big Island;* Hoolehua and Kalaupapa on *Molokai;* and *Lanai.* Call (800) 323–3345 from the mainland; (800) 652–6541 or (808) 833–3219 in Hawaii. Charter flights can be arranged.

(Also see Costs in this chapter.)

BUSINESS HOURS AND HOLIDAYS: So that you can part with your money at your convenience, shopping malls and quite a few stores on main drags remain open in the evenings. Retail stores, especially those in hotels, rarely take Sundays off. Banking hours are usually from 8:30 a.m. to 3 or 3:30 p.m., Monday through Friday. (However, some banks stay open until 6 p.m. on Thursdays or Fridays.) Businesses are generally open from 8 a.m. or earlier to 4 or 5 p.m. Most post offices open at 8 or 8:30 a.m. and close at 4:30 p.m. during the week; on Saturdays, hours are often 8 a.m. to noon. The main post office in Honolulu is open from 7:30 a.m. to 4:30 p.m. Monday through Friday and 7:30 a.m. to noon on Saturdays.

Stores, banks, and most businesses are closed on the main U.S. national holidays (Christmas Day, New Year's Day, Easter Sunday, Thanksgiving). Although banks and most businesses will be closed, a few stores stay open on Presidents' Day (third Monday in February), Prince Kuhio Day (March 26), Memorial Day (last Monday in May), King Kamehameha Day (June 11), the Fourth of July, Admission Day (third Friday in August), Labor Day (first Monday in September), Columbus Day (second Monday in October), and Veterans' Day (November 11).

BICYCLES: Many airlines allow bicycles on board as oversize luggage for a nominal extra charge. If you prefer, you can rent a bike on Oahu and other major islands. One of Maui's most popular activities is riding a mountain bike down the volcano. Several companies organize these excursions. For information about overnight bicycle tours, see Adventure in "The Best Places For . . . ."

CAMPING AND HIKING: You'll need to obtain a permit to camp in Hawaii. For **state parks,** contact the State of Hawaii Department of Land and Natural Resources, Division of State Parks (1151 Punchbowl St., Room 310, Honolulu, HI 96813, (808) 548–7455). For **national parks,** contact The National Park Service (300 Ala Moana Blvd., Suite 6305, Box 50165, Honolulu, HI 96813, (808) 541–2653). Applications for permits must be received at least seven days in advance. Be sure to keep your permit with you at all times while in the park.

The longest you may stay under each permit at any one park varies from two to five nights. While campgrounds are open every night on the Neighbor Islands, on Oahu they are open only from Friday through Tuesday nights. There are no fees for parking at, entering, or picnicking in state parks. However, you will be charged if you choose to stay in a cabin or A-frame shelter.

Housekeeping cabins have kitchens, living areas, bathrooms, and one to three bedrooms. Linens, towels, dishes, and other cooking and dining utensils are provided. Group accommodations are also available in 8-person bunklike units with toilet facilities, hot shower, linens, and a communal recreation/dining room. In cool mountain regions, you'll keep warm with fireplaces or electric heaters.

When **hiking,** wear long pants, since thorny plants and jagged rocks aren't too kind to human skin. Be prepared for wide variations in temperature, even within a particular hiking area. The weather can be intensely hot during the day, then downright cold at night. If you're planning to hike in Haleakala (Maui), Mauna Kea, or Mauna Loa (the Big Island) volcanoes, be prepared for very chilly temperatures. You might even see a dusting of snow during winter months.

Be sure to take insect repellent, sunscreen, a visor or hat, rain gear, a waterproofed tent (if you're not staying in a shelter), and plenty of drinking water. It's best to carry gear weighing no more than 35% of your body weight, especially when hiking in difficult areas such as Na Pali Coast on Kauai. The only place you'll need a hiking permit is Kahana Valley State Park on Oahu.

For hiking maps, contact the Hawaii Geographic Society (217 South King St., Suite 308, Honolulu, HI 96813 (808) 538–3952) or the State Parks Outdoor Recreation Office (151 Punchbowl St., Honolulu, HI 96813, (808) 548–7455). Another good source of highly detailed information is the *Hiking Hawaii* series of books by Robert Smith. Before settling into your hiking and/or camping adventure, note the location of the closest telephone. No alcohol is allowed in parks, by the way.

(Also see Roughing It and Budget-Conscious Travel in "The Best Places for . . . .")

CAR RENTAL: See Transportation in this chapter.

CLIMATE: Weather in Hawaii can be divided neatly into two seasons: winter and summer. During the winter, which runs from about mid-October through April, daytime temperatures are in mid-70s to low 80s. At night, the mercury dips by about ten degrees. There is generally more rain at this time of year, especially in November and December. The driest places to be during the winter are Waikiki on Oahu (although crowds here are at their largest during these months); Makena, Wailea, and Kihei on Maui; Kona and Kohala on the Big Island; and Poipu on Kauai.

Summer lasts from about May through mid-October. Daytime temperatures hover in the mid-80s. Evenings cool off by about five or ten degrees. Rain is less frequent, and when it does fall, it is usually in brief snatches.

Hawaii's busiest tourist season goes from Christmastime to mid-April, despite the possibility of wetter days. May through June and September through mid-October are actually the best times to go, since the islands are less crowded, the weather is driest, and the trade winds are at their most refreshing.

No matter what time of year, higher elevations are much colder than sea level. The northeast section of each island gets the brunt of inclement weather when wind and rain come. The southern and western areas of each island tend to be sunniest and driest. It's not unusual for people to be sprawled out on a beach in the blazing sun on one side of an island while the heavens have opened up on another.

Hurricanes and **earthquakes** are few and far between. **Volcanic eruptions** are periodic on the Big Island. However, not only are they safe, but viewing them up close is a favorite pastime. Note that although a haze called ''vog'' hangs in the air after eruptions, the sun manages to shine through.

COSTS: While package deals can be quite economical, they are only worth the saving if they take you where you want to go and if you can stay where you want to stay. Often, **hotels** that are part of packages are those that don't sell out easily because they aren't of the best quality, or aren't in the most desirable locations. Be sure you are clear about exactly what is included in the price of the package (airport transfers, lei greeting, meals, tours, cruises, etc.).

Before you talk to a travel agent, do some homework. Read through the descriptions of accommodations in this book. Scour newspaper travel sections for ads for moneysaving deals. Travel agents should be able to advise you on flights that are discounted depending on the time of year, day of week, and time of day you want to travel. They should also provide inside information on getting the best rates for rental cars.

Honeymoon packages may not be much less expensive than other packages. But your VIP treatment might include a lei greeting, airport pick-up in a limo, chilled champagne and fresh fruit upon arrival, room upgrade, a helicopter ride. Money-saving sports packages are common during less popular times of year.

Escorted and independent **fly-drive-hotel packages** are available through hotels themselves or through various airlines and tour companies. Some of the most popular are *American Express Vacations* (800) 637–6200, *Pleasant Hawaiian Holidays* (800) 242–9244, *Club Perillo*

(800) 431–1515, *Delta Dream Vacations* (800) 221–1212, *United* (800) 241–6522, and *AmeriWest Vacations* (800) 874–0747. In addition to **cruise and cruise-land packages,** *American Hawaii* (800) 765–7000 also offers **all-land vacations,** including room, rental car, and interisland flights.

You might consider making your hotel reservations yourself. If so, refer to the "Accommodations Quick Reference Charts" at the back of this book. In addition to toll-free numbers, you'll find approximate daily rates for double rooms in high season.

Accommodations in Hawaii add a 5% hotel tax and a 4% sales tax to the room rates, for a hefty total of 9%.

As far as **attractions** go, it's generally cheaper to shop around for good tour deals once you arrive in Hawaii than to prebook through a travel agent or your hotel activities desk. You can save 20% to 40% if you go directly to tour agents. Tax will usually be added to the quoted price for cruises, horseback riding, helicopter tours, and other excursions. Tour guides are tipped 15% to 20%.

(Also see Transportation in this chapter.)

CRUISES AND INTERISLAND FERRIES: These days, the only way you can sail to Hawaii from the mainland or from other Pacific locales is to board a cruise ship that calls briefly on Hawaii as one of its ports. However, once you fly to Hawaii, you can certainly take an interisland voyage.

Cruises • Two ships are based in Honolulu year-round: the S.S. *Independence* and the S.S. *Constitution* (**American Hawaii Cruises,** 550 Kearny St., San Francisco, CA 94108, (800) 765–7000). The two American Hawaii ships sail from Honolulu every Saturday for three-, four-, or seven-day voyages, stopping at Kauai, Maui, and the Big Island. Combination cruise/land packages are also available. While originally designed for 1000 voyagers, each vessel now carries 798 passengers, following extensive renovations in 1988. The S.S. *Constitution* was a favorite ship of the late Princess Grace of Monaco.

The cost of your cabin will be determined by its size, whether it has a porthole, and what deck it's on. Note that even though cabins on the higher decks are usually the most expensive, you'll find smoother sailing if your seafaring bedroom is closer to the surface of the ocean. Also, cabins closest to the center of the ship tend to afford the most comfortable rides, since the ship rolls and jerks less in the middle.

Booking and paying for your cabin as far in advance as possible can save you a healthy chunk of money. On the other hand, if you don't mind taking a chance, you can sometimes find a bargain by booking at the last minute when cruise lines are eager to sell any unused cabins.

Ask about roundtrip, reduced-fare air supplements and discounts for children traveling with full-fare adults.

Ferries • Running between Maui and Molokai (about $45 round trip), the 118-foot **Maui Princess** carries bikes, mopeds, scuba tanks, kayaks, canoes, or any other equipment at no additional cost. Be prepared, however, to load your own equipment. Also, be ready for a far-from-smooth 90-minute-plus ride, despite the boat's $60,000 stabilizers, which get rid of most of the rocking. If you tend to get seasick, talk to your doctor about preventive measures before your vacation.

Some ferries are packed with local workers traveling between home and their jobs, while others are filled with tourists planning to spend a day or a night on another island. Through **Tropical Rent-A-Car,** you can arrange to have complimentary pick-up and return. For ferry ticket information, or car-ferry or car-ferry-hotel packages, call (800) 833–5800 from the mainland; (808) 521–4157 on Oahu; (808) 661–8397 on Maui; (808) 653–5736 on Molokai.

(See individual Island chapters for half- or full-day cruises and other boating options.)

DIRECTIONS: If you're planning to drive in Hawaii, you'll have to get used to the local way of giving directions. If someone tells you to ''Go *diamondhead*,'' that means to drive southeast, toward Oahu's Diamond Head volcano. If you are east of Diamond Head, they might send you *Koko Head,* toward another easterly landmark. *Ewa* means to go northwest on Oahu, toward a region with that name. *Mauka* means to head inland, toward the mountains, while *makai* means to go toward the sea. Though all five terms are used on Oahu, only the last two are used on Neighbor Islands.

DRINKING AND DRUGS: The legal drinking age is 21 in Hawaii. You can buy beer, wine, and hard liquor in many supermarkets and delis, even on Sundays. Store closing times vary between 5 and 11 p.m. or so.

Be sure to follow safe drinking practices, just as you should at home. Particularly because you will be on unfamiliar territory, often on narrow, winding roads, it doesn't make sense to drink and drive. If you are planning to drink and drive anyway, allow an hour or more between your last alcoholic beverage and the time you hit the road. Call a cab if you or someone else thinks that you have had too much to drink. Your car won't mind being picked up the following day. Remember: The more alcohol you consume and the more quickly you consume it, the less you'll enjoy your vacation the next day.

Note that no alcohol is permitted in Hawaii's state or national parks.

In Hawaii, marijuana—said to be the state's largest cash crop—is known as *pakalolo*. As on the mainland, it's illegal. Anyone who possesses, smokes, sells, or grows it is subject to severe penalties. Possession of cocaine is far more serious. Enforcement of antidrug laws in Hawaii is becoming increasingly strict. Narcotics officers don't differentiate between residents and visitors who are "just having a little fun" on their vacation.

FESTIVALS AND SPECIAL EVENTS: Hawaii's various cultures have contributed many annual festivities. In addition to these, sporting events may also help you determine when to travel. Check with a Hawaii Visitors' Bureau (HVB) office for exact dates. (For HVB addresses and phone numbers, see Useful Contacts in this chapter, or in individual Island chapters.)

January

Narcissus Festival • The Chinese New Year is celebrated in Honolulu's Chinatown with an eruption of fireworks, dances, a ball, a beauty contest, and other happenings. This festival runs through March. For further information, call the Chinese Chamber of Commerce at (808) 533–3181.

Cherry Blossom Festival • *through March or early April* • With roots in Japan, this Honolulu event features lessons in the skillful craft of arranging flowers and preparing food that looks like modern art. The festival, which ends in late March or early April, also includes judo or aikido demonstrations, a January tournament at the Leilehua Golf Course, a beauty contest, and a coronation ball. For further information, call (808) 536–1218.

Hula Bowl Game • College football teams slug it out for the championship at Aloha Stadium in Aiea. Halftime is an elaborate production, with hula dances and Hawaiian music. For more information, call (808) 955–5541.

Annual Ala Wai Canoe Challenge • After an outrigger race on Honolulu's canal, paddlers compete in ancient Hawaiian games at Ala Wai Field. For further information, call (808) 923–1802.

Keiki Great Aloha Run • Hundreds of children try to best each other in this two-mile run around Oahu's McKinley High School track. For further information, call (808) 942–3786.

Big Board Surfing Classic • Master surfers head for this two-day contest at Makaha Beach in Oahu.

Makahiki Festival • Far better known to locals than to visitors, this revival of an ancient celebration of peace includes competitions in Hawaiian games, free food, and music. Molokai's Kaunakakai Park is the locale, and events are open to both children and adults. For more information, call (808) 553–3688.

February

The Captain Cook Festival • This all-out party held in Waimea, Kauai, honors Captain James Cook, the British explorer who brought Hawaii to the attention of his part of the world. For further information, call (808) 338–1226.

Hawaiian Open International Tournament • This PGA competition takes place at Waialae Golf and Country Club in Honolulu.

The Great Aloha Run • This eight-mile jog begins at Aloha Tower in downtown Honolulu and ends at Aloha Stadium in Halawa. Held each year on Presidents' Day, it is a benefit run for charities. The entry fee, about $16, is tax deductible. For further information, call (800) 3FUN–RUN or (808) 735–6092.

Pro Bowl • NFL stars play at Aloha Stadium in Honolulu.

Great Waikoloa Horse Races and Rodeo • Waikoloa on the Big Island is the locale of this rip-roaring rodeo.

Cherry Blossom Festival • See January.

March

Maui Marathon • Runners burn rubber from Maui Mall to Whalers Village.

Kamehameha Schools Songfest • *Oahu* • For information, call (808) 842–8211.

Prince Kuhio Day • *March 26* • With music and dance from the late 19th century and the early 20th, this statewide holiday honors the life and work of Hawaii's first Congressional representative. For further information, call (808) 546–7573.

Hawaiian Song Festival and Composing Contest • *Oahu* • For information, call (808) 521–9815.

Kite-Flying Competitions • This statewide event is held at Kapi-olani Park in Honolulu.

Scottish-Hawaiian Highlands Gathering • *Oahu* • For information, call (808) 523–5050.

St. Patrick's Day • Watch the parade in Waikiki.

Spring Renewal Festival • Sometimes the New Agers are indistinguishable from the hippies of the '60s at this retreat hosted by the YMCA camp in Keanae in Maui. A few hundred people gather here each year for yoga classes and meditation, fueled by vegetarian meals and absorption of the beautiful surroundings.

Cherry Blossom Festival • See January.

March/April

Merrie Monarch Festival • Sleepy Hilo, on the Big Island, perks up to honor David Kalakaua, Hawaii's last king, with a showdown between the state's premier hula schools. During his reign, Kalakaua revived the hula and other Hawaiian cultural traditions. You'll need to purchase tickets far in advance. For information about buying tickets by mail, call (808) 935–9168.

April

Buddha Day • Buddha's birthday is commemorated in temples throughout the islands.

Easter Sunrise Service • This inspiring ceremony is held at the tranquil Punchbowl National Memorial Cemetery in Honolulu. The views from this lofty site are fabulous.

Hawaiian Festival of Music • Classical, swing, jazz, and popular music is performed by musicians from all over the U.S. in this top-notch competition in Honolulu.

Cherry Blossom Festival • See January.

May

Lei Day • *May 1* • May Day is Lei Day on all islands, and no one would be caught dead without a fresh flower garland—or two, or three—around their neck. The coronation of the lei queen and lei-making contests are held at Kapiolani Park in Honolulu (call (808) 521–9815 for more information). In Kauai, the lei-making competition takes place at the Kauai Museum in Lihue ((808) 245–6931).

Pacific Handcrafts Guild Spring Fair • Ala Moana Park in Honolulu is the place to go to browse through all kinds of quality island-made crafts.

The Barrio Festival • A miniature Philippine village is put up on the lawn of the War Memorial Complex in Wailuku, Maui, for a glimpse into Filipino life.

Western Week in Honokaʻa • *The Big Island.* • For information, call (808) 775–7722.

June

King Kamehameha Day • *June 11* • All islands honor Hawaii's first king, the man who brought all of Hawaii under one rule. Happenings include hula performances, chant demonstrations, parades, and crafts exhibits. Dating back to 1872, this is the oldest state holiday. Most events take place on Oahu and the Big Island. Call (808) 935–9338 or (808) 536–6540.

King Kamehameha Hula and Chant Competition • This contest takes place in Ala Moana Park, Oahu. For information, call (808) 536–6540.

Festival of the Pacific • On Oahu, music, dance, and sporting competitions highlight the cultures of the Pacific. For further information, call (808) 833–0026.

Kapalua Music Festival • Chamber music is played by master musicians from all over the U.S. at the Kapalua Bay Hotel in Maui. For further information, call (808) 669–0244.

Mission Houses Museum Fancy Fair • Held on the lawn of the museum in Honolulu, this fair offers a striking array of handicrafts and other goodies, including Hawaiian foods.

Puna Cultural Festival • *The Big Island* • For information, call (808) 965–8936.

The O-Bon Dance Festivals • *late June through September* • Oahu and the Big Island. These traditional Buddhist ceremonies honor family members who have died. Performing in the yards of temples, Bon dancers dress in bright Japanese hapi coats or kimonos. They are accompanied by drummers, bamboo flutists, and vocalists. Colorful paper lanterns are strung through the yards. For further information, call (808) 945–3545.

Fiesta Filipina • *Oahu and other islands* • Celebrates the culture of the Philippines with music, food, and dance.

July

Rodeos • Paniolos (Hawaiian cowboys) have a field day in Makawao on Maui ((808) 877–5343) during Hawaii's biggest rodeo, and in Naalehu and on Parker Ranch on the Big Island ((808) 885–7655).

Naalehu Carnival • *The Big Island* • For information, call (808) 928–8326.

Tin Man Triathlon • Athletes swim, bike, and jog their way around Oahu.

Prince Lot Hula Festival • Bring a mat or a towel to sit on the grass among the other spectators in lush Moanalua Gardens on Oahu. For further information, call (808) 839–5334.

The Ukulele Festival • Few visitors know about this musical happening held in Kapiolani Park on Oahu. Performers come from various countries to show their stuff on their ukuleles. For further information, call (808) 487–6010.

The O-Bon Dance Festivals • See June.

July/August

Kona Hawaiian Billfish Tournament • *late July through early August* • Deep-sea fishing is king on the Big Island. People crowd the pier for the afternoon weigh-ins.

The O-Bon Dance Festivals • See June.

August

Na Hula O Hawaii Festival • *Oahu* • For information, call (808) 262–2397.

Macadamia Nut Harvest Festival • What can you do with macadamia nuts besides eat them? You'll find out at this fun-filled celebration that kids will enjoy in Honokaa on the Big Island during the third week of the month. For further information, call (808) 775–7276.

Establishment Day • The Big Island honors Hawaiian culture with music and dance performances and crafts workshops. For further information, call (808) 882–7218.

Hawaiian International Billfish Tournament • Crowds pack the shore when the marlin are weighed in at this fishing competition held in Kailua-Kona on the Big Island. For further information, call (808) 922–9708.

Slack Key Guitar Festival • This truly local concert showcases Hawaii's trademark style of playing the guitar. This event is held in the McCoy Pavilion in Ala Moana Park in Honolulu, Oahu. For further information, call (808) 536–4832.

West Kauai Summer Festival • *Kauai* • For information, call (808) 338–1226.

Molokai Riding Club Average • For information, call (808) 553–3569.

Samoan Flag Day • *Oahu* • For information, call (808) 545–7451.

The Keiki Hula Competition • Children compete in modern and ancient hula during this two-day event at the Kamehameha Schools Kakuhaupio Gymnasium on Oahu.

The O-Bon Dance Festival • See June.

September

Aloha Week Festival • This celebration of Hawaii is the state's most elaborate cultural event. The 27.5-mile canoe race from Molokai to Oahu is the highlight. The action lasts for a week on each of the main islands. Since the weeks occur successively, you can follow the crafts exhibits, luaus, and parades from island to island if you haven't had enough fun. Other activities include concerts, block parties, hula performances, and a grand ball. This festival was begun in 1946 by Hawaii Jaycees to put the depressing years of World War II firmly in the past. For further information, call (808) 944–8857.

Waikiki Annual Rough Water Swim • Everyone from *keikis* (children) to *tutus* (grandmothers) splashes through the waves in this swim race in Oahu.

Na Wahine O Ke Kai Molokai to Oahu Women's Race • For information, call (808) 525–5476.

O-Bon Dance Festival • See June.

October

Makahiki Festival • This is a reenactment of the ancient celebration of peacetime that was held each year to give folks a break from warfare. Oahu's Waimea Falls Park hosts this event, with Hawaiian music and games. For further information, call (808) 638–8511.

Chinese Moon Festival • *Oahu* • For information, call (808) 533–3181.

Kanikapila Hawaiian Music Festival • *Oahu* • For information, call (808) 948–8178.

Kamehameha Schools Festival • *Oahu* • For information, call (808) 842–8663.

Shinto Thanksgiving Festival • *Oahu* • For information, call (808) 945–3545.

Ironman Championship Triathlon • The swimming, biking, and running begins in Kailua-Kona on the Big Island.

Annual Orchid Plant and Flower Show • Some of Hawaii's most beautiful and most unusual flowers are on display in Blaisdell Center, Honolulu.

Bishop Museum Open House • This enjoyable fund-raising event for this fascinating Honolulu museum features planetarium shows, arts and crafts, and Pacific and Asian culinary specialties.

The Maui County Fair • A colorful parade kicks off this event, held at Kahului Fairgrounds in Maui. For further information, call (808) 877–5343.

Bankoh Molokai Hoe • *Molokai* • For information, call (808) 261–6615.

Outrigger Canoe Race • Strong arms paddle from Molokai to Oahu.

November

Kona Coffee Festival • Beginning after the harvest, this week-long celebration on the Big Island includes a coffee bean–picking contest, taste tests, and an elaborate parade with floats. For further information, call (808) 325–7998.

Na Mele O Maui • Hawaiian culture is brought to life through hula performances, arts and crafts, and luaus in Lahaina and Kaanapali in Maui. For further information, call (808) 879–4577.

Rodeo • On Oahu over Thanksgiving weekend, New Town and Country Stables hosts a rodeo that draws cowboys from all over the state as well as the mainland. For more information, call (808) 259–9941.

King Kalakaua Keiki Hula Festival • *The Big Island* • Hula performed by children. For further information, call (808) 329–8855.

Festival of Trees • *The Big Island* • For information, call (808) 935–7141.

Christmas Fair • You'll be checking off names right and left on your holiday gift list as you pick up all kinds of goodies for family and friends. The lawn of the Mission Houses Museum in Honolulu teems with craftspeople selling wonderfully imaginative wood carvings, wall hangings, clothing, jewelry, poetry, and other items.

December

Hawaiian Pro Surfing Championships • This surfing competition to end all surfing competitions takes place at the famed Banzai Pipeline on the north shore of Oahu.

Annual Honolulu Marathon • Runners begin at Aloha Tower and finish at Kapiolani Park.

Pearl Harbor Day • A service at the U.S.S. *Arizona* memorial commemorates the people killed in the attack that launched the U.S. into World War II.

Aloha Bowl Game • College football is played at Aloha Stadium in Oahu.

Hawaii International Film Festival • *Oahu* • Admission is free for all showings. Take part in screenwriting workshops or symposia on topics such as documentary filmmaking. For further information, call (808) 944–7200 or (808) 944–7666.

Festival of Trees • *Oahu* • For information, call (808) 547–4371.

Kauai Museum Holiday Festival • For information, call (808) 245–6931.

(Also see individual Island chapters.)

FISHING: You'll need a license for fresh water fishing. You'll also need one for deep-sea fishing if you're not on a charter boat. Make arrangements to charter a boat as far in advance as possible. Expect to pay about $400 for a full day (eight or nine hours) and to leave a 25% to 50% deposit when you make a reservation. You can buy and rent fishing gear at tackle shops. "Head boats" generally have gear and live bait for rent, while the price for charters includes gear.

For inshore or freshwater fishing tips, stop in at local tackle shops. Ask about hooking up (pun intended) with local guides. You'll find good fishing right off sandy or rocky coasts.

(Also see Fishing in "The Best Place For . . . .")

GETTING MARRIED: See "The Best Places For . . . ."

JET LAG: While most people suffer from jet lag after long flights, there are things you can do to take the edge off of it. First, to help you adjust psychologically, set your watch to the time of your destination (Hawaii or home) as you board the plane. Dehydration is a major contributor to the groggy, sapped feeling after hours in the air; during your flight, drink at least a glass of water per hour and avoid alcohol. Eat meals at times that are as close as possible to meal times of your destination (try to nibble a little, even if you're not hungry when served). Doing stretching exercises in your seat and taking periodic walks up and down the aisle will improve circulation. Get as much sleep as possible before and during the flight.

MAIL: You may want to make arrangements with your post office at home to have your mail held until you return from your trip. Most hotels in Hawaii sell stamps at the same price as in the post office. There doesn't seem to be a great deal of consistency in the length of time mail takes to travel between Hawaii and the mainland; allow anywhere from a week to ten days or more. Express Mail and courier companies such as Federal Express offer two-day service between the continental U.S. and the main islands. However, be forewarned that weekend pick-ups and drop-offs may not be available on Neighbor Islands, so those two days can turn into three or four. Many of the larger hotels have fax machines.

(Also see Business Hours and Holidays in this chapter.)

MEDICAL CONCERNS: Packing a small first-aid kit is a good idea. Also be sure to bring insect repellent, sun block, and sunglasses. While it's perfectly fine to drink tap water in Hawaii, don't drink from streams or natural pools since they may contain parasites. Fresh vegetables, fruit, and dairy products are also safe.

No matter how dark your skin is to begin with, be sure to use a good sunblock whenever you're outdoors. Don't spend your whole first day frying on the beach. Expose your skin to heavy doses of sun gradually, and avoid being in direct sunlight for long stretches between 10 a.m. and 2 p.m., when the rays are strongest. Don't forget that even on hazy days, the sun's powerful ultraviolet light comes through. However, if you do end up with a burn, stay out of the sun. Take a cool bath and apply a first-aid spray or lotion. Aloe is especially effective. Get medical help right away if your burn is so bad that you feel feverish, nauseated, dizzy, or have chills or a headache.

If you are in need of a doctor, the staff at your accommodation can help you contact one. Hawaii's largest hospital, Queen's Medical Center in Oahu, is one of the country's best medical facilities.

In case of emergency, dial 911 on Oahu, Maui, Kauai, Molokai, and Lanai. On the Big Island of Hawaii, you must call the local police directly (961–2211).

MONEY: While credit cards are widely used in Hawaii, not all establishments accept them and those that do don't necessarily honor all major cards. If you run out of money during your stay, you may be able to cash a personal check, get a cash advance, or arrange for someone at home to wire you money through offices of American Express or Western Union. (See individual Island chapters for locations.) Some of the larger hotels have American Express offices on the premises. You can use ATM (Automatic Teller Machine) cards at more than a few banks in Hawaii.

Traveler's checks are widely accepted. It is best to get at least a portion in small denominations ($10s or $20s) since some places have a limit on the amount they will cash. In case of loss or theft, be sure to keep your traveler's check receipt and a list of serial numbers separate from the checks themselves.

NEWSPAPERS: The state's daily newspapers are the *Honolulu Advertiser*, published in the morning, and the Honolulu *Star Bulletin*, which comes out in the afternoon.

PACKAGE TOURS: See Costs and Accommodations in this chapter.

PACKING: Keep your suitcase as light as you can. If at all possible, pack only what you can carry onto the plane. Then, while everyone else is waiting for their luggage in baggage claim, you'll be on your way to the beach.

By day Hawaii is an extremely casual place. You'll spend most of your time in bathing suits, shorts and T-shirts or sundresses, and sandals or rubber flip-flops (known as *zoris,* their Japanese name, or "slippers"). At night, dress can also be as casual as you want. However, if you're planning to splurge at any of Hawaii's excellent upscale restaurants, men should pack a sports jacket and women a few dressy outfits.

Be sure to bring plenty of sunblock and insect repellent, although you'll have no problem buying some once you arrive. If you'll be hiking, camping, or visiting high elevations (such as volcanoes), bring a sweater and windbreaker, long pants, gloves, and sturdy walking shoes or sneakers. Strong shoes also come in handy if you're going to be walking across lava (if you plan to search for petroglyphs or hunt for fallen coconuts on the Big Island).

SAFETY: While Hawaii may have the look and feel of paradise, it is still a part of the real world and crime is no stranger. Whenever you can, take advantage of hotel in-room safes or front desk safety deposit boxes. Carry as few valuables as possible when you go out, and never leave your things unattended—not even in the locked trunk of a parked car. Especially when you're on the beach or in a park, always keep your eye on your possessions. Do a little homework before you venture off the beaten path. Ask locals if you'll be comfortable in the areas you plan to visit. Fields of marijuana sprinkle the countryside and are often heavily guarded, either by less-than-friendly people or by booby traps. Never hitchhike.

In case of emergency, dial 911 on Oahu, Maui, Kauai, Molokai, and Laina. On the Big Island of Hawaii you must call the local police directly (961–2211).

(Also see Swimming and Sun and Medical Concerns in this chapter.)

SENDING HAWAII HOME: Everyone gets postcards from vacationing friends. But how many people receive unboxed, unwrapped coconuts in their mail boxes? I've tried **mailing coconuts** to the mainland on several occasions, and it actually works. Friends have gotten such a kick out of it. Be sure to find fallen coconuts that are brown (not green), with smooth surfaces. There should be a little liquid sloshing around inside. Use a thick, indelible marker to write the name and address directly onto the coconut. When you have it weighed at the post office, be sure that the stamps are firmly affixed. Some stores, such as those in Old Koloa Town on Kauai, sell coconuts for this purpose, but it is cheaper if you find and mail them yourself. One good place to look is under the coconut palms around the lava fields on the grounds of the Mauna Lani Bay Hotel on the Big Island. (Be sure to wear sturdy shoes, since the lava can be very rough.)

Inspected, boxed **pineapples** can be purchased at the airport or at fruit stands that deliver them to the airport in time for your flight or mail them directly to the mainland.

While in Hawaii, eat your fill of guava, passion fruit, mangoes, and avocados. The U.S. Department of Agriculture discourages people from bringing or mailing these fruits to the mainland since they can carry fruit flies and other destructive bugs. Visitors are urged to bake, can, dry, stew, or otherwise preserve fresh fruit before sending it to the mainland. Of course, this is only practical if you are staying in a private home or condominium with kitchen facilities.

If you're mailing boxes of **macadamia nuts** to the mainland, it is best to have them wrapped in plain brown paper. Otherwise, those flashy, attractive boxes may never reach their destinations.

SHOPPING: See shopping in ''The Best Places For . . . .''

SWIMMING AND SUN: The power of the Pacific is as awesome as its beauty. Always use caution in the ocean. Unless the water is calm, stick to a swimming pool. Be sure you know which of Hawaii's beaches are safe for swimming and which, because of rough waters or strong currents, are not. Some are better locales for sunbathing and picnicking than for taking a dip. Note that water conditions change with the season, so that calm beach of summer may be treacherous in winter. Heed weather or sea condition warnings. Never turn your back on the ocean. There are no lifeguards on Hawaii's beaches, so never swim alone. Don't overexert yourself by trying to swim great distances. Swim parallel to the shore if you get snagged by a rip current. Keep a close eye on children. Don't swim in the vicinity of surfers, since they can't always spot bathers.

Surfing and body surfing can be extremely dangerous. Try these sports only after you've had supervised instruction from someone who is highly skilled. When near coral reefs (which can give nasty cuts), wear protective shoes, such as reef slippers or diving booties. Avoid walking on partially exposed wet boulders, since a nearly invisible growth of algae can make them quite slippery.

When swimming in inland volcanic pools, be sure to note the locations of submerged rocks, which can be jagged. Even at pools where you see locals diving off ledges into the water, I don't recommend your trying this tricky feat.

Whether the natural color of your skin is pale eggshell or deep chocolate, use a strong, waterproof sunblock. You'll look and feel much healthier (now and in the future) if you allow yourself to get darker slowly. Sunglasses and a wide-brimmed hat will come in handy.

TELEPHONES: Hawaii's area code is 808. A local call is one that is made within an island. Calls to other islands or to the mainland are classified as long distance. Most hotels add a hefty surcharge to calls guests make from their rooms; a fee is often charged for access to a line even when a guest uses a telephone credit card.

TIME ZONE: Hawaiian Standard Time is two hours earlier than the Pacific Standard Time of the continental West Coast and five hours earlier than Eastern Standard Time. So if it's 9 a.m. in Hawaii, it's 11 a.m. in California, noon in Colorado, 1 p.m. in Illinois, and 2 p.m. in New York. That is, unless Daylight Saving Time (from the last Sunday in April through the last Sunday in October) is in effect on the mainland. In this case, since Hawaii does not observe Daylight Saving Time, the difference in time is increased by an hour.

TIPPING: As on the mainland, tipping is 15% to 20%.

TRANSPORTATION

Buses and Taxis • On islands other than Oahu, you'll need to drive if you plan to see more than your hotel. Oahu has a convenient public bus system, and taxis are plentiful in Honolulu. While cabs are available on other islands, they can be very expensive since distances can be great. Airport shuttle service can be arranged on the main islands. Many air-hotel package deals include transportation to and from the airport.

Renting Wheels • In comparing the charges of different car rental companies, make sure that you take into account factors such as the daily versus the weekly rate, the cost of insurance, whether you have to drop off/pick up the car at the airport, whether you'll be charged a flat rate or have unlimited mileage, etc. With unlimited mileage, a basic rental car with air conditioning is likely to run about $35 to $45 a day, plus insurance. Two- or three-day or weekly rates are quite economical. If you're going to be island hopping, you can rent a car ahead of time for all islands through one company. During the high season (winter), you'll need to reserve a car well in advance, and you'll find that rates are somewhat more expensive than during the summer. Note that some hotels and condominiums include car rental in their rates.

If you haven't rented a car before arrival, avoid those "$5 a day" and other too-good-to-be-true deals offered by people handing out flyers on the street, especially in Waikiki. Hidden costs can often make these "incredible" deals more expensive than others. Once in Hawaii, it is best to rent a car either at the airport or through your hotel.

It is against the rules of all car rental companies in Hawaii to drive regular vehicles on unpaved roads. You'll need to rent a four-wheel-drive vehicle to go to certain places, such as the summit of Mauna Kea or the green sand beach on the Big Island.

The national rental companies in Hawaii that usually offer the best deals are **Budget** (800) 527–0700 and **Dollar Rent-A-Car** (800) 365–5276. Others to check out are **Avis** (800) 331–1212, **Hertz** (800) 654–3131, **Alamo** (800) 327–9633, and **National** (800) 367–5140. **Tropical Rent A Car** (800) 227–7368 is an excellent statewide agency. Through some local firms, you can rent flashy sports cars, luxury sedans, or even used cars.

You'll get detailed driving maps at the rental company or your hotel. (See Directions, in this chapter, for Hawaii's unique names for north, south, east, and west). Before you leave, plan your route and note one-way streets, particularly in Honolulu. Avoid rush hours whenever possible. Find out locations of service stations, especially if you are beginning a long drive into a remote area. Also find out what the weather has been like in your destination and what Mother Nature has in store for the weather in the near future. A heavy rainfall one day can leave roads dangerously muddy the next, even if it's bright and sunny.

Since you never know when you might get snagged by an irresistible beach while driving, it's a good idea to take your beachwear, sunblock, hat or visor, sunglasses, and towel whenever you set out. So as not to cause accidents or anger residents, pull over into designated overlooks to enjoy scenic spots instead of driving slowly to absorb your surroundings. Always allow extra time to get wherever you're going (especially the airport). Never leave valuables in the car, even in a locked trunk. If you're one of the scores of vacationers driving a convertible, always put the top up when the car is parked so that an unexpected rainfall won't do any damage.

The law requires you always wear seatbelts and strap children under age three into car seats (which are available for rent).

For further information, refer to individual Island chapters.

Ferries • See Cruises and Interisland Ferries in this chapter.

TRAVEL FOR THE DISABLED: Wheelchair accessibility is improving in Hawaii, as it is in many parts of the world. Oahu is probably the best island in Hawaii for physically disabled travelers.

To help you plan your trip, contact an organization such as the **American Foundation for the Blind,** the **American Heart Association,** the **New York Diabetes Foundation,** the New York–based **Society for the Advancement of Travel for the Handicapped,** or **The**

Information Center for Individuals with Disabilities in Boston. In addition, Hawaii's Commission on the Handicapped has published the **Traveler's Guide for the Physically Handicapped** series, which covers Oahu, Maui, Kauai, and the Big Island of Hawaii. (Contact the Commission at Old Federal Building, 335 Merchant St., Room 353, Honolulu, HI 96813, (808) 458–7606.)

TRAVELING SOLO: Like most of the world's travel destinations, Hawaii is geared to couples. "Single supplements" cause what might be an economical hotel or tour package for two to be quite expensive for one. Especially at the larger hotels, the single traveler will pay more than half of the cost of a double room. Therefore, solo travelers will do well to seek out the least expensive ways to stay in Hawaii. Bed and breakfasts, small hotels, a YMCA, a YWCA, or campsites are good choices. These are also places where single travelers are most likely to meet people. Another option is to join a travel club that specializes in matching compatible single travelers. A good travel agent will be able to recommend such an organization in your area.

Single women should feel perfectly comfortable traveling alone in Hawaii. However, Hawaii is not immune to crime, so women (and men) should take the same precautions they would in any other nonutopia. Don't hitchhike; never turn your back on your belongings; don't go into remote areas at night; etc.

(Also see Singles in "The Best Places For . . . .")

TRAVELING WITH CHILDREN: See Families with Children in "The Best Places For . . . ."

USEFUL CONTACTS: The following are the main office of the Hawaii Visitors Bureau, in Honolulu, and continental U.S. HVB offices. See individual Island chapters for local HVB branches.

Main Office, Oahu
2270 Kalakaua Ave., Suite 801
Honolulu, HI 96815
(808) 923–1811

Chicago
180 North Michigan Ave., Suite 1031
Chicago, IL 60601
(312) 236–0632

Los Angeles
3440 Wilshire Blvd., Suite 502
Los Angeles, CA 90010
(213) 385–5301

New York
441 Lexington Ave., Suite 1407
New York, NY 10017
(212) 986–9203

San Francisco
50 California St., Suite 450
San Francisco, CA 94111
(415) 392–8173

Washington, DC
1511 K St., NW, Suite 519
Washington, DC 20005
(202) 393–6752

OAHU

To many outsiders who equate Oahu with Waikiki's high-rises, crowds, and kitschy-to-sophisticated stores and restaurants, it comes as a surprise that most of the island is countryside. Breezes ripple sugarcane fields and hibiscus petals. Jagged red cliffs plunge to royal blue waters edged in frothy white foam. Plump clouds lounge on the tops of rugged, jade-colored mountains. Master surfers balance their boards on mammoth curls. In some parts of the island, peacocks and jungle fowl freely strut their stuff. Even a small group of shy, wild wallabies hops around one area.

There is no question that Oahu is the most developed island in the chain. Yet, most of the development is contained on the southern coast, where Honolulu, the capital of the state, is located. The vast majority of the island's hotels (most of which are high-rises) are clustered in Waikiki. But this tourist haven is only a small (albeit jampacked) neighborhood within Honolulu, which in turn takes up only a small portion of the island's 608 square miles. Honolulu and its suburbs are along the leeward coast of Oahu. A pair of tunnels pierces the Koolau Mountains between the city and the windward coast, the far side of the island.

In the minds of some mainlanders, particularly those on the East Coast, Hawaii is somewhat of a paradisal blur. They know it is the home of Honolulu, Waikiki Beach, the extinct Diamond Head volcano, and the USS *Arizona* Memorial at Pearl Harbor. But they're not exactly sure which island these attractions are on. The fact that they're all found on Oahu is one of the reasons this is the state's most visited island. It is also the most populous chunk of the archipelago. However, it's not the largest. That honor belongs to the island of Hawaii, commonly known as the Big Island (and thus often mistakenly thought to be the main island). Following Maui in size, Oahu is only the third largest.

This island has grown on me over the years. In part, it's because I've become better acquainted with the Oahu that sprawls beyond Honolulu. There's a small town feel to much of the island. Mom-and-pop "plate lunch" restaurants and shave ice (snow cone) stands dot streets. Many police officers drive their own cars, removing the bubble light when they go home. But my feelings have also grown warmer toward

102

the busy capital itself, which is among the dozen largest cities in the U.S. This change of heart has everything to do with the beautification program that swept across Waikiki during the late 1980s. Tile-paved sidewalks, newly planted trees, improved traffic conditions, and the lessening of the hawking of leaflets advertising car rental companies and tourist attractions—this has all added up to a much more pleasant resort area than in earlier years.

If you're looking for action, you'll find plenty on Oahu. It would take ages to sample all the excellent restaurants, night clubs, discos, bars, and concerts. You can give your wallet a real workout in the stores and boutiques that hit you from all sides as you walk down Kalakaua Avenue and Waikiki's other streets or wander around your hotel. Oahu also has more than a few upscale shopping malls.

Riding the waves in an ancient Hawaiian-style outrigger canoe or learning to surf on Waikiki Beach are only the beginning of the many water- and landsports available. For fabulous (though crowded) snorkeling, few people pass up a trip to picturesque Hanauma Bay. Across the island from Waikiki, the North Shore, famed for its lush foliage, rural atmosphere, and beautiful beaches, seems to be in another world. During the winter, its excellent surfing conditions draw scores of sports enthusiasts, whether they come just for fun, to compete in one of the tournaments, or simply to watch the action (and all the bodies in skimpy bathing suits).

Oahu is a great place to bring children, since there are so many attractions to keep them occupied. In addition to the beach there is: a zoo, an aquarium, Sea Life Park, Paradise Park (with its trained bird show), the Maritime Center with its Children's Touch and Feel Museum, Kapiolani Park where kite flying is all the rage, a small amusement park, and even rodeos.

When you're ready to dig a bit below the surface of the island, visit the exhibits and recreated villages at the Polynesian Cultural Center. Explore unspoiled, flower-splashed Waimea Falls Park, on the site of an old Hawaiian settlement. Iolani Palace, the only royal palace in the United States is well worth your time. In Honolulu's Chinatown, the aromatic herbal shops are intriguing, and inexpensive restaurants serve a variety of Asian cuisines. Browse through the Bishop Museum, filled with Hawaiian artifacts, or Byodo-In Temple, a recreation of an ancient Japanese place of worship, surrounded by artful gardens.

Hawaiian Roots

Modern examples of old Hawaii are here and there throughout the island. After a storm, it is not unusual to see picknicking Hawaiian families walking stooped over along Ewa Beach, near Pearl Harbor. No, they aren't looking for shells; rather, they're collecting *limu* (edible sea-

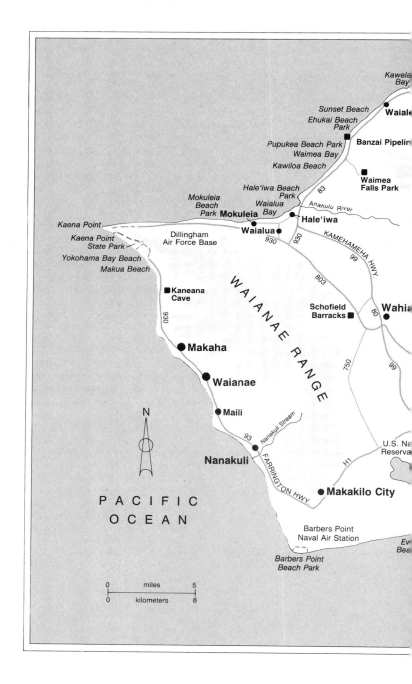

Kawela
Bay

Sunset Beach   Waiale
Ehukai Beach
Park
Pupukea Beach Park   Banzai Pipelin
Waimea Bay
Kawiloa Beach   Waimea
                            Falls Park

Hale'iwa Beach   83
Mokuleia   Park
Beach   Waialua   Anahulu River
Park Mokuleia Bay   Hale'iwa
Kaena Point   KAMEHAMEHA HWY.
                      Waialua
Kaena Point   Dillingham   930
State Park   Air Force Base   930
Yokohama Bay Beach   99
Makua Beach   803

■ Kaneana
Cave   W
                    A
                    I   Schofield   80
930   A   Barracks ■   Wahi
                    N
                    A
   ● Makaha   E   750
                    R   99
   ● Waianae   A
                    N
   ● Maili   G
                    E
N   Nanakuli Stream
                    93
                         FARRINGTON HWY.   U.S. Na
            Nanakuli   Reserva
                                H1
                            ● Makakilo City
PACIFIC
OCEAN
                    Barbers Point
                    Naval Air Station   Ev
                                          Bea
                Barbers Point
                Beach Park

0   miles   5
0   kilometers   8

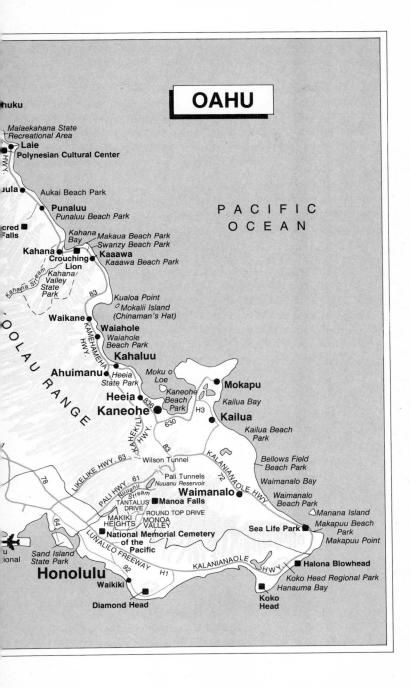

OAHU

huku

*Malaekahana State
Recreational Area*
Laie
Polynesian Cultural Center

Aukai Beach Park
uula

Punaluu
Punaluu Beach Park
cred
Falls
*Kahana
Bay* *Makaua Beach Park*
Swanzy Beach Park
Kahana **Kaaawa**
Crouching *Kaaawa Beach Park*
Lion
*Kahana
Valley
State
Park*

Waikane

Waiahole
*Waiahole
Beach Park*

Kahaluu

Ahuimanu *Heeia
State Park*
*Moku o
Loe*
*Kaneohe
Beach
Park*
Mokapu
Heeia
Kailua Bay
Kaneohe
H3
Kailua

*Kailua Beach
Park*

Wilson Tunnel
*Bellows Field
Beach Park*
Pali Tunnels
Nuuanu Reservoir
Waimanalo Bay
Waimanalo
*Waimanalo
Beach Park*
Manoa Falls
ROUND TOP DRIVE
*MANOA
VALLEY*
Manana Island
*Makapuu Beach
Park*
Sea Life Park *Makapuu Point*
**National Memorial Cemetery
of the
Pacific**
u
ional *Sand Island
State Park*
Halona Blowhead

Honolulu
Koko Head Regional Park
Hanauma Bay
Waikiki
**Koko
Head**
Diamond Head

Kualoa Point
*Mokalii Island
(Chinaman's Hat)*

PACIFIC
OCEAN

KAMEHAMEHA HWY.
KAHEKILI HWY.
LIKELIKE HWY. 63
PALI HWY. 61
KALANIANAOLE HWY.
LUNALILO FREEWAY
KALANIANAOLE HWY.
TANTALUS
DRIVE
MAKIKI
HEIGHTS
Nuuanu
Stream
KOOLAU RANGE
Kahana Stream

weed) brought in by the tide after having been uprooted by rough weather. Cooking with seaweed is a Hawaiian tradition that has been passed down for countless generations.

Among the people who make a noted difference on Oahu is acclaimed Hawaiian-Irish sculptor Rocky Kaiouliokahikoloehu Jensen. He works with Hale Naua III, the Society of Hawaiian Artists, to broaden the appeal and understanding of Hawaiian creativity and culture. Look for his totem pole–like tiki at the McDonald's in Waimanalo. Works done by Hale Naua artists—including feather creations, paintings, spears, and sculpture—are on display at Honolulu airport's interisland terminal and Fort DeRussy's U.S. Army Museum in Waikiki.

Na Hoa Hoala Kapa (Friends of the Reawakening of Kapa) is a group that continues the ancient tradition of making cloth from bark. It oversees everything from growing the trees to picking the plants for the dyes that create the designs. To learn about this complicated yet rewarding art, check local newspapers for the group's periodic demonstrations and lectures at the Bishop Museum, schools, and cultural festivals.

Now a musical institution in Oahu, Don Ho spent his early years in rustic Kaneohe, across the Koolau mountains from Honolulu, where he tended bar at his parents' restaurant. Graduating from the University of Hawaii with a degree in sociology, he became an Air Force pilot. Part Hawaiian, Chinese, and Portuguese, Don Ho has been a hot entertainer since the 1960s and his often sentimental songs have become synonymous with Hawaii for many people.

Millions of mainlanders who never set foot on Hawaiian soil were introduced to the Islands through his network television variety show that ran in the 1970s. He also toured the mainland continually, performing in glittery night clubs in Las Vegas, Los Angeles, and other cities. Some listeners may find his music a bit commercial or corny. But scores of other loyal fans never miss an opportunity to see and hear him in action.

Since 1981, he has spent six nights a week putting on a show at the Hilton Hawaiian Village Dome in Honolulu. His singing is sandwiched by a Polynesian revue and other Hawaiian entertainment. Nearly every night, he tells the audience that he hates "Tiny Bubbles," the song he's best known for. But then, of course, he sings it anyway, to the delight of the crowd.

Special Events

Oahu hosts many annual events in addition to the winter surfing championships on the North Shore. The state's largest cultural festival is Aloha Week, which takes place on the major islands each fall. The highlight is the 27.5-mile canoe race from the island of Molokai to Oahu. During halftime at the January Hula Bowl at Aloha Stadium, there's an elaborate performance of music and hula, as well as other entertainment. Tailgate parties crowd the parking lot with entire families barbecuing to a tangle of rock music from various and sundry radios.

Other happenings include the October reenactment of the ancient Hawaiian Makahiki Festival, a peacetime celebration with old games, at Waimea Falls Park; Chinese New Year and the Chinese cultural Narcissus Festival in Honolulu's Chinatown from January through March; the Japanese Cherry Blossom Festival from January through March: ukulele and slack key guitar festivals; rodeos; and kite-flying competitions at Kapiolani Park.

Getting Around

If you're based in Honolulu, driving can be far more trouble than it's worth. Thanks to a convenient public bus system, you won't need to rent a car on Oahu. In addition to traveling to many points in and around Honolulu, TheBus circles the island. Taxis are also convenient within Honolulu. Seeing the sights in Waikiki and downtown Honolulu is perfectly manageable on foot. There is even a fire engine–red trolley that takes tourists from Waikiki to surrounding attractions.

Whether you're walking or driving, you'll have to learn a new set of directions. On Oahu, *Diamond Head* means "east" (toward Diamond Head crater). *Koko Head* means "further east" (toward Koko Head crater). And *ewa* (pronounced "*ay*-vah") means "westerly" (toward Ewa Beach; memory key: the *w* should make you think "west," even though it's pronounced like a *v*). On both Oahu and the Neighbor Islands, *makai* (mahk-*eye*) replaces "southerly, toward the sea." And *mauka* (*mow*-kah) is Hawaiian for "northerly, toward the mountains, inland" (memory key: the first syllable sounds like that of "mountain").

By all means, get off the beaten path and explore. However, before you head into remote areas, talk to locals about whether or not you'll feel comfortable there. With tourism and tourists such a dominant force in Hawaii, some residents aren't especially pleased with the idea of their secluded neighborhoods being privy to outsiders too. In other cases, private property has been given over to marijuana fields and landowners may be less than friendly when it comes to protecting their income.

Waikiki

Waikiki may be a mere one and a half square miles in size, but its glitz and glitter get most of the attention given Oahu. Hundreds of hotels, restaurants, shops, night clubs, and bars are packed into its streets. ABC Drug Stores (which sell a whole lot more than drugs) are omnipresent— there are sometimes even two on a single block, anchoring it like book-

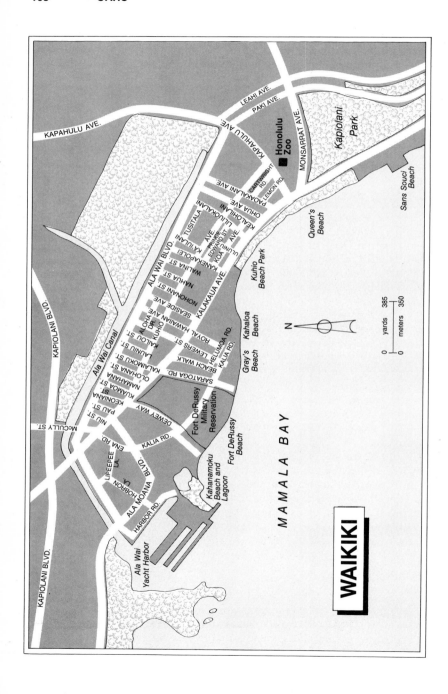

ends. The low profile of the rest of the island is fine with both residents and visitors who, leaving the hordes behind, escape to greater Honolulu and the rural regions. If you like mingling with locals, the only part of Waikiki to hang out in is Kapiolani Park. Otherwise, unless their employment brings them to this resort area, residents spend little time amid its forest of tourists.

Created by human hands (to rid the once swampy area of mosquitoes), the Ala Wai Canal forms Waikiki's north and west borders. Luxury condominiums with views of verdant hillsides stand along the shores of this glistening waterway. Canoe races take place on the canal in the evenings. In the east, Waikiki is bounded by Kapahulu Avenue, Kapiolani Park, and Diamond Head, the extinct volcano that has become an unforgettable landmark. Waikiki Beach and the Pacific Ocean command the southern coast.

From late 1986 to mid-1988, Waikiki underwent a $350 million transformation. What had degenerated into seedy tackiness by the 1970s—with advertising fliers scattered on sidewalks and plastic leis and palm trees in abundance—has now become downright respectable. Crosswalks on Kalakaua Avenue, the main thoroughfare, are decorated with Hawaiian kapa cloth designs. Visitors pour in and out of shops such as Tiffany, Gucci, Chanel, and Celine. Sidewalks have been widened, lined with flowers, outfitted with new benches, and repaved with bricks in warm earth tones. More trees, including Madagascar olive, monkeypod, and autograph, now provide a break from the sun. To lessen traffic congestion, pedicabs have been banned and street signs made more legible. Sidewalk distribution of commercial handbills has been cut down. (Don't be caught jay walking, by the way.)

The centrally located **Royal Hawaiian Shopping Center** takes up a chunk of Kalakaua Avenue. Out front, the **Waikiki Old Town Trolley** departs for tours of Honolulu. If you'd rather see the sights in a flashy car, check out one of the '50s and '60s or luxury car rental companies such as the one next to the Circle Hotel, the oil tank–shaped hotel across from the beach.

Timeshare booths around Waikiki offer big discounts, even freebies, on most major attractions. The catch is that you have to attend a two-hour sales presentation first. If you have time to spare, a little patience, and a lot of sales resistance (if you don't intend to buy any property), you could end up with free tickets for a Windjammer Cruise or other excursion.

Other shopping meccas include the crowded, open-air **International Marketplace** and **King's Village,** with its clocktower, both near Kalakaua and Kaʻiulani. King's Village is tucked behind the twin-towered Hyatt Regency Waikiki and across from the Princess Kaʻiulani Hotel. The cobblestone alleys and the appealing old architecture make this a pleasant place to stop, if only to see a Burger King in a most unlikely building. In addition to the restaurants and shops here, you can watch hula or candle carving demonstrations, among other activities. Every evening at 6:15, a Changing of the Guard Ceremony takes place here, with people dressed as they would have during the latter years of the Hawaiian monarchy.

If dignified, historic architecture is your thing, take a stroll through the Moana Hotel on Kalakaua. Built in 1901, it is Waikiki's oldest hotel. After undergoing a massive renovation, it has become part of the **Sheraton Moana Surfrider** complex. On the beach next to the Moana wing, colorful rows of surfboards stand on a rack, waiting to be taken out to play (for a rental fee). Look for the Wizard Stones on the beach here (near the showers), especially if you have an ailment. During the 16th century, these rocks were said to have been endowed with healing powers by four Tahitian prophets as a gesture of thanks after the stones were put there in their honor.

The queen of Waikiki is still the multi-tiered **Royal Hawaiian Hotel** (the second oldest), built in 1927 and known as the Pink Palace ever since. Stop for a drink at the hotel's outdoor beachside bar and watch life go by while Diamond Head crouches like a lion in the background. Waikiki hotels are a welcome mix of luxury, moderate, and low-budget accommodations. Quite a few luxury and some moderate hotels are directly on the beach. Hotels in all three categories are also near the beach or several blocks away. On the second floor of the twin-towered Hyatt Regency Waikiki, across Kalakaua from the beach, stop by **Hyatt's Hawaii** museum, with its display of Hawaiian arts, including antique quilts and artifacts. At the Waikiki branch of the **First Hawaiian Bank,** huge murals by Jean Charlot illustrate the history of the various ethnic groups that came to Hawaii.

Of course, grand **Waikiki Beach** is the focus of this resort. Different sections of this long sandy strip are known by various names. You'll note that some hotels that call themselves beachfront (and even have brochure photographs to ''prove'' it) are actually across Kalakaua Avenue from the ocean.

Catamarans glide across the water, taking visitors on sailing, snorkeling, and sunset cruises. Sunsets on Waikiki Beach are among Hawaii's best, by the way. (For a fabulous vantage point, after 5:30 p.m. take the glass elevator to the lounge at the top of the Ilikai Hotel.) Outrigger canoes bounce over the waves. But the main attraction is surfing. Everybody's into it. I first realized that age is no factor the moment I saw a slim, elderly, gray-haired woman in short shorts walk by with a surfboard tucked under her firm arm.

Waikiki Beach was one of the first areas in the Islands where Hawaiians began to surf. Certain beaches and kinds of surfboards were used only by the *alii* (aristocracy). This ancient sport was squelched by puritanical missionaries during the early 1800s. But it came back full force at the turn of the 20th century.

In the early days of Hawaii's tourism, "beachboys" taught visitors to surf. One of the best known was Duke Paoa Kahanamoku, a world championship surfer who maneuvered a 114-pound, 16-foot board made of koa wood. In 1915, he went to Australia to introduce the sport to hundreds of amazed onlookers. Waikiki's Kahanamoku Beach and Lagoon is named for this master athlete who was a champion Olympic swimmer as well.

Today "beachboys" (also serving as lifeguards) still teach the sport on Waikiki Beach. Some of the older ones made names for themselves in Hollywood movies, such as octogenarians Steamboat and Moon Doggie, who still guarantee you'll be standing on your board in half an hour. Even if you're not up for testing your skill, spend some time talking story with some of these men. However, if you're a woman who decides to enjoy the company of one of these "beachboys" after hours, know that you probably aren't the first tourist to succumb to their charms and it isn't likely you'll be the last.

Where oiled bodies now happily lie cheek by jowl, the land here was once rice paddies and swamps. After solidifying the ground with landfill, the sand for Waikiki Beach was brought in from other Hawaiian islands, California, Hong Kong, and the far side of Oahu. The main section of Waikiki Beach is especially crowded during the summer and again between December and March. Sun worshippers can escape the bustle by going to nearby **Diamond Head Beach** or **Kahala Beach,** further east.

In 1895, at the base of Diamond Head by **Sans Souci Beach,** a vicious four-day battle erupted between the businessmen who had pushed Liliuokalani off her throne and those who were loyal to the queen. The supporters of the Hawaiian monarchy lost and more than a hundred of them ended up behind bars. Among those imprisoned on charges of treason was George Lycurgus, the flashy hotelier who had opened the Sans Souci Inn on this beach.

Beginning inside **Diamond Head crater,** a well-defined trail leads to the top of this extinct volcano. Sunrises and sunsets are especially breathtaking from these heights. Attractive **Kapiolani Park** spreads itself out at the base of Diamond Head. Especially on weekends, it churns with people jogging; playing soccer, softball, frisbee, and tennis (on lighted courts); and flying kites (not just during the three-day kite-flying festival in March, either). Many Sunday afternoons at 2 p.m., the Royal Hawaiian Band gives free concerts at the bandstand.

David Kalakaua, who reigned as Hawaii's king from 1874 to 1891, was inspired to create this park by his visits to the mainland, where he saw large patches of green set aside for public pleasure. He dedicated this verdant spot in 1877, naming it after his queen. In those days, peacocks roamed freely and there were ponds stocked with gold fish. But these ponds were filled in during the 1920s. Horseracing thrived here for a while, until public distaste for the increasingly wild betting put an end to it.

Today, locals gather in clusters to hear each other strum ukuleles or slack key guitars. If you're visiting in July, consider attending the annual Ukulele Festival. Even the **Honolulu Zoo** (built in 1914) is here, and on Wednesdays and weekends its Monsarrat Avenue fence displays reasonably priced paintings by local artists. On Lei Day (May 1), the park is given over to all kinds of Hawaiian entertainment, including displays of leis and other arts and crafts, a lei-making contest, and the coronation of the lei queen. The **Waikiki Aquarium** is just across the street from the park.

Three times a week, visitors stream into the park for the **Kodak Hula Show,** which has been running since the 1930s. Concerts of Hawaiian, European classical, or popular music take place at the 8000-seat **Waikiki Shell,** an open-air amphitheater. If you follow the lead of locals, you'll buy lawn tickets and bring a picnic dinner and a blanket to spread on the grass, with Diamond Head looking down on you.

Any chance you're planning to return to Hawaii in the years 2026? You'll be just in time to see what the City of Honolulu buried here in a 50-year time capsule in 1976, as part of the U.S. bicentennial celebration.

Across the street from the park, right next to the Waikiki Aquarium, is the **Waikiki War Memorial Natatorium.** Built in 1927 in tribute to residents of Hawaii who had served in World War I, this stately oceanfront structure consists of a huge saltwater pool with a diving tower, and enough bleachers for 2000 people. In the middle of the bleachers, a tall, elaborately carved arch provides entrance.

In its glory days, the Natatorium played host to many swimming competitions. In one held during its first year, Johnny Weissmuller and Buster Crabbe broke world records. Hawaii's own Duke Kahanamoku, winner of four Olympic gold medals, trained in this pool. It also served as a social gathering spot for the general public. School children took swimming lessons here. Swimming and picnicking, families unwound at the end of the workday and on weekends. The two wading pools for children were eventually transformed into fish ponds, then later filled in and turned into volleyball and basketball courts.

Unfortunately, the Natatorium now stands neglected, crumbling, and strewn with trash, its bleachers sometimes serving as beds for homeless people and stray cats. The pipes through which the saltwater flowed into the pool became increasingly blocked and the pool water grew stagnant. The city and the Territory could never agree on whose responsibility it was to maintain the memorial, so it fell deeper into disrepair. Finally, in 1980, it closed.

Just as the Natatorium was on the brink of being torn down, it was declared a landmark. For many, allowing it to continue to decay would not only be insulting to the people who fought and died in WWI, but it would be sacrilege since this is such an impressive piece of architecture. Now the city and the state are locked in battle over who should take the initiative for its renovation. Meanwhile, a nonprofit organization called the Friends of the Natatorium is trying to raise enough money for its total restoration.

Some of the tall, modern buildings of Waikiki are built on top of old Hawaiian ruins and burial grounds. In the early 1800s, Waikiki was nothing to write home about. The beach was devoid of its coconut palms, the groves, which had grown thick, having been uprooted by a storm. Dilapidated grass huts were scattered here and there. The streams that ran through the swamps often overflowed, creating marshes that were homes to mosquitoes and rats. Hawaiians used these wetlands for planting rice paddies and taro patches and for building duck and fish ponds. The driest region was reserved for a banana grove.

Despite its seeming lack of appeal, Waikiki welcomed visitors, several of them noted writers. In 1848, Herman Melville jumped ship and earned a little cash picking up pins at a Honolulu bowling alley. Mark Twain spent some time here in 1866, and Jack London learned to surf along Waikiki Beach. Captivated by the beautiful Princess Ka'iulani, who lived in Waikiki with her parents, Robert Louis Stevenson passed many days sitting in the shade of the hau tree that still stands at the New Otani Beach Hotel. Along with Hawaiian *alii,* wealthy foreigners built themselves elegant waterfront homes in the driest areas. Small hotels began cropping up in the late 1880s. It wasn't until the 1920s that tons of coral were dumped into extensive marshlands, turning wet land into dry.

Many outsiders got their first taste of Hawaiian music from the popular "Hawaii Calls" radio program, which began in 1935, during the Depression, in an attempt to revive the tourist industry. Broadcast to the U. S., Canada, and Australia from the lanai of the Moana Hotel, it remained on the air until 1975. In 1936, the first travelers reached Honolulu by air: seven passengers flown in from San Francisco. If you think flights are tedious these days, be thankful you weren't on this 22-hour Pan Am Clipper trip. By the end of World War II, flying time between San Francisco and Honolulu had been shaved to a mere nine hours.

After the war, developer Henry J. Kaiser decided to breathe new life into Waikiki by building the Hawaiian Village, now with Hilton in front of its name. Especially after undergoing an extensive renovation in the late 1980s, this hotel—with its tile-covered Rainbow Tower, lagoon, theater, and shops—is still one of Waikiki's most impressive accommodations.

Once Hawaii became a state in 1959, tourism began to boom. James Michener's epic historical novel, *Hawaii,* was published that year, introducing the Islands to millions of mainlanders and whetting their appetites for first-hand looks. The 1970s saw a serious building frenzy, when most of Waikiki's present sky-scraping hotels and condominiums were born.

Greater Honolulu

When you're ready for a break from Waikiki (or wherever else you're staying), spend some time in the rest of Honolulu. While you'll need to drive or take public transportation to get to some parts of the city, seeing the sights in the heart of downtown Honolulu (about a ten-minute bus, taxi, or car ride from Waikiki) is perfectly comfortable on foot. At the far northwestern end of the city are **Honolulu International Airport** and **Pearl Harbor.**

Heading northwest from Waikiki, you'll pass **Kewalo Basin,** frequently called Fisherman's Wharf (which is really just the name of a restaurant there). Located at Ward Avenue, across Ala Moana Boulevard, this is the commercial harbor where many visitors board glass-bottom boats or catamarans for dinner and sightseeing cruises, set sail for Pearl Harbor, and charter deep-sea fishing boats. The upscale **Ward Center** shopping mall is nearby, along with the more ordinary **Ward Warehouse** mall. **Ala Moana Center** is noted for being one of the world's most humungous conglomerations of stores and restaurants and is a favorite among residents. Locals also flock to **Ala Moana Park,** a long beach bordered by grass and shaded by trees. The waves here are extremely gentle.

About a mile from Waikiki is **Ala Moana Farmers Market.** This makes a good stop for visitors who want a glimpse of traditional Hawaiian foods rarely seen at restaurants. Families shopping for luaus and everyday cooking mill around counters crowded with octopus, squid, piles of fresh fish, *lomi ʻoʻio* (chopped raw bonefish mixed with bits of seaweed), fish *poke* (bits of raw fish with seaweed), *kalua* pig, beef jerky, and containers of *poi* (mashed, fermented taro).

A number of worthwhile sights sit just outside the heart of downtown Honolulu. Not far from each other are the **Bishop Museum,** with its fabulous collection of Hawaiiana, and **Punchbowl** (the National Memorial Cemetery of the Pacific), with its commanding views of the city way below. **Foster Botanic Gardens,** blossoming with thousands of species of tropical flowers, trees, and plants, is also nearby. Graced

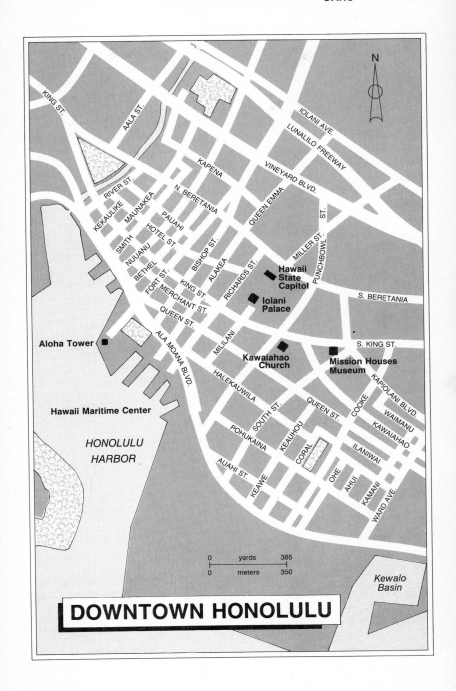

N

KING ST.
AALA ST.
KING ST.
IOLANI AVE.
LUNALILO FREEWAY
KAPENA
VINEYARD BLVD.
RIVER ST.
N. BERETANIA
QUEEN EMMA
KEKAULIKE
MAUNAKEA
PAUAHI
HOTEL ST.
MILLER ST.
PUNCHBOWL ST.
SMITH
NUUANU
BISHOP ST.
ALAKEA
RICHARDS ST.
Hawaii State Capitol
S. BERETANIA
BETHEL
KING ST.
Iolani Palace
FORT ST.
MERCHANT ST.
QUEEN ST.
S. KING ST.
Aloha Tower
ALA MOANA BLVD.
MILILANI
Kawaiahao Church
Mission Houses Museum
KAPIOLANI BLVD.
COOKE
Hawaii Maritime Center
HALEKAUWILA
SOUTH ST.
QUEEN ST.
WAIMANU
KAWAIAHAO
POHUKAINA
KEAUHOU
ILANIWAI
HONOLULU HARBOR
AUAHI ST.
KEAWE
CORAL
OHE
AHUI
KAMANI
WARD AVE.

0 yards 385
0 meters 350

Kewalo Basin

DOWNTOWN HONOLULU

with sunny courtyards and a variety of galleries, **Honolulu Academy of Arts** is also on many sightseeing lists.

Now bordered by condominiums and office buildings, **Thomas Square** sprouts sprawling banyan trees. In 1843, this was the site where Kamehameha III reclaimed the rule of his islands. For a few trying months, a British admiral had stolen power out from under the Hawaiian king. During the 1989 Bicentennial of the arrival of the Chinese in Hawaii, this square erupted with wild celebrations. The highlight was the 600-foot-long Chinese dragon snaking from Aala Park along King Street. This colorful, ferocious creature was 120 feet longer than the 1988 Singapore dragon that found its way into *The Guiness Book of World Records.*

Wearing your walking shoes, you'll be prepared to take a stroll around downtown Honolulu and Chinatown, where the captivating buildings, architecture, stores, and people tell a great deal about Hawaii's history. You may want to save **Mission Houses Museum,** on South King Street, for another day; you can spend a lot of time there, especially if a Living History Program or a crafts fair is in progress. One of the three buildings that make up the museum is a wooden house that is the oldest home in Hawaii. Built in Massachusetts, it was dismantled, then shipped to the islands and reassembled in 1821.

Just across the way is **Kawaiahaʻo Church,** the original permanent protestant church built by the missionaries of hand-cut coral stone in 1843. On the other side of King Street, **Honolulu Hale** (City Hall) was built in 1929 in Spanish/Moorish style. The beige, adobe building is topped by a red tile roof and surrounded by thick palms. If you happen by around noon, consider listening to one of the free daily concerts at the Skygate sculpture. Continuing west along King Street, you'll come to the white-columned **Hawaii State Library,** on the right.

Across the street, to the left, is **Kekuanoa,** a state government building whose exterior was featured as the Honolulu Police Department in the television series *Magnum P.I.* Nearby, the **Kamehameha I Statue** guards **Aliiolani Hale,** the Renaissance-style Judiciary Building that was built to serve as a royal palace in 1874. Ironically, the statue of the King who is heralded for having unified the Hawaiian Islands was based on an Italian model and made by an American. Not that most modern-day onlookers would notice, but the gold leaf clothing he is wearing is not historically correct.

A short stroll back to the right, on King Street, opulent **Iolani Palace** is the United States' only royal palace. Be sure to take a tour of this gracious building where Hawaiian monarchs reigned and where Liliuokalani, the island's last queen, was held prisoner while a group of American businessmen took over her country. Built above Hawaiian ancestral graves, on South Beretania Street, the modern **Hawaii State**

Capitol sports statues of Queen Liliuokalani and Father Damien, who selflessly helped improve the lives of those with Hansen's Disease (leprosy) who had been banished to the island of Molokai.

While the nearby governor's mansion, **Washington Place,** also on South Beretania Street, is not generally open to the public, passersby can look through the gates to try to catch a glimpse of the head of state. Built in 1846, this Greek Revival mansion has been home to Hawaiian governors since 1921. Before that, Hawaiian royalty, including Queen Liliuokalani, resided here.

On the same street is **St. Andrew's Cathedral,** with its stained glass windows illustrating notable events from Hawaii's past. Spend some time relaxing in the sunshine on nearby Richards Street at either **the Armed Services YMCA,** formerly the Royal Hawaiian Hotel, or the **YWCA** (near Iolani Palace), with its bright, peaceful courtyards.

A couple of blocks west of the Cathedral, **Tamarind Park** is a welcome oasis in the heart of the city. This flourishing patch of green was born of compromise. Much to the distress of many residents, the historic Alexander Young Hotel was torn down in 1981 to allow an office complex to grow. However, more than an acre of the land was saved for this trim park, which is now filled with trees such as monkey pod, shower, and, of course, tamarind. A stream flows through the foliage and a 12-foot Henry Moore sculpture is anchored in a reflecting pool. If you're lucky, you'll pass by during one of the periodic concerts, featuring big band music, or, every once in a while, slack key guitar.

Beginning just northwest of the statue of Kamehameha the Great, five-block-long **Merchant Street** was Honolulu's business district for nearly a century. The names behind these well-preserved 19th- and early 20th-century buildings are those of the haole families whose wealth was born in agriculture, blossomed with whaling, and later flourished through commerce. The melange of architectural styles ranges from Hawaiian Regional to European classical and contemporary.

Just off Merchant, on Bishop and near Queen, the 1929 **Alexander & Baldwin building** is one of my favorites. Headquarters of one of Hawaii's Big Five companies and topped by an Island-style double-pitched roof, this is a dramatic example of Hawaiian art deco. At the entrance, columns are carved with fruit and flower designs; round Chinese symbols are cut out above the door; lanterns hang from the ceiling and tiles turn walls into color-splashed murals of marine life. Bishop Street was once the most beautiful road in Honolulu. The mountains could be seen at one end and the water at the other. Now the harborview is obscured by buildings.

Back on Merchant, the **Stangenwald Building,** constructed in 1901, has Hawaii's first electric elevator. A central staircase sets off the upscale lobby, with its eye-catching mural. At six stories, this was once

Hawaii's tallest building. Near Bethel Street, the cannons protruding from the sidewalk in front of the old post office were once used as hitching posts. They came from the waterfront Fort of Honolulu, now replaced by **Irwin Park.** You can see some of the old fort's huge, dismantled coral stones in the water off the edge of the parking lot in front of where cruise ships dock at the harbor.

On the corner of Merchant and Bethel, the stone, Spanish Colonial-style **Honolulu Police Station Building** was built in 1930. Attractive tile work decorates the lobby, where photographs show the history of the building. One of Hawaii's most famous police cases was the 1930s Massie murder case. A group of Hawaiian and Japanese-American men was accused of beating and raping a white woman. When the defendants were acquitted, since there was not enough evidence to back up the claim, the woman's mother and naval lieutenant husband kidnapped and murdered one of the men. (See **U.S. Annexation (1893–1941)** in **Days Gone By.**) This dignified building now houses city services.

Across from here, on the same side of Bethel Street, the handsome brick and terra cotta **Honolulu Publishing Company** building began life in 1910 as the Yokohama Specie Bank. This Japanese financial institution opened in Hawaii to serve the influx of Japanese immigrants. The architecture of this stone and brick building, its facade decorated with intricate terra cotta work, reflects the period when admiration for things Western was strong in Japan.

At the end of Merchant, at Nuuanu, the impressive 1890 **Royal Saloon** has been transformed into Murphy's Bar and Grill. This brick and stucco building was once a popular waterfront hangout for many, even King David Kalakaua.

Our Lady of Peace Cathedral is planted at the Beretania Street (northeastern) end of Fort Street Mall, which outs across Merchant Street. Here Father Damien, who helped those afflicted with Hansen's Disease, was ordained a priest. Walking southwest, through a somewhat run-down area, you'll pass the **Blaisdell Hotel,** dating back to 1912. A block over from this promenade, on Bethel and Pauahai, **Hawaii Theater** was the Islands' premier stage before it became a movie house. Built in 1922 and now undergoing a long-term restoration, it is often one of the sites of the annual **Hawaii International Film Festival**. At the harbor end of Fort Street mall, 184-foot **Aloha Tower,** built in 1921, overlooks the water.

During the 1820s, in the old whaling days, more than 50 ships a year anchored off Honolulu, bringing many foreigners who decided to settle in this Pacific city. A century later, great numbers of tourists began to pour off ships here, welcomed by crowds of people selling leis and the music of the Royal Hawaiian Band. Now ten-story Aloha Tower is part of the **Maritime Center** museum, along with **Falls of Clyde,** a four-masted sailing ship, and the 60-foot *Hokulea* (a replica of an ancient Hawaiian vessel), which has sailed throughout the Pacific. Down Nimitz Highway, which now separates downtown buildings from the harbor, tours are conducted at the **Dole Pineapple Cannery**. Today an industrial zone, this area was once a red-light district.

Just off Nimitz Highway, **Chinatown** takes up about 16 blocks, bordered roughly by North Hotel, River, Beretania, and Nuuanu streets. Orange ducks hang in restaurant windows. Bakeries and stores selling homemade Chinese candy lure passersby inside. At herbal medicine shops, wooden drawers filled with natural ingredients line walls like library card catalogues. Dried lizard tails sit in jars, and the air is thick with incense, tiger balm, and ginseng. People go in and out of acupuncture offices. The streets are perfumed by fresh flowers from lei stands. Men gather at pool halls, while Chinese, Vietnamese, and Filipino restaurants do a brisk business. Many immigrants have also settled here from Cambodia and Laos. On North Hotel Street, popular **Wo Fat Chop Suey,** with its distinctive Eastern architecture, is Honolulu's oldest Chinese restaurant.

Especially on Saturday mornings, serious shopping takes place. At sprawling **Oahu Market,** on King and Kekaulike streets, boxes are heaped with live crabs attempting to claw their way out in slow motion. Counters are covered with whole suckling pigs, glistening fresh fish, chicken feet (for soup), and all kinds of cabbage, seaweed, ti leaves, fruit, and other vegetables. Built in 1904, the market was about to be sold to developers by its owners in 1984. Not only did the merchants get together to buy it, but they also raised thousands more dollars to renovate it. **Maunakea Market,** a newcomer at Maunakea Street between Hotel and Pauahi, is geared more toward tourists.

One of Honolulu's first neighborhoods, Chinatown got its name during the late 19th century, when Chinese immigrants began moving in. They took jobs as laundry workers, tailors, bakers, and grocers. During the 1890s, hundreds of prostitutes frequented Nuuanu and Pauahi streets. Many were Japanese wives or picture brides who had been abandoned by their husbands or intended spouses.

Ironically, notorious Bill Lederer's Bar at Hotel Street, is now a police station. King Kalakaua was known to have a drink or two at the old Pantheon Bar. In the 1880s, people could have a cocktail at this bar, take a horse-drawn trolley ride to Waikiki, get swimwear, a bath towel, and a cabana at the Longbranch Bath House—all for one price. Across the street, on the corner of Nuuanu and South Pauahi, the Blue Note Bar was where the first Hawaiian woman performed a strip tease act.

In 1900, the Board of Health ordered the fire department to burn down a block in Chinatown in an attempt to stem the spread of bubonic plague. While the plague may not have spread further here, the flames certainly did. The wind changed direction and suddenly nearly 40 acres of houses and businesses went up in smoke. More than 4000 people were left homeless. People in the area had had practice rebuilding their neighborhood. Back in 1886, another devastating fire, which started in a restaurant on the corner of Smith and Hotel streets, had left 7000 Chinese and 350 Hawaiians without shelter.

In January and February, the **Narcissus Festival** is in full swing in Chinatown. At the Queen Pageant, a talent and beauty competition, women take baby steps in their close-fitting *cheong-sam* gowns, embroidered with intricate Chinese designs. After the free Cooking Demonstration, the noted local and foreign chefs give their artful creations away as door prizes.

During the evening Chinatown Open House, the queen walks through the streets of Chinatown with her court of Chinese Chamber of Commerce officials. They visit stores, where the merchants give her *lishee* (gifts of money wrapped in red paper). Lion dancers accompany her: One dancer is at the head, the other at the tail. The **Chinese New Year** celebration erupts with a barrage of fire crackers. The dragon dance is often a highlight. It can take more than 70 people to bring the long, elaborate dragon costume undulating to life. For two nights, the **Cultural Plaza** (at Mauna Kea and Beretania streets, bounded by Kukui and River streets) is packed with food booths selling Chinese and other ethnic foods. Chinese music and the machine-gun pops of firecrackers mingle in the air. Jewelry shops and other stores around the plaza remain open.

Still somewhat scruffy today, Chinatown has been hit by a wave of gentrification. Architectural firms and a number of good art galleries have moved in. However, it remains best not to venture into the area alone at night. Through the Chinese Chamber of Commerce or the Hawaii Heritage Center, you can arrange to take a daytime walking tour of the neighborhood.

Honolulu may be crowded with tall buildings, but there is a great deal of leafy green at its fringes. Nestled in **Manoa Valley,** not far from Waikiki, **Paradise Park** is thick with all kinds of tropical vegetation and colorful birds. Its attractions include a performance of our feathered friends doing stunts such as riding bicycles on high wires. Manoa Valley is also home to the **University of Hawaii**.

Hiking is very popular among students and other locals in this area, particularly the short trek to **Manoa Falls,** for swimming and picnicking. In the early 1800s, the coffee that was to become the famous Kona was first planted here, before being grown on the Big Island of Hawaii. Imported from Brazil, this coffee was a big hit with sailors, whalers, and traders in port. Consider stopping at the small **organic vegetable market** in the valley. With acoustic jazz playing in the background, it's a great place to shop for a picnic when you're on your way to the North Shore.

Head for nearby Makiki Heights for the stunning, seven-mile **Tantalus-Round Top Drive**. City bus No. 15 takes this route. If you're doing your own driving, be sure to get very specific directions from a local. And don't forget a sweater. The drive is named for the two hills the loop crosses. You'll cut through dense tropical forest, where wild passion fruit, guava, and other natural sweets are begging to be picked. Some vantage points seem designed for sunset watching. From petite **Ualakaa Park,** you'll look down on the sprawling capital city and its harbor, as well as the Waianae Mountains, Diamond Head, and Koko Head. At night, when the city lights are twinkling, locals thinking romantic thoughts often make this winding drive.

A popular picnic spot, the Tantalus area is speckled with white and yellow ginger blossoms from June to December. Hikers found that the more they walked toward the 2013-foot peak of Tantalus Mountain, the farther away it seemed. So this region was named for the mythical Greek king. His royal punishment for displeasing the gods was to be forever submerged, thirsty and famished, in water up to his chin. Each time he bent his head in an attempt to drink, the water would suddenly drain away. And whenever he tried to pick the succulent fruit dangling from the overhanging trees, it would slip from his fingers as the wind shoved the branches aside. Today, the marked trails make reaching the mountain's peak none too difficult.

Taking the Pali Highway, one of the two roads that slice the Koolau Mountains, you'll come to **Queen Emma Summer Palace Museum,** the colonial mansion where Kamehameha IV lived with his bride. At the **Pali Lookout (Nuuanu Pali)** in 1795, Kamehameha I (of the Big Island) forced enemy soldiers (of Oahu) off the cliff in his successful (and bloody) drive to unify the Hawaiian Islands. Some say the 300 men were pushed, while others claim they hurled themselves over the edge instead of surrendering to the man who would be known as Kamehameha the Great. The view from the Lookout takes in nearly the entire windward coast.

The second way to cut across the mountains from Honolulu to the windward coast is to take Likelike Highway. When you emerge from **Wilson Tunnel,** a spectacular vista will be laid out before you: Peppered with houses, vibrantly green open spaces sweep to the foot of the mountains and to the water's edge. Banana trees and wild guava border the road. This side of the island is wetter and thus more lush than the leeward coast.

Eastern Oahu

Another way to get to windward Oahu is to head east from Waikiki, taking the coastal route. Even if you only spend a half day—going as far as Waimanalo and returning to Honolulu through the mountains on the Pali Highway—you will have seen some of Oahu's most impressive and varied scenery.

Passing the Honolulu Zoo, across from Waikiki Beach, you might catch a **windsurfing** championship in progress below Diamond Head Lookout. Frequently empty, Diamond Head Beach Park sits at the bottom of a cliff. While waves on the North Shore can build to more than 30 feet in height during the winter, five feet is considered high for this side of the island. In addition to a few scattered surfers, you might see people dragging fishing nets in. Molokai is anchored out in the ocean, with Maui silhouetted in the distance.

Bougainvillea sprinkles color everywhere and plumeria sweetens the air. In the Diamond Head, Kahala, and Hawaii Kai suburbs, Rolls Royces, Jaguars, and Lamborghinis wait outside multi-million dollar homes shaded by mango, monkeypod, purple-blossomed Jacaranda, and orange-blossomed African tulip trees. Millionaires tee off on the Waialae Country Club greens. Near the Hawaii Kai Golf Course, look for the rough dark stones of developer Henry J. Kaiser's **Rock Farm**. Many mainland celebrities live in these posh neighborhoods. While the luxurious **Kahala Hilton** is just a short drive from frenetic Waikiki, it seems to be on another island. Guests here escape the crush to enjoy tranquility and scenic beauty with lots of elbow room, yet all the action they could want is close by.

During the late 1980s, some of Honolulu's more expensive suburbs were swept up in the buying frenzy that had gripped many investors from Japan. Prices of houses and condominiums abruptly doubled and, in some cases, even tripled. Stories flew back and forth such as the one about the businessman from Japan who paid nearly $10 million for 10 houses in Kahala, then sold them all in Tokyo a couple of days later. Fleeing limited real estate options in Japan, investors also snatched up hotels and resorts in Hawaii. In a single year (1987), they spent more than $3 billion in Hawaiian real estate, more than in any other U.S. state or country. In fact, that year, the Japanese pumped more money into Hawaii than the total of foreign investment in the Islands in nearly three decades.

Makai of Hawaii Kai, gumdrop-shaped **Koko Head** ("Blood Hill") serves as a prominent landmark in this area. Neighboring **Hanauma Bay** is Oahu's premier (and therefore crowded) snorkeling spot. Cupped by mountains, the palm-fringed beach forms an almost complete circle. From the overlook high above, coral and smooth sandy patches are visible through the glass-clear blue water.

Across Kalanianaole Highway, the mountains give way to orange and brown earth. The greenery is alternately dusty and bright. Striated, craggy cliffs border the road on one side while the white surf from the navy blue ocean thrashes the rocky coast below. **Blow Hole,** where the water sprouts up through the rocks, is most dramatic when the waves are rough.

Body surfing and boogie board championships are held at nearby **Sandy Beach,** which is also a popular locale for kite flying. The whole windward coast unfurls itself from **Makapuu Lookout,** across the highway from **Sea Life Park.** Below the lava rock cliffs of Makapuu Point, boogie boarders and body surfers congregate at the beach. Sharks now breed in a cave at the bottom of Makapuu Point. But some say that people once could swim into the cave and find the entrance to a dry lava tube that would lead them all the way to Molokai!

You might see a group of schoolchildren on a nature walk along the cliffs or daring hang gliders swooping down from the Koolau peaks. The Makapuu Lighthouse, more than 600 feet above sea level, is said to have the world's largest lighthouse lens (13 by 9 feet). Made in France back in 1887, it has a 50-mile range.

Also called **Manana,** offshore **Rabbit Island** bears a mild resemblance to one of Bugs Bunny's relatives, with its ears pinned back. To me it looks much more like the head of a lioness. Some say it wasn't named for its appearance after all, but because rabbits were let loose on it by a Spanish friend of Kamehameha I. Ancient Hawaiians used the island to bury their dead, who were interned in the sand in a standing position. Today it serves as a nesting spot for thousands of seabirds and it is *kapu* (off limits) to human beings.

Although lush **Waimanalo** is an economically depressed area, it has an intriguing atmosphere and history. More than half the people who live here are Hawaiian. When the monarchy was overthrown by a mercenary group of American businessmen in 1893, Hawaiians in this area got busy. They rounded up as many rifles and guns as they could manage, intending to use them to restore Queen Liliuokalani to power. But before these loyal royalists had a chance to use their weapons, which they had hidden in the sand on Rabbit Island, their plans were exposed.

Baby Norfolk pines and bushy ferns decorate mountainsides. Bright red earth clings to cliffs, and flower nurseries thrive. Trucks park along the road selling fresh corn, which you shouldn't pass up if you're staying in an accommodation with cooking facilities.

This is *paniolo* (cowboy) country. Horses, cows, and wide-brimmed hats are everywhere. **The New Town Country Stables** puts on a rodeo every Thanksgiving weekend. A ranch sponsors the **Hawaiian Hoe-Down,** complete with hula and square dancing, country western music, and a meal of barbecued ribs, teriyaki chicken, and sweet local corn. A

polo field hosts matches every Saturday at 3 p.m. from March through August. There is even a golf course, backed by the massive **Koolau Mountains,** Oahu's most extensive range. Whenever it rains, the deep ridges become healthy waterfalls.

An old legend tells of a mysterious and disconcertingly beautiful woman, Kauholokahiki, who was only allowed to bathe in golden waters. A chief fell in love with her on sight, married her, then was devastated when she told him about the restrictions of her personal hygiene. He dreaded making the arduous journey to another island to search out yellow waters for his bride. If he failed to find them, he would have to give up the woman he loved. Then when she told him about the golden Waimanalo stream that flowed from the foot of the Koolaus, he was beside himself with joy.

In Waimanolo Town, **Frankie's Drive In,** which opened in the 1940s, is the oldest fast-food restaurant on Oahu. An inexpensive choice for Mexican food is **Bueno Nalo.** Be sure to try something from **Ken's Bakery,** where it's best to arrive early in the morning, before the tastiest items sell out.

Oahu's longest nonstop strip of white sand, three-and-a-half-mile **Waimanalo Beach,** stretches across Hawaiian Homestead Land. In 1921, a congressional law was passed returning certain sections of the Islands to Hawaiians. The most popular sandy expanse in the area is at **Bellows Field Beach Park,** on a military reservation. However, the public is welcome only on holidays and during weekends from noon on Fridays to midnight on Sundays. **Kailua Beach,** just north of here, is high on the list of Oahu's nicest.

The quiet hometown of entertainer Don Ho, **Kaneohe** ("Skinny Man") is where you emerge from the Koolau Mountains if you cut across the island from Honolulu on the Likelike Highway (Route 63). At low tide, a sandbar appears in **Kaneohe Bay.** This on-again-off-again island is a popular oasis among people on boats for picnics and relaxation. If you pass by on a weekend, you might see a few beach umbrellas on this tiny, treeless strip of sand far out in the deep.

Take Kahekili Highway (Route 83) to **Valley of the Temples**. Here you'll find **Byodo-In Temple,** a reconstruction of an ancient temple in Japan. Backed by the vertical cliffs of the Koolau Mountains, it is set amid delicately landscaped Japanese gardens. There is even a two-ton statue of Buddha and a carp-filled pond on the grounds.

Off **Heeia State Park, Coconut Island** is alive with flowers—from aromatic plumeria to ruffled hibiscus—which you can pick to your heart's content. From **Heeia Kai Boat Harbor,** arrange to take a glass bottom boat ride or to rent jet skis, go windsurfing, or canoeing. Outside a store called the **Pineapple Hut,** totem pole–like *tikis* guard the entrance. Ranging in height from small to very tall, several bear a suspicious resemblance to Spielberg's *E.T.* With one look, it's easy to see why some people are convinced that the filmmaker stole his idea for his loveable space creature from Hawaii.

A string of secluded beaches lie off Kamehameha Highway. Skip the **Coral Kingdom Market** in Waikane. This tangle of jewelry stalls is usually choked with passengers from tour buses. It was from the shore in this misty district that the *Hokulea* first set sail. This 60-foot replica of an ancient Hawaiian canoe first hit the water in 1975, off **Kualoa Beach,** with the Koolau Mountains gazing down. After sailing around the Hawaiian Islands, the *Hokulea* made several trips to Tahiti and other Pacific islands to illustrate the way the ancient Polynesians traveled great distances without benefit of modern navigational techniques. Kualoa was chosen as a launching site because in ancient times, it was one of Oahu's most sacred regions. When a chief was around, any canoe that passed by had to lower its masts out of respect.

You can arrange to participate in watersports at **Kualoa Ranch**. Many octopuses hang out around offshore **Mokolii Island,** more commonly known as **Chinaman's Hat** because of its shape. At low tide, you can stroll out to the island, but be sure to walk back before the tide comes in! **Fishing** is good in this area, as well as on most of this side of the island.

Kaaawa (yes, the word has a triplet of *a*'s, plus another for good measure) is another sleepy town. After passing more pleasant beach parks, watch for the **Crouching Lion** rock formation, overlooking mountain-enclosed **Kahana Bay**. Canoe races take place at the beach here, and people relax in the shade of its pine trees. Ancient Hawaiians once settled in Kahana Valley.

Unless you don't mind being caught up in masses of people pouring off tour buses, don't stop for lunch at **Pat's at Puanluu,** by **Punaluu Beach Park**. Inland, a slippery trail leads to **Sacred Falls Park**. After passing a few more beaches, you'll come to **Laie,** where the **Polynesian Cultural Center** is located. Run by Mormons, this center features a variety of authentic Polynesian villages and many exhibits. Visitors take canoe rides and attend a splashy musical show. Lunch or dinner is included in the entrance fee. Brigham Young University's Hawaii campus here is also run by the Mormons. Their eye-catching, white Mormon Temple stands at the end of a street lined with handsome Norfolk pines.

In the evenings, windsurfers can be seen in the bay at **Laie Point**. Out in the water, the surf crashes up against long, low-lying **Puka Rock,** which has a large, neat hole clear through it. Perhaps inspired by the hole in the rock, one of the many modern homes in this neighborhood is also round. Crabs scramble across the rocks at the edge of the churning water. If you're visiting during the winter, you might be lucky enough to spot migrating **whales** from here.

Near **Malaekahana State Park** beach, with its extensive strip of pines, the village of **Kahuku** is known for its sweet corn and watermelons, which are often sold at roadsides. If you're staying somewhere with a kitchen, look for **Cackle Fresh Eggs,** which sells inexpensive, unwashed eggs. Another place to check out is the **Amorient Aquaculture Stand,** on the *makai* side of the road. Here you can buy a take-out cup of fresh shrimp cocktail or fresh prawns, shrimp, or fish to cook. You'll recognize the area's prawn farms by the series of square ponds off the side of the road.

At the **Mill at Kahuku,** visitors wander around a turn-of-the-century mill, then stop for lunch at its eclectic restaurant. Locals joke that almost everyone in this neck of the woods has at least one of the following: a skate board, a surf board, a boogie board, and a bike. Not far north of here is the **Turtle Bay Hilton,** practically the sole hotel in the area, and certainly the only large one.

The North Shore and Central Oahu

Surfer's paradise begins with **Sunset Beach**. During the winter, this two-mile sandy expanse draws crowds of master surfers with its 20- and 30-foot waves. During the summer, when the water is "flat" (with waves a mere 10 feet tall), only experienced windsurfers and bodysurfers should attempt these sports. Even strong swimmers should not venture far from shore and no one should ever enter the water alone. Right off the road, the beach is backed by a thick row of pines.

Along with the other surfing meccas along the north shore, **Ehukai Beach Park** and the famed **Bonzai Pipeline** get their share of board masters during the winter. During the championships, a festive atmosphere prevails. Blaring rock music sails past busy photographers, judges, and tables stacked with T-shirts. Lines form at food trucks parked along the road.

At **Pupukea Beach Park,** a marine reserve next to Sunset, snorkeling could hardly be more exciting. When you need a lift after all your aquatic action, take a drive along one of the nearby steep, narrow roads that go up into the hills. In this area, dotted with small ranches and orchards, the Pacific Army trained for jungle warfare during WWII. During the summer, roadside fruit stand vendors sell all kinds of fresh pickings.

Many outsiders are surprised to learn that more than a few of the young folks who gather here to surf are non-smoking, drug-free, born-again Christians. As a matter of fact, the open-air services conducted by the North Shore Christian Fellowship are often a family affair. Beginning early on Sunday mornings, worshippers sit crowded under the sprawling awning that shades the Waimea Falls Park picnic area. While children fidget, guitar music accompanies hymns. Jungle fowl, peacocks, and pheasants wander around the field reminding everyone to be thankful for the beauty of nature.

Waimea Bay has a wide, especially attractive beach. Across from here, in the valley that was once one of Oahu's most sacred places, is **Waimea Falls Park** itself. Extensive botanical gardens spread through the grounds. Ancient Hawaii is brought to life here through shows in which divers plunge off cliffs to the base of waterfalls and men dance the early version of hula.

Haleʻiwa, the plantation town about an hour and 20 minute drive northwest of Waikiki, is the main settlement on the North Shore. Looking at this small, remote town today, it is hard to believe that it ushered in tourism before Waikiki did. In 1899, Benjamin J. Dillingham, a wealthy businessman, put a stately hotel here, christening it Haleʻiwa, meaning House of the Frigate Bird. This elegant Victorian lodging stood between the ocean and graceful **Anahulu River**. Fleeing Honolulu for seashore vacations, city residents climbed aboard the train that Dillingham had built for the surrounding sugar plantations and rode it here to the end of the line. Both the railroad and the hotel are long gone now. Hippies replaced the moneyed crowd for a while, then artists—many of whom remain—began setting up studios and galleries. Today most newcomers arrive with surfboards tucked under their arms and head for the appealing beach park.

In 1984, Haleʻiwa became a Historic, Cultural and Scenic District. However, this was just a few months too late for the rose-colored, art-deco Haleʻiwa Theater, which protestors could not save from being torn down. Despite the demise of this theater, the old feeling of the frontier town has been preserved and, in some cases, manufactured. Weathered wooden buildings—both old and new—house boutiques, health food stores, galleries, and a couple of restaurants. No new structures can look as though they were built after the 1920s. **Liliuokalani Church,** erected in 1932, is one of the town's earliest buildings. Named for the queen who worshipped there, it contains a whimsical wall clock, a gift from the monarch herself in 1892. Instead of numbers on this time piece, you'll see the 12 letters of the queen's royal name.

Spanning the river and dating back to 1921, the nearby concrete **Haleʻiwa Bridge** serves as a stationary diving board for children in the summer. During the popular August Haleʻiwa Lantern Festival, delicate paper lanterns are sent floating down the river by Japanese residents to honor their ancestors. To escape into the jungled interior, some people go **kayaking** along this serene waterway. Houses perch on stilts along its banks while chickens scurry around yards. Few people pass through town without stopping at **Matsumoto's,** a mom-and-pop general store, for a shave ice. Lilikoi, coconut, banana, and rainbow are the most-licked flavors. Red *azuki* beans or scoops of ice cream are often added to these snow cones. Don't be surprised if you have to wait on a wraparound line. At **Jameson's by the Sea,** near the island's narrowest bridge, diners can watch surfers navigate 20-foot waves. Sunsets give the restaurant a romantic glow.

Polo is all the rage at **Mokuleia Field,** beginning at about 3 p.m. on Sundays from early April through August. Here the Hawaii Polo Club battles teams from the mainland, South America, Australia, and Britain. If you don a big bonnet and a lei, you might blend in with the dignified ladies who make it their business to attend. People have picnics before the games. No one is bored between the two matches. They are too busy watching the sky divers, airplane stunts (provided by nearby Dillingham Airfield), people in fancy Hawaiian clothing riding horses, and other entertainment. If you'd like to try **hang gliding,** pay a visit to the Gliderport at the airfield.

The road dries up just west of Mokuleia, and a rigorous, two-mile hike to narrow, rocky **Kaena Point,** the end of the island, begins. Here, the desolate land sits high above the pounding surf. The point, which no longer has a road around it, can also be approached from the leeward coast.

Turning inland at Haleʻiwa toward acres of fields, you might pass a sugar cane truck piled high with cane brimming over its edges. Visitors have been stopping at **Dole Pineapple Pavilion** in Wahiawa since 1951. In addition to fresh pineapple, fudge and wooden bowls are for sale. Outside, various types of pineapple are labeled for the edification of passersby. **Delmonte's Pineapple Triangle** also has a garden growing pineapple in a wide variety of shapes, colors, and sizes. If you've ever wondered what the difference is between a Saigon Red and a Philippine Green, or how one from Samoa compares to one from Brazil, you'll find out here. If you're sorting through the neat rows of pineapple late in the afternoon, trucks packed with pickers might rumble by.

The U.S.S. *Arizona* at **Pearl Harbor** is Hawaii's number-one visitor attraction. In addition to hosting football and baseball games, 50,000-seat **Aloha Stadium,** nearby, also draws crowds for concerts. The giant water slides and other amusements at undistinguished **Castle Park,** across the street, are more popular with locals than visitors. If you happen by during the third weekend in July, stop at **Moanalua Gardens** to watch an annual hula festival on a historic site amid expansive monkeypod trees. In light traffic, **Honolulu International Airport** is about a 15-minute drive from downtown Honolulu and about 25 minutes from Waikiki.

The Western Coast and Kaena Point

Here the Waianae Mountains slide into lush valleys that slip into the ocean. Peaceful beach parks are scattered along Oahu's western shore. Overall, the swimming is pretty good during the summer when the water is calmest. Yet, since the Sheraton Makaha is the only hotel, this area draws far more locals than tourists.

A good surfing spot, **Nanakuli Beach Park** hugs the coast just off Route 93. The name, meaning "to look deaf," originates from the time when people in the area were too poor to share their food with pas- sersby, as was the custom. When they looked at strangers, they feigned deafness. Many Nanakuli dwellers are Hawaiians who are on the seem- ingly endless waiting list for Hawaiian Home Lands, which they can lease for $1 a year for 99 years. The delays are caused in part because, before homestead lots can be developed, they must undergo archaeolog- ical examination to make sure they contain no endangered animals, plants, or Hawaiian artifacts.

With two golf courses, the **Sheraton Makaha** is hidden in Makaha Valley, way off the beaten path. The drive from Honolulu takes about 1¾ hours. At **Makaha Beach,** about a mile from the resort, local fam- ilies and groups of friends arrive prepared to relax all day, whipping out barbecue grills, beach chairs, surf boards, ukuleles, and slack key guitars.

Route #93 comes to an abrupt halt near **Makua-Kaena Point State Park,** another good beach for surfing. **Kaena Point** itself, the island's northwest corner, can no longer be traveled by vehicle, not even motor- cycles or four-wheel-drives. The road that ran around the point until late 1988 had been built nearly a century earlier, in 1899, for a railroad line. The train chugged along here until the 1940s. Now the unrelenting surf has eroded about 30 feet of the old road. You can still circle the island, but you'll have to do this section on foot.

Oahu's leeward and windward coasts come together at Kaena Point, which can be reached from either the west or the North Shore. During the winter, some of the state's highest waves thrash the point, some- times jumping 40 to 50 feet into the air. Both onshore and offshore **fishing** is good here. Ask the ancient Hawaiians, who built a fishing camp at the tip of the point near the graffiti-covered lighthouse. You can still see the rocky remnants of the camp.

Along the shore, multicolored marine life thrives in tidepools. Among the shells and volcanic rocks you'll find along the sand dunes, you'll also see naupaka plants, with their white flowers. Half of each blossom seems to have been neatly lopped off. Look, but don't touch, since destroying the plant also destroys the land: Naupakas help secure the sand dunes.

Mynah birds and sea gulls putter about. Non-swimming frigates steal fish from other birds. Ancient Hawaiians believed that the soul of each dead person would come to Kaena, where a spirit would decide whether the time for death had truly arrived. If not, the soul would be sent back to the body. If ending life was appropriate, the spirit would guide the soul to the white boulder just east of Kaena Point, on the windward side. As the soul jumped off the rock into death, a god would decide whether it deserved to end up in *Kahiki* (heaven) or the place of never ending night.

Kaena is also said to be where the demigod Maui attempted to bring all the Hawaiian islands together. By tossing a giant coral fishhook over to Kauai and tugging, he tried to join it with Oahu. But he fell backwards to the ground when only a chunk of Kauai popped off, leaving the rest of the island anchored where it was. This chunk of Kauai, a small island known as Pohaku o Kauai ("rock of Kauai"), remains in the water just off the point. Using a far more violent strategy, Kamehameha I succeeded in unifying the Hawaiian Islands in 1810.

A Connecticut Yankee in King Lot's Court

Mark Twain visited Hawaii in 1866, during the reign of Lot, better known as Kamehameha V, the last of the royal Kamehameha line. A few Americans had settled in Honolulu, and they were already pressuring the United States to annex Hawaii, to secure their personal economic well-being. New England missionaries were hard at work in their continual battle to convert any Hawaiians who had slipped through the cracks and to bolster the faith of those who had already turned to Christianity. Twain remarked jokingly that he never met anyone in Hawaii who wasn't either a missionary or a whaling captain.

Serving as a reporter for the *Sacramento Union,* Twain sent his sometimes poetic, often humorous articles about the Islands to San Francisco by ship. While sightseeing on horseback, he discovered a Hawaii far different from that depicted by other members of the U.S. press. Although King Kamehameha V had been called a drunken, ruthless pagan by some American writers, Twain found him diligent, gentlemanly, and dignified.

Extolling the Islands' beauty, he said, "The good that die [in Hawaii] experience no change, for they fall asleep in one heaven and wake up in another." He was less kind to the Hawaiian staple called *poi,* however, saying, "An unseductive mixture it is, almost tasteless before it ferments and too sour for a luxury afterward. But nothing is more nutritious." Twain's *Letters from the Sandwich Islands* gives a fascinating glimpse into daily life in 19th-century Hawaii.

Princess Ka‘iulani: Almost a Queen

The niece of Liliuokalani, Hawaii's last queen, Victoria Kawekiu Ka‘iulani Lunalilo Kalaninuiahilapalapa (called Princess Ka‘iulani for short) was next in line for the throne. She was only 15 when named the royal heir. Her mother—Miriam Likelike, King Kalakaua's sister—had died, and neither Kalakaua nor Liliuokalani had any children. Born in 1875, Princess Kaʻiulani (the great-granddaughter of a first cousin of Kamehameha I) was one of few *alii* of her generation. Her father, Archibald Cleghorn, had come to Hawaii from Scotland in 1850.

Kaʻiulani grew up in Ainahau, a 10-acre Victorian-style estate in Waikiki. It was in the colorful surrounding gardens, where her beloved peacocks roamed, that the princess met Robert Louis Stevenson, one of the many guests at the estate. He was so taken with the beautiful young woman that he immortalized her in his poetry. Today skyscrapers stand where these landscaped gardens once grew.

To groom the delicate princess for her role as worldly queen, Kaʻiulani was sent off to study in England. Meanwhile, those who loved the monarchy and those who wanted the U.S. to annex the Islands battled it out in Hawaii. In 1893, when Kaʻiulani was 17 and still away in England, Hawaii was taken over by a group of American businessmen based in Honolulu. They created a republic of their own, in anticipation of the U.S. annexation that would take place several years later. Kaʻiulani traveled to the U.S. where she met with President Grover Cleveland and, in vain, begged him to restore the Hawaiian monarchy.

When the U.S. Congress turned Hawaii into an American territory, the princess fell into a deep depression. In a letter to her aunt Liliuokalani, the deposed queen, she wrote, "They have taken away everything from us and it seems there is left but a little, and that little our very life itself. We live now in such a semi-retired way, that people wonder if we even exist any more."

Kaʻiulani went to the Big Island for the wedding of a friend. After horseback riding in misty Waimea, she came down with a cold and fever. In 1899, at only 23 years old, Hawaii's almost-queen died of inflammatory rheumatism.

WHAT TO SEE AND DO

PERSONAL FAVORITES

The Polynesian Cultural Center, with its authentically recreated villages (see *Sights*).

Iolani Palace, where the Royal Hawaiian Band performs on Friday afternoons at the bandstand (see Sights).

The Maritime Center, where the *Hokulea* (the old-style canoe that retraced the journey of ancient Polynesians from Tahiti to Hawaii) is docked (see Sights).

The Saturday Living History Program at the **Mission Houses Museum** (see Sights).

*Honolulu **block parties,** held from time to time on Fridays after work, usually in the Merchant Square area between Nuuanu and Bethel streets (check local newspapers).

Kapiolani Park, a local hangout for flying kites; playing soccer, softball, and tennis; jogging; and listening to impromptu slack key guitar or ukulele jam sessions. The evening Hawaiian, pop, or European classical concerts at the Waikiki Shell turn the lawn into picnic grounds (see the Oahu introductory section and *Night Life*).

Walking tours through historic **downtown Honolulu** and **Chinatown** (see the Oahu introductory section; Sights; and Tours).

Kayaking in the ocean or on a river (see *Sports*).

Wonderful drives: One of the most dramatic is from Diamond Head past Makapuu Lookout to Waimanalo, then through the Koolau Mountains, along the Pali Highway, to Honolulu. Others are the mountainous Tantalus-Round Top Drive; and the beach-trimmed windward coast and North Shore (see the Oahu introductory section).

SIGHTS

Hawaiiana

Bishop Museum and Planetarium • *1525 Bernice St., Honolulu; 847–3511 or 847–1443* • Named in honor of Bernice Pauahi Bishop, the granddaughter of Kamehameha the Great, this museum is a must for anyone even remotely interested in Hawaii's heritage. When Charles Bishop met Princess Pauahi after he came to Hawaii from New York in 1846, she was engaged to Lot Kamehameha, who was next in line to take over Hawaii's throne. But her plans soon changed. The princess and her foreign husband went on to open Hawaii's first bank and he became a noted politician, entrepreneur, as well as a generous philanthropist.

Extremely proud of her culture, Bernice Bishop loved collecting Hawaiian arts and antiques. So it was only fitting that as a memorial to

*Off the beaten path

her after her 1884 death, Charles Bishop founded this museum in 1889. As the years passed, the collection snowballed and now encompasses items from many Polynesian cultures. The museum also serves as a center for research into anthropology and the Islands' natural history.

The two main galleries, demonstration and performance hall, Science Center, and planetarium are set on ten acres. The fascinating show at the planetarium vividly and visually explains how the ancient Polynesians sailed to Hawaii in canoes about 1000 years ago. Enter the old stone main building, and you'll step onto an intricately patterned tile floor leading to a beautifully carved central koa staircase. The lustrous native wood is a rich orange-brown. Portuguese laborers dug the volcanic rock used to construct this wing.

In the gallery to the right, two levels of wooden balconies overlook the main hall, with its glass-encased exhibits. A huge whale skeleton hangs from the ceiling. Displays include an old-fashioned grass *hale* (house); *kapa* (cloth made from pounded bark); a Hawaiian throne; elaborate royal feathered capes and headdresses; crowns worn by King Kalakaua and Queen Kapiolani; and paintings of members of the Hawaiian monarchy. Human teeth (of dead enemies) are artfully inlaid into wooden waste bowls. If you take a tour, you'll learn of old beliefs: For instance, human waste products had to be disposed of very carefully, lest they get into the hands of enemies, who could then pray for the death of the other person.

The museum also exhibits whaling implements, including a pot for boiling blubber; a sexy female figurehead from a whaling ship; a small insect zoo; and displays of Hawaii's volcanoes, plants, birds, and other animals.

Bishop Museum is about three miles from Waikiki. Departing from Waikiki, the Museum Shuttle Bus (922–1773) makes several round trips a day. You can also take Honolulu city bus No. 2 (be sure to board the "School Street" bus, not the one to "Liliha"), and get off at the Kam Shopping Center. Walk *makai* (toward the ocean) one block. If you're driving, head *Ewa* (west) on H-1 and get off at the Houghtailing Exit. Make a right turn onto Houghtailing and then take the second left, onto Bernice Street.

Open 9 a.m.–5 p.m. Mon. through Sat. Admission: $7.

Polynesian Cultural Center • *55–370 Kamehameha Highway, Laie (on the windward coast); 293–3333* • Wandering around authentic recreations of traditional villages from islands all over the Pacific, visitors get an intimate look at contrasting architectural styles and ways of life. The cultures of the indigenous peoples of Hawaii, Tahiti, the Marquesas, Tonga, New Zealand, Fiji, and Samoa come alive through musical performances, crafts demonstrations, exhibits of artifacts, and historical mini-lectures.

You might watch a group of Hawaiian women pounding out bark to make *kapa* cloth, a young Tongan walking almost effortlessly up a giant palm to lop off a coconut, or a Maori warrior sticking out his "tattooed" tongue to let his enemies know he means business. The canoe ride down the "river" is pleasant, and at the end of the day, visitors are serenaded by each village they pass along the way.

Wearing traditional dress, the people who work in the villages are actually from the islands they represent. Most of them are students at Brigham Young University, whose Hawaii branch is run by the Mormons who run the Polynesian Cultural Center. For the most rewarding part of visiting the Center, spend some time chatting with the staff between demonstrations. Many of them plan to return to their countries, while others end up marrying Americans and staying in the United States, some moving to the mainland. I talked to a Fijian grandmother who asked me to look up her daughter, who had married an American and moved to Philadelphia. She told me about old Fijian songs and legends that explained how these Pacific islanders had originally come from Africa.

After an afternoon of visiting villages, the buffet dinner is followed by a musical extravaganza incorporating dances from all the islands. This colorful outdoor show is complete with fire-breathing volcanoes. At the new theater—with a screen that is 70 feet tall and 130 feet wide—you will be able to see a 40-minute, multimillion-dollar adventure film that includes a shark hunt. Be sure to stop by the area where crafts from all the island are for sale.

Open 12:30–9 p.m. daily, except Sun. The admission price (about $40 for adults, and about $18 for children aged 5 through 11) includes all shows, tours, exhibits, and dinner or lunch.

Iolani Palace • *364 South King St. (at Richards St.), Honolulu; 522–0832* • Dignified Iolani, the United State's only royal palace, sits on a smooth patch of green in the midst of the capital's choking traffic and tall, modern buildings. A fence of gold-tipped spears encloses thriving pandanus, banyan, and flame trees, while a palm-lined promenade leads to the entrance. Its name meaning "bird of heaven," this four-story Victorian palace is Italian Renaissance in style.

Ironically, it was built in 1882 by King Kalakaua, who was revered by Hawaiians for reviving pride in Hawaiian culture. For example, he is credited with bringing back the hula, traditional music, and songs and poetry written in the Hawaiian tongue. All this had been sent underground by American missionaries. The first leader of *any* country to sail around the world, Kalakaua borrowed from the architecture that most impressed him during his visits with nearly a dozen heads of state, from Britain to Japan. Apart from its residents, the main Hawaiian presence in the palace was the ubiquitous prized native koa wood.

Moderation was a concept for which this king had little use. On at least one occasion, he threw a banquet for 5000 guests. He antagonized Honolulu's business community (most of whom were haole descendants of missionaries) by his extravagant spending. Bent on designing a regal mansion Hawaiians could be proud of, he cut no corners when he had elaborate Iolani Palace built.

The high-ceilinged interior is graced with intricately carved balustrades, plaster cornices with detailed designs, chandeliers, candlelabras, mirrors with gold leaf frames, and spacious bathtubs lined in copper. The furniture Kalakaua chose was custom made by a Boston firm that had built furniture for the American White House. Amid this splendor, King Kalakaua entertained many notable guests, including Robert Louis Stevenson.

After the king's sudden death in San Francisco in 1891, his sister, Liliuokalani, followed him to the throne. In 1893, she was deposed by a group of mostly foreign, Hawaii-based businessmen who turned Iolani Palace into the seat of their provisional government. In 1895, they convicted Liliuokalani of treason for being part of a widely supported attempt to restore her to power.

In a move that could hardly be more humiliating, the queen's accusers held her trial in the Throne Room, where she had once reigned. Upon entering the palace today, visitors don felt booties so as not to mar the glossy hardwood floors. They may wander into the velvet-draped Throne Room and the upstairs guest bedroom where the queen was imprisoned for nine months as punishment for wanting to continue leading her own country.

Under the new government, the Throne Room was used for legislative meetings. On display there today is a seven-foot-long twisted narwhal tusk topped with a gold ball. Given to Kalakaua by a whaling captain, the tusk served as a *puloulou*—a staff that was infused with *mana* (spiritual power) and thus ensured that the area surrounding the monarch was sacred. The Senate convened in the dining room, just across the hall. Silver, china, and crystal are now on display there.

During the 1930s, people on the mainland read newspaper articles about the eerie haunting of Iolani Palace. The state legislature actually suspended its work for a while, after a series of mysterious accidents was attributed to angry spirits in the mansion. Even today, some people swear that at night they sometimes see candlelight dancing in the window of the upstairs bedroom where the queen was imprisoned. Others say they hear the tinkling keys of the palace guards who once patrolled the mansion.

Iolani Palace housed the Territorial Government for more than 50 years and served as the capitol for a while after Hawaii became a state in 1959. Headed by Abigail Kawananakoa, Kalakaua's great-grandniece, a group of volunteers painstakingly restored the palace, locating and bringing back much of the original furniture that had been sold off. A rare early copy of *Legends and Myths of Hawaii,* written by Kalakaua, sits in the king's quarters along with his books in Hawaiian, English, German, and French. (You can pick up a new edition of *Legends* today in bookstores throughout the Islands.) In the entry hall, walls are hung with portraits of Hawaiian royalty, beginning with Kamehameha the Great.

At noon every Friday, the **Royal Hawaiian Band** gives a free performance at the bandstand in front of the palace. This band was established in 1847 by King Kamehameha III and has been playing ever since. Bring a picnic lunch and a mat or towel, don your lei, muumuu, or Aloha shirt, and you'll blend right in with the crowd. (Aloha wear is the dress code on Fridays on Oahu.)

See Tours if you're interested in taking a historical walking tour of the palace and grounds.

Open 9 a.m.–2:15 p.m., Wed. through Sat. The 50-minute tours begin every 15 minutes. Admission: $4 adults; $1 children ages 5–12.

Waimea Falls Park • *59–864 Kamehameha Highway, Haleiwa (North Shore); 638–8511* • Many weddings take place at these botanical gardens in a historical setting. Parrots flutter and peacocks parade around the colorful tropical flora, including one of the world's largest ginger gardens. The platter-sized lily pads on a pond look large and sturdy enough for a person to walk on. In one meadow, the immaculate flower beds resemble multicolored confetti at the edge of a plush grass carpet.

Visitors ride a tram through the gardens, getting on and off as they please. Few people miss the dive show, in which men plunge from cliffs to the base of a waterfall. Visitors are welcome to swim, but diving is strictly for those daring professionals. In addition to old grass huts and ancient agricultural terraces, people can watch demonstrations of early hula—when dancing was restricted to men.

Near the main parking lot, an ancient *heiau* (temple) has been renovated and reconstructed. Historians believe that it was dedicated to the god Lono, the divinity of the heavens. It is probably at least eight centuries old, making it one of the earliest in Hawaii. In honor of Lono, ancient Hawaiians held the annual Makahiki festival at the end of each harvest. All fighting was suspended during this time, and wild feasting and fun and games broke out. Each October, Waimea Falls Park hosts a reenactment of this festival, including old religious rites and Hawaiian games.

On the first Thursday of each month, the park sponsors a free Moonlight Walk and a Polynesian revue.

Open 10 a.m.–5:30 p.m. daily. Admission: $10 for adults; $6 for children aged 7–12; $2 for children aged 4–6.

Queen Emma Summer Palace • *2913 Pali Highway, Nuuanu Valley, Honolulu; 595–3167* • Built in 1848, this restored mansion, with its Greek columns and broad front lanai, was the home of Queen Emma and King Kamehameha IV. Now a museum, it houses an impressive collection of family furniture and memorabilia, including quilts, kapa cloth, calabashes, feather fans, silverware, koa cabinets, and the striking koa cradle of Prince Albert, the ill-fated heir to the Hawaiian throne. Lauhala mats cover the glossy wooden floors and mango trees shade the expansive grounds.

Queen Emma was much loved and is still revered for her compassion toward others. She built schools and hospitals, even caring for victims of a smallpox epidemic in her own home. Born Emma Rooke, she married Alexander Liholiho (Kamehameha IV) and inherited this home from her uncle, John Young II. Hanaikalamalama, as the palace was originally known, was built by John George Lewis (who was part Hawaiian, despite his Western name), after he bought the land from the government. He paid $800, then, a few years later, sold the estate to Young for $6000.

Prominent people, such as the Duke of Edinburgh, came often for dinner, dancing, and croquet on the lawn. The house remained empty for five years after Queen Emma died in 1885, since she had already buried her husband and young son, Prince Albert. In 1913, the mansion narrowly escaped being torn down and replaced by a baseball field. In stepped the Daughters of Hawaii, a historical preservation society, and the rest, as they say, is history.

In the Fall, the palace hosts an annual fundraising event, complete with food, arts and crafts demonstrations, and hula.

Open 9 a.m.–4 p.m. daily. Admission: $5 (except every Jan. 2, when the museum is free, in honor of Queen Emma's birthday).

Kodak Hula Show • *Kapiolani Park, Waikiki* • Since the 1930s, visitors have been coming to this outdoor theater three times a week to see performances of modern hula (done by women, as opposed to the earlier version done by men). To begin the show, a man dressed as King Kamehameha I calls out "Alo——hah!" and the audience responds in kind. Some of the ukulele-strumming, acoustic bass-plucking musicians are *tutus* (grandmothers) dressed in colorful muumuus, leis, and straw hats. Wearing traditional skirts made of ti leaves (glossy, forest green) and plumeria leis and crowns, a younger generation of women performs the hula, shaking feathered gourds (and parts of their bodies). The bright reds, yellows, greens, and other colors make snapping photos (with your Kodak film, of course) difficult to resist. Also included in the show are examples of Tahitian dances, which require much faster hip action than Hawaiian hula.

Showtimes: Tues., Wed., and Thurs. at 10 a.m. Free admission.

Puu O Mahuka Heiau • *off Route 83, 4 miles northeast of Haleiwa (North Shore)* • You'll notice that people still place offerings at this ancient temple, such as rocks wrapped with ti leaves. Oahu's largest heiau, Puu o Mahuka sits on a hill near Waimea Beach Park and Sunset Beach. This rectangular collection of stones is less than a mile up Pupukea Road (which should not be traveled during or immediately after wet weather). A stunning view is laid out from the bay side of this heiau. Declared a National Historic Landmark, it was once the site of human sacrifices. In 1794, several of Vancouver's crewmen had their lives snuffed out here.

Ula Po Heiau • *off Kailua Rd., Kailua (eastern windward coast)* • Time has reduced this heiau near a swamp to a rock pile. It's not easy to find, but you'll know you're on the right track when you see the YMCA, which is in front of it. If only one heiau is on your Oahu itinerary, make it Puu o Mahuka on the North Shore instead.

Keiawa Heiau • *Aiea Heights Dr., Aiea (west of Honolulu)* • A place of healing in old Hawaii, this crumbling temple is enclosed by low walls.

Royal Mausoleum • *2261 Nuuanu Ave., Honolulu; 536–7602* • Most members of the Kamehameha and Kalakauu royal families are buried on these three acres. While the mausoleum was built in 1865, the chapel wasn't added until 1922.
Open Mon. through Fri. from 8 a.m. to 4 p.m. and from 8 a.m. until noon on Sat. Closed Sun.

More of the Past

Mission Houses Museum • *553 South King St., Honolulu; 531–0481* • This museum is made up of three restored buildings that were once homes and headquarters of missionaries. In 1820, the one wooden house (the other two are of coral stone) was sent dismantled, all the way from Boston. It just didn't seem right to folks back home to have American missionaries living in grass houses while they did God's work. Adding local wood and old ship timbers to the pre-fab materials, the missionaries constructed a cozy four-bedroom house, now the Islands' oldest remaining wooden structure. As many as three or four families lived in this house at any given time!

Hawaiian chiefs came here, dressed in their new European clothes, to learn to read and write Hawaiian or take singing lessons in European music. Commoners also flocked to the house, for religious services and to get Western medicines to combat the new diseases foreigners had brought to Hawaii, which were devastating the indigenous population.

Missionary books, quilts, furniture, and other household items are on display.

The second oldest house, where the museum entrance is, was built in 1831. The third, dating back to 1841, is where the old hand-held printing presses are exhibited and demonstrated. The shelves in this building are piled with worn books and illustrations printed in the early 1800s with engraved plates or woodblocks.

In addition to taking a guided tour of these houses, on Saturdays visitors may participate in the Living History Program. Playing 19th-century missionaries and others, costumed actors are found cooking in the kitchen or in the parlor discussing social and political issues of the time. Visitors are invited to join in spirited conversations with people who've been dead for years—the driven, uncompromising Hiram Bingham, one of Hawaii's first and most influential missionaries; David Malo, the Hawaiian man of letters; Anthony Allen, the black Waikiki farmer; or whaling captains and other seamen. During the Thanksgiving program, visitors are asked to sample a 19th-century meal.

In late November or early December, the annual Christmas Fair takes place on the grounds. Food and all kinds of quality crafts are for sale. Various walking tours are offered, both of the museum and of the surrounding downtown Honolulu neighborhood (see Tours).

Open 9:30 a.m.–4 p.m. daily. Admission: $4 for adults; $1.50 for children age 6–15. The Living History Program is presented every hour on the hour from 10 a.m. to 3 p.m. every Sat.

Kawaiahaʻo Church • King St. • 14,000 coral blocks were used to construct this church, across the way from the Mission Houses Museum and down the street from Iolani Palace. While the porous coral may appear light in weight, each block would tip a scale at about 1000 pounds. Designed by famous missionary Hiram Bingham and built between 1837 and 1842, Kawaiahaʻo Church has a prominent clock tower. Services are conducted in both English and Hawaiian. Many people wear leis with their muumuus or jackets. Japanese weddings frequently take place here during the week.

On July 31, 1843, Hawaiian rule was returned to Kamehameha III after a brief stint under British control. For many years afterward, this day was considered a holiday of thanks. During the first service after Kamehameha was back in control of his country, he coined the phrase that turned into the motto of the land and that is now the state motto: *Ua mau ke ea o ka aina i ka pono* ("The life of the land is preserved in righteousness").

Outside, you'll see the tomb of Lunalilo, who became Hawaii's first elected king in 1873. To show how close he felt to his people, he walked barefoot to this church for his swearing in. Although his reign was brief, he was able to restore the vote for Hawaiian commoners and return to them their right to hold elective office. Instead of being buried at the Royal Mausoleum in Nuuanu Valley with the other alii, Lunalilo chose to end up here, with the regular folks.

The Damien Museum and Archives • *130 Ohua Ave., Waikiki; 923–2690* • This small museum is dedicated to the man who helped Hawaii's ostracized victims of Hansen's Disease (leprosy). Near the Hawaiian Regent Hotel and Saint Augustine's Catholic Church, its two rooms are brimming with memorabilia in tribute to Father Damien, the selfless Belgian Catholic priest who joined the exiles on remote Makanalua Peninsula on Molokai. The display includes old photographs of Kalaupapa, which the peninsula is commonly called, and of the people who were forced to move there, never to return to their families; old letters handwritten by Damien; a photograph taken of the priest the day he died—of Hansen's Disease; and a 20-minute video that fills in the gaps in his story.

Open Mon.–Fri., 9 a.m.–3 p.m. and Sat. from 9 a.m. to noon. No admission charge.

The State Capitol • *South Beretania St., between Punchbowl and Richards st. (near Iolani Palace), downtown Honolulu; 548–5420* • Built in 1969, above Hawaiian ancestral graves, this modern building took over the role of Capitol after Iolani Palace. Its architecture is heavy with meaning: The 60-foot pillars around the building suggest the Islands' coconut palm trees; the ceilingless central court brings the sky, one of nature's wonders, into the building; and circling the Capitol, reflecting pools represent the ocean that surrounds Hawaii.

On the grounds, the statue of Queen Liliuokalani clutches the *Kumulipu,* Hawaii's oldest and the most cherished creation myth; the proposed constitution of 1893 that was designed to maintain Hawaii's monarchy; and the music for famed *Aloha Oe,* the melancholy song written by the queen. In front of the building stands a statue of Father Damien, clearly suffering from Hansen's Disease, which he contracted while helping its shunned victims. Out of respect and admiration, people often decorate these statues with leis.

Hawaii Maritime Center • *Pier 7, Honolulu Harbor, near the foot of Punchbowl St.; 536–6373* • This maritime center has been established near where King Kalakaua's boathouse stood in the late 1800s. It was from here that the king, known as the Merrie Monarch, sponsored surfing meets and canoe races, reviving these Hawaiian pastimes. He also entertained friends at the boathouse with parties and performances that resuscitated hula and Hawaiian music. He and his friends spent so much time here that he installed Hawaii's first telephone line, between the boathouse and Iolani Palace.

The museum opened in 1988 on Nov. 16, the king's birthday. The highlight of the center is the Kalakaua Boathouse Museum, which resembles the original two-story building. Displays and videos celebrate Polynesian and Western maritime contributions as well as the monarch's love of the Hawaiian arts. Exhibits include everything from shark tooth tools and an intricately woven Hawaiian red and yellow feather cape to rotund iron caldrons first used to melt whale blubber, then later for boiling sugar or making *okolehao* (ti plant liquor).

Docked at pier 7, the **Hokulea** is a 60-foot replica of an ancient double-hull sailing canoe. Using only ancient navigational techniques, this vessel has traveled between Hawaii and Tahiti and throughout the Pacific, retracing the path of the ancient Polynesians. Also at this pier is the **Falls of Clyde,** a four-masted, square-rigged ship dating back to 1878. Board the ship and step into history.

Maritime Center open 9:30 a.m.–4 p.m. daily. Admission: $4.

Children's Touch and Feel Museum • *Pier 7, Ala Moana Blvd., Honolulu Harbor; 536–6373* • Part of the Maritime Center, this museum appeals to children—and many adults. The young at heart are invited to furl the sails on an al fresco reproduction of a ship's deck; to walk the plank and splash into an ocean of plastic bubbles; and to sit in a pseudosubmarine and play with its periscope and controls.

Open 9 a.m.–5 p.m. daily. Adults: $7. Children aged 6–17: $3.50.

Aloha Tower • *Pier 9, Honolulu Harbor, Honolulu* • This 10-story tower, a short walk from the Maritime Center, was once the tallest building in Hawaii. Built in 1926, it was turned over to the military for use during WWII. From the top floor observation deck, you can take in Honolulu Harbor, the city's forest of buildings, and the coast.

Arizona Memorial at Pearl Harbor • *U.S. Naval Reservation, Pearl Harbor, Honolulu; 422–2771* • More than 2000 Navy, Army, and Marine personnel and civilians died in the December 7, 1941, Japanese attack on Pearl Harbor that thrust the United States into WWII. More than 1000 people were wounded. Most of the American casualties occurred when the U.S.S. *Arizona* was bombed. Only about 150 of the 1200 or so bodies on board could be recovered from the broken, twisted battleship, so the sunken vessel became an aquatic grave for the remaining dead.

The white concrete memorial above the ship was built in 1962. It does not touch any part of the sunken wreck. The oil still seeps from its tanks after so many decades and creates a rainbow slick on the surface of the water. Across the harbor (which gets its name from the pearl oysters that were found in it), the Visitor Center houses a museum and a theater that shows a moving film about the attack.

Elvis Presley fans are proud to note that "The King" gave all of the money he made at his 1961 Pearl Harbor concert to the USS *Arizona* War Memorial building fund. This was the largest single donation.

Departing from the Visitor Center, you can take one of the free Navy shuttle boats across the harbor to stand on the Memorial (shuttles run from 7:45 a.m. to 3 p.m.); excluding the time you'll spend waiting on line, the tour lasts about an hour and 15 minutes. If you're driving, it's best to leave as early as possible. Other options are to pay to board one of the Pearl Harbor tour boats that depart daily from Kewalo Basin near Waikiki, or to take the *Arizona* Memorial shuttle bus. (See Tours.)

Pacific Submarine Museum • *next to the Pearl Harbor Arizona Memorial Visitor Center; 423–1341* • Here you'll see the U.S.S. *Bowfin* submarine, now a memorial to the 52 subs (and more than 3000 men who died in them) that were lost during WWII. Walk through the cramped vessel to see what life was like for the men.

Open daily 8 a.m.–4:30 p.m. Admission: $7 for adults; $1.50 for children aged 6–12.

Punchbowl • *2177 Puowaina Dr., Honolulu; 541–1430* • The military and their families are buried at scenic Punchbowl, officially called the National Memorial Cemetery of the Pacific. Headstones lie flat on the manicured lawns and small clusters of flowers decorate graves. High up winding roads, this peaceful locale has a lookout with a wraparound view of the mountains; Diamond Head, which seems to rise out of Honolulu's tall buildings; the avant-garde State Capitol; the Ala Moana Shopping area; and the Pacific Ocean. As tranquil and attractive as the grounds are, don't get any ideas about picnicking here. No food is allowed on the premises.

Open daily 8 a.m.–5:30 p.m.

U.S. Army Museum • *Battery Randolph, Kalia Rd., Fort De-Russy, Waikiki* • Housing artillery before World War I, this has been transformed into a museum with military displays concerning the U.S. Army's involvement in the Pacific.

Byodo-In Temple • *Valley of the Temples, Kaneohe, off Route 83, (eastern windward coast); 239–8811* • You'll drive through Valley of the Temples cemetery to get to this striking replica of an impressive ancient temple in Kyoto, Japan. The trim, surrounding gardens make the trip especially rewarding. A huge Buddha dominates a fish-filled pond.

Open daily 8 a.m.–4:30 p.m. Admission: $3 adults; $2 children under age 12.

Nature's Best

*   **Senator Fong's Plantation and Gardens** • *47–351 Pulama Rd.,
Kahaluu (southern part of the windward coast); 239–6775* • These botanic gardens are also a working plantation, with many different types
of fruit and nut trees. Trams amble through the 725-acre estate, taking
visitors on tours. Run by Hiram Fong, the first Asian-American to be
elected to the U.S. Senate, the gardens have a visitor center with a gift
shop and snack bar. Fong's father emigrated from China to Maui to
work in the sugarcane fields. His family struggling to stay afloat, Hiram
Fong began working (picking kiawe beans) when he was only four years
old. His industriousness landed him at the University of Hawaii. From
there, he moved on to Harvard Law School, and finally to the U.S.
Senate, serving under five presidents, from Eisenhower to Ford. About
a 40-minute drive from Honolulu, these gardens are near the Byodo-In
Temple.
   *Open 9 a.m.–4 p.m. daily. Admission: $7 for adults; $3.25 for
children.*

   Foster Botanic Gardens • *180 North Vineyard Blvd.; 531–1939*
• Paths wend their ways through nine acres and thousands of species of
tropical vegetation, including ferns, orchids, multi-colored bromeliads,
ginger, vanilla plants, pineapple, guava, and banana trees. Birds call
back and forth to each other throughout the grounds. Afternoon tours
are conducted three times a week (be sure to make reservations). Other
times, you're on your own to relax and wander as you please.
   Next to the garden, which is a 5-minute walk from the Chinese
Cultural Center, stands the **Kwan Yin Temple**. Here you can sit in the
sun on the veranda or spend a few pensive moments inside.
   Contact the Friends of Foster Botanic Gardens about the **hikes** they
lead on Oahu and Neighbor Islands.
   Open daily 9 a.m.–4 p.m.

   Paradise Park • *3737 Manoa Rd., Manoa Valley (at the fringes of
Honolulu); 988–6686* • Manoa is a quiet residential area flanked by
mountains, not far from downtown Honolulu. At the end of Manoa
Road, Paradise Park is deep in a flourishing rain forest (so be sure to
bring insect repellent). Paths give close-up looks at the varied flowers,
trees, and other greenery. In the amphitheater, uniformed schoolchildren crowd into the bleachers along with everyone else. The young set
stares in awe as cockatoos, macaws, and other birds perform amusing
tricks such as raising the American flag, pumping water, riding a scooter,
playing basketball, dancing, riding a bike on a high wire, mastering a
unicycle and a tandem bike.

Open 10 a.m.–5 p.m. daily. Admission: $7.50 for adults; $6.50 for children ages 13–17; $3.75 for ages 4–12.

The Arts

Honolulu Academy of Arts • *900 South Beretania St., Honolulu; 538–3693* • Especially if you're into Asian art (from furniture and bronzes to Japanese prints), don't miss this venerated museum. The collection also includes contemporary and traditional western works. Spend some time relaxing in one of the courtyards with tiled fountains. In a sunny, enclosed garden, you might come upon a class of art students busily sketching by a lily pond while birds provide background music.

Open 10 a.m.–4:30 p.m. from Tues. through Sat.; 1–5 p.m. on Sun. No admission charge.

The Contemporary Museum at Spalding House • *2411 Makiki Heights Dr.; 526–1322* • Art created since the 1940s is on display in this hillside estate.

Open 10 a.m.–4 p.m. Mon., Wed., Thurs., Fri., and Sat. On Sun., open noon–4 p.m. Admission: $4.

Animals

Sea Life Park • **Makapuu Point, Waimanalo (windward coast; southeastern Oahu); 259–7933** • Backed by horizontally streaked cliffs and with views of the ocean and offshore islands, this center of aquatic entertainment is in a gorgeous setting. Mock killer whales, porpoises, seals, and even a wholphin (half whale, half dolphin) perform amazing feats to the delight of the audience, even when they get splashed. Other marine exhibits include hammerhead sharks and other menacing creatures seen through glass in their natural habitats; and a display of license plates, hub caps, and old bottles—all removed from the stomachs of sharks!

Open 9:30 a.m.–5 p.m. daily, except Fri., when Sea Life closes at 10 p.m. Admission: $10 for adults; $8 for children ages 7–12; $4 for children ages 4–6.

Honolulu Zoo • *Kapiolani Park, Waikiki; 923–7723* • Built in 1914, this zoo has added nearly 1000 animals to its original half a dozen. Children enjoy the petting zoo, with more than 100 friendly animals. In the works is a $5-million savanna, where a couple hundred East African creatures will roam. On Wednesdays and weekends, look for art by local painters displayed, for sale, on the Monsarrat Ave. fence. During the summer, free musical shows are performed here on Wednesday nights.

Open 8:30 a.m.–4 p.m. daily. Admission: $1 for adults and chil-

dren between 13 and 17. The petting zoo is open 9 a.m.–2 p.m., Tues. through Sun.

The Waikiki Aquarium • *across from Kapiolani Park, Waikiki; 923–5335* • Though petite, this aquarium makes a worthwhile stop. It opened in 1904, making it one of the oldest in the country. Among the hundreds of species of Pacific marine life now residing here are seals, giant clams, sharks, sea turtles, lobsters, crocodiles, and a rainbow of fish.
Open 9 a.m.–5 p.m. daily. Admission: $2.50 adults; children under age 16 free.

Kualoa Ranch • **Kaaawa (central windward coast); 926–6069** • For a potpourri of action, head for Kualoa, a working cattle ranch where you can horseback ride in Kaaawa Valley, go snorkeling, take a helicopter tour, a dune buggy jaunt, and have lunch—all for one price.
Activities package: Mon. through Fri. Cost: $100.

~~~~~~

TOURS AND CRUISES

To get to the vast majority of Oahu's most impressive sights and attractions, you can leave the driving (and cruising or flying) to someone else. A rental car comes in handy for flexibility when you're outside Honolulu, but within the city it can be more of a headache than a convenience.

BY BUS: The least expensive, and often most interesting way to see the island is by city bus, since you'll be riding with residents going about their business. Some of the best coastal views of the island are from the Circle Island transit bus (#52 or #58); in about four hours, you'll travel practically the entire perimeter of the island. The next best choice is to be guided by one of the tour companies that use minibuses or vans (as opposed to slightly less expensive trips in full-size buses), such as **Akamai Tours** (971–4545 or (800) 922–6485) and **E Noa Tours** (599–2561 or 941–6608).
Departing from the Royal Hawaiian Shopping Center, the bright red, San Francisco–style **Waikiki Trolley** (526–0112) makes the rounds of central Honolulu's historical highlights. For $10, you can listen to this narrated tour, and climb on and off the trolley as often as you like between 8 a.m. and 3 p.m., spending as much time as you want at each site. Stops include Dole Cannery Square, Chinatown, Iolani Palace, Ka-

mehameha Statute, Academy of the Arts, Maritime Center, Hilo Hattie's (aloha clothing warehouse), Ala Moana Center, Ward Warehouse, Restaurant Row.

You can book a bus tour through a hotel activities desk or by contacting the company directly. Although there are many different companies, the various itineraries are relatively standard. The three types of **circle island tours** are the half-day trip around Oahu's southern shores; the all-day drive including the North Shore; and the all-day "grand circle," which takes in both. All half-day circle island trips cover Diamond Head; the ritzy neighborhood of Kahala; the Halona Blowhole; Hanauma Bay, a beautiful powdery crescent lapped by fish-packed waters; other beaches; Waimanalo farmlands; rainforests; and lookout points with overwhelming views. Some of these tours also include admission to Sea Life Park, the marine playland, or stops at Iolani Palace, Queen Emma's Summer Palace, or Punchbowl National Cemetery.

Grand circle island tours introduce visitors to the windward coast and North Shore, stopping at Japanese Byodo-In Temple, overlooked by the Koolau Mountains; the Mormon Temple in Laie; Sunset Beach (surfing heaven); beautiful Waimea Bay; and Waimea Falls Park, a botanical garden with Hawaiian cultural demonstrations. Some tours also include brief visits to the Polynesian Cultural Center (which is actually best left for its own day), lunch at a casual restaurant, or a beach picnic with enough time for swimming.

Note that guided tours to the **Polynesian Cultural Center** are available for those who want to see the evening musical extravaganza, but don't want to have to drive themselves back to their hotel at night. You can also get to **Pearl Harbor** on the *Arizona* Memorial Shuttle Bus ($2 per person each way).

Some **Honolulu city tours** stop at Pearl Harbor and the U.S.S. *Arizona* Memorial. Most include Punchbowl National Cemetery, Iolani Palace, the State Capitol, Washington Place (once the home of Hawaiian royalty and now the Governor's mansion), Mission Houses Museum, Kawaiahaʻo Church (the first mission church), the judiciary buildings guarded by the statue of King Kamehameha the Great, and Chinatown. With the exception of Pearl Harbor and Punchbowl, these sites are all easily covered on foot in one or two (very leisurely) days, so I don't recommend a bus tour of the city. If you'd like a guide, a better bet is to take one of the walking tours sponsored by the Mission Houses Museum, Iolani Palace, Chinatown Chamber of Commerce, and the Hawaii Heritage Center (see By Foot below).

Several companies sponsor tours with a twist: In its 17-passenger minibuses, **E Noa Tours** (above) offers one circle-island trip that takes visitors to plantations and introduces them to lei-making, hula, and Hawaiian music. One **TransHawaiian** (735–6467 or (800) 533–8765) half-day city tour includes a walking tour of Chinatown and glass-bottom boat and helicopter rides; another guides hikers up Diamond Head and takes them to a garden club. The Mysterious Orient Tour, organized by **Polynesian Adventure Tours** (922–0888) lets visitors take part in a Japanese tea ceremony and includes stops at Japanese gardens, a Thai pavillion, a Buddhist temple, a Korean Studies Center, and a Shinto shrine.

In addition to those mentioned above, other good tour companies are **Grayline** ((800) 367–2420), which offers a variety of tours, mostly in large buses; **Roberts Hawaii** (947–3939), which conducts tours in both vans and buses; and **Diamond Head Tours** (922–0544): guides are especially knowledgeable, since they all must take Hawaiiana classes sponsored by the Bishop Museum.

Most companies pick visitors up either right at their hotels or at neighboring accommodations. Drivers expect tips (of at least $1 per person), and in the vast majority of cases, they well deserve them.

BY FOOT: The best way to get to know Waikiki and downtown Honolulu is to put on some comfortable shoes and take a stroll. Various organizations offer informative guided walks.

The **Mission Houses Museum** (531–0481) and **Kapidani Community College** (734–9211) leads tours of the nearby historic sections of downtown Honolulu, as well as tours of the museum itself. During the Kamehameha Dynasty in Old Honolulu Tour, amblers learn about 19th-century Hawaii's struggle to maintain its independence despite powerful foreign outside influences. They even get a chance to discuss social, cultural, and political issues of the time with (costumed actors playing) the Reverend and Mrs. Hiram Bingham, missionaries who helped shape the Islands' history. Conducted once a month on Saturdays from 9 a.m. to 12 p.m., this tour costs $10 for adults and $4 for children, and includes admission to the museum.

Among the other walks is the Historic Crime Tour, conducted at night, in which participants are told about Hawaii's eerie supernatural heritage, including the Night Marchers, Chinese ghosts, Japanese folk monsters, and documented hauntings involving places such as Iolani Palace, Kawaiaha'o Cemetery, Queen's Hospital, and the State Capitol. Beginning around 6 p.m., this tour departs from the State Library on King Street.

Once a month, there's a tour called "A Musical Odyssey into Nineteenth Century Honolulu," which culminates in a noon concert by the Royal Hawaiian Band on the grounds of Iolani Palace.

Also once a month, **the Kapiolani Community College Office of Community Services** (735–8256) conducts a tour of Iolani Palace called Revolution! During this three-hour amble, strollers hear about the complex and controversial downfall of the Hawaiian monarchy. The cost is $10 for adults and $4 for children.

The Chinese Chamber of Commerce (533–3181) sponsors a three-hour walking tour of **Chinatown,** every Tuesday morning at 9:30 a.m. Lunch at Wo Fat restaurant follows. Cost: $5 plus $6 for the optional lunch. The three-hour Chinatown tours conducted by the **Hawaii Heritage Center** (521–2749) take place on Wednesdays and Fridays beginning at 9:30 a.m., and the cost is $5, plus lunch, if you like. While you walk and talk with your guide, you might learn about herbal medicine, Asian arts, or the differences among Buddhism, Taoism, and Shinto. As you go from store to store, there is time for shopping if the mood hits.

CRUISES: Most of Oahu's dinner and moonlight cruises, Pearl Harbor boat tours, and glass-bottom boat trips leave from **Kewalo Basin,** just beyond the *Ewa* (western) end of Waikiki. You can also arrange for deep-sea fishing charters here. Just across Ala Moana Boulevard, at the *makai* (ocean) end of Ward Avenue, this commerical harbor is often mistakenly called Fisherman's Wharf (there's a restaurant there with that name). For booze cruises and dinner excursions, you can often arrange free transportation to and from the boat so you don't have to worry about drinking and driving.

If you don't want to drive yourself or take a bus to **Pearl Harbor** to catch the free Navy shuttle boat to the U.S.S. *Arizona* Memorial, you can always pay to get there on one of the Pearl Harbor tour boats that leave Kewalo Basin a couple of times a day.

Dinner cruises are quite popular on Oahu. Aboard **Windjammer Cruises'** (922–1200) multi-deck *Rella Mae,* you can take either the standard $45 excursion, with an open bar and three shows, or the deluxe $60 dinner cruise, where the three shows are accompanied by better food and drinks, served by waiters. Choose between a 5:15 to 7:45 p.m. sunset cruise (which affords wonderful views of Honolulu) and an 8:45 to 11 p.m. moonlight cruise.

Most people give **Aikane** excursions (538–3680) high marks. Some swear by the sunset dinner cruise on a 75-foot catamaran, with its spirited musical show, dancing to a live band, dinner and open bar. The dance floor stays packed and the young hosts are extremely congenial. Young singles seem to enjoy the two-and-a-half-hour Rock Booze Cruise that includes loud music, pupus, and a bar that endlessly flows with drinks. Roundtrip transportation between the boat and Waikiki is definitely provided in this case. For a far more intimate experience, **Tradewind Charters** (533–0220) sets sail with a maximum of six people on a private yacht.

The ride is often bumpy on the inflatable boat that **Windward Expeditions** (263–3899) uses to tour Oahu's windward coast. But most passengers thoroughly enjoy the guides' running commentary about island history, traditions, and legends as the boat bounces past scattered offshore islands, even stopping at one that's a haven for seabirds. The one problem with this trip is that when the boat cuts into the cave where the birds nest, both the passengers and their feathered friends are almost choked with fumes from the motor.

Although being on a **submarine** is certainly exciting, a ride on Oahu's touring sub is an expensive affair (about $70 for adults and $36 for children for a 45-minute dip). I think your money would be better spent scuba diving or taking several snorkeling trips. But if you'd rather stay dry while you visit the depths, **Atlantis Submarine** (536–2694) can help you out. First you'll board a catamaran, at the Hilton Hawaiian Village dock in Waikiki. When you climb into the 65-foot sub, waiting a mile out in the ocean, you'll descend about 100 feet, seeing a sunken naval tanker amid the fish and coral. The submarine ride is only 45 minutes, but, including the catamaran shuttle, plan to spend 2 hours on this excursion.

HELICOPTERS: I recommend taking a helicopter ride on Oahu only if you're not going to Kauai, the Big Island, or Maui. Most flights are from 30 minutes (about $100) to an hour (about $200). **Papillon** (836–1566; or (800) 367–8047x142 from the mainland) has all bases covered with convenient take-offs from various parts of Oahu: Waikiki, the Turtle Bay Hilton, the Sheraton Makaha Resort, and Kualoa Ranch. If you only want a taste of what flying in a helicopter is like, take a six-minute whirl over Waikiki for only about $30 with **Hawaii Pacific Helicopters** (836–1566). Hawaii Pacific flights, which also come in longer versions, take off near the Ilikai hotel right in Waikiki. While you're comparison shopping, you might also give **Kenai Helicopters** (836–2071) a call.

FOR THE ACTIVE SET: If merely sitting in a van and looking at beautiful scenery just doesn't seem enough for you, try **Action Hawaii Adventures** (944–6754). In between riding around in a mini-van, you'll hike to Manoa Falls; learn about local vegetation; sample island fruit; swim and play with boogie boards at Waimanalo Beach Park (where you'll have a lunch that includes Hawaiian specialties); and snorkel at reef-enclosed Makapuu beach. You'll need to make reservations at least three days in advance for these tours that last from 8:30 a.m. to 5 p.m. The full-day excursion costs about $70. It's best not to bring children under age eight.

BEACHES

Oahu is rimmed with more than 50 beach parks, many of which have lifeguards, bathrooms, changing facilities, showers, and picnic tables. Only highly skilled surfers should enter North Shore waters during winter months, when the waves are massive. This shore is the site of winter surfing tournaments. At all beaches, heed warnings about surf conditions. Like any ocean, the extremely powerful Pacific must be handled with care.

Be sure to apply sunscreen before and immediately after going into the water. Let the rays darken your skin slowly. Don't spend your whole first day stretched out on the beach. It may not be a good idea to find shade beneath a palm tree, since falling coconuts can be very harmful if you happen to be in their path. Leave your valuables in your hotel or condominium safe. Unfortunately, theft is an all-too-common pastime at the shore, especially along the economically depressed Waianae Coast. While this western shore has some good beaches, it may not be a good idea to venture much beyond the Sheraton Makaha hotel, unless you are accompanied by local friends. Note that no alcohol is allowed on Hawaii's beaches.

Waikiki • *southeastern shore (leeward coast)* • The busiest and best-known beach in the entire state is actually a two-and-a-half-mile series of several beaches. Although it's often difficult to catch a glimpse of the sand between all the glistening bodies lying, walking, and playing on top of it, no one seems to mind the crush. At a string of concessions along the shore, "beachboys" make arrangements for people to sail on catamarans, ride outrigger canoes and aqua-bikes, go parasailing, and learn to surf, among other pursuits.

Swimmers looking for the calmest waves and the sandiest ocean floor gravitate toward **Kahaloa** and **Ulukou** beaches, facing the Royal Hawaiian ("the Pink Palace") and the Sheraton Moana Surfrider hotels. Many people consider this section the cream of Waikiki's crop. Even the police get to work from a station here. The beach in front of the Hilton Hawaiian Village is known as **Kahanamoku Beach and Lagoon**. Named after Duke Kahanamoku, Hawaii's beloved surfing champion and Olympic swimmer, this is a good spot for young children, since the waves are gentle. If you don't mind mixing with military personnel, try **Fort DeRussy Beach** (in front of the Hale Koa Hotel), the broadest section of Waikiki Beach. You might want to join a volleyball game here.

The Halekulani hotel overlooks calm, narrow **Gray's Beach,** once a Hawaiian retreat for spiritual healing. Surfers find great waves out past the reef. **Kuhio Beach Park,** by the Waikiki Beach Center, is an especially good spot for viewing the sunset. Although a seawall that protrudes into the ocean keeps waters relatively calm at shore, swimmers must be very careful since the ocean floor is potholed with unexpected drops. Surfing and bodysurfing are good on the ocean side of the wall. The sand becomes particularly powdery at **Queen's Beach,** near the Honolulu Zoo. This is a popular picnic site with the gay community, as well as with families. Locals and visiting singles flock to **Sans Souci Beach,** near the New Otani Kaimana Beach Hotel, for sunning, picknicking, and volleyball. The al fresco Hau Tree Lanai restaurant satisfies the hungry.

Ala Moana Beach Park • *just Ewa (west) of Waikiki; across from the Ala Moana shopping center* • Although this beach teems with families, couples, and singles swimming, playing volleyball, jogging, and just plain socializing, it is less crowded than Waikiki, which begins on the other side of the Ala Wai Yacht Harbor. Locals and visitors congregate here for picnics.

Diamond Head Beach Park • *near Waikiki, on the Koko Head side of Diamond Head crater* • Watched over by a lighthouse, this is not a good beach for swimming since the water is dangerously rough. But if you're into strolling and peering into tidal pools, consider stopping here.

Hanauma Bay • *near Oahu's southeastern tip* • You'll arrive here at the top of a hill, looking down on the palm-lined, mountain-backed C-shaped beach. This is one of Oahu's most beautiful settings. Even from above, you can see all kinds of coral through the transparent blue water. Walk down to the sand or take a jitney (for about 50¢ each way). Because snorkeling is so good here, the beach remains packed all day. If you don't own snorkeling gear, be sure to rent some before you come, or take a Hanauma Bay snorkeling excursion (see Sports).

Sandy Beach • *at the southeastern tip of the island, near Sea Life Park* • Look at but don't touch the water here. Despite the many body surfers who pack the shore, this part of the Pacific is *extremely dangerous,* even for champion swimmers. Very strong currents and jagged, hidden rocks create hazards not worth risking. Rock music blares from radios while young people show off their cars. Kites flutter high in the sky. At one of the food wagons parked across the street, consider sampling a **plate lunch** (generally teriyaki steak, chicken, or fish; two scoops of rice; a mound of macaroni salad; and *kim chee* (Korean pickled vegetables), or try **manapua,** a Chinese rice flour bun with meat or beans. Sandy Beach is sometimes referred to as Koko Head Beach Park.

Makapuu Beach Park • *southeastern tip of Oahu, across from Sea Life Park* • Body surfing and boogie boarding are big here, but should only be attempted by experts. Riptides can be life-threatening for the novice. However, the locale—a small cove at the bottom of impressive cliffs that serve as a jumping-off point for hang gliders—makes this a wonderful spot for soaking up the sun. Petite Rabbit Island is just offshore.

Waimanalo Beach Park • *southeastern end of the windward coast* • Locals fill the lawn here with barbecue grills, coolers, lawn chairs, and radios. They are sometimes less than pleased to see outsiders, so you might feel more comfortable if you come with a local friend or two. You'll feel less like an intruder on the beautiful beach, with its nonintimidating waves that draw boogie boarders and body surfers.

Bellows Field Park Beach • *southeastern end of the windward coast* • Because of the gentle waves, the swimming and body surfing are great here. Locals set up picnics in the shade of ironwood trees. Unfortunately, this U.S. Air Force beach is only open to the public from Friday afternoon until Sunday night, and on federal holidays.

Lanikai Beach • *southeastern windward coast* • Known to few outsiders, this beach is great for swimming. The tranquil setting is enhanced by the view of two silhouetted offshore islands. To find this beach, you'll have to take one of the lanes between the houses on coastal Mokulua Drive.

Kailua Beach Park • *windward coast, at Kailua* • Excellent for windsurfing and swimming, this palm-shaded beach is frequented by local families in addition to board sailors. Windsurfing equipment is available for rent in Kailua. Sailing and boating are also fine here (see *Sports*).

Leanani and Waiahole Beach Parks • *on Kaneohe Bay, windward coast* • The bay here is polluted, so the only reason to visit these parks is to relax or picnic on dry land.

Kualoa Beach Park • *north of Kaneohe Bay, windward coast* • Absorb the lovely setting. Views from the long, slim, often windy beach take in the bay and the Koolau Mountains. At low tide, you can walk out to Mokolii island, better known as Chinaman's Hat. Picnicking and camping are popular here.

Kaaawa Beach Park • *near Kaaawa, on the windward coast* • The swimming and snorkeling are quite good here.

Swanzy Beach Park • *near Kaaawa, on the windward coast* • This spot is far better for sunning than for swimming, since sharp and lumpy coral interfere with being in the water.

Kahana Bay Beach Park • *windward coast* • The shallow waters here make for better wading than swimming, so this is a good place to introduce toddlers and other children to the Pacific. This shady, picturesque site is also fine for a picnic or simple relaxation. Pandanus and ironwood trees provide ample shade. Boating and fishing are popular here as well. Not far from here is an ancient Hawaiian fish pond, which was still being used as late as the 1920s. See if you can find some ripe mangoes or bananas in lush Kahana Valley, across the road.

Punaluu Beach Park • *northern windward coast, near the Polynesian Cultural Center* • The swimming is good here, but the beach is often crowded in the afternoon with groups from tour buses that stop at Pat's at Punaluu restaurant for lunch.

Malaekahana Beach Park • *northern windward coast, between the Polynesian Cultural Center and the Turtle Bay Hilton* • Even though the beach is narrow, it is quite long and the waves are perfect for swimming and body surfing. When the tide is low, you can slosh all the way out to offshore Goat Island (but wear diving booties or other shoes to protect your feet from the jagged rocks). This shady beach park is a popular camp site with local families.

Ehukai Beach Park • *North Shore* • Home of the famous Banzai Pipeline, this is one of the North Shore beaches packed with master surfers during the winter. Even walking close to the water can be dangerous during winter months since 20- and 30-foot waves may suddenly come barreling further in than expected. Mother Nature does a dramatic about-face in the summer, when waves here become manageable for swimmers and snorkelers.

Sunset Beach • *North Shore* • In the winter, you can join the festive atmosphere while surfing contests take place here and at nearby North Shore beaches. Another dangerous spot during the winter for all but expert surfers, Sunset calms down enough during the summer to allow strong swimmers and good body surfers some safe fun. Look for food trucks, parked across the street, where you can buy plate lunches, shave ice, and beverages.

Waimea Bay • Swimming and snorkeling are good here during the summer, that is if you're a strong swimmer. Forget about entering the water during the winter. Don't even get close to the shore. Just watch the expert surfers doing their thing on 25-plus-foot waves. Right across the road from Waimea Falls Park, this beach is broad and has a shady picnic area.

Pupukea Beach Park • *North Shore* • Admire this beach from a safe distance during the winter. Strong swimmers can enjoy snorkeling here during the summer, when the water is kinder to humans.

Haleʻiwa Beach Park • *North Shore* • At funky little Haleʻiwa, the North Shore's only town, this beach is good for swimming and snorkeling during the spring and summer, but, like all North Shore beaches, should not be entered by anyone but accomplished surfers in the winter. Feel free to join a volleyball game or to toss a frisbee around.

Haleʻiwa Alii Beach Park • *North Shore* • Formerly known as Waialua Beach Park, this spot is good for swimming during the spring and summer only. Other times, surfing and watching (from a safe distance) should be the main activities.

Mokuleia Beach Park • *North Shore* • While this area draws many campers, the swimming is not good at all.

* **Yokohama Bay** • *just north of Makaha, on the Waianae coast* • Never crowded, this surfing beach lies at the northern end of the leeward coast road. (However, you won't be able to get to the North Shore from here unless you hike it, since there is no road for vehicles.) This frequently narrow and rocky beach is a prime fishing spot among locals. During the summer, when the water is "flat," children splash in the waves.

* **Ewa Beach Park** • *on the leeward coast, near Pearl Harbor* • Hawaiian families often choose this as a picnic locale. After a storm, it is not unusual to see people gathering uprooted *limu* (seaweed) to use in salads and other dishes. Hawaiians have been cooking with seaweed for generations. Asian immigrants have added their own seaweed recipes to Hawaii's culinary melange.

SPORTS

Watersports, the prime attraction for active travelers, can be arranged through most hotels and condominiums, even those not situated on the beach. Sports concessions and "beach boys" (life guards, surfing instructors, outrigger canoe paddlers, etc.) sprinkle Waikiki's sandy shore. You can also stop at the **Waikiki Beach Center,** adjacent to the Sheraton Moana Surfrider hotel. Some beaches or adjoining parks have **volleyball** courts. Details about water and landsports follow.

BIKING: Cycling on Oahu can be enjoyable, as long as you steer clear of Waikiki and the rest of Honolulu, where traffic is thick. Many airlines allow bikes on board for a small additional charge. If you haven't brought your own, you can rent one by the day (about $18) at **Aloha Funway Rentals** (942–9696) or by the week (about $47) at **University Cyclery** (944–9884), both in Honolulu. Ask whether insurance is included in the quoted rates. You'll need to give the cycle shop a deposit ($50 to $100) or a major credit card. If you have to leave your bike anywhere, always lock it. Be sure to wear a helmet and cycle gloves (for a safe grip). If you absolutely must ride at night (which I don't recommend *at all*), be sure your bike has a light and reflectors.

The Hawaii Bicycle League *(988–7175)* organizes rides every Saturday and Sunday that leave from the Kapiolani Park bandstand in Waikiki and wend their way to various parts of Oahu. Beginner rides cover less than 20 miles while the most experienced cyclists take 124-mile circle-island trips.

CANOEING: Along Waikiki Beach, "beach boys" compete for the chance to take tourists out in 30- to 40-foot outrigger canoes to ride the waves as the ancient Hawaiians once did. For about $5, paddlers will allow several good waves to push you toward shore. In this sport, sometimes called "canoe surfing," boats can travel faster than 25 miles an hour.

Guests at the 8-room Plantation Spa in Kaaawa on the windward coast may go canoeing along the Kahana River, gliding past the long, jumbled branches of hau trees to the tranquil place where the river pours into the ocean, and by the time-worn rocky walls of an old Hawaiian fishpond.

When Hawaiian kings, queens, and high chiefs used to ride their canoes or board surf, commoners knew to stay away from the beach, lest they sully these royal sports. When a kapu (taboo) was placed on a site reserved for alii at play, a commoner foolish enough to trespass might even be put to death.

After the 1820 arrival of American missionaries, canoe surfing, along with many other Hawaiian pastimes, was almost wiped out. The god-fearing haoles were appalled at all the glistening skin exposed—on both men and women—during water sports. By the end of the 19th century, aquatic games had begun making their comeback, thanks in large part to King David Kalakaua, who also revived the hula and other Hawaiian traditional arts. However, canoe surfing was never quite the same as it had been. In an attempt to preserve this disappearing segment of Hawaiian culture, Alexander Hume Ford started the Outrigger Canoe Club in Waikiki in 1908. A rival association, called the Hui Nalu Canoe Club, was put together in 1911 by a group consisting mainly of Hawaiians.

FISHING: **Kewalo Basin,** near Waikiki, is the place most visitors go to arrange full- and half-day excursions on charter fishing boats. Reliable companies include **Corene-C Fishing Charters** (536–7424); **Island Charters** (536–1555); **Sport Fishing Hawaii** (536–6577); **ELO-1 Sport Fishing** (947–5208); and **Tradewind Charters** (533–0220).

To share a boat for a full day (usually 7 a.m. to 3:30 p.m.), rates range from about $80 to $100 per person. For a half day, plan to spend $55 to $70 per person. To charter a boat, rates run from $450 to $575 for a full day, and from $330 to $390 for a half day. Rates include fishing gear, but you're expected to bring your own lunch. In most cases, the fish you catch go to the captain. Plan to tip the captain about $20. Ask about less expensive North Shore charters for tuna and marlin fishing.

Wahiawa Reservoir, not far from Schofield Barracks in central Oahu, is home to many big peacock and black bass. **Nuuanu Reservoir,** near the Pali Highway (Route 61), just outside Honolulu, is also good for small-boat freshwater fishing.

If you want to fish for sport, not for dinner, try some of the narrow streams and small ponds that drain and irrigate sugar cane and pineapple fields, such as those along **Kunia Road** going toward Waipahu, in southern central Oahu (near Pearl Harbor). The catch is, you must ask the landowner for permission. Remember that agricultural chemicals render these fish inedible.

Plenty of petite saltwater fish reside along **Kaneohe Bay,** near Kaneohe Beach County Park on the windward coast, making wade-fishing enjoyable here. However, these fish are not to be eaten. Also, you'll have to watch out for Portuguese Man-O-War and other jellyfish (apply meat tenderizer or urine if you do get stung) and be sure to wear good sunglasses, a hat or visor, sneakers, a long-sleeved shirt, and long pants.

Tidepools lie in waiting for those who slosh through the flats and climb over jagged reefs.

You may see locals fishing from cliffs at places such as a spot near Hanauma Bay, but I don't recommend your trying this yourself since it can be very dangerous. The edges of precipices can be extremely slippery and unexpectedly high waves can suddenly burst up from the ocean.

GOLF: Oahu has nearly 30 golf courses, the majority of which are open to the public. There are more courses here than on any of the Neighbor Islands. However, since Oahu receives more visitors, many greens tend to be crowded. Completed in early 1990, the 18-hole championship **Ko Olina Golf Course** (676–5300) sprawls on the leeward coast about a half-hour drive from downtown Honolulu. The lakes, waterfalls, and rock gardens make this green especially picturesque. Because the municipal **Ala Wai Golf Course** (296–4653) is right near Waikiki, it is quite popular and often packed. Vacationers will probably do better at the **Hawaii Kai Executive Course** or the **Hawaii Kai Championship Course** (395–2358 for both), just east of Waikiki. Transportation from Waikiki is provided to and from the course at the **Sheraton Makaha resort** (695–9544), on the Waianae coast. Near the North Shore, this course is in a picturesque valley. Also a distance from Waikiki, **the Turtle Bay Hilton** (293–8811) has a course on the North Shore. Waikiki's **Hilton Hawaiian Village** (949–4321) offers golf packages in conjunction with Turtle Bay, including round-trip transportation, lunch, a cocktail, a T-shirt, and a chance to go swimming.

HIKING: Oahu is interlaced with many good hiking trails, several close to Waikiki. *Remember: it is always best to hike with at least one other person, no matter how experienced you are.* If you're traveling alone, or if you'd like to be part of a group, you can arrange guided hikes through organizations including the **Nature Conservancy of Hawaii** (537–4508); the **Clean Air Team** (944–0804); and the **Sierra Club** (538–6616).

From the summit of **Diamond Head** crater, your eyes will take in Koko Head, Honolulu, the Waianae and Koolau mountains, and the ocean, among other sights. The trail to the top is clearly defined. A flashlight will come in handy when it's time to enter the tunnel used by the military during WWII. For a leisurely pace, allow about an hour going up and 45 minutes coming down. The interior of the crater is surprisingly lush. Note that facilities, open from 6 a.m. to 6 p.m., include drinking water and bathrooms.

Other good trails near Waikiki are in the Makiki Valley, Tantalus Mountain, and Manoa Valley area. From the Paradise Park parking lot, you can begin a 45-minute hike through jungled vegetation to **Manoa**

Falls, a perfect spot for swimming and relaxing. Easily reached by bus, the **Kanealole Trail** starts in Makiki Valley, turns west onto the Makiki Valley Trail, which cuts across the valley, then goes north on the Nahuina Trail, eventually coming to the Manoa Cliffs. From here you can take the Puu Ohia Trail northeast and go down into Manoa Valley via the Aihualama Trail.

Manoa Falls is less than a mile from here. The wind makes an eerie, musical sound as it blows through stands of bamboo. Bordering the trail, the leaves and branches of koa trees form a ceiling overhead. The roots of banyan trees drip to the ground like hair. Right before you reach Manoa Falls, you'll be yanked back into modern times with a view of Honolulu peeking through the woods. The trail out of the valley is just under a mile. You can catch a bus back to Waikiki from the Paradise Park parking lot, or walk about three miles down Manoa Road to Waikiki.

Guava trees, red and pink **mountain apples,** and blood red **Surinam cherries** grow along the trails. Springs are hidden in the dense greenery off the paths. **Job's tears** are plentiful. Local people string this plant's white, black, and bluish-gray pellet-sized beans into rosaries and leis. Many birds hang out along the Manoa Cliffs Trail, including unusual native species such as the red and black *apapane* and the gray, black, and white *elepaio*. You'll see plenty of eucalyptus, paperbark, and bamboo trees on the Puu Ohia Trail. At the end of this trail, just beyond the turnoff for descending the Aihualama into Manoa Valley, you'll come to a dramatic sweeping view of Nuuanu Valley, the Pali Highway, and a reservoir.

Through **Action Hawaii Adventures** (944–6754) you can spend a day hiking to Manoa Falls, snorkeling at a quiet beach, boogey boarding, and picnicking.

Kaena Point, the northwestern tip of Oahu, can be reached from either the North Shore or the leeward (Waianae) coast. From the leeward side, the two-hour, three-mile hike begins at Yokohama Beach (also known as Keawaula), a popular surfing spot. With the craggy cliffs to your right, you'll pass natural arches, caves, and places where the ocean spurts into the air like water from a whale's spout. At Barking Sands Beach (Kepuhi Point and Keaau Beach), the sand squeaks underfoot.

Approaching Kaena from Mokuleia on the wetter windward (North) coast, you'll pass cliffs (to the left) that are much greener than on the leeward side, and many more colorful flowers. Dramatic rock formations are interspersed with indigenous plants, salt pans, tidepools, sandy beaches, and trails into mountain gulches. Look into the sky, and you might see hang gliders floating down from the cliffs.

If you're interested in one of the occasional hikes conducted into historic and spiritual Moanalua Valley, contact **Moanalua Gardens**

Foundation (839–5334). Highly experienced hikers may want to head (in pairs) for the Maakua Gulch Trail or Sacred Falls, on the windward coast. Some hikers attempt to protect themselves from falling rocks the traditional Hawaiian way: by wrapping stones in ti leaves as divine offerings.

You can obtain maps detailing many hikes by visiting **Hawaii Geographic Maps and Books** at 49 South Hotel St., Suite 218, in Honolulu; writing to them at P.O. Box 1698, Honolulu, HI 96806; or calling (800)323–3723.

HORSEBACK RIDING: With **Koko Crater Stables** (395–2628), the trail cuts across Koko Head crater, not far from Waikiki. At **Kualoa Ranch** (236–8515 or 926–6069), in lush Kaaawa Valley on the windward coast (across from Kualoa Beach Park), you can take trail rides or participate in the action package that combines horseback riding with a helicopter whirl, a dune buggy ride, snorkeling, and other fun. If you've always wanted to trot along a beach, try the **Turtle Bay Hilton** (293–8811) on the northern windward coast. You'll ride through 75 rolling green acres. Rates run about $18 per person for fifty minutes to an hour. **New Town and Country Stables** (259–9941), in Waimanalo, is also worth checking out.

JOGGING: A well-pounded 4.8 mile route circles **Diamond Head,** by Waikiki, passing the Diamond Head Lighthouse, and affording views of the ocean as well as of ritzy residential neighborhoods. Enclosing Waikiki like parentheses, **Kapiolani and Ala Moana parks** also attract many joggers. On Sundays from March through November, you're welcome to join runners preparing for the December **Honolulu Marathon.** Meet at the Kapiolani bandstand in the park at 7:30 a.m. If you're up to the Marathon itself, join the crush (734–7200). Running along the mile-and-a-half **Ala Wai Canal,** you might pass outrigger canoe teams preparing for competitions.

As far as the rest of Oahu goes, don't jog in remote areas, no matter how scenic. Call the **Running Room** (737–2422) for tips on the safest and most appealing routes.

KAYAKING: Try **Adventure Kayaking** (924–8898); **Island Adventure** (528–0987); or **Twogood Kayaks Hawaii** (235–2352), based in Kaneohe on the windward coast, which periodically hosts free demonstrations on Kailua Beach. Rates range from $25 for a half day, $30 a day, and $45 a weekend on the windward coast to $45 for a two-hour paddle in Waikiki or $95 to $130 for overnight or five-day camping/kayaking trips.

PARASAILING: One of the most thrilling experiences I've ever had, parasailing is available on Oahu through **Waikiki Beach Services** (924–4941), **Hawaii Kai Parasail** (396–9224), **Aloha Parasail** (521–2446), and **Hawaiian Parasail** (923–4434). Rates run about $45 to $50 for 10 minutes in the air. What's parasailing? It's being strapped to a parachute that is tied to a boat by a long rope and floating high into the sky as the boat takes off. Coming back to earth is no problem. The boat slows down and you simply have to walk forward as your feet touch solid ground.

SAILING: On Waikiki Beach, you can arrange to sail on catamarans through concessions and "beach boys." Many sunset, moonlight, and dinner cruises leave from Kewalo Basin, not far from Waikiki. Sailing lessons are available through **Tradewind Charters** (533–0220). To learn, plan to spend about $35 an hour for one person, plus $2 for each additional person, up to four. Transportation from Waikiki can be worked out. Tradewind also hosts a cozy three-hour sunset sail for up to six people for about $60 per person, including pupus, champagne, and non-alcoholic drinks.

(Also see Canoeing and Kayaking, above, Snorkeling below, and the Tours and Cruises section)

SAILPLANE FLIGHTS: Through the **Hawaii Soaring Club** (677–3404), you can take an exhilarating 15- or 20-minute sailplane ride from a field at Mokuleia, near the polo grounds, at Dillingham Airfield on the North Shore. Wrapped in silence (since there's no motor), you'll float over gentle hills, the rugged Waianae Mountains, deep valleys, sugar cane fields, and heads of coral peeking through the clear Pacific. The pilots explain the sights as you glide. You can generally see for more than 40 miles and sometimes as far as 80 miles, to the island of Kauai.

SCUBA DIVING: Contact **Destination Hawaii** P.O. Box 90295, Honolulu, HI 96835 to receive a copy of their booklet (about $4) describing dive sites throughout Hawaii. Some of Oahu's most exciting spots are along the Waianae coast, an area not frequented by tourists. **Leeward Drive Center** (696–3414 or (800)225–1574), based here, takes divers into the underworld by day and by night; transportation is available from Waikiki. You can learn to dive through **Dan's Dive Shop** (536–6181), which offers a five-day certification course for about $300, as well as a $60 dive excursion on a catamaran. The scuba course for beginners given by **South Seas Aquatics** (on Kapahulu Ave., 735–0438; on Ala Moana Blvd., 538–3854; (800) 252-MAHI; or FAX (808) 526–9550) runs about $100, including equipment. **Tradewind Char-**

ters (533–0220) also hosts scuba sails. Other good scuba operations are **Pacific Quest Divers** (638–8338 or (800) 367–8047) in Haleʻiwa; and **Aaron's Dive Shop** (262–2333 or FAX: (808) 262–4158) in Kailua. Based in Santa Cruz, CA, **Real Hawaii** ((408) 423–9923; (800) 367–5108; or FAX: (408) 423–0469) is a reputable dive package tour operator.

SNORKELING: Many hotels have snorkeling equipment for rent or loan. While this water sport may seem intimidating to the uninitiated, it is actually very simple. Anyone can catch on in just a few minutes. If you've never tried it, ask someone who has snorkeled before to demonstrate. Of, if you're vacationing between March and June, the **City and County of Honolulu Department of Parks and Recreation** (486–3310) gives inexpensive snorkeling lessons (about $7). Also, if you take a snorkeling cruise or other snorkeling excursion, you'll get a lesson that prepares you to take the plunge.

Hanauma Bay is Oahu's premier snorkeling site, which means it is always crowded (unless you arrive very early in the morning). This gorgeous, palm-studded crescent (its name means "curved bay") is cupped at the bottom of mountains. When you arrive, you'll be high above the water, but the plentiful coral, interspersed with smooth patches of sand, is clearly visible through the glasslike blue water. For 50¢, a tram will take you down to the beach, but most people choose to walk. Be sure to wear rubber shoes or dive booties in the water, because the coral can give nasty cuts.

Many small pools between coral reefs are packed with fish, from longnose butterfly fish and moorish idols to potter's angelfish and iridescent parrotfish. Surviving on a diet of frozen peas, popcorn, and bread nibbled from human hands, they all stay happily plump. Walk around a slippery ledge to the left of the path down to the water, and you'll come to the **Toilet Bowl,** a pocket where water "flushes" in and out with the tides. But be careful, since the rush of water can be powerful.

There are various ways to get to Hanauma Bay, in addition to driving yourself. The city bus (531–1611) will drop you off at the top of the hill for 60¢ or you can take the Red and Black Bus ($1), which will leave you right at the bay. Be sure to rent snorkel gear (from your hotel or at Waikiki Beach) before you get here. **Steve's Diving Adventures** (947–8900) runs a half-day trip to the bay, including transportation and gear, for about $8. A similar half-day trip hosted by **Waikiki Diving** (922–7188) costs about $13.

Dan's Dive Shop (536–6181) organizes a half-day snorkeling excursion for about $30; and **Tradewind Charters** (533–0220) offers an upscale half-day snorkel sail for about $60.

SPECTATOR SPORTS: If you really want to feel like a local, join the sidelines for some of Oahu's most exciting sports:

On the North Shore during the winter, watch the **Triple Crown Hawaiian Pro Surfing Championships**. Lasting for two days, this spectacle takes place in November or December, the days chosen depending on how the waves are behaving. The locale is usually the Banzai Pipeline and Sunset Beach, which turns into a big party. Newspapers will keep you up to date. Over two weekends every March, **Buffalo's Annual Big Board Surfing Classic** (696–3878) takes place on Makaha Beach, on the Waianae coast. The atmosphere is also festive, with food galore and Hawaiian music.

In Hawaii, surfing is not limited to boards. Canoe surfing is also a big deal. Held on the first day after May 1 that the surf reaches at least 10 feet, the **Annual King Kamehameha Cup/Canoe Surfing Championship** takes place in Waikiki. Waikiki is also the site of the Annual **Ala Wai Canoe Challenge** (923–1802) in January. After racing on the canal, paddlers take to land to compete in ancient Hawaiian games at the Ala Wai Field. In October, there's an **outrigger canoe race** from Molokai to Oahu.

Over Thanksgiving weekend, **New Town and Country Stables** (259–9941) puts on a raucous **rodeo** that draws cowboys from the rest of the state and from the mainland.

For more horse action, the **Hawaii Polo Club** (533–2890 or 637–POLO) hosts games every Sunday from March to August at the Mokuleia field on Oahu's North Shore, by one of the island's most attractive beaches. International teams battle it out while spectators picnic on the grounds. (You can buy food once you arrive, but most people prefer to bring their own.) Admission is about $6 for adults and children aged 12 to 17.

At Makapuu Point, near Sea Life Park at the southeastern tip of the island, you can watch daring folks **hang gliding** off the cliffs.

If you ever thought Hawaii was too exotic to be part of the United States, just wait until **football** season and you'll have no doubts about Oahu's American heritage. The cream of the NFL crop plays the **Pro Bowl** at Aloha Stadium in Honolulu a week after the Super Bowl. College teams knock each other around here during the December **Aloha Bowl**. The January **Hula Bowl** (488–7731) pits All-American college superstars against each other. Half-time erupts with hula and music, and tailgate parties flood the parking lot. During the season, the **University of Hawaii Rainbows** tear up the stadium, cheered by huge crowds. Express bus service is frequently offered from Kapiolani Park in Waikiki (531–1611).

Volleyball is big in beach parks, as well as from September to

December when you can watch college home games at **Klum Gym** in Honolulu (948–6376).

During the December **Honolulu Marathon** (734–7200), spectators cheer runners at the Kapiolani Park finish line.

The **Pan Am Hawaiian Windsurfing World Cup** is held in July at Kailua Beach on the windward coast. Check newspapers for periodic windsurfing competitions off Diamond Head Point.

Kapiolani Park plays host to the **Pan Am World International Rugby Tournament,** every other October.

Every February, the PGA **Hawaiian Open Golf Tournament** draws thick crowds to the upscale Waialae Country Club (734–2151), not far from Waikiki.

The country's best basketball players are divided into four teams for the **Aloha Basketball Classic** at Honolulu's Neal Blaisdell Center (948–7523) every April.

SURFING: On Waikiki Beach, "beach boys" hang out to teach people to surf for about $12 an hour. From time to time, free lessons are sponsored by the **Honolulu Department of Parks and Recreation** (527–6343). **Point Panic** is a popular surfing spot near Kewalo Basin (also referred to as Fisherman's Wharf.)

Most board-lovers agree that the best surfing in Hawaii is along Oahu's **North Shore,** from Haleʻiwa to Kahuku. However, only experts should attempt to handle these monster curls. Each winter this area is pounded by some of the tallest, most shapely waves anywhere. The international surfing masters flock here each December and January for the **Triple Crown.** Each of these three contests takes five days. The competitions kick off at the **Banzai Pipeline, Sunset Beach, Waimea Bay,** and/or other prime surfing spots. **Yokohama** and **Mahaka,** on the northern Waianae coast, are other good locales for the sport.

TENNIS: Hotels with tennis courts give guests first priority, but most are available for the use of nonguests as well. One of the seven courts at the **Ilikai Hotel** (949–3811) in Waikiki is lit for night play, and you can learn the game or improve your techniques at the frequent tennis clinics. Lessons are also available at the two courts of the **Pacific Beach Hotel** (922–1233) in Waikiki, as well as at the one court at Waikiki's **Hawaiian Regent Hotel** (922–6611). Also in the Waikiki area, **Ala Moana Park** (521–7664) has ten free public tennis courts; the **Diamond Head Tennis Center** (971–7150) has nine; and **Kapiolani Park** (971–7150) is home to four.

WATER SKIING: Try **Tropical Water Ski** (923–4434) or **Suyderhoud Water Ski Center** (395–3773).

WINDSURFING: One of the best places to rent equipment, take lessons, and go on group sails in **Naish Hawaii** (262–6068), based in Kailua, on the southeastern windward coast. This outfit is run by Robby Naish, a world champion windsurfer, and his family. You might also try **Windsurfing Hawaii** (261–3539), in Kailua as well; **Aloha Windsurfing** (926–1185) in Honolulu; or **Surf 'n Sea** (637–9887) in Haleʻiwa, on the North Shore.

WORKING OUT: If you want to keep up with your exercise program, consider staying at **Hilton Hawaiian Village** or the **Halekulani Hotel** (both in Waikiki), or the **Kahala Hilton** (nearby, on the eastern side of Diamond Head), which all have fitness centers for the use of guests. Programs and facilities include weight rooms, exercise bikes, and aerobics classes.

Otherwise, check out the **World Gym** (942–8171) in Waikiki, open 6 a.m. to 11 p.m. For about $10 a day, $36 a week, or $50 for two weeks, men and women can have use of Nautilus machines, Universal gyms, full free-weight facilities, and a pro shop. This gym does a brisk business among tourists. Or look into the **Clark Hatch Physical Fitness Center** (536–7205) in Honolulu, which lures the health-conscious set with its indoor pool, racquetball court, treadmills, weight-training machines, and aerobics classes. You'll pay about $8 a day here. Hours are 6 a.m. to 8 p.m. on weekdays, and 7:30 a.m. to 5:30 on Saturdays.

SHOPPING

Stores on Oahu are as varied as the island itself. Crowded, jumbled T-shirt shops share Waikiki streets with Gucci and Tiffany. Most of Oahu's stores are found in Waikiki, and these (whether in hotels or on the street) tend to be more expensive than elsewhere on the island. **ABC drug stores**—selling everything from food, juice, and liquor to suntan oil, beach towels, and *zoris* (rubber flip-flops)—are on practically every block. Many say that **Long's,** another drug store chain, has the best buys in macadamia nuts and Kona coffee. Note that the majority of the goods at the International Marketplace in Waikiki are not made in Hawaii. Locals spend most of their money at Oahu's shopping malls.

If you'd like someone to help you sort through all your options, consider taking a **Honolulu shopping tour** with Vicki DeVille (945–1028 or 396–7797). For about $30, she'll pick you up at 9 a.m. in an air-conditioned van and spend four hours taking you to some of the city's most appealing shops. Depending on what you're looking for, tours might concentrate on antique clothing, wood work, ceramics, jewelry, or art. These excursions are conducted from Monday through Friday.

There are so many shops on Oahu that you'll certainly stumble onto your own favorites. Starting with malls, here are a few of the stores and outlets that have made the greatest impression on me.

SHOPPING MALLS: Residents go to **Ala Moana Center** (1450 Ala Moana Blvd.), about five minutes from Waikiki by bus. Said to be the world's biggest open-air mall, this place is packed with nearly two hundred shops and almost two dozen restaurants. **Liberty House,** Hawaii's answer to Macy's, draws crowds here, and many enjoy browsing through **Shirokiya,** a Japanese department store filled with clothing, housewares, and food.

The upscale **Ward Centre** (1200 Ala Moana Blvd.) is not to be confused with the older, plainer Ward Warehouse a block away. The sophisticated shops and restaurants of Ward Centre are trimmed in oak, with brass railings, and are set off by hand-carved wooden signs, brick walkways, wooden columns, and stained-glass light fixtures and hanging lamps. On Fridays, once a month, you can shop to live jazz in the garden courtyard, with complimentary wine and pupus, from 5 to 7 p.m.

Stores include **Allison's Wonderland,** stuffed with stuffed animals; the **Honolulu Chocolate Company,** selling gourmet sweets handmade from imported Belgian chocolate blocks and local fruits; the **Honolulu Hat Company,** where most of the hats are hand-blocked and hand-stitched (Princess Diana and Smokey Robinson have had headpieces designed and made here); **Polo Ralph Lauren**; **Pappagallo**; art galleries; and a gourmet deli where you can gather royal picnic fixin's such as caviar and smoked salmon. *Open Mon.–Fri. 10 a.m.–9 p.m.; Sat. 10 a.m.–5 p.m.; Sun. 11 a.m.–4 p.m.*

Down the street, **Ward Warehouse** (1050 Ala Moana Blvd. at the corner of Ward Ave.) is across from Kewalo Basin. **Blue Ginger** has a wide and attractive selection of handblocked batik cotton dresses, shirts, blouses, bags, quilted jackets, and children's clothing. You can prepare for the lower depths at **South Seas Aquatics Dive Shop. Coffee Works** sells both Hawaiian coffee and tea, to drink in the cafe with pastry, or to buy (coffee beans or tea in bags or loose) to take home. **Pomegranates in the Sun** specializes in local, Asian, and South American women's fashions. Monthly entertainment is offered in the 300-seat amphitheater. Annual events include a Japanese cultural festival in June and the Hawaiian Anthurium Society Show each Easter weekend. *Open Mon.–Fri., 10 a.m.–9 p.m.; Sat. 10 a.m.–5 p.m.; Sun. 11 a.m.–4 p.m.*

ALOHA WEAR: While it's difficult to turn a corner without running into a store selling aloha shirts and muumuus, most stock the mass-produced polyester versions. **Reyn's** (at the Kahala Mall) sells aloha wear in toned-down colors and less busy designs. For high quality apparel, try **Bailey's Antique Clothing Shop** (2051 Kalakaua Ave.), where you'll find scores of tasteful designs by local shirtmakers. Vintage shirts can run you anywhere from $30 to $500. Old rayon prints with buttons made of coconut shells are the most expensive. **Hilo Hattie's Fashion Center** may try to snag you for a factory tour, but my advice is to leave this one alone. Not only is this polyester aloha wear very commercial-looking, but you end up paying more for it at the factory than you would elsewhere.

ART GALLERIES: Many of Honolulu's best art galleries are in Chinatown, which is slowly being gentrified. Galleries began moving in during the 1980s, since rents were low and rental units were more spacious than in other parts of the city. **The Pegge Hopper Gallery** (1160A Nuuanu Ave.) exhibits the work of one of Hawaii's most popular artists. Hopper's warm paintings of caramel-colored Hawaiian women dressed in mauve, oranges, purples and reds grace many a hotel wall, especially in the Neighbor Islands. Some works by other Island artists are clear examples that immitation is a synonym for flattery.

Across the street is the **Pollitt Gallerie,** where traditional and expressionist art is on display. Browse through paintings, sculpture, batiks, collages, weaving, and ceramics at the **Designer's Emporium** (1044 Nuuanu Ave.). The nearby **Ramsay Chinatown Gallery** (1128 Smith St.), with its tranquil garden, hosts group shows in a building that is a National historic landmark. The first floor of **Hawaii Artists Gallery** (at the end of Maunakea St., near the waterfront) is filled with Japanese antiques, from lacquerware and scrolls to screens and woodblock prints. The second floor is dedicated to the works of well-known local artists. **The ArtLoft** (1186 North King St.) also showcases many local artists in solo and small group exhibitions. Whimsical handmade **jewelry** is sold here as well.

BEACH WEAR: Among the many boutiques vying for the attention of the beach-going crowd, **Local Motion** (1714 Kapiolani Blvd.) stands out with its brightly colored bathing suits, shorts, and tops guaranteed to bring smiles to many faces.

CRAFTS: In June, around July 4th, and in late November or early December, Honolulu's **Mission Houses Museum** hosts wonderful crafts fairs. You'll find everything from silk-screened or tie-dyed T-shirts and dresses, Hawaiian quilts, delicate hand washable silk scarves, and ethnic foods (such as German sausages) to koa wood necklaces (selling for $65 and $85) and Niihau shell necklaces ($3000 to $5000!). Check newspapers for the **Pacific Handcrafters Guild** fairs, held four times a year in Honolulu. Five days a week, there's a major **flea market** by Aloha Stadium. The Pearl City bus will take you there. Kam Drive-In, another popular flea market, is 20 minutes from Waikiki on the Pearl City bus.

If you've been searching high and low for knicknacks in the shape of food, try **Something Special** (Kahala Mall or Windward Mall) or various crafts fairs. You'll find ceramic sushi, manapua (Chinese rice pastry), and fortune cookies. **Mejiro Enterprises** (P.O. Box 61704, Honolulu, HI 96839; 941–9754) creates fortune cookie message holders and manapua paperweights from handmade molds. Most items cost under $25. **Magnets by Ruthie** (P.O. Box 1217, Kaneohe, HI 96744, 235–5068) is responsible for the sushi magnets, pseudo shave ice, and other realistic looking goods. Prices for these items range from about $4 to $12. (Also see Pillows and Pottery.)

HAWAIIAN ART DECO: The bold colors and tropical flora and fauna designs of the 1920s and '30s live on in etched glasses, china vases, glass platters, decorated sheet music, jewelry, old travel posters, and worn newspaper ads sold in various Oahu stores. An appealing selection of art deco goods is on sale at **As Time Goes By** (Kilohana Sq., 1016-B Kapahulu Ave., Honolulu, 732–1174) and **Corner Loft** (666 Keeaumoku St., Honolulu, 943–1788). If art deco reproductions will do, check out **Hollywood Hawaii** (619 Kapahulu Ave., Honolulu, 737–2731). For Hawaiiana, clothing, and jewelry, **Bailey's Antique Clothing** (2051 Kalakaua Ave., Honolulu, 949–8172 or 764 Kapahulu Ave., Honolulu, 734–7628) is worth a shot. Also try **Linda's Vintage Isle Antiques** (373 Olohana St., Honolulu, 942–9517). If you're in the market for jewelry, **Past Era** (701 Bishop St., Honolulu, 533–6313) is a good choice.

HAWAIIAN QUILTS: Nineteenth-century Hawaiian women took what American missionaries taught them and added their unique Island stamp to quilt making. Antique quilts are collectors' items and museum pieces. New ones can cost thousands of dollars. **Quilts Hawaii** (2338 South King St., Honolulu; 942–3195) has some quilts in stock, but much of its business comes from commissioned bed covers and wall hangings. Queen-size quilts begin at $3800, while one for a king-size bed can run you $4500 to $5000. Expect to wait up to two years for completion. But once you've laid out the money and the time, you'll have a beautiful piece of usable artwork, something to be passed down for countless generations. (Also see Pillows.)

JEWELRY: For reasonably priced necklaces (plus a few earrings, rings, and bracelets) made with semi-precious stones, try **Gems and Things** (334 Seaside Ave. in Waikiki or 1120 Bishop St. in downtown Honolulu; 923–6335). Browse through accessories made with hematite, rose quartz, amethyst, onyx, jade, and lapis lazuli, among others. (Also see Hawaiian Art Deco and Art Galleries.)

KITES: With hundreds of different designs, **High Performance Kites** (711 Keeaumoku St., Honolulu, 942–8799 and 1450 Ala Moana Blvd., Honolulu, 947–7097) has kites that range in price from $5 to more than $200. On weekends, it is not uncommon to find the store owner or staff members giving demonstrations and kite repair assistance at Sandy Beach Park. Just across the street from Kapiolani Park in Waikiki, **Kite Fantasy** (2863 Kalakaua Ave.; 922–5483) gives free kite-flying lessons, even to non-buying patrons.

KOA WOOD PRODUCTS: Native koa is probably Hawaii's most prized wood. Its rich burnt-orange color and beautiful grain make it especially attractive for hand-crafted clocks, bowls, pencil jars, jewelry boxes, and, of course, furniture. Places to shop for koa goods include **Martin & MacArthur** (841 Bishop St., Honolulu, 524–4434); **Artist Guild** (The Ward Warehouse, 1050 Ala Moana Blvd., Honolulu, 531–2933); **Hawaiian Heritage** (2870 Ualena St., Honolulu, 839–6656); and **Irene's Hawaiian Gifts** (Ala Moana Center, Shop #1251, 1450 Ala Moana Blvd., Honolulu, 946–6818).

KONA COFFEE: **Long's** and **ABC** drug stores have good prices on a variety of blends, as well as pure Kona.

LEIS: These fresh-flower garlands may seem corny or touristy to outsiders, but among residents of Hawaii these fragrant necklaces are worn and taken quite seriously. Some of the best are found at the stands sprinkled throughout Chinatown, such as **Sweetheart's Lei Shop** (65 North Beretania). You'll also see lei shops all over Waikiki.

MACADAMIA NUTS: Macadamia nuts are sold everywhere in Hawaii, from hotels to drug stores. The **Long's** and **ABC** chains keep their prices comparatively low. **The Hawaii Country Store** (2201 Kalakaua Ave., Waikiki) also has good prices and stocks a wide variety of macadamia nuts, from candy coated and chocolate dipped to naked.

PILLOWS: Hand-crafted pillows appliqued with Hawaiian flowers make good gifts—even to yourself. Bonnie Lum incorporates the colors and shapes of anthuriums, hibiscus, orchids, bird of paradise, torch ginger, and other tropical flowers into her designs. She uses a combination of machine and hand stitching. You may run across her work at crafts fairs. If not, you can obtain a brochure by contacting **The Pillow Lady,** (P.O. Box 3340, Mililani, HI 96789, (808)623–0574). The 12″ or 19″ square pillows, which run about $20 to $65, can be shipped to the mainland. **Quilts** and wall hangings done in floral patterns begin at $150.

PINEAPPLES: At **Fresh From Hawaii** kiosks, scattered around Waikiki, you can arrange to have freshly picked, boxed pineapple delivered to the airport upon your departure or sent straight to the mainland. To have three pineapples waiting for you at the airport, plan to pay about $8.75. It will cost you about $24.50 to have three sent to the mainland; they'll travel by air-courier and will arrive within two or three days.

POSTCARDS: **P.S. Write Soon** (374 Kalaimoku St., Honolulu) is the place to go for cards made from black and white photos of days gone by in Hawaii. You'll also find copper postcards embossed with Hawaiian-themed designs and reproductions of works by Island artists.

POTTERY: Some of Oahu's most distinctive kind of ceramics is **raku,** a 400-year-old Japanese art. The tradition is being carried on by **Pokai Pottery** (on Pokai Bay Street in Waianae; 696–3878), created by Bunky and Gail Bakutis, a husband-and-wife team. In addition to plates and vases, the Bakutises make jewelry and sculpture, among other items. Their work is sold in outlets including **Pauahai Nuuanu Gallery** in downtown Honolulu; **Following Sea** at Kahala Mall; **Art a la Carte** at the Ward Centre; and the **Elephant Walk** at Ala Moana. For more personalized shopping, contact the Bakutises at Pokai Pottery to see if they're having one of their three annual open houses while you're in town.

T-SHIRTS: With half a dozen Waikiki outlets packed with amusing, imaginative, and colorful designs, **Crazy Shirts** gets lots of attention, even in T-shirt City (a.k.a. Waikiki). Another good place to buy T-shirts is the large **flea market** in the Aloha Stadium parking lot. It's open five days a week, and you can get there by the Pearl City bus.

UNUSUAL CLOTHING: At **Montsuki** (1217 Hopaka Street, in an industrial Honolulu neighborhood called Kakaako; 537–3702), Janet and Patty Yamasaki, mother and daughter, design and make women's and men's clothing incorporating traditional kimono fabric that is anywhere from 15 to 25 or even 100 years old. In a marriage of styles from the East and West, they use silk and satin, sometimes combining the material of two or three different kimonos in one outfit. Most of the cloth comes from Japan, but they also import fabrics from India and other countries, always keeping an eye out for unusual natural materials.

NIGHT LIFE

In Waikiki and the rest of Honolulu (where Oahu's clubs, discos, and bars are concentrated), life after dark is frantic every night of the week. If you make some local friends, they might invite you to *holo-holo* (hop from nightspot to nightspot) and "suck 'em up" (toss down a few drinks). There are plenty of Polynesian revues, luaus, loud bars, rock and pop concerts, and video dance clubs with confetti sprinklers and laser lights. Many hotels have their own night clubs and lounges, featuring everything from throbbing disco music to romantic old-time big band combos and ukulele-strumming Hawaiian singers. There is also no scarcity of good local theater companies. There are even seasonal symphony concerts, chamber music, ballet, and opera. For details about sunset, dinner, and moonlight cruises (most of which leave from Kewalo Basin near Waikiki), see Tours.

Here are a few of the most popular places to be after dark:

Hawaiian Style

Many hotels and independent companies regularly host **luaus,** some in dramatic oceanfront settings. Although these feasts, with entertainment, will certainly give you a taste of Hawaiian food, music, dance, and traditions, these crowded, touristy affairs don't appeal to everyone. I prefer to steer clear of the larger feasts. Instead, I check the newspapers for fund-raising luaus sponsored by local churches, civic groups, or hula schools.

Jubilee Nightclub • *1007 Dillingham Blvd., Honolulu; 845–1568* • When you're ready for some real live Hawaiian music, without the commercial trappings, try this local night spot where the atmosphere could hardly be more laid back. *Open from 8 p.m. to 4 a.m.*

Don Ho • *The Dome, Hilton Hawaiian Village, Kalia Rd., Waikiki; 949–4321* • According to many, Don Ho is the king of Hawaiian music. Mainlanders will remember him from his network television variety show during the 1970s. With some help from dancers and other singers, he puts on a splashy Las Vegas–style Polynesian revue six nights a week. After all these years, he still (sometimes grudgingly) sings his trademark tune, "Tiny Bubbles." Dinner or cocktail shows are performed Sunday through Friday nights.

The Brothers Cazimero • *Monarch Room, Royal Hawaiian Hotel, Waikiki Beach; 923–7311* • At this beachfront night spot, singer-songwriters Robert and Roland Cazimero put their own special stamp on Hawaiian songs, both old and new. Hula dancers spice up the performance. Dinner shows take place from Tuesday to Saturday, while cocktail shows are on Friday and Saturday nights.

Al Harrington • *Polynesian Palace, Reef Towers Hotel, 247 Lewers St., Waikiki; 923–9861* • This Hawaiian singer has been a crowd pleaser for many years. Musicians and dancers are part of this popular revue. Dinner or cocktail shows are hosted from Sunday through Friday.

Danny Kaleikini • *Kahaha Hilton Hotel, Kahala; 734–2211* • For more than two decades, Danny Kaleikini has been crooning Hawaiian tunes to audiences sandwiched between hula dancers and other musicians. In this popular show, he amuses his listeners with the lively anecdotes he intersperses with song.

The Polynesian Cultural Center • *in Laie, windward coast; 293–3333* • This lavish production, performed by students from Brigham Young University's Hawaii campus, is an exciting way to close a day of visiting the Center's recreated villages. The show even includes a fiery volcano. In living color, you'll see the differences and similarities among the dances and music of various Polynesian islands. The show follows dinner, which starts being served at 4:30 p.m. (See *Tours* for details about guided transportation.)

The Ainahau Showroom • *the Sheraton Princess Ka'iulani Hotel, 2342 Kalakaua Ave., Waikiki; 922–5811* • Some say this is one of Oahu's strongest Polynesian revues. The stage is brought to life by energetic dancers from Fiji, Samoa, New Zealand, and Tahiti.

Sea Life Park Hawaiian Revue • *Makapuu Point, southeastern tip of Oahu; 259–7933* • After spending an afternoon at this worthwhile marine park, consider staying on for the imu (underground oven) ceremony and the Polynesian show, performed on Thursdays and Sundays at 8:30 p.m. The cost of the show is included in the park admission price (about $9). You're welcome to buy yourself dinner at the Galley Restaurant. You can get to Sea Life Park from Waikiki on Bus No. 58, and a shuttle (about $4) takes people back to Waikiki at the end of the show.

The Hawaiian Hoe-Down Country Barbecue • *Heeia Park, Kailua area, southeastern windward coast; 922–3377* • A truly hybrid affair, this cookout is accompanied by live country & western music, square dancing, and hula-dancing paniolos (cowboys). Held on Tuesday and Thursday evenings, the fun begins at 5:30 p.m. The $40 price tag includes dinner and round-trip transportation from Waikiki.

Local Hang Outs and Happenings

Studebaker's • *Restaurant Row, 500 Ala Moana Blvd., Honolulu; 526–9888* • Opened in 1988, this night club takes patrons back to the 1950s and '60s, with both its music and its neon-lit decor. Dressed as cheerleaders, waitresses have been known to dance on the tables. Pupus are complimentary from 4 to 8 p.m., Monday through Friday. Only people over age 23 are admitted. *Open Mon. through Sun. until 2 a.m.*

Scruples • *Waikiki Market Place, 2310 Kuhio Ave., Waikiki; 923–9530* • If you're in the mood to party with more locals than tourists, try this disco, where you'll dance to Top 40 songs, between 8 p.m. and 4 a.m.

Rumours • *Ramada Renaissance Ala Moana Hotel, 410 Atkinson St., Waikiki; 955–4811* • Residents flock here after work, some remaining until the wee hours. Flashing lights slice through the crowd on the dance floor, which is set off with videos. If you happen by on a Big Chill night, you'll shake it up to oldies from the '60s and '70s. *Open Sun. through Thurs. from 5 p.m. to 3 a.m., and on Fri. and Sat., until 4 a.m.*

The Wave Waikiki • *1877 Kalakaua Ave., Waikiki; 941–0424* • The music at this disco ranges from hard rock to boogie, both live and recorded. *Open until 4 a.m.*

Fast Eddie's • *52 Oneawa St., Kailua; 261–8561* • Let your hip bones slip to Top 40s tunes or pounding rock music played by live local bands or, occasionally, groups from the mainland. Some women are turned on by the famous **Male Revue,** Fri. and Sat. from 8:30 to 10:30 p.m. *Club open nightly 8 p.m.–4 a.m.*

Ryan's Parkplace Bar and Grill • *Ward Centre, 1200 Ala Moana Blvd., 523–9132* • Luring residents after work, this is where singles mingle while sipping beer and munching pupus and other snacks.

Anna Banana's • *2440 South Beretania St., Honolulu; 946–5190* • Slightly on the raunchy side, this smokey, high-decibel club plays host to reggae bands, blues singers, and other quality live music (9 p.m. to 2 a.m., Wed. through Sun.). Name-brand performers (such as Taj Mahal) show up from time to time to entertain enthusiastic crowds. *Open nightly until 2 a.m. (recorded music on Mon. and Tues.).*

Chuck's Steak House • *Manoa Marketplace, Honolulu; 988–7077* • This attractive lounge is a good place to listen to live jazz groups. *Monday through Thursday, 9 p.m. to 12 a.m.*

Buzz's Original Steak House • *2535 Coyne St., Honolulu; 944–9781* • On Friday and Saturday nights, between 8 p.m. and 11:30 p.m., this restaurant lounge turns into a night club featuring live jazz and folk music. On Sunday nights, from 9 to 12, the accent is on ukulele music spiced with the singer's observations and reminiscences about Hawaii.

The Hawaii International Film Festival • *1777 East-West Rd., Honolulu; 944–7666* • This week-long festival is both a cultural and a social event. Important movies from the U.S., the Pacific, and Asia are shown during the day and evenings at various Oahu theaters. The free films, workshops, and lectures draw people from all over the state.

Kumu Kahua Theater Company • *grounds of St. Andrew's Cathedral, 224 St. Emma Sq., Honolulu; 599–1503* • If you're interested in what makes Hawaii tick, consider attending one of the productions by this theater company, which uses the 50th state as a theme for its plays and shows. *Tickets: about $7.*

American Theater Company Hawaii • *599–5122* • Professional actors from Hawaii as well as Broadway take part in plays presented in different parts of Oahu.

Honolulu Community Theater • *520 Makapuu Ave., Honolulu; 734–0274* • In the shadow of Diamond Head, right in Waikiki, this company puts on very good musicals, dramas, comedies, and the classics throughout the year. *Tickets: $8 to $14.*

John F. Kennedy Theater • *University of Hawaii's Manoa campus, Honolulu; 948–7655* • In addition to American musicals, this theater stages Chinese opera, Kabuki, and Noh.

The Manoa Valley Theater • *988–6131* • These actors may not be professionals, but they infuse lots of spirit into these productions that run from Sept. through June. *Tickets: $10 to $15.*

Honolulu Comedy Club • *1777 Ala Moana Blvd.; 922–5998* •
Local and mainland comics go for the funny bone at this popular club.
*Show times: Tues., Wed., Thurs., and Sun. at 9 p.m.; Fri. at 8 and 10
p.m.; and Sat. at 7, 9, and 11 p.m.*

Noodle Shop • *Waikiki Sand Villa Hotel, Ala Wai Blvd., Waikiki;
922–4744* • More comedy is in store here, often spoofing the various
ethnic groups that have peopled Hawaii. *Wed. through Sun., 9:30 and
11 p.m.*

The Aliis • *Alii Showroom, Waikiki Plaza Hotel, 2045 Kalakaua
Ave., Waikiki; 955–6363* • Following the lead of locals, visitors have
discovered the talents of this singing group that also performs dance and
instrumental pieces. Dinner and cocktail shows take place from Tues.
through Sun.

Rock and Pop Concerts • Especially when internationally acclaimed artists or groups are in town, young folks pack the stands at
Aloha Stadium (488–7731) and Neal Blaisdell Center arena (521–2911)
in Honolulu.

Honolulu Symphony • *Blaisdell Concert Hall, Ward Ave. at King
St., Honolulu; 532–2911* • On Tues. evenings and Sun. afternoons from
Sept. to April, the Honolulu Symphony (sometimes joined by well-known
international musicians) makes sweet music. The Symphony on the Light
Side performs on Fri. evenings during these months.

Kapiolani Park Concerts • *Below Diamond Head, Waikiki* • During the summer, the Honolulu Symphony holds its Starlight Series in
the park. Locals buy lawn tickets, pack picnic baskets, and spread blankets on the grass.

The Hawaii Opera Theater • *the Blaisdell Concert Hall, Honolulu; 537–6191* • Local and mainland opera singers come together on
stage in February and March, accompanied by the Honolulu Symphony
and the Hawaii Opera Chorus. *Tickets: $16–$40; to charge them on
MasterCard or Visa, call 531–2161.*

Chamber Music Hawaii • *531–6617* • Throughout the year, concerts take place at the Honolulu Lutheran Church at 1730 Punahou St.;
Honolulu Academy of Arts on Beretania St. and Ward Ave.; and other
places on Oahu.

European Dance • *The Honolulu Symphony (537–6161)* • brings
the San Francisco Ballet to Hawaii in the fall. Ballet Hawaii (988–

7578), a home-grown troupe, performs *The Nutcracker* each year at Christmastime at the Mamiya Theater (3142 Waialae Ave., Chaminade University, Honolulu).

Other Night Clubs and Discos

Society of Seven • *Outrigger Waikiki Hotel, 2335 Kalakaua Ave., Waikiki Beach; 922–6408* • The multi-talented members of this group know their way around songs, dances, musical instruments, and hilarious impersonations. Two shows are performed Mon., Tues., Thurs., Fri., and Sat. nights, with only one show on Wed.

Flashback • *Hula Hut Theater Restaurant, 286 Beach Walk, Waikiki; 923–8411* • Get here early to see stars such as Marilyn and Elvis brought back from the dead by look-alikes. Dinner and cocktail shows take place from Mon. through Sat. evenings.

An Evening at La Cage • *Genesis Nightclub, 2888 Waialae Ave., Honolulu; 734–3772* • The packed audience practically rolls on the floor with laughter while the male and female impersonators poke fun at stars such as Michael Jackson, Prince, and Aretha Franklin. Dinner and cocktail shows are performed every night.

Rascal's • *2301 Kuhio Ave., Waikiki; 922–5566* • The lip-sync band is loads of fun. Every night at 9, an All-Male Revue plays up to women (about $20). Then, from 10:30 p.m. to 4 a.m., the place turns into a disco (about $5), complete with flashy videos, for the under-30 set.

Black Orchid • *Restaurant Row, 500 Ala Moana Blvd., Honolulu; 521–3111* • You may not run into partial owner Tom Selleck at this snazzy restaurant and club, but you'll hear live jazz and other music in the evenings.

Moose McGillycuddy's Pub and Cafe • *310 Lewers St., Waikiki; 923–0751* • Beer is the beverage of choice at this casual hangout where live bands play from about 9 p.m. to 1:30 a.m.

Jazz Cellar • *205 Lewers St., Waikiki; 923–9952* • Despite the name, it's the nightly live rock music that packs them in. The inexpensive drinks certainly add to the club's popularity: On Mon. nights, alcoholic beverages go for less than a dollar and there's a happy hour from 2 to 4 a.m., when the Jazz Cellar closes its doors.

Pink Cadillac • *478 Ena Rd., Waikiki; 942–5282* • Here you'll dance to hard rock. *Open nightly 9 p.m.–2 a.m.*

Masquerade • *224 McCully St., Waikiki; 949–6337* • This disco is complete with blaring music—mostly punk and disco—and wild videos. *Open from 9 p.m. to 2 a.m. from Sun. to Thurs. and until 3:30 a.m. on Fri. and Sat.*

Bobby McGee's Conglomeration • *2885 Kalakaua, Waikiki; 922–1282* • This disco draws mainly people in their 20s. *Open until 2 a.m.*

Cilly's • *1900 Ala Wai Blvd., Waikiki; 942–2952* • Mostly disco music is heard at this club, which is quite popular with a young crowd. Happy hour drink specials can cost under a dollar.

Tropics Surf Club • *Hilton Hawaiian Village, 2005 Kalia Rd., Waikiki; 942–7873* • There is nothing simple about the decor of this disco, with its confetti and fog machines. Waiters and waitresses entertain by doing more than serving drinks. *Open from 9:30 p.m. to 2 a.m.*

Nick's Fishmarket • *Waikiki Gateway Hotel, 2070 Kalakaua Ave., Waikiki; 955–6333* • This upscale, romantic restaurant and club is one of Waikiki's most appealing. The place is filled with music and dance between 5:30 and 1:30 every night.

Genesis Nightclub • *2888 Waialae Ave., Waikiki; 734–3772* • Disco music and a packed dance floor follow the dinner show here, beginning at 10:30 p.m. and lasting until 4 a.m.

Nicholas Nickolas • *Ala Moana Americana Hotel, 410 Atkinson Dr., Waikiki; 955–4466* • Put on a snazzy outfit, take in the wonderful view, and shake a leg to some great music. The dance floor wakes up Sun. through Thurs. from 9:30 p.m. to 2:00 a.m.; and Fri. and Sat. from 10 p.m. until 3 a.m.

Annabelle's • *Ilikai Waikiki Hotel, Ala Moana Blvd., Waikiki; 949–3811* • Ride to the top of the hotel to this relaxed disco, which overlooks the twinkling lights of Honolulu. *Open until 4 a.m.*

Trappers • *Hyatt Regency Waikiki, 2424 Kalakaua Ave., 922–9292* • When you're in the mood to dress up a bit and listen to live New Orleans jazz or fusion, this is a good place to visit. *Open 5 p.m.– 2 a.m.*

CULINARY OAHU

Hotel restaurants are some of the best places to eat in Hawaii. Not only do they keep visitors pouring in, but locals make a habit of returning often to their favorites as well. Honolulu boasts Hawaii's widest choice of restaurants. Both in and outside of hotels, they range from (good) greasy spoons to dining rooms bathed in top-drawer elegance. Waikiki restaurants tend to be the most expensive in the state, particularly for dinner.

If you want a taste of traditional Hawaiian food but aren't in the mood for a crowded luau, try the thatched-roof **Willows,** which has been around since 1944, in Honolulu. Head to **Chinatown** in downtown Honolulu for Vietnamese, Filipino, and (what else?) Chinese cuisine in small, family-run eateries. Thai food is big on Oahu, and **Keo's,** at two Honolulu locations, is king in this department. For Korean creations, many people enjoy Honolulu's **Kim Chee No. 2.**

Of course, there are also many places to have American and continental dishes. Among both residents and visitors, the most popular include **Bagwell's 2424** at the Hyatt Regency Hotel, **La Mer** at the Halekulani, **The Third Floor** at the Hawaiian Regent, and **Michel's** at the Colony Surf (all in Waikiki), and **John Dominis** at Kewalo Basin in greater Honolulu. Note that these are also some of the state's most expensive places to dine.

Several good (if somewhat trendy) dining spots are found along **Restaurant Row,** at 500 Ala Moana Boulevard in Honolulu. During the week, you can get here from downtown Honolulu on a free shuttle, which operates between 11:20 a.m. and 1 p.m. Between 5:30 and 9:15 p.m. from Thursday through Sunday, trolley service runs between Waikiki and Restaurant Row.

While some visitors dress up at dinner time just for the fun of it, men are required to wear jackets at only a handful of restaurants. For the most part, casual chic is the way to go.

Hawaii's pervasive Japanese influence shows itself in the deli-like stores that do a brisk business in sushi, tempura, and plate lunches. A hybrid culinary institution in the Islands, a fast-food plate lunch generally includes a teriyaki or curried meat or fish entree, two scoops of rice, and macaroni salad. **Zippy's,** a fast-food chain restaurant popular among locals, serves *saimen* and other Japanese and Chinese dishes, as well as burgers.

Selling goodies such as *manapua* (Chinese steamed rice-flour dough stuffed with pork or black beans), *lunch wagons* parked near beaches cause lines to form. A stroll through Chinatown can be a gustatory adventure. The peanut-rice squares and custard pies gather no moss at **Lin Fong** on Maunakea Street. **Shung Chong Yuein Chinese Cake Shop** tempts passersby with candied papaya, coconut, pineapple, lotus root, and ginger. Black sugar donuts and moon cakes are specialties at **Ting Yin Bakery.**

Dave's Hawaiian, at the Ward Warehouse in Honolulu, is known for its wonderful ice cream, in flavors such as Kona coffee candy with macadamia nuts, coconut macadamia, and vanilla dotted with fresh berries. Many people headed for a day at the beach stock up at **Ruffage** on Kuhio Avenue in Waikiki. The thick fruit shakes go well with the vegetable, turkey, or fish sandwiches on highly textured multi-grain bread. To pick up ethnic Island food, try **Ala Moana Farmers Market,** not far from Waikiki. You'll find all kinds of Hawaiian favorites such as *poi, imu*-cooked pig, *limu* (seaweed), and coconut pudding.

Residents with a taste for some of the island's most delicious *malasadas* (Portuguese donuts without the holes) go to **Leonard's Bakery** on Kapahulu in Honolulu. If potato chips are your thing, you'll risk becoming a slave to thick, crunchy **Original Maui Kitch'n Cook'd Potato Chips,** widely available in supermarkets and delis. But if the calories don't give you pause, perhaps the hefty price tag will. A 7-ounce bag can run more than $4. However, if you buy these chips on the mainland, you'll pay nearly twice as much (when you can find them).

Few people pass through Hale‘iwa, the little surfing town on the North Shore, without stopping at **Matsumoto's** for a shave ice. Known as snow cones in other parts of the world, the Hawaiian version comes doused with mango, passion fruit, coconut, and other tropical syrups. **Flavormania Ice Cream,** at the Hale‘iwa Shopping Plaza, makes dozens of varieties of rich ice cream on the premises. Also in Hale‘iwa, **Celestial Health Food Store** is a good place to gather fixings for a picnic lunch.

Greater Honolulu

The Willows • *901 Hausten St., Honolulu; 946–4808* • This historic open-air restaurant just north of Waikiki is truly Hawaiian in decor and some of its cuisine. With a braided palm roof and rough wooden beams, it has tables overlooking a once-royal fish pond churning with tangerine-colored carp and encircled by thick greenery. Ceiling fans cool the air. At night, a group of Hawaiian musicians (playing the bass, guitar, and ukulele) stroll from party to party taking requests. The special Hawaiian luncheon or supper comes with poi, roast pork, lomi salmon, a seaweed ball, steamed laulau, Hawaiian rock salt, and haupia. Sri Lankan curries are also on the menu, along with cream of avocado soup, pasta, roast turkey, knockwurst, mahimahi, and wilted spinach salad. The Sunday brunch buffet gives diners a chance to sample goodies across the board. Dessert is worth saving room for: try the apple crepes, raspberry mousse, or huge slabs of pie. A children's menu is available.

In the 1850s, this property was owned by Princess Victoria Kamamalu, granddaughter of Kamehameha I, and sister of Kamehameha IV and V. Being invited to one of her outdoor banquets here was considered a high honor. The restaurant was built around a pond once used for supplying drinking water and fresh fish, as well as for bathing. These waters were believed to contain healing powers, so people came from great distances to fill jugs to take back home. In the 1930s, the property was sold to the Hausten family, whose daughter turned it into a restaurant in 1944. The establishment is now owned by Randy Lee. *(Moderate)*

Ono Hawaiian Foods • *726 Kapahulu Ave., Honolulu; 737–2275* • There are only ten tables at this unassuming local favorite. Entrees include kalua pig, laulau, poi, butterfish, and that Hawaiian staple, SPAM. Other popular choices are chicken long rice and stir-fried sliced steak with vegetables. Portions are quite generous; after lunch here, you may not feel like having dinner. *(Inexpensive)*

Sekiya's Restaurant & Delicatessen • *2746 Kaimuki Ave. (across from Kaimuki High)* • Some residents say Sekiya's prepares the best plate lunch on Oahu. Whether they eat it in or take it out, patrons also enjoy the teriyaki beef, *chow fun* (warm noodles with vegetables), shrimp or vegetable tempura, breaded butterfish, fried SPAM, and sushi. *Closed Mon. (Inexpensive)*

Keo's • *625 Kapahulu Ave., 737–8240; and Ward Centre, 533–0533 (both in Honolulu)* • Celebrities beat a path to the original Kapahulu Avenue Keo's, decked out with Asian antiques, Tiffany lamps, and fresh flowers. In an attractive garden setting, the restaurant at Ward Centre is set off with orchids and other blossoms. Keo Sananikone continues to build on his reputation with spicy Thai dishes such as ulua fish with black bean sauce, crispy fried shrimp rolled in lettuce and cucumber with a delicious dipping sauce, and vegetarian spring rolls with mint leaves. Peanuts, basil, lemongrass, and other flavors wake up the palate. For a fruity, coconut cocktail, try the Evil Princess. *(Moderate to Expensive)*

Restaurant Sada • *1432 Makaloa St., Honolulu; 949–0646* • Ask a Honolulu resident to direct you to her favorite sushi bar, and chances are you'll find yourself at this Japanese restaurant, behind the Ala Moana Center. *(Inexpensive* to *Moderate)*

Roy's • *6600 Kalanianaole Highway, Hawaii Kai, Honolulu; 396–7697* • About eight miles east of Waikiki, in the ritzy suburb of Hawaii Kai, Roy Yamaguchi has made a culinary splash. Before coming to Hawaii, he began by thrilling diners in Los Angeles with his imaginative creations that married the East to the West. This duplex restaurant gazes out at Maunalua Bay. The bar, with its outdoor tables, is downstairs. The upstairs dining room, with its tall picture windows, is always packed. In the center of the room, the gleaming white-tile and stainless-steel kitchen is open to full view of the diners at the surrounding tables. The ever-changing menu might include steamed pork dumplings served with a mustard and soy vinaigrette dressing; seafood-filled potstickers in a sauce made from sesame seeds and butter; beef stir-fried with roasted macadamias, fresh mint, and Maui onions; scallops flavored with ginger and basil. Pizza here is for the adventurous, coming with such toppings as marinated Chinese chicken, Japanese sprouts, or shitake mushrooms. *(Moderate* to *Expensive)*

Maile • *The Kahala Hilton, Kahala, Honolulu; 734–2211* • The muted earth tones of the decor cast an orange glow on this elegant dining room at dinner. Appetizers might be quail on a mixed salad with raspberry vinaigrette, escargot in puff pastry, pan-fried foie gras on asparagus tips with green peppercorns, or fresh sashimi. Diners choose among soups such as truffle, onion au gratin, and chilled melon. Good selections for entrees are the filet of Hawaiian sunfish with saffron butter sauce and lobster dumplings in spinach leaves and black linguine; boned lamb loin; and duckling with lychees, peaches, bananas, and mandarin slices. Allow 45 minutes for the gingerbread or chocolate dessert souffles, or try the poppy seed parfait with hazelnut sauce. *(Expensive)*

Chiang-Mai • *2239 South King St., Honolulu; 941–1151* • This dining spot may be low on atmosphere, but it is certainly high on delicious Thai specialties, including a wide selection of vegetarian dishes. *(Inexpensive)*

Cafe Cambio • *1680 Kapiolani Blvd., Honolulu; 942–0747* • Popular among locals for business lunches, this upscale bistro serves very good pizza and pasta. *(Inexpensive* to *Moderate)*

Kim Chee No. 2 • *3569 Waialae Ave., Honolulu; 737–0006* • Of the three Kim Chee restaurants, this is the closest to Waikiki. Served in a down-to-earth atmosphere, the highly seasoned Korean fare includes barbecue chicken, spare ribs, and, of course, kim chee (spicy cabbage or other vegetables). This makes a good lunch stop. *(Inexpensive)*

Saigon • *1344 Kapiolani Blvd., Honolulu; 955–5040* • Light, crispy summer rolls (made with pork, shrimp, mint, and chives) and spring rolls (without the pork) are served at this Vietnamese restaurant, as well as noodle or fish entrees and garlicky soups. *(Inexpensive)*

Irifune • *563 Kapahulu, Honolulu; 737–1141* • Long-time residents love the delicate stir-fried entrees that combine crisp vegetables with tofu, chicken, or fish. The plain but homey atmosphere adds to the appeal. *(Inexpensive)*

John Dominis • *the foot of Ahui St., at Kewalo Basin, Honolulu; 523–0955* • The excellent food is neck and neck with the wonderful ocean view. Surfers ride the waves in the distance while fishing boats pull up to shore. Seafood is the specialty here, and the location—right near the Honolulu Fish Market—could hardly be more convenient. A lobster-filled pond meanders through the restaurant. Treats from the sea are prepared in a variety of tasty ways, from broiled in butter to steamed with ginger. Save room for a slice of macadamia nut creme pie.

This upscale restaurant borrows its name from John Owen Dominis, the son of an Italian ship captain. Dominis married Hawaii's last queen, Liliuokalani, in 1862 and later became governor of Oahu. *(Expensive to Very Expensive)*

The Prince Court • *Hawaii Prince Hotel, Ala Wai yacht harbor, Honolulu; 956–1111* • Here diners will find the same good food and service that travelers to Maui have come to know at the restaurant of the same name at the Maui Prince hotel. Tall windows afford views of the harbor. The inspired American regional cuisine includes artful creations such as a souffle of ahi and salmon with three caviars and sesame toast; pan-seared venison with pine nuts and a date and apricot chutney; kiawe-grilled free range chicken; and prawns and slipper lobster in coconut saffron sauce served with wild rice studded with pecans. *(Expensive)*

The Black Orchid • *Restaurant Row, at 500 Ala Moana Blvd., Honolulu; 521–3111* • Make your reservations early to enjoy the American regional cuisine at this art deco restaurant, partially owned by Tom Selleck. Dining is inside or al fresco. The gourmet selections include black linguini alfredo with salmon caviar; charred ahi with mango; lamb sausage with spaghettini; smoked trout en croute; and warm duck salad. The breads and pasta are freshly made. In the evenings, live entertainment draws many. A 10-minute walk or a shuttle ride from the Honolulu business district, this restaurant can also be reached by a 10-minute taxi or trolley ride from Waikiki. *(Moderate)*

Sunset Grill • *Restaurant Row, at 500 Ala Moana Blvd., Honolulu; 521–4409* • Enclosed in glass, the wood-burning Italian rotisserie is the focus of this restaurant, turning out grilled vegetables, fish, chicken, and beef. The fresh pastas and desserts are also delicious. For that special picnic lunch, visit the take-out deli counter. *(Moderate)*

Rose City Diner • *Restaurant Row, at 500 Ala Moana Blvd., Honolulu; 524–7673* • This cafe takes diners back to the 1950s, with its roller-skating waiters and Hawaiian mementos from the days before these tropical islands turned into a state. *(Inexpensive)*

Fisherman's Wharf Restaurant • *on the harbor at Kewalo Basin, Honolulu; 538–3808* • This seafood restaurant is so popular that many people call Kewalo Basin, the jumping-off point for many sightseeing and party cruises, Fisherman's Wharf.

Woodlands • *1289 South King St., Honolulu; 526–2239* • This no-frills storefront eatery serves good Chinese dumplings, soups, and noodles. *(Inexpensive)*

Rainbow Drive-In • *3308 Kanaina Ave., Honolulu; 737–0177* • Locals come here for some of the best plate lunches around. *(Inexpensive)*

Crepe Fever • *Ward Centre, across from Ala Moana Beach Park, Honolulu; 521–9023* • This is a good place for a filling, inexpensive lunch. Although the emphasis is on Mexican-influenced ''health food,'' ham and chicken can be found among the vegetarian choices. You might try cream of potato soup, a salad, and a cheese and vegetable crepe. Thick sandwiches come on whole grain bread. Waiters are happy to serve you gourmet coffees, espresso, and cappuccino from **Mocha Java,** across the way, which shares the same management. *(Inexpensive)*

Il Fresco • *Ward Centre, across from Ala Moana Beach Park, Honolulu; 523–5191* • Stiff white linen adorns the tables at this highly praised Italian restaurant, where you can eat in an attractive courtyard or inside. Whether you're in the mood for pasta with a delicate freshly made sauce, gourmet pizza prepared in a wood-burning oven, or kiawe-grilled chicken, you'll find it here. *(Moderate)*

Yum Yum Tree • *Ward Centre, across from Ala Moana Beach Park, Honolulu; 523–9333* • Appealing to families, this homestyle restaurant serves steak, seafood platters, omelettes that diners "design" themselves, and pasta salad. It may take forever to decide which of the twenty or so different pies to choose for dessert: macadamia nut creme, blueberry apple, English toffee, Pumpkin crunch, and peach Bavarian are just a few. At brunch, people munch waffles, pancakes, French toast, and all kinds of eggs. *(Inexpensive to Moderate)*

Monterey Bay Canners • *Ward Centre, across from Ala Moana Beach Park, Honolulu; 536–6197* • This seafood restaurant features an all-you-can-eat salad, soup, and hot potato bar from Monday through Friday, 11 a.m. to 3 p.m. Ono (wahoo), mahimahi (dorado) and other fish are on the menu for lunch and dinner. The Sunday brunch is popular. The restaurant also has a Waikiki location, in an Outrigger hotel. *(Moderate)*

Compadres Mexican Bar and Grill • *Ward Centre, Honolulu; 523–1307* • This large, attractive restaurant draws a young, lively crowd. Dine outside on the balcony or indoors. Along with the usual Mexican fare, you'll find hamburgers, great margaritas, and T-shirts and sweatshirts emblazoned with the restaurant logo for sale. In addition to lunch and dinner, Compadres serves breakfast. *(Moderate)*

Big Ed's Deli and Restaurant • *Ward Centre, across from Ala Moana Beach Park, Honolulu; 536–4591* • For filling breakfasts, overstuffed Reubens and other sandwiches at mid-day, and broiled meat at dinner, try this casual dining spot. *(Inexpensive)*

Chez Sushi • *Ward Centre, across from Ala Moana Beach Park, Honolulu; 536–1007* • At this Japanese cafe with the atmosphere of a French bistro, sushi comes a la francais. Before eating your Japanese entrees, begin with a French appetizer. *(Moderate)*

Horacio's Steak and Seafood Grill • *at Ward Warehouse, Honolulu; 521–5002* • Overlooking Kewalo Basin, this restaurant provides upscale food and atmosphere for downscale prices. The attractive dining areas are spacious and ceiling fans circulate the air. The emphasis is on salads, soups, sandwiches, and seafood. Try the mahimahi stuffed with shrimp and crab, stir-fried chicken, quiche, or pasta. Wine is served and there's a wide selection of beer. As far as desserts go, Horacio's is known for its burnt cream (a custard). The chocolatey coffee toffee pie is excellent. At night, there's live music. *(Inexpensive to Moderate)*

Honolulu Hard Rock Cafe • *1837 Kapiolani Blvd., Honolulu; 955–7383* • Like the other Hard Rock Cafes around the world, this casual restaurant is plastered with gold and platinum records, famous guitars, and other musical paraphernalia, with a few aloha shirts and surfboards once used by celebrities thrown in. Hamburgers, fish sandwiches, and ribs are on the menu. *Reservations taken for lunch only. (Inexpensive)*

Wo Fat • *115 North St., Chinatown, Honolulu; 533–6393* • Founded in 1882, this Chinese restaurant has risen from ashes twice to become Chinatown's most famous landmark. First it was burned to the ground along with neighboring buildings in a major fire in 1886. Then it was destroyed again in the flames of 1900. Today this auditorium-sized restaurant, with its green-tiled eaves, high ceilings, and decorative Chinese symbols, serves chop suey, chow fun, won ton, noodles, and the like. *(Inexpensive)*

Ha-Bien Vietnamese Restaurant • *King and River St., Chinatown, Honolulu; 531–1185* • This large corner restaurant, located in what was once the red light district, pulls in a steady stream of diners, mainly Vietnamese immigrants. *(Inexpensive)*

Ken Fong • *Hotel St., Chinatown, Honolulu; 537–6858* • This small plain restaurant is especially popular among Chinese residents.

Young's Noodle Factory • *Chinatown, Honolulu; 533–6478* • The noodles are made on the premises of this dining spot that has been around for a long time. *(Inexpensive)*

Pearl City Tavern • *Pearl City, northern Honolulu; 455–1045* • Serving Japanese and American food since 1944, Pearl City has a truly local following. Try the fish misoyaki (cooked with soybean paste), beef sukiyaki, Maine lobster, or ahi sashimi. At the Monkey Bar, live, glass-enclosed monkeys entertain each other. Take a peek at the upstairs bonsai garden. *(Inexpensive)*

Waikiki

La Mer • *The Halekulani Hotel, on Kalia Rd.; Waikiki; 923–2311* • Tables in this elegant dining room—done in warm rusts, golds, and browns—are spaced so that everyone has a view of the ocean. At night, patrons can look out to the catamarans taking the partying crowd on dinner cruises. While the walls are decorated with Hawaiian carvings, the accent of the food is French. Try the kumu (a local fish) baked in parchment with seaweed, mushrooms, and other vegetables. For dessert, the delicious chocolate souffle resembles a beehive hairdo. *(Very Expensive)*

Orchid's ● *the Halekulani hotel, Waikiki; 923–2311* ● Right at the edge of the beach, with a view that takes in Diamond Head, this restaurant serves three meals a day. Hardwood floors, white table cloths, and a profusion of orchids and greenery make this a particularly pleasant locale. The seafood and homemode pasta are fast-moving menu items, and the pastry department outdoes itself daily with its fresh cakes and other sweets. *(Moderate* to *Expensive)*

The Third Floor ● *Hawaiian Regent Hotel, toward Diamond Head end of Kalakaua Ave., Waikiki; 922–6611* ● An elegant, award-winning restaurant, the Third Floor is widely considered one of Hawaii's best places to dine. Not that their taste buds are superior to anyone else's, but celebrities such as Anthony Quinn, Elton John, and Carol Burnett often pass through these doors. Tall rattan chairs add to the privacy of each well-spaced teak table. In the center of the room, carp dart across a glistening pond. During dinner, a trio plays background music, from lilting Hawaiian standards to Spanish folk songs.

The gourmet continental cuisine is complimented by an impressive wine list. Naan (cushiony, thick Indian charcoal-cooked bread) accompanies dinner. Among the entrees, you might find filet mignon topped with Canadian bacon and Swiss cheese; a casserole of lobster, opakapaka, shrimp, and scallops in a fennel sauce; or medallions of veal with mushrooms. Complimentary bonbons (balls of vanilla ice cream encased in brittle dark chocolate) are served after the main course, but this stops few from ordering dessert. Macadamia or chocolate souffles are popular, along with French pastries and Viennese cakes. *Jackets requested for men. Reservations recommended. (Expensive* to *Very Expensive)*

Bagwells 2424 ● *Hyatt Regency Waikiki (third floor of the Ewa Tower); 922–9292* ● Named for developer Chistopher Bagwell Hemmeter, the Donald Trump of Hawaii, this is one of Oahu's top restaurants. The multi-level seating, at banquettes, booths, and free-standing tables, is both private and clearly part of the general elegant surroundings. (People reserve intimate table 21, ideal for a group of four, at least two days in advance.) While three separate dining rooms are each enclosed with translucent etched-glass panels, they are also open to the rest of the room. The tweedy upholstery, in beige tones, is complimented by whitewashed oak, marble and granite, large Chinese vases, bursts of fresh flowers, and a waterfall. At night, soft music comes from a piano in the center of a black marble floor, making the instrument appear to be sitting in the middle of a deep pool. Chances are, you'll find the service, by male and female waiters, attentive yet unobtrusive.

The food here is celebrated for its delicious (sometimes rich, sometimes delicate) sauces on many items from appetizers to desserts. Try the baked duck sausage, creamy lobster chowder, and spinach salad with Maui onions and salmon marinated in lime. Follow it up with charbroiled beef tenderloin with duck liver and oranges, steamed filet of opakapaka, or angel hair pasta with smoked and fresh salmon. In addition to a la carte choices and special set menus, diners can also try the Grazing Menu, consisting of smaller portions for sampling a variety or simply eating light. There's an extensive selection of coffees and teas and a variety of fruit and pastry for dessert. *Reservations required. Jackets suggested for men. (Expensive* to *Very Expensive)*

The Hau Tree Lanai • *New Otani Kaimana Beach Hotel, at the foot of Diamond Head; 923–1555* • Right on the beach, this appealing restaurant is built around the same hau tree that shaded the Victorian home that stood on this spot in the early 1900s. Breakfast might consist of a coconut smoothie, papaya muffins, and thick Belgian waffles topped with crunchy macadamia nuts. This is one of the few Oahu restaurants that also serves an authentic Japanese breakfast including fish, rice, and miso soup. Good choices for lunch are turkey pesto fettucine and broiled ahi steak with tomato chili sauce. At night, in the dancing light of blazing torches, diners enjoy smoked duck salad with raspberry vinaigrette, soft shell crabs fried in beer batter, and veal with smoked mushrooms, all accompanied by rye bread sweetened with molasses. *(Inexpensive* to *Moderate)*

Parc Cafe • *Waikiki Parc Hotel; 921–7272* • This brightly lit hotel dining room serves delicious gourmet creations three meals a day. The breakfast buffet includes pancakes and French toast with guava or maple syrup, fresh fruit, muffins, croissants, eggs, bacon and sausage, and other goodies. Sunday brunch is more elaborate, with ginger chicken, eggs Benedict, grilled fish, and sesame beef. Lunch might begin with gazpacho, followed by an avocado and alfalfa sprout sandwich. Flavorful pastas, seafood, lamb, and other meats are artfully arranged on their plates. The duck and salmon are smoked by the chef himself. The house bread, spiced with basil, oregano, and thyme, comes with dinner. Given enough advance notice, the chef will be happy to prepare vegetarian dishes or other special foods. *(Moderate)*

Kacho • *Waikiki Parc Hotel; 921–7272* • An excellent Japanese restaurant, Kacho serves a traditional breakfast that includes seafood and vegetable appetizers, broiled fish, pickled and braised vegetables, steamed rice, miso soup or *okayu* (rice soup), plus *natto* (fermented beans). For lunch and dinner, the Kyoto-style cuisine consists of sushi and sashimi, a variety of soups, tempura, and marinated dishes such as eel, octopus, and shrimp. No jeans, shorts, or flip-flops are allowed at dinner. *Reservations are recommended. (Moderate)*

Michel's • *The Colony Surf Hotel, Waikiki Beach; 923–6552* • This romantic restaurant opens onto the beach at Diamond Head. The early American decor includes oil lamps, ceiling fans, chandeliers, sterling silver vases and stemware, and gold-trimmed china. Beveled mirrors in the back reflect the ocean view, giving the feeling of being encircled by water. At breakfast, diners gaze out to early morning swimmers and the surf pounding the shore. Orange juice comes in a sterling silver bowl of ice, and blackberry, strawberry, and orange marmalade preserves are served in three silver bowls with three silver spoons. For the first meal of the day, you might try a chicken hash crepe or a belgian waffle. A variety of salads, such as crabmeat, lobster, and spinach, are served at lunch, along with souffles, breast of duckling, steak, and curried shrimp. Brought to your table by waiters in penguin attire, dinner might open with vichyssoise or lobster bisque and hearts of palm salad, then move on to chateaubriand or veal piccata. *(Expensive)*

Hanohano Room • *Sheraton Waikiki, 2255 Kalakaua Ave.; 922–4422* • A glass elevator glides from the lobby thirty floors up to this elegant restaurant. The sweeping view encompasses Diamond Head, especially dramatic at sunset, and the city lights of Honolulu. Crystal chandeliers sparkle while (from 9:30 p.m. to 12:30 a.m.) the mellow sounds of a combo pull diners onto the dance floor. For starters, try the chilled Alaska king crab legs with cognac or the duck crepe suzette in a sauce made with port wine. The creamy clam chowder and the French onion soup are also delicious. Also popular is the papaya and duck salad with pine nuts. Bonbons are served after appetizers to clear the palate. Good choices for entrees include New York steak broiled with truffles; rack of lamb; and tiger prawns stuffed with crab and served over saffron rice. On the dessert menu you'll find cheese cake with passion fruit sauce, seasonal berries, and crepe suzette. *Dinner only. Reservations required. Jackets and ties recommended for men. (Very Expensive)*

Momoyama Japanese Restaurant • *Princess Ka'iulani Hotel, Waikiki; 922–5811* • Among the selections at this traditional, teppan style restaurant is the special that includes a lobster tail, broiled New York steak, miso soup, wafu salad, pickled vegetables, rice, ice cream, and green tea. *Dinner only. (Moderate)*

Kyo-Ya • *2057 Kalakaua Ave., Waikiki; 947–3911* • The Japanese food here is cooked right at your table. Try the sukiyaki or the shabu-shabu (thinly sliced beef in a noodle and vegetable broth). *(Moderate)*

Hamburger Mary's Organic Grill ● *2109 Kuhio Ave., Waikiki; 922–6722* ● This open-air bar and grill serves gigantic hamburgers and overflowing sandwiches. *(Inexpensive)*

Islander Coffee House ● *247 Lewers St., Waikiki; 923–3233* ● Not far from the fancy Halekulani and Waikiki Parc hotels, this modest coffee shop is always busy, filled with the sound of clattering silverware and animated conversation. For breakfast, the Portuguese sweet bread French toast is delicious, and the waffles are also good. Sandwiches include mahimahi, barbecue pork, hot turkey, and bacon and avocado. Among the complete dinners (served with soup or salad, potatoes or rice, and hot orange bread) are teriyaki steak, fried fish platter, grilled ham steak, and stir-fried chicken with vegetables. All kinds of ice cream are served here, from malts to sundaes in which the ice cream, atop a chocolate chip cookie, is smothered in hot fudge, whipped cream, and macadamia nuts. *(Inexpensive)*

Top's Restaurant On The Beachwalk ● *Beachwalk and Kalakaua Ave., Waikiki;* ● The atmosphere is pleasant at this friendly diner that serves homestyle American food twenty-four hours a day. Waitresses quickly learn your name and use it. Breakfasts are hearty. For lunch, the grilled mahimahi platter comes with fresh beets, tomatoes, a hard-boiled egg, and cottage cheese. The steak and eggs with fries and prime rib are also hot items. *(Inexpensive)*

Nick's Fishmarket ● *Waikiki Gateway Hotel, 2070 Kalakaua Ave.; 955–6333* ● In a dark, candlelit setting, this restaurant serves some of the best seafood around. The Monterey abalone and the filling bouillabaisse are signature creations. This is a sister restaurant to the Black Orchid (on Restaurant Row in Honolulu), partially owned by Tom Selleck, once one of Nick's Fishmarket's most frequent patrons. *Reservations required. (Expensive)*

The Golden Dragon ● *the Hilton Hawaiian Village, Waikiki; 946–5336* ● A gourmet Chinese restaurant, the Golden Dragon is on the lagoon side of the hotel's landmark Rainbow Tower (with its colorful mosaic design). As you enter between golden Chinese horses, you'll see a large tropical fish tank. Waiters roll food to tables on carts that resemble Chinese chariots.

Dai Hoy Chang opened this restaurant in 1958. Although he was born in Honolulu, he grew up in Canton, China, where his culinary skills were perfected. To secure new recipes and fresh menu ideas, he travels often. If you catch him at a rare free moment, he might tell the story behind his famous cold ginger chicken: this dish was born when he was about to serve a platter of hot chicken, but was interrupted by an urgent and lengthy telephone call. Other good selections are smoked spare ribs, bird nest or sharkfin soup, seafood egg rolls, and lobster with curry and haupia (Hawaiian coconut pudding). For the delicious Peking duck with plum sauce, you'll need to place your orders twenty-four hours in advance. *(Moderate)*

The Lobster Tank • *2139 Kuhio Ave., Waikiki;* • To be sure, there are plenty of live Maine lobsters waiting for diners here. But the menu also offers mahimahi with bananas, alligator with pecans, snapper in black bean sauce, and Cajun dishes such as blackened steak and shrimp with cayenne, cinnamon, and garlic. For dessert, try the sweet potato pie, chocolate mint tarts, or rose petal pikake ice cream. *(Moderate)*

California Pizza Kitchen • *Kahala Mall, 4211 Waialae Ave., Waikiki; 737–9446* • Near Diamond Head, this cafe serves lunch and dinner. Pastas and salads are on the menu along with pizzas topped with goodies such as Thai chicken and peanuts. *(Inexpensive)*

Elsewhere on Oahu

Bueno Nalo • *Waimanalo, southeastern windward coast; 259–7186* • Despite the startlingly bright, somewhat gaudy decor of this modest joint, people often line up outside to sample the delicious Mexican food. You can order nearly any combination of tacos, tamales, chile rellenos, and enchiladas. Dress in cool clothes—not only is the food nice and spicy, but there is no air conditioning. Bring your own liquor. *No reservations or credit cards accepted. (Inexpensive)*

Haiku Gardens • *Kaneohe, southeastern windward coast; 247–6671* • Kiawe-grilled meats are the trademark of this lovely restaurant in a glorious garden setting, complete with jungled greenery and lily ponds. Dining in the open air, you'll see the Koolau Mountains laid out before you. Hawaiian dishes, such as lomilomi salmon, kalua pig, chicken long rice, and haupia are on the menu. *Closed Mondays. (Moderate)*

Crouching Lion Inn • *Kaaawa, central windward coast; 237–8511* • Dine inside or outside to gaze at the crashing Pacific. This is a good place for hearty soups (such as turkey vegetable), seafood platters, and steaks. Vegetarian entrees are available. *(Moderate)*

Paniolo Cafe • *Kamehameha Highway, Punaluu, windward coast; 237–8521* • Portions at this Tex/Mex restaurant seem to be designed for giants. The mammoth hamburgers are large enough for two. Mai Tais, beer, and other drinks come in 16-ounce Mason jars. *(Inexpensive* to *Moderate)*

Jameson's By The Sea • *Haleʻiwa, North Shore; 637–4336* • Along with well-prepared seafood, evening diners are treated to fabulous sunsets at this oceanview restaurant. *(Moderate)*

Steamer's • *Haleʻiwa Shopping Plaza, Haleʻiwa, North Shore; 637–5071* • Seafood, burgers, and generous salads are served at this restaurant, not far from Waimea Falls Park. The Sunday and Tuesday buffets have a healthy following. *(Moderate)*

Kemoo Farms • *Wahiawa, central Oahu; 621–8481* • The rural decor and ambience of this restaurant complement the hearty meals that come with soup and salad. While gazing out at the lake from this building that dates back to 1915, diners enjoy the roast duck stuffed with macadamia nuts and the signature rainbow trout. *Reservations recommended. (Moderate)*

Smitty's Pancake House • *46077 Kamehameha Highway; 247–8533* • Although the pancakes are delicious, this restaurant is not just for breakfast. In addition to hamburgers and French fries, you'll find a few Hawaiian entrees on the menu. *(Inexpensive* to *Moderate)*

WHERE TO SLEEP ON OAHU

Especially in Waikiki, Oahu accommodations are so competitive that many are continually being renovated and refurbished in an attempt to convince travelers to choose them over others. Both on and off the beach, there is a broad range of types of hotels and condominiums. When Mark Twain visited Honolulu in 1866, he and his companions paid about six dollars a week for their furnished rooms in a cottage in the middle of town. Their weekly meals ran them a mere ten bucks. While times have certainly changed, you can still find some decent bargains. Available in price categories across the spectrum, hotels appeal to the all-I-need-is-a-room-with-a-bed vacationer as well as to the visitor who says, "I'm into nonstop action but I don't want to have to leave my hotel to find it."

If you're looking for an isolated, self-contained resort, your choices are pretty much limited to the Turtle Bay Hilton on the northern wind-ward coast and the Sheraton Makaha, nestled in a valley on the leeward coast. For seclusion with few diversions other than the beach and watching polo matches, try Mokuleia Beach Colony on the North Shore. If you'll settle for tranquility without the isolation, consider the plush Kahala Hilton, a short drive from Waikiki. Those who don't need many dis-tractions beyond beautiful inland scenery gravitate toward intimate Manoa Valley Inn, just two miles from Waikiki.

Big spenders splurge at the dignified, beachfront Halekulani. Here spacious, peaceful grounds make it easy to forget that this resort is in the heart of a bustling tourist center. Other favorites among those with deep pockets are Hilton Hawaiian Village, the Hyatt Regency Waikiki, and the Hawaiian Regent.

Some hotels in frenetic Waikiki have dizzyingly similar names, so be sure you know exactly which one is yours before you try to get a taxi driver to take you there. The Outrigger chain has a slew of Waikiki hotels, most of which appeal to people with beer budgets and some of which also draw those with champagne taste. Sporting many reasonably priced rooms, the Outrigger Reef (not to be confused with the Outrigger Reef Towers or the Outrigger Waikiki) is on one of the best sections of the beach. The Aston and Sheraton chains also have some good hotels for non-sheiks.

For bed and breakfast contacts, see the Accommodations Charts at the back of the book

Outside Waikiki

★★★★★ **Kahala Hilton** • *Kahala, Honolulu* • While this plain white high-rise may seem unassuming as you approach it from the driveway, you will quickly discover it is actually one of Oahu's most elegant resorts. Film stars, musicians, and international models often book the suites and plush rooms at this beachfront hotel. The location, on the peaceful side of Diamond Head, is fabulous. Whenever you crave crowds and a tangle of stores and restaurants, Waikiki is just a 10-minute drive away (shuttle service is provided).

Guest rooms come with parquet floors or wall to wall carpeting, sitting areas, minibars, his-and-hers dressing rooms, and thirsty bath-robes. Every other room has a balcony, some of which are huge. Views take in the water or the rolling bright green hills dotted with houses, the palm-studded golf course, and Koko Head in the distance. On a placid bay, the beach invites snorkeling with its coral reefs just off-shore. Rafts for lounging float in the water. Cared for by trainers from Sea Life Park, dolphins put on three shows a day in the lagoon, near the swimming pool. Sea turtles and huge bright blue fish move through the ponds around the grounds. *(Very Expensive)*

☆☆☆ **Ramada Renaissance Ala Moana Hotel** • *410 Atkinson Dr. Honolulu* • A ramp leads from this hotel to the popular Ala Moana Shopping Center next door, and Ala Moana Beach Park is just a block away. Each with a lanai, rooms look out to the ocean, the Koolau Mountains, or Diamond Head. Private safes and credit card–like electronic door keys are high-tech features of rooms. If you'd like to be pampered with extras such as a spa and complimentary breakfast and newspapers brought to your room each morning, ask about the special suites. Guests gather around the white grand piano in the lobby lounge for live entertainment. *(Moderate)*

★★★ **The Manoa Valley Inn** • *Manoa Valley, Honolulu* • Two miles from Waikiki and down the street from the University of Hawaii, this former private home is now a bed and breakfast inn. In a flourishing, breezy valley, it has a mere seven guest rooms plus a private cottage that sleeps four. The handsome main house, with its eaves and gables, was built in 1912. Now refurbished, it is listed in the National Register of Historic Places. The inn is decorated with oriental rugs, hand-carved tables, and other eye-catching antiques—even a nickelodeon that still works. Breakfast and an afternoon fruit and cheese buffet are served on the lanai overlooking Diamond Head. If you've been to any of Hawaii's popular Crazy Shirts stores, you may be surprised to learn that Manoa Valley Inn is owned by the T-shirt king himself, Rick Ralston. Some rooms share baths. *(Moderate)*

☆☆☆ **Holiday Inn Airport** • *Honolulu International Airport* • If you're just passing through Oahu on your way to or from a Neighbor Island, consider staying at this pleasant and convenient retreat. The last time I checked in, I stood in line behind a mainland woman who was greeted by the desk clerk like an old friend. She explained to me that she was a frequent traveler and found this hotel so pleasant she booked a room here instead of going into Waikiki whenever she was in transit. Guest rooms are spacious and contemporary, with remote control color TV, a refrigerator, attractive, sturdy hard wood furniture, and sitting areas. Service at the restaurant and bar is friendly and efficient. In addition to a swimming pool, there's a T-shirt–packed gift shop on the premises. *(Moderate)*

★★★ **The Plantation Spa** • *Kaaawa, on the windward coast, halfway between Kahuku and Kaneohe* • Opened in 1988, this intimate spa never hosts more than twenty people at once, and usually only from six to fifteen. It is located on Oahu's quiet northeast shore, 24 miles from Honolulu International Airport and 26 from Waikiki, so a rental car is a necessity. Housed in the historic six-acre Hale Kamalu estate, the Plantation Spa is watched over by the hulking Koolau Mountains.

Decades ago, people would stop here to water their horses in the midst of long journeys.

Guests, many of whom are women in their forties and fifties, stay for at least six days. Bodil Anderson, originally from Sweden, leads them as they revitalize both their bodies and souls. The old carriage house has been transformed into a workout room, for aerobics or using the exercise machines. Rates include either three daily gourmet vegetarian meals or the European juice and broth fast, served family style. Smoking, of course, is as kapu (taboo) as eating meat.

Also part of the package are one herbal wrap, one massage, hikes, canoe trips, yoga, badminton, volleyball, use of the swimming pool and heated whirlpool, health-related lectures, and exercises (both on land and in the water). Long windows look out to the ocean from each of the massage rooms and a waterfall dribbles into the swimming pool. Evening entertainment ranges from songs and music performed by staff members to Hawaiiana demonstrations done by people from the nearby Polynesian Cultural Center. Guests head to the remodeled orchid house for pedicures, manicures, and facials, given at an additional cost. *(Very Expensive)*

☆ **Laniloa Lodge** • *Laniloa St., Laie, northern windward coast* • Near the Polynesian Cultural Center, this modest accommodation is the only game in town. Some people choose to stay here before or after the long drive from Honolulu to the Center or the North Shore. The Polynesian-themed studio units are equipped with air conditioning and color television. Lanais have views of the swimming pool. *(Inexpensive)*

☆☆☆☆ **Turtle Bay Hilton And Country Club** • *Kahuku, northern windward coast* • Far off the beaten path, near the famous surfing beaches of the North Shore, the Turtle Bay Hilton is a pleasant, self-contained resort. While the beaches are beautiful here, the waters can be dangerous for swimming. Visitors spend most of their aquatic time in either the oval or the free-form pool. However, people do snorkel and take scuba certification classes. There are ten tennis courts and an 18-hole golf course. Horseback riding is also available on the lush, expansive grounds. The spacious, attractive lobby is home to some tempting shops and boutiques where Polynesian woven baskets and exotic flower leis are on sale. While not every room has a lanai, they all contain a color television, refrigerator, and clock-radio. Moderate in size, they are decorated in rattan accented with mauve, aqua, and ivory. Nonsmoking rooms are available upon request. Guests are urged to leave their valuables in the safe at the front desk. At mealtimes, guests choose between two restaurants. *(Very Expensive)*

☆☆ **Mokuleia Beach Colony** • *Waialua, North Shore* • An hour drive from Waikiki, this out-of-the-way condominium rests on the North Shore, famed for its surfing. The closest town is about 15 minutes away. Unpeopled beaches sprawl for miles. However, the coast fronting the condo is thrashed by waters too rough for swimming, so you'll have to seek out nearby placid coves or stick to the oval pool. There's one tennis court and during the summer, polo matches take place on a field nearby. Duplex and one-story cottages contain one-bedroom apartments with televisions, kitchens (with dishwashers), and large lanais, some of which are enclosed by screens. Rooms vary in their proximity to views of the water, gardens, and pool. A minimum stay of two weeks is required at Christmas time and one week during the rest of the year. *No credit cards are accepted. (Inexpensive)*

The Sheraton Makaha Resort And Country Club • *on the northern leeward coast* • A 90-minute drive from Honolulu, this hotel sits in a flourishing valley about a mile from Makaha Beach. Low-rise buildings are topped with tall A-frame roofs. The decor incorporates rich woods and earth tones. Each air-conditioned room has its own lanai, as well as a color television and refrigerator. Golf enthusiasts give high marks to the hotel's two courses. Many people enjoy taking the guided horseback ride to an ancient Hawaiian sacrificial heiau. Families are pleased to discover that there's a summer program for guests aged five to twelve. Activities include hula classes, Hawaiian arts and crafts lessons, photography excursions, and supervised restaurant dining. At nearby Makaha Beach, local families and groups of friends come prepared to relax all day with barbecue grills and beach chairs. Someone might absentmindedly strum a ukulele or a slack key guitar, the music mingling with surrounding conversations. *(Moderate to Expensive)*

Waikiki

Here's a rundown of the best of the bunch, beginning with waterfront hotels and condos, then moving away from the beach:

On Ala Wai Yacht Harbor

☆☆☆☆ **Hawaii Prince Hotel** • *100 Holomoana St., at edge of Ala Wai Yacht Harbor* • This recent addition to Waikiki stands on the site of the old Kaiser Medical Center. In fact, footage of the hospital's 1987 demolition made its way into an episode of the *Magnum P.I.* television series. Overlooking the harbor, this $150 million luxury hotel is within walking distance of the Ala Moana Shopping Center. The Hawaii Prince's two pinkish glass and stone towers poke 32 stories into the sky. Slate walkways bordered by thriving greenery cut through the grounds.

More than 50 of the 500-plus guest rooms are one- and two-bedroom suites. Each room—accented with marble, wood, and natural fabrics—has an ocean view through floor-to-ceiling windows. Room service is available around the clock. Beds are turned down at night and complimentary newspapers are available each morning. Travelers who have been to the sister hotel, the Maui Prince, will be pleased to encounter the same high, unobtrusive quality of service. They'll also find two of the same gourmet restaurants: the Prince Court (regional American food) and the Hakone (Japanese cuisine). Along with a fifth-floor pool deck with a striking waterfront view, a variety of lounges and shops also keep guests occupied. *(Very Expensive)*

☆☆☆ **The Ilikai** • *Ala Moana Blvd. on the Ala Wai Yacht Harbor* • At the western edge of Waikiki, this huge hotel attracts many business travelers. Its two towers are located next door to Ala Moana Beach Park, which is popular for swimming and jogging, and it shares a beach with neighboring Hilton Hawaiian Village. Two pools and five tennis courts also lure the active set. Every evening, a torch lighting ceremony takes place in the busy lobby. The large rooms are complete with either full kitchens or extended dressing areas with safes, mini bars, refrigerators, toasters, and coffee machines. Those without kitchens have full bathrooms, while those with kitchens have showers instead of tubs. The color scheme includes shades of blues and grays. Little elephants form the bases of lamps, and white-washed rattan and marble-topped tables add to the attractive decor. Popular lounges provide entertainment at night. *(Expensive)*

☆☆ **Aston Waikikian On The Beach** • *Ala Moana Blvd.* • A rare bird in Waikiki, this hotel is a low-rise. It stands right next to Hilton Hawaiian Village. The name is slightly misleading, since the Waikikian is not actually *on* the beach. However, it does overlook a lagoon and the lagoon shares a sandy shore with Duke Kahanamoku Beach. The old-fashioned Polynesian architecture, with its high-pitched roofs, is reminiscent of the '60s and '70s. The newest wing, the Tiki Tower, is air-conditioned. Windows look out onto pathways winding through lush gardens. In addition to a swimming pool, there is a restaurant and cocktail lounge. *(Moderate to Expensive)*

On the Beach

★★★★ **Hilton Hawaiian Village** • *Hilton Hawaiian Village off Kalia Rd.* • This is one of those resorts that many guests don't leave until it's time to go home. Thanks to its 1988 $100 million personality

change, Hilton Hawaiian Village has been transformed from not especially distinguished to splashy. In the grandiose, open-air lobby, hand-
somely uniformed porters push gleaming gold luggage carts through the
whirl of activity. More than 2500 rooms and scores of shops and restaurants are located in and around its four towers, the most distinctive of
which (at least from the outside) is the mosaic-covered Rainbow Tower,
a Waikiki landmark.

In the Rainbow Bazaar, few can resist photographing the Thai temple or the 400-year-old farmhouse that was brought from Japan in pieces
and put back together here. Don Ho, perhaps the best known of Hawaii's entertainers, performs at the Dome six nights a week. The split-
level swimming pool rambles over 10,000 square feet and is bordered
by colorful blossoms and lava rock waterfalls. The grounds are also
graced with fish ponds, streams, Japanese sculpture on marble and granite pedestals, palm trees, and a profusion of other tropical greenery.

Guest rooms, in varying degrees of luxury, come with and without
ocean views. In the Diamond Head Tower, for instance, all rooms above
the 14th floor are suites that look out to the Pacific. Open-air hallways
provide vistas of gardens, mountains, the ocean, and marina. Features
of all rooms include lanais, mini bars, refrigerators, remote control color
cable television, and baths with double sinks. The executive suites in
the Alii Tower are individually decorated, with special touches such as
vanities with retractable shaving mirrors and mini-TVs, silver ice buck-
ets, and cut crystal glasses. Guests here receive complimentary continental breakfast and pupus in the afternoon. Non-smoking rooms are
available in every tower.

At the Travel Service Center, guests set up their itineraries, from
cruises and horseback rides to tours and car rentals. Pedi-boats, snorkeling equipment, canoes, hobie cats, surf boards and other water sports
equipment are rented on the beach. A fitness center with a pool and
Jacuzzi is also available. *(Very Expensive)*

☆☆☆ **Waikiki Shore Apartments** • *Fort DeRussy Beach Park* •
Apartments in this beachfront condominium with front desk service are
individually decorated. Each has its own lanai, running the width of the
unit, with views of the ocean, the mountains, and the wonderful sunsets. The apartments also have full kitchens and washers and dryers.
The location of this accommodation is prime. *(Moderate* to *Very Expensive)*

★★★ **Outrigger Reef Hotel** • *Kalia Rd., next door to the
Halekulani* • Perhaps Waikiki's best choice for a moderately priced yet
highly attractive beachfront hotel, this accommodation is often referred
to simply as The Reef so as not to be confused with other Outriggers.
The dignified lobby—once a cluttered tangle of garish souvenir stalls—

is now graced with a rock and water sculpture, stone tile floors, and round columns. The bordering stores have tasteful facades. Furnished in ivory and pastels, guest rooms are contemporary, with private lanais, refrigerators and color television with pay movies. Suites feature honor bars, wet bars, kitchenettes, microwave ovens, and two bathrooms each. Extensive water sports are the draw by day and lounges and restaurants provide entertainment at night. *(Moderate)*

★★★★★ **Halekulani** • *Kalia Rd., at Lewers St.* • It's difficult to believe this gracious, tranquil hotel is right in the heart of Waikiki, at the edge of the state's most crowded beach. Potted silver cup bromeliads and pink cactus blossoms decorate the white-columned porte cochere. A sweeping staircase fringed with waterfalls leads to the lobby and garden. Adjoining towers topped with pyramid-shaped roofs enclose a grassy, palm-studded courtyard, a popular locale for weddings. The hotel's dazzling color scheme is white—in seven shades, that is—set off by the teak-stained wood of shopfronts and louvered doors. Best viewed from a balcony, one million tiles have been laid out to form a huge orchid on the floor of the oceanfront swimming pool.

The Halekulani is full of personal touches. Guests are escorted to their rooms, where they are registered in plush privacy and shown around. They are greeted with complimentary chocolates freshly made in the hotel's pastry shop. In the bathroom, floor-to-ceiling mirrors slide open to the closet, which contains a safe and is separated from the bedroom by sliding louvered wooden doors. Although there's a stall shower, the deep tub also has a hand-held, snake-neck nozzle. The sink is surrounded by red marble and thick terry cloth robes are provided to be used by guests during their stay. One of each room's three telephones is conveniently located in the bathroom. Lanais are very large and most look out to Diamond Head (the most impressive view) and/or the ocean. In addition to the expected color TV and mini bar/refrigerator, there are marble vanities, and fresh flowers and newspapers appear daily. When visitors order breakfast room service, a toaster is brought to the room.

Upstairs in the hotel's elegant original wing (built in 1931) is La Mer, for fine dining. Orchid's is a wonderful spot for an oceanfront breakfast, complete with views of surfers and outrigger canoes. Head to the fitness center to work off any unwanted calories. All tours and sports activities are arranged by the concierge. For early arrivals or late departures, two hospitality suites provide changing rooms, showers, color TV, and complimentary refreshments. If you're planning to book a room in December or January, you'll need to make a reservation at least six months in advance, and send your deposit in at least two months before your vacation. *(Very Expensive)*

☆☆☆☆ **Sheraton Waikiki** • *Kalakaua Ave.* • Many guests return to this beachfront hotel, with its two connected towers forming a V.

Especially because of its coveted location, it is the world's number one revenue producing Sheraton. Special rates are given for extended stays. The lobby is dressed in oak, with blue and green accents, and it's constantly but quietly busy. Decorated exactly alike, the attractive rooms differ in price according to view. A glass elevator whisks diners up to the Honohano Room, a rooftop restaurant with a great view. One of the two swimming pools is shaped like the head of a mushroom, while the other is round. There are three non-smoking floors and 12 wheelchair access rooms. Honeymooners should ask about the limo service to and from the airport. *(Very Expensive)*

★★★★ **The Royal Hawaiian** • *Kalakaua Ave.* • Affectionately known as the Pink Palace, this low-lying, Moorish hotel dates back to 1927, making it the second oldest in the Islands. It was built on the site of King Kamehameha V's summer cottage, which stood here in the mid-nineteenth century. In the early days, it catered to wealthy tourists who, with their servants in tow, sailed to Honolulu by steam ship, often remaining for months at a time. The first registered guest was Princess Kawananakoa, who would have become queen of Hawaii had the monarchy survived.

The roomy lobby is decorated with marble, crystal chandeliers, and sparkling mirrors. Picture windows draw shoppers into stores. Rooms contain colonial style furniture, including twin cherrywood beds, refrigerators, mini-bars, a sitting area, cut-glass light fixtures, and plush baths with pink marble. Having cocktails at the beachfront cafe is a popular pastime. The oval swimming pool also faces the water. In the evenings, the Monarch Room comes alive with the original Hawaiian music of the Brothers Cazimero *(Very Expensive)*

☆☆ **Outrigger Waikiki** • *Kalakaua Ave.* • Busy day and night, this large, modern hotel is the best known of the Outriggers. The management seems to have a great tolerance for noise, whether it comes from rambunctious children or late partiers. The lobby is cluttered with souvenir, T-shirt, and designer wear shops, as well as restaurants and cocktail lounges. Guests traipse by in bathing suits. The Society of Seven, a local group that blends song and humor, is one of Oahu's most popular acts. Rooms have private lanais with varying views, refrigerators, color TV with pay movies, and safes. Suites also come with mini bars, wet bars, kitchenettes with microwave ovens, and two baths. The sparse furnishings are rattan and wood veneer, in ivory and pastels.

For a daily fee (about $20 to $30, depending on the season), you can join the Kuhio Club for penthouse pampering that includes a private concierge and food service, a sun deck, fitness center, assorted fruits and pastries, and national newspapers any time of day. Many enjoy the oceanview Monterey Bay Cannery, one of the many restaurants, which features seafood and steak broiled over kiawe wood and live nightly entertainment. The extensive sports facilities begin with the pool and beach. *(Moderate* to *Expensive)*

★★★★ **Sheraton Moana Surfrider** • *Kalakaua* • Of these two hotels that became one, the Moana is the more intriguing. Built in 1901, it is Hawaii's oldest. Its first guests paid a whopping $1.50 a night. This four-story Italian renaissance building, once one of Hawaii's tallest, has been on the National Register of Historic Places since 1976. "Hawaii Calls," the famous radio program, was broadacast from the 1930s to the '70s from the Banyan Court, near where the swimming pool now sprawls. It was beneath the huge banyan tree that still spreads itself here that Robert Louis Stevenson spent so much time. Nearly two years of painstaking restoration in the late 1980s, to the tune of $50 million, brought back much of the Moana's original elegance. Copies of turn-of-the-century antiques were made from prized native koa wood. One lobby sofa was actually owned by a Hawaiian monarch back in the 1800s. To see nearly a century of Moana memorabilia, stop by the hotel's Historical Room.

If you want to be surrounded by old-fashioned architecture, be sure to request a room in the Banyan Wing, which includes the Moana portion of the complex. In quiet pastels, rooms are decorated with wood and wicker. Each has an armoire with a television, refrigerator, mini bar, and safe hidden inside. Baths are modern, with art deco touches. Cotton *yukatas* (Japanese robes) are provided for guests to use during their stay. Newspapers are delivered to guests every day and room service is available all day and night. Rooms throughout vary greatly in size, decor, and view, so make sure you know what you're getting when you make your reservations. *(Very Expensive)*

★★★ **The New Otani Kaimana Beach Hotel** • *Sans Souci Beach, across the street from Kapiolani Park* • At the quieter eastern end of Waikiki Beach, this hotel sits at the foot of Diamond Head, at the edge of Waikiki. When Robert Louis Stevenson visited in 1893, he spent five weeks at the Sans Souci Inn, which stood near where the Otani Kaimana is found today. Prominent local haole families once built private homes in this area. Kaimana is the Hawaiian word for "diamond," and the elegance of such a gem is what you'll find when you enter the marble-floored lobby, done in cream, mauve, lavender, and gray. With only 125 guest rooms, this hotel is refreshingly small. Guests particularly enjoy the al fresco dining at the oceanfront Hau Tree Lanai restaurant. For Japanese cuisine, the hotel has the Miyako. The beach is alive with kayaking, sailing, and snorkeling. There's a park just across the street. The hotel is a convenient jumping off point for hiking to the summit of Diamond Head, for expansive views of Oahu. *(Moderate* to *Expensive)*

★★★ **The Colony Surf** • *Diamond Head area, at Waikiki's fringes* • Since this small, attractive hotel does so much repeat business, the cordial staff makes a point of remembering not only names, but guests' likes and dislikes from visit to visit. Appealing to moneyed visitors, the one-bedroom suites and studios are actually apartments, with complete kitchens and comfortable living areas. Another big draw is the Colony Surf's location, away from the wildest part of Waikiki Beach. Reserve early to dine at Michel's, the famed French restaurant in a fabulous open-air oceanfront setting. The Colony Surf East, under the same management, is similar in character, but its rooms are less spacious. *(Very Expensive)*

☆☆☆ **Diamond Head Beach Hotel** • *eastern end of Waikiki Beach, at the edge of Waikiki* • If you'd like to be on Waikiki Beach, but can do without the crowds, this small hotel is a good choice. Guest rooms are comfortable and attractively done. Families often book the units with kitchenettes. A light breakfast is included in the rates. *(Expensive)*

Across from the Beach   No buildings are between these hotels and the ocean.

Waikiki Surfside • *2452 Kalakaua Ave.* • The convenient location, right across from the beach and in the thick of Waikiki action, draws some young, budget-conscious travelers to this small, run-down hotel. All of the no-frills rooms are air-conditioned, with color TVs and lanais. Mattresses are on the thin-hard-and-lumpy side and your TV may or may not be working. Some views take in the ocean, while less expensive rooms gaze out at the garage. The lobby resembles the tiny customer service office at a Meineke muffler shop—rickety vinyl reupholstered chairs separated by a cigarette vending machine, a calendar give-away from Chow-Ling's Haberdashery on the wall. *(Inexpensive)*

Waikiki Circle Hotel • *2464 Kalakaua Ave.* • You can't miss this tall, tubular hotel. However, despite its intriguing and unusual shape, it's a good choice only if money is an object. You'll be right across Kalakaua Avenue from the beach—although from the purposely misleading photo on the brochure, you'd think the ocean waves lapped at the hotel's front doorstep. The hallways are indeed circular and the oddly-shaped, plain rooms, though small, come with lanais (facing the beach or the Koolau Mountains). There are also TVs and stall showers. A restaurant and lounge are on the premises, but most guests prefer to venture out. *(Inexpensive)*

☆☆☆ **Pacific Beach Hotel** • *Kalakaua Ave.* • These two towers offer views of and easy access to the beach. The lobby, with marble and brass touches as well as a mirrored ceiling, has been resurfaced in granite. All rooms have private lanais and safes. Kitchenettes include 3-burner stoves, ovens, and 10-cubic-foot refrigerators. The Pacific Beach boasts about its huge indoor oceanarium, a 280,000-gallon, three-story tank showcasing more than 60 different species of marine life, visible from three separate dining rooms. Visitors come from everywhere to watch the scantily clad female diver feed the deadly barracuda, stingray, angel fish, and other sea creatures. Two of the hotel's restaurants, The Neptune and The Oceanarium, feature a view of one of three daily shows. Stonework surrounds the swimming pool area and snack bar. A whirlpool and fitness center help vacationers unwind or work off tension. The two tennis courts rarely lack players. *(Expensive)*

★★★★ **Hawaiian Regent** • *Kalakaua Ave.* • Just across Kalakaua Avenue from the water, this five-acre resort is a huge complex. Appealing mostly to mainland yuppies and Japanese tourists, it encompasses a mall of shops and designer boutiques, a tennis court, two swimming pools, several restaurants and night spots, and two hospitality suites. Much like its sister hotel, the Mauna Lani Bay on The Big Island, the Hawaiian Regent is an example of the Japanese style of meticulous attention to detail. Seashell designs are stamped in the sand in ashtrays throughout the hotel. Fresh anthuriums, bamboo orchids, and sprays of yellow, white, and orange blossoms are everywhere. Ivy cascades down ivory walls. An elegant lobby, spacious and open-air, is decorated with unusually woven rattan chairs and loveseats and a carefully crafted fresh water fountain. The walls serve as a gallery of saleable fine art created by local artists. Each with a private lanai, guest rooms are pleasantly upscale with many extras, such as robes, and marble basin tops and granite-tiled floors in baths. The Third Floor is the hotel's signature restaurant. *(Expensive)*

☆☆☆ **Holiday Inn Waikiki** • *Kalakaua Ave.* • Right next door to the Honolulu Zoo, Kapiolani Park, Waikiki Aquarium, and a slew of fast food restaurants, this is an especially good choice for families traveling with children. It is also the best Kalakaua Avenue location for viewing both the June 11 King Kamehameha Day Parade and the Aloha Week Parade in September. People fight to get seats on the terrace of the Captain's Table Restaurant, the hotel's main dining room.

The beach across the street is the quieter end of Waikiki's sandy strip. Hawaii's only heated swimming pool is just off the lobby, which is one flight up from the ground floor. Since hotel towers keep most of the sun off the pool during the day anyway, many prefer to swim in the evening when other guests are out on the town. Some of the small, crowded guest rooms have no lanais at all, while others have either large balconies or standing lanais (just big enough for a couple of pairs of feet). The largest rooms are those that face Diamond Head. Ocean-front and junior suites come with refrigerators, and two rooms are set up for people in wheelchairs. *(Moderate* to *Expensive)*

Near the Beach

☆ **Outrigger Royal Islander** • *corner of Saratoga and Kalia rds.* • While you can't see the beach from the hotel grounds, a short path leads to it. This budget accommodation is just across the street from the beachfront Waikiki Shore Apartments. Standard rooms are small but perfectly comfortable. All rooms are air-conditioned and have TVs, refrigerators, lanais, and baths with stall showers. *(Inexpensive)*

Malihini Hotel • *217 Saratoga Rd., just off Kalia Rd.* • In an unusual display of honesty in marketing, the postcard/brochure says it best: "Small, plain hotel with no extra frills. Just a place to stay in an excellent location." A (very) modest apartment hotel, this accommodation is a short stroll from the beach. The 30 studios and one-bedroom units, all with kitchenettes, are cooled either by ceiling or table fans. Televisions are available for rent. *No credit cards or checks are accepted. (Inexpensive)*

☆ **Outrigger Edgewater** • *2168 Kalia Rd. near Beach Walk* • A small hotel in a forest of highrises, the modest Edgewater is a somewhat tranquil alternative to Waikiki's more popular accommodations. The beach is a few steps away and the Trattoria makes a good stop for Italian food. *(Inexpensive* to *Moderate)*

☆☆ **Outrigger Waikiki Tower** • *Lewers St. and Kalia Rd.* • Not to be confused with the countless other Outriggers, this one is across from the plush oceanfront Halekulani Hotel, in one of Waikiki's busiest areas. Bordered by stores, the lobby is pleasant enough, especially when compared to the cluttered public rooms of some of its neighbors. Rooms are comfortable and all kinds of street action is on view from the Waikiki Broiler Restaurant. *(Inexpensive* to *Moderate)*

★★★★ **Waikiki Parc** • *2233 Helumoa Rd., at Kalia Rd.* • If this tasteful hotel appears to be an understated Halekulani (the ultra-luxury beach resort across the street), it's because it's owned and operated by the same corporation. Opened in 1988 with just under 300 rooms, it is considered small by Waikiki standards. The spare, modern lobby is done in pastels and various shades of white, greeting guests with uncrowded charm.

Built above and around the parking lot, the bright, comfortable rooms are studies in blue, beige, and eggshell. On one side, lanais and standing balconies look out to the ocean, while the other three sides have views of parking lots and other tall buildings. Each chicly decorated room has one telephone at bedside and another in the bathroom; a refrigerator/mini-bar; a 19" color remote control cable television; an AM/FM clock radio; and a safe. Feet tread on carpets and ceramic tiles. For those who like to sleep in, shutters keep the sun from pouring through the sliding glass balcony doors.

Room service is available from 6 a.m. to 10 p.m. Guests have the use of washers and dryers. Eight rooms are equipped for wheelchairs. When it's time to play, beach activities can be arranged through the hotel. Ask to be on the eighth floor if you don't want to have to take an elevator from your room to the pool. Two excellent restaurants, the Parc Cafe (continental and American regional) and Kacho (Japanese) serve three meals a day. *(Moderate* to *Expensive)*

☆ **Outrigger Reef Lanai** • Some rooms in this economy hotel have kitchens, and at least one has a microwave. All simply decorated, they vary in size from cozy to spacious, some with stall showers and adjoining walk-in closets. When guests aren't out enjoying Oahu, they can lie in bed and watch television. *(Inexpensive* to *Moderate)*

☆☆ **Outrigger Reef Towers** • *240 Lewers St.* • The convenient location—on a palm-lined block near the beach and in the thick of Waikiki hurly-burly—makes this mid-level hotel a good choice. There isn't much to see from the windows of the comfortable guest rooms, but who cares? Just step outside, and you can see (and do) as much as you'd like *(Inexpensive* to *Moderate)*

★★ **The Breakers Hotel** • *250 Beach Walk* • Stretching from Beach Walk to Saratoga Avenue, and halfway between Kalia Road and Kalakaua Avenue, this hotel is close to both the ocean and the main shopping thoroughfare. The Breakers is a pleasant surprise along a strip of low-budget hotels. Shingled roofs cover a handfull of buildings. Banana trees, palms, and other tropical greenery add color to the pool patio. Attractively furnished in rattan, bright guest rooms surround the pool. Each air-conditioned unit has a kitchenette, color TV, and safe. Some are two-room suites that sleep four. Staff is happy to arrange tours around Oahu or sightseeing excursions to Neighbor Islands. *(Inexpensive* to *Moderate)*

☆☆ **Hawaiiana Hotel** • *Beach Walk* • While this small hotel is rather plain in decor, it is not far from Fort DeRussy Beach. Its low-rise wings surround colorful gardens, which sit just outside guest room doors. Most of the air-conditioned rooms have lanais, and all contain kitchens and safes. You'll be treated to fresh pineapple when you arrive. In the mornings, juice and coffee are served on the patio, and complimentary newspapers are available. Guests are welcome to use the free washers and dryers. *(Moderate)*

☆☆☆ **Waikiki Beachcomber** • *2300 Kalakaua Ave.* • It may be called the Beachcomber, but it's not on the sand. Instead, you'll find it on busy Kalakaua Avenue, across from the Royal Hawaiian Shopping Center and next to the Waikiki Movie Theater. To get to the beach, you'll have to walk a block or so along Kalakaua. Head to the pool terrace if you'd rather swim closer to home. On the street below the hotel, awnings shade the large display windows of glitzy Fifth Avenue–style stores. An escalator takes guests up from the ground floor to the shop-filled but pleasant looking lobby. Wicker chairs define seating areas and store windows are wood-trimmed. All guest rooms come with private lanais, refrigerators, safes, color TVs that show pay movies, either half or full bathtubs, and ironing boards (you call for an iron). Furniture is done in blond wood. Oceanview rooms look out to the water way across Kalakaua Avenue. If you're too lazy to go out at night, order the pizza package, which includes a selection from the movie channel. *(Moderate* to *Expensive)*

☆☆☆ **Sheraton Princess Ka**ʻ**iulani** • *Kaʻiulani Ave., off Kalakaua Ave.* • Her handsome portrait prominently displayed in the entrance to the lobby, the namesake of this hotel died, heartbroken by the overthrow of the Hawaiian monarchy, at the tender age of 23. Picturesque King's Village mall is across the street and the beach is about a block away. Inlaid carpet and tiles, bleached oak, and tasteful fabrics adorn the lobby. Tables are topped with protea blossoms in glass bowls. You'll pass a patina dolphin on a pedestal on your way from the lobby to the oval pool. The cozy poolside lounge is alive with greenery. A few expensive shops and boutiques are discreetly tucked away in the rear of the lobby. Rooms vary greatly according to size, view, and decor. While they are perfectly nice, some of the smaller ones have a 1960s feel. Along with marble vanities and oak furniture, a number of them have twin beds and no lanais. Other more modern rooms contain king-sized beds and writing desks. Rooms for non-smokers and people in wheelchairs are available. *(Moderate)*

☆☆☆ **Hyatt Regency Waikiki** • *Kalakaua Ave., off Kaʻiulani* • Across Kalakaua from the Sheraton Surfrider Moana and Queen's Beach, famous for its soft sand, this hotel takes up an entire block. Just look for the two connected towers. In the congested lobby, gleaming with rich koa wood, a labyrinth of dozens of stores and boutiques brings to mind the Galleria shopping mall in Dallas, Texas. It may take a day or two to become oriented. We have heard many guests asking directions to the front desk or to their elevator bank after roaming around in frustrating attempts to find it on their own. Once located, elevators seem to take ages to come. Other hotel services can also be quite slow, often delivered by impersonal staff.

Guests who can afford it would probably do best booking rooms in the deluxe Regency Club. Its pampered members have exclusive use of its rooftop sundeck, with its wonderful panorama of the mountains and the Pacific. There's also a cooler here filled with beer and soft drinks for the taking. All hotel rooms are done in light colors with furniture of rattan, whitewashed oak, or glass topped wrought iron. Chinese and other Asian influences are apparent in the decor. Rooms offer a variety of views, with Diamond Head/partial ocean front being the most popular. The swimming pool provides an alternative to a stroll to the beach. Hawaiian quilts dress up the walls in some public hallways. For more Hawaiiana, visit Hyatt's Hawaii, a collection of historic artifacts and cultural items. *(Very Expensive)*

☆☆ **Aston Waikiki Beach Tower** • *2470 Kalakaua* • The beach is just down the street from this all-suite hotel. A spacious lanai runs on two sides of each one- and two-bedroom unit. The most expansive vistas are from floors twenty and above. Apartments sport full kitchens and wet bars, and concierge service is available. *(Inexpensive)*

★★★ **Outrigger Prince Kuhio** • *Kuhio and Ohua Ave.* • While the Prince Kuhio, the top of the Outrigger line, is just a block from the beach, it's away from the most congested sections of Waikiki. Unlike other large hotels, each of the 600-plus rooms here has its own character. Special features include marble baths and wet bars. For the best view, request a room on a high floor on the Diamond Head side, or opt for special pampering in the Kuhio Club. With just a few stores, the spacious, open lobby is a pleasant place to relax in the morning over complimentary coffee that flows from a silver urn. *(Moderate to Expensive)*

☆☆ **Kaimana Villa** • *near the Honolulu Zoo* • Ask about room/car packages at this accommodation, which offers comfortable one- and two-bedroom air-conditioned suites that have full kitchens with dishwashers, as well as washer/dryers. Partial ocean and Diamond Head views are available. Kapiolani Park is a brief stroll away. *(Moderate)*

★★★ **Waikiki Joy Hotel** • *320 Lewers St.* • One of the areas's newest and smallest accommodations, the Waikiki Joy opened in 1988. The suites and individual rooms here suit a wide range of wallets. Each unit comes with an ocean-view or partial ocean-view lanai, a high-tech stereo system with a bedside control panel, and a Jacuzzi. Some also sport kitchens, while others have refrigerators or wet bars. *(Moderate to Expensive)*

☆ **Royal Grove Hotel** • *Uluniu Ave., near Kuhio Ave.* • At this six-story, bright pink, low-cost hotel, you'll be taken under the wing of the owners, the Fong family. Despite the lack of scenic views, the studios and one-bedroom units are perfectly acceptable—that is if you don't mind wood veneer dressers and plastic-covered chairs. Most kitchenettes are in good working order, and all rooms have private baths and either black and white or color TVs. While the larger, standard rooms are air-conditioned and have double beds plus a twin, the twin-bedded smaller rooms have no AC. There are narrow lanais off some of the larger units. The most-requested rooms are those above street level, overlooking the flower-studded pool area. Waikiki Beach is about a block away. *(Inexpensive)*

Waikiki Lei Apartments • *Ka'iulani Ave., off Kuhio* • A few blocks from the beach, this modest, four-story accommodation offers rooms equipped with kitchens. If you'd like an air-conditioned unit with a television, be sure to mention it when you make your reservations. After a point, the daily rate descends with each additional day you stay. Note that there is no elevator and that the staircase is outside. *(Inexpensive)*

☆ **Continental Surf Hotel** • *Kuhio Ave.* • The plain, air-conditioned rooms are fine here at this high-rise located a couple of blocks from the beach. Each contains a color TV and some have kitchenettes. But this is not the place to come for pleasant views or lanais. *(Inexpensive)*

Edmunds Hotel Apartments • *on the Ala Wai Canal, off Ka'iulani* • There are waterfront views here, to be sure, but not of the Pacific. All of the small, plain but comfortable rooms look out to the attractive Ala Wai Canal, distant Manoa Valley, and verdant mountains. The building is hugged by long lanais. Units come with kitchens and televisions. The beach is about four blocks away. Unfortunately, traffic on Alai Wai Boulevard can be annoyingly loud at times. *(Very Inexpensive)*

OAHU DETAILS

SAVING MONEY: Some airlines offer economical package deals. For example, **Delta Dream Vacations'** Oahu excursion includes

- round trip flights
- a fresh flower lei greeting upon arrival
- round trip airport transfers (including baggage handling and tips)
- hotel stay (including taxes and porterage)
- a continental breakfast the first morning
- half price tickets for a catamaran cruise and for the Bishop Museum

To depart from Los Angeles for an 8-day/7-night stay at the Princess Ka'iulani Hotel would cost $575 and up, per person, double occupancy. From Dallas/Ft. Worth it would begin at $775, and from Atlanta, $875. Staying the same length of time at Hilton Hawaiian Village or the Sheraton Moana Surfrider would begin at $725 from Los Angeles, $975 from Dallas/Ft. Worth, and $1055 from Atlanta. Delta also arranges for travelers to spend their vacations on two or more islands. Call (800) 872–7786 for further information.

GETTING TO AND FROM THE AIRPORT: Honolulu International Airport, near Pearl Harbor, is *ewa* (west) of downtown Honolulu and Waikiki, where most hotels are located. The 20-minute drive can turn into 45 minutes during rush hours. Especially when rooms are booked as part of fly/stay package deals, **complimentary airport shuttle** service is often provided to hotels. Both the far-flung Turtle Bay Hilton and the Sheraton Makaha Resort pick guests up and drop them off at the airport at no additional cost.

By Bus: The least expensive way to get to Waikiki is by the 60¢ **public buses** (#19 or #20), which depart from the airport baggage claim exits every 20 minutes or so. Light packers can take advantage of this, since passengers may only carry on one bag each and they must ride with their luggage on their laps. For $5 per person, both **Airport Express** (949–5249) and **Gray Line** (834–1033) shuttle vacationers to and from various hotels and condominiums.

By Taxi: The ride into Waikiki should cost about $16 plus tip and 25¢ per bag.

By Limousine: For $35 to $55 per hour, some couples, especially honeymooners, treat themselves to limo rides between the airport and Waikiki or elsewhere. Most companies require a two-hour minimum, so vacationers can take a scenic whirl before arriving at their destination. Good outfits include **Five Star** (595–3077 or (800)367–4753), **Silver Cloud** (524–7999 or (800)992–9918), and **First Class** (839–0944 or (800)248–5101).

By Car: Rental agencies located at or near the airport provide complimentary shuttle service from the baggage claim area to and from their offices. You'll see courtesy phones for contacting them.

GETTING AROUND OAHU: **By Car:** Within Honolulu, driving a car is more trouble than it's worth. Public and tour buses travel all over the island. However, for the greatest degree of freedom, you might consider renting an auto for explorations beyond the capital city. Many of the national and state-wide car rental agencies have offices at the airport, as well as in Honolulu and other parts of Oahu. **Tropical** (836–1041 or (800)367–5140) is an excellent state-wide rental company, with good prices. In addition to the major companies, a variety of smaller local agencies appeal to people who want a car for just a few days. Convertibles are very popular among visitors. For those with deep pockets who like to hit the road in style, try **Cruisin' Classics** (531–1954) on Kuhio Avenue: **Aloha Funway** (942–9696 or (800)367–2686) on Kalakaua Avenue; or **Ferrari Rentals** (942–8725) also on Kalakaua, all in Waikiki. You'll choose among Ferraris, Jaguars, Rolls Royces, Porsches, Maseratis, Lamborghinis, and exclusive 1928 Model A Fords with 6-cylinder Mustang engines, among other exotic beauties. Some companies, such as **Nifty Fifties** (922–5060), next to the Circle Hotel on Kalakaua and at Gateway to Waikiki on Kalakaua, specialize in attention-grabbing cars from the 1950s, '60s, '70s.

Driving Tips: In the morning and afternoon, traffic is especially thick between Honolulu and its suburbs, such as Mililani and Hawaii Kai. Unless you don't mind moving at a crawl, avoid the Pali Highway going into the city from Kailua on Monday through Friday mornings and going toward Kailua after the workday. During the winter when the North Shore waves are ready for individual surfers and annual surfing championships, the line of cars become particularly lethargic between Haleʿiwa and Laie.

Watch out for the long, low mongooses (no, not mongeese) that zip across the road near sugar cane fields.

By Bus: Efficient Honolulu City buses, called TheBus, travel between and within Waikiki and downtown Honolulu, as well as around Oahu. The fare is 60¢. For schedule information, call 531–1611.

Physically **handicapped vacationers** can arrange to be transported by **Handi-Van Service** (524–4626).

RENTING VIDEO CAMERAS: If you haven't brought your own video camera, you can rent one at some of the **Dollar Rent A Car** offices in Waikiki (926–4200).

TOURIST OFFICES: The state's main office of the **Hawaii Visitors Bureau** is located on Waikiki's thoroughfare at 2270 Kalakaua Avenue, 8th floor, Honolulu, HI 96815; 923–1811. Hours are 8 a.m. to 4:30 p.m., Monday through Friday.

POST OFFICES: The branch closest to most hotel is the one in Waikiki's Fort DeRussy on Saratoga Ave. Some shopping centers, such as the Royal Hawaiian on Kalakua Ave., and some hotels have P.O. branches as well. Most post offices are open from 8 a.m. to 4:30 p.m. For the branch nearest you, call 423–3990.

AMERICAN EXPRESS AND WESTERN UNION OFFICES: If you run out of cash, don't panic. Through American Express or Western Union, you can arrange to have money wired to you quickly from someone at home or through your credit card or bank account. Some of the larger hotels have American Express offices on the premises; call 946–7741 for the most convenient location. For Western Union, call (800)325–6000.

SURF REPORT: Call 836–1952.

ALCOHOLICS ANONYMOUS: Call 946–1438 for information about participating in local meetings.

WEIGHT WATCHERS: Call 955–1588 to participate in local meetings.

EMERGENCIES: Dial 911.

MEDICAL ATTENTION: You don't need an appointment to be seen by one of the physicians participating in the 24-hour **Doctors on Call** program. If necessary, doctors will come to your hotel or condo. Clinics are set up in the Reef Towers (926–0664), the Hyatt Regency (926–4777), and the Hawaiian Regent (923–3666), three Waikiki hotels.

Hospitals are **Queen's Medical Center** (1301 Punchbowl Street, Honolulu; 547–4311); **Straub Clinic** (888 South King Street, Honolulu; 522–4000); and **Kapiolani Medical Center for Women and Children** (1319 Punahou Street, Honolulu; 947–8633).

For dental care, make an appointment with the **Waikiki Royal Hawaiian Dental Group** (Waikiki Medical Building, 305 Royal Hawaiian Avenue, suite 209; 926–5732). Hours are 8:30 a.m. to noon on Mondays; 8:30 a.m. to 5 p.m. on Tuesdays, Thursdays, and Fridays; and 1 to 8 p.m. on Wednesdays.

Those who wish to try acupuncture, the highly successful ancient Chinese healing technique, should make an appointment at the **Waikiki Acupuncture Clinic** (305 Royal Hawaiian Avenue, suite 208, Waikiki; 923–6939).

MAUI

The second largest member of the Hawaiian archipelago, at roughly 729 square miles, Maui is also the second most visited. It is named for the demi-god who stood on the rim of 10,023-foot Haleakala volcano and snared the sun with a long rope to slow its journey across the sky. This Maui did because the fiery yellow ball sped by too swiftly for anyone to put in a good day's work. For instance, night always fell before the kapa cloth that women pounded from water-soaked bark had had a chance to dry.

Maui has quickly become the most built-up of the Neighbor Islands. It is now home to more millionaires than almost anywhere else. Drawing quite a few affluent travelers, some of its most luxurious accommodations are attractions in themselves. Many vacationing mainlanders—from surfing bums to yuppies and middle-aged couples—have turned into residents over the years.

Once actually two separate islands, Maui consists of two volcanic peaks divided by lush valleys thick with sugarcane and pineapple fields. From the air, it looks as if a pair of mountainous cookies, one much smaller than the other, had been placed too close together when they went into the oven. Maui's shape is often described as the head and torso of a woman in profile. Her head forms West Maui, dominated by the West Maui Mountains. Her neck is the six-mile isthmus that slopes gently toward Mount Haleakala, which commands larger East Maui—her bust, shoulder, and side.

Along with prime scuba and snorkeling sites, buff-colored beaches ring the island. Many young, fitness-oriented travelers are lured by the mountain bike excursion down Haleakala volcano, horseback riding in the crater, scenic hiking trails, good camp sites, and excellent surfing waves and windsurfing breezes. Health food stores and fruit stands do big business in avocado/alfalfa sprout sandwiches and smoothies (those California shakes made from fresh fruit and yogurt).

During the winter, Maui is the whale-watching capital of the state. Year-round, the historic, picturesque port town of Lahaina offers a glimpse into Hawaii's 19th-century whaling days. Maui also boasts quite a few

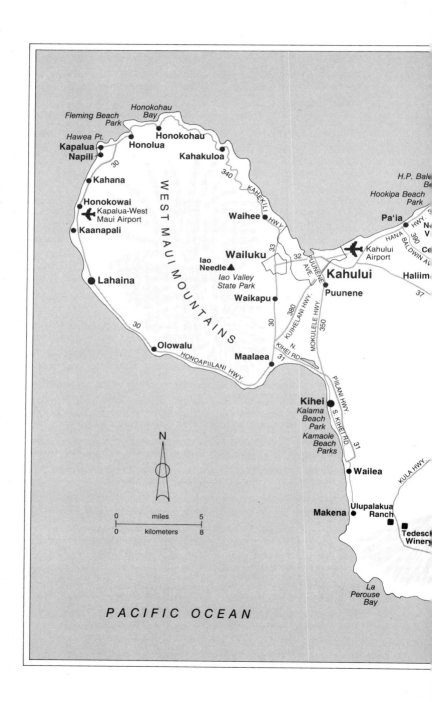

Fleming Beach Park

Honokohau Bay

Hawea Pt.

Kapalua
Napili

Honolua

Honokohau

Kahakuloa

30

Kahana

W
E
S
T

340

KAHEKILI HWY.

Waihee

Honokowai
Kapalua-West
Maui Airport

Kaanapali

M
A
U
I

Iao
Needle▲

Wailuku

33

32

Kahului
Airport

N.

M
O
U
N
T
A
I
N
S

Iao Valley
State Park

Waikapu

Lahaina

30

30

380

KUIHELANI HWY.

MOKULELE HWY.

350

PUUNENE AVE.

Kahului

Puunene

Haliim

37

Olowalu

HONOAPIILANI HWY.

Maalaea

31

KIHEI RD.

H.P. Bal
B

Hookipa Beach
Park

Pa'ia

390

N
V

HANA HWY.

BALDWIN AV

Ce

N

PIILANI HWY.

S. KIHEI RD.

Kihei
Kalama
Beach
Park

Kamaole
Beach
Parks

Wailea

31

KULA HWY.

Makena

Ulupalakua
Ranch

**Tedesc
Winery**

La
Perouse
Bay

0   miles   5
0   kilometers   8

PACIFIC OCEAN

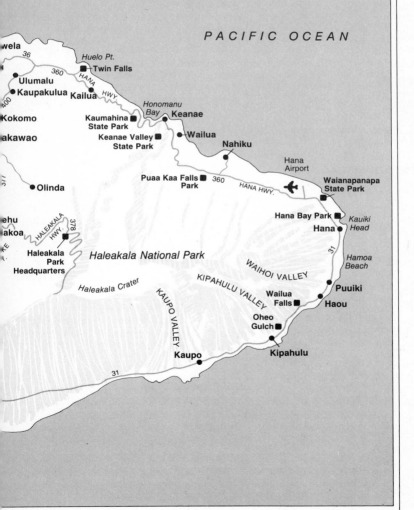

MAUI

PACIFIC OCEAN

wela
36
Huelo Pt.
Twin Falls
360
Ulumalu
HANA
Kaupakulua Kailua
HWY
Kokomo
Kaumahina
State Park
Honomanu
Bay
Keanae
akawao
Keanae Valley
State Park
Wailua
Nahiku
Olinda
Puaa Kaa Falls
Park
360
HANA HWY.
Hana
Airport
Waianapanapa
State Park
ehu
HALEAKALA
378
Kauiki
akoa
HWY
Hana Bay Park
Head
KE
Haleakala
Park
Headquarters
Haleakala National Park
WAIHOI VALLEY
Hana
31
Hamoa
Beach
Haleakala Crater
KIPAHULU VALLEY
KAUPO VALLEY
Wailua
Falls
Puuiki
Oheo
Gulch
Haou
Kaupo
Kipahulu
31

worthwhile art galleries, as well as a vineyard where wine tasting takes place in an old converted jailhouse.

The busiest sandy crescent, palm-studded Kaanapali Beach, is a younger, far less congested version of Oahu's Waikiki. Most of Maui's action—by day and by night—takes place here and in neighboring La-haina, on the northern west coast. There's a wide array of restaurants, hotels, and condominiums, along with excellent golf courses and tennis courts. The only problem with all these convenient diversions is that during the most popular seasons (the summer and Christmas through Easter), Kaanapali and Lahaina are jam-packed with tourists.

Those who find these vacation playgrounds too crowded can choose among several other quieter, less developed resort areas. To the north are Kapalua and Napili, while Kihei, Wailea, and Makena lie to the south. Many of these resorts come complete with their own tennis courts and golf courses. And it's not difficult at all to find unpeopled strands along the miles of tranquil, beautiful beaches that stretch from Maalaea, on southern West Maui, to Makena, on southern East Maui. For the utmost in seclusion, head to remote Hana, on the far eastern coast of the island.

Hawaiian Roots

Despite the influx of mainlanders and other outsiders, pockets remain on Maui where Hawaiian is still the language of choice. Many Hawai-ians live in and around flourishing Hana, isolated from the tourist cen-ters. However, most remnants of the indigenous culture are found un-derground—literally. The earliest artifact dug up on the island, on the south side of East Maui, dates back to about the 6th century A.D.

Here, as well as on other Hawaiian Islands, periodic battles erupt among developers, archaeologists, and Hawaiians over building on and/ or unearthing ancient burials and other sacred sites. A descendant of a missionary family, local developer Colin Cameron was born on Maui. The chairman of the Maui Land & Pineapple Company, of which the Kapalua resort is a subsidiary, he had been known to contribute healthy sums of money to cultural causes and conservation projects. However, in 1986, he began making plans to build a beachfront hotel, a Ritz-Carlton, at Honokahua, near Kapalua, on the northwest coast, at a well-known Hawaiian burial site. The Kapalua Land company started quietly conducting the archaeological study required before any building is done. The intent was to remove all the contents of the graves. It was only by accident that the public got wind of this project.

After a period of heated controversy, local Hawaiian activist groups finally gave in to the disinterment. Along with the Office of Hawaiian Affairs, they came to an agreement with the developers about the care and treatment of each artifact and set of bones. But once exhumations began, the remains of nearly 900 people were uncovered, some of whom had probably been buried as far back as 1200 years ago. Also discovered were fish hooks, *ulu maika* (lawn bowling) stones, and rare shell jewelry. When the news of the number and antiquity of burials reached the Hawaiian community, outrage over the disturbance of the graves was refueled.

In late 1988, Hawaiians from all islands poured into Maui to participate in a 24-hour vigil at the site. The following week, a ceremony of mourning was held, highlighted by prayers and chants. It was not that other buildings hadn't been planted on sacred ground. But this project had become a symbol for what indigenous people would no longer tolerate. After another 24-hour vigil was held, this time in front of the Honolulu home of Governor John Waihee (Hawaii's first Hawaiian governor), the head of state called for a cease-fire, and work on the project stopped. Finally, in February 1989, Hannibal Tavares, Mayor of Maui County, reported that the activists and Colin Cameron had reached a new agreement. The site of the hotel would be moved inland, away from the burial mound, so that no more bones would be touched. The skeletons that had already been dug up would be reburied and the mound restored. This explains why the Ritz-Carlton Kapalua hotel, scheduled to open in 1992, will be set back from the ocean.

Whale Watching

From November through June, migrating humpback whales bound through Hawaiian waters. Maui provides the state's best vantage point. Growing as long as 45 feet and weighing as much as 40 tons, these are the fifth largest of the great whales. Scientists believe that they travel the 3000 miles from Alaska to breed in Hawaii's warmer climate, giving birth 12 months later. While whale-watching cruises depart several times a day from Lahaina and Maalaea harbors, conservationists encourage people to view these aquatic giants from land (and with a good pair of binoculars, you'll do just fine). They fear that the sound of so many people-packed boats interferes with the whales' mating. If you're determined to view the whales by sea, try the two-and-a-half hour cruise run by the Pacific Whale Foundation on its research vessel. The money from your ticket will go toward the foundation's work. (See Sights in "What to See and Do.")

Maui Arts

While commercial, touristy art can certainly be found on Maui, the island is better known for its many accomplished artists producing quality work. Maui sports more than three dozen galleries, mostly in Lahaina. Art exhibits and other cultural events take place throughout the year. Vacationers can participate in **Maui Art Tours.** They'll spend a day riding in a stretch limo between visits to the studios and homes of artists. Guests will watch them at work and chat with them over tea or coffee. A few hotels are virtual museums, such as the Westin Maui (with all kinds of antiques and its oversized marble Asian and European replicas) and the Hyatt Regency Maui (where an 18th–century Burmese Buddha is only one item in the hotel's multi-million dollar collection). Both of these resorts are on Kaanapali Beach.

Begun in 1934 by a group of women headed by socialite Ethel Baldwin, the **Hui Noeau** is Maui's original art collective. Today it resides in Baldwin's Kaluanui estate and has become a significant educational and cultural outlet with a few hundred members. Visitors are welcome to absorb island art in glorious surroundings or to purchase hand-painted clothing, ceramics, posters, and other works.

After two decades of planning, the **Maui Community Arts and Cultural Center** has opened in Kahului. Its two theaters—one seating more than 1000 people, the other, 200—are expected to draw national touring companies as well as local drama groups. Art exhibitions are held in the 3500-square-foot gallery.

Special Events

Perhaps Maui's most amusing annual event is the summer SPAM cook-off. Since 1987, the 50th anniversary of this canned meat, both professional and home-trained chefs have competed for prizes, each trying to create the tastiest and most imaginative dish. While mainland noses may turn up at SPAM, here in Hawaii this pressed meat is a staple, happily consumed for breakfast, lunch, and dinner. If you're interested in seeing what all the fuss is about, write to Tana Mitchell, the Maui Mall, P.O. Box 156, Kahului, HI 96732; or call (808)877–5523.

It's not surprising that some people refer to Maui as Southern California, especially when you consider the Spring Renewal Festival, held in March. During this event, a few hundred New Agers gather at the scenic YMCA camp in Keanae for yoga classes, meditation, and vegetarian meals. As part of the Barrio Festival in May, a miniature Filipino village is set up on the lawn of the War Memorial Complex in Wailuku.

On King Kamehameha Day, in June, the whole state honors the great warrior responsible for uniting the Hawaiian Islands. Also in June, the Kapalua Music Festival brings a bit of European culture to this beautiful, tranquil resort area, with chamber music played by masters from all over the United States.

If you're vacationing around July 4th, be sure to catch the raucous annual rodeo at Makawao, in upcountry Maui, where paniolos (Hawaiian cowboys) do their thing. Aloha Week, in September and October, is the state's largest celebration of Hawaiian culture. For some local flavor, make a point of attending the October Maui County Fair, kicked off by a parade and held at Kahului Fairgrounds. Hula performances are the highlight of Na Mele O Maui, a festival held in Lahaina and Kaanapali in November, which also includes arts and crafts and luaus.

Getting Around

Most travelers fly into Kahului Airport, just east of the neighboring towns of Kahului and Wailuku. Grayline-Maui transports travelers by bus between the Kahului Airport and Kaanapali. However, the smaller, newer Kapalua-West Maui Airport is convenient for many visitors since it is close to both Kaanapali and Kapalua and provides free round-trip shuttles. Some vacationers take the shuttles to their hotels and condos, then return to the airport later to pick up their reserved rental cars when traffic is not so congested.

Traffic along the road between Lahaina and Kaanapali is particularly sluggish during rush hours. Although Maui has no island-wide public transportation system, shuttle service is available to guests of various hotels. In Kaanapali, these buses run between accommodations, Whaler's Village Shopping Center, and the town of Lahaina. Kapalua and Wailea also offer local bus service within each resort.

You'll need to rent a four-wheel-drive vehicle to get to some of Maui's most scenic hideaways, such as Polipoli State Park, on the slopes of Haleakala Volcano, and La Perouse Bay, south of Makena resort.

West Maui

Created before Mount Haleakala in the east, the rugged West Maui Mountains have had more time to become expertly sculpted by the elements. Their last volcanic eruption probably occurred some 5000 to 10,000 years ago, while Haleakala crater is thought to have spewed lava as recently as 500 to 1000 years ago. West Maui is the busiest section of the island. It is home to Kaanapali, the major resort area; jungled Iao Valley (great for hiking) with its prominent Iao Needle; and the adjoining towns of Kahului (the island's port) and Wailuku (its administrative center). From Kaanapali Beach, along the west coast, there are striking views of Molokai and Lanai.

The North: Off a bumpy section of the Honoapiilani Highway, east of Kapalua, the picturesque fishing village of **Kahakuloa** is one of Maui's first settlements. Hikers and others in the mood for rugged but worthwhile hideaways will come upon quiet beaches and good snorkeling spots along this eastern coast.

Near the Kapalua-West Maui Airport, **Kapalua** draws vacationers with truly upscale tastes—and pocketbooks. The smooth, bright green expanses between the volcanic peaks and the beige shore are peppered with dark green Norfolk pines. A plush hotel—the sprawling Kapalua Bay—beachfront and inland condominiums, and comfortable villas are scattered across 750 artfully planned acres. The locale for celebrated chamber music festivals and wine symposia, serene Kapalua is also known for its gourmet restaurants and chic boutiques. There's no need to be a golfer to enjoy the stunning vistas of duck-filled ponds and rolling hills on the two Arnold Palmer–designed fairways. And tennis buffs have a hard time staying off the courts.

A small, laid-back, upper-income community of residential and beachfront condos, **Napili** is about a 15-minute drive north of bustling Kaanapali. There's a handful of petite stores, boutiques, and restaurants in the area. The Kahana Manor Shops include A to Z Grocery Store, Kahana Clothing Co. (selling resort wear), and Dollie's Cafe (for pizza and cappuccino). While this region is picturesque, some of the coastline is rocky and the beaches aren't especially good for swimming. **Kahana** and **Honokowai Beach** are two more quiet condominium communities just north of the main tourist center. On Monday afternoons and Thursday mornings, Kahana hosts a **Farmer's Market,** packed with all kinds of freshly plucked fruit and vegetables.

Kaanapali: If you arrive in Maui during the winter and drive to Kaanapali (''rolling cliffs'') from Kahului Airport, you might spot **whales** from the sea cliffs along northwest West Maui. Cars may be pulled over while people stand on the nearby bluffs to get good looks at the mammoth mammals. Once vacationers reach Kaanapali, many park themselves in the resort and never budge. After all, the palm-fringed beach is gorgeous. Kaanapali is also Maui's center for surfing, renting jet skis, water-skiing, and windsurfing (whether you want to take lessons or just rent equipment). In the morning, rainbows often shimmer above the Pacific.

Deluxe hotels and condominiums gaze across the electric blue water to the islands of Molokai and Lanai. At the Hyatt Regency Maui, parrots flap around an atrium ablaze with elaborate flower arrangements in tall vases. At the Westin Maui, swans glide across carp-filled ponds; larger-than-life Buddhas line walkways; and weathered South Pacific art decorates corridors. Kaanapali also boasts a good selection of restaurants, space-age discos, Polynesian revues, waterfront luaus, shops, and tennis courts. *Mauka* (inland) of the three-mile beach, the rich green golf courses (two, 18-hole), and patchwork land slope up ever so gently toward the West Maui Mountains, crowned with plump white clouds. Along with shuttle buses, the **Lahaina-Kaanapali and Pacific Rail Road** (also called the **Sugar Cane Train**) runs between here and Lahaina, about four miles away.

With Hawaii's original capital in neighboring Lahaina, the Kamehamehas—the islands' most celebrated royal family—used Kaanapali as their playground. In these waters they fished, maneuvered their immense koa wood surfboards, and raced their outrigger canoes. On land, they satiated themselves at banquets and entertained each other with hula performances. Along the lowlands now covered by the **Royal Kaanapali Golf Courses,** the alii also played ancient games such as *ulu maika.*

As resorts go, Kaanapali is still a pup, born in 1962. During the 1950s, the board of directors of AmFac, owners of Kaanapali and most of its adjacent sugarcane fields, came up with the idea of turning the area into a resort. To discuss their plans, they got together for a luau on the beach at **Puu Kekaa** (a.k.a. **Black Rock**), a peninsula used as a diving platform by Maui's King Kahekili. (Today, every evening as the sun slips into the ocean, a diver reenacts these skillful leaps over the craggy rocks.) According to ancient tales, Puu Kekaa was also the departure point for the fire goddess, Pele, who left to seek a new home elsewhere in the islands. At the time when the AmFac businessmen dreamed up the resort, the new residents of drowsy Maui earned their living either picking pineapple or cutting cane. After the demise of the whaling business, seamen had virtually deserted Lahaina, where streets were now lined with many broken-down, weather-beaten, and boarded-up buildings. The seat of the Hawaiian monarchy had left here to relocate in Honolulu.

Today, the Royal Lahaina Resort stands where Kaanapali's first 31 vacation cottages were built in 1962. The Sheraton Maui, erected at Puu Kekaa—the site of AmFac's brainstorming feast—held its grand opening in 1963. Rooms went for a mere $15 a night. Now transformed into the splashy Westin Maui, the Maui Surf followed. Other hotels and condominiums sprouted during the 1960s, '70s, and '80s. Until 1981, Kaanapali had a horse-racing track. **Whaler's Village** is an open-air, oceanfront shopping center, with the worthwhile **Whaler's Village Museum** and several good restaurants.

Lahaina: Just south of Kaanapali, much of Lahaina (the first royal capital of the Hawaiian Islands) has now been declared a National Historic Landmark. It was a flourishing whaling port during the 19th century. Herman Melville, of *Moby Dick* fame, was among the hundreds of sailors who passed through. Kaahumanu, Hawaii's regent and the favorite wife of King Kamehameha I, worried that the transient, unruly seamen would have a bad effect on residents. Coming from Oahu and the mainland to assist the queen, American missionaries helped pass laws against such undesirable behavior as spitting in public, and wanton sex between foreigners and Hawaiians both on land and at sea.

Lahaina began to fall into decay around 1843, when Hawaii's whaling business started to slip and the islands' capital was officially moved to Honolulu. Today, with tourism, sugar, and pineapple Maui's main industries, much of the old town's charm (but little of its bawdiness) has been restored. Drunken sailors no longer pug it out on the shore or join rowdy packs in search of willing or unwilling Hawaiian women. Sunlight glints off the windows of the refurbished or re-created wooden Front Street buildings that now house a jumble of restaurants, cafes, T-shirt shops, jewelry stores, and clothing boutiques. Take the time to wade through the touristy souvenirs and you'll find a welcome array of quality goods. Most of Maui's major **art galleries** are in Lahaina, many along the main street.

The town was named for the relentless sun (la haina) that can be especially merciless in the afternoon. However, afternoon is also the time when you're likely to see rainbows, if you look *mauka* (toward the mountains). The town is most crowded during the cooler, earlier part of the day. Don't even think about trying to find a parking space then. Opt for the **Sugarcane Train** (for some reason, this is particularly popular among Japanese tourists) or one of the shuttles that run between town and accommodations in neighboring Kaanapali. Lahaina is comprised of only about four mile-long streets, which run parallel to the waterfront. Most of the sights are found on or adjacent to a half-mile section of Front Street. Plan to spend a couple of hours poking around here. At the **Baldwin House Museum,** on Front Street, you may want to get a copy of the pamphlet called *Lahaina: A Walking Tour of Historic and Cultural Sites.* The name of a prominent local family with missionary roots, Baldwin crops up frequently in Hawaiian history and on contemporary places of interest. The *Maui News* is owned by this clan, which has built schools, parks, and other public institutions. The Baldwins are respected for giving generously to the islands that gave them their wealth. Next door to the museum is the **Masters' Reading Room,** which was constructed in 1833, making it Maui's oldest building. Now headquarters of the Lahaina Restoration Foundation, it was once a mission storeroom and place of relaxation for the crews of visiting ships.

The harbor is the jumping-off point for most of Maui's sailing charters and cruises to the nearby island of Lanai and elsewhere. Here at the **Ocean Activity Center,** arrangements can also be made for scuba trips, snorkeling excursions, parasailing, and other water sports. Docked offshore, the *Carthaginian II,* a striking replica of a 19th-century square-rigged ship, is a museum. Along the seawall near the ship, look for the orange and black Hawaii Visitors Bureau warrior marker that points to a cluster of rocks in the water. Ancient Hawaiians believed that the **Hauola Stone** here, roughly resembling a chair, had a curative effect on the infirm who sat in it and let the waves bathe them. Facing the harbor are the foundations of King Kamehameha I's **Brick Palace** and the place where a royal taro patch once thrived. Missionaries built nearby **Spring House** above a freshwater spring. Now surrounded by the **Wharf Shopping Center,** the building shelters a large lighthouse lens that directed ships to safety in the old days.

Set back from the water, the red-roofed **Pioneer Inn**—with its creaky porch and walls hung with whaling relics and turn-of-the-century signs —dates back to 1901. The bar here makes an intriguing stop for a cool drink. Just across the street, the expansive **banyan tree** was planted in 1873 to celebrate the 50th anniversary of the arrival of Protestant missionaries in Hawaii. Thrown wide like many open arms, the branches drip vertical shoots that grow into additional trunks resembling elephant legs. Since it covers nearly an acre, it is difficult to believe this is only one tree. There are plenty of benches and plenty of shade. However, sit at your own risk, unless you have an umbrella to protect yourself from the droppings of the mynahs and other talkative birds.

The historic **Lahaina Courthouse** stands on Wharf Street, in front of the banyan tree. It contains both the District Court and the **Lahaina Art Society,** which displays some of its paintings in former jail cells in the basement. A portion of the **Old Fort,** built on these grounds in the 1980s, has been reconstructed near the courthouse. Walking south along Front Street, you'll come to **Holy Innocents Episcopal Church,** where a Hawaiian madonna adorns the altar. Kamehameha III's palace and Princess Nahienaena's grass house were once near here. Turning left on Shaw Street and left again onto Wainee, you'll find **Waiola Church and Cemetery.** It is built on the site of Wainee, Hawaii's first stone church, which was damaged in a storm in 1858, then set ablaze in 1894 by Hawaiians enraged by the American-backed overthrow of their monarchy. Members of Hawaiian royalty are buried in the cemetery, including Queen Keopuolani, one of the wives of Kamehameha the Great and the first high-ranking Hawaiian to convert to Christianity.

Just north along Wainee Street, Lahaina's largest Buddhist congregation holds services at the **Hongwanji Temple.** On Prison Road, right off Wainee Street, **Hale Paahao** (Old Prison) was built during the 1850s by convicts themselves to contain the overflow of disruptive, law-breaking foreign sailors. To learn about Maui's Chinese heritage, pay a visit to the **Wo Hing Society** (further north on Front Street), which began as a temple back in 1912. During the 1830s, King Kamehameha III used to entertain himself and others in the building that later became **Seamen's Hospital,** another block north. It now houses **Lahaina Printsellers,** where you can browse through antique maps and other nautical items.

A short drive from the center of town, **Lahaina Jodo Mission** is a restful, blossom-filled Japanese cultural park that is definitely worth a stop. About two miles up a slope *mauka* (inland) of Lahaina, the campus of **Lahainaluna School** treats visitors to a panoramic view of pineapple and cane fields, the harbor, and the islands of Lanai and Molokai. This is the oldest public school west of the Rockies. On the grounds, visit **Hale Pai,** a restored printing house that is now a museum. To get here, hike or drive toward the huge white L (for Lahainaluna, of course) near the mountain's summit.

South of town, narrow **Olowalu Beach** is a great snorkeling spot just off the road. **Honolua Bay,** a winter surfing area in the Lahaina District, played a pivotal role in recent Hawaiian history. In 1976, the *Hokulea,* a replica of a double-hulled ancient Polynesian sailing canoe, set off from here with a 17-person crew for a two-month journey to Tahiti and back. The point of the excursion was to prove that Hawaii's ancient Polynesian settlers not only could have sailed but did sail to Hawaii on purpose and without the benefit of modern navigational techniques. The day the *Hokulea* reached Tahiti was declared a national holiday as a huge crowd of Tahitians welcomed their long-lost cousins.

Kahului and Wailuku: Kahului, Maui's commercial and industrial center, is about 23 miles (or a 35-minute drive) from Lahaina. The island's main airport is just outside town. If you've packed a pair of binoculars, you might want to stop at **Kanaha Pond Wildlife Sanctuary,** between Kahului and the airport. This is one of the most active waterfowl preserves in Hawaii. Also not far from the airport, **Alexander & Baldwin Sugar Museum** (in a former plantation house in Puunene) illustrates the importance of sugarcane to Hawaii's economy and cultural history. Sugar and pineapple headed for the mainland depart from busy, crowded Kahului Harbor in town. On Kaahumanu Avenue, the main drag, the **Kaahumanu Center** is Maui's largest shopping mall. **The Maui Community Art and Cultural Center,** a $16-million theater and visual arts complex, has recently opened. While Hawaiian flowers certainly bloom at the **Maui Zoological and Botanical Gardens** (on Kanaloa Avenue, off Kaahumanu), the main attraction is the children's zoo, which counts some members of endangered species among its ranks.

To the west, the adjoining town of Wailuku is older, greener, hillier, and generally more attractive than Kahului. Over a third of the island's population lives in these two towns, which are separated by Wailuku Gulch, spanned by a bridge. Especially if you're staying in a condo or private home, consider taking care of your grocery shopping in Kahului or Wailuku, where prices are the lowest on the island. Sitting in the foothills of the West Maui Mountains, Wailuku is the administrative center of Maui County (which includes the islands of Molokai, Lanai, and Kahoolawe). Houses in this town range from tin-roofed plantation-style cottages to suburban-style homes surrounded by lovingly landscaped grounds.

The art-deco architecture draws a great deal of attention to **Iao Theater,** built in 1927, on North Market Street in Wailuku's historic district. On Sundays starting at 9 a.m., the sound of hymns sung in Hawaiian floats out from the parishioners seated in the koa wood pews at nearby **Kaahumanu Church.** This house of worship is generally closed to the public at other times. A small stone building set against the mountains, it was named for the favorite wife of Kamehameha the Great. Beside the church, two white, red-roofed buildings, their entrances decorated with lively tiles, make it difficult not to take photos of the whole scene. **Hale Hoikeike** (also known as Bailey House, for its early owner, or the Maui Historical Society Museum) is a 19th-century missionary home containing Hawaiiana (some from before the arrival of Europeans) as well as missionary furniture and other household items.

Stop for a quiet picnic in **Iao Valley**'s pleasant **Kepaniwai Park and Heritage Gardens,** where typical houses of Hawaii's various ethnic groups stand in honor of the islands' diversity. During the late 18th century, a vicious battle was waged in this area: Kahekili of Maui practically wiped out the whole army of Kalaniopuu, and bodies clogged Wailuku Stream. The translation of Kepaniwai is "damning of the waters," and Wailuku, downstream, means "bloody river." At a bend in Iao Valley Road (Hwy. 32) in the Black Gorge area, tour bus drivers are fond of pointing out the mountainside rock formation that resembles **John F. Kennedy's Profile.** While driving along this scenic road, you'll see the dramatic lime and forest green West Maui Mountains looming in the distance.

The highway dries up at **Iao Valley State Park.** The valley began as the crater of the West Maui volcano and was enlarged by wind and rain. Rising 1200 feet from the ground, **Iao Needle** points to the sky like a giant green finger. There are about ten major botanical zones on Maui, ranging from desert to soggy, from the tropics at sea level to an alpine region at the summit of Mount Haleakala. Each area contains a different group of plants. In tropical Iao Valley, bathed by about 150 inches of rainfall a year, the variety of plant, animal, and insect life is greater than anywhere else on the island. This is a wonderful area for hiking, especially if you enjoy picking fruit. Apple bananas, mangoes, guava, and coffee trees grow wild. This last plant produces red coffee berries in the fall. Remove the skin from the berry and suck on the two beans in each. The coating has a candylike flavor. But don't try to eat the beans! If you happen to be hiking in July or August with dirty hair, look for the three-inch red bulbs of the shampoo ginger plant, which contains a clear liquid that can serve as a natural shampoo; there won't be any suds, but it will leave your hair soft and silky. (The Paul Mitchell hair care company has even marketed it commercially.)

East Maui

Maui's larger, eastern section attracts the active vacationer not content simply to lounge on a beach. The dormant Haleakala volcano begs to be explored inside and out, whether you hike or take a horseback ride into its crater, or coast 38 miles on a bicycle down its outer slopes.

You'll find everything in this part of Maui from cowboys and rodeos to a vineyard, eucalyptus and redwood trees, and Charles Lindbergh's grave. Offshore Molokini crater captivates snorkelers and divers with its whirl of fish and other marine life. Getting to remote Hana—at the end of a winding, cliffside road way over on the isolated east coast—is an adventure in itself. This drowsy town has a greater concentration of Hawaiians than most other parts of Maui.

While there are all kinds of outdoor activities in East Maui, those who care to do nothing more than bask in the sun can choose among miles of little-used beaches, starting at Makena and continuing up along the western coast. Great for swimming, many of these beaches are also perfect for surfing and boardsailing. During the winter, this is the first part of Hawaii visited by migrating whales. Dotted with condos and hotels, Maui's quieter resorts have sprouted along this shore. It is also the driest section of Maui. Landlubbers entertain themselves with several golf courses and a host of tennis courts (many of which are free). While the islands of Lanai and Kahoolawe are anchored out in the Pacific, Haleakala, propping up the clouds, looms in the background off the side of the main road. This massive volcano slopes gradually upward, changing from pale green to black-green.

Kihei: About nine miles (a 20-minute drive) from Kahului, residential Kihei is far more laid back than Kaanapali up north. It stretches for about six miles along both sides of South Kihei Road. Stay at a condo here, and you'll be right near one of the sunny **Kamaole waterfront parks** that attracts snorkelers, scuba divers, and big-game fishing enthusiasts. Oceanside baseball and soccer games in **Kalama Park** offer many opportunities to mingle with locals.

After Kaanapali, Kihei was the first of Maui's other vacation playgrounds to spring up. In sharp contrast to Kaanapali, Wailea, and Makena, it clearly was not a planned resort. There seems to be no question that each developer did as he pleased. Randomly scattered amid clumps of condos and hotels are a couple of shopping centers, a few restaurants (from Hawaiian plate lunch stands to Mexican or steak and seafood spots), and individual stores selling beachwear, souvenirs, and watersports equipment. Yet despite the undistinguished looks of the community, some of the comfortable condos here are quite attractive—and they are less expensive than in swankier parts of the island. There is also far more of a local feeling to this area. The person next to you on the beach or in a restaurant is likely to live on Maui. Some residents are happy to share directions to their favorite island eateries or hideaways.

Wailea: Just south of Kihei, Wailea is about a 45-minute drive from Lahaina and Kaanapali, and about 35 minutes from Kahului. If you're looking for a spacious, meticulously laid out resort, you'll find it here. The artfully designed hotels, condos, and **Wailea Shopping Village** complement each other and the beautiful sandy coastline. Wailea is much greener than Kihei, thanks not to Mother Nature, but to an extensive sprinkler system. Two of Maui's best golf courses spread themselves out here. **The Wailea Tennis Center,** near the Maui Inter-Continental Hotel, boasts Maui's only public grass tennis courts. Wind-surfing, boogie boarding, and scuba diving are popular in this area and lessons are available. Wailea was built in the early 1970s by Alexander & Baldwin, one of Hawaii's Big Five companies whose wealth dates back to the islands' plantation and missionary days.

Makena: About a 50-minute drive from Kaanapali and 30 minutes from the Kahului airport, Makena is Maui's newest and most tranquil resort. This is the best place to stay if you want to be in a deluxe hotel off the beaten path, but within striking distance of mainstream action. The sleek, Japanese-owned Maui Prince, the first of Makena's accommodations, opened its louvered sliding doors in 1986. Now there is also a plush condominium, two 18-hole golf courses, and tennis courts. Don't be surprised if you see cacti along the road in this arid region.

Hippie colonies once thrived at **Makena Beach.** Snorkeling is as good as it ever was off **Makena Landing,** where black pebbles are underfoot. In 1874, just a few days after becoming king, David Kala-kaua arrived at Makena Landing with Queen Kapiolani aboard the S. S. *Kilauea.* They had come to pay a visit to Captain James Makee, the governor of the region and the owner of a large ranch in neighboring Ulupalakua. Makee often entertained his guests in a big way: When the royal couple reached the shore, they were met by about 150 dancers, singers, and horsemen, and nearly 100 torchbearers who accompanied their carriage to the ranch.

Near the landing, you might pass a wedding in progress at small but popular **Keawalai Church.** Off the cactus-bordered road not far from here is wide, long, **Big Beach** (a.k.a. **Oneloa**). This beige strip of sand is backed by Puu O'Lai ("cinder cone"), a petite gumdrop-shaped hill. The beach is studded with kiawe trees, which have huge gnarled trunks bent to one side by the wind. Nude bathers gather on a small section of this shore. You'll find some **petroglyphs** at the far end of the beach (to the left if you're facing the water). Friends of mine who recently honeymooned in Kaanapali said, as gorgeous as their hotel beach was, they drove nearly an hour every day to this beautiful beach. They loved the tranquility and found it easy to get into conversations with locals here. Offshore are uninhabited Kahoolawe, and **Molokini Crater,** a wonderful snorkeling and scuba diving spot. (Make arrangements at your accommodation to take a cruise there.) From November to April, you might even see **humpback whales** in these waters. You'll need to rent a four-wheel-drive vehicle to get to **Ahihi-Kinau Natural Reserve** (also called **Cape Kinau**), a Hawaiian archaeological site created by the lava flow from Haleakala's most recent eruption (back in 1790); or to picturesque **La Perouse Bay,** which takes its name from the first European to visit Maui (a French adventurer who arrived in 1786).

Upcountry Maui: The region between about 3000 and 7000 feet up along the north, west, and southwest slopes of Haleakala is known as upcountry Maui. However, exploring this area and driving to the volcano's summit should be done on separate days. The land here is given over to cool breezes, agriculture, small towns, rodeos, and ranches for cattle, sheep, and horses. Although upcountry sits just above the beach resorts of Kihei, Wailea, and Makena, people coming from those areas must take the one paved route through Kahului. Makena even lies along the lower slopes of Ulupalakua, but this upcountry ranch must still be reached in the same roundabout (though scenic) way. At press time, the unpaved road that connects Makena to upcountry is closed indefinitely.

After leaving Kahului, Hwy. 37 wanders up through rippling sugarcane fields, past pineapple plantations, and by patches of cabbage, onions, tomatoes, cucumbers, and flowers sprouting from the burnt orange earth. To the north, Kahului Bay glistens in the sun, while Maalaea Bay shimmers to the south. Guava bushes and avocado trees border roads. Winding Piiholo Road is overhung with old eucalyptus trees, which emit a soft, sweet fragrance. They are anchored on top of low, earthen roadside walls, with their roots peeking through the dark orange soil. East of Hwy. 37, suburban-looking **Haliimaile,** with its huge jacaranda trees, was once a pineapple plantation village.

Not far south of Haliimaile, rustic 19th-century **Makawao** is well known for its *paniolos* (Hawaiian cowboys), and its annual July 4th rodeo and parade. Any time of year, it is not unusual to see people riding horses through the pretty, residential streets, lined with low wooden buildings. Not only does Makawao have a public park with a horse ring, but hitching posts are planted by parking spaces in town. Hibiscus and bougainvillea splash color all over. At the **Hui Noeau** visual art center on Baldwin Avenue, visitors are welcome to take lessons in various disciplines, or attend exhibits or lectures. The modern Buddhist temple and the Makawao Library also make intriguing stops. Few people pass up a visit to **Komoda's Store and Bakery** (also on Baldwin Avenue), famous for their cream puffs and other goodies. Some people travel long distances to eat at **Polli's,** a reasonably priced Mexican-plus restaurant on Makawao Avenue.

Residential **Pukalani** ("hole in the heavens"), just southwest of Makawao, fills the eye with more pretty homes, flowers, horses, and fields. The only upcountry golf course and a handful of eateries and stores call this town home. The **Kula** district begins here. Kula itself is about a 45-minute drive from Kahului. Just after you pass Pukalani, along Hwy. 37, you'll see an octagonal church on a hillside, with impressive Haleakala at its back. Dating from 1897, the **Church of the**

Holy Ghost was constructed especially for Portuguese immigrants who had come to Maui to work on its upcountry ranches and farms.

Kula, sprawling from 1000 to 4000 feet up the slopes of Haleakala, may be known for its patches of onions, cabbage, and lettuce, but its real fame comes from its flourishing protea farms. More than 200 acres here (over 70 percent of Hawaii's total protea-growing land) are given over to this colorful blossom that is native to the southern regions of Africa and Australia. At the **University of Hawaii Kula Experimental Station,** visit the garden to see many different kinds of protea, varying in diameter from two to 12 inches. Near where Route 37 becomes 377, **Kula Botanical Gardens** flourishes with all kinds of trees, flowers, and plants growing around streams and a pond. This is a good place to stop for a picnic at the tables provided. At **Sunrise Protea Farm,** about 3 miles beyond the turnoff for Haleakala National Park, you can have these exotic flowers sent to the mainland. You might also pay a visit to **Upcountry Protea Farm. Kula Lodge,** on Haleakala Highway (Route 37), makes a pleasant choice for a filling lunch. It's also very popular for breakfast among those returning from watching the sun rise over Haleakala crater. The fabulous views from the restaurant are free. Also in the Lodge you'll find the **Curtis Wilson Cost Gallery,** where paintings of pastoral Kula landscapes are on display. Even if the $3,300 to $60,000 price tags are out of your range, this is worth some of your time.

Polipoli Spring State Recreation Area sprawls along the southwest slopes of Haleakala, just above Makena. However, not only will you have to get there from Makena by going north, then doubling back, but you'll also have to rent a four-wheel-drive. If you're into unspoiled natural beauty, hiking trails, and wouldn't mind seeing some redwoods and sweeping views of the island, you won't be disappointed. Since the park is so large and only four-wheel-drives can make the trip, it is usually very quiet. When the weather cooperates, you can see as far as the Big Island of Hawaii. Polipoli ("mounds" or "breasts") is a good place for day trips as well as overnight hiking and camping jaunts.

This lofty park is part of the Kula and Kahikinui Forest Reserve. In the 1920s, during a reforestation and conservation project, the state planted a cluster of California redwoods and hundreds of cedar, ash, cypress, and sugi. Pines and cypress shade **Polipoli Campground,** where the free campsites have facilities including tables, water, flush-toilets, and burners for cooking. Groups of up to ten people can find inexpensive shelter in a state housekeeping cabin. Although there is no electricity or refrigeration here, the cabin does have gas lanterns, a gas stove, cooking and eating utensils, beds, bedding, and cold showers. The view from here is spectacular, especially at sunset.

To get to Polipoli, take Route 37 past Kula, turn left on Route 377 for just under a half mile, then turn right onto rugged, bouncy Waipoli Road and take it about ten and a half miles to its end. Some people hitchhike to the summit of Haleakala (even though hitchhiking is illegal in Hawaii) and then hike eight miles down the Skyline Trail (which begins on the south side of Science City) to Polipoli park.

Also in the southwest, and sharing its slopes with Makena, **Ulupalakua** is a cattle and sheep ranch where the smell of eucalyptus wafts through the air. A wonderful site for a picnic, this area offers panoramic views encompassing the West Maui Mountains, the ocean, and tiny Molokini island. This is where you'll find Hawaii's only vineyard, **Tedeschi Winery.** Ulupalakua was a sugar plantation known as Rose Ranch during the 19th century. The former jailhouse here now serves as a wine tasting room.

Haleakala National Park: The largest dormant volcano in the world, massive Haleakala (''House of the Sun'') rises two miles into the sky. It hasn't erupted since 1790. This mountain ensures that Maui's climate is schizophrenic: lush in the north and east, parched in the southwest. Pushed across Maui by northeasterly tradewinds, rain clouds bump up against Haleakala. Moving up along the slopes into the cooler air, they let loose their water on northern and eastern Maui. By the time the clouds make it to the southwestern portion of the island, they have spent most of their rain.

Haleakala Highway (Rt. 37) winds through upcountry Maui. The 30-mile drive from Kahului to the crater should take about 1½ hours. Before making this trip, be sure to check weather conditions, visibility, and the exact times of sunrise and sunset (call 572–7749). (Visibility is best early in the day, by the way.) Especially if you're heading up to watch the sunrise, don't forget to bring some *very* warm clothing (a jacket and/or thick sweater, gloves, a hat, long pants, heavy socks, etc.). The high altitude often means the temperature at the top is as much as 30 degrees cooler than in coastal areas. Also, it is not uncommon for the weather to be dry and sunny at sea level while rain pours down at the summit.

After going about a dozen miles through picturesque upcountry Maui, make a left onto Route 378, the steep Haleakala Crater Road. At the entrance to the park, each car pays about $4 and each bicycle about $1.50. There is no charge for senior citizens. Right inside the entrance, a side road on the left will take you to **Hosmer Grove,** about a half mile away. Picnic tables are found in this campground, along with a quiet trail that wends its way past non-native trees such as fir, juniper, cypress, and eucalyptus. Open daily from 7:30 a.m. to 4 p.m., **Park Headquarters** are located about a mile from the entrance to the park. This is where visitors obtain camping permits and oral or written information about the volcano. Ask about guided walks along the crater rim (conducted sporadically in summer months). Outside the headquarters, toward the back of the building, you'll see some *nene gueese,* Hawaii's state bird.

The first crater viewing spot is **Leleiwi Overlook,** at 8800 feet. If you happen to be at the rim here in the late afternoon, you might catch a glimpse of your shadow looming against the clouds down below, perhaps even surrounded by the arc of a rainbow. This phenomenon is known as Brocken's Specter among Westerners and *aka-ku-anue-nue* ("the seeing of one's soul") among Hawaiians. The 3000-foot-deep, 19-square-mile crater itself could swallow the entire island of Manhattan.

Kalahaku Overlook, at 9325 feet, is one of few places where you can see rare **silversword.** Resembling a cone-shaped, gray or purple sea anemone, this delicate yet hearty plant thrives where few others can, at high altitudes with extreme temperature fluctuations. Even when the thermometer hits the 90s here during the day, snow can fall that night. Kalahaku's silverswords are protected from goats and humans by a stone wall. They take anywhere from 10 to 20 years to reach maturity and their full 8- or 10-foot height. These plants die after blooming only once and scattering their seeds. The best time to see them is from May, when the flowers begin to look like silver puffs, through August, when the stalk has grown and the blossoms have sprouted yellow and magenta. From this overlook, there are thrilling views of the stark, lumpy crater.

Ten miles from Park Headquarters, the glassed-in **Haleakala Visitor Center** is perched at 9745 feet. It is generally open from 6:15 a.m. to 3:30 p.m. This is the place to be for the most spine-tingling views of the crater's lunar landscape. It's a prime spot for sunset watching. The ebony lava looks like petrified molasses and the cinder cones resemble licorice gumdrops. Rocky formations come in chocolate brown, reds, oranges, sooty black, golden, charcoal gray, and even some greens. Throughout the day, the sun alters the crater's hues. (The view is especially intense during the morning or late afternoon.) Each hour from 9 a.m. to 12 p.m., the ranger conducts talks about the volcano. Among other interesting tidbits, you'll learn that the crater is so deep that even if the 110-story World Trade Center buildings were placed on the top of each other, they would still stand 300 feet below the crater rim. From the Visitor Center, people can hoof it a few hundred yards to the **White Hill Overlook.** Along the way, they'll pass stone shelters where ancient Hawaiians once bedded down while visiting Haleakala.

Unless you're in a plane or a helicopter, you can't get any higher than the **Puu Ulaula** observation point, at Haleakala's 10,023-foot summit. When the weather is clearest, the wrap-around view takes in the crater, the rest of the island, Lanai, Molokai, the Big Island of Hawaii, and Oahu. The nearby domes of Science City, which is not open to the public, house a research and communications center for scrutinizing the sun and moon, tracking satellites and missiles, and testing lasers.

During his 1866 visit, Mark Twain delighted in pushing boulders from the summit down the sides of the crater. He watched with glee as they hit the steep walls with explosions of dust, sometimes bouncing 300 feet into the air, shrinking in size until they vanished from view. However, that was then and this is now. Today Haleakala National Park prohibits visitors from moving any rocks, dirt, animals, or plants. Don't even think about *touching* silversword, since human contact can easily destroy these endangered plants.

A better way to have fun is to **hike** or **horseback ride** into the crater or to coast down the outside of Haleakala on a **mountain bike** (see Sports). The most exciting version of the bike ride begins with a view of the sunrise over the crater. You'll start down the mountain bundled up in jackets, sweaters, gloves, and long pants. By the time you reach the end of your ride, you will have peeled off layer by layer to T-shirt and shorts. You'll whiz along hairpin curves, through sweet-smelling eucalyptus forests that give way to plumeria trees, pineapple fields, and sugarcane plantations. When you pass the sugar mill, the smell of molasses will fill your nostrils. The ride culminates in a hearty breakfast or lunch at a restaurant.

While horseback riding or hiking in the crater, you'll have close up views of silversword and other plants as well as of goats, mongooses, boars, partridges, and the brown and beige Hawaiian *nene goose* (which grows to two feet in length). The heavy silence—punctured only by the swirling wind and the crunching of rocks and stones underfoot—has a presence of its own. You'll discover that many of those cinder cones that looked like small gumdrops from above are actually several hundred feet high. Ancient Hawaiians once worshipped their gods in sacred Haleakala. Down in the crater, you'll stumble upon the crumbling altars and shelters they left behind. Along the **Halemauu Trail,** you'll come to the 10-foot-wide, 65-foot-deep **Bottomless Pit,** where early Hawaiians tossed the umbilical cords of newborns to ensure that children would become worthy adults.

Hana Bound: Tucked away on the isolated east coast of East Maui, Hana is removed from the rest of the island by far more than geography. "Fight Smog. Buy a Horse," suggests one of the bumper stickers sold at the general store in the drowsy town. When the population is not swelled by itinerant tourists, it hovers around a mere 1000. Many residents are Hawaiian and most people earn their living through fishing or ranching. The jagged mountains, green expanses, and explosion of flowers seem to have changed little since the ancient Polynesians called this area home. Today, verdant Hana has attracted celebrities such as Richard Pryor, Kris Kristofferson, George Harrison, and Jim Nabors, who all bought houses in the vicinity. This is also where Charles Lindbergh chose to be buried.

Surprisingly, the mention of Hana elicits contrasting opinions from veteran travelers. Some insist "You've just *got* to go" while others dismiss the trip as a waste of time, saying "All that driving—and then there's nothing much to see when you get there." True, the drive is long and not for the faint of heart, and the diminutive town is completely devoid of sights that scream "tourist attraction." But those who are disappointed have misunderstood the point of the journey. At least half the excitement is in the trip itself—along a dramatic, scenic "highway."

While you can get to Hana by small plane or helicopter, the most thrilling way is to drive (or be driven along) the 52 twisting, turning, climbing, cliff-edge miles from Kahului on Route 36 (Hana Highway). The one-way trip can take anywhere from 2½ hours to a leisurely 3½ or 4, depending on your speed and number of stops. Since the driver spends much more time concentrating on the narrow, snaking road than gazing at the magnificent scenery, many travel companions let one person take the wheel in one direction and another on the way back. Other people choose 12-hour van tours so that no one has to worry about negotiating the road.

Hana Highway came into being when the feet of ancient Hawaiians pounded out a path. Convicts broadened it during the 1920s, but it wasn't paved until 1962 and couldn't accommodate regular traffic until it was further improved in 1982. Washouts aren't uncommon and the damp weather is hard on the road. In some places, vehicles creep along at 10 miles an hour or less. Hundreds of precarious curves lead to dozens of one-lane bridges over rocky streams and past quiet settlements, thick rainforests, waterfalls, swimming holes, a riot of blossoms, and flourishing state parks where people pause for picnics. The road hugs the edge of a precipice, high above dark sand beaches, pitch black boulders, and deep blue waters with vigorous white surf. Hit with about 100 inches of rainfall a year, this coast is extremely lush. The air is perfumed by wild ginger, plumeria, orchids, eucalyptus, and mangoes ripening on trees. Ferns, bamboo, and monkeypods decorate the roadside. Just off the highway, many trails are popular with hikers, some of whom spend three or four days camping in the area.

The other half of the fun of Hana lies in the more subtle pleasures of unwinding, talking story with locals, and absorbing remnants of Hawaiian history once you arrive. Consider carrying your towel and bathing suit so you can take advantage of a mountain pool or one of Hana's beaches. Completing the round-trip drive in a single day can be extremely exhausting since, if you spend any time at all in Hana, it can take more than 12 hours. In addition, it is difficult to get a real feel for the town in the couple of hours alloted by most visitors. A far more rewarding way to appreciate this flourishing region of Maui is to stay at one of the handful of accommodations for a couple of days. This way, you'll get a taste of the intoxicatingly low-key ambience that blankets Hana before and after the day-trippers swarm the town.

Near Kahului, **Pa'ia** is the last town you'll come to before reaching Hana, so it's your last chance to fill up on gas or any other necessary supplies. The historic main street in this former sugar plantation town is lined with a collection of old and new low-rise buildings. Some of the original turn-of-the-century structures have been converted into boutiques, eateries, and galleries, such as Maui Crafts Guild. Mama's Fish House and Dillon's are two restaurants that do booming business. Look for the tiny white courthouse/police station. Across the street from a Protestant church, the **Manto Kuji Soto Buddhist Temple** is backed by the water. Don't be surprised if you see some fruit and cans of 7-Up or beer in the graveyard. People customarily place the deceased's best-loved food or drink on tombstones.

In 1880, Samuel T. Alexander and Henry P. Baldwin opened the sugar mill in Pa'ia, boosting the town's economy by turning it into a plantation community. Residential camps sprang up around the mill. As with plantations throughout Hawaii, each of these settlements was populated by a different ethnic group made up of foreign immigrants. The twin sections of Upper Pa'ia and Lower Pa'ia developed a half mile apart. During WW II, when thousands of U.S. Marines and other servicemen were stationed nearby, the town flourished further. After the war, faced with labor union demands for better wages and more humane working conditions, Alexander & Baldwin began closing down some of its camps. In the 1950s and '60s, hundreds of plantation families started leaving Pa'ia after buying new homes in Dream City, a Kahului housing community developed by Alexander & Baldwin. This left Pa'ia's plantation camps empty and its streets virtually deserted by the mid '60s. Then, in the late '60s and early '70s, a new breed of folks began to fill the town—hippies from the mainland. Today, the flower children have given way to people attracted to nearby Hookipa and Spreckelsville beaches. **Hookipa Beach County Park** is one of Maui's premier surfing and windsurfing spots, with waves often reaching 15 feet.

After Hookipa, the road cuts through sugarcane and pineapple fields backed by bright swards of green. It then begins to meander rollercoaster style over hills and through valleys. At almost every turn, a new waterfall and swimming hole appears. **Maliko,** a particularly lush valley studded with palms, is the site of an old Hawaiian village. Wispy pines line one side of the road while banana plantations stand on the other. Along with the more familiar kind, you'll see the small, firm apple bananas (also called Chinese bananas). From time to time, tiny depressions—miniature valleys—dip away from the edge of the road. Locals will tell you that the very tart fruit of the lilikoi vines and trees (a.k.a. passion fruit) will make you pucker up when you bite into it. The buttercuplike blossoms of hau plants open yellow in the morning and turn red as the day goes by. Thick ferns form roadside walls and the wind whistles through stands of bamboo. One of the most striking trees you'll see on the way to Hana is the rainbow eucalyptus, whose smooth bark is vertically striped with red, yellow, green, and brown, as if someone had sat in its branches and poured paint down the trunk.

Grazing beef cattle add clumps of brown and beige to the many shades of green. You'll pass a lone house or church here and there. Some of the homes in this area have windmills for generating power. An island resident told me that one house even has bicycle-generated power: the people who live there spend part of each day pedaling away. Rusty roadside mail boxes and flower-filled front yards mark residential neighborhoods, such as **Kailua,** an old plantation town. As the road climbs, panoramic views open up. While you'll come to a pipe at the edge of the highway that always spouts fresh spring water, I wouldn't recommend stopping for a drink. The water is wonderfully clear and refreshing, but it's near a tricky curve where traffic could be a problem if you stopped.

The highway's first bridge is about 13 miles from Pa'ia, at **Twin Falls,** which is just what its name implies: a pair of waterfalls. To find them, park your car and walk along the right side of the stream until you reach the pool at the base of the cascades. Continue walking to the left for a bit and you'll discover a more impressive fall, also with a pool that is fine for swimming. You'll see many cars parked by **Puahoka-moa Falls,** which thunders into a rocky stream, bordered by picnic tables. But you may want to resist the temptation to stop here since even more spectacular waterfalls await you further along.

Kaumahina State Park is about 24 miles from Hana. The name means "the rising moon," and I'm told that if you stick around after dark, you'll see the lunar orb coming up over the ocean. In addition to picnic tables and shelters, you'll find drinking water and flush toilets here. The crunch of tourists usually thins out by 3 p.m. or so. To **camp** here, you'll need to obtain a free permit. Like the bony, interlacing fingers of dozens of hands, roots cover the ground, so be careful when walking. Across the road from the park, a lookout point affords a sweeping view of the royal blue Pacific and **Keanae Peninsula.** A quilt of taro patches spreads across this flat jut of land, the site of a Hawaiian village.

After another mile, massive **Honomanu Valley** sprawls to the right, with its 3000-foot cliffs and plummeting waterfall. Bright African tulips dapple the highway's greenery with reddish-orange blossoms. Dipping down to sea level, the road passes unpeopled **Honomanu Beach,** where the waves are excellent for **surfing.** Mountain apple trees are abundant along this stretch. The small, red pear-shaped fruit has a delicious white pulp inside. Hana Highway then takes a steep climb before coming to

Keanae Aboretum, where you can splash in **Piinaau Stream.** A hike into the arboretum, filled with many native as well as introduced plants, will give a glimpse of pre-modern, natural Hawaii. Various kinds of taro grow in patches and tropical trees provide shade. The **Keanae Overlook,** a favorite among shutterbugs, is near mile marker 17. You'll gaze down on smooth, rectangular taro patches and the ocean. Haleakala volcano is visible in the distance. Almost a mile after mile marker 20, **Wailua Lookout** provides a vista of Wailua Canyon and small Wailua Village, with its tiny church.

There are many fruit stands around here. When the vendors are absent, it's not unusual for them to leave the fruit beside an honor box where customers are trusted to drop in their money. Back along the craggy lava coast, you might see local fishermen casting nets into the ocean just as ancient Hawaiians did. Distinctive monkeypod trees, bright red hibiscus, and yellow and white plumeria are plentiful in this area. If you hike or drive into **Keanae village,** you'll get a close-up view of the missionary church that was built in 1860, allowed to deteriorate, and then reconstructed by locals in 1969. About a half mile from Wailua Lookout, **Waikane Falls** are considered by many to be the most picturesque in the region. At **Puaakaa State Park,** the road passes two more waterfalls with inviting pools. White angel trumpet flowers dangle from branches like Christmas tree ornaments. Hawaiian strawberries, which turn white when they ripen, grow wild. You'll also see heliconia, also known as lobster claws because of their shape and orange color, and yellow poincianas, whose fluffy blossoms have inspired people to nickname them ''scrambled egg trees.''

Next you'll come to oceanside **Waianapanapa State Park,** where you can camp out on a rise overlooking a black sand beach or stay in a cabin. Pronounced *Why*-ah-*nah*-pah-*nah*-pah, the name means ''glistening water.'' The swimming is good and there is an abundance of hiking trails and wild fruit waiting to be plucked. There are caves here you can hike to and swim in. According to a legend about one aquatic grotto, a Hawaiian princess fled from her jealous husband. She made the mistake of hiding on a ledge in a cave that was known to be used by lovers for secret rendezvous. Her frenzied husband ran everywhere searching for his wayward wife. While he was catching his breath by the cave, he caught something else as well: a glimpse of her reflection in the water at the grotto's entrance. Convinced that she must have gone there to meet another man, he flew into a rage, bashing her head against the walls and killing her. Locals say that it is the princess's blood that, even today, turns the cave pool red every April. Some claim you can still hear the echoes of her terrified shrieks. However, according to others, the water turns crimson from the tiny red shrimps that multiply in the pool in the spring and the ''shrieks'' are the sound of the wind whooshing in and out of the grotto. Exploration of Waianapanapa's caves is best left to divers or extremely strong swimmers. Everyone else can swim off the striking black sand beach.

Just outside Hana, 60-acre **Helani Gardens** is worth a stop, especially if Howard Cooper, the man who runs it, is around to give a bit of commentary on some of the more unusual plants and flowers. Admission is a couple of dollars. (For exact directions, call 248–8274.) There are quite a few other nurseries for exotic flowers in the area.

The coastal, agricultural town of **Hana** itself lies about three miles south of Waianapanapa State Park. It was from this area that King Kamehameha the Great first set out, in 1795, to conquer the rest of the Hawaiian Islands (a mission he didn't accomplish until 1810). Some of the first Polynesians to arrive in Hawaii settled in Hana. Today it is home to a larger percentage of Hawaiians than most other parts of the island. You won't find any city lights here. The air is frequently filled with the squawks of mynah birds or hymns sung in the Hawaiian language wafting from a church. Petite corrugated-roof houses are surrounded by bright flowers and expanses of ranchland. The only bank, the Bank of Hawaii, opens for 90 minutes a day from Monday to Thursday, then for a whopping three hours on Friday. Mount Haleakala's lower slopes are given over to thick forests.

In its heyday, before Europeans came to Hawaii, Hana bustled with some 45,000 to 75,000 people. By the 1830s, the population had shrunk to about 11,000. Beginning in the 1860s, sugar plantation workers were hustled in from China, Japan, Portugal, and the Philippines. The mills kept the economy healthy, especially during the 1920s and '30s. Then, after WW II, the plantations began to close down and massive unemployment swept through the area. To stave off disaster, Paul Fagan, a San Francisco entrepreneur, purchased sugar plantation land and turned it into a ranch for Herefords. In an equally daring move, he built a cluster of low-rise buildings and opened one of Hawaii's earliest non-Waikiki resorts. Thanks to this visionary, both the ranch and the resort, now called **Hotel Hana-Maui,** remain Hana's economic backbone. As a matter of fact, they are virtually the only game in town as far as jobs go. If you wonder about the large **white stone cross** on a hill overlooking Hana, it was planted there by Fagan's wife to honor her husband after his death in 1960.

Until it was sold in the late 1980s, Hotel Hana-Maui was caught in a steady decline. The new owners pumped goo-gobs of money into it, doing extensive renovations and also buying 4500 acres of ranch land. Today it is one of Hawaii's most exclusive, expensive, and isolated resorts. Across from the two nearby public tennis courts, **Wananalua Church** dates back to the 1830s. In an intertwining of heritage, much of the volcanic stone used to build this European-style church was taken from the remains of ancient Hawaiian *heiau* (temples). And the mortar was ground from coral that was collected by Hawaiians who dived from old-style Polynesian canoes.

Up the road from the hotel, **Hana Bay** is a good place to stumble into conversations with locals. People swear by the teriyaki hamburgers at **Tutu's Snack Bar** in Hana Beach Park across from the bay. The stand also served good *saimin* (noodle soup) and *haupia* (coconut) ice cream. The beach here has grayish sand, a combination of pulverized coral and volcanic ash. The calm waters make swimming pleasant. A short trek from the bay will take you to the **Lighthouse on Kauiki Head.** In the old days, people would stand on top of the hill and let the rest of the village know when they spotted schools of fish so they could cast their nets. A legend explains why clouds so often hover so close to the top of this cinder cone: The demi-god Maui united a pair of lovers here for eternity by turning one into the hill and the other into the mist above it. **Red Cinder Beach,** which has drawn nude bathers for quite some time, lies over Kauiki hill. Celebrated for having inspired so many Hawaiians to convert to Christianity, Queen Kaahumanu (a wife of King Kamehameha the Great) was born in one of the caves near Kauiki in 1768.

Few people pass through Hana without stopping at **Hasegawa's General Store.** With a tangle of miscellaneous merchandise cluttering its shelves, it won't get any points for neatness. But whether you're looking for a T-shirt, a whimsical bumper sticker, baby food, barbed wire, or film, you're likely to find it here.

Several miles south of Hana, **Oheo Gulch** lies near the coastal edge of Haleakala. Frequently referred to as "Seven Pools" or "Seven Sacred Pools," these volcanic swimming holes are actually closer to 30 in number. From a bridge, you'll look down on a handful, and depending on when you arrive, you'll see people cooling off in or diving into the holes in the charcoal colored rock. I don't recommend your following the lead of locals and diving in, since hidden rocks can be deadly if you're not familiar with the holes. The best time to visit Oheo Gulch is early in the morning, before the van- and car-loads of tourists arrive.

A couple of miles further along the narrow, bumpy road, **Kipahulu** is the site of **Charles Lindbergh's grave.** Extremely fond of Hana, this master aviator chose to be buried here, at difficult-to-find **Palapala Hoomau Congregational Church.** On your way here, you'll pass houses ranging from plush to small and weather-beaten, **St. Paul's Church,** and the tall chimney (partially obscured by vegetation) of a crumbling sugar mill. Just beyond the mill and a pasture, you'll come to a steel gate and a road that leads to the church. Inside, you might find a program from a recent service containing hymns written in Hawaiian. This plain, one-room house of worship was built in 1864 on a cliff high above the Pacific. You'll find Lindbergh's tombstone in the small graveyard. Of the many places he had been around the world, he is said to have found Hana the most beautiful. Against his doctor's advice, he left his sick-bed in New York and returned to Hana to die in 1974.

Just past this church, the road from Hana dries up. If you're traveling in a four-wheel-drive vehicle, consider turning onto nearby **Kaupo Road.** This slim, rugged stretch is rocky and desolate in parts. But it offers breathtaking cliffside views of the ocean far below. Some 5 miles from Lindbergh's grave (about 15 miles from Hana), you'll come to the small, crowded Kaupo general store, which sells everything from groceries and cold sodas to fishing tackle. Also along this route, a weathered graveyard where many Hawaiians are buried surrounds **Hui Aloha Church,** a small wooden building. The road ends near Makena.

WHAT TO SEE AND DO

PERSONAL FAVORITES

The spectacular drive from Kahului to **Hana** (see Maui introductory section)

Driving through **Upcountry Maui** (see Maui introductory section)

Exploring the paniolo (cowboy) town of **Makawao** (see Maui introductory section)

*Visiting **Hui Noeau Visual Arts Center** in Makawao (see Maui introductory section and More About Sights below)

Watching the sun rise over **Haleakala Crater** (see Maui introductory section and Biking in Sports)

Exploring **Haleakala National Park** (see Maui introductory section)

The **mountain bike ride** down Haleakala volcano (see Sports)

Whale watching (see Maui introductory section and More About Sights, below)

Wandering through the historic whaling port of **Lahaina** (see Maui introductory section)

*Indicates little-known treasures or places that are off the beaten path.

Snorkeling or scuba diving at **Molokini Crater** (see Sports)
*Swimming at **Oneloa Beach,** also called **Big Beach** (see Beaches)
Hiking in **Iao Valley State Park** (see Maui introductory section)
*Picnicking or camping in **Polipoli Spring State Recreational Area**
(see Maui introductory section and Sports)

SIGHTS

Hawaiiana

Hale Hoikeike • *2375-A Main St. (Route 32), Wailuku; 244–3326* • Also referred to as Bailey House and Maui Historical Society Museum, this old missionary house was built of lava rock in 1833. It contains Maui's most extensive public collection of Hawaiian artifacts. On display as well are furniture and clothing used by missionaries. *Admission: $2 for adults, 50¢ for children 11 and younger. Open 10 a.m.–4:30 p.m. daily.*

Hana Cultural Center Museum • *Hana, eastern East Maui; 248–8622* • The second name of this museum, Hale Waiwai 'O Hana, means "House of Treasures of Hana." Among the relics of days gone by here are photographs of Hana's sugar mill era during the early 1900s and everyday Hawaiian implements such as poi pounders.

The Hawaii Experience Omni Theater • *824 Front St., by Lahainaluna Rd., Lahaina; 661–1111* • Near Longhi's and Kimo's restaurants, this theater features a 45-minute film about Hawaii with a presentation similar to that of the multimedia New York Experience. Tucked among the old-style buildings along Front St., the Omni sports a 60-foot domed screen, which almost seems to surround the audience. With flashing lights and 8-channel sound, the movie is truly entertaining. The adjacent souvenir shop sells unusual T-shirts and beach bags, among other items. *Admission: $7 for adults; $5 for children.*

More Remnants of the Past

Alexander & Baldwin Sugar Museum • *3957 Hansen Rd., Puunene (just south of Kahului); 871–8058* • One of Hawaii's "Big Five" companies, Alexander & Baldwin has its roots in the islands' early New England missionary families. The corporation, now one of Maui's main landowners, is responsible for planting thousands of acres of sugarcane. Built in 1902 adjacent to the company's sugar mill, this museum originally served as the home of the plantation overseer. Today its displays concerning sugar production and immigrant life outline the importance of cane to Hawaii's economy and cultural history. In addition to a working model of a sugar processing machine and a restored 1882 steam locomotive, you'll see old photographs; a field worker's uniform (protective hat, scarf, and gloves); and a reproduction of a labor contract, written in Hawaiian, that dates back to 1876. *Admission: $2 for adults; $1 for children 6–17. Open 9:30 a.m.–4:00 p.m. Mon.–Sat.*

Baldwin Home Museum • *Front St., near Dickenson, Lahaina (next door to the Master's Reading Room); 661–3262* • This is a good place to stop as soon as you get to Lahaina, since members of the Lahaina Restoration Foundation supply free walking tour maps of the historic town. The 19th-century home of the Reverend Dwight Baldwin, M.D., this whitewashed stone building contains furnishings that once belonged to this missionary physician. From the mid-1830s through the late 1860s, Dr. Baldwin and his family welcomed countless patients, fellow missionaries, whaling captains, and members of the congregation who came to chat or to seek medicine or advice. Today visitors are invited to take a look at the living room, with its Steinway piano; the imported china on display in the dining room; the gleaming four-poster koa wood bed in the master bedroom; and Maui's first toilet in the bathroom. On Lei Day, the second and last Thursday of every month, local women string aromatic flower garlands out front. *Admission: $2 for adults; $1 for children (or free if accompanied by a parent). Open 9 a.m.–4:30 p.m. Mon.–Sun.*

Pioneer Inn • *at Hotel and Wharf Sts., Lahaina; 661–3636* • A red-roofed, multiwinged building, this hotel, bar, and restaurant is one of Lahaina's most distinctive landmarks. The forest green wooden structure is set off with white railings around the first-floor veranda and the second-floor balcony. Dating back to 1901, the inn consists of a creaky original wing with tiny, dim, airless guest rooms and a newer wing (1966) with more comfortable accommodations. The bar and restaurant (popular among non-guests) are decorated with nautical implements and other artifacts. Some amusing old rules are displayed by the reception desk: "Women is not allow in you room. If you wet or burn you bed you going out. You are not allow to gambel in you room. You are not allow in the down stears in the seating room or in the dinering room or in the kitchen when you are drunk. You must use a shirt when you come to the seating room." Things have calmed down here considerably since the days when these rules were vigorously enforced. Just across the street is the sprawling old **banyan tree.**

Carthaginian II • *Lahaina Harbor, in front of the Pioneer Inn; 661–8527* • The original square-rigged *Carthaginian* (featured in *Hawaii*, the movie based on James Michener's novel) was anchored at the harbor here until 1972. It was replaced by the current replica of a 19th-century brig, and turned into a floating museum. Built in Germany during the 1920s and later transformed into the type of ship the missionaries sailed in from New England to Hawaii, the *Carthaginian II* underwent extensive renovations in 1989. A video presentation on whales and the sounds they make is a highlight of the small exhibit below deck. (For information about where and when to spot whales, check with the **Whale Report Center** on the dock next to the ship.) *Admission: $2 for adults; $1 for children (or free if accompanied by a parent). Open 10 a.m.–4 p.m. Mon.–Sat. and 11 a.m.–4 p.m. Sun.*

Wo Hing Society • *858 Front St., Lahaina; 661–3262* • In 1912, immigrant Chinese plantation laborers constructed this building as a temple home and recreational center for unmarried men who had fallen on hard times. The Lahaina Restoration Foundation has since turned it into a museum celebrating the contributions of the Chinese to the island. Films about Hawaii dating back to the late 1890s are shown here and Chinese artifacts are on display. You'll find Maui's only public Taoist altar upstairs. *Admission to temple: $1.50 adults; free for children accompanied by parents. Open 9 a.m.–4:30 p.m. Mon.–Sat.; noon–4:30 p.m. Sun.*

Lahaina Whaling Museum • *865 Front St., Lahaina; 661–4775* • All kinds of whaling artifacts are displayed at this museum started by T-shirt king Rick Ralston (owner of the Crazy Shirts chain). You'll see weathered harpoons, old photographs, and intricately carved ivory. *Free admission. Open 9 a.m.–10 p.m. daily.*

The Seamen's Cemetery • *next to the cemetery of Maria Lanakila Church at Wainee and Dickenson sts., Lahaina* • Buried here are many sailors whose presence as a group in Hawaii helped shape the islands. One, for example, is Thomas Johnson, a black seaman who traveled on the whaler *Acushnet* with Herman Melville. Only a couple of tombstones are left in this 19th-century graveyard.

The Seaman's Hospital • *1024 Front St., Lahaina; 661–3262* • King Kamehameha III held his royal bashes here after this house was built in the 1830s as a place for the monarch to entertain. In later years, the U.S. government turned it into a hospital for seamen from whaling ships. Today it houses **Lahaina Printsellers,** which stocks old maps and nautical charts. *Open daily 10 a.m.–4 p.m.*

The Lahaina Courthouse • *Wharf St., Lahaina (by the banyan tree)* • King Kamehameha III never finished building the palace he began near this site. After a storm destroyed the partial structure (which had been serving as a courthouse), the stones, wood, and other materials were used to create this new courthouse in 1859. Now the District Court is found here, along with the **Lahaina Art Society,** which displays some of its paintings in the cells of the old jail. *Open from 10 a.m.–4 p.m. daily.*

Wailoa Church and Cemetery • *Wainee St., near Shaw St., Lahaina* • This small house of worship stands on the site of Wainee, the first stone church built in Hawaii (in 1832). It could accommodate as many as 3000 parishioners. However, apparently the gods were not with Wainee. It was badly damaged in a storm in 1858. Then in 1894 it was set ablaze by Hawaiians furious at the overthrow of their monarchy and the U.S. annexation of the islands. Not only did the church represent foreign influence in Hawaii, but Wainee's minister believed that the American takeover had been a good move. Another church was built here, but it too suffered a fire and then was tousled in a storm. The church that stands here today was built in 1953. Poke around the graveyard, and you'll discover the tombstones of Hawaiian *alii,* commoners, and missionary families. Queen Keopuolani, a wife of King Kamehameha the Great, was laid to rest here. One of the earliest members of the *alii* to convert to Christianity, she played a major role in spreading missionary influence by convincing other Hawaiians to follow suit.

Hale Paahao • *Prison Rd., off Wainee St., Lahaina* • Near the Baldwin Mission House, a.k.a. Baldwin House Museum, this prison was built in 1852 to give rowdy, drunken whalers a place to spend the night while thinking about changing their disruptive ways. Seamen who found themselves confined to "Stuck-in-Irons House" were guilty of such crimes as not getting back to their ships by the curfew at sunset. *Open 9 a.m.–4 p.m. daily.*

***Lahaina Jodo Mission** • *Ala Moana St., close to Mala Wharf, outside the main part of Lahaina* • The imposing bronze Buddha that commands this tranquil, flower-filled park was put here in 1968 to commemorate the centennial of the arrival of Hawaii's first Japanese immigrants. The pagoda, with its trio of roofs, serves as a sacred memorial to the dead. Both the pagoda and the small temple are closed to the public, but you're welcome to look inside.

***Lahainaluna School** • *about 2 miles up Mt. Ball, which backs Lahaina; 661–0313* • Touted as the oldest secondary school west of the

Rockies, Lahainaluna opened its doors as a mission school in 1931. The majority of the first students were Hawaiians. The missionaries had only recently turned the islands' language into a written one, by developing a 12-letter alphabet and printed material in Hawaiian was scarce. Within three years, the school was printing the island's first newspaper—in Hawaiian. *Hale Pai* ("printing house"), in the oldest building on campus, was soon producing text books on grammar, history, and a variety of other subjects. Classes were taught in Hawaiian until the 1870s. David Malo, the school's most celebrated graduate, was a member of the first class. He went on to become a teacher, minister, and author of highly respected scholarly works. Today when the school year draws to a close, the students take part in an annual performance of music and dance and they play ancient Hawaiian sports, all in Malo's honor.

Whaler's Village Museum • *Whaler's Village, Kaanapali Parkway, Kaanapali; 661–5992* • In an open-air, waterfront shopping center, the displays at this small museum include 19th-century whaling implements, photos, the skeleton of a 30-foot sperm whale, and an old whaling boat. Videos provide additional information about Maui's lucrative whaling years. *Free admission. Open 9:30 a.m.–10:30 p.m. daily.*

Church of the Holy Ghost • *Route 37, near Pukalani, in Kula, upcountry* • Along the road to to the summit of Haleakala, you'll pass this distinctive church. Octagonal in shape, it sits on a hill, the volcano looming behind it in the distance. It was constructed in 1897 for Portuguese immigrants who labored on upcountry farms and ranches.

Nature's Best

Oheo Gulch • *Route 31, Kipahulu district of Haleakala National Park* • After the long drive to Hana, many visitors continue for 10 miles to the swimming holes of Oheo Gulch. Often called Seven Sacred Pools, they actually number more than two dozen and no one ever considered them sacred. As it heads for the ocean, the Oheo Stream flows down the valley, spilling into a series of volcanic holes in the rocks. Especially during midday, many travelers cool off here. To avoid the hordes, come early in the morning or late in the day. Some locals take dangerous dives into the holes from overhanging ledges, but I don't suggest you try this stunt. The setting is quite appealing, with its smoky gray rocks and expansive green slopes that end up at the edge of the royal blue Pacific. The energetic can hike to upper pools and waterfalls. Makahiku Falls is about a half mile from the parking lot, while Waimoku Falls is about a mile and a half farther.

Maui Tropical Plantation • *Route 30 at Waikapu; 244–7643* • These 120 flourishing acres are a working plantation. Take a narrated tram tour and you'll learn about both agriculture and aquaculture on Maui. You'll also have a chance to taste freshly cut sugarcane and various tropical fruits. Protea, orchids, and anthuriums blossom in the flower nursery. Fresh fruit and gifts are on sale in the plantation's market. Stay for lunch or a barbecue dinner. *Open 9 a.m.–5 p.m. daily.*

Kepaniwai Park and Heritage Gardens • *Iao Valley Road (Route 32), Iao Valley* • Traditional homes from various cultures stand in this peaceful county park in tribute to the people who have come together to create a present-day Hawaii. You'll see a Hawaiian grass shelter, a Portuguese villa, and a New England salt box, among buildings from other locales.

Kula Botanical Gardens • *Route 37; 878–1715, upcountry* • Streams snake across attractively landscaped mountain slopes in this trim, verdant oasis. This land once belonged to Princess Kinoiki Kekaulike. Complete with picnic tables, the grounds also contain a picturesque pond, bridges, rare native koa trees, bamboo, stately Norfolk pines, and an array of orchids and other colorful flowers. *Open 9 a.m.–4 p.m. Admission: $4 for adults; 75¢ for children ages 6–12.*

Sunrise Protea Farm • *Route 378, upcountry, 3 miles past the Haleakala National Park turnoff; 878–2119* • After admiring these exotic proteas at this farm 4000 feet above the Pacific, you can arrange to have cut flowers sent to the mainland. *Open 7:30 a.m.–4 p.m. daily.*

Wine Tasting

Tedeschi Vineyards and Winery • *Ulupalakua Ranch, upcountry (off Route 37); 878–6058* • Take a tour of the birthplace of the only wine produced on Maui. The tasting is done in a former jail that was once also used as a ladies' card room. Try the pineapple wine or the Maui Blanc de Noirs brut champagne. Begun as a sugar plantation in 1850, this ranch once had a billiard hall, a bowling alley, and the only swimming pool in Hawaii. Both King Kalakaua and Robert Louis Stevenson visited often. The poet has written that he was stunned by the amount of champagne the monarch was able to consume while he relaxed in this upcountry getaway. *Free admission. Open 9 a.m.–5 p.m. daily.*

Animals

Whale Watching • *Nov. through Mar.* • Humpback whales—which can be 40 feet long and weigh 40 tons—also appear along the coasts of other Hawaiian islands. Maui, however, is recognized as the whale watching capital of the archipelago, since the bulk of these massive visitors come to its shores. You'll get the most out of your vigil if you've packed a pair of binoculars. **The Pacific Whale Foundation** (879–8811) sponsors cruises, with a marine biologist on board, to raise money for research and preservation of the endangered humpbacks. Many other whale watching cruises depart from Lahaina. In recent years, some ecologists have urged people to cut down on the large number of boats that go searching for whales. These crafts can be disruptive to breeding and the general comfort of the animals. Instead of traveling by sea, they suggest you choose a vantage point on land, such as the top of the cinder cone at Big Beach in the Makena area. You'll still have a great view as these giant mammals fluke (lift their tails into the air), breach (jump partially out of the water), and spurt water from their blowholes. Check with the **Whale Report Center** on the dock next to the *Cartha-ginian II* in Lahaina for up-to-date information about the best places to spot whales.

Kahana Pond Wildlife Sanctuary • *Route 396, between Kahului Airport and Kahului* • Bird lovers won't want to miss this waterfowl preserve where migratory fowl and native birds mingle. They flutter around the serene pond peppered with tiny grassy islets.

The Arts

*****Hui Noeau Visual Arts Center** • *2841 Baldwin Ave., Makawao; 572–6560* • A nonprofit art institute, Hui Noeau was begun in 1934 by a group of 21 women, headed by Ethel Baldwin, a prominent member of one of Maui's leading families. Located upcountry in the paniolo (cowboy) town of Makawao, it is housed in Mediterranean-style Kaluanui, the old Baldwin estate built in 1917. This gracious, sunny two-story building, now a historic landmark, rests on the upper slopes of Haleakala volcano, providing a perfect vantage point for a panoramic vista of the island. Near the entrance to the driveway, you'll see the ruins of one of Maui's first sugar mills. The nine acres of grassy grounds are studded with tall Cook Island pines and camphor trees. A reflecting pool sets off a scrupulously trim garden.

Its name meaning "Club of Skills," Hui Noeau was born as a casual gathering of women who painted, sketched, and made pottery in the gardens of various homes, including Kaluanui. One of the other meeting places was the Baldwin beach house at Spreckelsville, where Ethel Baldwin's grandson, Colin Cameron (president of the multimil-lion-dollar Maui Land and Pineapple Company) now lives. Today, ex-hibits and classes are open to visitors. Lectures throughout the year might be given on weaving; hand papermaking with fibers; Japanese woodblock printing; or raku and the art of tea ceremony ceramics. The ceramics studio, by the way, is housed in the former stables and tack rooms out back. Workshops might be held on lei-making, Chinese calligraphy, photography, jewelry-making, and sculpture. The Hui currently has more than 600 members, from Hawaii, Australia, the mainland, and Canada. Every spring, **Art Maui,** the island's most acclaimed art show, is held here. An annual Christmas craft fair also takes place on these grounds. After wandering through the stately home, stop at the gift shop, which carries baskets, local posters, ceramics, hand-painted clothing, and other imaginatively rendered items. *Free admission. Open daily, 10 a.m.–3 p.m.*

TOURS AND CRUISES

If you'd rather leave the driving, sailing, flying, or guiding to someone else while you ramble around Maui, here are some of the best ways to get acquainted with the island and its surrounding waters. Most transportation is air-conditioned.

BY CAR: When friends of mine recently returned from a vacation on Maui, they couldn't stop raving about **Guides of Maui** (877–4042), a personalized tour company based in Kahului. A guide will meet you at your hotel or condo and, in your rental car, drive you wherever you want to go. Guides are happy to share their favorite hideaways—secluded beaches and other little-known scenic spots. If you like, they'll take you to meet residents (perhaps with similar interests, hobbies, or professions) at their homes. Begun by a part-Hawaiian woman, this behind-the-scenes manner of getting to know Maui has really caught on. *Cost: about $140 for a full day for two people; about $10 for each additional person.*

BY BUS, VAN, OR LIMOUSINE: The transportation offered by Maui's main tour companies ranges from hulking motorcoaches to minivans and cozy limousines. Visitors are picked up either at their hotels or nearby. Be sure to ask about the size of the vehicle, the number of passengers, and the locations and number of stops so that there are no surprises once you climb aboard. The driver keeps up a constant commentary while you cruise along the road. Sometimes the jokes he or she must have told hundreds of times can wear on your nerves. On one bus tour, I thought I would scream if the driver asked us to repeat "Alo————HAH" one more time as we boarded and reboarded. However, visitors can usually cull intriguing and amusing bits of information from the drivers' good-natured chatter. Most people tip them about $1 per passenger.

There are four basic kinds of tours. Sometimes called the Circle Island Tour (even though none of these actually circles this expansive island), the first is a full-day excursion. It might include Iao Needle, the historic attractions in the town of Wailuku, and other parts of West and Central Maui. Other tours make stops at Haleakala volcano and upcountry, while still others throw in some good snorkeling. These tours cost about $30 to $50 for adults, half-price for children.

If you'd like to confine yourself to Haleakala and upcountry, these half-day tours—which usually include stops at Tedeschi Vineyards and Winery and a protea farm—cost about $42 for adults and $21 for children.

One of the most popular trips is the 6-hour Haleakala Sunrise Tour, which begins in the dark of night. By the time you reach the summit of the volcano, the sun will be ready to start coming up over the crater. A continental breakfast, sometimes with champagne, is served atop the mountain by some companies. The cost is about $45.

The van tours to Hana, the remote village at the end of a spectacular jungled cliffside highway, can last nearly 12 hours. While these excursions can be exhausting, the scenery along the way is fabulous and you don't have to worry about dealing with the tricky twists and turns yourself. These tours cost about $50 to $65 per person.

Maui's tour companies are based in Kahului. One of the state's most experienced is **Gray Line** (245–3344 or (800) 367–2420, Mon.–Sat., 6 a.m.–5 p.m). The tours it offers are to Haleakala, Iao Valley/Lahaina, highlights of the whole island, upcountry Maui, or Hana. Lunch is not included in the price of tours. **No Ka Oi Scenic Tours** (871–9008) conducts a popular Hana tour, including lunch. Other good outfits that run a variety of excursions are **Robert's Hawaii Tours** (947–3939); **Polynesian Adventure Tours** ((800) 622–3011); **Trans Hawaiian Services** ((800) 533–8765); and **Akamai Tours** ((800) 922–6485).

BY FOOT: To get the most out of a stroll around Lahaina, pick up a **walking-tour map** at the Baldwin Home Museum at 696 Front St. (661–3262).

BY SEA: Like motorcoach tours, most of Maui's cruises put you in the center of a huge group of fellow tourists. **Trilogy** (661–4743 or (800)874–2666), based in Lahaina, runs a very good ½-day snorkeling excursion to fish-filled Molokini islet, actually a partially submerged volcanic crater. To take advantage of the best (calmest) sea conditions, the tour departs at 6:30 a.m. Delicious home-baked cinnamon rolls help wake up drowsy passengers. Costing about $65, this cruise leaves from Maalaea Harbor. From December to April, Trilogy conducts **whale**

watching trips for about $35. Other cruises take vacationers to the island of Lanai (a 1½ hour ride) for a day of snorkeling at a marine preserve, riding kayaks, taking a glass-bottom boat trip, or cooling out in hammocks strung between coconut palms in the $4-million beach park known as **Club Lanai.** There are good hiking trails and activities also include volleyball, biking, and treasure hunts. An open bar sits on a mini-island in the middle of a pond. A continental breakfast is served, as well as a barbecue lunch that might include goodies such as teriyaki chicken; Korean-style ribs, mahimahi, pasta salad, and garlic bread. **Club Lanai Cruise** (871–1144; $100 per person) and **Captain Nemo's** (661–5555 or (800)367–8088; about $75 for snorkelers, $90 for certified divers, and $100 for non-certified divers. $ per person) also sail to this plush playground on this largely undeveloped island. The Trilogy tour to Lanai, which costs about $125, leaves from Lahaina Harbor at 6:30 a.m. and returns at 4:30 p.m. No alcohol is served, but you may bring your own.

From December to April, **humpback whales** migrate to Hawaii's waters to give birth, especially around Maui. A variety of cruises operate out of Lahaina for close-up views of the majestic members of this endangered species. In addition to Trilogy, whale watching excursions are run by the **Pacific Whale Foundation** (879–8811), based in Kihei; **Captain Zodiac Raft Expedition** (667–5351) in Lahaina; **Seabern Yachts** (661–8110) in Lahaina; and **Ocean Activities Center** (879–4485) in Kihei. The cost is about $32 for adults and $16 for children.

Hordes of young people climb aboard catamarans and other boats for dinner and sunset cruises, many of which feature open bars and dancing. You'll sit down to dinner on the 65-foot, 119-passenger **Spirit of Windjammer** schooner (667–6834; about $48), accompanied by live entertainment. The 2½-hour sunset sail on a 58-foot catamaran run by **Captain Nemo's Ocean Emporium** (661–5555; about $33) features champagne, beer, and pupus (appetizers). For a more intimate experience, try a 2½-hour gourmet dinner sail on a luxury yacht with **Genesis Sailing Charters** (667–5667; about $58). There are never more than 20 passengers at once.

BY HELICOPTER: Since these whirls are so expensive, you should choose your tour carefully. The most exciting tour on Maui is the 90-minute flight over Hana and Haleakala (about $140 per person). Less interesting is the 30-minute tour of West Maui (about $80 to $100). If you can afford it, the 2-hour tour of the whole island (about $200) will introduce you to inaccessible, flourishing valleys, and thundering waterfalls, as well as stark Haleakala volcano. If you are planning to visit the Big Island of Hawaii or Kauai, I recommend that you wait to take a helicopter tour over one of those islands.

Maui's leading helicopter companies include the following:

Papillon (669–4884 or, from the mainland: (800)367–7095). Most flights depart from Kapalua Hills Heliport, about a 10-minute drive north of the Kaanapali resort area. Some flights also leave from Kahului Airport. Among its tours, Papillon offers a West Maui/Molokai trip for about $200, with views of Molokai's sea cliffs and Kalaupapa Peninsula; a one-hour sunset flight for about $180; a 60-minute Haleakala sunrise tour plus a 30-minute touch-down for a continental breakfast for $220; and a 7-hour Hana whirl for $325.

A tour of West Maui and the north shore of Molokai costs about $180 (65 minutes), through **Kenai** (871–6463 or (800) 367–2603)

Maui Helicopters (879–1601 or (800)367–8003) runs sunrise and sunset flights; a tour to Hana over upcountry Maui's farms and ranches; an excursion above Haleakala crater; and a whirl above the whaling town of Lahaina and the Kaanapali Beach resort of West Maui. Rates range from about $120 to $215. Maui Helicopters also offers fly/drive packages to Hana—a 40-minute helicopter flight one way and a van ride in the other direction—for about $185.

Two other good companies offering a variety of tours are **South Seas Helicopters** (871–8844) and **Hawaiian Helicopters** (669–4884).

BY RAIL: Especially popular among Japanese tourists, the steam-driven **Lahaina Kaanapali & Pacific Railroad** (661–0089) takes passengers on a 12-mile round-trip ride through thick sugarcane fields. It was inspired by the turn-of-the-century trains that carried cane to the mills. Six round-trip excursions run daily between Puukolii and Lahaina. Free transportation is provided to Lahaina Harbor and the historic section of Front Street in a double-decker bus. The train ride costs about $9 round trip and $6 one way for adults; half price for children.

ADVENTURE TOURS: Based in Makawao (cowboy country), **Adventure Island Tours** ((800) 234–HIKE) takes the energetic trekking through remote, natural parts of Maui. Also in Makawao, **Outer Island Adventures** ((808) 572–6396) specializes in hikes and hike/bike trips complete with gourmet lunches. They also offer sightseeing tours in air-conditioned vehicles. For mountain bike rides down Haleakala volcano, as well as horseback riding and other hiking tours, see Sports.

ART TOURS: With **Maui Art Tours** (572–8374 or 572–7132), you'll spend a half or a full day being whisked around in a stretch limo to the homes and studios of some of Maui's most prominent artists. You'll discuss their work and their particular field in general over coffee or tea. Each full-day trip, two to five passengers at a time visit three or four different artists. Together visitors and the guide decide what types of art they would like to see in progress—from basketry and painting to sculpture and ceramics. The day includes a catered picnic lunch—you'll dine with crystal and china—on the scenic grounds of Makawao's visual arts center. The meal features such gourmet treats as asparagus mousse with caviar and passion fruit cheesecake. Arrangements to participate can be made through your hotel activities desk or by calling directly. Please give at least 48 hours' notice. *Cost: about $150 per person for a full day; $75 for a half-day excursion.*

BEACHES

Two of Maui's most beautiful beaches are at the island's extremes: Kaanapali in northwestern West Maui and Oneloa (Big Beach) in southwestern East Maui. Spend some time driving around the island to see the variety of sandy (or sometimes rocky) shores.

Kaanapali • *northern West Maui* • This is where most of Maui's visitors congregate—and with good reason. A broad, 3-mile, palm-edged crescent, Kaanapali (Maui's premier resort area) is lined with attractive hotels and condominiums. All kinds of watersports facilities are available here. There's also a healthy selection of restaurants and shops, both in accommodations and in oceanfront Whaler's Village Shopping Center.

Oneloa • *in Makena, East Maui* • Often called *Big Beach,* this 100-foot-wide, 3000-foot-long beige sandy strip faces the islands of Kahoolawe and Molokini. Even though a honeymooning couple I know was staying in gorgeous Kaanapali, they took the 45-minute drive to this beach every day. They explained they loved the low density of fellow bathers, especially during the week. Most of the people who use this beach are locals, and my friends said they enjoyed getting into conversations with residents here. During the '60s, Oneloa was a favorite hangout for hippies, who lounged in and around the tents they pitched. People can still camp out here. The area is full of cacti, jade plants, and kiawe (mesquite) trees, with huge gnarled trunks bent over by the wind. Like an overgrown gumdrop, Puu O'Lai (cinder cone) stands guard over the beach. On the other side of this volcanic hill is **Little Beach.** This isolated pocket lures nude bathers even though police periodically remind them that public nudity is illegal in Hawaii.

Honolua • *Route 30, north of Napili and Kapalua, West Maui* • Surfing and windsurfing are excellent at this picturesque beach.

D.T. Fleming State Park • *northern West Maui, off Route 30, just north of Kapalua Resort* • Another beach that is quiet on weekdays, this one has picnic tables, grills, rest rooms, and showers. However, the tides can be quite powerful, so swimming is recommended only to the strongest of swimmers.

Napili Beach • *northern West Maui, just outside Napili Kai Beach Club* • This tranquil sandy crescent is a good choice for escape. The facilities of the condominium, however, are for guests only.

Honokowai Beach • *just north of Kaanapali, West Maui* • Although this beach is rocky, you can splash around in the volcanic pool. Picnic tables and showers are provided.

Lahaina Beach • *West Maui* • This slim stretch of sand, ending at Lahaina's small boat harbor, borders waters calmed by an offshore reef.

Puunoa Beach • *just north of the Lahaina harbor, West Maui* • Another beach that is enclosed by reefs, this one extends to the old Mala Wharf.

Olowalu Beach • *off Route 30, south of Lahaina, West Maui* • There are no facilities here and you'll have to park at the edge of the road, but this sandy beach is one of the island's best snorkeling spots. Petroglyphs are found in the Olowalu area.

Papalua State Wayside Park • *south of Olowalu, West Maui* • The offshore reef ensures calm waters and good snorkeling at this sandy stretch bordered by kiawe trees.

Awalua Beach • *near Olowalu, West Maui* • Locals flock here for the swimming and new surfers try to hone their craft.

Kamaole Beaches • *Kihei, East Maui* • If you want to mingle with locals, these three beach parks are a good place to start. You might stumble upon a soccer game or see families flying kites.

Wailea Beaches • *west coast of East Maui* • In this peaceful region—a far cry from the bustle of Kaanapali—five appealing crescents claim two coastal miles.

Hookipa • *near the town of Paʻia, not far from Kahului, East Maui* • Many people stop here on their way to Hana, but most come for the windsurfing and surfing, which boardsailors swear by. You can rent sports equipment in shops in the town of Paʻia. Championship international competitions in both sports are held here each year. If you plan to hike on the way to Hana, this is a good place to fill your water bottles.

Baldwin Beach Park • *near Pa'ia, East Maui* • Named for one of Maui's oldest, wealthiest, and most influential families, this beach is a local favorite. Camping tents are pitched along this shore.

Spreckelsville Beach • *near Pa'ia, East Maui* • This beach is great for windsurfing.

Hamoa Beach • *just past Hana, toward Kaupo, East Maui* • An unspoiled stretch of salt and pepper sand backed by thick greenery and rolling hills, this beach is lapped by exceptionally clear blue water. The Hotel Hana Maui uses this beach, and its facilities are reserved for guests. However, as with all of Hawaii's beaches, the sand and water are public property.

Black Sand Beach • *Waianapanapa State Park, near Hana, East Maui* • This ebony sand was created when hot lava hit cold water.

*Kaihalulu Beach • *Hana, East Maui* • Also called **Red Cinder Beach,** this is one of Maui's most remote coves. The rugged path that leads to it begins near the community center and a Japanese cemetery. However, it isn't marked, so you'd do well to ask a resident to point you in the right direction. You'll walk around Kauiki Hill, with meadows and hills in the distance. The coastline in this area is rocky and the ocean quite rough. When you arrive at the beach, you'll see that the cove is enclosed by 300-foot-tall rust-colored, iron-rich cliffs. As more visitors stumble upon this beach, the nudists that used to sunbathe here are dwindling in number.

SPORTS

Maui offers a host of ways to keep in shape, most of them aquatic. At the **Ocean Activities Center** (879–4485 or (800) 376–8047, ext. 448; 715 Front St., Lahaina; or The Wailea Shopping Village), you can rent Windsurfers, wave skis, outrigger canoes, Hobie cats, snorkel gear, and boogie boards. Lessons are also available. In addition, arrangements for sailing and fishing charters can be made at the Lahaina harbor, as well as for scuba and snorkeling excursions, para-sailing, and cruises to watch whales or to visit neighboring Lanai and Molokini. If you're interested in renting jet skis, surfing, or water skiing, head to Kaanapali Beach, which also has excellent golf courses and tennis courts.

BIKING: One of the most enjoyable things to do on Maui is cycle 38 miles down Haleakala volcano, especially after watching the sun rise over the crater. The temperature, landscape, and aromas all change dramatically from top to bottom. Cold, rocky, and brown at the summit, the volcano gives way to expanses of wheat-colored grass and the air grows warmer. Views of the West Maui Mountains and patchwork farmland open up in the distance. With each hairpin turn, more tufts of green appear. Mail boxes stand in front of houses set back from the road. A wonderful fragrance envelopes bikers as they pass through a eucalyptus forest. The sweet perfume of plumeria blossoms wafts by. Everyone is glad to have visors to pull down (helmets are mandatory) when they are hit by a barrage of tiny bugs as they zip through pineapple fields. The smell of molasses from sugarcane mills greets cyclers when they come to cane fields. Suddenly everything is green and the steep mountain slopes have flattened out considerably. With heads bent to the ground, lethargic cows and horses stand in pastures behind fences made of branches and wire. By the time they reach the bottom, the bikers—who shivered in hats, gloves, sweaters, and windbreakers at the summit—have stripped down to shorts and T-shirts.

Several companies operate these mountain bike excursions. Most offer two versions: the sunrise expedition and the later morning trip. You'll be picked up in the middle of the night (around 3 a.m.) if you plan to get to the summit before the sun does. Vans carry passengers and the mountain bikes you'll be given at the top. It's freezing up there, so even though the bike companies provide windbreakers and gloves, be sure to bring your own warm layers as well. A breakfast of pastries is served while the sun starts to bathe the crater in light. After riding down, you'll have a picnic or brunch at a restaurant. Those who don't want to drag themselves out of bed can take the later morning trip, which also ends with a picnic or meal in a restaurant. Most of the riding is coasting so it's more fun than hard work. The leader keeps in touch by walkie-talkie with the driver of the van, who follows the train of bikers, watching to make sure everyone is okay. Through hand signals, the leader tells riders to slow down, stop, or pull over when necessary. If anyone gets tired, they are welcome to ride in the van.

The companies that lead these excursions are **Maui Downhill** (871–2155 or (800)535–2453); **Maui Mountain Cruisers** (572–0195 or (800) 232–MAUI); and the pioneering outfit, **Cruiser Bob's** (667–7717 or (800)654–7717). Rates average about $90 per person.

Outer Island Adventures (P.O. Box 996, Makawao, HI 96768; 572–6396) conducts seven-night biking and hiking excursions on Maui.

If you'd simply like to rent a bicycle, note that it is safest not to venture onto Maui's two-lane highway or other narrow main roads. It's best just to ride in the immediate vicinity of your accommodation. **Let's Rent a Bike** (661–3037) in Kaanapali will let you have one for about $5 an hour, while rates at **AA Go Go Bike Hawaii** (661–3063) in Lahaina are about $10 an hour.

CAMPING: On the road to Hana, **H.P. Baldwin Beach Park,** one of the county parks on Maui's east side, is especially popular among the outdoor set. Facilities at Hawaii's county campgrounds include water, toilets, cold-water outdoor showers, tables, and grills. For information about various county sites, permits, and fees (which are minimal), contact the **Department of Parks and Recreation,** (War Memorial Gym, Kaahumanu Ave., Wailuku, HI 96793; 244–9018).

Two pleasant state parks are also found in eastern Maui: **Waianapanapa State Park** (about 20 miles from the Kahului Airport), on a precipice high above a beach with striking ebony sand (park caretaker: 248–8061); and **Kaumahina State Wayside Park** (25 miles east of the airport), on a palisade above the coast. **Polipoli Springs,** another state park, spreads along the lofty slopes of Haleakala volcano. It's a good choice for day trips as well as overnight adventures. In addition to a stand of California redwoods, you'll find one cabin and campgrounds. The cabin is reserved far in advance, so make your plans early if you want ready-made shelter here. From many lookout points, you'll have wonderful panoramic views of Maui. All of Hawaii's state parks are free. For camping permits and cabin reservations, contact **State Parks Camping,** (Division of State Parks, P.O. Box 1049, Wailuku, HI 96793; (808)244–4354).

Haleakala National Park, about 10 miles south of Hana and 60 from Kahului Airport, is also free. In this moonscape of a park, the silence—broken only by the wind and the crunching of rocks and stones underfoot—is intense. There is no water or other facilities, except the three multibunk cabins on the crater floor. These dirt-cheap lodgings are always booked—months in advance, in fact. To secure a bed, you'll have to enter a lottery by sending your choice of dates to **Haleakala National Park** (P.O. Box 369, Makawao, HI 96768. For further information, call 572–9177 or 572–9306). The cabin bunk fee includes firewood, but you'll have to bring your own food, sleeping bag, and light. Even though it is quite chilly at this altitude, the sun is surprisingly strong, so be sure to bring sunglasses and sunblock. Light rain gear will also come in handy.

If you're interested in a guided, individualized camping and hiking trip, try **Personal Maui** (P.O. Box 1834, Makawao, HI 96768; 367–8047); or **Outer Island Adventures** (572–6396).

(Also see Hiking in this chapter.)

FISHING: Deep-sea fishing enthusiasts on Maui are rewarded with catches of mahi-mahi, Pacific blue marlin, tuna, and other game fish. No licenses are required. The harbors in Lahaina and Maalaea (southern West Maui) are the places to make arrangements for charters. Trips are usually four or eight hours and boats provide all gear, including bait and ice. Try the **Aloha Activity Center** (667–9564) in Lahaina or **Excel Charters** (661–5559) in Maalaea.

For shore fishing, the most sheltered spots are along the southern coast. Many locals enjoy fishing from piers at Kahului Harbor or off beaches and in ponds not far from Kahului Airport. Although people are no longer permitted to fish from Hamoa Beach (used by the Hotel Hana-Maui), the fishing off Hana Beach State Park is quite good. Many of Maui's best shore fishing spots are at the end of rugged roads that require four-wheel-drive vehicles and are difficult to find. The **Hawaii Visitors Bureau** should be able to hook you up with a shore fishing guide who is familiar with the places where cliffs and the surf are safest.

GOLF: Maui has quite a few top-rated championship greens, in both East and West Maui. Hugging the lower mountain slopes of West Maui, the **Royal Kaanapali North Golf Course** was designed by Robert Trent Jones, Sr. It is the longest course on the island. Both this green and its sister, **Royal Kaanapali South Golf Course** (661–3691 for either), are graced with wonderful ocean and mountain scenery. Green fees are about $75 for both resort guests and the public. I'm not a golfer, but I could spend hours on the two gorgeous Arnold Palmer courses at the **Kapalua Golf Club** (669–8044). The fourth hole on the Bay Course here is in a stunning location atop a lofty peninsula enclosed by the ocean. Complete with duck-filled ponds and rolling hills, these courses are very challenging. Along with its neighboring Village Course, this Kapalua gem is considered among the world's best by the pros. These two courses play host to a popular annual tournament. Green fees are about $60 for Kapalua Bay Resort guests and $90 for the public.

At the **Wailea Golf Club Orange Course,** the lava rock walls were built more than a century ago. Another course here is the **Wailea Golf Club Blue Course** (879–2966 for both Orange and Blue). Maui's public courses are less expensive, but their views are no less expansive. **Pukalani Country Club** (572–1336) sprawls in Kula, upcountry Maui. Note that the high altitude may make you somewhat light-headed. Green fees are only about $45. In an arid part of the island, **Silversword Golf Course** (874–0777) sits in Kihei near Wailea. Fees are also about $45. At **Waiehu Municipal** (243–7400) by the beach at Wailuku, fees are a mere $20 or so for a round during the week and $25 on weekends. If you want to learn the strokes, you can take lessons at any of Maui's courses or contact **Sunseeker Golf Schools** (667–7111) at the Royal Kaanapali or **Maui Parbusters** (572–8062) at Puakalani. To find out about golf **tournaments,** contact Rolfing Productions at (669–4844).

HIKING: Maui is criss-crossed with countless scenic hiking trails, some near resort areas. Many people enjoy walking in the tropical rain forest of **Iao Valley** in West Maui, with its prominent green Iao Needle rock formation. At **Olowalu,** south of Kaanapali, you can take the 30-minute trek to the **petroglyphs** not far from the Olowalu Store. After taking a road through the sugarcane fields into Olowalu Valley, you'll spot the ancient rock carvings on a promontory about 25 feet above the path. On the far side of the cinder cone at **Oneloa Beach** (a.k.a. **Big Beach**) in Makena in southern East Maui, a trail leads from **Little Beach** 360 feet to the top of the cone. Any time of year, the views from this wooded site are exceptional. During the winter, this is a wonderful vantage point for **whale watching.**

The extremely hardy may want to hike into stark, eerie **Haleakala Crater,** with its three dozen miles of steep trails. Keep in mind that the high altitude will make you tire more quickly than usual and you may become light-headed. Periodically from June through August, national park rangers lead morning nature walks starting at the Visitor Center or Hosmer Grove (call 572–9306 for details). **Sliding Sands** is one of the volcano's least rigorous trails. Beginning at the summit, it dips about four miles to the crater floor. Plan to spend twice as much time getting back up as going down. Even if you don't go all the way to the bottom, you'll still get more than a taste of Haleakala's rugged appeal. Be sure to dress warmly and to bring lightweight rain gear. However, you'll also need sunglasses and sunblock.

Few avid hikers can resist the trails along the **Hana Highway.** You'll need at least three or four days of hiking and camping to truly appreciate this jungled region. Hookipa Beach County Park, a popular surfing and windsurfing hangout, is a good place to stop to fill water bottles. First you'll come to **Twin Falls** about 20 miles from Kahului Airport. The four-mile round-trip trail begins by the turnoff right before Hoolawa Bridge. Follow the jeep road through meadows and by Hoolawa Stream. Wild guava is plentiful, both the common yellow type and the smaller, red, strawberry variety. Various trails off the jeep road lead to small pools. At one pool, about a half mile along the trail, you might see locals diving off the rocky lava ledge over which a waterfall crashes into a pool. Residents also swing into the water from the rope tied to a branch of a banyan tree. This is a popular site for skinny dipping. Whenever you're swimming in natural pools, be careful of submerged rocks. The jeep road roughly follows the river for another mile before you reach an irrigation ditch. After about 100 yards along the bank of the ditch, you'll see the first of the Twin Falls. Take the trail on the right around this fall to get to the second fall. Take a refreshing dip in the pool below either waterfall.

About six miles beyond Twin Falls on the highway, the **Waikamoi Ridge Trail Nature Walk** is some two miles round trip. You'll know you've come to the beginning of the trail when you see a parking area and a picnic table on a cliff overlooking the highway to the right. Passing through a bamboo forest, this trail also goes by mahogany, tree ferns, guavas, and many other kinds of vegetation. Roughly halfway between Kahului and Hana, **Kaumahina State Park** provides flush toilets, drinking water, shelters, and picnic tables. The crowd of tourists here usually disappears by 3 p.m. or so. This park sits on a bluff with a dramatic view of the Keanae Peninsula. If you hike into the **Keanae Arboretum,** beyond Kaumahina State Park and Honomanu Beach, you'll find all kinds of labeled native and imported plants, as well as many varieties of taro growing in patches. Hiking about a quarter mile to the caves at **Waianapanapa State Park,** near Hana, is a popular pursuit. At **Oheo Gulch** (a.k.a. Seven Pools or Seven Sacred Pools), beyond Hana, don't stop at the lower pools that are usually crowded with visitors. The first of the upper falls is only about a half mile from the parking lot.

One of the best outfits for guided treks is **Hike Maui,** run by Ken Schmitt, who leads half-day, full-day, and overnight rambles along coasts, through rain forests, or into the mountains. Swimming is often part of the trip. A naturalist, botanist, geologist, and anthropologist, Schmitt has also studied history, zoology, mythology, and classical languages. Along the way, he identifies plants, flowers, birds, and animals, plucking fruit for hikers to sample. A picnic lunch is always included, as well as round-trip transportation from central Maui. Day hikes range from 5 to 12 hours, including driving time, and prices run from about $60 to $100 per adult, less for children.

The hikes conducted by **Outer Island Adventures** (572–6396) range from easy to difficult and last from a few hours to all day. Prices run from about $60 to $135 for adults, with discounts for children under age 14. Picnics or gourmet lunches are part of the package. Many trips include stops for swimming. Another good company to try is **Personal Maui** (P.O. Box 1834, Makawao, HI 96768; 367–8047).

For more information about various trails, contact **State Parks Camping,** Division of State Parks, P.O. Box 1049, Wailuku, HI 96793; 244–4354.

(Also see Camping in this chapter.)

HORSEBACK RIDING: For an upscale horseback excursion, try **Adventures on Horseback** (242–7445). You'll have a choice in where you'd like to go and you'll mount and dismount to explore the coast and rain forest. A five-hour tour with a gourmet lunch costs about $110 per person. Through **Makena Stables** (879–0244), you can go horse-back riding on Ulupalakua Ranch, and to Tedeschi Winery for a catered picnic. **Pony Express** (667–2200), based in Kula, specializes in rides into Haleakala crater. One of these trips runs from 9:30 a.m. to 2 p.m. (about $95 per person) covering 7½ miles to and from the crater floor, where riders unsaddle themselves for a picnic lunch. The other excursion lasts from 9:30 a.m. to 5 p.m. (about $125 per person), and in addition to visiting the crater floor, riders are treated to many more natural wonders. Pony Express also offers a leisurely ride through the rolling hillside and through a eucalyptus forest about a mile below the entrance to Haleakala Crater. Pony Express keeps its groups small, so be sure to make reservations at least three days in advance.

In Hana, **Charlie's Trail Rides and Pack Trips** (contact Charlie Aki, c/o Kaupo Store, Kaupo, Maui, HI 96713; (808) 248–8209) presides over horseback riding. Mr. Aki takes two to six adventurers on two-day jaunts that depart from Kaupo Gap for camping in Haleakala crater. The cost is about $150 per person for four to six people or $200 for two to three people. A $75 deposit is required.

PARASAILING: To be gently lifted into the air by a parachute, contact **Wailea Parasail** (879–1999) in Kihei or **Para-Sailing Hawaii** in Lahaina (661–5322).

SAILING: Many of the larger hotels run their own catamaran or glass-bottom boat cruises or sailing trips. I've heard good reports about the **Lin Wah II** (661–3392 or (800) 833–5800), a 65-foot Chinese glass-bottom junk. Serious sailors with a taste for luxury yachts will want to contact **Seabern Yachts Sail Charters** (661–8110) in Lahaina. Up to only six passengers take each of these cruises, which range in length from a two-hour sail to an overnight charter and include sailing instruction and snorkeling. Other reputable companies are **Island Marine Activities** (800) 833–5800 in Lahaina; **Genesis Yacht Charters** (667–5667) in Lahaina; and **Sail Windward Sea Yacht Charters** (235–2984) based in Kaneohe, Oahu.

(Also see Tours and Cruises.)

SCUBA DIVING: In addition to Maui's coasts, there are some wonderful dive sites off neighboring Lanai and Molokai. Although it's not on the water, the lovely neo-Victorian **Plantation Inn** (667–9225; (800) 433–6815; or FAX: (808) 667–9293) in Lahaina has an excellent dive program with economical week-long scuba packages. Full certification (about $275 for the four-day course) is available on Maui in PADI, NAUI, and SSCI training programs. Among the most experienced dive operators are **Ed Robinson's Hawaiian Reef Divers** (879–3584; (800) 635–1273) in Lahaina; **Capt. Nemo's** (661–2059); **Hawaiian Reef Divers** (667–7647) in Lahaina; **Central Pacific Divers** (661–8718; (800) 551–6767; FAX: (808) 667–9293) in Lahaina; **Lahaina Divers** (667–6280; 667–7496; (800) 367–8047; FAX: (808) 661–5195); **Ocean Activities Center** (879–4485; (800) 367–8047; FAX: (808) 879–7427) in Kihei and Lahaina; the **Dive Shop** (879–5172 or (800) 367–8047) in Kihei; **Maui Dive Shop** (661–5388); **Extended Horizons** (667–0611) and **Scuba Schools of Maui** (661–8036).

Some of Maui's best diving is at **Molokini,** a partially submerged volcano whose crater just breaks the surface of the ocean. Also great for snorkelers, depths here range from 10 feet to more than 60 at the dropoff. A variety of companies offers scuba trips to this location, including the **Ocean Activities Center** (879–4485) and **Lahaina Divers** (667–6280). The sail to the islet takes about 45 minutes. Schools of yellow butterfly fish and others swarm snorkelers and divers, who often feed them bread crumbs. Porpoises often frolic in these waters. From November to April, there's a good chance you'll also spot humpback whales. Even if you don't see one of these gigantic mammals, you may hear them calling out to each other when you're under water.

SNORKELING: **Molokini Crater,** off the Makena coast, is Maui's mecca for snorkelers as well as scuba divers. The 3½-hour **Trilogy Snorkeling Cruise** (661–4743 or (800) 874–2666) is one of the most enjoyable ways to get here. Masks and fins are provided. You'll see all kinds of multicolored fish, including triggerfish, yellow tang, orangespine, and bluespine, unicornfish, bluestripe snapper, pinktail durgeon, arc-eye hawkfish, and even white-tip sharks, octopi, and zebra moray eels. Since the catamaran departs early (about 6:30 a.m.) when the water is calmest, you'll be treated to a breakfast of homemade cinnamon rolls with coffee or tea. Lunch might consist of pineapple-glazed chicken, tossed green salad, corn on the cob, and freshly baked bread. Other snorkeling excursions are conducted by the nonprofit **Pacific Whale Foundation** (879–8811); **Hawaiian Reef Divers** (667–7647); and **Ocean Activities Center** (879–4485).

You can also snorkel right off the beach, in places including **Black Rock** (also called Puu KeKaa) in front of the Sheraton Maui on Kaanapali Beach; **Honolua Bay, Kapalua Beach, Olowalu Beach, Makena Landing,** on the small bay (which is covered with black lava pebbles); and **La Perouse Bay.**

SURFING: **Hookipa Beach** is probably the most popular surfing (and windsurfing) spot on Maui. Championship surfing competitions are held here every year. **Honolua Bay,** in northern West Maui, also has excellent waves, which can rise up to 15 feet during the winter. For an overview of the hot-dogging surfers, drive down the red dirt road at Lipoa Point. You'll cut through pineapple fields before reaching the 200-foot cliffs that serve as a perfect vantage point for the surfers' aquatic ballet. Surfing lessons are given through hotels in Kaanapali, Wailea, Kapalua, and Makena. Look for the stacks of boards, which rent for about $9 to $11 an hour. Places that specialize in instruction include **Lahaina Beach Center** (661–5762); **Maui Surfing and Windsurfing School** (871–6231); and **Maui Beach Center** (667–4355 and 661–4941).

TENNIS: There are tennis courts all over Maui, in hotels, condos, and elsewhere. The **Wailea Tennis Center** (879–1958) has the greatest number: 3 grass courts, nearly a dozen hard surface courts, and a 1000-seat tennis stadium. The **Royal Lahaina Tennis Ranch** (661–3611) at Kaanapali boasts 11 courts, 6 of which are lighted. **Kapalua Tennis Garden** (669–5677) has ten lighted courts on which tennis attire is required. The six-court **Makena Tennis Club** (879–8777) is one of Maui's newest. Court time generally runs about $10 a day per person; resort guests get discounts. Private lessons cost about $50 an hour and are widely available (as well as cheaper group lessons). You'll find two lighted public courts at **Lahaina's Civic Center** (661–4685) and two in **Hana.**

WATERSKIING: The only game in town is **Lahaina Water Ski** (661–5988). Rates run from about $28 for 15 minutes for one person to $78 an hour for one to five people.

WINDSURFING: Maui's best beach for boardsailing is **Hookipa Beach,** in northern East Maui, about 35 miles from Lahaina. International competitions take place here throughout the year. Windsurfing gear is sold at stores in nearby Paʻia. Wind and wave conditions are also excellent at **Honolua Bay,** in northern West Maui. Most of the larger hotels give windsurfing lessons, and many won't charge you for the land demonstration on a simulator. Instruction begins at about $40. You'll pay from about $20 to $40 an hour to rent boards without taking lessons. In addition to hotels, lessons are given by **Maui Surfing and Windsurfing School** (871–6231); **Ocean Activities Center** (879–4485); **Lahaina Beach Center** (661–5762); **Kaanapali Windsurfing School** (667–1964); **Hawaiian Sailboard Techniques** (871–5423); **Maui Magic Windsurfing Schools** (877–4816); **Windsurfing West** (871–8733); and **Hi-Tech Sailboards** (877–2111).

WORKING OUT: For weight machines, aerobics classes, and massage, try the **Lahaina Health Club** (2805 Honapiilani Hwy., Lahaina; 667–6684) or the **Kahana Gym** (4310 Lower Honoapiilani Hwy., Kahana; 669–7622). You don't have to be a hotel guest to use the weight room or take aerobics classes at the **Maui Marriott** (667–1200) in Kaanapali, but you will be charged a fee of about $4. One of the island's best health clubs is at the **Westin Maui** (667–2525) in Kaanapali, but, alas, its weights, aerobics classes, and massages are only for hotel guests. Ditto for the health spa in the **Hyatt Regency** (661–1234) in Kaanapali. In Wailea, daily aerobics classes are conducted at the Stouffers Wailea hotel and the **Maui-Inter-Continental Wailea** (879–1922).

SHOPPING

While the larger hotels have clusters of boutiques on the premises, it is more fun (and more economical) to wander in and out of the small stores along Front Street in Lahaina. If you're in the market for locally produced ceramics, jewelry, clothing, candies, and other items, keep an eye out for the **Made on Maui** logo. Shopping centers tend to stay open later (9 a.m.–9 p.m.) than stores elsewhere (usually open 9 a.m.–5 p.m.). Here are some of my favorite spots to part with money:

SHOPPING CENTERS: To go where the locals go, head for the **Kaahumanu Center** (275 Kaahumanu Ave.; 877–3369) in central Kahului. Here among some five dozen shops and restaurants are Hawaii's two main department stores: **Liberty House** and **Shirokiya**, a Japanese contribution to the islands. The indoor, air-conditioned **Lahaina Cannery** (1221 Honoapiilani Hwy., north end of Lahaina; 661–5304) resembles the 1919 Baldwin Packers pineapple cannery that once stood on this site. Three of its most intriguing shops are **Hobie Sports,** with its exhibit of heavy old Hawaiian surfboards contrasted with the modern lightweight variety; **Reyn's,** which sells a better than average selection of aloha shirts; and **Kite Fantasy,** whose name says it all. Toward the south end of Lahaina are **The Wharf** (658 Front St.; 661–8748) and **505 Front Street** (667–2514).

Right on Kaanapali Beach, **Whaler's Village** is an open-air collection of boutiques and waterfront restaurants. There's also a small (free) whaling museum. In addition to a branch of **Liberty House** department store, you'll be able to browse through shops including **Maui on My Mind, Silks Kaanapali, Crazy Shirts, Lahaina Scrimshaw, ACA Joe's,** and the omnipresent **Benetton.**

ALOHA WEAR: I wouldn't bother with highly commercial **Hilo Hattie's** (1000 Limahana Pl., in Lahaina) in West Maui, at least not for aloha wear. However, they also sell the popular **Banana Butter** produced at the Maui Jelly Factory in Makawao. **The Clothes Addict** (579–9266) was born as an antique clothing store; although it has been transformed into a surf shop for the most part, it does still stock vintage aloha shirts (ranging from about $100 to $400, mind you). For other well-made aloha shirts, poke around **Reyn's** (661–5356 at the Lahaina Cannery Shopping Center and 669–5260 in Kapalua). **Liberty House,** with a handful of branches in hotels and elsewhere on Maui, has a healthy choice of moderately priced floral print muumuus and shirts.

ART GALLERIES: There's something about Maui that gets creative juices flowing. Witness the large number of galleries, exhibits, and artists' cooperatives on the island. For details about the work of various artists or items in specific mediums, contact the **Art Information Desk of Maui** (122 Lahainaluna Rd., Lahaina; 667–6224). Throughout the year, exhibits showcase the paintings, ceramics, sculpture, and basketry of an array of local, national, and international artists. Hosted by the Hui Noeau Visual Arts Center every spring **Art Maui** (572–6560) is the island's most celebrated show, featuring the work of the most accomplished local artists. The efforts of island marine artists are displayed for **The Ocean Arts Festival,** held from January through March at Lahaina Galleries (661–0839 or (800) 228–2006) to benefit the Pacific Whale Foundation, a nonprofit research group. Perhaps the best known of these aquatic artists is Robert Lyn Nelson, whose surreal paintings and sculptures combine views from above and below the ocean's surface. Lahaina Galleries has four branches on Maui. The Cousteau Society receives some of the proceeds from the **Maui Marine Art Expo,** held annually from February through March at the Maui Inter-Continental Hotel in Wailea (879–1922). If you'd like to visit artists in their studios, consider taking a **Maui Art Tour** (see Tours for more information).

No art lover should pass up a chance to visit **Hui Noeau Visual Arts Center** (2841 Baldwin Ave., Makawao; 572–6560) in an elegant old estate in paniolo (cowboy) country. (See Sights for details about exhibits and classes.) When the **New Coast Gallery** (Maui Inter-Continental Wailea Hotel, Wailea; 879–2301) isn't hosting the annual Maui Marine Art Expo, it exhibits sculpture, prints, and paintings covering a variety of themes. **Grycner Gallery** (758 Front St., Lahaina; 667–9112) is the only place in Hawaii where you'll be able to purchase the work of R. C. Gorman, famed for his renderings of Navajo women. However, why come all the way to Hawaii to buy a Gorman? See if you like the work of Pegge Hopper, a local painter whose omnipresent works of Hawaiian women seem to have been heavily influenced by Gorman.

Lahaina Printsellers (the Old Seamen's Hospital, 1024 Front St., Lahaina, 667–7843; the Wharf, Lahaina, 661–3579; and Whaler's Village, Kaanapali, 667–7617) stocks antique maps and engravings, some done as early as the 16th century (every item is certified). The old hospital that houses the main Front Street shop once nursed infirm and injured whalers back to health. Ask to see the 18th-century engravings done from the sketches made during the voyages of British Captain James Cook, the first recorded European to visit Hawaii. The gallery can frame the work you buy in gleaming native Hawaiian koa wood. A cooperative called the Lahaina Art Society runs the **Old Jail House Gallery** (649 Wharf St., Lahaina; 661–0111) on the waterfront. More than a few misbehaving whalers were sentenced at this historic former court house and lock-up. **The Village Gallery** (1287 Honoapiilani Hwy., Lahaina; 661–3280) sells much local artwork, from oil paintings to reasonably priced hand-crafted jewelry.

In Pa‘ia, a small frontier town on the road to Hana, an artists' community flourishes. The **Maui Crafts Guild** is located here, along with **Local Woods and Crafts,** and the studio of **Eddie Flotte.** This Philadelphia transplant with a keen eye for everyday details has preserved many a Pa‘ia street scene in watercolor renditions: the town's weathered historic buildings; a group of old men playing cards and drinking soda.

(Also see Crafts.)

BEACH WEAR: Begun as an antique clothing shop, **The Clothes Addict** (579–9266) now concentrates on swimwear and sportswear. Other good choices are **Paradise Clothing** (Whaler's Village, Kaanapali; 661–4638); **Foreign Intrigue** (Whaler's Village, Kaanapali; 667–6671); **Kramer's Men's Wear** (Lahaina Cannery Shopping Center, Lahaina, 661–5377; and Kaahumanu Center, Kahului, 871–8671).

(Also see Aloha Wear and Distinctive Clothing.)

BOOKS: **Wharf Books** (the Wharf Shopping Center, 658 Front St.) stocks a good selection of Hawaiiana titles.

CHOCOLATE: Chocoholics should investigate the chocolate-covered roasted coffee beans at **Escape to Maui** (at the Wharf as well as Lahaina Cannery shopping centers); and more goodies at **Rocky Mountain Chocolate Factory** (Lahaina Cannery).

CRAFTS: The goods sold at **Maui's Best** shops are all made on the island by local artisans and craftspeople. You'll find everything from sweatshirts and bamboo flutes to macadamia nut popcorn and tea. Also on sale are stuffed animals, candles, koa wood bowls, shell jewelry, and silk-screened T-shirts. The original Maui's Best outlet resides at the Kaahumanu Center in Kahului (877–2665) and there's another branch in Kihei (879–4734). **Maui on My Mind** (667–5597 at Lahaina Cannery Shopping Center and 661–5643 at Whaler's Village in Kaanapali stocks stenciled Christmas ornaments, koa wood jewelry boxes, and pillow covers done in Hawaiian quilt designs. At the **Maui Crafts Guild** (579–9697), in the small town of Paʻia on the northern coast of East Maui, you might find intricately woven baskets, handpainted raw silk bags, and sculptures created from handmade paper. Another good Paʻia stop for arts and crafts is **Paʻia Gallery and Gifts** (579–8185).

(Also see Art Galleries, Koa Wood Products, and Distinctive Clothing.)

DISTINCTIVE CLOTHING: **Silks Kaanapali** (667–7133) has a great selection of handpainted women's apparel, as well as kimonos, scarves, belts, and unusual jewelry. More hand-adorned clothing, scarves, jewelry, and handbags are found at **The Painted Lady** (Whaler's Village, Kaanapali; 661–5383). All are original designs by local artists or craftspeople from California. **Apparels of Pauline** (Lahaina Market Place, 770 Front St., Lahaina; 661–4774) and **Maui Four Winds** (820 Front St., Lahaina; 667–7174) both also sell hand-painted shirts and other clothing. For attractive 100% cotton sportswear for men, try **Kula Bay Tropical Clothing** (Lahaina Market Place, 770 Front St., Lahaina; 667–5852). If your head is feeling left out, poke it into **Maui Mad Hatter** (The Wharf Shopping Center, 658 Front St., Lahaina; 661–8125), where you'll find scores of caps and other hats.

FRUIT AND VEGETABLES: At **Paradise Fruit** (1913 Kihei Rd., Kihei; 879–1723) you can buy boxed, inspected pineapples, coconuts, and Maui onions. **Take Home Maui** (121 Dickenson St., Lahaina; 661–8067) does not charge extra for delivering some of the island's nature treats to your hotel or to the airport upon your departure.

HAWAIIAN INSTRUMENTS: For handmade traditional musical instruments, try **Happy Hula Supply** (P.O. Box 238, Wailuku, Maui, HI 96793; 242–4442).

HAWAIIAN MUSIC: **Bounty Music** (Kahului; 871–1141) is the place to go for Hawaiian records and tapes.

HAWAIIAN QUILTS: Introduced by 19th-century New England missionaries, quilts took on a unique life of their own in Hawaii. Instead of the patchwork American style, local quilts have a large, symmetrical single-color design that is appliqued onto a solid-color background. The cut out designs are reminiscent of the snowflake patterns snipped from folded paper by schoolchildren. Since stitches on Hawaiian quilts are minuscule, these bed covers and wall hangings are very time-consuming to create and thus quite costly. A quilt for a double bed could run you

$2200 to $7000 or more. Wall hangings can cost between $450 and $1000 and pillow shams, about $75 to $150. Not only do you need deep pockets to invest in these future family heirlooms, but you also need a lot of patience: A commissioned quilt can take from six months to two years to complete. Try the **Quilt Connection** (572–0537) or contact artist **Wailani Johansen** (250 Front St., Lahaina; 661–0731).

(Also see Crafts.)

JEWELRY: Wales & Co. (661–8885) is a fine jewelry store specializing in Hawaiian heirloom jewelry, which comes with a lifetime guarantee. Silver bracelets run about $250 and gold bracelets begin at about $500. Special orders are welcome. Brass or turquoise and silver antique pieces can be found at **Yoki Boutique** (579–9249). Both **Silks Kaanapali** (667–7133) and **Madeline Michaels Collectibles** (708 Front St., Lahaina; 661–4198) have good selections of jewelry you won't find anywhere else. Try **Crown Pearls International** (667–7839 at Whaler's Village and 661–8234 on Front St.) for top quality pearls, coral, emeralds, and other fine gems and stones at good prices.

(Also see Crafts and Distinctive Clothing.)

KITES: Try **Kite Fantasy** (661–4766) at the Lahaina Cannery Shopping Center on Honoapiilani Hwy. in Lahaina.

KOA WOOD PRODUCTS: In upcountry Maui, **John of Maui & Sons** (100 Haiku Rd., Haiku; 575–2863) should have some koa wood items among its carved bowls, plates, boxes, and other crafts. Note that this lustrous native Hawaiian wood is becoming more scarce and thus more expensive than in years past.

(Also see Crafts.)

KONA COFFEE: For Kona and other blends of Hawaiian coffee (which is grown on the Big Island of Hawaii), try **Sir Wildred's** (the Lahaina Cannery, Lahaina; 667–1941) or **Take Home Maui** (Dickenson St., Lahaina; 667–7056).

MACADAMIA NUTS: These are grown on the Big Island of Hawaii, but you'll have no problem finding them at most grocery stores and many other shops.

MAUI POTATO CHIPS: You'll pay more than you might expect, but the thick, flavorful **Original Maui Kitch'n Cook'd Potato Chips** are worth every penny (and every calorie). Quite a few other brands with similar names vie for your dollars, but locals swear by the real McCoy. Bags of these crispy spuds are available in most grocery stores.

MAUI WINE: **Tedeschi Vineyards and Winery** (upcountry Maui; 878–6058) produces the state's only local wine. You can taste-test Maui Blush, Maui Blanc (pineapple wine), or Maui Brut-Blanc de Noirs (homegrown bubbly) before buying at the winery or pluck a bottle from one of the grocery shelves around the island.

MICKEY MOUSE ITEMS: Talk about specializing . . . Everything at the **Maui Mouse House** (661–5758)—from towels, shirts, baby clothes, and stuffed animals to Christmas ornaments, watches, and stamps—comes with Mickey Mouse's face or body on it.

PERFUME: If you'd like to take Hawaiian aromas home, stop at **Island Tan** (760 Front St., Lahaina, 661–8296; and Whaler's Village, Kaanapali), which sells locally produced fragrances in addition to cosmetics.

SCRIMSHAW: More scrimshaw is sold in Maui than anywhere else in the world (even New England). This art form dates back to Maui's 19th-century whaling days. These new or antique etched bones, teeth, and tusks are sold in many Lahaina shops. At **Lahaina Scrimshaw** (845 Front St., Lahaina; 661–8820), prices range from under $10 for key chains and pendants to thousands for antiques or carved elephant tusk sculptures.

T-SHIRTS: While you'll encounter scores of stores selling T-shirts, **Crazy Shirts**—with its quality tailoring and wide variety of designs—is the king. This statewide chain store has several locations in Lahaina, including the Front Street and Lahaina Cannery branches. Also worth checking out is **Sun-Tees Hawaii** (Limahana Rd., Lahaina; 667–1995), which stocks silk-screened shirts with imaginative and unusual designs.
  (Also see Crafts and Beach Wear.)

NIGHT LIFE

   When the stars come out, most of Maui's partying crowd heads for bars, discos, night clubs, lounges, luaus, and dinner cruises in and around Kaanapali, Lahaina, and Wailea. Some restaurants turn into local hangouts, with music and heavy-duty socializing. Many hotels have some kind of entertainment, at least on weekends, perhaps a contemporary combo or a single Hawaiian singer strumming a ukulele and crooning haunting traditional melodies. For sunset and dinner sails, turn to Tours and Cruises. When you're in the mood to see a side of Maui most visitors miss, find out what's doing at Kahului's Maui Community Arts and Cultural Center. In addition to two theaters, this complex has a spacious gallery.

Hawaiian Style

Most luaus, all with plentiful authentic Hawaiian (and modified Hawaiian) foods, feature lively Polynesian revues. I've heard good things about the luaus at the Inter-Continental Wailea Hotel (the setting is a lawn at the edge of the Pacific) and the Hyatt Regency Maui in Kaanapali. However, I recommend checking newspapers for the occasional local luaus hosted by civic groups or other community organizations to raise money for various causes. Many people find these usually smaller-scale affairs more enjoyable than the crowded, commercial shebangs hosted by or near hotels. For a comfortable balance between commercial and intimate, try the beachfront Old Lahaina Luau (505 Front St., Lahaina; 667–1988). Guests may choose between sitting at tables or on tatami mats. *The cost for adults is about $40 and for children under age 13, about $18.*

Maui Tropical Plantation's Hawaiian Country Barbecue • *Wailuku; 244–7643* • When cowboys came to Hawaii from South America, Hawaiian tongues turned the word ''Espanol'' (Spanish) into ''Paniolo.'' This paniolo (Hawaiian cowboy) party is kicked off with a narrated tram tour of acres of the state's most important agricultural crops. Then appetites are satisfied with a filling barbecue dinner, accompanied by an open bar, a Hawaiian-style country-and-western musical performance, and square dancing.

Hosted Mon., Wed., and Fri. from 5:30 p.m. to 8:30 p.m., this affair runs about $40 for adults, $30 for children aged 5 to 12, and $6 for children under 5.

Makai Bar • *Maui Marriot Hotel, Kaanapali; 667–1200* • Try this night spot for Hawaiian entertainment with an ocean view.

Local Hangouts and Happenings

Nanatomi's • *667–7902* • Local bands draw crowds at this night club.

Banana Moon • *Maui Marriott, Kaanapali; 667–1200* • You'll hear top 40 music at this flashy disco that attracts a youthful crowd of locals and tourists over age 21. *Open 9 p.m.–2 a.m. nightly.*

Blackie's Bar • *Blackie's Boat Yard, Honoapillani Hwy., La-haina; 667–7979* • In a distinctive octagonal building, this jazz club spotlights live trios and other groups. This isn't a place for the late night set, since the live music usually ends by around 8 p.m.

Maui Community Theater • *Iao Theater, Wailuku; 242–6969* • This local theater group may be moving into the new Maui Community Arts and Cultural Center in Kahului. Dating back to the turn of the century, it is one of Maui's earliest. The group puts on about half a dozen productions a year, from Broadway musicals to variety shows. *Tickets run about $11 for adults, and less for seniors and children under age 17.*

Baldwin Theatre Guild • *Kahului; 242–5821* • Various come-dies, dramas, and muscals are put on by this group each year. *Tickets cost about $7 for adults, $4 for students, and $5 for seniors.*

Kapalua Music Festival • *Kapalua Resort; 669–5273 or (800) 367–8500* • Every August since 1982, the soothing sounds of European clas-sical music have floated through the air in northern Western Maui dur-ing this festival. Renowned musicians come from the New York and Chicago Philharmonic Orchestras, Julliard, and other parts of the main-land and the world. The glorious, verdant grounds of the Kapalua Re-sort make this a particularly appealing setting. *Tickets cost about $12 for adults and $8 for children aged 6 to 12.*

Maui Symphony Orchestra • *244–5439* • One of the symphony's most popular performances is the July 4th concert, which takes place on the picturesque Kaanapali Golf Course. Fireworks punctuate the mu-sic. In addition to a Christmas concert, the symphony also plays two al fresco pop performances, a European classical concert, and an opera event. *Tickets begin at about $4 for adults and $1 for children.*

International FIlm Festival • *Kaahumanu Center, Kahului; 944–7200 (Honolulu headquarters)* • Films from the U.S., the Pacific, and Asia are screened from the end of November to the beginning of De-cember.

Other Night Spots and Discos

Spats II • *Hyatt Regency Maui, Kaanapali; 667–7474* • This Ital-ian restaurant is transformed into a disco at 10 p.m. From Sun. to Thurs. it remains open until 2 a.m., until 4 a.m. on Fri. and Sat. Geared toward a 30-something crowd, Spats II is furnished with antique reproductions and elegant decor. People generally dress up for this club.

El Crab Catcher ● *Whaler's Village, Kaanapali; 661–4423* ● Live music is served up along with the seafood, from 9:30 p.m. to 12:30 a.m. every night. A Hawaiian group frequently plays.

Inu Inu Lounge ● *Maui Inter-Continental Wailea, 879–1922* ● Attracting a young crowd, mainly from the nearby resorts, this lounge features oldies or live rock and big bands. *Open 9 p.m.–2 a.m.*

CULINARY MAUI

Maui's restaurants are concentrated in West Maui and northwestern East Maui. Kahului and Wailuku are home to a selection of good, casual eateries patronized mainly by locals. Some of them serve Hawaiian cuisine. You'll notice that, unless you're at a luau, contemporary "Hawaiian food" usually includes items such as Spam and eggs, Portuguese sausage, and saimin (noodle soup with vegetables and meat)—a reflection of the islands' varied ethnic influences. **Chung's,** in Wailuku, packs them in for real local breakfasts. **Takamiya's,** also in Wailuku, and **Casanova Deli,** in Makawao, are good places to stop for picnic fixin's if you're headed upcountry. **Ming Yuen** serves generous Cantonese meals in Kahului. With many delicious vegetarian entrees, **Polli's** is a popular Mexican restaurant (located both in Makawao and Kihei). On your way to Hana, stop at **Uncle Harry's Fruit Stand; Charley's,** in Paʻia, for pasta and pizza; or **Picnics,** also in Paʻia, for tofu burgers, spinach and nut sandwiches, cappuccino, and smoothies (yogurt shakes). Maui's top-rated restaurants include **The Plantation Veranda** and **The Bay Club** at the Kapalua Bay Resort; **Longhi's, Avalon,** and **Kimo's,** all on Front Street in Lahaina; **Gerard's,** on the veranda of the Victorian-style Plantation Inn on Lahainaluna Road in Lahaina; cozy **Chez Paul,** in Olowalu, just south of Lahaina; **The Prince Court,** at the Maui Prince hotel in Makena; and **Haliimaile General Store,** in upcountry Maui.

The **Dairy Queen** in Kihei sells hot malasadas (Portuguese donuts without holes). Nearby is **Paradise Fruit,** a popular pit stop on Kihei Road for yogurt fruit shakes and sprouts-and-avocado-on-whole-grain-bread-type sandwiches. Head to **Komoda Store** in Makawao for delicious creampuffs. Affectionately known as Maui Potato Chips, **The Original Maui Kitch'n Cook'd Potato Chips** fly off supermarket shelves, despite their hefty price tag (sometimes more than $4 a bag). These famous crunchy chips have many competitors (such as Maui Style

Potato Chips and Hawaiian Potato Chips), but you should try to stick with the originals. Cut from unpeeled potatoes, they are surprisingly thick, delicately salted, pleasantly ungreasy, and preservative-free. A Japanese American couple that had been interned on the mainland during WWII began making these chips on Maui during the 1950s. Not long after mainland companies got wind of this delicious, quiet revolution, they began imitating these snacks.

Tedeschi Winery and Vineyards on Ulupalakua Ranch in upcountry Maui produces the state's only **local wines,** from a pineapple variety to bubbly. For those with beer budgets, Aloysius Klink, originally from Germany, began brewing **Maui Lager** in 1986. If it's 3 a.m. and you have a craving for Dutch cheese, imported beer, sushi, or other gourmet treats, head for the 24-hour **Safeway** market in the Lahaina Cannery Shopping Center. Other grocery stores in Lahaina are **Foodland** and **Nagasako's.** Maui's least expensive supermarkets are in Kahului and Wailuku.

Kapalua

The **Plantation Veranda** • *Kapalua Bay Hotel; 669–5656* • Aptly named, this attractive restaurant stirs visions of 19th-century Hawaii, with its pink country-style wooden furniture, glossy mahogany floors covered with throw rugs, and slow-moving ceiling fans. Walls are brought to life by Pegge Hopper's trademark murals of round, brown Hawaiian women. A harpist often plays at dinner. Entrees range from duck, spring lamb, and chateaubriand to bay scallops, shrimp, and local fish. *Reservations required. Jackets required for men. A, M, V, C, D. (Expensive)*

The **Bay Club** • *Kapalua Bay Hotel; 669–5656* • One of Maui's most attractive restaurants, the Bay Club sits in a wooden building with its own pool and deck, and a glorious view of Molokai and Lanai. Open to the palms and the ocean, the room is refreshed by breezes from outdoors. While it's a wonderful spot for lunch, flickering candlelight and the quiet tunes of a pianist also make it appealing in the evening. Large ceiling fans rotate above high-backed rattan chairs and handsome panelled walls. The menu features delicious nouvelle cuisine selections. *Reservations required. Jackets requested at dinner. A, M, V, C, D. (Expensive)*

Kaanapali Area

Swan Court • *Hyatt Regency Maui, Kaanapali Beach; 661–1234* • Swans float past tables near the lagoon in this elegant open-air dining room that has been dubbed "Most Romantic Restaurant" by the *Lifestyles of the Rich and Famous* TV show. Your feelings about the show notwithstanding, this truly is an exceptional place to dine, whether for dinner, lunch, or the breakfast buffet. The chef has won awards for his veal chops and Baked Alaska. Other good selections include chicken cooked in bourbon and fish with mushrooms and capers. *Reservations recommended. Jackets required at night. A, M, V, C, D. (Expensive)*

Sunset Terrace • *Hyatt Regency Maui, Kaanapali Beach; 661– 1234* • Dinner is accompanied by the Drums of the Pacific Polynesian Revue. A complimentary mai tai is served with each meal. Diners choose among teriyaki chicken, sauteed ono, sweet and sour pork, teriyaki steak, and a combination of all of the above. Everyone is served macadamia nut pie for dessert. Arrive early to get a good seat. *Reservations required. (Moderate to Expensive)*

Sound of the Falls • *Westin Maui, Kaanapali; 667–2525* • This al fresco restaurant by the hotel's huge waterfall-fed swimming pool is a good choice for an elaborate Sunday buffet brunch. *(Moderate)*

Nikko • *Maui Marriott, Kaanapali Beach; 667–1200* • If you've ever been to Benihana of Tokyo, you'll know what to expect at this Japanese steakhouse. Diners sit at communal tables where the food is cooked by a chef who tells a stream of jokes while catching bowls of rice he has tossed behind his back, throwing shrimp over his shoulder onto the grill, and juggling huge razor-sharp knives. *Reservations required. A, M, V, C, D. (Moderate)*

Leilani's on the Beach • *Whaler's Village, Kaanapali; 661–4495* • You may have a long wait for a table on weekends, but most of the food is worth it. Decorated with local art, some walls are panelled in golden brown wood. Others are made of exposed rugged lava rock. Many enjoy dining on the curved terrace overlooking the water. Friends and I have had the best luck with the char-broiled teriyaki tuna with Chinese vegetables and rice; ginger chicken; deep-fried Malaysian shrimp; Cajun-style fish; and baby back pork ribs. Downstairs at the seafood bar, tables are lit by the dancing flames of torches. *(Moderate)*

El Crab Catcher • *Whaler's Village, Kaanapali; 661–4423* • The eclectic menu at this popular restaurant features Mexican quesadillas and nachos, Chinese shredded wonton salad, hamburgers, mahi-mahi sandwiches, Hawaiian chicken, broiled fish, and prime rib. Among the many tropical drinks are a chi chi (coconut cream with pineapple and vodka) and a relaxer (guava nectar, lilikoi juice, orange juice, rum, brandy, and gin). *(Moderate)*

Chico's Cantina • *Whaler's Village, Kaanapali; 667–2777* • The usual Americanized but zesty Mexican fare is served here: chimichangas, nachos, quesadillas, tacos, enchiladas, tostadas, burritos, fajitas, and the like. Children's portions are available. *(Moderate)*

Erik's Seafood Grotto • *Kahana Villa Condominiums, Kahana (3 miles north of Kaanapali), 669–4806; and Kamaole Shopping Center, 2463 S. Kihei Rd., Kihei, 879–8400* • Early bird specials are served between 5 and 6 p.m. at this attractive, casual dining spot. For appetizers, try sashimi, yakitori (marinated chicken), crab-stuffed artichokes, or steamers. Tasty selections for the main course include seafood curry, baked stuffed prawns, king crab legs, broiled local fish, Louisiana catfish, and a steaming bowl of bouillabaisse. Landlubbers don't despair— steak is also on the menu. Cocktails have been christened with amusing names, such as lava flow (fresh bananas, pineapple juice, coconut syrup, cream, grenadine, and rum) and passionate grog (local rum, lilikoi— passion fruit—and orange juices). Kona coffee ice cream and coconut pie top the dessert menu. *Reservations recommended. A, V, M. (Moderate)*

Lahaina

Gerard's • *the Plantation Inn, Lahainaluna Rd.; 661–8939* • Attracting more than its share of celebrities, this casual French restaurant began as a small bistro near Front Street. It is now ensconced in plusher digs in a wonderful turn-of-the-century-style inn. At the helm is French chef Gerard Reversade, who cut his teeth in Parisian restaurants before coming to Hawaii. The inner dining room is graced with stained glass over French doors, brass, and oak. White wicker chairs are set off with floral cushions in pinks and greens. The lanai, filled with white garden furniture, is enclosed by Victorian pillars, an elegant balustrade, and delicate latticework. Pink umbrellas fringed in white shade outdoor tables while fluffy hanging plants rustle in the breeze. The chef combines cooking styles of various regions of France with fresh Maui and Eastern ingredients, creating innovative concoctions such as ahi with bearnaise sauce and bean sprouts spiced with ginger; and rabbit with prunes. A hearty breakfast here might consist of thick Belgian waffles; paper-thin crepes with fresh fruit; or eggs Florentine and duck sausage. *Reservations required. A, V, M, D, C. (Moderate to Expensive)*

Kimo's • *845 Front St.; 661–4811* • Each entree at this steak and seafood restaurant comes with fresly made carrot muffins and French rolls, salad, and herb rice. The selection of local fish is broad, from *hapu* (Hawaiian sea bass) and *ulua* (deep-sea pompano) to *aʻu* (broadbill swordfish) and *ahi* (Hawaiian big game yellowfin tuna). Preparation of the fish is your choice, from broiled in lemon butter to grilled spicy Cajun style. Also on the menu are teriyaki sirloin steak, hamburgers, and Koloa pork ribs glazed with plum sauce. Children's portions are available. If you leave room for dessert, try the macadamia nut ice cream or the lilikoi (passion fruit) sherbet. *(Moderate)*

Longhi's • *888 Front Street; 667–2288* • The accent is on the Italian at this popular, noisy waterfront dining spot that sells T-shirts emblazoned with its logo. A great vantage point for **whale watching** during the winter, this is also a good place for gazing at dramatic sunsets. Instead of handing out written menus, the waiters sit down with diners to present the mercurial choices orally. Most of the ingredients are Maui-grown. The pasta, breads, and pastries are all made on the premises. Some say that lunch is better than dinner here. The midday menu might feature king crabmeat or Greek salad, crab and chicken canneloni, or pasta marinara. Breakfast begins with freshly squeezed orange juice and freshly ground Kona coffee. There's a dance floor on the upstairs level and jazz is often played on weekends. *Reservations not accepted. A, V. (Moderate)*

Sam's On the Beach Pub and Restaurant • *505 Front St.; 667–4341* • The continental seafood and other selections at this waterfront restaurant have received mixed reviews from patrons. *(Moderate)*

Avalon • *844 Front St.; 667–5559* • Step into 1940s Hawaii at this colorfully decorated restaurant that brings together cuisines of Hawaii, California, Japan, China, Mexico, Thailand, and Indonesia. Try the grilled chicken breast in a ginger sesame dressing served with crunchy rice noodles, macadamia nuts, and Hawaiian field greens; the prawns in black bean sauce; or the steamed Chinese dumplings. Guacamole is prepared tableside. If you're into celebrity watching, this is a good choice. *Reservations recommended. A, V, M, D. (Moderate)*

Musashi • *Lahaina Shopping Center, 667–6207* • Lunch and dinner are served at this informal Japanese eatery complete with a sushi bar. Try the salmon teriyaki, sukiyaki, the tempura, or one of the noodle dishes. If you're on the run, order a Bento Box lunch (Hawaii's answer to McDonald's). Call ahead if you'd like to take advantage of the complimentary transportation provided from hotels between Kaanapali and Kapalua. *(Inexpensive* to *Moderate)*

Alex's Hole in the Wall • *834 Front St.; 661–3197* • The pasta and sausage are made on the premises of this homey, if cluttered, Italian restaurant. The lasagne, made with a variety of cheeses, gets raves. *Reservations not accepted. A, V, M. (Inexpensive* to *Moderate)*

La Bretagne • *562-C Front St.; 661–8966* • Near Lahaina's famous banyan tree, this small French restaurant in a house built in 1920 is always crowded. As you taste the rack of lamb or seafood in puff pastry, you may get the feeling that you are dining in someone's living room. Espresso flows from a highly polished brass machine. *Reservations recommended. A, M, V. (Expensive)*

Olowalu

Chez Paul • *Olowalu, West Maui (Hwy. 30, about 4 miles south of Lahaina); 661–3843* • With just over a dozen tables—each sparkling with china and crisp linen—this is one of Maui's finest restaurants. It is set against the West Maui Mountains. The imaginative French menu is always changing. One day you might find veal cooked with apples and Calvados while another you might run across local fish poached in white wine, bathed in a creamy sauce with capers and shallots. The only problem with Chez Paul is that single diners are not welcome. This is because this small restaurant wants to use all its seats at all times; it sounds like discrimination to me. *Reservations required. Dinner served at either 6:30 p.m. or 8:30. A, V, M, C. (Expensive)*

Wailuku/Kahului

The Chart House • *500 Puunene Ave., Kahului; 877–2476* • I've gotten lukewarm reports from friends who've eaten here. However, this waterfront steak and seafood restaurant is quite popular with residents. Fish flit about in oversized aquariums. Try the charbroiled yellowfin tuna in a lemon sauce. *Reservations recommended. A, V, M. (Moderate)*

Chung's • *Wailuku* • A local eatery especially popular for breakfast and lunch, Chung's serves pancakes, Portuguese sausage, and Spam and eggs. The saimin is also excellent here. *(Inexpensive)*

Yori's • *Wailuku* • This funky old restaurant is a good choice for contemporary Hawaiian cuisine—at least a slew of locals think so. *(Inexpensive)*

Saeng Thai • *Wailuku; 244–1567* • Many residents come here for the spicy homestyle cuisine. *(Inexpensive)*

Tasty Crust • *Wailuku; 244–0845* • Locals swear by the pancakes and saimin served here. *(Inexpensive)*

Ming Yuen • *162 Alamaha St., Kahului; 871-7787* • Generous portions of Cantonese and Szechuan dishes are served at this informal spot that always has a local crowd. Try the mooshu pork or the chicken with peanuts, Chinese vegetables, hot peppers, and garlic. *Reservations recommended. A, V, M, D. (Inexpensive)*

Ichiban • *Kahului Shopping Center, 2133 Kaohu St., Kahului; 871-6977* • You'll find many Japanese diners at this casual restaurant that serves delicious sashimi, tempura, sukiyaki, and teriyaki. *V. (Inexpensive)*

Paʻia Area

Mama's Fish House • *799 Poho 579-9672* • Just outside Paʻia, popular Mama's Fish House is located along the Hana Highway. While it is something of an institution, some diners have thought it overpriced and touristy, and a few say it serves up more hype than good food. However, you would probably do well to try the sweet potato fries, the fish filet stuffed with shrimp, or the smoked fish mousse. *Reservations required for dinner. A, V, M. (Moderate to Expensive)*

Dillon's • *89 Hana Hwy. (on the main road in Lower Paʻia); 579-9113* • Run by New York transplant Nancy Powell, this popular restaurant is known for its bagels, burgers with kosher dill pickles, pepper steak, and hero sandwiches. People also flock here for cocktails and pupus. Good breakfast selections are French toast with Kahlua, eggs benedict, and pancakes with fresh local fruit. Begin the day with a guava sunrise or a steaming cup of Kona coffee. *A, M, V. (Inexpensive to Moderate)*

Kihata's • *Paʻia; 579-9035* • This eatery, complete with a sushi bar, serves good Japanese cuisine. *(Inexpensive)*

Makawao Area

Kitada's • *Makawao; 572-7241* • This rustic diner lures many Portuguese cowboys. It serves an excellent plate lunch, and saimin is on the menu—even for breakfast. Patrons refill their own coffee cups and soda glasses. *(Inexpensive)*

Polli's • *1202 Makawao Ave., Makawao, 572-7808; and 101 N. Kihei Rd., Kihei (on the beach), 579-9672* • The Buffalo chicken wings get good reports at this mostly Mexican restaurant that once served only vegetarian food. There is still a good selection of meatless enchiladas, tostadas, burritos, and tacos. Few patrons pass up a chance to sample one of Polli's margaritas. A champagne brunch is also served. *Dinner reservations required. A, V, M. (Inexpensive)*

The Haliimaile General Store • *900 Haliimaile Rd., Haliimaile; 572–2666* • Located upcountry, this restaurant snags many residents as well as vacationers on their way to and from Haleakala crater. This gourmet dining spot seems just a bit out of place in the middle of pineapple fields. Born as a plantation store back in 1925, it was turned into a restaurant in 1988 by a successful local caterer, Beverly Gannon, and her husband, Joe. Try the grilled chicken served with local pineapple chutney; the pasta with pine nuts, brie, and sundried tomatoes; or the lamb chops with mint, goat cheese, and a wild rice pancake. For dessert, don't miss the Kona coffee cheesecake. *Reservations required. Closed Mon. Open 11 a.m.–3 p.m. and 6–9:30 p.m. A, V, M. (Moderate)*

Kula

Kula Lodge • *about 3½ miles south of the Pony Express Stables; 878–2517 or 878–1535* • Perched on the edge of a cliff upcountry, this rustic dining spot yields a fabulous view of the island. Good choices are the shrimp curry, cold teriyaki chicken, and especially the mahimahi sauteed with ginger, served in a light cream sauce, and sprinkled with seaweed. There's a healthy selection of vegetarian dishes, as well as wines. If you're on your way back from watching the sun rise over Haleakala crater, this is a good place for breakfast. Try the Belgian waffles with fresh raspberries or mangoes, topped with coconut syrup. *(Moderate)*

Grandma's Coffee House • *878–2140* • A family-run bakery and restaurant, this eatery serves coffee that is grown on Maui and roasted by owner Al Franco himself. He uses a roaster that was passed down from his great-great grandmother and is more than a century old. The recipes for the delicious baked goods have also been around for generations. Other crowd pleasers are the sandwiches, chili, and Portuguese red bean soup. *Open 7 a.m. to 5 p.m. daily except Monday.*

Kihei and Wailea

Raffles • *Stouffer Wailea Hotel, Wailea; 879–4900* • Named for Sir Stamford Raffles, the British founder of Singapore, this elegant, dimly lit restaurant is done in dark woods and Oriental rugs, set off by etched crystal, linen tablecloths, and artfully arranged fresh flowers. Consider the tender baby lamb or the opakapaka (Hawaiian pink snapper) with fresh chives and grapes in a vermouth sauce. At the lavish Sunday brunch, you'll have the opportunity to design your own omelette, or choose a filling salad, a tropical fruit plate, or Beef Wellington. Although this restaurant has won more than a few awards, some patrons have felt it overrated. *Reservations required. Jackets requested. A, V, M, D, C. (Very Expensive)*

Paradise Fruit • *Kihei; 879–1723* • You may think you're in Southern California when you step into this roadside eatery that serves fruit shakes, yogurt shakes, fruit salads, and vegetables-and-sprouts sandwiches. You can sit out front or get your goodies to go. *(Inexpensive)*

La Familia • *2511 S. Kihei Rd., Kihei, 879–8824; and 2119 Vineyard, Wailuku, 244–3904* • This Mexican restaurant was started, then sold, by the same woman who opened Polli's. *A, V, M. (Inexpensive)*

Eric's Seafood Grotto • *Kihei* • (see Kaanapali Area)

Polli's • *on the beach in Kihei* • (see Makawao Area)

Makena

Prince Court • *Maui Prince Hotel; 874–1111* • The delicious American regional cuisine is further enhanced by the setting—flickering candles, windows with louvered shutters that open to a string trio in a courtyard graced with a Japanese rock garden. Many of the vegetables and spices are grown by the chef himself. Corn bread is served with dinner. On the menu, you might find black bean soup; slipper lobster hush puppies with a dressing of honey, lime, mustard, and macadamia nuts; seafood sausage with basil; or kiawe roasted chicken breast with apple corn cakes. Dessert specialties include macadamia nut brittle flan and chocolate peanut butter souffle. *Reservations required. A, M, V. (Expensive)*

Hakone • *Maui Prince Hotel; 874-1111* • At this restaurant with a sushi bar, more than gifted chefs were imported from Japan. Most of the materials used to build Hakone were also brought from the East, including the wooden floor boards and the wall hangings. The bright, spare decor is in keeping with Japanese tradition, as is the delicious food. *A.M.V. (Moderate to Expensive)*

Hana

Hana Ranch Restaurant • *248–8255* • Everyone from ranch hands and hotel workers to vacationers dines here. Portions of T-bone steak, chicken, and fried wild mushrooms are large. The wine list is surprisingly good for such a remote dining spot. *Dinner served Fri. and Sat. only. (Moderate)*

WHERE TO SLEEP ON MAUI

Some of Hawaii's most expensive accommodations can be found on Maui, where the majority of places to stay fall into the luxury category. However, before you turn to another island, note that there are also quite a few inexpensive-to-moderate sleeping quarters, including hotels, condominiums, B&Bs, and housekeeping cabins. In addition, even the more costly hotel rooms and condos can be quite economical if shared with friends. Maui has more condos than anywhere else in Hawaii. These homelike units with kitchens are popular among many travelers, especially families. While most don't have restaurants or night spots, many condo complexes are on the beach and the majority come complete with pools and other hotel-style facilities and services. In most cases, these apartments are individually furnished by their owners, so units within a single complex may vary greatly in decor.

Maui's tourism development began in earnest in the 1960s with the Kaanapali beach resort in West Maui. The two 18-hole Royal Kaanapali Golf Courses, the many tennis courts, and the profusion of water sports remain big draws. West Maui is the busiest visitor center today. Up north are the condos and hotels of upscale Kapalua and more down-to-earth Napili. Just south of Kaanapali, other accommodations are found in Lahaina, the picturesque old whaling port. Far quieter than Kaanapali and Lahaina, Wailea is a meticulously planned resort area in East Maui. Though not nearly as pretty to look at, the accommodations in neighboring Kihei are less expensive than those elsewhere on the island. In arid, southern East Maui, posh Makena is the youngest resort. Apart from lush, isolated Hana, it is Maui's least developed tourist mecca.

Speaking of Hana, as remote and sleepy as it is, this town is home to one of the island's most exclusive resorts, the refurbished **Hotel Hana-Maui.** Those seeking tropical luxury and wide-open spaces head for the **Kapalua Bay Resort,** which has two excellent golf courses. Although it's not on the beach, the small, Victorian-style **Plantation Inn** in Lahaina is one of my favorite hotels in the state. The much-loved Gerard's (a French restaurant) resides here, and the moderately priced inn offers a good scuba program. Two pleasant, inexpensive places to stay are the

Maui Lu Resort and the **Mana-Kai Maui,** both in Kihei. A find in the mid-level price range is the **Coconut Inn** in Napili. Whether or not they are staying at the **Westin Maui** in Kaanapali, many vacationers roam around its luxurious grounds, replete with waterfalls, larger-than-life statues, and Oriental vases, rugs, and sculpture. Also in Kaanapali, the **Hyatt Regency Maui** is another eye-opener, with its exotic uncaged birds and plentiful Polynesian art and artifacts. The nearby **Sheraton Maui** was the island's first major hotel. Hawaii's Sheraton chain runs a good children's program for guests from June through Labor Day. Every unit in the **Embassy Suites Kaanapali Resort** is a one- or two-bedroom state-of-the-art suite. Two of Maui's newest (and most upscale) hotels are the **Four Seasons** and the **Grand Hyatt Wailea,** both in Wailea. The **Stouffer Wailea Beach Resort,** also in Wailea, and the **Maui Prince,** in Makena, are other top accommodations.

The larger hotels have restaurants, shops, and night spots on the premises. Golf, honeymoon, and rental car packages are available through many hotels and condos. For details about B&Bs, private homes, and housekeeping cabins, see the entries at the end of this section.

Kapalua

★★★★ **Kapalua Bay Club** • Nestled at the shore in an area where tall pines stud grassy slopes, the Kapalua Bay Club is one of Maui's most tasteful resorts. Vines hang from the concrete beams of the very high ceiling of the open-air lobby, which looks out to the butterfly-shaped pool and the ocean. Boutiques are found in a breezy arcade. The manicured grounds are set off by palms, bright flowers, a waterfall-fed stream, and a wooden footbridge over a pond. Parties are often held at the coconut grove by the beach. Guests enter their attractive, spacious rooms through wide double wooden doors. Those who don't like air-conditioning can turn on the wooden ceiling fans. Baths are done in marble and (as is the trend with many of Hawaii's more expensive properties) are thoughtfully designed for simultaneous use by two people who don't want to get in each other's way: the twin sinks are opposite each other; there are both a tub and a stall shower; and the toilet is in a separate room within the bath. Two of Maui's best restaurants are on the premises: the Plantation Veranda and the Bay Club. The resort is also adjacent to two of the island's most challenging golf courses, and tennis courts are available. A shuttle bus provides transportation around the grounds. *(Very Expensive)*

★★★ **Kapalua Villas** • Looking like residential suburbia, three groups of villas are scattered across the sprawling grounds of this condominium complex. Some of the one- and two-bedroom units are elevated on verdant slopes, while others are closer to the water or the golf course. Handsome furnishings, modern kitchens, lofty ceilings with exposed beams, and spacious bathrooms make these apartments a pleasure to come home to. Guests are welcome to use all facilities of the Kapalua Bay Club hotel, including the beaches, pools, golf courses, tennis courts, and shuttle bus. Room service is available in the condos. *(Expensive* to *Very Expensive)*

Napili

☆☆ **Napili Point** • In each of these one- and two-bedroom Aston condominium units, a private lanai affords a view of the ocean. While apartments aren't air conditioned, ceiling fans and tradewinds do the job just fine. Vanity areas and small bathrooms are adjacent to bedrooms, and ironing boards are provided. Kitchens contain bars, dishwashers, blenders, and coffee makers. Sports facilities include a freshwater swimming pool. For tennis, guests are invited to the Aston Kaanapali, about 4 miles away, but they have to arrange their own transportation. Kaanapali's golf courses are nearby. Inquire about car/condo packages. *(Moderate* to *Expensive)*

☆☆ **Napili Shores Resort** • These large studio and one-bedroom condominiums are situated at an attractive beach. Some units have views of the colorful gardens. The Orient Express, a popular restaurant, serves spicy Thai and Chinese food at good prices. *(Moderate)*

☆☆ **The Coconut Inn** • The walls and towels may be thin and the beach may be about a 10-minute walk away (that is, when the tides haven't swallowed it up), but many people highly recommend these spacious, breezy studio and one-bedroom apartments. You'll find a swimming pool in the nicely landscaped grounds, which are surrounded by a pleasant residential neighborhood. Served every morning at breakfast, the homebaked banana bread draws raves. The Napili Shores Resort, with its Orient Express restaurant, is nearby. *(Moderate)*

☆☆☆ **Mahina Surf** • During high season, you'll need to reserve one of these one- or two-bedroom plain but comfortable condos at least three months in advance. All provide full ocean views, except for a handful with partial ocean views. Ceiling fans cool the air instead of air-conditioning. Full kitchens are equipped with microwaves and dishwashers. All units come with radios and color televisions, and some also have cable and VCRs. The two-story horseshoe-shaped building housing these apartments encloses a swimming pool. Also on the premises are barbeque grills, laundromat, and a lending library. A sandy beach is about a 5-minute stroll away. Golf courses and public tennis courts are about 3 miles from here. The front office remains open from 7 a.m. to 7 p.m. *(Moderate)*

★★★ **Napili Kai Beach Club** • The Japanese touches in rooms are part of what makes this small, bayside hotel stand out in the crowd. For instance, paper screens slide open to the lanai and views of the water. Located in low-rise buildings, rooms come with kitchenettes. (Room service isn't available.) Guests choose among four swimming pools, a Jacuzzi, two tennis courts, two putting greens, and the nearby golf courses at the Kapalua resort. Every week they mingle at the manager's mai tai party and book ringside seats for the Polynesian show. *No credit cards accepted. (Expensive)*

Kaanapali

All of Kaanapali's accommodations are convenient to the Royal Kaanapali Golf Courses, tennis courts, and the beach. Shuttle service is available within the resort as well as to Lahaina.

On the Beach:

★★★ **Aston Kaanapali Shores** • Actually located in Honokowai, just north of Kaanapali, this apartment hotel is often booked more than six months in advance for the November-December season. The unusual lobby with textured clay walls opens to a lush, jungled courtyard with waterfalls, red ginger, and palm trees. While there is certainly activity in the lobby, it is never too noisy or crowded. A garden foot path winds along a fish-stocked pond. Lanais of first-floor rooms lead to the beachwalk. Ceilings are high and living rooms (in the one- and two-bedroom apartments) are spacious. Studios are also for rent. Laundry facilities, storage closets, cable TV, and kitchens with dishwashers are features of units. Furnishings include rattan couches with thick floral cushions, bamboo and glass coffee tables, and end tables. Non-smoking rooms (in which you don't have to worry about the stale odor from previous puffing guests) are available, along with rooms with wheelchair access. An outdoor play area for children and a good-sized swimming pool make this resort especially appealing to families. The three lighted tennis courts are open until 10 p.m. and the closest golf course is only about 3 miles away. *(Expensive)*

★★★ **Papakea Beach Resort** • There's plenty of elbow room between the low-rise buildings that house the condo units at this spacious resort in Honokowai, just north of Kaanapali. The homelike studios and one- and two-bedroom apartments are cooled by ceiling fans instead of air-conditioning. Ponds churning with fish, paths bordered by flowering bushes and bamboo, and classes in subjects such as the proper way to cut a pineapple never let you forget you're in Hawaii. Facilities include two swimming pools, a whirlpool, and tennis courts. *(Moderate)*

★★★★ **Embassy Suites Kaanapali Resort** • Each unit in this Honokowai resort is a luxurious suite, with one or two bedrooms, a living room, two telephones (two separate lines, no less), a lanai, and a kitchenette. Culinary gadgets include a microwave oven and coffee maker, and there's also a wet bar. The bedroom-sized baths are decked out with two marble vanities, a stall shower, and a tub. For indoor entertainment, suites are equipped with 35″ remote control color TVs, VCRs (the resort has a video library), stereos, and cassette decks. Room service is available from 11 a.m. to 11 p.m. Most suites have views of the ocean. On the lanais of the two presidential suites, telescopes allow visitors to zero in on whales as they glide by during the winter. Guests are invited to indulge themselves in a complimentary full breakfast every morning and the manager's al fresco cocktail party every afternoon. Small bridges span streams filled with fish. Lilies, bird of paradise, and hibiscus flourish in gardens. A 12-foot waterslide ensures that giggles accompany the act of getting into the one-acre swimming pool. After a workout in the fitness center, sore muscles can be soothed by the whirlpool, sauna, or a massage. While this resort is hardly for those on a budget, two people can turn a one-bedroom gardenview suite into a very good deal by sharing it with another couple. *(Expensive* to *Very Expensive)*

☆☆ **Royal Lahaina** • Reminiscent of totem poles, Polynesian tikis welcome guests to this lava rock Outrigger chain complex, Kaanapali's second oldest hotel. Cluttered souvenir shops lead the way to the lobby, panelled in dark wood, where more stores are found. Appealing to conventions and large groups, this hotel has a commercial, busy feel. Even the birds chirp loudly all over the property. In the main wing are the medium-sized, individual rooms. The well-spaced low-rise cottages are more attractive, even though their interiors may put you in mind of motel rooms. Set on a grassy, tree-shaded lawn with a nearby gazebo, these shingle-roofed buildings have either one or two stories. Some oceanview rooms open to dramatic coastal vistas. In the afternoon, hot and cold pupus accompany the live music in the indoor/outdoor lounge overlooking the flourishing main pool area and the picturesque sandy beach. Other swimming pools and the 11-court Royal Lahaina Tennis Ranch are among the facilities. The hotel borders one of Kaanapali's golf courses. *(Moderate* to *Expensive)*

☆☆☆ **Sheraton Maui** • On the rugged Black Rock peninsula (a.k.a. Puu KeKaa) and adjacent to one of the golf courses, this was the first hotel built in Kaanapali. Outside the entrance, shops are clustered in a circular glass-walled structure. The circular lobby is frequently crowded with groups checking in or out. The multilevel property extends along the longest, widest section of the beautiful beach. Snorkeling is excellent off the peninsula. Sports facilities include three tennis courts, lit for night play, and two freshwater pools. At the end of each day, cocktail hour begins as divers jump off Black Rock into the ocean as part of the torchlighting ceremony. Oceanfront cottages are available in addition to individual guest rooms. During the summer (June–Labor Day), guests aged 5 to 12 are invited to take part in the free children's program. Supervised by counselors, the younger set is taught such things as lei-making, other Hawaiian arts and crafts, and sand castle building. *(Expensive)*

☆☆ **Kaanapali Beach Hotel** • Centrally located, this modest hotel dating back to the '60s is a good choice if you're looking to save money. Rough, chocolate-colored lava stone columns stand at the entrance. The crescent of low-rise buildings cups a palm-shaded patio that gives way to the broad beach. Live Hawaiian music hangs in the air by the Polynesian-style wooden roofs that resemble the bows of ships. A swimming pool is a short walk across the lawn. Rooms (which vary mainly in terms of their views) are quite spacious, with rattan chairs, a couch, louvered sliding doors, a dressing room, refrigerator, ironing board, and lanai. Hotel activities include lei-making, ti leaf skirt making, hula lessons, and pool aerobics. For a small fee, guests may play tennis at the Sheraton Maui or in Lahaina. *(Moderate)*

★★★ **The Whaler** • Whaler's Village shopping center and the two Royal Kaanapali championship golf courses across the street make convenient neighbors for the Whaler. The difference between this condominium and a full-service hotel is barely detectable. Sunlight streams into the open-air lobby, which has a granite floor. There's a beachfront swimming pool, whirlpool, five tennis courts with a pro shop and a teaching pro, a general store, an exercise room, and a sauna. The studio and one- and two-bedroom apartments are found in two 12-story towers. While waiting for the elevator, guests stand on sea blue tiles and gaze out at the mountains, ocean, and courtyard. Special touches in units include marble baths, full kitchens with parquet floors, and $12' \times 2'$ closets. *(Expensive to Very Expensive)*

★★★★★ **The Westin Maui** • Next door to Whaler's Village shopping center, this flamboyant resort is an attraction in itself. Some consider it overdone and overwhelming, while others revel in its lavish touches. It was developed by Chris Hemmeter, Hawaii's version of Donald Trump. The hotel's motto seems to be, "Why have one waterfall when 16 will do?" The first splashes across from the entrance to the breezy lobby, which is dressed in muted beiges and pale pinks. Other water-falls pour over rocky outcroppings into swan-filled ponds and the enor-mous swimming pool. Guests delight in swimming under the cascades and whizzing down water slides into the pool. The multimillion-dollar international art collection turns the grounds into an al fresco museum. Mammoth Chinese statues, tremendous urns, and columns not much smaller than redwood trees line corridors. Huge bronze horses and other animals seem to hulk around every corner. After the grounds, most guest rooms are surprisingly small. This is because the Westin Maui was another, more modest hotel in its earlier incarnation. Each elegantly appointed room has a wet bar and refrigerator. Accents include marble- and glass-topped tables and heavy, wide chaise lounges. Guests are in-vited to take advantage of the fitness center and a full range of beach activities. *(Expensive* to *Very Expensive)*

★★★★ **Kaanapali Alii** • The waiting list for the Christmas holi-days and other peak seasons can be nearly a year long for these upscale condos. Artfully landscaped grounds surround freshwater swimming pools. Jacuzzi, exercise room, and saunas. Unlike in many condos, the front desk is open 24 hours. A concierge is on hand to arrange sports, tours, and other activities. The four buildings have six one- and two-bedroom apartments on each floor. Rooms look out to the mountains, the garden, and/or the ocean. In the two-bedroom units, every master bedroom has a whirlpool and a sunken patio. Baths come with separate vanity areas and are equipped with bidets. Other facilities include microwaves, dish-washers, trash compacters, blenders, and coffee makers. Guests also have the use of washers and dryers. In Building #3, oceanfront two-bedroom apartment #1006 is fabulous. The full ocean view provides excellent whale watching from the lanai, especially at sunset. A special security key is necessary to enter buildings. A 3-night minimum rental is required, except during Christmastime, when guests must remain at least 10 nights. *(Expensive* to *Very Expensive)*

☆☆☆ **Maui Marriott** • The concrete block architecture gives this hotel the feeling of a deluxe motel. Toward the southern end of Kaan-apali, it contains relatively standard rooms, though they are nicely dec-orated with wicker and rattan. Twenty-four–hour room service is available. *Very* long open-air hallways form balconies enclosing a court-yard that sprouts tall palms. Depending on where your room is, you may be in for a *long* walk every time you get off the elevator on your floor. Most rooms gaze out to the ocean. Palm trees also grow up from the spacious lobby, with its unobtrusive shops. At Nikko, a popular

Japanese steakhouse, chefs turn cooking into a humorous performance at the grills at tables where patrons are seated together, family style. Three of the 5 tennis courts are lit at night and the hotel has a resident tennis pro. There are also two large swimming pools with waterfalls, a pair of whirlpools, and a weight room. Watersports are easily arranged. The popular Banana Moon disco, with its flashing videos, is on the premises. *(Expensive* to *Very Expensive)*

★★★★★ **Hyatt Regency Maui** • Until the Westin Maui came along, this was Kaanapali's most elaborate showpiece. Developer Chris Hemmeter created the Hyatt before trying to outdo himself with the Westin. Many people prefer the Hyatt's more understated approach. The lobby is panelled in orange-brown wood. Parrots and macaws perch uncaged on brass rings. Buddha heads and other sculptures stand on pedestals. Near the Napili wing shops, a glass-covered coffee table serves as a showcase for New Guinea headdresses, headbands, and shell necklaces. Art and artifacts from Burma, Thailand, and China, among other places, are displayed here and there. Rotund penguins waddle and huge carp dart around various pools. A swinging rope-and-wood-plank bridge spans a section of the swimming pool. Corridors outside guest rooms are decorated with glass-enclosed pieces of art. In rooms, the TV and minibar are hidden in handsome armoires, and dressing areas are spacious. Yukatas (Japanese robes) are provided for guests to use during their stay. Traditional Chinese furniture has clearly inspired some pieces in rooms. *(Very Expensive)*

Near the Beach:

★★ **Maui Kaanapali Villas** • An Aston property, this hotel/condominium is within shouting distance of the sand. In addition to individual rooms, guests may stay in studios or one-bedroom suites. Hotel-style rooms have refrigerators, while the large units come with full kitchens. Three swimming pools are found on the spacious, pleasantly landscaped grounds. *(Moderate)*

☆☆ **Kaanapali Plantation** • This condominium resides on the other side of the tracks—the Lahaina-Kaanapali & Pacific Railroad tracks, that is. Apartments, all with electric kitchens, range in size from one to three bedrooms. Each unit has a private entrance. Even the smallest apartments have two baths each, while the 3-bedroom condos have 1½. Facilities include a swimming pool and tennis court. Maid service is provided every day except Sunday. *(Moderate* to *Expensive)*

☆☆ **Maui Eldorado** • Some of these low-rise condominium units are separated from the beach by a palm-studded golf course while both a street and a golf course lie between the water and others. If you're not in the mood to walk to the beach, take the hourly shuttle. For those who forgo the Pacific, three swimming pools are on the premises. The 11-court Royal Lahaina Tennis Ranch is next door. Each of the large studio, one- and two-bedroom apartments has a private lanai. Some of the one-bedrooms and all of the two-bedrooms have two baths. The tub and toilet are separated from the vanity and sink area. Kitchens have dishwashers and ice-making machines. Groceries, wine, and other liquor are sold in the lobby. *(Moderate)*

☆☆ **Kaanapali Royal** ● A golf course, ponds, and Kaanapali Parkway stand between this condominium and the beach. Whaler's Village beachfront shopping and dining complex is a short stroll away. On the grounds are a pool, Jacuzzi, sauna, and two tennis courts. Some of the baths in these two-bedroom, two-bath apartments have their own private lanai gardens. Each unit is equipped with a washer, dryer, and full kitchen. *(Expensive)*

Lahaina

Shuttle service is available between here and Kaanapali.

★★★ **Plantation Inn** ● *Lahainaluna Rd.* ● This cozy Victorian-style inn makes up for its non-beach location with a myriad of extra touches. Although this two-story building was born in the 1980s, it draws travelers into the turn of the century. The individually decorated guest rooms feature stained glass windows, Tiffany-esque lamps with fringed shades, floral wallpaper, brass and canopy beds with ruffled coverlets, wicker rockers, old-fashioned long-neck telephones, and hardwood floors. Remote-control color TVs, VCRs, and refrigerators are discreetly tucked away in period oak armoires. While rooms are centrally air-conditioned, they also have ceiling fans. Most open to lanais. Baths are highlighted by brass fixtures and rounded free-standing porcelain sinks. When combined, rooms turn into suites. Lush plantings surround the artfully tiled swimming pool and Jacuzzi. Meals are served at indoor/outdoor Gerard's, a French restaurant and one of the best places to eat on Maui. Ask about room/car or scuba diving packages. *(Moderate)*

☆☆☆ **Lahaina Shores** ● *475 Front St.* ● Conveniently located at the end of Lahaina boardwalk, this six-story condominium is the only accommodation in town that is on the beach. While a medley of stores and restaurants are nearby, this is one of the least crowded parts of Lahaina. The large, white plantation-style building has tall columns and a beautiful arched porte cochere. Trimmed in oak, the attractive lobby is spacious and simply furnished. As in major hotels, someone is on duty at the front desk 24 hours a day. The swimming pool is just off the lobby. Public tennis courts and a basketball court are across the street, while a 10-minute drive will take you to the closest golf courses. Although the studio and one-bedroom oceanview or mountainview apartments are not as eye-catching as the rest of the hotel, they are perfectly comfortable. Guests have a choice of restaurants on the premises. *(Moderate)*

Pioneer Inn • 658 Wharf St. • Set back from the waterfront on a lawn, this red-roofed wooden hotel dates back to 1901. Lanais surround the U-shaped building, which faces a tangle of masted boats in the harbor. The lobby, Old Whaler's Grog Shop (the bar), and dining room are decorated with all kinds of relics from Maui's whaling days. Compasses, lanterns, model ships, glass buoys, and timeworn cooking utensils hang from walls or perch on rafters. The plain but comfortable guest rooms in the new wing are air-conditioned, some with king-sized beds, others with a queen plus a twin; all have private baths. Although lanais in this wing are separated by partitions, guests from different rooms are in clear view of each other when on their balconies. An old sign by the creaky wooden staircase leading up to the original wing reads, "Anyone on this floor after 6 p.m. who is not a registered guest (or with same) will be arrested for trespassing." Rooms in the old wing are small, dark, and not air-conditioned; bathrooms are shared. The last time I passed through, this wing seemed more like a flophouse than a hotel, with transient-looking men lying on sagging twin beds during the afternoon. *(Inexpensive)*

★★★ **Puunoa Beach Estates** • *two blocks from town* • Each of these two- and three-bedroom condo apartments have beachfront lanais, a party-sized whirlpool tub in the master bedroom, two color TVs, a cassette deck, VHS recorder, and ceiling fan. Upon arrival, refrigerators and bars are stocked with welcoming goodies. Each individually furnished unit is accented with koa wood and etched glass windows. Some have high-pitched natural wood ceilings. You might find sleep-inducing armchairs, Asian vases, Japanese screens, or reproductions of Chinese carpets. Facilities include a swimming pool, paddle tennis courts, a sauna, and washer and dryer. Every day, the newspaper appears at each suite.

Kula

☆☆ **Kula Lodge** • *upcountry Maui* • Nestled in a forest and with crackling fireplaces, this rustic mountain lodge isn't exactly what travelers envision when they think of Hawaii. Two wooden cabins house the five units, three of which have fireplaces, and four of which have lofts. From this height, the views—stretching out to the Pacific—are spectacular. Note that even though cabins don't have kitchenettes, the restaurant (which serves breakfast and lunch every day) serves dinner only on weekends. *(Moderate)*

Kihei

☆☆ **Aston Kamaole Sands** • Somewhere between a condominium and a hotel, this large accommodation offers 24-hour front desk service, an Activities Desk, and restaurant. However, there's no air-conditioning in the one-, two-, and three-bedroom apartments housed in the 10 four-story buildings, which are across the road from the beach. Facilities include a swimming pool, a wading pool, tennis courts, and barbecue grills. *(Moderate)*

☆☆ **Maui Sunset** • These one- and two-bedroom oceanfront condo units come with a swimming pool, a Jacuzzi, and tennis courts. There's also an exercise room. Guests are welcome to use the laundry facilities and maid service is available upon request. *(Inexpensive* to *Moderate)*

☆☆ **Hale Kamaole** • Across the road from Kamaole Beach Park Three (which has a very nice stretch of sand), the grassy grounds of this condominium are filled with flowers. A minimum stay of four nights is required, and many repeat guests book the split-level two-bedroom apartments. One-bedroom units are also available. All units come with blossom-draped lanais and electric kitchens with dishwashers, but only some are equipped with telephones. There's a tennis court in addition to two swimming pools. Maid service is provided at an added cost. Rates here are especially attractive during the summer. *(Inexpensive* to *Moderate)*

☆☆ **Mana Kai-Maui** • The location on a wonderful expansive beach makes up for the unexciting architecture and guest rooms of this modest eight-story hotel/condominium. A rental car, which guests pick up at the airport, is included in the rates. A swimming pool is on the premises along with a bar, restaurant, and a couple of stores. Watersports enthusiasts may arrange their schedules here at an office of the Ocean Activities Center. Lanais are open to the ocean. While some rooms are petite and have no kitchens, the price is certainly right. *(Inexpensive* to *Moderate)*

☆☆ **Maui Lu Resort** • Built in and around a former private home, this plain but comfortable accommodation has buildings on both the inland and beach sides of the road. Guests will have to walk a bit to get to the sandiest part of the shore. The superior rooms are good choices and the one-bedroom cottages are quite spacious. Palms and other trees shade the grounds. Along with a pool and tennis, there are shops, a restaurant, lounge, and evening entertainment. Many travelers comment on the friendliness of employees. *(Inexpensive)*

Wailea

Shuttle service is available to area golf courses, tennis courts, a gym, and a shopping center.

★★★★ **Stouffer Wailea Beach Hotel** • On each side of the entrance, a long relief sculpture hugs the wall above fountains and pools. This raised mural depicts the escapades of Maui, the demigod. Perhaps the most dramatic of the Hawaiian-themed lobby art is the wall-hanging made of straw, yarn, and cloth in a riot of reds, blacks, whites, and oranges that represents a fiery volcanic eruption. One of Maui's nicest luaus takes place on these lush grounds by the ocean. Rooms, decorated with distinctive handcrafted koa wood furnishings, all have private lanais and cable TV with HBO (the television set is secreted away in an attractive koa armoire). All of the plush suites—accented with rattan, louvered doors, and floor-to-ceiling sliding mirrored closet doors—are oceanside. Snorkeling is excellent by the lava rocks off the beach to the left. The main swimming pool is free-form and guests may take the plunge in three Jacuzzis. Catering to executives and celebrities, some rooms are reserved for the Mokapu Beach Club: members have their own swimming pool and receive complimentary continental breakfast served in their rooms, terry cloth bathrobes, and a welcome gift. The Mokapu Beach Club grounds also offer the best vantage point on the property from which to see whales during the winter. Raffles, the hotel's fine dining room, has continually won awards. Parents who want some time off from their kids can send the little ones to Camp Wailea, a supervised children's program run during Easter week, the summer, and Christmastime. *(Expensive* to *Very Expensive)*

☆☆☆☆ **Maui Inter-Continental Wailea** • The first hotel in the area, this is a group of scattered low-rise units with a seven-story main building. Rough, dark brown lava rock walls in the lobby are set off by wicker chairs and tall potted plants. At the art gallery in the lobby, you might see a Japanese woodblock, a 1641 Rembrandt, a koa wood bowl, or a painting by Hawaii's celebrated Pegge Hopper. Most guest rooms face the ocean and are decorated with marble-topped desks, wooden armoires that contain TVs and mini bars, and commodious dressing rooms. Floor-to-ceiling mirrors serve as sliding closet doors. The L-shaped junior suites are especially nice. Guests spend much of their time in the three swimming pools, award-winning La Perouse restaurant, and the Polynesian-style Inu Inu Lounge, which is especially popular at sunset.

In addition to lei-making classes and other crafts demonstrations, a weekly luau is held at the water's edge. *(Expensive)*

☆☆☆ **Wailea Villas** • Only two of the complexes in this trio of condominiums are on the beach, but all are surrounded by flourishing, well-tended, sprawling grounds. Swimming pools are here for those not in the mood for the sand. Wailea Elua is where you'll find the most attractive—and most expensive—apartments. A concierge is on hand to see to guests' needs. The upscale apartments come with one, two, or three bedrooms. *(Expensive)*

Grand Hyatt Wailea • With nearly 800 rooms (all of them ocean-view), this addition to Hawaii's megaresort family is scheduled to be open by the time you read these words. The hotel stands on a beach, but the ocean almost seems mundane next to the other bodies of water here. The main swimming pool, set off by a fountain that is lit after dark, takes up 15,000 square feet. A 2000-foot-long river pool boasts the world's first river elevator; gushing water pushes a basket-like cubicle through a tube with rock on three sides and a glassed-in aquarium on the fourth. For those who would like to begin their honeymoons with nuptials in Hawaii, there's a wedding chapel on the grounds. Vacationers have a choice of five restaurants, including an authentic Japanese dining room and a seafood restaurant on a pier. The spacious health spa tempts visitors to keep in shape. Guest rooms—which each have a private lanai, three telephones, a remote control TV, and a bathroom with a tub and separate shower—are quite large. *(Expensive to Very Expensive)*

★★★★ **Four Seasons Wailea** • Completed in the spring of 1990, the beachfront Four Seasons Wailea has just under 400 rooms, about half the number of its fellow newcomer, the Grand Hyatt Wailea. Each of the appealing, commodious guest rooms has a private lanai; a king sized bed, two doubles, or twins; remote control TV; and a VCR (there's a VCR library at the concierge desk). The larger swimming pool, with a fountain, is the focal point of the hotel. The smaller pool is free-form in shape. A health club, two tennis courts, a library, and three restaurants also keep guests pleasantly occupied. This resort is a good choice for families. Children aged 5-12 are invited to participate in the well-supervised activities in the Kids for All Seasons program. For no additional charge, parents staying at the hotel can drop off the younger set for as long as they want between 8 a.m. and 5 p.m. daily. For special pampering, book a room on one of the Concierge floors. *(Expensive to Very Expensive)*

Makena

★★★★ **Maui Prince** • The high standard of service, the unobtrusive staff, and the spare, stylish decor all reflect the Japanese ownership of this attractive beachfront hotel. In the open-air lobby, tall wooden louvered doors are pushed back by day to expose the central octagonal courtyard below. Gaze down, and you'll see a Japanese rock garden with a waterfall, streams, and lush plantings. At night, a string trio plays Baroque music here, outside the Prince Court, the hotel's signature American regional restaurant. Complete with a sushi bar, Hakone is an excellent Japanese dining spot. Each morning guests find fresh Japanese designs stamped into the sand of hip-high ashtrays around the hotel. The two round pools near the golf course are disappointingly small and shallow, but the beach is just across the way and other beaches are nearby. Tennis (on six Laykold courts) and horseback riding can also be arranged. The al fresco corridors outside guest rooms overlook the garden courtyard and the volcano propping up clouds in the distance. Most rooms have views of the Pacific from their lanais. Special touches include remote-control color TVs; VCRs; refrigerators; slippers and yukatas (Japanese robes) for guests' use during their stay; hand-held shower nozzles; and separate rooms for toilets. Room service is always available. Ask about the sports and activities package. *(Expensive* to *Very Expensive)*

★★★ **Makena Surf** • The one- and two-bedroom beachfront condos here are roomy and pleasantly decorated. You'll have lots of elbow room in the swimming pool and lounge and you won't have to wait long to play a game of tennis. Guests are required to book at least three nights at this upscale accommodation, Makena's first condominium. *(Very Expensive)*

Hana

★★★★ **Hotel Hana-Maui** • Painstakingly renovated and upgraded during the late 1980s, the post-WWII Hotel Hana-Maui is now considered one of the island's premier places to stay—among those with a taste for rustic elegance, that is. Don't go looking for all the trimmings you'd expect at other equally expensive hotels: There are no TVs or radios in guest rooms and room service isn't available; ceiling fans stand in for air-conditioning; and a good beach is about 2½ miles away. Yet pampering is no stranger. Travelers sleep in individual rooms, suites, cottages, and a restored turn-of-the-century plantation house that rests on a hilltop. Terry cloth robes await guests, along with mildly perfumed soaps and other toiletries. Some bathtubs have views of gloriously colorful gardens. Hulking rattan furniture stands on bleached hardwood floors and counters are topped with stone. Replicas of traditional Hawaiian quilts cover beds, and walls are decorated with original local art. Rooms also have refrigerators, ice-machines, and wet bars. Hot tubs are found on some lanais. The salt-water swimming pool doesn't get much action. There are also two tennis courts, a three-hole putting green, and a jogging trail that follows the route of a famed ancient Hawaiian runner. The hefty rates include three meals and the hotel operates its own charter service between the Hana-Maui and the island's main airport in Kahului. *(Very Expensive)*

☆☆ **Hana Kai-Maui** • If you want to be on a beach in Hana, this condominium is the place to stay. Unfortunately, however, the picturesque shore here is rocky and thus better for sunbathing than swimming. A spring dribbles into the lava rock swimming pool. All with large lanais and kitchens, the commodious apartments face the water. Don't expect telephones, radios, or TVs. *(Moderate)*

★ **Heavenly Hana Inn** • At the entrance, two stone lions stand as sentinels at an elaborate Japanese gate decorated with Japanese lanterns. Public rooms are cluttered with Japanese knickknacks. The four modest two-bedroom apartments are outfitted with Japanese screens, a variety of Asian art, and antique-looking furniture. Since this inn is two miles out of town, you'll need a car if you plan to do any exploring. Those who'd prefer to be in town should inquire about the one-bedroom beach cottage and the other larger cottage that are rented by Heavenly Hana. *No credit cards accepted. (Moderate to Inexpensive)*

☆☆ **Aloha Cottages** • Almost as if you were staying in a bed & breakfast, you'll get to know the friendly owner, Fusae Nakamura. She rents a studio along with three two-bedroom apartments. There's nothing fancy about the decor, but the rooms are perfectly comfortable. *No credit cards. (Inexpensive)*

BED AND BREAKFASTS AND PRIVATE HOMES

One of the best ways to get to know the real side of Maui is to stay in a bed & breakfast. Some offer separate cottages while others accommodate guests in rooms in the owner's house. Daily rates range from dirt cheap (under $40) to very expensive (around $160). A minimum number of nights may be required. Try the following companies:

- **Bed & Breakfast Maui-Style** • Box 886, Kihei, Maui, HI 96753; (808) 879–2352 or (808) 879–7865
- **Bed & Breakfast Kilohana** • 378 Kamehameha Rd., Kula, Maui, HI 96790; (808) 879–6086
- **Bed & Breakfast Honolulu** • 3242 Kaohinani Dr., Honolulu, HI 96817; (808) 595–7533 or (800) 288–4666
- **Bed & Breakfast Hawaii** • P.O. Box 449, Kapaa, Kauai, HI 96746; (808) 822–7771 or (800) 675–7832

To rent a private home in Hana, contact **Hana Bay Vacation Rentals** ((800) 248–7727). A three- or four-night minimum stay may be required. For private homes and cottages elsewhere on Maui, try **Bed & Breakfast Pacific-Hawaii** (19 Kai Nani Pl., Kailua, Oahu, HI 96734; (808) 262–6026). Prices range from moderate to expensive.

HOUSEKEEPING CABINS

Some people book cabins in Maui's parks more than a year in advance, so make your reservations as far ahead of your trip as possible. Near Hana, **Waianapanapa State Park** is a good choice for spending a few nights after the gorgeous 52-mile, twisting, turning drive from Kahului. The 12 cabins sit on a precipice above a striking black sand beach where the body surfing is often quite good. Only very strong swimmers should attempt to explore the freshwater caves. On the other hand, the four-mile trail to Hana isn't too rigorous a hike. As many as six people can sleep in each shelter. Cabins come complete with electricity, hot water, stoves, refrigerators, cooking and eating utensils, showers, beds, bedding, and towels. For two adults sharing a cabin, the cost would be about $9 a night (half price for children) and about $7 per person for six adult bunk mates.

Six thousand feet above sea level on a slope of Haleakala Volcano, **Polipoli State Park** offers a solitary three-bedroom cabin that accommodates up to ten people. There is no electricity or refrigeration, but cooking and eating utensils, beds, bedding, and towels are all provided, along with wood and gas lanterns. You may have to remind yourself that you're in the tropics when you enter the forest, dense with cedar, ash, Monterey cypress, and a stand of California redwood trees. It also gets quite cold up here. Along the many hiking trails, you might come across such birds as quail or ring-necked pheasants. If you happen to be here in June, look for ripe Methley plums. The cost for two adults sharing a cabin would be approximately $9 a night (half price for children) and about $7 per person for six adults. To make reservations for a cabin at either of these parks, write to **Polipoli and Waianapanapa Cabins** (Division of State Parks, P.O. Box, 1049, Wailuku, HI 96793).

Rugged, experienced campers can consider the three cabins in the volcanic crater in stark, eerie **Haleakala National Park.** Kapaloa Cabin rests nearly 6 miles down from the trailhead at the volcano's summit. The hike down to Holua Cabin is almost 7½ miles long. And you'll have to trek just under 10 miles to reach Paliku Cabin. For about $7 per person per night, each shelter can provide drinking water, a wood-burning stove, and cooking and eating utensils. Firewood runs an additional $3.50 or so. While cabins are furnished with beds, you'll have to provide your own blankets or sleeping bag. Remember: It gets *mighty* chilly at the summit and in the crater. Keep an eye out for silversword, the rare and delicate endangered plant; wild goats; and the nene goose, Hawaii's state bird. To make reservations for a cabin, write to **National Park Cabins** (Haleakala National Park, P.O. Box 537, Makawao, HI 96768).

(Also see Camping and Hiking in Sports).

MAUI DETAILS

SAVING MONEY: You'll spend less if you book a package deal such as one of those offered by **United Airlines** (800) 328–6877). For example, United's seven-night excursions to Maui include round-trip flights, hotel, a compact car, and tax. To leave from San Francisco, the cost would begin at about $726 per person, double occupancy, at a moderate hotel near the beach. For an expensive beachfront resort, it would start at about $1168. From Chicago, prices range from about $1096 to $1420 and up. From New York, vacations begin at around $1130 for moderate properties and $1454 for deluxe beachfront hotels.

GETTING TO AND FROM THE AIRPORTS: Most planes (including jumbo jets) touch down on Maui at Kahului Airport (877–0078). The drive from here to Kaanapali, where the majority of hotels are located, is about an hour; to Kapalua and Napili, also about an hour; to Lahaina, about 35 minutes; to Kihei, about 20; to Wailea, about 35; and to Makena, about 45. The smaller, newer Kapalua-West Maui Airport (669–0228) is only about two miles from Kaanapali and Kapalua, and just over five miles from Lahaina. Small planes also fly into Hana

Airport, from Kahului as well as from other Hawaiian islands. Room rates at Hotel Hana-Maui include pickup and delivery at this airport.

By Bus: Grayline-Maui (877–5507) charges about $18 each way between Kahului Airport and Kaanapali. **Robert's Hawaii** (871–4838) provides similar transportation to and from the airport. Free shuttle service is available to and from Kapalua-West Maui Airport for vacationers staying in Kaanapali.

By Taxi: If you can't find a cab at the airport, try **Kaanapali Taxi** (661–5285); **West Maui Taxi** (667–2605); **Kihei Taxi** (879–3000), which also serves Wailea and Makena; **Alii Cabs** (661–3688); or **Yellow Cab** (877–7000). Plan to spend about $38 from Kahului Airport to Kaanapali; $35 to Lahaina; $30 to Kihei; $35 to Wailea; and $40 to Makena.

By Limousine: Contact **Alii Limousine Service** (874–6402) or **Carey Limousine** (836–1422 or (800) 336–4646).

By Car: Rental agencies located at or near the airport provide complimentary shuttle service from the baggage claim area to and from their offices.

GETTING AROUND MAUI: While shuttle buses run in Kaanapali and other resort areas, you'll need a car for exploring the rest of Maui.

By Car: Maui's car rental companies are quite competitive, so you can get away with paying under $25 a day for a compact car. Make your reservation as far ahead of your arrival as possible, expecially if you are vacationing during the summer or between late December and the end of February. In addition to the major national rental agencies, Maui has some other good companies. Among them are **Tropical** (661–0061 or (800) 352–3923); **Convertibles Hawaii** (877–6543 or (800) 367–5230); **Rainbow Rent-A-Car** (661–8734); **Rent-A-Jeep** (877–6626); **Trans Maui Rent-A-Car** (877–5222 or (800) 367–5228); and **Rent-A-Wreck** (877–5600 or (800) 367–5230). (Also see "Nuts and Bolts.")

Driving Tips: During rush hours, the traffic on roads between Lahaina and Kahului is especially lethargic. There is no road, at least not a driveable one, that will take you around the whole island of Maui. Therefore, you will find yourself doing a fair amount of back tracking if you plan to do extensive touring.

By Shuttle: Various bus services operate within and between Maui's resorts. The free **Kaanapali Shuttle** stops at each hotel in the area and at condos upon request; it also makes periodic runs to and from Lahaina. **Aston Hotels** provides complimentary shuttle service for its Kaanapali area guests wishing to go to Whalers Village Shopping Center and Lahaina. The **Kaanapali-Lahaina Shuttle** (about $1.75) carries visitors between the Royal Lahaina Hotel in Kaanapali and the Wharf Shopping Center in Lahaina. Free shuttle service is also available within both Kapalua and Wailea. Your accommodation will have copies of schedules.

By Taxi: See Getting To and From the Airport.

Getting to Hana: Through **Dollar Rent-A-Car** (248–8237), travelers can arrange to take this beautiful but demanding drive one way and leave the car in Hana. Reservations must be made at least three days in advance. Vacationers can also travel in small planes between Hana and Kahului or Kapalua-West Maui airports or other Hawaiian islands. Another way to end up in this lush eastern region of Maui is to take a helicopter. **Papillon Hawaiian Helicopters** ((800) 367–7095) and **Maui Helicopters** ((800) 367–8003) both run dropoff and pickup charters.

INTER-ISLAND FERRIES: The Maui Princess cruises between Lahaina and the island of Molokai. Bicycles are carried free of charge.

RENTING VIDEO CAMERAS: Inquire at the **Dollar Rent-A-Car** office in Kaanapali or **Point 'n Shoot Video** (879–1811) in Kihei.

TOURIST INFORMATION: The **Maui Visitors Bureau** (871–8691) is located at 111 Hana Hwy., Kahului.

POST OFFICES: For information about the branch closest to you, call 667–6611 in Lahaina.

EMERGENCY CASH: If you need some money in a hurry, contact **Western Union** ((800) 325–6000) or the main office of **American Express** on Oahu (946–7741).

WEATHER: 877–5111

TIME: 242–0212

ALCOHOLICS ANONYMOUS: Call 244–9673 about participating in local meetings.

WEIGHT WATCHERS: Call 955–1588 for details about local meetings.

EMERGENCIES: Dial 911.

MEDICAL ATTENTION: **Maui Memorial Hospital** (244–9056) is located in Wailuku. In other parts of the island are **Kula Hospital** (878–1221) in Kula and **Hana Medical Center** (248–8294) in Hana. In West

Maui, **Doctors on Call** (667–7676) is based at the Hyatt Regency Maui; **Whaler's Village Clinic** (667–9761) is at the shopping mall in Kaanapali; and the office of **Maui Physicians** (667–7001) is at the Lahaina Square Shopping Center in Lahaina. In East Maui are **Kihei Clinic** (879–1440) in Kihei; and **Wailea Medical Services** (879–7447) in Wailea.

Thatched roof *hales* reflected in a lagoon, Coco Palms Resort, Kauai

Horseback riding along the slopes of Haleakala volcano, Maui
MARY ANNE HOWLAND

The pine-studded landscape of Lanai, with Molokai across the water

A "floating" urn at the Westin Kauai hotel   RACHEL JACKSON CHRISTMAS

Puuopelu, an elegant home and museum on Parker Ranch, the Big Island of Hawaii
MARY ANNE HOWLAND

Hanauma Bay, Oahu's mecca for snorkelers
RACHEL JACKSON CHRISTMAS

Kenya? Nope. Molokai Ranch Wildlife Preserve   MARY ANNE HOWLAND

Surfboards parked in front of a house, Molokai   MARY ANNE HOWLAND

Waikiki Beach, with Diamond Head in the background, Oahu   OUTRIGGER HOTELS HAWAII

Iolani, the only royal palace in the United States, Honolulu, Oahu   THE FRIENDS OF
IOLANI PALACE

Mauna Kea golf course and the Mauna Kea Beach Hotel, the Big Island of Hawaii

KAUAI

If I had to choose my favorite Hawaiian island, Kauai would probably win. My opinion certainly wouldn't be in the minority. Even many Oahu residents are quick to name Kauai as their most loved Neighbor Island. Therefore, one afternoon while I was relaxing in a hot tub at the sumptuous Westin Kauai hotel, I was startled out of my serenity by a conversation I overheard between a pair of fellow soakers. Draining her mai tai with a slurp, one woman told another, "I went driving up north yesterday and there was nothing to see. I should have just stayed here." I was flabbergasted. *Nothing to see?* In my book, jagged mountains, smooth green cow-studded meadows, craggy cliffs, waterfalls, rainbows spanning bays, and deserted sandy crescents hardly constitute "nothing." Perhaps this woman was so dazzled by the elaborate human-made pleasures of the island's first megaresort that, as far as she was concerned, nature's handiwork paled by comparison. It's good that this vacationer didn't do the location scouting for *South Pacific,* Michener's *The Hawaiians,* Elvis' *Blue Hawaii, Sadie Thompson, Raiders of the Lost Ark, The Thorn Birds,* or *Fantasy Island.* These and other well-known film and television productions would have looked mighty different without the scenes that were shot on Kauai.

Much of Kauai's beauty comes from its age. The oldest of the main Hawaiian Islands, it has had plenty of time to be sculpted by the elements. Its 553 square miles are embellished by some of the state's most stunning scenery, from meandering rivers and streams to the breathtaking, 4000-foot cliffs of the Na Pali Coast and 10-mile-long, 2-mile-wide, 3600-foot-deep Waimea Canyon (dubbed the "Grand Canyon of the Pacific" by Mark Twain). Rising more than 5000 feet, Mt. Waialeale (why-ollie-ollie) stands at the center of the nearly round island.

This extinct volcano is considered the wettest spot on earth. Almost 500 inches of rain (about 40 feet!) fall on this misty mountain each year, and its dark green slopes are striped with white cascades. No wonder its name means "overflowing water." But this precipitation is surprisingly localized. Just a few miles west, there's an arid region that receives a mere six inches of rain a year. On the mountain, lava tubes

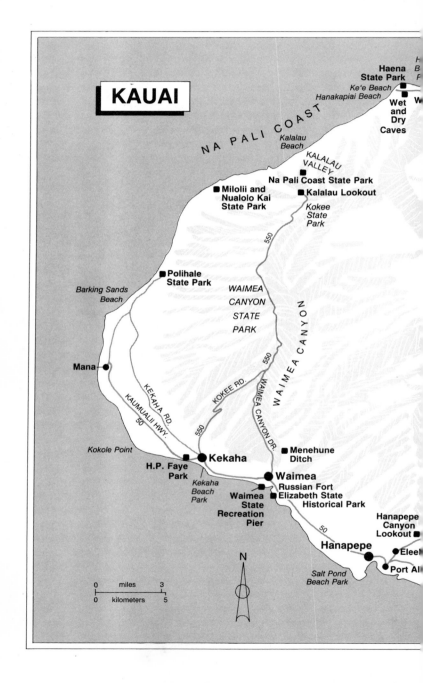

KAUAI

Haena
State Park

Ke'e Beach
Hanakapiai Beach

Wet
and
Dry
Caves

NA PALI COAST

Kalalau
Beach

KALALAU
VALLEY

Na Pali Coast State Park

Milolii and
Nualolo Kai
State Park

Kalalau Lookout

Kokee
State
Park

Polihale
State Park

Barking Sands
Beach

WAIMEA

CANYON

STATE

PARK

550

WAIMEA CANYON

Mana

550

KOKEE RD.

WAIMEA CANYON DR.

KEKAHA RD.

KAUMUALII HWY.

50

Kokole Point

H.P. Faye
Park

Kekaha

Menehune
Ditch

Waimea

Kekaha
Beach
Park

Waimea
State
Recreation
Pier

Russian Fort
Elizabeth State
Historical Park

Hanapepe
Canyon
Lookout

50

Hanapepe

Elee

Port All

Salt Pond
Beach Park

N

0   miles   3
0 kilometers 5

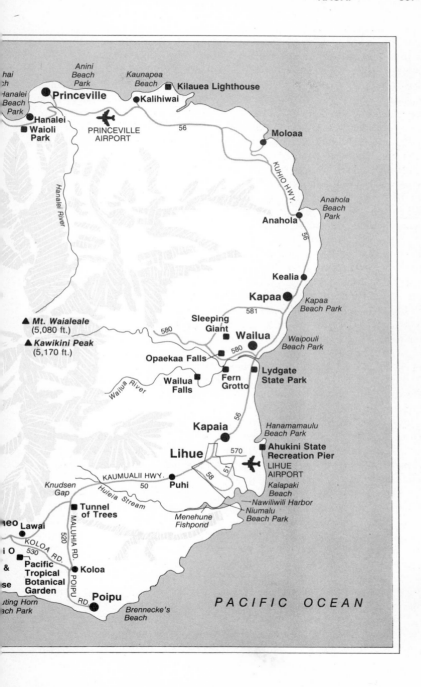

PACIFIC OCEAN

spew miniature rivers. The water pouring down the slopes has carved out the Na Pali Coast and other cliffs. At the misty summit, strong winds prevent ohia trees from growing more than *six inches* off the soggy ground! Consider taking a helicopter tour over this mountain. Elsewhere on Kauai, human hands have further enhanced the island's striking vistas with taro patches, rice paddies, pineapple fields, sugar-cane, and somnolent rural towns.

The northernmost of Hawaii's inhabited islands, Kauai and tiny neighboring Niihau are the only major members of the archipelago that can't be seen from any of the other islands. Eighty miles of rough, churning ocean lie between Kauai and Oahu. In fact, Kamehameha the Great found Kauai so difficult to reach that he was unable to conquer it in battle as he had the other islands. He finally managed to bring it under his rule, thus uniting the Hawaiian Islands, but only after tricking Kauai's chief into handing it over.

Kauai is *not* for people who thrive on crowds or night life. While it does have its share of resort hotels, shopping centers, and good restaurants along with a smattering of museums, art galleries, and night spots, its main draws lie outdoors. Hiking, camping, and scuba diving are all excellent here. At the end of a winding dirt road in the west, Polihale is the island's longest beach, stretching more than 15 miles. The sandy shores in the north are also eye-pleasing, but during the winter their waves are much too rough for swimming, snorkeling, or diving. At this time of year, head to Poipu, in the south, or the east side of the island, where the water remains much calmer throughout the year.

Thanks to the fact that Kauai receives more rain than the rest of Hawaii, it is covered with a multitude of flowers and other flourishing vegetation. Shrouded in mist, lopsided mountain peaks and verdant expanses take on a mystical beauty when showers hit. The sunniest regions are along the southern coast, where the Poipu resort area is located, and the western shore, where Polihale beach is found. Hanalei and Princeville, in the north, are the resorts where rain is most frequent. Thus the north is wonderfully green.

Hurricane Iwa, which tore through Kauai in 1982, was one of the island's worst natural disasters. A great deal of land and many buildings were heavily damaged. Hard times followed. A renewed push toward tourism on this relatively undeveloped island helped pull Kauai out of the economic slump. New luxury hotels and condos sprouted. More upscale restaurants opened. Sightseeing companies increased rubber raft excursions, whale-watching cruises, and helicopter tours. Yet tourism does not seem to predominate on Kauai today. There are still plenty of places that appear unchanged by the visitor industry.

Poipu remains the island's most popular resort area, especially among the young set. Its sandy beaches are good for swimming and bodysurfing throughout the year. If you choose to stay in quiet Waimea, west of Poipu, you'll get a taste of day-to-day life for residents. At the lodge in the cool forest of lofty Kokee State Park, you can curl up in front of a crackling fireplace at night. Chances are your plane will land in Lihue, Kauai's capital, where the island's main airport is located (the other one is at Princeville). The splashy Westin Kauai hotel is near town. Known as the Coconut Coast, the beach-rimmed strip north of Lihue (encompassing Wailua and Kapaa) is studded with more hotels and condominiums. This area is rich in Hawaiian history. Golfers are drawn to tranquil Hanalei and Princeville in the north. When you're ready to explore, allow at least three days for leisurely touring—one for Poipu up the east coast to Kapaa; another for Kapaa up along the north shore through Hanalei and Princeville to Haena, where Kuhio Highway (Route 56) ends; and the third for the southern coast west of Poipu, up to Waimea Canyon, Kokee State Park, and Kalalau Lookout. You may want to spend another day or an afternoon on Polihale beach on the west coast.

Hawaiian Roots

Kauai is famous for its tales of *Menehune,* the race of miniature people who were the Hawaiian version of European leprechauns or trolls. The difference is that the Menehune may have truly existed. According to a census taken toward the end of the 1700s, 65 Menehune living in Wainiha Valley were under the domain of Kauai's King Ka-umu-alii. These hirsute, white-skinned people were said to be a mere two or three feet tall, with red faces, wide noses, overhanging foreheads, and scraggly straight hair. Fond of dining on poi and shrimp, the Menehune weren't big on conversation—but when they *did* speak, their deep gravelly voices sounded like dogs growling. They got a real kick out of playful activities such as rolling down hillsides into the ocean. With their compact, muscular bodies, they were well suited for their celebrated stone masonry. For instance, impressive Menehune Ditch, in southwestern Kauai, is believed to have been built by members of this nocturnal race in just one night. The Tahitian word for "Menehune" means "commoner." Some historians theorize that the Menehune were inhabiting Tahiti when the Polynesians first arrived there and that these little people eventually made their way to Hawaii. Legend says that when their chiefs began to worry that too much interbreeding with Hawaiians would dilute their race, the Menehune sailed away on a floating island.

In residential Waimea, west of Poipu, you're likely to hear the Hawaiian language spoken and Hawaiian music that isn't played in exchange for tourists' dollars. More Hawaiiana is found along the Coconut Coast, from Lihue north. At the Kauai Museum in Lihue, displays include ancient Hawaiian featherwork, *umeke laau* (carved wooden bowls), and elaborate necklaces made of tiny shells or braided human hair and whale bone. In Wailua, Highway 580 is also known as King's Highway, since in the old days Hawaiian regents were carried along this road so that their royal feet were not sullied by touching the ground. Off this highway, Pohaku Ho'Ohanau is a sacred heiau where ancient Hawaiians used to make sacrifices to the gods. At the edge of the Wailua River, you'll find Kamokila, a restored ancient Hawaiian village where visitors can watch poi being pounded and learn traditional Hawaiian crafts and games. The lagoons at the nearby Coco Palms Resort were built for Queen Deborah Kapule, Kauai's last reigning monarch, who once lived on the grounds. The thick coconut grove here is especially scenic. Another coconut grove, at Lydgate State Park, once served as a place of refuge for law-breaking Hawaiians. They could escape punishment—often death—if they reached this beach before being caught.

Farther north along the east coast, you'll come to Anahola Beach Park. During the late 1980s, Hawaiians and other sympathetic residents camped out in tents to demonstrate the need for decent, affordable housing. They protested the taking of land from Hawaiians, specifically this 1.5-acre beach park, which, along with ten adjoining acres, is managed by Kauai County. They pushed for native Hawaiian businesses to be developed at the park. Although the government had set aside land for native Hawaiians, these Kauaian Homelands have poor or nonexistent roads, water and drainage systems, and utility lines. In addition, waiting lists for parcels of this land are years long.

At Ke'e Point on the Na Pali Coast, just after the road ends on the north shore, an ancient stone hula shrine still stands. This altar honors Laka, the goddess of hula. Before each dance, performers would decorate the shrine with lama wood wrapped in yellow kapa cloth and strands of maile vine and other plants. The dancers' chants would ask Laka to allow her spirit to slip into their bodies so their movements could be as artful as hers. After each performance, they would remove their colorful leis and some of their costumes, leaving them in back of the altar. Today, some hikers are lucky enough to pass the shrine when offerings have been placed here or even when a hula *halau* (school or group) is dancing at this time-honored site.

Seventeen miles off Kauai's southwestern coast, Niihau is often referred to as "the Forbidden Island." Until the late 1980s, only people with Hawaiian blood were welcome here (with the exception of the haole family that owns the island). It was 1864 when Elizabeth Sinclair, a wealthy widow from Scotland, bought the narrow 19-mile-long land mass from King Kamehameha for $10,000. Over the years, her descendants, the Robinson family, have made sure that old Hawaiian traditions are maintained here. Niihau is the only place in Hawaii where Hawaiian is the primary language. Plumbing, electricity, telephones, cigarettes, alcohol, and guns are all alien to its 200 or so residents. Most people work on the Robinson's cattle and sheep ranch or sell honey or charcoal. Another lucrative though time-consuming industry is the making of leis comprised of tiny, rare Niihau shells. These intricate necklaces, sold throughout Hawaii, can cost hundreds or even thousands of dollars each.

Some residents of the state commend the Robinsons for their success in keeping a piece of old Hawaii alive in the present. However, other people believe that this haole family is exploiting the people of Niihau for cheap labor. In 1988, helicopter tours were begun from Kauai to supplement the cost of using the whirlybird for medical emergencies. However, the flights don't go near the town of Puuwai, so sightseers don't get a peek at areas where people live. Many tourists have complained that a glimpse of barren, deserted land, no matter how "forbidden" it once was, just isn't worth the hefty price of these flights.

Special Events

On Lei Day (May 1), everyone decks themselves out with floral garlands, and a fierce lei-making competition is held at the Kauai Museum in Lihue. The museum also hosts a holiday festival in December. Aloha Week, the state-wide celebration of Hawaiian culture, featuring street fairs, hula performances, and crafts demonstrations and sales, occurs in September or October.

Perhaps Kauai's most colorful annual event is the Japanese O-Bon Festival which runs from mid-June through August. Rooted in Buddhism, this series of weekend ceremonies and dances pays homage to the ancestors. After a brief religious service, live drums accompany taped Asian music. Inside a roped-off circle, people of different races dressed in colorful kimonos and happi coats dance gracefully. The *chochin* (Japanese paper lanterns) hanging above their heads are believed to light the path of the souls of the deceased, who are thought to come home every summer. Waiting to buy local specialties—such as *yakatori* (skewered chicken cooked over charcoals), *mochi* (steamed squares of sweetened, pounded rice), shave ice (snow cones), pronto pups (corn dogs), and flying saucers (a hamburger between two slices of bread)— spectators cluster around food stands. There is usually a "ball throw" booth as well as "dime toss" and "ring the bottle" concessions and dart games. Each bon dance ends promptly at midnight.

Hosted by Kauai's Koloa Jodo Mission, a special tradition takes place following sunset on the Sunday after the Saturday night O-Bon dance. Residents and tourists crowd Kukuiula Small Boat Harbor, while members of the temple launch a boat stocked with food. Trailing behind it are rafts carrying cho-chin. Each paper lantern has been bought from the temple by a different family so that each clan will be represented. In this way, participants symbolically send the souls of the departed back to the Buddha Land of Peace. The food ensures that the souls won't grow hungry.

Getting Around

Kauai's main airport is at Lihue, a five-minute drive from town. Wailua and Kapaa hotels and condos are about 15 minutes away. The drive to Hanalei and Princeville, in the north, will take about 1¼ hours from Lihue. The smaller Princeville Airport is only five minutes from the hotel and condos of Princeville, and 15 minutes from the town of Hanalei. From Lihue Airport to Poipu, in the south, the ride should last about 15 minutes. Plan to spend a least two hours on the road to get to the lodge in wooded, mountainous Kokee. Princeville hotels and condos offer free shuttle service to and from Princeville Airport. Some accommodations in other parts of Kauai provide complimentary shuttle service to and from Lihue Airport. Otherwise, Gray Line Hawaii and Shoppe Hoppers shuttle buses and vans run between the airport and accommodations. Of course, taxis and rental cars are also available at the airport, and you can arrange to be picked up by a limousine.

Although there is no public bus system on Kauai, Shoppe Hoppers vans take visitors to various stores and attractions. You can also travel to specific sights by tour bus. Taxis, which can be painfully expensive, are best left as a last resort. The most convenient way to get around is by rental car. Kauai has one main road, but unfortunately it just falls short of making a complete circle around the island and no roads cut all the way across the rugged interior. This means that you'll have to backtrack during your touring, unless you plan to move from a hotel in one part of the island to an accommodation in another. However, Kauai's scenery is spectacular coming *and* going. You'll probably find it useful to have a four-wheel drive for a trip to Polihale beach or to Kalalau Lookout.

The South

Heading west on Highway 50 toward Poipu on your way from Lihue Airport, don't be discouraged if you can't make out **Queen Victoria's Profile** near the top of the Hoary Head Mountains to the left. Not everyone agrees that this rocky configuration looks like Her Majesty. To the right, Mt. Waialeale slopes upward. When you turn south onto Highway 520, a.k.a. Maluhia Road, you'll cut through the **Tunnel of Trees,** a dramatic passageway lined with stately eucalyptus whose branches reach out to each other overhead.

Established in the 1830s, Kauai's first sugar plantation once thrived where **Old Koloa Town** now stands. You'll see the timeworn smokestack and other remnants of the mill. Attractively refurbished or re-created 19th-century wooden buildings give the town a Western frontier look. The boutiques and galleries housed inside are better for browsing than for buying, since the upscale jewelry, clothing, and other goods come with (very) upscale price tags. Across the street from the mammoth monkeypod tree, sugarcane has been planted to illustrate the variety of strains. Nearby, you'll see a monument with bronze bas-reliefs of members of the different races and nationalities whose back-breaking work made Hawaii's sugarcane fields so prosperous. The town also sports a post office, some restaurants, and a gas station next to a food stand selling good plate lunches and saimin.

Once a private estate, **Kiahuna Plantation Resort and Gardens** is ablaze with thousands of different types of plants and flowers, such as hibiscus, orchids, aloe, and plumeria. Tours are conducted of the gracious grounds, which include lava-rock pools and a garden with herbs and other plants used by early Hawaiians. **Poipu,** Kauai's sunniest resort area, is known for its string of good beaches and appealing collection of hotels and condominiums. Swimming and boogie-boarding are all the rage here. Ancient Hawaiian *petroglyphs* can be found at **Poipu Beach Park.** The waves are perfect for bodysurfing at **Brennecke's Beach.** Other good sandy stretches in this neighborhood are **Mahaulepu** and **Shipwreck's Beach,** both refreshingly tranquil and uncrowded. Nearby **Prince Kuhio Park,** on Lawai Road, marks the birthplace of one of Hawaii's most cherished politicians. Water gushes into the air as if from a geyser at **Spouting Horn,** at the end of this road. Forced into a lava tube, waves have nowhere else to go but up. Don't venture off the paved walkway, since the rocks can be dangerously slippery.

Just north of Poipu, **Lawai** farmland yields a healthy selection of tropical fruit. You'll need to make reservations to visit the **Pacific Tropical Botanical Garden** in Lawai Valley. Tours of the flourishing grounds include a visit to a neighboring 100-acre garden estate that boasts a commanding view of Lawai Bay. Here you'll see the vacation cottage used by Queen Emma, wife of King Kamehameha IV, during the 1880s. Ancient Hawaiian taro terraces and stone walls remain. Back on Highway 50, you'll come to the picturesque village of **Kalaheo.** Most of the people who live in the attractive homes of this settlement are Portuguese immigrants who came to Hawaii to fish and work on the plantations. If you're carrying picnic fixin's, consider stopping at **Kukuiolono Park,** with its Hawaiian display, Japanese gardens, and golf course. The view from this lofty height is wonderful.

More beautiful blossoms await visitors at 12-acre **Olo Pua Gardens,** about a half mile up a private road just past Kalaheo. This plantation estate dating back to the 1930s features a pond in the shape of a hibiscus. Along Highway 50, **Hanapepe Overlook** brings cars and tour buses to a halt. Lush vegetation and bright green geometric plots of farmland cover deep Hanapepe Valley. Smooth hills roll gently in the distance. In stark contrast, the dramatic canyon cliffs are a vivid orange. Here in this chasm in 1824, the son of Kauai's King Ka-umu-alii was the leader of the island's final military maneuver. Weathered wooden buildings border the streets of **Hanapepe,** which is reminiscent of an old Western town on the mainland. Chickens do their jerky dash back and forth across the road. A few upscale shops struggle to keep afloat on the often deserted streets. This agricultural town once bustled with energy. Then came a highway that bypassed it, and a shopping center was built nearby. Along the makai (ocean) side of the main highway, **Kauai Soto Zen Temple** makes an eye-catching landmark. At the end of Lele Road, you'll come to **Salt Pond Beach Park,** where salt is still dried in the sun as it has been for generations. From nearby **Burns Fields,** arrange to take off in a glider plane or a helicopter.

The West

A few miles west of Hanapepe, the overgrown ruins of 19th-century **Fort Elizabeth,** more commonly called the **Russian Fort,** sit on a rise above the Waimea River. A German adventurer working for a Russian trading company bamboozled Kauai's King Ka-umu-alii into having it built. He gave the Hawaiian monarch his worthless word that Czar Nicholas would help overthrow Kamehameha the Great, thus restoring Kauai's independence. Across the Waimea River Bridge and about 2½ miles up Menehune Road, **Menehune Ditch** is an aqueduct said to have been constructed by Kauai's legendary race of little people. Archaeologists have lent credence to this theory by pointing out that the stones were cut and put together in a manner that bears no resemblance to any other construction done by Hawaiians. They also note that markings have been found here that seem to have no connection with early Hawaiian drawings, symbols, or designs.

Not far from the Russian Fort is the site where British Captain James Cook first landed in Hawaii in 1778, at Waimea Bay. The unassuming **Captain Cook Monument** stands on the roadside in the rural town of **Waimea**. Cows laze in the shade of trees. Some houses are flanked by the bushy, dwarfed variety of palms; no need to climb them for coconuts—just reach up. If you're headed to Waimea Canyon, Kokee State Park, or Kalalau Lookout, turn *mauka* (inland) up **Waimea Canyon Drive.** Those who would prefer a less rugged route should continue west on Highway 50 to Kekaha, then turn mauka onto wider, smoother **Kokee Road** (Highway 550).

Sugarcane fields stretch for miles along much of Highway 50. Outside the mill in the plantation town of **Kekaha,** a sign reads, "Sorry, absolutely no factory tours.'' However, anyone is welcome to watch the machinery heaving the stalks onto trucks that seem about to buckle under the weight of all the cane. The smell of molasses mingles with the perfume of the plumeria and other flowers that border the area's handsome wooden homes. West of Kekaha, dune buggies often roar down the sand of **Kekaha Beach Park,** off Highway 50. Overlooked by commanding sea cliffs, **Polihale** is Kauai's longest beach. On weekends, this broad stretch of sand also draws the dune buggy crowd, but it is practically deserted at other times. You'll reach the beach after driving to the end of Highway 50, then turning *makai* (left) onto a rutted, rocky dirt road that snakes through sugarcane fields toward the Pacific.

Waimea Canyon Drive and Kokee Road meet each other near **Waimea Canyon Lookout,** about 3400 feet in the sky. Along the way you'll be treated to panoramic views of Niihau, the town of Waimea, and the bright blue Pacific. Especially during winter months, a sweater will keep you comfortable at these cool, breezy heights. Growing deepest in color toward the end of the day, the gorge's burnt oranges, mauves, and jades continuously change in intensity. The vastness of the rugged chasm is hard to believe.

Some 45 miles of Hawaii's most rewarding and extensive hiking trails crisscross 4435-acre **Kokee State Park,** beginning at around 3000 feet. Allow at least a full day if you're planning to hike. Trails range from comfortable strolls to challenging treks. For instance, the path to scenic Kawaikoi Stream is not long, while more extensive, more rugged routes will take you through dense forest to waterfalls or a cluster of California redwoods. If only sightseeing is on your agenda, half a day will suffice. All kinds of rare birds and plants flourish in this region. Goats perch precariously at the nearly vertical edges of Waimea Canyon. Delicious lilikoi (passionfruit), blackberries, and local Methley plums grow wild. Vistas take in the imposing cliffs of the Na Pali Coast, beaches, jungled valleys, and even a swamp.

Kokee's misty forests were once a prime source of lustrous koa wood, which was cut into surfboards, canoes, paddles, and weapons. Ancient Hawaiians also came here armed with nets and poles smeared with a gluelike substance. They caught the most brilliantly colored birds, plucked their feathers, then released the animals. The plumes were fashioned into ceremonial helmets, robes, and leis to be worn by the alii.

You may hear Kokee's *(moa)* wild fowl conversing loudly with each other. The ancestors of these chickens arrived in Hawaii by canoe with the early Polynesian settlers. Kauai is one of the only parts of the state where these birds still thrive. On other islands, they were virtually wiped out by the mongooses imported by sugar planters to get rid of the rats in the cane fields. An old story explains why the mongooses did not decimate Kauai's wild chickens by eating their eggs as they did elsewhere: A crate packed with these small, furry, long-tailed creatures was delivered to each island. While the inspector from Kauai was examining the cargo at the dock, one of the animals bit him. Enraged, he threw the crate into the water, and the mongooses all drowned.

The ancient Polynesians also carried the ancestors of Kokee's *pua'a* (wild pigs) when they sailed across thousands of ocean miles from Tahiti. Early Hawaiians often killed and buried pigs to appease the gods. These animals were almost as weighty a sacrifice as human beings. Pigs served other purposes as well: Their meat was eaten—but only by men— and boar tusks were transformed into jewelry. Unfortunately, hunting of wild boar, deer, and some game birds is permitted in Kokee at various times of year, so *be careful*. Rainbow trout fishing is allowed in a variety of streams in Kokee State Park. However, this sport is limited to August and September, and anglers need to obtain freshwater fishing licenses.

During the 1930s, when Kokee's hiking trails were originally laid out, cabins were built where **Kokee Lodge** now stands. The weather can be downright chilly up there, so the fireplaces in the guest rooms get lots of action. In addition to a good restaurant and a gift shop, the inn sports **Kokee Museum.** An old legend explains how the meadow facing the lodge came into being. This verdant open expanse once sprouted as many trees as the rest of the area. A trans-island trail to Kalalau Valley cut through these dense woods. Residing in this forest was a terrifying *akua* (spirit), who got his kicks from hiding behind trees and then roughing up, even sometimes killing, unsuspecting travelers. The people of Kauai begged one of their gods to do away with this cruel spirit. But the evil akua paid no attention to the god's orders to cease and desist. The deity became so infuriated at the spirit's disrespect that the god swooped down and tore up all the trees by their roots. He piled them up, set them ablaze, and decreed that trees would never again grow here and thus akua would have no place to hide.

When the weather cooperates, the **Kalalau Lookout,** at about 4000 feet, affords views of mountains, waterfalls, treetops in the sprawling valley, and the beach-rimmed ocean. A rewarding hiking trail starts here. In ancient times, Kalalau was one of Kauai's major settlements. The crumbling heiau where religious sacrifices were made and the agricultural terraces where taro and other crops once grew are virtually all that remain of the villages today.

The East

After driving north of Poipu through the **Tunnel of Trees** and heading east, you'll come to **Kilohana,** not far from Lihue. Since 1986, this Wilcox family sugar plantation estate has welcomed the public to its 35 landscaped acres. Art galleries, jewelry stores, crafts shops, and other boutiques fill the rooms of the handsome old house. A flower-lined courtyard has been transformed into an attractive restaurant. Agricultural displays and rides in a carriage drawn by Clydesdales also entertain visitors. Across the road, **Kukui Grove Shopping Center** is one of Hawaii's many malls.

About five minutes outside Lihue, 19th-century **Grove Farm Homestead** is still a working farm. Its 80 acres also serve as a living museum, giving travelers a glimpse of old Hawaii. Every week, cruise ships sidle up to shore at **Nawiliwili Harbor,** Kauai's main port. This commercial dock is also the place to board boats for sightseeing, fishing, and snorkeling excursions. Not far from here in **Kalapaki Beach,** a serene cove at the edge of the **Westin Kauai** hotel. With its extensive Asian and Pacific art collection, dramatic sprawling swimming pool, and selection of restaurants, this lavish resort is worth investigation.

Huleia Stream spills into Nawiliwili Harbor. Although it is fed by rain-drenched Mt. Waialeale, its average depth is only four feet and it is no more than ten feet at its deepest. It meanders through densely jungled **Huleia National Wildlife Refuge,** where the opening scenes of *Raiders of the Lost Ark* were filmed. Mynah birds screech and egrets perch amid the tangle of mangroves along the shore. Fiery red ginger, monkeypod and mango trees, hibiscus, and elephant ear plants also border this 18-mile waterway, only three miles of which are navigable. Some part of the stream swirl around boulders. While the wildlife sanctuary is closed to the public, you can see it from a kayak (a *wonderful* experience) or by small boat. Another place to catch a glimpse of the refuge is from the **Menehune Fishpond Overlook** on Niumalu Road, a quiet, mountainous thruway.

Also called **Alakoko** (''rippling blood''), this fishpond was believed by ancient Hawaiians to have been built by the Menehune, Kauai's legendary elflike race. The aqueduct stretches 900 feet along Huleia Stream. Watched over by the craggy Hoary Head Mountains, this pond is still used for raising mullet, as it has been for centuries. According to early Hawaiians, the Menehune agreed to construct this stone-enclosed fishpond for a young prince and princess. However, they made it clear to all that absolutely no one would be allowed to watch them at work. In just one night, they built the pond. The heavy stones were transported to the stream by passing them from person to person in a line that stretched for 25 miles. When the job was almost done, the royal pair could no longer resist taking a look at the industrious little people. Catching them on their hillside perch, the Menehune turned the two into the twin stone pillars that you can see today on the ridge above the pond.

In **Lihue,** the county seat for both Kauai and Niihau, all kinds of Hawaiiana is on display at the **Kauai Museum.** Lihue Airport is just outside town. The shore from Lihue north is known as the Coconut Coast, for its many palms. As you drive along Kuhio Highway (Highway 56), you'll be treated to great views of Kauai's trademark open land. As you travel north, the color green seems to come in an increasing number of shades, from lime to forest. You might see a few horses, their heads bent to the grass, then pass a huge pasture with a single cow.

From Highway 583 or from Maalo Road (off Highway 56), gaze down on **Wailua Falls.** These dramatic 80-foot cascades were used in the opening of the defunct *Fantasy Island* television series. The cliff over which the water tumbles into a pool served as a diving platform for daring alii. A nearly vertical hiking trail leads down to the falls. In **Wailua** (''sacred water''), remnants of the Hawaiian past have made their way into the present. Nothing much remains of **Holo Holo Ku Heiau** beyond a flower garden marking the small grassy area. However, human sacrifices were once made at this site. In more recent history, hippie types were living here, unbeknownst to the authorities until there was a fire in the stone structure and pots and pans were discovered inside. Hawaiian women once went to the neighboring heiau, **Pohaku Ho-Ohanau,** to give birth to ensure that their children would become kings or chiefs. Fronted by a small lawn, these rocky ruins sit by the side of the road.

Coco Palms Resort is the kind of hotel most people envision when they think of Hawaii. Thatched-roof bungalows sit at the edge of a lagoon near a thick palm grove. The lagoons were built for Queen Deborah Kapule, Kauai's last reigning monarch, who once lived on the grounds. The coconut grove was originally planted during the mid-19th century by a German physician. As the trees have become elderly (palms don't live much more than 100 years), they have been replaced by new ones. Each time the resort plants a palm, it is given a plaque honoring one of Coco Palms' better-known guests (such as local athletes, James Michener, and Bing Crosby).

Visit the small **Palace Museum and Library** at Coco Palms, with its impressive display of old furniture, books, quilts, and other items. The hotel's caged monkeys hoop and holler each time bells ring on the grounds. The bells announce the frequent weddings that take place at the cozy chapel built for Rita Hayworth in her *Sadie Thompson* role. If you happen by just before sundown, be sure to stay for the torch-lighting ceremony. Clad in loincloths, well-muscled young men run along the lagoon leaving a trail of flames behind them. While this isn't exactly an authentic Hawaiian ceremony, it's fun to watch.

Off Highway 580 is the lookout for **Opaekaa Falls** (''rolling shrimp falls"). The namesake crustaceans once lived at the bottom of these mammoth cascades. Across the road and far below, the **Wailua River** wends it way between the mountains. You can look down on the thatched roofs of **Kamokila,** a re-created Hawaiian village on the banks of the river. From the waterfall overlook, vans transport people down to the village, where they can watch poi pounding and other demonstrations of ancient arts and traditions. At the end of Highway 580, **Keahua Arboretum** is a good place for a picnic or a hike to a private swimming hole.

Boats leave from Wailua Marina, off Highway 56, for **Fern Grotto,** three miles up the Wailua River. The leisurely ride, between mountains and past hau trees and other vegetation, is almost as picturesque as the fern-covered cave. My only problem with going to this lava tube is that you have to do it with a boatful of other people. The companies that take tourists there have the river sewn up. Along the way, a band plays and passengers are coaxed into ensemble hula lessons. Scores of weddings take place at the cave each year. Next to Wailua Marina, luaus are held at **Smith's Tropical Paradise,** a pleasant, expansive botanical garden with models of Polynesian, Japanese, and Filipino villages. From **Wailua Bridge,** the view of the river, palms, jagged mountains, and beach is spectacular. **Lydgate State Park,** at the mouth of the Wailua River, attracts strong swimmers and snorkelers with its lava pools. Ancient Hawaiians found refuge at this beachfront coconut grove when they have committed crimes against the gods.

You'll find some good boutiques and restaurants at the **Coconut Plantation Market Place.** This attractive open-air mall in **Waipouli** (whose border blurs with Kapaa's) is part of a development that includes a group of hotels on a rocky beach. The mountain ridge known as the **Sleeping Giant** is visible from Waipouli and the town of Kapaa. Hawaiian legend has it that the overgrown Puni fell into his slumber after a hard-fought battle. Another story explains that the giant simply gorged himself at a luau and never woke up from his nap. From Kapaa, it will take about an hour to hike to Puni's chin. A picnic table invites trekkers to relax a spell. Between June and October, the guavas are ripe for plucking off their trees. If you take the left-hand path just before the trail ends, you'll come to an overlook with a sweeping view of Kauai's eastern shore.

Tourists are far outnumbered by residents in **Kapaa.** Along the main street, stores and restaurants reside in handsome restored buildings that date back to the 19th century. The shops and eateries of **Waipouli Town Center** draw a local crowd. Across from a Catholic cemetery, **Kealia Beach** is better for sunbathing than swimming, since the undertow can be dangerous. Calmer waters are found at **Anahola Beach Park**. This tranquil, shady strip has been the site of demonstrations protesting the poor condition of Hawaiian Homestead Lands in the area. The road-side **Duane's Ono-Char Burger,** in Anahola, is a favorite place for a snack among locals.

Kauai's countryside is especially dramatic in this northern region. The many shades of green are set off by the iron-rich rust-colored earth, the orange blossoms of African tulip trees, aromatic white and yellow plumeria petals, and the spidery red and yellow flowers of Australian silky oaks. Open expanses give way to papaya and banana groves. The distinctive, narrow peaks of Anahola Mountain loom in the distance.

The North

The northern coast is my favorite part of Kauai, perhaps even of the whole state. Both despite and because of the amount of rain this region receives, it is stunning in its lushness. Towering above all the wild greenery, farm plots, and secluded beaches, mountaintops form abstract scupture against the sky. If you are staying elsewhere on Kauai, plan to spend a full day in and around Hanalei and Princeville, about an hour's drive from Wailua and an hour and 40 minutes from Poipu. This doesn't include time for hiking along the dramatic cliffs of Na Pali or viewing these promontories from a helicopter or boat.

North of Anahola, Kilauea Bridge will take you into the town of **Kilauea.** Unusual in shape, round **St. Sylvester's Catholic Church** is nestled amid red lobster claw plants, crotons, and mango and avocado trees. At one point, a group of hippies turned themselves into squatters in this modern house of worship. The stained-glass windows of **Christ Memorial Church,** built of lava rock in the 1940s, were imported all the way from England. On Saturday afternoons at the **Hawaiian Art Museum** on Kolo Road, **Hawaiian Appreciation classes** are given in chanting, hula, folklore, and history as well as art (call 828-1309). Many travelers can't resist stopping at **Banana Joe's,** a produce stand along Highway 56 that does a brisk business in fresh fruit, dried fruit, fruit shakes, fruit salad, fresh corn, and other vegetables. If you're visiting between December and May, you might spot a humpback whale from **Kilauea Point,** a promontory with wraparound views. Turquoise, electric blue, and jade water churns white as it thrashes the bottom of the cliffs. The bird sanctuary here by **Kilauea Lighthouse** is a nesting place for frigates, boobies, and other seabirds.

The view from **Kalihiwai Valley Overlook** takes in the flourishing dale and a waterfall. Kalihiwai Road leads to Anini Road, which runs into **Anini Beach.** Novice windsurfers and snorkelers cut their teeth on these waves. **Kalihiwai Bay,** a tranquil curve of sand, is also part of the quiet, residential community. Back on Highway 56, you'll pass **Princeville Airport,** which mainly provides commuter service. Area helicopter tours also take off from here. Horseback riding can be arranged at nearby **Pooku Stables.**

Developed as a vacation resort, the community of **Princeville** is one of Kauai's most scenic regions. Sprawling across the tops of cliffs, the 11,000 acres overlooking valleys are sprinkled with upscale condominiums, private homes, and the beautiful **Sheraton Mirage Princeville Hotel.** Made up of three 9-hole greens designed by Robert Trent Jones, Jr., the **Princeville Makai Golf Course** is considered one of the best in the world. The 18-hole **Prince Golf Course** is another top place for teeing off. From many parts of town, the striking Makana mountain peaks can be seen. Immortalized in *South Pacific,* they are still commonly known as **Bali Hai.**

This area was once a sugar plantation belonging to Robert Crichton Wyllie. Originally from Scotland, he became Minister of Foreign Affairs for the Hawaiian kingdom in 1798, holding the position for nearly seven decades. He chose the name Princeville for his plantation in honor of young Prince Albert, the child of Kamehameha IV and Queen Emma. Wyllie was known for his no-holds-barred entertaining. In 1862, he threw the four-year-old prince a royal birthday party, highlighted by a grand parade of 200 costumed Hawaiian men and women on horseback. Sadly, he died of an illness before his fifth birthday. Following Wyllie's death, Princeville passed into the hands of the Scotsman's nephew. But the plantation was beset by so many financial problems that the new owner committed suicide. In 1895, Albert Wilcox, a member of a missionary family originally from Connecticut, bought the land. He rescued it from total ruin by curtailing the failing sugar crops, turning the highlands over to cattle ranching, and renting the lowlands to Chinese rice farmers.

Princeville Shopping Center sits across the road from the **Hanalei Valley Overlook.** The breathtaking view encompasses many taro patches. A river cuts through the tapestry of farm plots, which carpet the valley against a background of irregular mountain ridges. Also down below, the **Hanalei National Wildlife Refuge** offers 900 acres of protection for endangered waterfowl. On its way into the valley, Highway 56 passes along a creaky, arched, one-lane bridge that was built in 1912. Despite its elderly appearance, residents are too attached to it to replace it. Kayaking is common on the river here and cows graze in a pasture along the bank.

Hanalei was one of the earliest areas settled by the ancient Pacific voyagers who first came to Hawaii. Whey they arrived, the region was covered with marshes. After they were through with it, the mushy terrain had been turned into thriving farmland, complete with dams and irrigation ditches. According to ancient Hawaiians, Kauai's last Menehune resided here. Some present-day locals say that *mo'o* (giant lizard gods) still live in Hanalei's mountain pools. Many rainbows decorate this lush part of Kauai. An old story explains how these colorful arcs came to be: A stranger arrived with sheets of kapa dyed in various hues. He threw the bark cloth into a pool at the base of a waterfall and the colors were forever reflected in the mist. Hanalei ("crescent bay") aptly describes the namesake sandy cove cupped by mountains. This narrow roadside beach is good for swimming and snorkeling near the pier, where the water is calmest.

In the small, pretty town, **Waioli Mission** is where one of Kauai's wealthiest and most influential haole families got its start. This was the home of Abner and Lucy Wilcox, a missionary couple who came to Hawaii from Connecticut in the 1840s. Now a museum, this old house displays koa wood furniture and other belongings that characterize their early spartan lifestyle. The Wilcox mansion, built on Hanalei Bay once their fortune had grown, is still the family home. A dearth of workers for Kauai's plantations brought contract laborers from China, then from Japan. As the Asian community grew, taro patches gave way to rice paddies. The building that now houses the **Hanalei Museum** was originally the home of some of the area's first Chinese immigrants, the Ho family. Displays bring old Hanalei in particular and old Hawaii in general to life. The Chings are another early Chinese family whose legacy lives on, in **Ching Young Village** shopping center. In 1896, Ching Young and his wife, Man Sing, immigrated to Hawaii. Here they had eight children, bought a rice mill, and opened a general store. Today this general store is where you'll find the petite **Native Hawaiian Museum** and some arts and crafts shops.

Artists, poets, and other creative types are drawn to these and other boutiques and galleries in Hanalei. Perhaps the town's artistic leanings are a holdover from the early 1970s, when Hanalei was flooded with hippies, mostly from the mainland. The area's serene atmosphere changed drastically when some 60 of these transients began camping out in nearby Haena, on land owned by Howard Taylor, brother of actress Elizabeth Taylor. They fancied themselves "getting back to nature." Shelters thrown together with old lumber and sheets of plastic went up both on the ground and in trees. Some of these flower children earned their living by doing odd jobs in and around town. Others went on welfare or grew and sold marijuana. Local residents were disgusted and angered by the lifestyle of these young people. Finally, after years of fighting it out through the legal system, the state purchased the land, turning it into Haena State Park, and the hippies were sent packing. In Waipa Valley, just west of Hanalei, pick up some fresh fruit or vegetables from one of the farmers and spend some time talking story.

Before you reach Haena from Hanalei, you'll cross some more scenic one-lane bridges and come to **Lumahai Beach**. It was on this lovely mile-long cliff-enclosed stretch that Mitzi Gaynor sang about washing a man out of her hair in *South Pacific*. Travelers can gaze down on this cove from the road or carefully pick their way down the steep trial to the sand. Boats and rubber rafts leave for cruises along dramatic Na Pali coast from nearby **Tunnels Beach.** This broad stretch of sand, where the water is relatively calm, affords wonderful views of the cliffs.

Farther along Highway 56, **Maniniholo Dry Cave** gapes at the side of the road. You can walk deep inside this high-ceilinged grotto that is nearly as large as a football field. Lunch wagons wait to serve people at **Haena State Park,** across the road from the cave. **Haena Beach,** great for shelling, is also good for strong swimmers when the water is calm. Local children and adults swim in the rocky stream by the Haena State Park sign on the roadside. A waterfall trickles into the natural pool here. By the old houses in this area, you might see goat and pig skins hung out to dry like laundry, with birds perched on the lines. Some people believe that **Waikapalae** and **Waikanaloa Wet Caves** were scooped out by Pele, the fiery volcano goddess. Although the stagnant water is no longer safe for swimming, the caves are visually impressive.

Highway 56 dries up at **Keʻe Beach State Park,** where the 11-mile **Kalalau Trail** along the Na Pali Coast begins. From the beach, you'll have a fabulous view of the cliffs. The climactic scene in *The Thorn Birds* TV mini-series in which a young woman and a priest finally express their love for each other was filmed on this shore. Even Pele, the volcano goddess, could not resist Keʻe's romantic charms. She transformed herself into a beautiful mortal so she could join a hula festival here. Human desires suddenly overcame her, and before she knew it, she had fallen deeply in love with the island's dashing Chief Lohiau. A trail from the beach leads to **Lohiau's Dance Pavilion.** This stone shrine honors Laka, the hula goddess. Present-day hikers sometimes come across offerings left at the altar by contemporary dancers and worshippers.

Meaning "the cliffs" in Hawaiian, the **Na Pali Coast** is accessible only by foot. However, spectacular views of it can be enjoyed from both the air and the sea. Whether this ruggedly beautiful coastline is seen from a boat or raft, through a helicopter window, or while hiking along it on the Kalalau Trail, no traveler should miss an opportunity to visit the region. About two miles along the hiking trail, picturesque **Kanakapiai Beach** is a favorite stopping-off point for trekkers. Although the beach is at its widest and the waves at their calmest during the summer, the water here can be dangerous for swimming year-round. When the water is calm enough (in the spring and summer), sightseeing-boats cruise by 4000-foot precipices and past old valleys. (Some cruises include lunch and snorkeling.) Rafts skirt waterfalls and zip into the caves behind the cascades. Towering over small sandy coves, the striated mountains and cliffs are a melange of greens, oranges, and browns. Huge patches of red earth are visible where chunks of the cliffs have broken off and tumbled into the sea over the centuries. The tiny moving figures boaters see in valleys and along the trail are goats and hikers. Sometimes following boats, pairs of dolphins show off by spiraling out of the water in unison or rolling on their backs and slapping their tails on the ocean's surface. Huge sea turtles poke their heads out of the Pacific.

Old superstitions remain about the region. Fishermen will tell you that if the mood hits, the fickle Na Pali spirits can make it difficult for certain travelers on particular days. Stories are passed around about mysterious happenings that tell adventurers to come another day instead. People have arrived at the trailhead minus that backpack of food and supplies they were positive they put in the trunk of their car. Others have set out in a boat in prime condition only to have it break down out of the blue. But visitors need not worry—all they have to do is heed the warning signs.

Historians believe that Na Pali was the first part of Kauai to be settled, probably around 989 A.D. The fertile land was well-suited for all the agricultural terraces the early Hawaiians built, and fresh water streamed down mountainsides. Villages were peppered with heiaus. Since each valley was surrounded by virtually impenetrable cliffs, it was difficult for hostile outsiders to reach this isolated region. Thus Na Pali was far more peaceful than the rest of the island. The Reverend Hiram Bingham, the head of the original group of missionaries in Hawaii, was the first Westerner to visit Na Pali, where he settled in 1822.

Especially in **Kalalau Valley,** hikers can stumble upon ancient, crumbling heiau, house sites, food pits, and taro terraces. When horses were brought here by boat in 1864, children were terrified by the strange, massive beasts. Taro farmers and their families lived in this valley until around 1919. Coffee and *ti* plants (for making *okolehao*—Hawaiian whiskey) were grown commercially in nearby valleys until the 1920s. During the latter part of that decade, two men were said to have moved all the way from Honolulu to one of Na Pali's secluded nooks so that they could distill bootleg alcohol.

A triplet of peaks known as the **Three Sisters** watches over Kalalau Valley. According to legend, a storm ripped through a coastal village in Kalalau, sweeping away homes and taro fields. Three goddesses who lived in mountain caves behind the valley felt sorry for the poor mortals below. They turned themselves into human beings and went down to help the villagers. With this divine aid, the results of the storm's vicious handiwork were repaired in just one day. While the villagers rejoiced, grateful for this superhuman assistance, the father of the sisters fumed. How dare his daughters lower themselves by fraternizing with mere mortals? To punish the wayward goddesses, he transformed them into the pillars of stone that still stand.

A smattering of people make their home in this flourishing valley today, living off the land and the sea. Locals will tell you about "the Hermit of Kalalau," a doctor who moved into one of the caves by the beach during the late 1950s. In the late 1960s and early '70s, mainland hippies joined him in the valley. Kauaians were scandalized to discover that these young people were living on and around sacred, historic heiau, house sites, and taro terraces. Although locals complained about this lack of respect, most of the hippies remained in Kalalau until the late 1970s, when they were finally evicted by the state along with those living in Haena.

WHAT TO SEE AND DO

PERSONAL FAVORITES

Cruising and snorkeling along the spectacular cliffs of the **Na Pali Coast** (see Kauai introductory section and Tours and Cruises).

Wandering around wonderfully green **Hanalei** and **Princeville** (see Kauai introductory section).

Visiting vast **Waimea Canyon** (see Sights).

*Basking on long, quiet **Polihale Beach** (see Beaches).

Taking a **helicopter ride** over Na Pali, Waimea Canyon, and Mt. Waialeale (see Tours and Cruises).

Cruising along the Wailua River to **Fern Grotto,** a gaping cave decorated with jungled foliage (see Sights and Tours and Cruises).

Learning about old Hawaii at the **Kauai Museum** and the re-created village of **Kamokila** (see Sights).

***Hawaiian Appreciation Classes** at the Hawaiian Art Museum (see Kauai introductory section).

*Off the beaten path.

Shopping at gracious **Kilohana,** a handsome old plantation house (see Sights and Shopping).

Bird-watching at **Kilauea Lighthouse** (see Sights).

Most Scenic Drive: along the historic east and verdant north coasts. (See Kauai introductory section.)

~~~~~~

SIGHTS

Hawaiiana

Kamokila Hawaiian Village • *6060 Kuamoo Rd., Wailua; 822–1192* • On the bank of the Wailua River, this re-created Hawaiian village is around the bend from Fern Grotto. It was built near the overgrown ruins of an old settlement not far from where Kauai's King Kaumu-alii had his war canoes constructed. Among the grass huts are an herbalist's house, an oracle tower, an eating house, and a sleeping shelter. Visitors watch demonstrations in ancient arts and crafts, salt making, hula, Hawaiian quilt making, and pounding taro root to make poi (the Hawaiian dietary staple). There are plots of taro and other plants used for food or medicine. Artifacts on display include a kukui nut pounder (to extract oil used for lamps), birth stones, and petroglyphs (rock carvings).

Admission: $6 for adults; $2 for children aged 6–12. Open 9 a.m.–4 p.m. Mon.–Sat. Across road from Opaekaa Falls, get shuttle bus down to village. Free shuttle bus service for some Wailua and Kapaa accommodations.

Kauai Museum • *Rice St. (Albert Spencer Wilcox Bldg., Lihue; 245–6931* • Cultural, artistic, and geological exhibits highlight the pasts of Kauai, Niihau, and the rest of Hawaii. The feather helmets and cloaks here are particularly striking. Polynesian sailors got the idea for the intricate craft of fashioning clothing from feathers during their travels in South America. Once worn by the alii during battles, these centuries-old garments remain bright in color. Ancient Hawaiians could tell a person's rank by the length and design of his cloak—the longer the cape, the more lofty his social position. Warriors carefully guarded their helmets, which they believed contained their *mana* (power) and that of their ancestors. They proudly passed their helmets down to their sons, unless, of course, these prized possessions had been taken from them during wars.

The museum also contains an intriguing display of calabashes, both wooden *(umeke laau)* and gourd *(umeke pohue)*. The shape of a plate or bowl indicated the kind of food that would be served in it. Dog meat and pork were presented on long shallow platters, while poi was put into round bowls. Water was boiled by putting hot rocks into water contained in high calabashes with thick bottoms. Beautifully grained though it was, native koa wood was not used for cooking or dining dishes since it poisoned food. Instead, containers made of this prized wood were reserved for storing shells, kapa cloth, feathers, and other dry household goods. Woods that floated, such as wiliwili and hau, were carved into storage containers for fishing gear on canoes. The neighboring island of Niihau was known for its elaborately decorated gourds. Decaying leaves and dark mud were mixed into ink, which was used to paint the hollowed-out and dried containers.

Niihau is also famous for its shell leis, examples of which you'll see at this museum. The tiny, intricately patterned shells are found on the beach only during certain months, so it can take years to gather enough to make a necklace. Thus these leis, sold today in stores throughout Hawaii, are very expensive. Another necklace exhibited is the *lei niho palaoa*. Only alii of the highest status were allowed to wear these leis made of tiny strands of braided human hair, usually adorned with an ivory pendant. On May 1 (Lei Day), a lei-making contest is held at the museum—for garlands made of flowers, not hair. Be sure to check out the Hawaiian quilts that were inspired by New England missionary women.

Open Mon.–Fri. 9 a.m.–4:30 p.m., and Sat. from 9 a.m. to 1 p.m. Admission: $4 for adults, free for children under 18.

Native Hawaiian Museum • *Ching Young Village, Hanalei* • Remnants of the heritage of Hawaii's indigenous people are on display in this small museum housed in what was originally a general store.

Fort Elizabeth • *Hwy. 50, just southwest of Waimea River Bridge* • You might say that the remains of this fort stand as a reminder of the tricks that could be pulled in the days before airplanes, telephones, Express Mail, and fax machines. Commonly called the Old Russian Fort, it was built around 1816. While in the employ of Baranov's Russian American Trading Company of Alaska, Georg Anton Scheffer arrived in Hawaii. Pretending to be a heart specialist, he cared for the infirm King Kamehameha I. In exchange, the grateful monarch gave him some prime oceanfront land. Scheffer began building a fort there. When the king saw that he had put up the Russian flag over the foundation, he promptly took the land back and continued building the fort for himself.

Then Scheffer heard that the king of the island of Kauai was tired of being ruled by King Kamehameha. He sailed to Kauai and convinced King Ka-umu-alii that the czar would help him regain Kauai's independence. In addition, he promised Russia's help in ousting Kamehameha so that Ka-umu-alii and the czar could split the rule of the other Hawaiian islands. After receiving more waterfront land and a royal gift of 30 Hawaiian commoners, Scheffer began building Fort Elizabeth, again flying the Russian flag. The charlatan's downfall finally came when the commander of a Russian naval ship arrived in Hawaii. Word reached King Ka-umu-alii that Scheffer was nothing but an imposter and that the czar had absolutely no desire to control or do battle with Hawaii. The Kauaian king quickly threw Scheffer off the island and sent a message to King Kamehameha asking him to disregard anything he might have heard about Ka-umu-ali being disloyal to the kingdom. If only the king of Kauai could have checked Scheffer's references . . .

More Remnants of the Past

Kilohana • *Hwy. 50, Lihue; 245–5608* • Whether you're in the mood for upscale shopping or not, this boutique-filled former plantation estate is worth some time. A carriage drawn by Clydesdale horses takes people for spins around the spacious grounds. Opened to the public in 1986, the main house has been carefully restored, gleaming with Douglas fir and Northern California pine. In the entryway stand two huge, highly polished calabashes made of beautifully grained monkeypod wood. These cask-shaped containers were used for storage. Receptions and weddings are held in the long, wide living room. The handsome koa wood bench here is more than a century old, and exposed beams cross the high ceiling. The war clubs were imported from New Guinea. Shops selling paintings, ceramics, Japanese antiques, clocks, jewelry, Hawaiian artifacts, and clothing now occupy the nine bedrooms, some of the nine bathrooms, and many of the closets. Oriental rugs decorate wooden floors. The guest cottage out back has been converted into Stones at Kilohana, a store carrying Pacific handiwork. From Gaylord's, the restaurant in the flower-lined courtyard, you'll have a view of Mt. Waialeale.

Shops open daily 9 a.m.–5 p.m. Gaylord's open for dinner.

Grove Farm Homestead Museum • *Hwy. 58, a mile southeast of Lihue; 245–3202* • Established in 1854, this sugar plantation was in operation until 1978. Still a working farm, the homestead and grounds are now an 80-acre living museum. Visitors learn about the plantation life of the Wilcox family, one of Kauai's wealthiest clans. The plantation was started by George Wilcox, one of the sons of missionary teachers Abner and Lucy Wilcox, who had moved to Hawaii from Connecticut during the 1840s. Armed with a Yale University degree, Wilcox was among those who revolutionized agriculture in the islands. In the days when it took a ton of water to produce a pound of sugar, he was one of the first people who began using irrigation ditches, railcars instead of oxcarts, and plows that were powered by steam instead of oxen.

Admission: $3 for adults and $1 for children 5–12. Tours conducted at 10 a.m. and 1 p.m. on Mon., Wed., and Thurs. Reservations required.

The Palace Museum and Library • *Coco Palms Hotel, Wailua; 822–4921* • During the 1890s, a group of American businessmen living in the islands overthrew the Hawaiian monarchy and placed Queen Liliuokalani under house arrest in Iolani Palace. Many of her underground supporters secretly made flag quilts, one of which is exhibited here. On one side is a bold flower design, while the Hawaiian flag is depicted on the other. Those loyal to the throne could quickly flip their bedcovers if they got an unexpected visit from a representative of the new government. Also on display at this small museum are antique wooden furniture, books, and portraits.

Hanalei Museum • *Hanalei* • This 19th-century plantation-style house has been turned into a museum highlighting the town and honoring Kauai's various ethnic groups. The home originally belonged to the Ho family, who were among Hanalei's first Chinese immigrants. When he was only 14, Ho Pak Yet came to Hawaii as an indentured laborer, accompanied by his teenage wife. Together, they saved enough money to buy a rice farm in Hanalei. The museum's displays include rice implements, old photographs of Hanalei, furniture, a bowl used for poi, weathered wooden surfboards, and an antique muumuu.

Waioli Mission House Museum • *Hwy. 56, Hanalei; 245–3202* • The plain koa wood furniture on display reflects the lifestyle of Abner and Lucy Wilcox, Connecticut missionaries who moved to this home during the 1840s. This husband-and-wife team spent more than two decades teaching at a school for Hawaiian boys from Kauai and Niihau. Abner had a reputation for being extremely strict with his students, while Lucy was known for her softer, gentler touch. They raised seven of their own sons, and their children and grandchildren went on to become prosperous, leading citizens. George Wilcox, for example, built a vast fortune from his Grove Farm surgarcane plantation near Lihue (now a living museum). Albert became wealthy by buying and selling Princeville Plantation. The Wilcox mansion on Hanalei Bay, still the family home, was built by him.

Donations appreciated. Open 9 a.m.–3 p.m. Tues., Thurs., and Sat.

Kokee Natural History Museum • *Kokee Lodge, Kokee State Park; 335–6061* • This small museum containing Kokee memorabilia is worth a few moments.
Open daily, 10 a.m.–4 p.m. No admission charge.

Nature's Best

Waimea Canyon • *up Waimea Canyon Dr. or Kokee Rd.* • Especially during winter months, be sure to take a sweater when you visit what Mark Twain called "The Grand Canyon of the Pacific." This 10-mile-long, 2-mile-wide, 3600-foot-deep chasm is a study in pinks, reds, oranges, greens, browns, and golds. The intensity of color changes with the moving sun. Goats move effortlessly along the rocky, nearly vertical edges of the cliffs. You can see this vast natural wonder by helicopter, by driving to the Waimea Canyon Lookout, or by hiking to other vantage points in and around Kokee State Park. Along the road up to the lookout, cacti are scattered across the dry hills. Yellow tufts of grass sprout from the prairielike terrain. After some hairpin curves, the ocean and the island of Niihau reveal themselves in the distance. The road continues to snake uphill, past silky oak trees with their bright red-and-yellow blossoms, the pink flowers of passion fruit vines, pines, and koa trees (once used to make canoes). Consider stopping at rustic Kokee Lodge, further up, for a meal. You may also want to continue climbing to the **Kalalau Lookout,** with its sweeping view of a historic Hawaiian valley.

Fern Grotto • *up the Wailua River* • The only way to see this gaping cave dripping with ferns and other vegetation is to take a commercial cruise from Wailua Marina. Packed with people on long rows of seats, the flat-bottomed boats ease along the river. They pass jagged mountains and cliffs with orange earth showing through the greenery. The ridge known as the Sleeping Giant gazes down on the water. Lining the banks are "scrambled egg trees," with their fluffy, butter-colored flowers, and blossoming hau trees, with their tangle of low-growing, criss-crossed branches. As passengers walk along the path to the cave, wild chickens parade by. Their long red and orange feathers look too bright to be real. Other fowl rustle through the bushes of this extremely lush forest.

When sightseers reach the cave, musicians from the boats perform "The Hawaiian Wedding Song" to show off the acoustics of the grotto. The song is quite appropriate, since dozens of weddings take place here each year. For evening ceremonies, torches are lit along the path. Couples are transported to and from the grotto in a special wedding boat. Hundreds of ferns grow from the cave walls and water trickles from above. Even on sunny days, the light is dim here, so be sure to bring fast film if you plan to take photos. While this is a wonderfully primordial setting, it would be much more pleasant if you didn't have to see it in the company of so many other people.

Cost: $10 for adults; $5 for children. (See Tours and Cruises for further details.)

Kilauea Point Wildlife Refuge • *Kilauea* • Bring your binoculars or a telephoto lens for eyeball-to-eyeball views of red-footed boobies, frigates, laysan albatross, and red-tailed tropic-birds. More seabirds nest along the rugged cliffs of this promontory than anywhere else in the main Hawaiian islands. Called *a* in Hawaiian, red-footed boobies usually build their homes in shrubs or small trees. These birds are two feet long and white in color. *Iwa,* or frigates, like to swoop down on boobies and other birds in flight to steal the fish they're carrying. Big, black-and-white *moli,* or laysan albatross, pass most of their time hunting for squid and fish. They only step on dry land when they're ready to court or breed. Until these birds mature, they can spend as many as *six years* on and above the open ocean without touching terra firma. Thus, they are less than graceful on land. Their slow, goofy-looking waddle makes them an easy catch for wild dogs and other predators.

Kilauea Point, high above the crashing ocean, is also a great place for spotting dolphins, monk seals, green sea turtles, and—from December to May—humpback whales. If you're very lucky, you'll see one of these 45-foot mammals jump completely out of the water. The lighthouse here was erected in 1913. Its beam could be seen for 20 ocean miles and planes could spot it 90 miles away.

Open noon–4 p.m. daily, except Sat.

Smith's Tropical Paradise • *next to Wailua Marina, Wailua; 822–4654* • Freckles Smith began his career as a busboy at nearby Coco Palms Resort. Today he's the president of Smith's Motorboat Service, which runs tours to Fern Grotto and operates this 30-acre botanical park. Paths wind past many-hued tropical plants and scenic lagoons. You can see the grounds by foot or take a guided tram tour. Luaus followed by international musical revues are held Monday through Friday evenings. A highlight of the feast is watching the steaming imu pig being removed from its earthen oven (a hole in the ground filled with red-hot lava rocks).

Costs: For botanical garden—$5 for adults, $3 for children. For tram ride—$8 for adults, $4 for children. For luau and show—$40 for adults, $25 for children age 11 and under. For show alone—$11 for adults, $6 for children.

*Pacific Tropical Botanical Garden • *Lawai Valley; 332–7361* • Little known by people who aren't botanists or conservationists, this flourishing 186-acre garden is a good place for anyone who appreciates the beauty (and the importance) of natural splendor. Some experts predict that no tropical rain forest will survive the year 2000 in Central and South America, having fallen victim to the economic promise of the lumber and cattle business. In addition to killing off many resident species of plants and animals, this will have a devastating effect on the ozone layer and on oxygen production worldwide. This garden serves as a center for the preservation and protection of the world's tropical plants.

Visitors take a van ride along a curving, bumpy road down into Lawai Valley. Giant green lily pads cover practically the whole surface of a pond. They are said to be strong enough for a human being to walk on. Along Lawai Stream are strands of bamboo, kukui nut trees, monkeypods, and palm trees. Double-coconut trees take more than 70 years to mature, and then seven more before their unusual nuts reach their full weight (sometimes 50 pounds).

Cost: $16. Reservations required. Open daily. Narrated shuttle and walking tour (2½ hours) given Mon.–Fri. 9 a.m. and 1 p.m.; Sat. 9 a.m.; and Sun. 1 p.m.

TOURS AND CRUISES

Travelers who decide to be taken around by someone who knows Kauai intimately will have a variety of options. I highly recommend the helicopter rides on this island and the cruises along the Na Pali Coast (in either a Zodiac rubber raft or a larger boat). Another exciting tour is conducted by kayak along Huleia Stream, through Huleia National Wildlife Refuge. One of the best van excursions is the historical and cultural tour run by North Shore Cab Company.

BY BUS, VAN, OR LIMOUSINE: You'll cover a lot of territory by taking the full-day Wailua River/Fern Grotto/Waimea Canyon tour offered by most companies. Part of the day will be spent cruising up the river to the fern-covered cave. Other sightseeing hightlights on this trip include Opaekaa Falls, Menehune Fishpond, and Fort Elizabeth (a.k.a. the Old Russian Fort). **Gray Line** ((800) 367–2420) uses both vans and large tour buses, while **Chandler's** (245–9134) uses only vans. Those who like riding in style should check out **First Class Limousines** (839–0944 or (800) 248–5101); **Kauai Island Tours** (245–4777), which carries sightseers in stretch limos and Cadillacs; and **Roberts Hawaii Tours** (245–9101), which also has stretch limos in its fleet. **Trans Hawaiian**

Services ((800) 533–8760) and **Polynesian Adventure Tours** ((800) 622–3011) are other reputable companies.

If you're interested in an excursion that zeroes in on sights involving Kauai's myths, legends, and history, consider the 2½-hour van tour offered by **North Shore Cab Company** (826–6189), based in Hanalei. You'll hear how various dramatic natural formations came to be, according to ancient Hawaiians, as well as tales about Kauai's New England missionaries, the hula goddess, and the Menehune (the legendary race of miniature people). You'll also see where scenes from several movies were shot. Pick-ups are available at Lihue Airport or at north or east coast hotels. The cost is about $36.

For an in-depth look at wooded Kokee State Park and spectacular Waimea Canyon, **Kauai Mountain Tours** (245–7224 or (800) 222–7756) uses small four-wheel-drive vans to travel the back roads of Kauai's western region. A full-day trip with lunch will run about $78. Half-day tours are also conducted.

BY BICYCLE: The full-day excursion organized by **North Shore Bike, Cruise, and Snorkel** (822–1582), based in Kapaa, begins with a cycling tour followed by a cruise to a pair of snorkel sites and a barbecued lunch (about $68). Groups are rarely larger than a dozen people (more often six or so). Transportation is provided to and from hotels on the northeastern coast.

BY SEA: When north shore waves are at their calmest, during the summer, many sightseers cruise in rubber rafts along the stunning Na Pali Coast. Contact **Captain Zodiac** (826–9371 or (800) 422–7824), sometimes also called Na Pali Zodiac. Don't let the word "raft" put you off. These motor-powered craft are actually just small boats. Your Zodiac might slip into a roofless cave, past a waterfall at its mouth. You might spot dolphins or huge sea turtles. Both the 3½-and 5-hour trips include snorkeling. Passengers on the longer excursion are also taken to a secluded beach and given lunch. During the winter, these excursions are offered if the weather and ocean conditions are good. However, at this time of year, the trip can be especially bumpy, something like riding on a trotting horse, and the water may be too rough for the raft to enter sea caves. Zodiacs are boarded at Tunnels Beach, not far from Hanalei, where the Captain Zodiac office is located. One advantage of a winter cruise is that you might spot whales, which come to Kauai around mid-November and leave in mid-May. If you'd prefer to see the Na Pali Coast from a larger boat, with a deck or two, try **Lady Ann Cruises** (245–8538). This company's whale watching and snorkeling cruises are popular. Other outfits to consider are **Blue Water Sailing** (822–0525) and **Na Pali Kauai Boat Charters** (826–7254 or (808) 367–8047).

One of the most exhilarating activities in Kauai is to paddle a kayak along tranquil Huleia Stream through the jungled Huleia National Wildlife Refuge. **Island Adventure** (245–9662 or (800) 331–8044) leads daily three-hour morning or afternoon tours (about $32). Each person gets his or her own kayak. The group might consist of anywhere from five to three dozen people. At the end of the scenic excursion, paddlers are shuttled over land back to their cars. This company also guides people on half-day kayak trips in the ocean, for about $48 including a picnic lunch.

Smith's Motor Boat Service (822–4111) and **Waialeale Boat Tours** (822–4904) conduct cruises up the Wailua River to **Fern Grotto** (about $9 for adults; half price for children under age 12). The ride is beautiful, as is the cave and its flourishing surroundings. My only problem is that each flat-bottomed boat is packed with more than 100 tourists. Such an appealing setting would be best viewed with fewer people around. The outside of the fern-covered cave is dim, even on sunny days, so be sure to bring a flash or fast film. As you glide along the river, you'll be told about the passing sights, serenaded with live guitar and ukulele music, and coaxed into taking group hula lessons. Since Fern Grotto is frequently the site of weddings, you might see a bride and groom in their own special boat. Smith's offers an evening cruise with a luau at Smith's Tropical Paradise ($30 for adults; $21 for children under age 12). Waialeale's dinner cruise includes a barbecue ($45). All excursions depart from Wailua Marina.

BY HELICOPTER: If your wallet is amenable, don't miss an opportunity to take a helicopter tour on Kauai. Prices range from about $90 per person for a 30-minute flight to $165 for a 65-minute whirl. Trips including drop-offs are more expensive. While Waimea Canyon, Hanalei Valley, and Kalalau Valley can all be seen from lookout points on land and the cliffs of the Na Pali Coast can be seen by boat, there's nothing like getting an aerial view of these spectacles. And unless you're a bird or in a low-flying plane, the only way to see lush Mt. Waialeale Crater is by helicopter. Most flights take off from Princeville, but a few depart from Lihue Airport. Some companies provide complimentary ground transportation from hotels to take-off points.

Papillon Helicopters (826–6591 or (800) 367–7095) whets passengers' appetites before flights with a slide presentation that includes views from above. This is the only company that is licensed to make mountain landings. One of their excursions includes a 50-minute flight and a 1-hour drop-off in a mountainous area where you can go swimming in a freshwater stream and hiking ($152). Honeymooners and other loving couples particularly enjoy the private 50-minute flight that includes a 2-hour drop off with a picnic lunch complete with Cornish game hens and champagne ($250). Other companies to consider are

Kenai Helicopters (245–8591 or (800) 662–3144), **ERA Helicopters** (245–9555), **Ohana Helicopter Tours** (245–3996), **Gilligan's Charters** (822–7007), and **Menehune Helicopters** (245–7705).

Until the late 1980s, only people with Hawaiian blood were allowed on neighboring Niihau. Today **Niihau Helicopters** (338–1234 or 335–3500) takes sightseers to the "Forbidden Island." These flights don't go anywhere near where people live, and are not especially scenic or educational. Your money would be be better spent on other helicopter tours—that is, unless you feel like contributing to a worthy cause: These tours were started to support the island's emergency medical helicopter service. Flights (which range from $140 to $240) leave from Burns Air Field, a mile and a half from Hanapepe.

BY GLIDER PLANE: To soar quietly over Hanapepe Valley and Port Allen in western Kauai, contact **Tradewinds Gliders** (335–5086). A 20-minute flight will cost $100 for two people and $85 for one. A 40-minute flight will run $160 for two people and $135 for one.

BEACHES

Generally speaking, in the winter, beaches along the south shore are calm and thus good for swimming, while north shore beaches are too rough for swimming but fine for expert surfers. Summer months bring good surfing and bodysurfing waves to the south shore and flatten most northern waters enough for safe swimming. The waters along the eastern shore are often not good for swimming since they can have high waves and strong currents. Some of the quietest beaches are along the western shore, past Kekaha. These strands are also frequented by locals.

*Polihale • *west coast* • Mid-summer is the safest time to swim in these waters. During the rest of the year, the long, broad beach watched over by soaring Na Pali sea cliffs is best used as a sunbathing and picnic spot. Dune buggies kick up the sand on weekends, but the beach is refreshingly empty and quiet at other times. Since there are no trees, there is no natural shade—just a few picnic shelters by the base of the cliffs. You may want to bring an umbrella. Restrooms and showers are provided. Camping is permitted here in tents. When you turn left at the end of Highway 50, you'll be on a bumpy dirt road that winds through seemingly endless sugarcane fields. Looming ahead, the horizontally striped cliffs bear a strong resemblance to Mount Rushmore. Note that some car rental agencies prohibit drivers from taking the vehicles onto dirt roads.

Kekaha Beach • *southwest shore* • The sound of dune buggies often slices the air along this long, narrow, sandy stretch off Highway 50. The undertow is strong and there are usually many breakers. But when the water is calm enough, this is a popular spot for teaching local children to surf. Picnic tables are provided. Camping is permitted.

Waimea Beach • *southwest coast* • This strip is popular among locals and vacationers who want to get away from the crowds.

Salt Pond Beach Park • *Hanapepe, south shore* • Families gravitate to this spot, since the relatively flat waters are fine for swimming. Take advantage of the picnic tables.

Brennecke's Beach • *Poipu, south shore* • Bodysurfing is all the rage here. Waves increase in height during the summer. Lifeguards are on hand to keep an eye on the crowd. Showers and restrooms are provided. If you don't feel like bringing your own munchies, head to one of the take-out places across the road.

Prince Kuhio Park • *Poipu, south shore* • Although this beach is on the rocky side, it's a pleasant place to spend some time.

Poipu Beach Park • *south shore* • Very busy on weekends, this is an excellent surfing beach. Snorkeling is also rewarding here, and waves are usually manageable for bodysurfing. Lifeguards scan the water. Showers and restrooms are available. Be sure to take a spin in this neighborhood—you'll see some beautiful homes.

Kalapaki Beach • *Nawiliwili Park, southeast coast* • The swimming is excellent at this sandy curve fronting the lavish Westin Kauai Resort. Windsurfing is popular among locals here.

Ahukini • *east coast* • Stop here if you're in the mood for some good snorkeling.

Hanamaulu Beach Park • *east coast* • Campers enjoy this waterfront park where nice shells can often be found. However, in the past, this beach has had problems with polluted water.

Lydgate State Park • *Wailua, east coast* • In the old days, Hawaiians who had broken *kapus* (taboos) fled to the Place of Refuge here, thus avoiding punishments that could include death. Swimmers and snorkelers enjoy splashing around in the rock-enclosed natural pool that's about the size of a football field.

Wailua Beach • *east coast* • When the waves are small enough, this is a good spot for swimming or for novice surfers to get the hang of hanging ten.

Kapaa Beach Park • *east coast* • The swimming and fishing are generally good here. This is mainly a local hangout. Picnic tables and barbecue pits are provided.

Anahola Bay • *northeastern shore* • With mountains in the background, this curving sandy strip is fine for swimming. Waters are calmest at the southern end and by Anahola Stream at the northern extreme. Restrooms and showers are provided. The adjacent state park is popular with campers.

Anini Beach • *north shore* • This protected beach is one of the best north shore strands for swimming during the summer. Windsurfers enjoy this spot. During the winter, waves should be left to master surfboarders.

Hanalei Beach Park • *north shore* • Taking a dip here is safest by the old landing. The surfing is particularly good during the winter.

Lumahai Beach • *north shore* • Famous for is role in *South Pacific,* this beautiful beach is not safe for swimming. However, it's a great place to spend some quiet time sunbathing, picnicking, or searching for olivine crystals in the sand.

Tunnels Beach • *north shore* • If you plan to cruise along the Na Pali Coast, you'll board your boat or Zodiac raft here. The view of the cliffs is wonderful, especially in the late afternoon. Since the waters are protected, swimming and snorkeling are fine here during the summer.

Keʿe • *north shore* • This pristine crescent near the beginning of the Kalalau Trail was the setting for the seduction of a young woman by a priest in *The Thorn Birds,* the television mini-series. A path leads to an ancient hula platform, where the blessings of Laka, the hula goddess, are still sometimes invoked. You might see offerings left by recent dancers. You'll know you've found this beach when Highway 56 grinds to a halt.

Haena State Park • *north shore* • Swimming is recommended here only for the strongest of swimmers and only when the water is *very* calm. However, the shelling and fishing are good. Picnic tables and barbecue pits are provided.

Hanakapiai • *Na Pali Coast, northwest shore* • Hikers reach this picturesque strand after trekking about two miles along the Kalalau Trail. While it's a scenic place to relax, the currents can be treacherous, so swimming is not advised. A freshwater stream adds to the beauty of the setting. However, sometimes during the winter, the beach vanishes beneath the high tide.

SPORTS

Hiking, camping, scuba diving, and fishing are all excellent on Kauai. Snorkeling excursions and other watersports are easily arranged through hotels.

BIKING: Cycling is particularly rewarding on this largely rural island. Mountain bikes can be rented at **Outfitters Kauai** (742–9667). In addition, two-wheelers are available at **South Shore Activities** (742–6873) and **Pedal and Paddle** (826–9069). Plan to spend $16–$22 a day. (Also see Tours and Cruises.)

FISHING: Arrange ocean charters through **Sportfishing Kauai** (742–7013) in Koloa; **Gent-Lee Fishing** (245–7504) or **Gilligan's Coastal Charters** (822–7007) in Lihue; **Seabreeze Sportfishing Charters** (828–1285) in Kilauea; **Alana Lynn Too Charters** (245–7446) in Anahola; or **Seascape Kauai** (826–1111) in Hanalei. A full day of shared charter fishing runs from $130 to $160, while a half day goes for about $90. If you'd prefer to charter a boat for your own group, a full day will cost from about $575 to $700, while a half day will run $350 to $475.

For freshwater fishing, you'll need to obtain a license through **Aquatic Resources** (Box 1671, Lihue, HI 96766; 235–4444). The folks at **Bass Guides of Kauai** (822–1405) in Lihue or **Cast & Catch Freshwater Bass Guides** (332–9707) in Koloa can show you the best fishing spots. Black and peacock bass are found in Kauai's streams and ponds. In Kokee State Park streams, a rainbow trout season runs on certain days in August and September. For small jacks and reef fish, try the reefs near Hanalei Bay. Be extremely careful, however, since the tide can be quite strong here. There's also good fishing for barracuda, small ula, and jacks off the end of the breakwater at Nawiliwili. At night, locals wade out at Anini Beach on the north shore to spear lobsters and fish. If you'd like to join a group of local fishermen, you may be able to make arrangements through the **Chamber of Commerce** (245–7363) or **Lihue Fishing Supply** (245–4930).

GOLF: Serious golfers stay in Princeville on the verdant north shore. Made up of three 9-hole greens, the renowned **Princeville Makai Golf Course** (826–3580) was designed by Robert Trent Jones, Jr. Fees, including shared carts, are about $55 for resort guests and $70 for nonguests. The 18-hole **Princeville Prince Golf Course** (826–3580) is another good place to tee off in the area. Winter fees, which also include shared carts, are about $30 for people staying in the resort and $38 for outsiders. Summer rates are lower. Down south in Kalaheo, the 9-hole **Kukuiolono Golf Course** (332–9151) charges only $6 for green fees and $6 for carts for those playing 9 holes and $11 for those playing 18. To play on the 18-hole **Wailua Municipal Golf Course** (245–8092 or 245–2163) in Wailua, plan to spend $11 during the week and $12 on weekends.

HIKING AND CAMPING: Some 45 miles of hiking trails cut through mountainous, forested **Kokee State Park,** at the edge of the Na Pali Coast. Before setting out, be sure to stop at the ranger station for trail maps and information about current trail conditions. To get the most out of the park, plan to spend at least three days, camping or staying in one of the cabins at Kokee Lodge. Some trails lead to exhilarating cliff-edge views of vast Waimea Canyon. Appearing to defy gravity, goats perch along the sheer edges of the chasm. Other trails lead to waterfalls, swimming holes, or deep into the forest, where you can find a stand of California redwood trees. Nude bathers are a common sight in the pool below Waipoo Falls No. 1. A favorite spot for relaxation and a picnic is Waipoo Falls No. 2, which overlooks the canyon. Families should consider trying the two-mile hike along the Puu Ka Ohelo-Berry Flat Trails. In addition to California redwoods, they'll pass Australian eucalyptus, Japanese Sugi pines, and other striking trees. Hikers should look out for Methley plums and vines laden with ripe lilikoi (passion-fruit). Banana lilikoi is a favorite snack for Kokee's wild pigs.

The **Na Pali** region is also best appreciated in a leisurely three days or so. Be very careful of the sheer cliff edges. Erosion can cause them to be quite dangerous. The 11-mile Kalalau Trail, which runs from Haena Beach Park to Kalalau Valley, can be especially hazardous between October and May, and during June rains. Some hikers say you'll pass the most impressive scenery in the first mile. Hanakapiai, with its flourishing foliage and small beach, is about an hour's hike (two miles) from Haena Point. You'll see one of Na Pali's many waterfalls in the valley here. When you reach Kalalau Stream, you can play Tarzan—just grab the hanging ropes and swing across the water. Kalalau is Na Pali's largest valley, and perhaps its most beautiful. The beach here has lovely ivory sand. Listen out for Kamapuaa, the hog man, who is said to live in several of Na Pali's valleys. He frequently changes form—one moment he might be rain and the next he might turn himself into an ocean wave.

Tent camping is permitted at various state and county parks and other scenic locales, including the following: Anahola State Park on the northeast coast, Anini Beach on the north shore, Haena Beach Park on the north shore, Hanalei Beach Park on the north shore, Hanamaulu Beach Park on the southeast coast, Kapaa Beach Park on the eastern shore, Kekaha Beach Park in the southwest, Kokee State Park in the mountains in the west, Polihale State Park on the west coast, and Salt Pond Beach Park on the southern coast. Campers must obtain free permits for state parks from the **Department of Land and Natural Resources, State Parks Division** (3060 Eiwa St., Lihue, HI 96766; 245–4444) or, for county parks, from the **Kauai War Memorial Convention Hall** (4191 Hardy St.). These offices can also supply them with maps and further details.

HORSEBACK RIDING: In the Princeville area, **Pooku Stables** (826–6777 or 826–7473) conducts trail rides along seacliffs high above the churning Pacific, through wide open fields, and in Hanalei Valley, with its patchwork of farm plots. The one-hour valley ride costs about $22; the two-hour shoreline ride, $42; and the three-hour waterfall picnic excursion, $68 including lunch. Every August, Pooku Stables hosts a wild **rodeo,** called the Hanalei Stampede, complete with music and dancing. **CJM Country Stables** (245–6666) in Koloa leads one-hour rides for $22; two-hour rides for $42; and three-hour beach and breakfast rides for $58.

KAYAKING: Through **Island Adventures** (245–9662 or (800) 331–8044) in Lihue, you can arrange to kayak along Huleia Stream, in a wildlife refuge. Each sightseer makes this scenic journey in his or her own kayak, which is actually a *Royak* (a combination of a kayak and a canoe). The trip is one-way. Paddlers are picked up by shuttle at the end of the excursion and driven back to their cars. This three-hour excursion costs around $32. Kayaking on the ocean can also be arranged.

SAILING: For sunset dinner cruises, moonlight sails, winter **whale watching** trips, Na Pali Coast tours, and other group excursions, try **Na Pali Coast Cruise Line** (335–5078), **Na Pali Kai Tours** (335–5044), **Lady Ann Cruises** (245–8538); or **Kauai Charterboat Service** (245–7502). Charters can be arranged through **Blue Water Sailing** (822–0525). (Also see Snorkeling.)

SCUBA DIVING: Since Kauai is the oldest of Hawaii's main islands, the coral below its waters has had more time to build colonies on top of colonies. Thus, its reefs are some of the state's most complex and beautiful. Most of Kauai's best diving is along the southern, protected coast. Many good south shore dive sites are just 10 to 30 minutes away from Port Allen and Kukuiula Harbor. One of Kauai's best cave dives, called Sheraton Caverns, is just offshore from the Sheraton Kauai Hotel in Poipu. Lobster and sea turtles hide out in the various underwater grottos that range from 35 to 60 feet in depth. The 65- to 80-foot-deep General Store is a U-shaped reef filled with an unusual variety of marine life. Shrimp, lobster, and red squirrel fish reside in its two caves. This site also boasts a wrecked 19th-century steamship.

Koloa Landing is a good place for new divers to test the waters. The reef here at this old boat landing slowly descends to 25 feet. All kinds of fish swarm around, including butterfly fish and blue-striped snapper. Divers get a kick out of feeding the moray eels here. Diving along Kauai's north shore is excellent, but the waters are calm enough only during the summer. There are some striking underwater lava tubes and archways in this region. Along the eastern shore, divers can explore the Wreck of the *Lukenbach,* a German freighter that sank in a storm in 1951. Some of the ship's plates, dishes, silverware, and bottles remain in the galley.

To arrange dives or to take scuba classes or lessons in underwater photography, inquire at **Fathom Five Divers** (742–6991) in Koloa; **Aquatics Kauai** (822–9213 or (800) 822–9422), based in Kapaa; **Sea Sage Diving Center** (822–3841) also in Kapaa; and **Ocean Odyssey** (245–8681) at the Kauai Hilton.

SNORKELING: Most of the Na Pali cruises include snorkeling. Sea turtles and dolphins are often spotted in this area. During most of the winter, when the water is rough along the north shore, the majority of cruises are conducted along other coasts. Try **Captain Zodiac Raft Expeditions** (826–9371 or 826–9772) in Hanalei; **Whitey's Boat Cruises** (826–9292) in Hanalei; **Playtime Charters** (335–5074) in Hanapepe; **Ocean Ventures** (828–1447) in Kilauea; **Captain Andy's Sailing Adventures** (822–7833) in Koloa; or **Na Pali Kauai Boat Charters** (826–7254) in Princeville.

SURFING: The best surfing is along the north shore during the winter and in the Poipu area in the summer.

TENNIS: Kauai has no shortage of tennis courts. In addition to some 70 hotels courts, there are nearly two dozen public courts lit for night play. Some resorts charge guests from $4 to $8 to play, while others offer free tennis. Nonguests are charged anywhere from \$5 to \$9. **The Hanalei Bay Resort** (826–6522) has 11 courts terraced down a slope toward the ocean. There are three clay courts and six hard at **Coco Palms Resort** (822–3831) in Wailua. **The Sheraton Coconut Beach Hotel** (822–3455) in Kapaa has three courts, while there are four at the **Kauai Hilton and Beach Villas** (245–1955), just south of Wailua, and six at **Stouffer Poipu Beach Resort** (742–1681).

WATER SKIING: Contact **Kauai Water Ski & Sports** (822–3574) in Kapaa or **Adventures Unlimited** (245–8766) in Lihue.

WINDSURFING: Also called boardsailing, this sport can be arranged through **Nawiliwili Marine** (245–5955), **Garden Island Windsurfing** (826–9005) in Hanalei, or **Hanalei Sailboards Kauai** (826–9732). Both lessons and equipment rental are available.

SHOPPING

Like the other major islands, Kauai has a variety of shopping centers, some with a good selection of worthwhile stores. A few of these malls stay open until about 9 p.m., to catch the dinner crowd, while others close at 5 p.m. Shops are also found in hotels (there are some wonderful boutiques in the Westin Kauai, for example), but prices are quite high. While Old Koloa Road (in Koloa, near Poipu) is lined with tempting shops, prices are hotel-steep. Outside of resort areas, Kauai offers some moderately priced family-run stores, where patrons can spend some time talking story with the owners. If you want to rub elbows with locals, head to Kapaa, Waimea, Eleele, or Lihue. Here are some of Kauai's most memorable shops:

SHOPPING CENTERS: One of Kauai's most attractive places to spend time and money is **Kilohana** (3–2087 Kaumualii Hwy., Puhi), a converted plantation estate. Bedrooms, bathrooms, and closets in the gracious old main house have been transformed into upscale showcases for Japanese antiques, Hawaiian and South Pacific crafts and artifacts, clothing, jewelry, paintings, and ceramics. Shoppers are invited to take horse and carriage tours around the grounds. (Also see Sights.) Across the road is **Kukui Grove Center** (3–2600 Kaumualii Hwy.; 245–7784), the island's largest mall. Complimentary shuttle service is provided from some areas. Locals are the main patrons of the **Rice Shopping Center** (4303 Rice St., Lihue). Those with wallets to match their expensive taste should wander around the **Kiahuna Shopping Village** (2360 Kiahuna Plantation Dr.) in Poipu. Locals prefer **Waimea Canyon Plaza** (Hwy. 50, Waimea) and modest **Eleele Shopping Center** (Hwy. 50, near Hanapepe).

There's more local flavor at **Waipouli Town Center** (4–901 Kuhio Hwy.) at the southern end of Kapaa. You'll find fast-food restaurants such as the **Yogurt Place; Foodland,** a 24-hour supermarket; a jewelry story, and clothing boutiques. Shoppers are entertained with hula dancing and music during the afternoon at flower-filled **Kinipopo Shopping Village** (356 Kuhio Hwy., Kapaa). If you're staying at Coco Palms Resort, this is a pleasant walk along peaceful Papaloa Road, just east of busy Kuhio Highway. North of here, **Coconut Plantation Market Place** (4–484 Kuhio Hwy., Kapaa) is an eye-pleasing open-air mall. The weathered shingle-roofed buildings enclose a courtyard with fountains and plants. Pipes, pumps, wheels, cranks, and other plantation machinery are painted bright red, yellow, and green. The restaurants and shops (selling handmade jewelry, Niihau shell necklaces, scrimshaw, T-shirts, resort wear and other goods) are open late.

On the north shore, **Princeville Center** (5–4280 Kuhio Hwy., Princeville) has a healthy selection of boutiques and restaurants for the monied set. More down-to-earth, **Ching Young Village** in nearby Hanalei offers crafts shops, clothing stores, restaurants, and the Native Hawaiian Museum. **Pua & Kawika's Flowers** (826–9193) specializes in maile, ginger, and pikake **leis,** all made fresh daily.

ALOHA WEAR AND USED GOODS: Collectibles and Fine Junque (338–9855), on Highway 50 in Waimea, stocks a good variety of vintage aloha shirts. Made of rayon and with coconut shell buttons, they date back to the 1940s and 1950s. The patterns are more muted in tone than contemporary floral prints. Racks are also hung with vintage silk clothing from China and Japan, as well as new fashions. Amid the jumble of furniture, tables are piled with cut-glass dishes, old violins, oil paintings, Pegge Hopper prints, stained-glass lamps, old books, battered Hawaiian license plates, costume jewelry, and Beatles albums. Perfect for the beach or for relaxing at home, brightly colored Polynesian *pareus* (sarongs) are sold at **Tahiti Imports** (Coconut Plantation Market Place in Kapaa; 822–9342). (Also see Hawaiian Quilts.)

ART GALLERIES: Photographer Diane Ferry handtints her photos, which she sells at **Kauai Images Gallery** (937 Kuhio Hwy., Kapaa; 822–1950) along with original works by other notable local artists. At **Montage Galleries** (Princeville Shopping Center, Princeville; 826–9151), paintings, limited edition prints, and posters by some of the state's best-known artists are displayed. Niihau shell jewelry and handmade gold pieces are also sold here. You'll find more wall decorations at **The**

Poster Shop (5424 Koloa Rd., Koloa; 742–7447), which boasts the work of Pegge Hopper, one of Hawaii's premier painters. Owned and operated by local artists, the **Artisans' Guild of Kauai** (Ching Young Village, Hanalei; 826–6441) sells everything from basketry, ceramics, and woodwork to batiks and hand-painted clothing.

A Christmas gift show is held every December at **Stones at Kilohana** (Kilohana Plantation, near Lihue; 245–6684). Year-round, this gallery carries striking masks, hula implements, wood carvings, baskets, and other artful crafts from Hawaii and the South Pacific. Also at this attractive plantation are **Kilohana Galleries** (245–9352), which carries locally produced sculpture, ceramics, and glass work; and **The Hawaiian Collection Room** (245–9452), which has an impressive assortment of Niihau shell leis, antique ivory, scrimshaw, and 19th-century Hawaiian stamps, coins, and documents. Next door to Kintaro, an excellent Japanese restaurant, **D.S. Collection Gallery** (4–370 Kuhio Hwy., Kapaa; 822–3341) is known for its block prints, paintings, carved ivory, and porcelain from Japan, China, and Hawaii.

BEACHWEAR AND T-SHIRTS: Many people like the lively sportswear and bathing suits at **M. Miura Store** (4–1419 Kuhio Hwy., Kapaa; 822–4401). (Also see Distinctive Clothing.).

BOOKS: For Kauai's best selection, try **Waldenbooks** (Kukui Grove Center, ouside Lihue; 245–7162).

CRAFTS: **Kauai Crafts in Progress** (1384 Kuhio Hwy., Kapaa; 822–7558) is known for its handpainted tiles framed in koa wood, among other items. **Stones at Kilohana** (Kilohana Plantation, outside Lihue; 245–6684) stocks South Pacific artwork including Fijian tapa cloth (like Hawaiian kapa cloth), woodcarvings, and wall hangings. **The Station** (Hwy. 50, Hanapepe; 335–5731), which began life as a gas station, now pumps out local crafts, including island needlepoint. A second branch has opened in Poipu (2827A Poipu Rd.; 742–1202).

DISTINCTIVE CLOTHING: **Art to Wear** (1453 Kuhio Hwy., Kapaa; 822–1125) carries a wide assortment of hand-pained bathing suits, T-shirts, dresses, bags, and even shoes and silk earrings, for both children and adults. **Canefield Clothing Co.** (Kilohana Plantation, outside Lihue; 245–5020) sells hand-painted batik wear and other appealing garments. At **Tropical Shirts** (Coconut Plantation Market Place in Kapaa, 822–0203; and Kiahuna Shopping Village in Poipu, 742–6691), hand-embroidered or silk-screened shirts, dresses, and other fashions for women, men, and children are on sale. **See You in China** (Kukui Grove Center, near Lihue; 245–8474) stocks clothing from Asia.

FRUIT AND VEGETABLES: The roadside **Farm Fresh Fruit Stand** (4–1345 Kuhio Ave., Kapaa; 822–1154) is packed with fresh pineapple, coconuts, papayas, mangoes, and bananas. You can even buy fresh sugarcane here (which some people like to chew on), ginger (great for spicing up fish and vegetables), and locally produced honey, jams, and jellies. If you'd like to take some of Kauai's juicy pineapples home, you can arrange to have an inspected and certified box of two, three, six, or eight delivered to the airport for your departure. You'll need to give at least 24-hours' notice. Major credit cards are accepted. Boxed, inspected pineapples are also sold at the airport, but prices may be a bit higher for the convenience. Fresh produce and other goods are also available at **Sunshine Market** (Koloa Baseball Field, Koloa) every Monday from noon to 3 p.m. This is a good place to mingle with residents.

HAWAIIAN QUILTS: Inspired by New England missionaries, Hawaiian women put their own spin on the American quilting tradition. You'll find examples of this distinctive island art form at **Kapaia Stitchery** (Kuhio Hwy., near Lihue; 245–2281). This shop also sells other kinds of original needlework, as well as muumuus and aloha shirts made to order from tropical fabrics.

JAPANESE ANTIQUES: For beautifully preserved old prints, inlaid wooden boxes, silk kimonos, and ceramics, browse around **Half Moon Japanese Antiques** (Kilohana Plantation, near Lihue; 245–4100).

JEWELRY: Kauai is the best part of the state to buy Niihau shell leis, since they are somewhat cheaper here than elsewhere. Niihau is the only island where these minuscule shells, decorated with delicately detailed natural designs, wash ashore in significant quantities. Each lei takes anywhere from 20 to 200 hours to complete, since the tiny shells must be picked out of the sand, sorted by size, shape, and color, and then cleaned, drilled with holes, and strung into intricate patterns. This painstaking work, the scarcity of the shells, and the beauty of the necklaces account for the hefty price tags (they may cost hundreds, sometimes thousands of dollars each). The rarest colors are red and deep pink. These necklaces are sold, among other places, at **Kilohana Plantation** near Lihue; and **Kauai Gold Limited** (Coconut Plantation Market Place, Kapaa; 822–5281), which also carries scrimshaw and gold jewelry. (Also see Art Galleries.)

If you're in the market for Hawaiian heirlooms, try **Capricorn Fine Gems** (Kukui Grove Center, near Lihue; 245–6233). **Jim Saylor Jewelers** (1318 Kuhio Hwy., Kapaa; 822–3591) stocks an unusual collection of designs (handmade on the premises), along with rare gems from a variety of countries. At **the Goldsmith's Gallery** (Kinipopo Shopping Village, 356E Kuhio Hwy., Kapaa; 822–4653), some of the handcrafted gold jewelry is quite imaginative.

MACADAMIA NUTS: Prices tend to be lowest at **Star Market** (245–7777) and **Long's Drugs** (245–7771), both in the Kukui Grove Center just outside Lihue.

NIGHT LIFE

On Kauai, life after dark is far quieter than on either Oahu or Maui. The island does have a couple of discos. However, most evening entertainment is centered around restaurant bars and hotel lounges, where live music often accompanies pupus and conversation. Those who don't mind being part of a crowd of fellow tourists should consider taking an evening cruise or attending a luau. While the Sheraton Coconut Beach Hotel in Kapaa and the Stouffer Waiohai Beach Resort in Poipu both host luaus, many visitors prefer to attend the feasts held outside hotels.

Hawaiian Style

Smith's Tropical Paradise • *Wailua Marina, Wailua; 822–4654* • The 30 tropical acres of flowers, plants, and trees make visitors feel as though they have stepped into old Hawaii when they attend the luau given here. While riding on the tram or walking through the grounds, they'll pass several lily ponds. The first is huge, with a large rocky fountain. Royal palms, banana trees, crotons, and bougainvillea surround the water. Hundreds of birds flutter around the rain forest garden, filled with stalks of bamboo, red ginger, scarlet lobster claws, pineapples, and papaya trees. Before the feast, everyone observes the outdoor *imu* ceremony: The boned kalua pig, the centerpiece of the meal, is removed from its oven—a hole in the ground that has been heated by red-hot rocks. Featuring Hawaiian, Maori, Samoan, Tongan, Japanese, and Chinese music and dances, the performance takes place on a stage across a lily pond from the audience. The Samoan fire dancers are a big hit. While the bleachers are covered, the stage is open to the sky. Luaus take place here from Monday to Friday, beginning at 6 p.m.

Tahiti Nui • *Kuhio Hwy., Hanalei; 826–6277* • Up on the quiet north shore, this family-run luau is hosted by a convivial group of folks. The singing, dancing, and telling of anecdotes is done in a truly down-

to-earth manner—sans glitz. The casual atmosphere and Polynesian decor of this restaurant capture Hawaii as it once was. Of course the menu
includes the usual filling luau fare—kalua pig, lomilomi salmon, taro,
poi, sweet potatoes, and haupia (a jiggly coconut pudding). Luaus are
hosted here three nights a week.

Polynesian Revue • *Sheraton Kauai Hotel, Poipu; 742–1661* •
Twice a week, the Outrigger Room (decked out with a huge outrigger
canoe) erupts with the music and dance of peoples of the Pacific. The
energy of the performers and the oceanviews through the windows make
up for the average food.

Na Kaholokula • *Sheraton Coconut Beach Hotel, Kapaa; 822–
3455* • Hula hips swirl gracefully and traditional Hawaiian tunes are
performed during this twice-weekly show.

Local Hangouts and Happenings

Park Place • *Harbor Village Shopping Center, 3501 Rice St.,
Nawiliwili; 245–5775* • There are usually more men than women at this
local gathering spot near the entrance to the Westin Kauai Resort. Many
patrons come from Kauai's military base, and the crowd can get a tad
rough on occasion. Most of the time, however, people are simply busy
chewing the cud, dancing to Top 40 tunes, or watching others shake a
leg. Happy hour doesn't end until midnight on Wednesdays. The club
closes at 4 a.m. nightly.

Club Jetty • *Nawiliwili Harbor, Nawiliwili; 245–4970* • Live bands
sometimes play at this waterfront disco that appeals to the younger generation. More often, a D.J. plays taped music. *Open 10 p.m.–3:30 a.m.,
Wed.–Sat.*

The Paddling Club • *Westin Kauai, Kalapaki Beach, Nawiliwili;
245–5050* • Speakers throb with American rock 'n' roll and pop at this
splashy, multilevel disco. Huge screens alternate between music videos
and live-action videos of people on the dance floor. Mirrors are everywhere. High, narrow counters made of glossy wood provide just enough
room for elbows or drinks. When it's time to rest your feet, sink into a
padded booth. The liveliest time to come is Employee's Night (Wednesdays). Sunday through Thursday, wearing shorts and sandals is fine, but
on Friday and Saturday nights, people are expected to dress up. *Open
until 2 a.m. during the week and 4 a.m. on weekends.*

Gilligan's • *Kauai Hilton, north of Lihue; 245–1955* • Until the
Paddling Club came along, this upscale spot was *the* disco on Kauai.

Music, usually Top 40 tunes, is recorded. The crowd is thickest on Mondays (Employee's Night). People are asked to dress up.

The Kauai Community Players • *822–7787* • Call or check newspapers to find out when and where this local theater group is performing.

Other Night Spots

Buzz's Steak and Lobster • *Coconut Plantation Market Place, Kapaa; 822–7491* • Catering mainly to tourists, this restaurant offers both live Hawaiian music and American pop nightly from 8:30 to 11:30. The daily happy hour (from 3 to 5 p.m.) is quite popular as well.

Drum Room • *Sheraton Kauai, Poipu; 742–1661* • Featuring live bands that often play tunes for slow dancing, this lounge draws everyone from young folks to the 40-plus crowd.

Charo's • *between Hanalei and Haena; 826–6422* • The dinner show at this beachfront restaurant owned by the Latin dancer and guitarist includes hula and flamenco. Some folks enjoy the show, but most people find the food disappointing. Charo only performs every once in a while. But if you want to see her, all you have to do is step into the gift shop outside the restaurant. There's a picture of this less than modest woman on nearly every item in the store. Inquire about transportation from Princeville and its surroundings.

Evening Cruises

Paradise Adventure Cruises • *Kuhio Hwy., Hanalei; 826–9999* • For an intimate sunset cruise (a far cry from most of Hawaii's other more populous ocean excursions), try this outfit. You'll sail on a 25-foot Boston Whaler that carries only six passengers.

Na Pali Coast Cruise Line • *Port Allen, Hanapepe; 335–5078* • Sailing along the scenic southern coast, this three-hour dinner cruise includes drinks, a sit-down dinner of either fish or prime rib, and wonderful views.

Playtime Charters • *Port Allen, Hanapepe; 335–5074* • Mai Tais are the beverage of choice on this two-hour sunset supper sail. The 32-foot boat takes about two dozen people along the south shore.

CULINARY KAUAI

Kauai may not be famous for its culinary expertise, but it has enough good restaurants to keep most vacationers—and residents—satisfied. Among the best (and most expensive) gourmet dining spots are **Tamarind** at the Stouffer Waiohai in Poipu; **Plantation Gardens** in Poipu; **Inn on the Cliffs** and **Prince Bill's,** both at the Westin Kauai near Lihue; and **Gaylord's,** outside Lihue. Two excellent Japanese restaurants are **Tempura Gardens** at the Westin Kauai and **Kintaro** between Wailua and Kapaa. Delicious Italian food is served in an al fresco setting at **Casa di Amici** in Kilauea. At the other end of the monetary spectrum, a few Lihue eateries draw a steady local crowd: **Eggbert's** and **Ma's Family Restaurant** pack them in for breakfast, while **Hamura's** and **Yokozuna Ramen** serve some mean saimin. **Duane's Ono-Char Burger,** a roadside stand in Anahola, snags many locals and visitors on their way to and from the north shore. Note that some restaurants serve dinner only. Dress is casual at all but a couple of places.

Created by Walter Lappert to combat the idleness he found in retirement, **Lappert's Ice Cream** is manufactured near Hanapepe. You can buy some at the stand there, at Lappert's Ice Cream Parlor at the Coco Palms Hotel in Wailua, or at restaurants and stores around the island. Fresh local fruits are incorporated into this smooth, rich treat, such as lilikoi (passionfruit), guava, coconut, papaya, mango, pineapple, and litchi.

Hanapepe's **Kauai Kookie** is another good stop. For mouth-watering pastries and breads, try **Jacques of Kauai,** a bakery in Kilauea. In the same town, **Banana Joe's** stand specializes in fresh fruit, dried fruit, and fruit shakes. Sold in most grocery stores and delis throughout Kauai, **Waimea Taro Chips** are a refreshing alternative to potato chips. Tiny purple threads decorate each crisp, delicious chip. This snack is made from the same root that when mashed and fermented becomes poi. But unlike this ancient Hawaiian staple, these chips win over the uninitiated with one bite. Another winner is locally produced **Kukui Nut Guava Jam.**

The West and South

Kokee Lodge • *Kokee State Park; 335–6061* • Nestled in thick wilderness 3600 feet above Kauai's tropical coast, this rustic mountain lodge serves hearty meals. A 16-foot plank of koa wood, from a tree felled by Hurricane Iwa in 1982, runs along the bar. Dinner might consist of Korean-style ribs, teriyaki steak, broiled mahimahi, or boneless Cornish game hen. For lunch, Portuguese red bean soup, hamburgers, and chili with honeyed corn bread are good choices. Lilikoi pie and silk chocolate pie top the list for dessert. Fresh fruit, eggs, pancakes, and French toast are on the breakfast menu. *Breakfast and lunch served everyday. Dinner, Fri. and Sat. only. A, V, M, D, C. (Inexpensive)*

Kinipopo Pizza & Stuff • *Kekaha; 337–1811* • Originally located near Kapaa on the east coast, this casual eatery serves pizza in 16 different configurations. You'll also find submarine sandwiches. Some of the combinations are vegetarian. After ordering, flip through one of the While You Wait albums, filled with cartoons from *The New Yorker*, the Peanuts series, and other sources. Patrons are invited to bring their favorite comic strips to add to the collection. *(Inexpensive)*

Wrangler's • *Waimea; 338–1218* • Paniolo (cowboy) themes are strong in the decor. The menu (featuring Mexican, Texan, Korean, Japanese, and Chinese-style dishes) caters to carnivores. The beef, from southern Kauai, comes in various forms, including pan-fried steak smothered in mushrooms, peppers, and onions. Pork chops are cooked in garlic butter, while the stir-fried pork, shrimp, and vegetables has a tomato base. *Closed for lunch on Sun. A, V, M, D, C. (Inexpensive)*

Green Garden • *Hanapepe; 335–5422* • Many locals recommend this family-oriented dining spot for its steak, fish, and shrimp. The emphasis is on homestyle Chinese and American cooking. However, Green Garden should be avoided at lunchtime, when busloads of tourists pour in on their way to and from Waimea Canyon. The name is a perfect description of the restaurant—all the potted and hanging orchids and other plants and flowers give diners the feeling they are outdoors. *Dinner reservations recommended. Closed Tues. nights. A, V, M, D, C. (Inexpensive)*

Omoide • *Hanapepe; 335–5066* • A very local crowd gathers at this deli every day for generous portions of homestyle Japanese, Chinese, and American food kept hot on steam tables. *Lunch only. (Inexpensive)*

Brick Oven Pizza • *Kalaheo; 245–1895* • Many residents consider this the best place to come for pizza on Kauai. *M, V. (Inexpensive)*

Lawai Family Restaurant • *Kalaheo; 332–9550* • While enjoying homestyle Hawaiian, Chinese, Japanese, and American food, talk story with the folks at the next table. This casual eatery is known for its sweet and sour pork and saimin. If you're on the run, stop in for a shave ice. All three meals are served daily. *(Inexpensive)*

Plantation Gardens • *Kiahuna Plantation, Poipu; 742–1695* • In an old plantation manor house, this restaurant is surrounded by footpaths winding through gardens dating back to 1938. Guests dine on the parlor floor and wide lanais. If you'd like to sit on the porch, arrive about 5:30 p.m. for a cocktail, and you can remain on the lanai for your meal. But even if you're seated inside, you'll still be dining al fresco. Ceiling fans and small peacock chairs contribute to the pleasant atmosphere. Seafood is the main attraction on the menu. The fish stuffed with crabmeat, linguini with baby clams, crab salad, and abalone sauteed with lemon butter are all delicious, as are the veal with asparagus and the filet mignon. If you have room for dessert, try the macadamia nut ice cream with chocolate sauce and whipped cream. *Dinner only. A, M, V. (Moderate* to *Expensive)*

Mango's Tropical Restaurant • *Old Koloa Town; 742–7377* • The land and the sea come together here, both on the menu and in the decor. Nautical accents and potted tropical plants complement the polished wood and gleaming brass. It may take you a while to wade through the extensive menu, which has borrowed preparation styles and ingredients from China, Japan, Europe, and the mainland. *Reservations recommended. A, M, V, D, C. (Moderate)*

Brennecke's Beach Broiler • *Poipu; 742–7588* • Diners may watch the chef in action at this popular restaurant overlooking the water. Tables on the second floor have the best view of the shore. Distinctively flavored *kiawe*-grilled meat and seafood are house specialties. Freshly made tropical fruit sherbet provides a refreshing ending to any meal here. *Reservations recommended. M, V. (Moderate)*

Poipu Beach Club • *Stouffer Poipu Beach Resort, Poipu; 742–1681* • Prices could hardly be better for breakfast, especially for the Poipu/Koloa resort area. The macadamia nut rolls and the omelets are particularly good. Along with a filling meal, you'll have an eye-opening view of the Pacific and the hotel's pool and colorful gardens. For dinner, fish is prepared in a variety of styles. Beef, pork, and chicken are also on the menu. *Only breakfast and dinner served. Dinner reservations recommended. A, V, M, D, C. (Moderate)*

Tamarind • *Stouffer Waiohai Hotel, Poipu; 742–9511* • Among Kauai's top restaurants, this award-winning dining room is set off with mirrors, bronze pillars, and comfortable banquettes. The menu is varied and imaginative. Appetizers range from lobster ravioli; Beluga caviar; and sausage of venison, boar, and duck with green peppercorn mustard to sashimi accompanied by silver chopsticks. The fresh papaya bisque comes in an edible papaya bowl. Entrees include roast lamb; ono broiled with black bean ginger sauce; and quail cooked in pastry and stuffed with crabmeat and mushrooms. The souffles and fresh fruit are good choices for dessert. *Dinner only. Jackets or dress shirts required for men. Reservations recommended. A, M, V, D, C. (Expensive* to *Very Expensive)*

The Waiohai Terrace • *Stouffer Waiohai Hotel, Poipu; 742–9511* • Sunday champagne brunch here is so popular island-wide that you may need to make reservations several days in advance. You'll have a choice of dining areas at this oceanview restaurant: outside in the warm sun, in the shade of a sea-grape tree, or inside. In addition to waffles, eggs, and other ordinary breakfast fare, you'll find shrimp, lamb chops, and *poke,* a Hawaiian dish made with raw tuna and pounded *limu* (seaweed). Other meals include light, low-cholesterol entrees such as pasta primavera and smoked chicken with sesame ginger sauce. *Reservations recommended. A, M, V. (Moderate)*

House of Seafood • *Poipu Kai Resort, Poipu; 742–6433* • Every night, the menu changes at this popular restaurant decorated with wicker and potted plants. Tropical vines drip from the exposed beams of the high ceilings. Whether you order fish, shrimp, lobster, or scallops, your meal will include chowder or salad, rice pilaf, vegetables, and rolls that are straight from the oven. *Dinner only. Reservations recommended. A, M, V, C, D. (Expensive)*

The East

Gaylord's • *Kilohana Plantation, Puhi (outside Lihue); 245–9593* • In a flower-filled courtyard at the back of a 19th-century plantation main house, this restaurant has a wonderful view of smooth lawns and Mt. Waialeale in the distance. While lunch is served, some patrons have found the food better at dinner. If you arrive before the sun goes down, you can take advantage of the scenery and wander around Kilohana's boutiques. You might even take a spin in the carriage drawn by a Clydesdale horse. The dinner menu includes such creative entrees as grilled duck with mango sauce (in season, the mangoes come from Kilohana's trees) and poached filet of ono in a carmelized cream sauce with ginger. End the meal with a cup of espresso from the restaurant's old Italian coffee machine. *Reservations required. A, M, V, D, C. (Moderate to Expensive)*

Oar House Saloon • *Nawiliwili; 245–4941* • Near the Westin Kauai and Kauai Chop Suey shopping center, this dimly lit, casual bar and grill has the feeling of a British pub. Locals hang out here in the late afternoon and evening to play pool and darts. The grill is always sizzling with burgers and steaks. Sandwiches are on the lunch menu. *A, V. (Inexpensive)*

Inn on the Cliffs • *Westin Kauai, Lihue; 245–5050* • You may have to make reservations a day or two in advance to dine at this split-level waterfront restaurant. Overlooking Nawiliwili Harbor and the mountains, the expansive wooden deck upstairs is great for sunset watching over cocktails. Downstairs, the dining room is graced with high ceilings, tall square columns, and a huge fireplace. While pastas are the highlight of the menu, the seafood and chicken are also quite good. *Reservations required. A, M, V. (Expensive)*

Prince Bill's • *Westin Kauai, Lihue; 245–5050* • Perched on top of the hotel's Surf Tower, this casually elegant dining room has a wonderful view. If you're dining after dark, the indoor surroundings (blond wood, tile floors, attractively set tables) are just as pleasant. Ahi, ono, and other seafood is served, along with filet mignon and lamb chops. The salad bar—which includes everything from shrimp to octopus salad—comes with each entree. Both the coconut bread and the macadamia nut bread are scrumptious. *Reservations required. A, M, V. (Expensive to Very Expensive)*

Tempura Gardens • *Westin Kauai, Lihue; 245–5050* • Kyoto-style Japanese food, including sashimi, sushi, and tempura, is served in a lovely garden setting. Guests dine to the sounds and sights of ponds churning with koi, conversational birds, and waterfalls. *Reservations recommended. A, M, V. (Moderate to Expensive)*

Eggbert's • *4483 Rice St., Lihue; 245–6325* • With a serious local following, this modest restaurant does big business, especially at breakfast. In addition to French toast, a variety of omelets, and other egg dishes, the morning menu includes banana pancakes and Portuguese sausage. Fish, chicken, beef, and pork are served at other times. *(Inexpensive)*

Kauai Chop Suey • *Lihue; 245–8790* • Many residents give high marks to the Chinese food served at this local spot. *(Inexpensive)*

Ma's Family Restaurant • *Lihue, 245–3142* • Pancakes made with bananas or papaya are a specialty for breakfast at this modest eatery that is popular with locals. The Kauai Museum is nearby. *(Inexpensive)*

Hamura's Saimin Stand • *Lihue, 245–3271* • After visiting the Kauai Museum, consider stopping at this restaurant around the corner for lunch. The heaping bowls of saimin are filled with homemade noodles. *(Inexpensive)*

Yokozuna Ramen • *Lihue, 246–1008; Kapaa Shopping Center, 822–2563* • At two locations, this friendly Japanese restaurant serves excellent saimin and tempura. *(Inexpensive)*

Club Jetty • *Nawiliwili; 245–4970* • There's nothing fancy in the decor of this Chinese restaurant that overlooks Nawiliwili Harbor. Try the pineapple shrimp or the abalone with black mushrooms. Stick around after dinner, and you can party with the club crowd. *Dinner only. Reservations recommended. A, M, V, D, C. (Inexpensive)*

Rosita's • *Kukui Grove Center, Lihue; 245–8561* • When you're in the mood for spicy food, consider this popular Mexican-style restaurant decorated with bright pinatas. In addition to nachos and tacos, you'll also find lasagne and chicken cooked with tomatoes, green peppers, and onions. *A, M, V. (Inexpensive)*

Casa Italiana • *Lihue; 245–9586* • For a taste of northern and southern Italy, this is a good choice. Posters of Italy add to the European atmosphere of this spacious, two-story restaurant. The delicious pasta is all homemade, and the veal dishes are also good. A salad bar and crunchy garlic bread complement the entrees. *Dinner only. Reservations recommended. A, V, M, C. (Moderate)*

Hanamaulu Cafe • *Hanamaulu, just north of Lihue; 245–2511* • You can choose between Japanese and Chinese food at this attractive teahouse set off with a gurgling stream, ponds, and landscaped gardens. While there's a sushi bar, some Japanese selections are cooked on an open grill. Cantonese entrees include sweet and sour spareribs, crab claws, and chop suey. *Reservations required. V, M. (Inexpensive* to *Moderate)*

Seashell • *Wailua Beach, Wailua; 822–3632* • Just across the road from the Coco Palms Hotel, this seafood restaurant overlooks flourishing gardens and the Pacific. Happy hour is the perfect time to enjoy the view while mingling with other guests. A favorite appetizer is *dim sum* (dumplings) stuffed with shrimp. Freshly caught fish comes broiled, bathed in sauce, or in bubbling stews. Entrees include the salad bar. *Dinner only. Reservations recommended. A, V, M, D, C. (Moderate)*

Kintaro • *between Wailua and Kapaa; 822–3341* • Sit at the sushi bar and watch the chefs at their artistic craft, or dine at a table. Either way, the sushi, sashimi, tempura, and other fresh Japanese specialties are excellent here. The Coconut Plantation Market Place is just up the road, and Coco Palms Hotel is also nearby. *(Moderate)*

Bull Shed • *Waipouli; 822–3791* • The portions are generous at this often crowded oceanfront steak and seafood restaurant. Patrons dine family style at large tables. The huge slabs of teriyaki sirloin and prime rib move quickly. Rack of lamb is another popular choice. Meals include an unspectacular salad bar. *Dinner only. Reservations recommended. A, V, M. (Inexpensive to Moderate)*

Norberto's • *Kapaa; 822–3362* • Probably the best place on Kauai for Mexican food, Norberto's serves a wide variety of fajitas, burritos, tacos, tostadas, and enchiladas. Chips, salsa picante, soup, and rice and beans accompany entrees. *Dinner only. A, V, M. (Inexpensive)*

Kapaa Fish & Chowder House • *Kapaa; 822–7488* • Spicy Cajun-style fish and shrimp are served at this attractive restaurant, along with seafood fettuccine and Alaskan crab legs cooked in beer. Entrees for landlubbers are also well prepared. *Dinner only. Reservations recommended. A, V, M. (Moderate)*

Aloha Dinner • *Kapaa; 822–3851* • When you're ready for some authentic Hawaiian food, come to this no-frills eatery. In addition to poi (made from mashed, fermented taro root), you'll be able to sample lomi-lomi salmon (chunks of the salted fish mixed with chopped onions and tomatoes), kalua pig, fried akule (a dried fish), and poke ahi (raw yellowtail tuna and seaweed in sesame oil), among other dishes. There might be some haupia (coconut jellied pudding) for dessert. *(Inexpensive)*

Kountry Kitchen • *Kapaa; 822–3511* • Locals pile in for breakfast, which is the best of the three meals served here daily. Friendly waiters and large portions make up for the plain decor. *(Inexpensive to Moderate)*

Ono Family Restaurant • *Kapaa; 822–1710* • I've never understood the popularity of this roadside restaurant. The casual, pleasant decor—wooden booths and tables with cane-back chairs—is nice enough. However, french fries, grilled cheese, and other dishes seem greasier than necessary. The outdoor dining area looks pleasant, but it's filled with the sound of cars whizzing by along the main road. Perhaps if I liked buffalo, I'd change my tune. Yes, burgers made from ground buffalo meat are prepared here in ten different ways, such as with pineapple and teriyaki sauce or mushrooms and cheese. If you're not adventurous enough for this, regular beef burgers also come with a variety of toppings. Otherwise, try the chili or sandwiches. For breakfast, consider omelets, hash and eggs, or French toast. *(Inexpensive)*

Dragon Inn • *Kapaa; 822–3788* • Some residents consider this Kauai's best Chinese restaurant. Try the shrimp and black bean sauce. *(Inexpensive)*

Duane's Ono–Char Burger • *Anahola; 822–9181* • Not to be confused with Ono Family Restaurant in Kapaa, this is a roadside stand. ''Ono'' means delicious in Hawaiian, and these burgers are just that, according to many residents who rarely pass by without stopping to munch. This is a good lunch spot along the way to the north shore. If you'd prefer not to eat on the run, take a seat at one of the round tables in the shade of the royal poinciana trees. The house specialty is the avocado burger, which also comes piled with alfalfa sprouts, cheddar cheese, and lettuce, and is smothered in teriyaki sauce. *(Inexpensive)*

The North

Casa di Amici • *Kilauea; 828–1388* • In a quiet part of Kauai, this al fresco restaurant serves some delicious Italian food. Fluffy plants hang from the high open-beam ceiling. Latticework dividers define dining areas. Italian music plays softly in the background. Try the pasta with walnuts in a Romano cheese cream sauce. The pesto and alfredo sauces are also good, as are the veal, beef, and chicken dishes. Half portions of pasta are available. *Reservations recommended. A, M, V, D, C. (Moderate)*

The Lanai • *Makai Clubhouse, Princeville; 826–6226* • Half of the pleasure of dining at this open-air restaurant is the view—of the flourishing countryside and cliffs. So try to arrive before the sun goes down. The other half is the imaginative continental cuisine. Broiled pepper steak and ono (a fish) with tomatoes and garlic are two of the tastiest dishes. Coffee with liqueur brings the meal to a delicious close. *Dinner only. Reservations recommended. A, V, M, D, C. (Moderate)*

Papagayo Azul • *Ching Young Village, Hanalei; 826–9442* • The accent is Mexican at this plant- and flower-filled roadside restaurant. Guacamole, burritos, enchiladas, and other spicy specialties are good choices. If you have a taste for barbecued chicken or ribs, this is also the right place. The banana fritters make a filling dessert. *(Inexpensive)*

Hanalei Dolphin • *Hanalei; 826–6113* • Set at the water's edge, this seafood restaurant lures many with its fried calamari and blackened fish. The soy and ginger chicken is another specialty. *Dinner only. Reservations recommended. A, V, M, D, C. (Moderate)*

Foong Wong's • *Ching Young Village, Hanalei; 826–6996* • Located one flight up in the shopping center, this Chinese restaurant serves generous dinner specials. The seafood dinner might include almond shrimp, scallops with snow peas, sweet and sour mahi-mahi, and shrimp fried rice. Vegetarian dishes are also available. The pupu platters are popular with groups. *A, V, M. (Inexpensive)*

Charo's • *Hanalei Colony Resort, Haena; 826–6422* • Although this oceanfront restaurant is usually crowded for its dinner show, I have found the food nothing to get excited about. The Thai spring rolls, sashimi, fried zuccini, teriyaki steak, macadamia fried shrimp, and stuffed chicken cooked in sake and coconut milk all sound far better than they taste. The dining rooms have the look and feel of a 1960s tourist trap. Large photos of owner Charo, the Latin "coochie coochie girl," decorate walls. She occasionally performs during the last 15 minutes of the shows. *Reservations recommended. Inquire about transportation from Princeville. A, M, V, D, C. (Moderate)*

WHERE TO SLEEP ON KAUAI

Where you stay on Kauai may depend on what you plan to do. Poipu, along the southeast coast, is the island's driest resort area. The beaches are excellent here, especially during the winter when those along the north coast are too rough for swimming. During the summer, Poipu's shores are great for surfing—both body and board. This area is close to Lihue, the capital, and attractions such as Kilohana Plantation, Grove Farm Homestead, Waimea Canyon, and Pacific Tropical Botanical Gardens. Because of rocky shores or strong currents, some east coast beaches are not as good for swimming as others. Many are sandy and all are fine for sun worshipping, picnicking, and strolling. Along this shore, hotels in Wailua and Kapaa are near the 18-hole Wailua Golf

Course and Coconut Market Place shopping center. Also nearby are sights including ancient *heiau* (temples), both Opaekaa and Wailua waterfalls, Wailua River, Fern Grotto, and Kamokila (the re-created old Hawaiian village). In the north, Hanalei and Princeville, where refreshing showers aren't unusual, attract serious golfers to various courses. Lovers of verdant tranquility are also drawn to this region. As gorgeous as they are to look at, the waters off many of the beaches along this coast should be avoided during the winter. Sights in this area include the impressive Na Pali cliffs, stunning valleys covered with taro patches, the distinctive peaks known as ''Bali Hai,'' several small museums, and wet and dry caves.

Kauai offers a healthy selection of hotels, condominiums, and B&Bs. Until the arrival of the opulent **Westin Kauai** in Lihue during the late 1980s, they were all either comfortably low-key, such as Kapaa's **Kauai Beachboy,** or elegantly understated, such as Poipu's **Stouffer Waiohai.** Now **the Hyatt Regency Kauai** in Poipu has joined the ranks of Hawaii's megaresorts. When the **Sheraton Mirage Princeville** on the north shore finally reopens early this year, it is expected to resume its place among Hawaii's most attractive places to stay. With its palm grove, cottage-lined lagoon, and sinks made of giant clam shells, **Coco Palms** Resort in Wailua has a truly Polynesian flavor. Those who like remote rustic settings should consider the mountain cabins of **Kokee Lodge,** high in a cool, thick forest. Another good place for escape is **Waimea Plantation Cottages,** on the southwest coast, where the renovated beachfront dwellings housed sugar plantation workers at the turn of the century.

Families traveling with children should note that **Sheraton** hotels (three of which are on Kauai) host a free summer program for kids aged 5 to 12. Supervised by counselors, children play games such as beach paddle ball and learn lei-making, sand castle building, and Hawaiian arts and crafts. Evening activities are sometimes offered. Families are also drawn to Kauai's many apartmentlike condos. Rooms in most are individually furnished by owners, so decor may vary from unit to unit within a complex. For details about housekeeping cabins, renting private homes, or additional B&Bs, see the entries at the end of this section. Guests at condos, private homes, and B&Bs may be required to book a minimum number of nights.

Princeville and Hanalei

The beaches along this coast can be too rough for swimming during the winter.

☆☆ **Hanalei Colony Resort** ● Near Haena and next to Charo's restaurant and gift shop, these two-story wooden buildings sit along the beach in a remote part of the island. Palms and other vegetation border golf course—smooth lawns. Facilities include a swimming pool and whirlpool hot tub. Each decorated differently, the homelike condo apartments have full kitchens, spacious lanais, and ceiling fans. The decor of some has a dated 1970s feel. In yours, you might find wicker bar stools at the kitchen counter and straw mats and baskets decorating the walls. Bedrooms are defined by partitions, so they aren't sound-proof. While units aren't equipped with air conditioning, TVs, phones, or dishwashers, alarm clocks are available from the office. Here guests can book boat, raft, helicopter, scuba, and snorkeling excursions. Linens and towels are exchanged daily at the housekeeping window, and guests may use the coin-operated washer and dryer. *(Moderate)*

★★★ **Hanalei Bay Resort** • Banana trees, palms, and other tropical foliage flourish throughout the extensive grounds of this clifftop Princeville resort. While it's a condominium complex, it feels more like a hotel. In addition to a restaurant, there are 11 tennis courts (three lit for night play), a swimming pool, and two saunas on the premises. Transportation is provided around the property, to or from the beach (about a five-minute walk away), and around Princeville. Guest quarters are quite spacious. Hotel rooms (without kitchens) are available as well as studios and one-, two-, and three-bedroom suites. Lanais come with absorbing views. The top-floor units of these low-rise buildings have lofts. However, since ceiling fans and trade winds stand in for air conditioning, these lofts can get rather warm. Hotel rooms share coin-operated laundry facilities while suites have their own laundry and ice machines. *(Moderate* to *Very Expensive)*

☆☆ **Sandpiper Village** • The two-bedroom, two-bathroom cottages at this Princeville condominium resort are perfect for families and groups of friends. Cooled by ceiling fans and decorated with rattan furniture, units have high airy ceilings, kitchens equipped with dishwashers, and washing machines. From the large windows, guest have wonderful views of the gardens and mountains. A swimming pool and sauna are on the premises. *(Moderate)*

Sheraton Mirage Princeville • This resort is terraced into a cliff above the beach and bay. After closing for a multimillion dollar renovation in the spring of 1989, it is scheduled to reopen under new ownership by the spring of 1991. When I heard this stunning hotel was about to undergo a major transformation, my reaction was, if it ain't broke, why fix it? Guests were greeted by bellmen in belted white tunics and white safari hats. Done in pastel blues, pinks, and greens, the Victorian-style lobby was decorated with tall lanterns, white wicker, stained glass, and gingerbread balustrades. Hawaiian quilt patterns were reflected in the design of the carpets and inlaid wooden ceiling. Each American Colonial-style guest room came with a teddy bear, a jar of homemade brownies, and antique reproductions.

It remains to be seen how many of these special touches will be retained. Plans call for enhanced views of the water and "Bali Hai" peaks from the lobby and redone restaurants. Marble and glass will be used extensively. The swimming pool and some of the rooms will be enlarged. Whirlpools will be added to selected baths. For those in the most expensive rooms, butler service will be available around the clock. Complimentary transportation will be provided to the golf course, tennis courts, shops, and Princeville Airport. *(Very Expensive)*

★★★ **The Cliffs** • Gazing down on the ocean from its lofty perch, this Princeville condominium accommodates guests in one- to four-bedroom apartments. Oak and rattan furniture decorates the spacious units, some of which have two-story living rooms and sleeping lofts. While apartments come with cable TV, they don't have telephones. Balconies off the master bedroom and living room look out to gardens or the Pacific. For a game of pool or Ping-Pong, head to the recreation center, which also sports a whirlpool and fireplace. Both a swimming pool and tennis courts are on the grounds and other activities may be arranged through the front desk. *(Moderate to Expensive)*

★★★ **Puu Poa** • All of these upscale Princeville condo units have extensive ocean views. Done in whites and beiges, rooms are bright and sunny. The two-bedroom, two-bathroom apartments come with hot tubs. On the grounds are a swimming pool and a tennis court. A path leads to the beach. Maids tidy up apartments about every three days. *(Very Expensive)*

Kapaa and Wailua

While the beaches along this coast are aesthetically pleasing, not all are swimmer-friendly.

☆☆ **Aston Pono Kai** • After the unassuming front desk, actually a small open-air counter, the manicured, pine-studded grounds come as a surprise. Two- and three-story wooden buildings stand along the beach. Lanais face the water, with its continual breakers. Some of these one- and two-bedroom condos have shag rugs and other furnishings reminiscent of the 1970s, while more modern apartments come with rattan tables and chairs and tiled patios. Units are equipped with cable TV, air conditioning, and ceiling fans. Facilities include a swimming pool, tennis courts lit for night play, a sauna, and garden barbecue grills. Coconut Plantation Market Place and the Wailua Golf Course are nearby. *(Expensive)*

☆☆ **Kapaa Shore Condos** • These modest condos across from Waipouli Plaza shopping center all have lanais. The beach in front of the property is good for sunbathing, but swimming is not recommended since the water is rough. Be sure to make reservations well in advance for the resort's sole tennis court. The Wailua Golf Course is just over three miles away. Guests may arrange other activities at the front desk, which is open from 8 a.m. to 5 p.m. After hours, they can contact the staff by using the pay phone (there are no phones in rooms). The pool and Jacuzzi are open from 8 a.m. to 10 p.m., and there are two gas barbecue grills. *(Moderate to Expensive)*

☆☆☆ **Sheraton Coconut Beach** • At Coconut Plantation and on Waipouli Beach, this hotel has a commercial but pleasant look. Palms, breadfruit trees, ironwoods, and flowers thrive around the grounds. There's a hot tub by the pool and sundeck. In addition to tennis courts, scuba diving lessons and windsurfing equipment rentals and lessons are available. River kayaking excursions may also be arranged. A fish pond with a waterfall is the centerpiece of the bright lobby, which is decorated with tapestries and stained glass. Pu pus are served in the lounge in the afternoon. All with cable TV, sitting areas, and lanais, the spacious rooms differ mainly by location and view. Many look out to the ocean. In-room safes are available for a minimal daily fee. This hotel hosts a popular luau. *(Expensive)*

☆☆☆ **Plantation Hale** • Now managed by the Outrigger chain, this all-suite condominium offers three swimming pools, tennis courts, a putting green, and a shuffleboard court. Situated at Coconut Plantation in Kapaa, it is near all kinds of shops and restaurants. Waipouli Beach is within walking distance. Done in mauve and peach, rooms are pleasantly furnished with white rattan and glass-topped tables. They all have lanais, small living rooms, full kitchens, TVs, ceiling fans, closet safes, and baths with dressing areas. *(Moderate to Expensive)*

☆ **Coral Reef Hotel** • A plain but comfortable beach accommodation, this hotel attracts economically minded travelers. The well-kept rooms are pleasant enough. Oceanfront units come with private lanais and some rooms have refrigerators. Nearby beaches are better for taking a dip than the waters directly in front of the Coral Reef. There are a pool and tennis court. Shops and restaurants are not far. *(Inexpensive)*

☆☆ **Kauai Beachboy** • On Waipouli Beach, this group of three-story buildings is near the Coconut Plantation Market Place. All rooms in the hotel have lanais that face the ocean. TVs and refrigerators are provided. In addition to a restaurant, lounge, and shops, there's a beachfront courtyard with a swimming pool, tennis courts, and shuffleboard. This is a good choice for budget-conscious travelers who want to be on the water. *(Moderate)*

☆ **Kauai Sands** • This no-frills hotel sits right on the water. The modest rooms are perfectly comfortable, and some have kitchenettes. While a restaurant and lounge are on the premises, a wide selection of shops and restaurants is nearby. *(Inexpensive)*

★★★★ **Coco Palms** • With historic palm groves, lagoons bordered by thatched roof *hales* (bungalows), and flaming torches at night, this Wailua resort wraps visitors in old Hawaii. The grove once belonged to Queen Deborah Kapule, Kauai's last monarch. Sounding strangely like cats, peacocks on the grounds call out to each other while caged monkeys give sporadic cheers. Church bells announce the frequent weddings at the small wooden chapel built for Rita Hayworth in her *Sadie Thompson* role. Near the chapel, the Palace Museum and Library houses antiques that belonged to King Kalakaua and Queen Liliuokalani. Opened in 1953 as a 12-room inn, this hotel still retains some of the '50s feeling in its patterned carpets and dark-wood Polynesian architecture.

Done in blues and aquas, many of the rooms in the three-story main buildings have whimsical, cartoonish frog or fish motifs on wallpaper and bathroom tiles. Sinks are made from giant clam shells imported from Micronesia. Some of the shuttered rooms have twin beds while others have kings. The plush lagoon-side cottages are especially popular among honeymooners. Elvis Presley, who filmed *Blue Hawaii* at Coco Palms, is said to have favored the King's Cottages, with their outdoor lava whirlpools, sculpturelike carved headboards, and chandeliers resembling palm fronds. Begun with the blowing of a conch shell and the beating of a drum, a torch-lighting ceremony takes place at the lagoons every night. Carrying dancing flames, young men in *malos* (loin cloths) run along the water. In addition to three swimming pools, a roomy Jacuzzi with a waterfall, and Wailua Beach across the main road, this resort has a nine-court tennis center (three clay and six Laykold hardsurface). *(Moderate* to *Expensive)*

☆ **Kay Barker's Bed & Breakfast** • For a taste of Kauai behind the scenes, consider booking one of the four rooms at this inland bed & breakfast not far from Coco Palms Resort in Wailua. Each has a private bath. Continental breakfast is included in the rates. Visitors mingle and talk story with their host in the sitting rooms of the house. *(Inexpensive)*

★★★ **Aston Kauai Resort** • In the lobby, coffee-colored lava rock columns provide an appealing contrast to the rose, lime, and lavender couches and armchairs. This spacious reception area with its high-pitched beamed ceiling leads to a Japanese garden out back. Peacocks roam the grounds while carp add orange and white to ponds. A footbridge takes guests to one of the two swimming pools, and facilities also include tennis courts. A rough but attractive beach is a five-minute-walk away. All of the chicly decorated guest rooms have cable TV, refrigerators, and safes, but none open to lanais. The studios with kitchenettes and one-bedroom cottages appeal to families. Both children and adults may take part in the Hawaiian crafts demonstrations. Every weekend, there's live island entertainment in the lounge. *(Expensive to Very Expensive)*

★★★★ **Kauai Hilton and Beach Villas** • Located in Hanamaulu, between Wailua and Lihue, this beach resort offers both individual hotel rooms and apartments with complete kitchens and laundry facilities. Rose-colored tiles and huge ginger jar vases decorate the spacious lobby, which is sprinkled with pleasant sitting areas. Featuring a cave and waterfalls, the main pool, divided into sections, is sprawling. Multicolored flowers surround the water. At sunset each day, torches are lighted around the pool. Found in red-roofed white buildings, the comfortable rooms all have lanais that look out to the ocean, the gardens, or the mountains. Guests have a choice of restaurants and lounges. Gilligan's Disco, with its large-screen TV, is a popular hangout among the younger crowd. Tennis courts are on the premises. *(Very Expensive)*

Lihue Area

★★★★★ **Westin Kauai** • This megaresort made a big splash when it landed on Kalapaki Beach in 1987, replacing the old Kauai Surf Hotel. Guests descend to the massive lobby on escalators. The walk to rooms can be long, but there is much to keep the eyes occupied on the way. As with Hawaii's other hotels built by developer Christopher Hemmeter, this resort has a multimillion dollar art collection that includes pieces from China, Japan, Taiwan, and the South Pacific. Circling an island, the huge round swimming pool is bordered by Jacuzzis. In these whirlpools separated by waterfalls and white marble columns, visitors chat with each other over drinks by day or night. Tall oriental vases appear to be floating on the surface of the reflecting pools that overlook the swimming pool.

In another sprawling body of water, guests may watch swans being fed in the morning. People move around the extensive grounds by foot, by elegant carriages drawn by Clydesdale, Percheron, and Belgian horses, and by sleek Venetian launches made of African mahogany. Monkeys, wallabies, pink flamingoes, pheasants and other animals roam freely on islands in the lagoons. At the water's edge, an octagonal chapel with handsome columns is a popular wedding site. Along with watching daily demonstrations in Hawaiian basket weaving, lei making, and quilting, guests entertain themselves on the tennis courts, two 18-hole golf courses, and at the European-style spa. Most of the guest rooms have lanais and ocean views. However, after the rambling splendor of the public areas, some visitors are disappointed by the small size of the rooms in the wings that were part of the old hotel. *(Very Expensive)*

Hale Lihue Motel • The antithesis of the Westin Kauai, this unassuming accommodation is found right in town. It is convenient to Lihue's popular local restaurants, the Kauai Museum, and sights along the south and east coasts. Rooms, some of which have kitchenettes, may be on the spartan side, but are well kept. *(Inexpensive)*

Poipu

Hyatt Regency Kauai • Scheduled to open by the time you read these words, this lavish beach resort will give the Westin Kauai some serious competition. There's a secluded feel to this bayside spot since the other Poipu hotels can't be seen from here. Beyond the resort, there's nothing but sugarcane fields and mountains. Wicker, ceiling fans, and the extensive use of wood (even in bathrooms) create a mood reminiscent of Hawaii's old plantations. Double-pitched tile roofs top the low-rise buildings. Those who forgo the "action pool"—extravagantly designed with slides, waterfalls, and a children's area—can relax in the Jacuzzi at the quieter pool.

In addition to horseback riding and four tennis courts with a pro shop, there will also be an 18-hole Robert Trent Jones, Jr., golf course. Massage rooms at the spa open to gardens, and other spa facilities will include saunas, a weight room, a lap pool, and a juice bar. The artwork around the resort, all by local artists, will stress Hawaiian themes. Instead of the more commercial entertainment found at some hotels, a local *hula halau* (hula group) will be hired to perform. Island "old timers" will be enlisted as musicians. One of the several restaurants will sit on an island in the main lagoon. *(Very Expensive)*

★★★★ **Stouffer Waiohai Beach Resort** • Subtly elegant, the Waiohai sits on a beautiful stretch of beach. In addition to an array of other watersports, outrigger canoe rides can be arranged here. Underwater cameras—both still and video—may be rented at the Beach Services Center. Those who can do without the sand can plunge into one of three swimming pools. Six Laykold tennis courts are on the premises, and the 18-hole Kiahuna Golf Course, designed by Robert Trent Jones, Jr., is just across the street. During botanical walking tours around the lush grounds, guests learn about the history and uses of dozens of Hawaiian plants. In the summer, parents are invited to give themselves a real vacation by dropping their children off at the supervised children's programs.

The breezy lobby, done in beiges and creams, sports four-story windows. Home of the Tamarind, one of Kauai's best restaurants, the Waiohai also boasts The Terrace, where the Sunday brunch draws residents and visitors from all over the island. Each with a lanai, the chic rooms come with mini bars, wet bars, refrigerators, and remote control TV. Second telephones are found in the baths, which also have gold sinks, marble counters, and built-in vanities with three-sided moveable mirrors. *(Very Expensive)*

☆☆☆ **Stouffer Poipu Beach Resort** • I highly recommend this hotel to families and those who don't want to spend an arm and a leg to be on a great beach. Guests at this small, unpretentious accommodation are invited to use many of the facilities at the neighboring Waiohai hotel, including the tennis club. An 18-hole golf course is across the street. Rooms at the Poipu Beach Club have kitchenettes, cable TV, and lanais. One of the two swimming pools is reserved for children. The young set may also take part in the children's program run during the summer and other busy seasons. The restaurant is one of Poipu's best (and least expensive) breakfast spots. Tall windows look out to the pool and ocean. Try the fried, batter-dipped ahi with eggs and hash browns or rice. *(Moderate)*

☆☆☆ **Kiahuna Plantation** • Set amid 35 acres of landscaped grounds, beachfront cottages and low-rise buildings contain one- and two-bedroom apartments. With lanais and high ceilings, these cozy condos are decorated with rattan furniture, louvered windows, and ceiling fans. The small kitchenettes are equipped with microwaves. A variety of watersports may be arranged at the beach. Mori Gardens features over 100 varieties of cacti from all over the world. At Hawaiian Gardens, next to the lagoon, guests are invited to participate in poi making, coconut husking, and Hawaiian games. In the original plantation manager's house, the Plantation Gardens, one of three restaurants on the premises, is known for its delicious seafood. *(Very Expensive)*

★★★ **Sheraton Kauai** • Many guests return year after year and more than half of the staff has worked here since the hotel opened in

1968. If the Sheraton doesn't look its age, it's because much of it was rebuilt after a tangle with Hurricane Iwa in 1982. Huge chandeliers made of white shells hang in the lobby, which is open to a carp-filled pond and lush foliage. Bridges cross lagoons and torches light tiled paths at night. A children's pool is adjacent to one pool, while another adjoins a Jacuzzi. The snorkeling is good just off the curving beach, and all kinds of watersports are available here. Twice a week, luaus take place on the deck at the edge of the beach, where the kalua pig is roasted. From the Drum Lounge, where live bands draw people in the mood for dancing, sunsets reveal themselves through the picture windows. This is also a good perch for spotting whales during the winter. Naniwa, where Japanese food is prepared tableside, is one of several hotel restaurants. All with lanais, the commodious guest rooms look out to the ocean, lagoons, or gardens. Most have refrigerators and mini bars. Some are equipped with safes, telephones, and double sinks in baths, and bedside panels with remote controls for TV, air conditioning, and lights. In these rooms, you can even press buttons to find out the time in various cities around the world. *(Very Expensive)*

★★ **Koloa Landing Cottages** • This small accommodation appeals to vacationers looking to escape the crowds. It offers a mere two studios and two two-bedroom cottages, with exposed beam ceilings and cable TV. Fruit trees on the grounds provide guests with delicious snacks. Beaches are a stroll away and a variety of restaurants is also nearby. The owners give guests as much—or as little—personal attention as they need. *(Moderate)*

☆☆ **Garden Isle Cottages** • In a quiet section of Poipu, these studios and one- and two-bedroom apartments are located in various cottages. Some are closer to the water than others. The nearest swimming beach is a five-minute drive away. Restaurants are not far. Sections of the grounds are pleasantly overgrown with banana trees, bougainvillea, and hibiscus. Weekly maid service is provided for some units, while none is available for others. *(Inexpensive)*

☆☆ **Kuhio Shores** • The lanais of each of these homey one- and two-bedroom condo apartments face either the small beach or the harbor. Guests are also treated to wonderful sunsets. Modern kitchens are complete with dishwashers, microwaves, and garbage disposals. *(Moderate to Expensive)*

★★★ **Poipu Kapili** • Across the road from the water, these sprawling low-rise balconied buildings are set amid artfully landscaped grounds. A pool and tennis courts are on the premises and good swimming beaches are not far. All of the one- and two-bedroom apartments and penthouse units have high ceilings, ceiling fans, and louvered wooden sliding doors leading to lanais. In the two-bedroom apartments, modern dishwasher-equipped kitchens with stools at their counters open onto tremendous living/dining rooms. A tub is in one bath while the other has a stall shower. *(Very Expensive)*

★★★ **Whaler's Cove** • Although this attractive condo complex is on a rocky shore, it's a great place for winter whale watching and the beach is only a five-minute drive away. Facilities include a swimming pool. All suites have two bedrooms and two baths, but some units are larger than others. Cooled by ceiling fans instead of air conditioning, these modern apartments have TVs, high ceilings, huge walk-in closets, cushiony carpets, and rich brown koa moulding and doors. In some master baths, there's a whirlpool tub along with two free-standing sinks and a hand-held shower. Patios are large and shaded by palms. Kitchens are decked out with microwave ovens, dishwashers, and washers/dryers. The 18-hole Kiahuna golf course is nearby, as are tennis courts and other Poipu attractions. *(Very Expensive)*

Lawai

★★ **Victoria Place** • With only three guest rooms and a studio apartment, this hillside bed & breakfast gazes down on lush foliage, undulating sugarcane fields, and the ocean. Guest rooms look out to the pool deck, enlivened by gardenia, bougainvillea, ginger, and hibiscus. One room is set up for wheelchair access. With a private entrance, king-sized bed, living room, and kitchen, the studio is called Victoria's Other Secret. The hearty continental breakfast includes homemade breads and four or five tropical fruits. Vacationers receive personal attention from the gregarious proprietor, Edee Seymour, who steers them to little-known restaurants, beaches, and scenic hideaways. She is also happy to make restaurant reservations and arrangements for rental cars, helicopter tours, and horsebacking riding. Poipu beaches are only about a ten-minute drive away. Twenty minutes behind the wheel will take you to Lihue. Kukuiolono Golf Course and the boutiques and restaurants of Old Koloa Town are each about five minutes away. *(Inexpensive)*

Waimea

☆☆☆ **Waimea Plantation Cottages** • Dating from 1910 to 1930, these rustic beachfront cottages were once the homes of sugar plantation workers. Spare but comfortable, they now have one to four bedrooms, full kitchens, cable TV, telephones, cassette players, and radios. All are on the ocean side of the road, but some are closer to the water than others. The sand is dark on this tranquil beach, due to silt from the river that runs into the ocean. However, there's a swimming pool on the grounds and a more picturesque beach is about a mile west of here, in Kekaha. Away from south shore crowds, this secluded accommodation is an excellent place to unwind. Grocery shopping is nearby in the town of Waimea. *(Inexpensive* to *Moderate)*

Other Bed & Breakfasts and Private Homes

Staying in a B&B or renting a private home can give you more than a glimpse of Kauai beneath the surface. Many of these accommodations, all run and decorated with a personal touch, are in residential communities. Daily prices for double rooms run from about $30 to $125. Most are in the $60 to $80 range. A minimum number of nights may be required. If you'd like to find out about B&Bs in addition to those described above, or about renting private homes and cottages, contact the following companies:

Bed & Breakfast Hawaii • P.O. Box 449, Kapaa, Kauai, HI 96746; (808) 822–7771 or (800) 367–8047.

Bed & Breakfast Pacific-Hawaii (also handles private homes and cottages) • 19 Kai Nani Pl., Kailua, HI 96734; (808) 262–6026 or (808) 263–4848.

Bed & Breakfast Honolulu • 3242 Kaohinani Dr.; Honolulu, HI 96817; (808) 595–7533 or (800) 288–4666.

Housekeeping Cabins

Kokee Lodge • High in the mountains of Kokee State Park, 3600 miles above sea level, these simple cabins are halfway between spectacular Waimea Canyon and Kalalau Lookout. The cool misty air in these thick woods is sweet with the smell of eucalyptus and pine. Here on a tropical island, blankets and fireplaces get much use (wood is available at an additional cost). Each of the one- and two-bedroom cabins (sleeping from three to seven people) contains a refrigerator, electric stove, cooking and eating utensils, beds, blankets, pillows, linens, and a hot shower. In season, hikers enjoy picking wild plums and fishing for rainbow trout in streams (freshwater fishing licenses are required). In the main building, the restaurant serves filling breakfasts and lunches daily, and dinner on weekends. There is also a gift shop, a convenience store, and the petite Kokee Natural History Museum. The Lodge is 40 miles from Lihue Airport, at least a 90-minute drive. *(Inexpensive)*

KAUAI DETAILS

SAVING MONEY: Economical package deals are offered by tour companies and airlines. Through **American Airlines** ((800) 321–2121), for example, you can book a 7-night vacation that includes round trip flights, coupons for either in-flight movies or cocktails, an economy rental car, and taxes. Vacationers are flown to Honolulu, where they change to a flight on either Hawaiian or Aloha Airlines. To leave from San Francisco during peak season, the cost would be about $1010 per person, double occupancy, in a standard room at the moderately priced Stouffer Poipu Beach Resort. A stay in an oceanfront room at the more upscale Stouffer Waiohai would run around $1400 per person. To depart from Chicago, the cost of staying at the moderate hotel would be about $1120, while it would be around $1600 at the expensive accommodation. From New York, the moderate hotel package would run about $1130 and the more expensive excursion would be about $1610.

GETTING TO AND FROM THE AIRPORTS: Kauai's main airport is just outside Lihue, the capital. Those staying on the north shore should fly into Princeville. Find out if your accommodation provides complimentary transportation to and from either airport. If not, you can get where you're going by bus, van, taxi, limo, or rental car.

By Bus and Van: Make reservations to travel with **Gray Line Hawaii** ((800) 367–2420), which runs between Lihue Airport and hotels. The cost should be about $5 to the Lihue area, $9 to Poipu, and $6 or $7 to Wailua or Kapaa. **Shoppe Hoppers** airport shuttle (332–7272) charges about $5 to the Wailua/Kapaa area and $7 to Poipu.

By Taxi: Akiko's (822–3613) is a good cab company in the Poipu/Lihue area. The fare from the main airport to Poipu should be about $28. The **North Shore Cab Company** (826–6189) charges about $12 from Princeville Airport to Hanalei.

By Limousine: To ride to or from the airport (or to sightsee) in style, contact **Limo Limo Limousine Service of Kauai** (822–0393) or **First Class Limousines** (839–0944 or (800) 248–5101).

By Car: The major rental agencies have desks at Lihue Airport. Guests are transported in vans to and from the cars. (See Getting Around Kauai, below, and Nuts and Bolts.)

GETTING AROUND KAUAI: Just one main road goes around most of Kauai. Since it doesn't encircle the island completely and since no roads cut all the way across the interior, you'll have a second chance to see whatever you missed the first time you passed it.

By Bus: While there are no public buses on Kauai, **Shoppe Hoppers** (332–7272) vans take visitors from their hotels to various stores and attractions. The fare depends on the destination. Tour buses visit all of Kauai's major sights.

By Car: In addition to national and statewide rental agencies, the following are reputable local companies: **Westside U-Drive** (332–8644) based in Kalaheo; **Adventures Jeep & Car Rentals** (245–9622) in Lihue; and **Rent-A-Wreck of Kauai** (245–4755) also in Lihue.

Driving Tips: During morning and afternoon rush hours, avoid Lihue and the road between Lihue and Kapaa, unless you don't mind moving at a crawl. When you're going on sightseeing drives (such as to Waimea Canyon), it's best to leave as early as possible so that you don't end up stuck behind tour buses.

By Taxi: Cabs are only practical for short rides on Kauai, or for travelers who have money to burn. (See Getting To and From the Airports, above.)

By Limousine: See Getting To and From the Airports, above.

By Bicycle: See Sports.

RENTING VIDEO CAMERAS: Try **Gilligan's Video Camera Rental** ((800) 222–7756) in Kapaa or **Kauai Video** (245–7675) in Lihue, Kapaa, Waimea, and Kalaheo. Scuba divers should note that underwater video cameras are available for rent at the **Stouffer Waiohai** Beach Services Center in Poipu.

TOURIST INFORMATION: Contact the **Hawaii Visitors Bureau** (3016 Umi St., Suite 207, Lihue, HI 96766; 245–3971), **The Kauai Visitor Center** (Coconut Plantation Market Place, Kapaa; 822–0987), **Poipu Beach Resort Association** (Box 730, Koloa, Kauai, HI 96756; 742–7444), or the **Coconut Coast Visitor Association** (P.O. Box 1454, Kapaa, Kauai, HI 96746; 822–0293).

POST OFFICES: To find the location of the branch closest to you, call 245–4994.

EMERGENCY CASH: If you've spent more than you planned, you may be able to get money quickly through **American Express** (246–0627 at the Westin Kauai; ask about other locations) or **Western Union** (245–9437 in Lihue; 822–9473 in Kapaa; and 826–7331 in Princeville).

TIME: Call 245–0212.

WEATHER: Call 245–6001.

ALCOHOLICS ANONYMOUS: Call 946–1438 in Oahu for information about participating in meetings on Kauai.

WEIGHT WATCHERS: To find out about participating in local meetings, call (800) 535–6296.

EMERGENCIES: Dial 911.

MEDICAL ATTENTION: Contact **Wilcox Memorial Hospital** (245–1010) in Lihue; **Kauai Veterans Memorial Hospital** (338–9431) in Waimea; or the **Kauai Medical Group** (245–1500 in Lihue; 245–5651 in Kukui Grove; 742–1621 in Koloa; 822–3431 in Kapaa; 828–1418 in Kilauea; and 826–6300 in Princeville).

HAWAII: THE BIG ISLAND

Alternatively lush and stark, the island of Hawaii is one of the most unusual-looking and diverse places I've ever seen. Its striking appearance is due in part to the fact that it is still growing. Kilauea, the world's most active volcano, continues its periodic spurts of lava, which solidifies and adds to the island's land mass. From safe lookout points and helicopters, people watch the magnificent pyrotechnics. Called "vog" (volcanic fog), a haze hangs in the air for a few days after each of these intermittent eruptions. However, the sun shines through. Recent and ancient lava flows, ebony or chocolate in color, and moonscapes of volcanic craters stretch for miles in some regions. In other areas, waterfalls plunge into jungled valleys and mist clings to rolling hills. Flower nurseries, macadamia nut orchards, and coffee plantations thrive in the rich volcanic soil. With its *paniolos* (cowboys), rodeos, and herds of Herefords, Parker Ranch is the largest privately owned cattle ranch in the United States. Mauna Kea, a dormant volcano 13,796 feet above sea level, and active Mauna Loa, 13,677 feet above the ocean, are the world's tallest mountains (if measured from their aquatic bases). During winters when there is enough snow, experienced skiiers can actually whiz down the slopes of Mauna Kea.

So as not to be confused with the whole state, Hawaii is commonly referred to as the Big Island. And, at about 4000 square miles in size, big it is: Even if all the main islands in the chain were placed within its borders, they each would have plenty of elbow room. Some outsiders are under the mistaken impression that, because of its size and name, Hawaii is the main island in the chain and thus the home of the capital, Honolulu (which is actually on Oahu). For such a huge place, the Big Island is sparsely populated and has a great deal of undeveloped land. It is nearly twice as large as the other main islands combined, yet only about ten percent of the state's residents call it home. Although it was the first part of the archipelago to be inhabited, it is the geological baby of the bunch. It's only been around for about a million years, as opposed to the first main island, Kauai, which was created more than five million years ago. Thus, the Big Island hasn't had time to develop as many beaches as its older siblings. However, sandy shores here come in a variety of colors: eggshell, pitch black, salt and pepper, and (believe it or not) even bright green (from olivine crystals).

The best beaches are along the 40-mile Kohala Coast, in the northwest. This side of the island is treated to the least amount of rainfall in all of the inhabited Hawaiian chain. The Big Island's most expensive resorts are found here. Following the lead of the Mauna Kea Beach Resort, some of these hotels are virtual museums of art and artifacts from the Far East, the South Pacific, and Hawaii. Many remnants of Hawaii's past remain in this area, which is peppered with *heiau* (temples), *petroglyphs* (ancient rock carvings), and royal fishponds. Hotels including the Mauna Lani Bay and Kona Village have incorporated some of these fishponds and petroglyphs into their grounds. Northern Kohala is the birthplace of Kamehameha the Great, the ruthless Big Island king who brought the whole archipelago under his rule. The kingdom's seat of government was moved from the Big Island to Lahaina, Maui, in 1820, and finally to Honolulu in 1845.

To the south, the town of Kailua-Kona is a jumping off point for excellent marlin fishing and the headquarters for international fishing tournaments. There are few beaches here along the Kona Coast, where the dramatic shore is trimmed in craggy black lava set off by green lawns and palms. However, some of the island's best snorkeling sites can be found along here. The many hotels and condominiums in this area are close to a wide selection of shops and restaurants. On the other side of the island, not far from alternately flourishing and desolate Volcanoes National Park, Hilo is the island's capital and largest town. While this residential community does have some hotels, agriculture and shipping contribute far more heavily to its economy than tourism does. This is because the few nearby beaches are rocky and Hilo receives a great deal of rain. Even when the weather is dry, the sky is often gray. However, this eastern side of the island is wonderfully lush, sprouting papayas, sugar cane, and thousands of varieties of orchids.

Hawaiian Roots

Big Island residents often ask visitors not to offend Pele, the volcano goddess, by taking any rocks or sand. Many vacationers who scoff at this warning have nothing but bad luck after returning home with their stash. Post offices regularly receive rocks that have been mailed back by travelers desperate to undo their insult to the fiery-tempered goddess. Shells, on the other hand, make fine souvenirs, since they are part of the sea, not the land. Some contemporary Hawaiians believe, as their ancestors did, that Pele has lived in every volcano in the archipelago

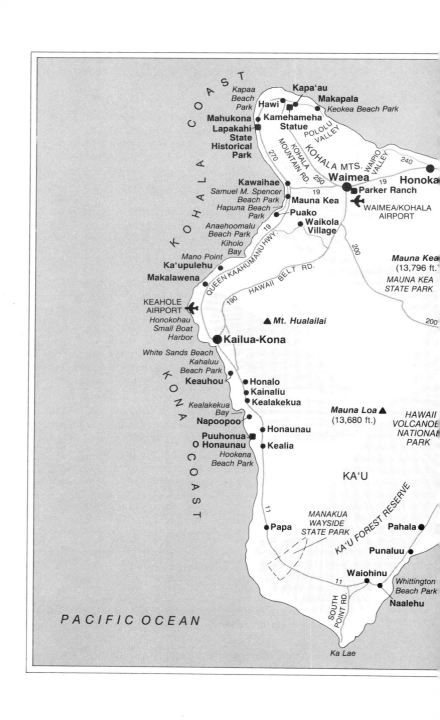

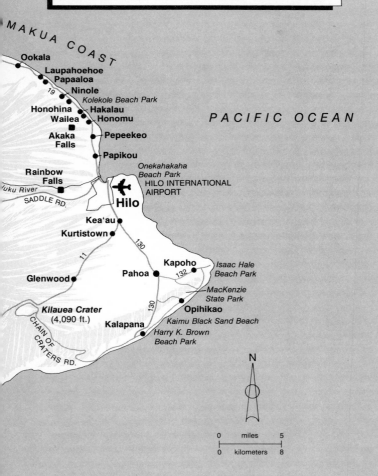

HAWAII: THE BIG ISLAND

MAKUA COAST

Ookala
Laupahoehoe
Papaaloa
19
Ninole
Kolekole Beach Park
Honohina — Hakalau
Wailea — Honomu
Akaka — Pepeekeo
Falls
— Papikou

PACIFIC OCEAN

Rainbow
Falls
Onekahakaha
Beach Park
HILO INTERNATIONAL
AIRPORT
Juku River
SADDLE RD.
Hilo

Kea'au
Kurtistown
130
11
Kapoho   *Isaac Hale*
Pahoa   *Beach Park*
132
Glenwood
— *MacKenzie*
State Park
130
Opihikao
Kilauea Crater
(4,090 ft.)   Kalapana
Kaimu Black Sand Beach
CHAIN   *Harry K. Brown*
OF   *Beach Park*
CRATERS RD.

N

0   miles   5
0   kilometers   8

and now resides in the Big Island's Halemaʻumaʻu Crater in Kilauea Caldera. She is said to have chosen Hawaii as her home after being run off Kauai by her sister, Na Maka, goddess of the sea, escaping to Oahu, and then fleeing to Maui. Ancient Hawaiians were known for their keen understanding of their environment. Thus it is not surprising that Pele's journey parallels the births of the Hawaiian islands, from the oldest to the youngest, according to present day geologists.

Pele is a vibrant and mysterious part of the lives of more than a few Hawaiians today. She is said to spend much of her time wandering near volcanoes. People frequently report seeing a long-haired woman who suddenly vanishes when observers get too close. In 1988, worshippers of Pele became embroiled in a legal battle with developers of a proposed geothermal energy plant. The Hawaiians believed that their religious rights would be violated if the plant were built as planned near Kilauea volcano, on what they considered sacred land. They feared that its construction would lead to Pele's demise. The Hawaii Supreme Court ruled that the plant would not prevent people from having access to this sacred region and that it would not infringe on religious rights. The Court noted that the original development site had been moved several miles away from the area that has traditionally been considered Pele's home. However, this project remains controversial.

Ancient Hawaiians had their own version of sledding, but they didn't use snow. Called *holua,* this adult sport was the highlight of the Makahiki Festival, the annual season of peace. The holua runs were made from piled, packed lava rocks that were cushioned with grass, leaves, and mats, then wet with hundreds of gallons of water. Clinging to narrow wooden sleds, called *papa,* competitors zoomed headfirst down the runways. Remnants of several holua runs remain on the Big Island, in Kona. The one in Keauhou, just south of Kailua-Kona, was declared a National Historic Landmark in 1964. It was probably built by King Kamehameha around 1814. Like a steep highway, it went all the way down to the coast, about a mile from its start. The upper ¾ mile portion is still intact. Fifty feet wide, it rises as high as eleven feet above the hillside in some sections. The lower quarter mile has given way to condos and a golf course.

According to one legend involving a Big Island holua contest, Kahawali, the chief of Puna, in the east, was about to enter a match. Dancers and musicians were keeping the crowd occupied while they waited for the competition to begin. Itching with curiosity about the reason for all the partying, Pele descended from her Kilauea home. She disguised herself as a local chieftess and demanded that Kahawali race her down the hill instead of the man he'd planned to challenge. Tickled by the boldness of this woman, the chief agreed. But the holua was far more difficult than Pele had expected, and she was soundly beaten by Kahawali.

Shouting that the contest must have been rigged in his favor, she insisted on a rematch. Someone must have damaged her borrowed papa, she told him. He agreed to another bout. But then she demanded that they switch papas so that all would be fair. He dismissed her request, climbed onto his papa, and began whizzing down the slope. An infuriated Pele jumped up and down, waving her fists in the air, sparking a volcanic eruption. Riding the red-hot river of lava, she pursued Kahawali down the hill. It made no difference to her that the dancers, musicians, and onlookers were being swallowed up by the fiery cascade. Horror swept over the chief as he realized who his competitor really was. Leaving his entire family to the lava flow, he scrambled into his canoe and paddled as fast as his arms would move, fleeing to Maui, Lanai, Molokai, and finally hiding out at the home of his father on Oahu.

Perhaps because Pele, such a powerful female god, is at the helm, the Big Island is where women first won more equal footing with men. After the death of Kamehameha the Great in 1819, Kaahumanu, his favorite wife, convinced Liholiho (Kamehameha II) to end the kapus against women dining with men and eating certain foods (such as coconuts, bananas, and pork). This led to an overthrow of the old, restrictive Hawaiian gods. However, soon the arrival of American missionaries brought a new form of restraint to the islands. Yet, despite the many changes Hawaii's spirituality has gone through, Pele has survived.

To see well-preserved ancient heiau, petroglyphs, and royal fishponds once off-limits to commoners, visit the Kohala Coast in the northwest. The larger of the two rocks in front of Hilo's library, on the eastern side of the island, is known as the Naha Stone. As a teenager, Kamehameha the Great is said to have moved this 7000 pound monolith. In doing so, he fulfilled the prophecy that the man who could budge it would someday unify the Hawaiian islands. Hilo is also known for its prestigious annual Merrie Monarch Festival, during which *hula halaus* (hula groups) from all over the state take part in competitions (see Special Events, below). If you're interested in the ancient art of *kapa* (bark cloth) making, see if any civic groups or the Hilo campus of the University of Hawaii are hosting seminars by Kanae Keawe. This master craftsman has tried to recapture this lost art through research, but he has had to rely mostly on trial and error. Kanae Keawe is also an expert in traditional *lauhala* (pandanus frond) weaving, woodcarving, featherwork, and lei-making.

Special Events

One of Hawaii's most popular annual events is the Merrie Monarch Festival, a week-long hula competition held in Hilo each April. Those who don't purchase their tickets far enough in advance (usually several months ahead) must be content to watch the graceful evening performances on television. The festival also includes free activities such as midday hula shows; a parade with floats and marching bands; a Hawaiian cultural fair with crafts, music, and food booths; and displays of Hawaiian quilts, artifacts, historic photographs, and antique furniture. The program is named for Hawaii's last king, David Kalakaua, dubbed the Merrie Monarch for his love of the arts and of having an all-out good time. During his 1874 to 1891 reign, he was largely responsible for bringing back the hula and other Hawaiian traditions that had been banned by American missionaries. They believed that the expressive body and hand movements were too sexually suggestive.

When this festival began during the 1960s, only women's *halau* (hula groups) competed. The event soared in popularity after a men's hula division was added in 1976. (Men, by the way, were the original dancers of hula in ancient Hawaii.) Today, it features both *kahiko hula* (ancient) and *auana hula* (modern) styles, accompanied by *mele* (ritual chants). Some halau spend years on the waiting list to participate. While most groups are from the various Hawaiian islands, some come all the way from the mainland. Throughout the year, visitors on all islands should keep an eye out for any fundraising luaus hosted by hula halau to cover the cost of the costumes, leis, food, and transportation they'll need to take part in the festival. These luaus tend to be more down to earth than the more commercial affairs hosted by hotels and other tourist-oriented groups.

Vacationers can immerse themselves in more Hawaiiana at the Puuhonua O Honaunau National Historical Park Annual Cultural Festival, held at the end of June or early July on the Kona coast. In June, in addition to the Kamehameha Day Parade in Kailua-Kona, there is also a celebration in Hawi (North Kohala) during which the statue of King Kamehameha I is draped with a multitude of long, colorful leis. Other festivals that highlight hula, lei-making, music, and Hawaiian games include the August happening at Puukohola Heiau on the Kohala Coast; Aloha Week, a major island-wide celebration in late September or early October; and the Annual West Hawaii Makahiki Festival, based on an ancient peace and harvest-time event, in Keauhou-Kona in October. Famous for its beautiful blossoms and other vegetation, Hilo hosts Annual Orchid Shows in June and July, the Annual Big Island Bonsai Show in July, and the Annual Hawaii Anthurium Association Show in August. In November, the Annual Kona Coffee Festival, held in Kailua-Kona, honors the harvest of the only coffee that is grown commercially in the U.S.

There are many Big Island events for those who like watching or participating in sports. In July, Mauna Kea Beach Hotel is the place to be for the Annual Pro-Am Golf Tournament, held on one of the world's top courses according to *Golf Digest* and other golf magazines. Complete with paniolos, Parker Ranch is the site of the Rodeo and Horse Races on July 4th and a Round-Up Rodeo in September. More than 200 people race a mile through churning waves in the Hapuna Rough Water Swim held on the Kohala Coast in July. At Honokohau Harbor, just outside Kailua-Kona, men and women begin a three-mile outrigger race during the Annual Kai E Hitu Long Distance Canoe Race in August. More than 1200 athletes from all 50 states and dozens of other countries compete in the rigorous 2.4 mile swim, 112-mile bike ride, and 26.2 mile marathon during the annual Ironman World Triathlon, which begins in Kailua-Kona in October.

Many competitions revolve around one of the Big Island's most cherished sports: Fishing. The July Kona Ahi Jackpot Fishing Tournament and the Pacific Game Fish Research Foundation Light Tackle Tournament take place in Kailua-Kona. In Kailua-Kona in August, during the Kona Hawaiian Billfish Tournament, American teams are chosen for the annual week-long International Billfish Tournament, the island's most celebrated angler's competition, held later that month. In both events, fishing enthusiasts race to spots where they think they'll find the greatest number of marlin and yellowfin tuna. For good luck, some still carry on the ancient traditions of bringing Hawaiian salt tucked securely in a *ti* leaf and ensuring that no bananas have found their way on board. Every afternoon (around 4 or 5 p.m.), the catch is weighed before a crowd of spectators at the pier by the King Kamehameha Hotel or at the Fuel Dock. Parades and parties are part of the festivities. Toward the end of August, children can get in on the act during the Annual Keiki Fishing Tournament, also in Kailua-Kona.

Getting Around

To really appreciate the Big Island of Hawaii, you'll need to stay at least a week. You may want to divide your time between a hotel on the Kohala Coast (if you can afford it), one in Kona, and one in Hilo.

The Big Island's two main airports are Hilo International Airport (a.k.a. General Lyman Field) in the east and Keahole Airport in Kona on the west coast. Hilo International is barely five minutes from most of Hilo's hotels and about 30 minutes from Volcano. Many commuters who live in the Waimea area fly into Kamuela Airport, up north. From Keahole, the drive is about 35 to 50 minutes to Kona-Kohala hotels, 10 minutes to Kailua, and 20 to Keauhou. Some accommodations on the Kohala Coast and in Kailua and Keauhou provide transportation to and from Keahole Airport for less than the cost of a taxi. Many first-time visitors are struck by the landscape they see as they swoop down on Keahole Airport, which is built on top of a desert-like lava flow. The black runways cut through ebony and dark brown expanses punctuated by tufts of dry yellow grass. Along the roads to and from the airport, the green palms and purple, red, and orange bougainvillea provide a stunning contrast to the dark, barren terrain.

It's certainly true that at 93 miles at its longest and 76 miles at its widest, the Big Island lives up to its name. But it is possible to drive all the way around it in a day. Companies such as Gray Line and Hawaii Resorts Transportation give "circle island" as well as half-day tours in buses and limousines. However, many visitors prefer to explore the island at a more leisurely pace on their own. There is no island-wide bus system on the Big Island. But Hele-On Buses travel between Kailua-Kona and Hilo twice a day (except Sunday when there is no service) for about $7 each way. In Keauhou and Kailua-Kona, complimentary shuttle buses take guests of hotels and condos to the Kona Country Club golf course and shopping centers.

Rental cars provide the most flexibility. It's best to reserve autos well in advance of your arrival, especially if you plan to travel between November and March, during August, early in April (when the Merrie Monarch Festival takes place in Hilo), or in October (during the annual Ironman Triathlon). Remember, sights and attractions can be far apart on the Big Island. Used to the long distances, many residents have no problem with driving 50 miles just to visit a friend for an evening or to eat at a particular restaurant.

One main road goes around the southern portion of the island. Two roads cut across the northern segment: Saddle Road runs from Hilo to South Kohala, where it joins Highway 190 to head north to Waimea or south to Kailua Kona; and after following the Hamakua Coast in the east, Highway 19 heads inland, then meets Highways 250 and 270 for the journey to North Kohala, or follows the western coast (on Queen Kaahumanu Highway) down to Kailua-Kona. The drive from Kailua-Kona to Hilo should take about 2¼ hours via the northernmost route and 3¼ hours via the southern route. Driving from Kona to Hilo on Saddle Road (the middle route) will take roughly 2¼ hours. Some vacationers choose to spend a night or two in Hilo when they're ready to visit Volcanoes National Park and the Hamakua Coast. Volcanoes National Park is only a 45-minute drive from Hilo, while it is 2½ hours from Kailua-Kona. The Black Sand Beach at Kalapana is about 45 minutes from Hilo. Waimea is approximately 1¼ hours from Hilo and 50 minutes from Kailua-Kona.

The Kohala Coast and Kamuela (Waimea)

From royal fishponds and burial caves to heiau and petroglyphs, intriguing remnants of Hawaii's past are well-preserved along the sunny, beach-rimmed Kohala Coast. Some of the ponds and rock carvings have been incorporated into the grounds of luxury hotels. Kohala is the birthplace of Kamehameha the Great, the celebrated unifier of the Hawaiian islands. The beaches along this coast were once frequented by Hawaiian monarchs at play. Also called the King's Trail, Ala Mamalahoa is a path that has been pounded by generations of royal feet into a gleaming black line through the rough lava. Some hotels lead jogging jaunts along this ancient trail, part of which was later broadened for travel on horse-back.

Heading north from Kailua-Kona or Keahole Airport on Queen Kaahumanu Highway (named for Kamehameha I's feisty, favorite bride), you may think you're driving through a vast wasteland. No buildings or even gas stations border the road. As far as you can see, stark lava flows sprawl on both sides of the highway. Here and there the barren charcoal landscape is interrupted by hay-like pili grass, kiawe trees, and cascades of colorful bougainvillea, which create a brilliant contrast. The Big Island version of graffiti also decorates the roadsides. Kids use white coral rocks to spell out phrases such as "Fred loves Noelani" on the black lava expanses, most of which resulted from the last eruption of Mt. Hualalai in 1801.

What could Laurance Rockefeller possibly have been thinking when he decided to build the Mauna Kea Beach Hotel in this desolate area in 1965? Well, his idea caught on, and many other developers have fol-lowed suit. From most of the road, there's no sign of these plush re-sorts. They are tucked neatly out of sight at the water's edge, beyond the lava flows that stretch between the highway and the Pacific. Despite the ruggedness of the region, the grounds of these well-spaced hotels are startlingly green, with flowers in every hue and smooth lawns and golf courses. While the expensive Kona-Kohala coast has a (very) long way to go before it even begins to resemble Oahu's Waikiki or Maui's Kaanapali, some residents and loyal vacationers are dismayed by the plans for building additional splashy hotels along this coast.

The Kohala district begins at **Anaehoomalu,** where a curving white sand beach gives way to a shallow bay. Regular folks weren't allowed to fish at the royal ponds by the adjacent **Royal Waikoloan** hotel, but contemporary commoners are welcome to tour these picturesque bodies of water. The meandering fishponds at the **Mauna Lani Resort,** further north, are also quite impressive. At the **Hyatt Regency Waikoloa,** the human-made sights are so lavish that guests may not notice that there is only a rocky shore and a small, artificial lagoon beach. Sleek boats cruise canals and long, columned corridors are lined with museum-like displays of Asian and Polynesian art and artifacts.

Further north in the **Puako** area, the craggy shore is riddled with tidal pools that make perfect swimming holes for kids (even the adult variety). You'll also find petroglyphs here. Between Mauna Lani Resort and Mauna Kea Beach Hotel, **Hapuna State Recreation Area** has a beautiful strip of white sand and camping cabins set back from the water. Many consider this and neighboring **Kuanoa Beach,** where the Mauna

Kea Beach Hotel is located, the most attractive shores on the Big Island. Kohala's hotel art craze began with the **Mauna Kea,** where tours of its fabulous collection are conducted twice a week. One way to get to the upscale ranching town of Kamuela (a.k.a Waimea) is to turn *mauka* (inland) not far from here, onto Kawaihae Road (Highway 19). This route will also take you across to the east side of the island, down the lush Hamakua Coast and to Hilo, the Big Island's largest (albeit often waterlogged) town.

Back on the Kohala Coast, **Samuel M. Spencer Beach Park,** just north of the Mauna Kea hotel, draws many local families for picnicking and camping out. From the park, you'll have a good view of **Puukohola and Mailekini heiaus,** both within walking distance. In an ironic twist, Kamehameha I built the first of these ancient temples to honor his family's war god, while the second was constructed to celebrate 40 decades of peace between the Big Island and Maui. Before setting out to conquer the Hawaiian Islands, Kamehameha sacrificed 15 men at Puukohola. One of them was a rival chief, whom he invited to the dedication of the heiau, then promptly had killed. At night, people sometimes still pray and leave offerings here (but no longer in human form). The snorkeling is good off **Lapakahi State Historical Park.** Here a path leads to the ruins of an old fishing village and exhibits tell a bit about Hawaiian life in the past.

At the island's extreme northern tip, near Upolu Airport (which serves private planes), little-visited **Mookini Heiau** has stood since about 400 A.D. This was probably where the birth rituals befitting a high-born child were performed for Kamehameha I, who began life nearby. People are said to have known early on that he would be a powerful and influential man. When his mother was nearly at the end of her pregnancy, she was overtaken by a constant craving for tiger shark eyes. That same month, Halley's comet crossed the sky. The child became the first of the Kamehameha line of rulers. As a young man, he prepared for his life as a warrior by dodging spears hurled at his chest.

In green North Kohala, pastures speckled with Holstein cows are now far more prevalent than the sugarcane fields that once blanketed the area. At one point, five sugar plantations flourished in Kohala. The quiet streets of **Hawi,** the northernmost town on the Big Island, are lined with low clapboard houses and shops. To get a real feel for this old plantation community, chat with patrons or the merchant at **M. Nakahara General Store,** where you'll find everything from rubber sandals and hardware to fabric and children's clothing. The shelves of neighboring **Nakahara Grocery Store** are piled with foods that reflect the tastes of Hawaii's many nationalities: salted duck eggs, fresh poi, spicy dried squid, imported Japanese crackers and cookies, seaweed salad, shrimp chips, octopus *poki,* and *laulau* (leaves wrapped around ground pork or fish). If you're feeling adventurous, you might find some fixin's for a picnic here.

East of Hawi, **Kapaau** is the site of the imposing 1878 **King Kamehameha Statue,** which stands in front of the North Kohala Civic Center. On King Kamehameha Day in June, residents drape the monarch with scores of brightly colored leis. The statue bears a striking resemblance to the one in front of the Judiciary Building in Honolulu. This is because that statue was copied from this one. Intended for Honolulu, the original was modeled by an American sculptor in Italy, cast in Paris, and lost during a shipwreck off the Falkland Islands. So the replica, which now stands in Honolulu, was made. Then the original turned up. It seemed appropriate to erect it near the birthplace of the first ruler of the Hawaiian Kingdom. Just east of here, a winding scenic drive through meadows and a residential neighborhood will take you to **Keokea Beach Park.** At the end of a rust-colored dirt road, you'll have a panoramic view of the frothy surf thrashing the shores of a rocky cove. On this eastern side of the North Kohala peninsula, the main road grinds to a halt at **Pololu Valley Lookout.** Awe-inspiring cliffs drop into deep valleys where wild boars, goats, pheasants, and horses roam freely. A rugged hiking trail dips into Pololu and eventually makes its way to distant Waipio Valley, where Kamehameha I was raised.

The 20-mile drive from Hawi south along the **Kohala Mountain Road** (Highway 250) to Kamuela is one of the island's most scenic routes. An eerie mist often hangs over the towering ironwoods, open fields, and country lanes. You'll pass **Kahua Ranch,** which sports a windmill. The paniolos here are as likely to round up cattle on motorcycles as on horseback and as adept at growing carnations as they are at raising sheep. At nearby **Kohala Ranch,** visitors are welcome to watch matches at the **Arena Polo and Equestrian Center,** or even to take polo lessons. Before you reach the town of Kamuela, you'll come to a lookout point from which you'll have an extensive view of the Kohala Coast.

Kamuela, also called **Waimea,** has its roots in land that Kamehameha I left to his granddaughter, Kipikane. She married John Palmer Parker, a sailor from Massachusetts, and together they established **Parker Ranch,** in 1847. It remains the largest privately owned cattle ranch in the U.S. Hawaii's first cowboys were Mexicans, Spaniards, and Indians from the mainland. *Paniolos,* as cowboys are now known in Hawaii, is a corruption of the word *Españoles* (the Spanish). Wild rodeos are periodically hosted by the ranch. Tours of its historic homes and grounds (including calf feedings, round-ups, and other operations) begin at the **Parker Ranch Visitor Center and Museum** in the center of town.

Waimea was the ancient Hawaiian name for the area, but it was dubbed Kamuela (the Hawaiian version of Samuel) after Colonel Sam

Parker, the son of John Palmer Parker. However, many people continued to call it Waimea and since there are Waimeas on both Oahu and Kauai, the U.S. Post Office requested that the name be officially changed. So much for officialdom: This town is still commonly known by both names. At the crossroads of the island's main highways (routes 250, 19, and 190), it rests in the Kohala Mountains. Nearly 3000 feet above the dry, sunny Kohala Coast (a 45-minute drive away), it is about an hour's drive from Hilo (along Saddle Road). Rainbows often span its verdant fields where horses graze, enclosed by fences made of stones or rough logs. Horseback riding past cattle in open fields or into forests thick with ferns and aromatic ginger is a popular pastime. The stables of the Mauna Kea Beach Hotel are located here. Houses with gingerbread trim are complemented by neat, colorful gardens. Small churches coexist peacefully with modern mini-malls.

Kamuela/Waimea was born as a shopping and services area for ranch employees. As drowsy as this village is, development is happening too quickly for many long-time residents. They complain about the new homes and shopping centers that keep cropping up. Others are pleased with the changes. One tasteful shopping center is **Hale Kea,** which used to be the main house and outbuildings of Laurance Rockefeller's ranch. More than a few people from Honolulu and other busy parts of Hawaii have relocated to Waimea. They've been lured by the prospect of living in the country, yet being able to take advantage of Waimea's chic boutiques, smattering of gourmet restaurants (several of which are owned by former chefs at some of Hawaii's most upscale resorts), and art galleries. **Nikko Gallery,** for instance, is in a former home dating back to the 1880s. If you ask about the ''Boy Blue'' that's scratched into the glass of the door, locals will tell you that Prince Kuhio etched his nickname there with a diamond in 1889. The gallery has an impressive collection of Japanese antiques and Hawaiian koa woodwork. Over the years, another draw for affluent families has been private Hawaii Preparatory Academy, which is one of the best schools in the state. It was founded in 1949 by an Episcopal bishop. Two of its four campuses—an elementary school and a middle school—are in central Waimea, and one (the high school) sprawls across more than 80 acres of Parker Ranch land.

At the **Kahilu Theater,** you might catch a classical concert, a hula performance, or a Broadway play. Richard Smart, the sixth-generation owner of Parker Ranch, is largely responsible for the existence of the theater. He even appears in some of the local productions. He is also the person who began the extensive tours of Parker Ranch. These bus excursions include visits to his elegant family home, **Puuopelu,** to see its international display of renowned paintings, porcelain, and antique furniture; and to **Mana,** the simple koa wood building where the ranch founder once lived. You can see another impressive koa interior at **Im-**

iola Congregational Church, where wooden calabashes are suspended from the ceiling. Most of the varied displays at **Kamuela Museum** consist of Hawaiian implements and furniture. Albert Solomon runs the museum with his wife, Harriet (a descendent of John Palmer Parker), and tells some good stories about old Hawaii. Would-be astronomers should stop in at the **Keck Control Center,** to learn about the powerful telescopes at the summit of Mauna Kea.

Moonwalking—Well, Almost

More than 1600 years ago, Polynesians used their knowledge of astronomy to guide them over thousands of miles of open ocean to Hawaii, first landing on the Big Island. Today, the world's largest optical-infrared telescope, at Keck Observatory on the 13,796-foot summit of Mauna Kea, helps contemporary scientists learn more about the heavens. The dry, generally cloud-free weather here on Hawaii's loftiest peak creates such prime conditions that scientists from Great Britain, the Netherlands, France, and Canada, as well as NASA, have built their country's major telescopes here. More than 90 percent of all the stars visible from anywhere on the planet can be seen from this perch.

Since the telescopic observation is done after dark, you'll have to go at night to see the stars. However, some tour companies lead daytime excursions to the bleak (sometimes snow-covered) lunar-like summit to see the massive and complex equipment. Even though companies provide parkas, travelers should still wear warm clothing. People may make the long trip on their own, but they'll need to rent four-wheel-drive vehicles. However, be forewarned that some people (like me) experience altitude sickness (dizziness, headache, fatigue, nausea). If these symptoms are relatively mild, ask for a few inhalations of pure oxygen through a tube at the summit. Otherwise, turn around and go back down. Children under age sixteen are not allowed to make the trip at all. Don't be surprised if your bags of potato chips or other snacks burst from the pressure of the altitude, as ours did.

After climbing through Parker Ranch lands along Saddle Road, you'll turn onto Summit Road, with about 15 more miles to go until you reach the top. Some of the scattered *mamane* trees you'll see began growing 200 or 300 years ago. With the introduction of cows and sheep, the trees are dying out, since these animals eat the seeds, buds, and flowers. At these high elevations, you might catch a glimpse of native birds such as the *nene goose* (the state bird) and the small, bright yellow *palila.*

Mauna Kea scientists live in a building resembling a Swiss chalet, on a mountainside near the **Mauna Kea Visitor Center.** Open from Friday through Monday with limited hours, the center is dedicated to Ellison Onizuka, the astronaut from Hawaii who was killed in the *Chal-*

lenger explosion. (Restrooms are always open.) Only four-wheel-drive vehicles are permitted beyond this point. Once the vegetation disappears, you'll come to the desert-like **Valley of the Moon,** where Apollo astronauts trained to get the feel of lunar life. In the distance, you may be able to spot piles of rocks jutting up from a flat area. Dating back to around 200 or 300 A.D., these are shrines constructed by ancient Hawaiian stone workers. Finally, you'll come to the telescopes, housed in domed white buildings that resemble huge igloos. Thus, from the stone age to the space age, Mauna Kea spans the development of humankind.

Kailua-Kona and the Kona Coast

Although it caters primarily to tourists, the lively town of **Kailua-Kona** is a pleasant place to spend some time. Most of its low buildings are found along the mile or so segment of oceanfront Alii Drive between Hotel King Kamehameha in the north and the Kona Hilton in the south. Many of its boutiques and restaurants are housed in a variety of shopping arcades (some rather atmospheric). Visitors wander in and out of stores selling island specialties such as macadamia nuts, jewelry made from coral and shells, billowy color-splashed muumuus, guava jelly and lilikoi (passion fruit) jam, ceramic chimes, and, of course, gourmet Kona coffee grown in surrounding plantations. A prime al fresco perch for lunch or evening sunset watching is the waterfront **Kona Inn,** with its peacock chairs, Oriental rugs, ceiling fans, and rich wood panelling. In August, Kailua-Kona is mobbed by anglers taking part in the Kona Hawaiian Billfish Tournament and the Hawaiian International Billfish Tournament. October lures hundreds of muscled bodies to compete in the Ironman World Triathon Championship, which begins in town. However, Kailua-Kona also offers several attractions that played important roles in Hawaii's history.

Alii Drive is shaded by immense gnarled banyan trees with dripping shoots, and branches that reach all the way across the street. This area was once the summer haunt of Hawaiian royalty. For a trip into the regal past, visit **Hulihee Palace,** which now has an intriguing collection of antiques used by monarchs, many of whom spent six months of each year here. Across the street, spired **Mokuaikaua Church** was built by missionaries and is Hawaii's oldest Christian house of worship. With its tangle of commercial lobby shops, Hotel King Kamehameha stands on the site of **Kamakahonu,** the king's royal compound. Nearby **Kailua Wharf** is the departure point for yacht charters, glass-bottom-boat cruises, sunset sails, submarine sightseeing rides, para-sailing, and fishing charters. The catch is sometimes weighed here at the end of the day, most often during fishing tournaments. Local fishermen still cast their lines or nets from the seawall along Alii Drive, where women often sell hats, bags, mats, and other lauhala weavings. At the entrance to **Kailua Bay,** look for the totem pole–like *tikis* of restored **Ahuena Heiau.**

Holualoa, on the *mauka* (inland) outskirts of Kailua-Kona, is known for its art galleries. In addition to other buildings, both an old home and a former church have been converted into showplaces. Although many of the artists are from the mainland, there is also a great deal of Hawaiian art on display, from calabashes to pick boards (large serving trays used at luaus). You'll also find block prints and oil paintings depicting old legends, carved ivory, silver and brass jewelry, and fabrics tie-dyed with island-style designs.

About a mile south of Kailua-Kona, you'll come to **Magic Sands Beach** (also called **Disappearing Sands** and **White Sands**), next to tiny St. Peter's Catholic Church. The beach is so named because, during the winter, the tides wash it away. The swimming and snorkeling are o.k. here in the summer. A better beach for these pursuits—except when the surf is high—is **Kahaluu Beach Park,** farther on. Throngs of people pack the sand and pavilion on weekends. As Alii Drive continues south, the profusion of flowers is spectacular, with peach, fuchsia, yellow, white, and orange blossoms bordering the road. This is where you'll see some of the area's more upscale hotels and condominiums. Beaches remain scarce, but swimming pools and green lawns artfully landscaped into the craggy black lava coast make up for the lack. In **Keauhou** ("kay-OW-hoe-oo"—"New Beginning"), transportation is available from area accommodations to **Keauhou Shopping Village** and **Keauhou-Kona Country Club Golf Course.** If you're passing by on a Saturday, check out the **flea market** held next to the **Botanical Gardens** across from the Keauhou Beach Hotel. If you're in the market for macadamia nuts, you'll save a bundle by buying a bag of broken bits and pieces (just as scrumptious as whole nuts) and you'll find discounted Kona Coffee as well. This is also a good place to pick up a handsome lace-trimmed muumuu.

In Hanalo, **the Daifukuji Mission,** a picturesque Buddhist temple, reminds visitors of Hawaii's multi-cultural heritage. The **Kona Historical Society Museum,** in nearby Kealakekua, gives some background on this rural village that has turned to business and banking. At **Kealakekua Bay,** a monument honors Captain James Cook, the first European to arrive in these islands. This fish-packed cove is a popular snorkeling site for catamarans and other pleasure boats. Inland, the road winds through coffee country, along the lower slope of Mauna Loa volcano. Hawaii is the only part of the U.S. where coffee is grown commercially. Stop at the **Kona Coffee Mill Museum** and have a steaming cup. It was 1825 when coffee—soon to be Hawaii's black gold—first found its way to the islands, along with a sad cargo. The coffee plants, picked up during a stop in Brazil, arrived at Kona on the British warship that was carrying the bodies of King Kamehameha II and Queen Kamamalu. The royal couple had been visiting London when they both caught measles and died. First the coffee was planted in Manoa Valley on Oahu. Then, in 1828, farmers tried it on the Big Island. Kona's dry climate provided perfect conditions and it flourished as never before. Large-scale coffee growing eventually fell victim to rising labor costs, droughts, and dropping world coffee prices. Then in the late 1970s, people around the globe began developing a voracious taste for gourmet coffee, and the market began to soar once again. Highway 11 cuts through fertile land, with many different kinds of trees along the road: macadamia nut, wide-leafed breadfruit, mango, and tall, skinny papaya.

In the town of **Napoopoo,** not far from Kealakekua Bay, a memorial celebrates the life of Henry Opukahaia, who convinced the first missionaries to come to Hawaii from New England. In the spirit of religious pluralism, this memorial is near **Hikiau Heiau.** At this Hawaiian place of worship, Captain Cook was honored as a god, which Hawaiians believed he was when he turned up in 1778. Also in the area is **St. Benedict's Painted Church,** a small gothic building on a hill with a view of the South Kona coast. At the turn of the century, a Belgian priest painted all the Biblical scenes that adorn the walls and ceilings to teach Christianity to Hawaiians, some of whom did not know how to read. On the waterfront, **Puuhonua O Honaunau** provided religious and political asylum for 12th century Hawaiians. Also called City or Place of Refuge, this site has been restored and filled with indoor-outdoor exhibits. You'll see a *konane* board (for Hawaiian checkers), thatched roof *hales* (houses), and tall tikis guarding the water's edge. Wear sturdy shoes, since the paths along lava flows can be quite rugged.

Kaʻu and Ka Lae (South Point)

Much of the land is desert in the **Kaʻu** region, the southern portion of the Big Island. However, **Manuka State Wayside Park,** near the lower end of the Kona Coast, flourishes with an arboretum and trails through trim, colorful gardens. Picnic pavillions make this a relaxing stop and camping in shelters is allowed, with permits. **Ka Lae** (South Point), with its unusual green sand beaches, is the southernmost tip of the United States. As Hawaiians have always believed, historians have concluded that this is the part of the archipelago where the ancient Polynesian settlers first stepped ashore. Some experts say that these original inhabitants arrived between 700 and 750 A.D., while others point to evidence that indicates they were here as early as 300 A.D. or even 150 A.D.

The Kamehamehas were frequent visitors to Ka Lae. Kamehameha I spent a great deal of time fishing for ahi here, while Kamehameha II enjoyed surfing off the point. When Kamehameha I fought (and won) a vicious battle with Keoua, the high chief of Kaʻu, warriors and civilians alike hid in the lava tubes that ran between their village and the ocean. Now Kaʻu is sparsely populated, but in its heyday, more people lived here than anywhere else in the island chain. Just 30 miles offshore, by the way, a new volcanic island, Loihi, should break the ocean's surface in a few thousand years.

For exploring the area, you'll fare best in a four wheel drive. About six miles west of Naalehu, a narrow road branches off Highway 11. This road heads south for 12 bumpy miles to Ka Lae. Along the way, you'll pass herds of cattle, horses, and a wind farm that generates electricity by taking advantage of the air's constant motion. **Papakolea** (or **Green Sands Beach**) is three rough miles (more than a two-hour hike) from where the side road ends. While four-wheel-drive trails will take you closer than the road, the walk is still long. But if you've never seen olivine crystals before, it's worth the trek. These green grains were created when the fiery lava from an 1886 eruption of Mauna Loa surged into the chilly ocean. The green sand, the multi-hued blue of the Pacific, and the orange earth create a vibrant collage. Unfortunately, strong currents generally make the water too dangerous for swimming. Fishing for tuna, on the other hand, is almost as popular here as it was in the old days. Ancient fishermen knew how to prevent their canoes from being carried away by the rough tides. They tied the boats to ropes that were secured in holes in the rocks on shore. Some contemporary anglers continue this practice.

Kaʻu was used by the U.S. Army during WWII. Along with environmentalists and archaeologists, residents of Kaʻu are overwhelmingly against the proposed building of a space center in this historic area. They believe it would be dangerous to their health and safety and that it would interfere with a prime fishing site. Proponents of the spaceport say it could bring hundreds of jobs to this economically depressed region, but residents are convinced that these highly technical positions would be filled by outsiders anyway. Whether or not the space center is given the go-ahead, there will be some industrial development in Kaʻu, such as a facility that makes organic fertilizer from algae. There are also plans in the works for constructing two large resort hotels in the area.

If you fancy the idea of being in the boonies, book a room at the **Shirakawa Motel** in Waiohinu. Look for **Mark Twain's monkeypod tree.** The original, planted by Twain in 1866, lost a battle with a 1957 storm. However, a new tree grew from its roots. Colonial-style **Kauahaao Church** dates back to the 19th century. Flat, pretty **Naalehu,** a former sugar plantation town nearby, is backed by scenic hills. Stop at a food stand here for *malasadas,* Portuguese hole-less doughnuts. Although Naalehu is known as the most southern town in the U.S., you won't hear any drawls. A thrill for many visitors is stretching out under a palm on the coal black sands of **Punaluʻu Beach,** just northeast. If you'd like to spend some time in this area, try the **Seamountain at Punaluʻu** condominiums. On a hill overlooking the village here, a small church honors Henry Opukahaia (the same man commemorated in Napoopoo), who urged the missionaries to bring Christianity to Hawaii. In the early days, the *kauwa* (enslaved class) were kept in an area near Punaluʻu. To distinguish them from everyone else, they were forced to wear tattoos around their eyes or on their foreheads.

Hawaii Volcanoes National Park and the Hilo Area

The Big Island is the only part of Hawaii where volcanoes are still active. As you drive through **Hawaii Volcanoes National Park,** you may wonder what planet you're on. After witnessing an eruption of 4090 foot Kilauea, Mark Twain remarked, "I have seen Vesuvius since, but it was a mere toy, a child's volcano, a soup-kettle, compared to this." Even if Madame Pele doesn't see fit to treat you to a fiery display, the vast craters, natural steam vents, lunar landscape are awesome enough. Highway 11 cuts through the park. Aptly named **Chain of Craters Road,** which leads from **Kilauea Crater** to the coastal region, has been closed from time to time since a new series of periodic eruptions began in 1983. Although a haze called vog (volcanic fog) hangs over the island during and after an eruption, this volcanic dust helps create some of the state's most dramatic sunsets (along the Kona-Kohala Coast). The park is interlaced with 150 miles of hiking trails and scenic drives. One brief stroll takes visitors through gigantic **Thurston Lava Tube** and into a dense, ginger-scented fern forest. It surprises many travelers to know that, in addition to camping shelters, picnic grounds, and a restaurant, the park contains a hotel, a golf course, an art center, and a museum.

With its small towns and coastal regions, **Puna,** in the east, is bright with anthuriums, orchids, ginger, and yellow *mamani*. While it also sprouts macadamia nuts, the district is best known for its delicious papayas. Here on the east rift of Kilauea volcano, **Wao Kele O Puna** ("Green Forest of Puna") is the last large tropical rain forest in the United States. One of the world's biggest geothermal power plants is under construction on forest land. The plant will use steam from below the erupting volcano to generate electricity. Worshippers of Pele—the goddess who Hawaiian tradition says resides in Kilauea's caldera—aren't the only people disturbed by the plan. Environmentalists believe it is ecologically dangerous (and unnecessary) to destroy any part of one of the world's scarce rain forests.

Just over two miles from Pahoa, **Lava Tree State Park** is an eerie reminder of the power of Pele. In a 1790 volcanic eruption, lava surged through an ohia forest, leaving black molds of the trees in its wake. At **Cape Kumukahi,** the island's easternmost tip, you'll see the lighthouse that was miraculously spared by a 1960 flow. Now looking like rushing water that was suddenly frozen, the lava passed on both sides of the lighthouse without knocking it down. Directly south of Pahoa, palm-shaded **Kaimu Black Sand Beach** has been perhaps the island's most picturesque stretch of dark sand. At press time, however, this shore is in the direct path of a fiery lava flow. Most of the town of Kalapana has already gone up in flames. Fortunately, though, all residents have been evacuated and the beloved **Star of the Sea Painted Church** has been moved.

The verdant rolling hills, flamboyant blossoms, carpet-like lawns, and grassy plains tell you that rain is no stranger to this side of the island. At the **Mauna Loa Macadamia Nut Orchard,** on the outskirts of Hilo, macadamia trees line one side of the long entry road and stately pines border the other. While touring the grounds, visitors learn how these fattening nuts are processed. Then they are invited to taste-test the different varieties before buying a can or two. Nearby **Panaewa Rain Forest Zoo** makes a good stop for children. When the sun cooperates, a colorful shimmering arc is caught in the mist at **Rainbow Falls,** in Wailuku River State Park. The best time to visit is early in the morning.

Thirty miles from Volcanoes National Park, **Hilo** is a quiet water-front town with a handful of hotels. Had it not been for the bravery of Princess Ruth Keelikolani in 1880, it might not exist today. Once when it seemed certain that Hilo would be overrun by lava from an eruption of Mauna Loa, the princess traveled all the way from Honolulu. Standing at the edge of the red-hot flow, she gave offerings to Pele and recited chants that had been passed down through the generations. In just a few hours, the liquid rock stopped moving.

If you're driving along the highway from Volcanoes National Park between June and December, you'll be treated to a fragrant explosion of white and yellow ginger growing wild. Although most of Hilo's shores are rocky and its skies are more often gray than blue, its proximity to east coast attractions make spending some time here worthwhile. The town does receive a lot of rain, but most of it falls either at night or in brief showers during the day. Many of Hilo's easygoing residents are descendants of the Filipino, Japanese, and Chinese laborers who immigrated to work on the surrounding sugar plantations, once the foundation of Hilo's economy. In some of the cluttered, tin roof stores, merchants use abacuses instead of—or to double check—vintage cash registers. While cane fields remain, some have been replaced by macadamia nut farms and the omnipresent flower nurseries that bloom with orchids, anthuriums, and ginger. Visitors are welcome to tour the grounds of some of the nurseries and to buy inspected plants, cuttings, or seeds to mail to the mainland. The **Nani Mau Gardens** has one of the state's most extensive ginger gardens. **Hirose Nurseries, Orchids of Hawaii,** and **Hilo Tropical Gardens** are other good places to stop.

The cultural heart of the Big Island, Hilo is the site of the annual Merrie Monarch Festival, held each March or April at the Edith Kana-kaole Tennis Stadium. Plays, concerts, and other local performances take place at the University of Hawaii-Hilo campus. The college, which has an art gallery, also sponsors periodic lectures and demonstrations on kapa making, lauhala weaving, and other Hawaiian traditions. Inquire about the annual courses in the school's Elder Hostel Program designed for senior citizens visiting from the mainland.

Most of Hilo's hotels are clustered along **Banyan Drive,** where the old Chinese trees, dripping hairy shoots, were planted by notables such as Amelia Earhart and Cecil B. De Mille during the 1930s. A thick wall of coconut palms stands across from the stores along **Hilo Bay,** which is bordered by parks and gardens. In 1946, an Alaskan earthquake set off a *tsunami* (tidal wave) that quickly moved toward Hawaii. Traveling across the open ocean at perhaps more than 600 miles an hour, the series of waves slowed down—but grew in height—as the ocean floor rose toward shore. Gathering steam, the first wave suddenly sucked the water out of Hilo Bay. Some people ran into the dry seabed, delightedly scooping up the fish that had been stranded. Then, in a flash, the monster wall of water hit the shore. One hundred and fifty-nine people lost their lives and 163 were hurt. The tsunami also caused more than 25 million dollars in property damage. Another tidal wave struck Hilo in 1960. Today, however, a very sensitive scientific warning system has been devised and is used throughout the state.

A small footbridge from Banyan Drive will take you across to tiny **Coconut Island** in Hilo Bay. Studded with palm trees, it's a popular setting for picnics and plain relaxation. Off Banyan Drive, tranquil **Lil-iuokalani Gardens,** named for Hawaii's last queen, is filled with Japanese-style pagodas, bridges, and ponds. Spend some time in the shade of a flat-topped monkeypod tree and you might see people fishing or a local wedding party having their pictures taken. Early risers should check out **Suisan Fish Market,** at the edge of the Wailoa River near the Banyan Drive hotels. Every morning (except Sundays) at about 7 a.m., returning fishermen lay out glistening 50- to 100-pound ahi (yellow fin tuna) in neat rows along with other tropical fish. In Pidgin and at least a couple of other languages, they auction off their catch.

At adjoining **Wailoa State Park,** fishermen take to Waiakea Fish Pond in rowboats. Picnic tables and a shelter make this park a popular local hangout. At the octagonal **Wailoa Center,** on the grounds, you can see exhibits of the work of area artists. Visitor information is also available here. If you'd like to hear what the Hawaiian language sounds like, attend a service at **Haili Church** on Haili Street (sermons are also given in English). Built by Protestant missionaries from New England, it dates back to 1859. Many Hawaiian artifacts and exhibits highlighting Hawaii's other major ethnic groups are on display at **Lyman Mission**

House and Museum on the same street. The immense **Naha Stone,** which Kamehameha the Great is said to have moved as a teenager, stands in front of the Hawaii Public Library on Waianuenue Avenue. Beside it is the smaller **Pinao Stone,** which once guarded the entrance of a heiau. When the weather is right, locals head for **Onekahakaha Beach,** about three miles outside town, toward the eastern end of Hilo Bay. This is one of the area's few sandy shores.

The Hamakua Coast and Waipio Valley

The lush, rural **Hamakua Coast** is one of the island's most stunning regions. If you'd like to explore it at a leisurely pace, consider staying at one of its small accommodations near Honokaa. You can approach it from the Kohala Coast or from Hilo. About six miles north of Hilo, you'll come to **Old Mamalahoa Highway Scenic Drive** (off Highway 19), after passing through endless cane fields that melt into the verdant mountains. This four-mile stretch is bordered by royal palms, poincianas, breadfruit and African tulip trees. Flourishing ravines come into view and bridges span rocky streams. The road passes weathered sugar plantation towns, with old fashioned movie theaters, tin-roofed houses, and wooden-frame churches. Stop at the bluff that gazes down on **Onomea Bay,** with its distinctive rocky formations. If you'd like to visit **Hawaii Tropical Botanical Garden,** at the bay, get your ticket (or any visitor information you might need) at the little yellow church. From here, you'll ride down in a van.

At the **Honomu Plantation Store,** old photographs will give you a glimpse of what Hamakua once looked like. This is a good place to pick up fresh pineapples, Kona coffee, or macadamia nuts. You can even have your loot mailed to the mainland. At nearby **Akaka Falls State Park,** water plummets more than 400 feet over a volcanic cliff. (This setting is far more spectacular than Hilo's Rainbow Falls, by the way.) Especially in the late afternoon sun, **Laupahoehoe Point** is a beautiful spot. Its name means "leaf of lava," and indeed this is a narrow lava peninsula that is lapped by the Pacific. Local families enjoy a barbecue in the stone pits here. Picnic tables and shelters are also provided. At the edge of the water is a monument to the 20 schoolchildren and their teachers who were killed here by the 1946 tidal wave.

Just beyond Paauilo, you'll come to flourishing **Kalopa State Park,** another good picnic locale. On the slopes of Mauna Kea, this 600-acre recreation area is filled with sweet-smelling eucalyptus, ohia trees, and koa forests. Camping facilities and cabins are on the premises. The drowsy town of **Honokaa** is the king of macadamia nut production. Hawaii's first macadamias were planted here back in 1881. More nuts come from this town than from anywhere else in the world. If you haven't yet seen how they're prepared for your palate, visit the **Ha-**

waiian **Holiday Macadamia Nut Co.** and munch on the free samples.

One of my favorite places in all of Hawaii is **Waipio Valley,** cupped by 2000 foot-cliffs. Kamehameha the Great spent his formative years here. Located just northwest of Honokaa, it can be reached from both the Hamakua and Kona-Kohala Coasts (a 90-minute drive from either Hilo or Kona). At six miles long and a mile wide at the shore, this is the island's largest valley. In its heyday, 40,000 people called it home. Now, barely a few dozen live here, most of them taro farmers. A visit here makes an invigorating day trip. You can get down the bumpy, nearly vertical entry road on the **Waipio Valley Shuttle,** through a tour company, or on foot. Some of the tours include horseback riding, picnics, and/or swimming. Down below, the roads are rocky riverbeds, bordered by aromatic jasmine and ginger, mango and guava trees, taro fields, and edible fern shoots. You might catch a glimpse of wild horses.

By the **black sand beach,** look for the white naupaka flowers that also grow in the mountains. Half the petals of each blossom seem to be missing. Legend has it that these flowers were once lovers whose families forbade them to marry, banishing one to the seashore and the other to the mountains. While the ocean is too rough for swimming here, it's fine to take a dip in the freshwater stream that bisects the ebony beach. (However, don't take a drink without first boiling the water for at least five minutes.) A narrow waterfall pours down one of the cliffs. The beach, scattered with driftwood, is backed by pines. Arrive early enough and you might see local surfers in action. If you'd like to absorb the valley's beauty slowly, camp out overnight or bed down in **Tom Araki's hotel.** Often referred to as "The Waipio Hilton," this five-room accommodation has cold showers and no electricity.

WHAT TO SEE AND DO

PERSONAL FAVORITES

*Jungled **Waipio Valley,** on the northeast coast, where you can take a horseback ride along its rocky riverbeds and cliff-enclosed black

---

*Off the beaten path.

sand beach. (See Hawaii: The Big Island introductory section, Tours, and Sports.)

Mookini*, **Puukohola, and Mailekini heiaus,** impressive ancient stone temples in Kohala. (See Sights.)

Parker Ranch, with its *paniolos* (cowboys) in Kamuela/Waimea, where horseback riding is a pleasant pasttime. (See Sights and Sports.)

Hulihee Palace, in Kailua-Kona, where Hawaiian royalty once vacationed. (See Sights.)

Puuhonua O Honaunau, on the Kona Coast, also known as the City or Place of Refuge, with its ancient *tikis,* thatched roof shelters, and lava trails. (See Sights.)

***Ka Lae** (South Point), where hikers can visit a green sand beach (See Hawaii: The Big Island introductory section and Sports.)

Hawaii Volcanoes National Park, especially when Kilauea is erupting (See Sights.)

The petrified forest of **Lava Tree State Park,** in the volcanoes area (See Hawaii: the Big Island introductory section.)

Suisan Fish Market, in Hilo, where fish are sold in a lively, multilingual auction. (See Hawaii: The Big Island introductory section.)

Akaka Falls and its surrounding rain forest, on the Hamakua Coast. (See Sights.)

Wonderful Drives: One is along the agricultural **Hamakua Coast,** from Hilo to the Waipio Valley Lookout. Another is the inland route along the **Kohala Mountain Road** (Highway 250) between Waimea/Kamuela and Hawi, including the Pololu Valley Lookout.

SIGHTS

Hawaiiana

***Mookini Heiau** • *Hawi, North Kohala; 944–6922* • Perhaps few vacationers visit this ancient temple for fear that its past will catch up with them. Built for human sacrifices (among other uses), Mookini was the first site in the state to be listed with the National Register of Historic Places. Kamehameha I was born nearby, during the late 1750s, and he underwent royal birth rituals at this heiau. A rugged unpaved road not far from Upolu Airfield leads to the timeworn remains of the 20-foot stone walls on a hill. This large heiau is believed to have been constructed from rocks passed from worker to worker from a valley 14 miles away.

Lapakahi State Historical Park • *North Kohala; 548–6408* • Dating back to the late 1300s, this fishing village was established on a rugged, isolated segment of the coast. Wear sturdy shoes to wander along the trails through the remains. You'll see old canoe sheds, house sites, and some of the stone tools and utensils the ancient residents used. The peaceful grounds make a pleasant place for picnics and snorkeling offshore is quite rewarding.
Open 8 a.m.–4 p.m.

Puukohola Heiau National Historic Site • *about a mile southeast of Kawaihae, near the Mauna Kea Beach Hotel, Kohala; 882–7218* • Kamehameha the Great built this hilltop temple to honor his family war god, Ku, in 1791. He invited his cousin (who also happened to be an arch rival) to attend the dedication, then killed him as soon as he arrived, sacrificing his body to Ku. Kamehameha was then prepared to begin his bloody attempts to bring all of the Hawaiian islands under his control. Where once there stood thatched roof shelters and carved wooden statues, a huge stone platform is all that remains of this heiau today. In an ironic juxtaposition, Puukohola overlooks 13th century **Mailekini,** a heiau constructed to celebrate four centuries of peace between the Big island of Hawaii and Maui.

Kamuela Museum • *at intersection of Rts. 19 and 250, Kamuela/ Waimea; 885–4724* • This museum is run by Harriet Solomon (a descendant of the man who founded Parker Ranch) and her husband. The mishmash of haphazardly grouped items comes from Hawaii, other Pacific islands, the mainland, and China. You'll see everything from Hawaiian stone weapons, kapa cloth, fish hooks made from human bones, and a portrait of Queen Liliuokalani to a Nazi flag and a stuffed iguana.
Open 8 a.m.–5 p.m. daily. Cost: $3.50 for adults; $1.50 for children under age 12.

Eva Parker Woods Cottage • *Mauna Lani Bay Hotel, Kohala Coast; 885–6677* • Mauna Lani's renowned Francis Iʻi Brown Golf Course is named after the high-living kamaaina who used this beach cottage for vacationing and entertaining. His many guests arrived by boat from various parts of the world. Built in the 1930s, the cottage sits at the edge of fishponds once reserved for alii. Today it is a museum of Hawaiian artifacts and local treasures.
Visits arranged upon request.

Hulihee Palace • *75–5718 Alii Dr., Kailua-Kona; 329–1877* • Made of coral and lava, this two-story palace stands at the edge of Kailua Bay. It was built in 1838 for Johan Adams Kuakini, governor of the island. Over the decades, many members of Hawaiian royalty spent several months a year relaxing at this vacation home. King David Kalakaua later bought it and had it remodeled and enlarged. He filled its rooms with Victorian furniture, imported rugs, and delicate china. After its new owner died in 1914, the palace fell into ruin. The Daughters of Hawaii, a group of women whose foreparents had been Hawaii's first American missionaries, convinced the territorial government to buy the building. In 1927, the Daughters themselves took over its restoration and turned it into the museum it is today. Along with featherwork and kapa cloth, much of Hulihee's original furniture is on display. Its prize pieces include a table inlaid with nearly two dozen different kinds of native wood and an artfully carved four-poster bed whose posts once resided in Kamehameha's grass palace. It is clear from the size of some of the chairs how large Hawaiians were. Kamehameha I is thought to have been nearly seven feet tall. Both Queen Kamamalu and rotund Princess Ruth Keelikolani were said to have been a towering six feet. The missionary influence is apparent in the architecture and furnishings. Just across the street, Mokuaikaua is the oldest Christian church in Hawaii.

Admission: $5 for adults; $1.50 for students; 75¢ for children aged 6–12. Open 9 a.m.–4 p.m. daily.

Ahuena Heiau • *adjacent to Hotel King Kamehameha, Kailua-Kona; arrange tours through the hotel: 329–2911* • From 1813 until his death in 1819, Kamehameha I ruled the Hawaiian kingdom from this restored thatched-roof structure. The surrounding area was reserved for the residences of his wives and close relatives. Ahuena Heiau was constructed to honor the god Lono. Whether it was used for human sacrifice is up for debate. However, there is no question that Liholiho, Kamehameha's son and the person who would become Kamehameha II, studied here, learning all about politics, navigation, fishing, sailing, and farming. When Kamehameha the Great died at this heiau, his body received the traditional rites of passing: it was placed in a pit where the flesh was cooked off the bones and buried. So that no one could steal the great leader's *mana* (spiritual power), the bones were hidden (somewhere in North Kona). When the first missionaries arrived aboard the *Thaddeus* in 1820, they found the heiau in shambles. After the king's demise, it had been trashed by jubilant crowds when Liholiho, who had become Kamehameha II, had declared the ancient Hawaiian gods and their restrictive kapu system null and void. The missionaries were more than happy to step in with their own brand of religion.

Puuhonua O Honaunau (Place or City of Refuge) • *Honaunau, Kona Coast, south of Kailua-Kona; 328–2326* • For ancient Hawaiians, *kapus* governed everything from dietary habits and sexual relations to land ownership. These taboos were believed to be divine will and going against the gods could have far reaching consequences for all Hawaiians. Therefore, the punishment for transgressors could be severe—often death. However, people who broke these sacred laws could be spared if they reached Puuhonua O Honaunau before being caught. Refugees were protected here by the *mana* (spiritual power) that remained in the bones of the dead chiefs who were buried in nearby heiaus. Through a ceremony performed by a *kahuna* (priest), the lawbreaker would be absolved of all guilt. This refuge is adjacent to the ancestral home of the Kamehameha line. After a fight with Kamehameha I, Kaahumanu, his number one wife, is said to have hidden from him at Puuhonua O Honaunau, only to be given away by the barking of her pet dog. As usual in their tempestuous relationship, the loving couple finally made up. The land remained in the hands of Hawaii's royal family until the late 19th century, when it was bought by Charles R. Bishop. Also called Place (or City) of Refuge, this 180-acre site—the most revered of Hawaii's religious sanctuaries—was restored and turned into a national historic park in 1961.

Sights include the Kaahumanu stone (where the regent hid during her tiff with Kamehameha), a reconstructed heiau, old-style thatched roof *hales* (houses), burial caves, a stone for playing *konane* (a royal game something like checkers), a royal fishpond, and a royal canoe landing. Be sure to wear sturdy shoes if you plan to walk through the lava fields to see the petroglyphs. Exhibits cover various aspects of ancient life, and traditional skills and crafts are demonstrated by staff members. Over the weekend closest to July 1, a three-day cultural festival is held in the park. Transformed into royalty, the staff is decked out in elaborate feather capes and helmets. Vacationers are invited to try their hands at lei making, lauhala weaving, poi pounding, and tying fishing nets. They can even help pull in a load of fish. Young folks particularly enjoy the La Paani festival, held the first Friday in February and November, during which local school children compete in Hawaiian games such as spear throwing, dart sliding, and arm wrestling.

Admission: $2 for adults; free for children 16 and younger. Visitor Center open 7:30 a.m.–5:30 p.m. daily. Drawing picnickers and fishing enthusiasts, park remains open until midnight.

Lyman House Memorial Museum ● *276 Haili St., Hilo; 935–5021* ● Built in 1839, restored Lyman House was once the home of Hilo's first Christian missionaries, the Reverend David and Sarah Lyman. The museum next door, which opened in 1973, displays antiques from the days of Hawaii's monarchy and items from the early 1900s. Some pieces date back to the time before Westerners arrived. In addition to Hawaiiana, exhibits also spotlight missionary life and the various ethnic groups that populated the islands.

Admission (including guided tours): $4 for adults; $3 for children 13–18; $2 for children 6–12. Open 9 a.m.–5 p.m. Mon.–Sat.

More of the Past

*Greenbank • *Halawa, North Kohala; 883–9254* • Located in the neighborhood where Kamehameha the Great was born, the grounds of this estate sprawl across acres of gardens, deep ravines, and a tropical rain forest. The home, which dates back to the early 1800s, belonged to James Wight, a botanist and physician from Scotland who was shipwrecked in Hawaii. There's no telling when ironwood trees and orchids would have reached the island if he hadn't brought them.

Visits, with tours, arranged by reservation.

Parker Ranch • *Parker Ranch Shopping Center (Visitor Center and Museum), Kamuela/Waimea; 885–7655* • When John Palmer Parker, a sailor from Newton, Massachusetts, jumped ship in Hawaii in 1809, he found a job cleaning fish ponds for Kamehameha I. In 1816, he married Princess Keliikipikaneokaloahaka. Called Kipikane for short, she was the granddaughter of the king. Thus, the New England haole became a member of the Hawaiian royal family. Back in 1788, Captain George Vancouver had come to the islands with Captain James Cook, the man who let Europe know that Hawaii existed. When Vancouver returned in 1793, he brought Mexican longhorn cattle as a gift for Kamehameha. The king put a kapu on killing cows, decreeing that anyone who disobeyed the law would be put to death. But the cows reproduced so rapidly, trampling and eating such great quantities of vegetation on Mauna Kea's slopes, that they soon threatened nearby communities. Kamehameha hired his American grandson-in-law to control and shrink the herd. In exchange, he gave Parker two acres of land. In 1847, the ex-sailor and his wife established Parker Ranch.

Today, at 250,000 rolling acres, this is the largest privately owned cattle ranch on U.S. soil. Cowboys from Mexico and South America were brought in as ranch hands, and the word *paniolo* (a corruption of *Espanoles*) entered the Hawaiian vocabulary. After Parker's death, ownership of these lands fell into the hands of a 14-year-old descendent, Thelma Parker. She grew up to be the mother of Richard Smart, the great-great-great-grandson of the founder and the current owner of the ranch.

Tours begin at the Parker Ranch Visitor Center. The Museum here was started by Thelma Parker Smart. On display are her jewelry, her well-used bible, and the blue gown she wore to the opera at Covent Garden in England when George V was crowned king in 1911. Exhibits also include old saddles, bridles and bits, branding irons, iron pots, brass plates, and an old wind-up telephone mounted on the wall. Portraits, photographs, and a short film tell the history of the ranch and the Kamehamehas, as well as of other relatives and family friends. One part of the museum is dedicated to Duke Kahanamoku, an Olympic swimming champion who introduced surfing to Australia in 1912 and served as sheriff of Oahu for 25 years.

Arriving at the Visitor Center every few minutes, shuttle buses pick up sightseers for tours of the ranch. (The less expensive half-day tour is enough for most people.) Visitors may get on and off as frequently as they please. They visit Puukalani Stable (where they might catch a calf feeding in progress), the adjoining horse-drawn carriage museum, and the two Parker family historic homes. They might pass a round-up or a branding, inoculation, or horse-training session. Whenever they have a free moment, the paniolos (some of whom are second- and third-generation cowboys) are happy to talk story.

The living room of opulent **Puuopelu,** the home of Richard Smart, glitters with chandeliers hanging from skylights that flood the room with sunshine. Among the many original paintings are works by Degas, Renoir, and Chagall. Chests and tables are topped with stone camels and horses from China's Tang and Ming dynasties, Japanese vases, brass gondola ornaments from Venice, jade ranging in color from rose to bright green, Venetian glass, and Marie Antoinette and Louis XVI plates. In contrast, **Mana,** the older family home that was relocated next door, is a small, rustic affair, built in 1847. Its glossy walls, floors, and ceilings are made of rich brown koa. This gleaming wood was also used for the calabashes on display and the amazingly high headboard on the bed.

Admission to museum (open Mon.–Sat. 9 a.m.–4:30 p.m.): $5 for adults, $2.50 for children aged 4–12. Admission to historic homes (open Mon.–Sat. 9:30 a.m.–4:30 p.m.): $6 for adults, $3 for children aged 4–12. Cost of full-day tour (including museum, historic homes, trip to original site of Mana, and lunch): $40 for adults, $20 for children aged 4–12. Cost of half-day tour (including everything except lunch and the long drive to the original Mana homestead): $16 for adults, $8 for children aged 4–12.

Mokuaikaua Church • *across Alii Dr. from Hulihee Palace, Kailua-Kona; 329–0655* • This house of worship symbolizes the merging of two cultures: The lava stones in its walls came from an old heiau that was no longer in use. Founded during the 1820s, this building was the first Christian church in Hawaii. It was completed in 1837 by the original group of New England missionaries. Inside, be sure to take a look at the model of the *Thaddeus,* the ship on which these Americans arrived, and the copy of the writings of one of the missionary wives explaining how she felt about her new life.

Liliuokalani Park • *on Hilo Bay, off Banyan Dr., Hilo* • In addition to a friendly lunchtime bunch, this tranquil park attracts children who fish in the ponds with bamboo poles and local fishermen who catch *opae* (Hawaiian shrimp) with nets to use as live bait. Although the park is named after Hawaii's last monarch, it was actually designed as a tribute to Hilo's first Japanese immigrants, who arrived as laborers in the sugar cane fields. A visit to Kyoto, Japan, inspired the haole plantation managers to build this artfully landscaped Japanese garden. The many-tiered stone lanterns, one of them ten feet high, were given to the park by Japanese officials in the early 1900s. In Asia, they were first used to illuminate evening religious services, then later found their way into private homes. A symbol of wealth, they were carved from granite or marble. These sturdy treasures were about the only part of the pond- and bridge-filled park that was not washed away in the 1946 tsunami. The park was rebuilt, only to be swept away again in the 1960 tidal wave. Still some of the stone lanterns remained intact, if mud-covered. In 1968, to commemorate the 100th anniversary of the Japanese presence in Hawaii, the government of Japan donated a wooden *torii* gate, two stone lion gates, and thirteen more lanterns to the park.

Nature's Best

Onizuka Center for International Astronomy and Mauna Kea Observatory • *at the 9200 foot elevation of Mauna Kea; 935–3371* • The 13,796-foot summit of Mauna Kea volcano is one of the world's leading sites for research in astronomy. To understand why, visit this center, named for Ellison Onizuka, the Big Island astronaut who was killed in the explosion of *Challenger*. Exhibits illustrate the work of the scientists who use the massive telescopes at the top of the mountain. By calling in advance, you can arrange to take a free tour of the observatories at the summit. A four-wheel-drive vehicle is best for driving on Saddle Road (Highway 200), which will take you to this center. Before you decide to make the trip, note that some people get altitude sickness.
Open Fri.–Mon. Times vary, so call ahead.

Hawaii Volcanoes National Park • *Volcano (the southeast); 967–7311 (Visitor Center) or 967-7643* • Whether you're coming from Hilo or the Kona-Kohala Coast, plan at least a full day for this trip. A national park since 1916, the island's most visited attraction takes up over 344 square miles, encompassing Kilauea and Mauna Loa volcanoes. More than two million people pour into the park each year, the majority arriving when eruptions are in progress. The terrain ranges from moon-like craters, steaming firepits, and hissing fumaroles to thick rain forest. Picnic grounds, camping cabins, and 150 miles of hiking trails and scenic drives lure vacationers to this otherworldly landscape, about 4000 feet above sea level. The park even boasts a golf course and a hotel. During a visit here, Mark Twain quipped, ''The surprise of finding a good hotel in such an outlandish spot startled me considerably more than the volcano did.''

Kilauea's caldera alone is two and a half miles long, two miles wide, and 400 feet deep. Off 11-mile **Crater Rim Drive,** Halemaumau (the 300-foot-deep fire pit inside Kilauea) is where Pele, the hot-tempered volcano goddess, is believed to live. Kamehameha II abolished the islands' restrictive religion in 1819. However, many Hawaiians continued to worship the old gods, even after American missionaries arrived the following year and began converting people to Christianity. In 1824, Queen Kapiolani, who had readily converted, decided to prove to those who had not yet embraced Christianity that Pele did not exist. She stood at the rim of Halemaumau and ate some red *ohelo* berries, known to be sacred to the goddess, without offering any to Pele first. When the queen was not struck down on the spot, she told her people that this showed that there was no such thing as Pele, or any other Hawaiian god.

Yet some contemporary Hawaiians maintain that Pele continues her wandering, sometimes in the form of a wizened old woman, other times as a beautiful girl with flowing hair. From politicians and businesspeople to educators and reporters, residents have told of sightings of a mysterious woman just before eruptions. Thus, many people take very seriously the warning not to remove any rocks or volcanic sand from Hawaii, lest they anger the powerful goddess.

Kilauea's longest recorded series of eruptions began on New Year's Day of 1983. In early April, lava swept away the first house to be destroyed by the volcano in a quarter century. By the end of that year, more than a dozen homes and hundreds of housing lots had been smothered by the flow. Mauna Loa got in on the act in 1984, the first time it had erupted in nine years, and the first time both volcanoes had performed together in 65 years. Lava oozed onto the highway in 1986. Early the following year, just two months after the highway had been rebuilt, the road was swallowed by lava once again—to the delight of tourists with cameras. Along **Chain of Craters Road,** you'll see old sections of the highway that were partially covered with lava. During a fiery 1989 eruption, the former visitor center went up in smoke and a new one had to be built. By July of 1990, the lava flow had destroyed most of the town of Kalapana and threatened to ruin famed Kaimu Black Sand Beach. A trucking company volunteered to move the historic Star of the Sea Painted Church, whose walls and ceilings are covered with colorful religious murals done in 1931. Luckily, town residents have been safely evacuated.

All this talk of destruction may make you hesitate to visit the park—

or even the island for that matter. But bear in mind that, with a highly sensitive warning system, volcanic eruptions and the path of lava flows can be predicted. This means that sightseers are kept far away from any dangerous areas and homeowners are advised if they need to evacuate. Fatalities from Hawaii's volcanic eruptions have been scarce. Some of the last in recent history occurred in 1790, when a group of warriors battling Kamehameha I was wiped out by flying boulders, poisonous gases, and fire. A hiking trail from the highway by the western edge of the park leads to an area where footprints of members of the retreating army can still be seen in the petrified lava.

Across the street from **Volcano House** (the current hotel) is **Volcano Art Center,** in a building that began life in 1877 as the park's lodge. The work of local artists sold here includes wood carvings, photographs, and paintings done on T-shirts, silk, and canvases. Within walking distance of Volcano House, you'll find **steam vents** and the yellow, sour smelling **sulphur banks.** About four miles from the hotel, take a brief stroll through a rain forest thick with cushiony mosses and huge *hapuu* ferns, their long stems tightly curled into spirals at the top. Then you'll come to gigantic **Thurston Lava Tube.** This walk-through tunnel was created when hot lava continued to pour through an outer shell of cooled lava. A couple of miles west of the hotel, **Kipuka Puaulu** is a lush oasis that was spared by the surrounding lava. Also visit nearby **Tree Molds,** which were formed when lava covered trees, burned them to ash, then cooled and hardened.

Admission: $6 per car, $3 for bikers and hikers. Visitor Center open 7:45 a.m.–5 p.m. daily. Park open 24 hours a day, year round. Obtain updates on volcanic activity from the public information officer at Hawaii Volcanoes National Park (P.O. Box 52, Hawaii Volcanoes National Park, HI 96718; 967–7311 or 967–7643). For recorded eruption messages, call 967-7977. Maps are available at the Volcano House Visitor Center.

Thomas A. Jagger Museum • *Hawaii Volcanoes National Park (three miles past entrance); 967-7643* • On the rim of Kilauea Crater, this museum displays the highly accurate seismographs used to pick up volcanic activity, even far below the earth's surface. You'll also see videos of Kilauea's eruptions and lava rocks that visitors are welcome to touch. **Halemaumau Overlook** is about a ten-minute walk away.

No admission charge. Open daily from 8:30 a.m. to 5:00 p.m.

Rainbow Falls • *just off Wainuenue Avenue on Rainbow Dr., Wailuku River State Park, outside Hilo* • If you arrive when the sun is behaving, you'll see a dramatic rainbow shimmering on the mist of this waterfall. The best time to come is early in the morning. Just up the road, near Hilo Hospital, you'll come to **Boiling Pots.** These churning pools and series of cascades are created by the water rushing into large pits in the lava of the riverbed. The park here is a scenic spot for a picnic.

Hawaii Tropical Botanical Garden • *Onomea Bay, off the Four-mile Scenic Dr., Hamakua Coast (just north of Hilo); 964–5233* • This non-profit nature preserve in a tropical rain forest is filled with birds, marine life, jungled vegetation, streams, and waterfalls. The bright heliconias, bromeliads, and ginger are particularly striking. The garden sprawls along a craggy ocean coast.

Open 8 a.m.–5 p.m. Make reservations in advance. Required (tax deductible) donation: $9; senior discount offered. Hotel pick-ups from Hilo available (for at least two people) at additional cost.

Akaka Falls State Park • *ten miles north of Hilo, near Honomu Village* • If it's a choice between Rainbow Falls and these 400-foot-plus cascades, make this 66-acre park your destination. A long (sometimes steep) trail winds up and down through a thick rain forest, with towering bright yellow bamboo stalks, banyan trees, and flowers. Before you reach the main falls, you'll pass mini cascades that flow under bridges. Benches are placed at strategic locations for rest stops.

*Waipio Valley • See Hawaii: The Big Island introductory section, Tours, and Horseback Riding in Sports.

The Arts

Artist Community of Holualoa • *Holualoa, North Kona; Kona Art Center (322–2307), Holualoa Inn (324–1121)* • In its earlier incarnation, this flourishing art colony was a dilapidated coffee plantation. About 1300 feet above sea level and resting on the slopes of Hualalai volcano, it now vibrates with creativity. Old wooden buildings in this plantation town have been given new life as galleries, such as the Kona Art Center, Studio Seven, and Kimura's Lauhala Shop. Classes are offered at the Old Coffee Mill.

Animals

Swimming with Dolphins • *Hyatt Regency Waikoloa, Kona-Kohala Coast; 885–1234 or 228–9000* • If you're looking forward to getting in the water with these gentle, playful mammals, you'd better make arrangements before you arrive in Hawaii. This activity is booked up well in advance—and with good reason. There is something wonderfully exhilarating about swimming with such large, warm, smooth-skinned creatures and not having to be afraid. Underwater, you can hear their conversations, which sound like clicks and laughter.

Make reservations as far ahead as possible. Cost: $58.

*Panaewa Rain Forest Zoo • *just south of Hilo; 959–7224* • Not many visitors know about this small zoo where a few animals native to the rain forest live in relatively natural settings. Peacocks have the run of the grounds. You'll also see the *nene goose,* Hawaii's rare state bird, and parrots, monkeys, African pygmy hippopotamuses, and a tapir. Neighboring the zoo is the **Panaewa Equestrian Center,** with its rodeo/racetrack and horse stables.

Open daily from 9 a.m. to 4:30 p.m. No admission charge.

Whale Watching • Between December and April, you can catch glimpses of these massive creatures that migrate to Hawaii from cooler climes. Some tour companies take sightseers on jeep excursions to elevated vantage points while others take people out on the sea. The profits of the **Pacific Whale Foundation** (329–3522 or (800) WHALE–1–1), which conducts 2½ hour cruises, go toward research and the protection of whales. The cost is about $28 for adults and $18 for children between ages 3 and 12. You can book other ocean or land whale watching tours through hotel activity desks. If you'd like to strike out on your own, two good places for sightings are the Francis Iʻi Brown Golf Course on the grounds of the Mauna Lani Bay Resort on the Kohala Coast and the tip of North Kohala.

Parker Ranch • *Kamuela/Waimea* • See More of the Past.

TOURS AND CRUISES

Distances between attractions on the Big Island can be long, so you may decide to see some of the sights in your rental car, and others from a tour bus, jeep, helicopter, plane, or boat. You can even visit the underworld in a submarine.

BY BUS: Several bus companies offer circle-island tours ($36–$42) that include the Kona-Kohala Coast, Kamuela/Waimea, Hawaii Volcanoes National Park, Hilo, and the Hamakua Coast. However, these trips can last anywhere from nine to twelve hours and are extremely tiring. A more rewarding way to see the island is in segments. Bus companies offer tours to specific areas in addition to their more extensive excursions. For instance, **Gray Line** (833–8000 or (800) 367–2420) conducts tours to Hilo/Volcano/Kona; Hilo/Volcano/Kalapana black sand beach; Kona and Keauhou (including Puuhonua O Honaunau Historical Park, a.k.a. Place of Refuge; St. Benedict's Painted Church; and Kealakekua Bay, where Captain Cook landed). Gray Line uses both large buses and limousines.

Other good companies providing similar tours are **Roberts Hawaii** (947–3939); **Akamai** (329–7324 or (800) 922–6485), which transports sightseers in cozy vans and also offers a North Kohala tour; and **Hawaii Resorts Transportation** (885–7484), which takes vacationers to Kohala, Waipio Valley, the green sand beach at Ka Lae (where people can usually see turtles offshore), and the summit of Mauna Kea volcano. The **University of Hawaii's Institute for Astronomy** conducts free Mauna Kea Summit Tours. The special Saturday evening trips include an opportunity to look through the powerful telescopes that are used only after dark. How much you see will depend on the weather. The catch with this gratis excursion is that you must provide your own four-wheel-drive transportation to the Onizuka Center for International Astronomy (935–3371), 9200 feet up the slopes of Mauna Kea. From there you are driven to the observation domes on the 13,679 foot summit. Make reservations at least two weeks in advance. Note that some people suffer from altitude sickness on the way up to Mauna Kea. The drowsiness, headache, and nausea can have serious consequences if not treated right away—either with inhalations of pure oxygen or by turning around and going back down the mountain. Children under age 16 are not allowed to take the tour at all.

Big Island Tours (885–2883) also offers a Mauna Kea summit tour. This company carries visitors in vans that hold 25 passengers or fewer. The 25-passenger van is equipped with a video player so that, on the way home, sightseers can watch what they shot. In addition to a Waimea shopping trip and other tours, Big Island takes people on a 6-hour four-wheel-drive trip to the green sand beach at Ka Lae. If you like traveling in small groups, **Paradise Safaris** (322–2366) limits its tours to Waipio Valley and Mauna Kea to seven people each.

BY BOAT: During winter months, whale-watching excursions (offered by a variety of companies) are all the rage. Try **Pacific Whale Charters** (329–3522), based in Kailua-Kona. Many adults enjoy the dinner/moonlight sails run by **Captain Bean's Cruises** (329–2955). Vacationers depart from Kailua-Kona on a 142-foot Polynesian-style sailing canoe, complete with a live band, dancing, and open bar. Combination land and sea adventures are offered by **Captain Zodiac Raft Expeditions** (329-3199), which takes people on bumpy rides in rubber inflatables along the scenic Kona Coast. There's time for snorkeling at Kealakekua Bay, where Captain Cook was killed in 1779. Sightseers are dropped ashore at Puuhonua O Honaunau (Place of Refuge) and travel by van to St. Benedict's Painted Church, a macadamia nut factory, and a Kona coffee mill. Most cruises off Big Island shores include snorkeling at Kealakekua Bay. Among the best are **Fair Wind Sail** (322–2788), based in Keauhou-Kona, which uses a 50-foot glass-bottom trimaran (dinner cruises can be arranged); and Kailua-Kona-based **Captain Cook VII** (329–3811 or 329–6411), which entertains passengers on the 150-foot glassbottom boat with Hawaiian dancers.

BY SUBMARINE: I'd only recommend a dip in the **Atlantis Submarine** (329–6626) if you're not planning to snorkel or scuba dive during your vacation, or if you take it during the winter when you might spot whales. These trips in a 46-passenger sub are expensive (about $60 a pop). A slew of colorful fish—zebra-striped Hawaiian sergeants, monogamous butterfly fish, yellow tangs, balloon-like puffer fish, bluestripe snapper—swim right up to the portholes. However, the fish swarm around not because of plant-life (which is scarce) but because they are drawn to feeding stations (net bags) anchored to coral reefs. In other words, beyond the fish, there isn't much marine life to see along the path of the sub. The **Atlantis** descends from 40 to 60 feet. It's capable of going down to 150, but the scenery isn't particularly exciting at that depth. The boat that takes passengers to the sub leaves from Kailua Pier, by Hotel King Kamehameha (which is where people sign up for the trip).

BY HELICOPTER: If Kilauea (the most active of Hawaii's two active volcanoes) is erupting and you can afford it, take a helicopter tour above Hawaii Volcanoes National Park. You'll hear the bubbling, crackling, and hissing, and see red hot fountains of lava and ribbons of the fiery molten rock flowing from the crater. Actually, with its steaming pits, lunar terrain, and pockets of rain forest, this park is pretty spectacular even when the volcanoes are quiet.

All helicopter companies offer variations on the following routes: Kilauea or Mauna Loa (the island's second active volcano); the Kona coastline, the town of Kamuela/Waimea, Parker Ranch, the Hamakua Coast, Waipio and Waimanu valleys, black sand beaches, and remote white-sand coves. In the north, you might hover near sheer cliffs pocked with an ancient burial cave that still contains skulls and bones. Some flights combine the Kona Coast with a whirl above Puuhonua O Honaunau (Place of Refuge), Captain Cook Monument and Kealakekua Bay, and Hawaii Volcanoes National Park. Prices range from about $75 for a 30-minute ride to $275 for two hours. Shop around for the best deals. **Volcano Heli-Tours** (967–7578) is based right at the volcano. **Papillon** (885–5995 or (800) 367–7095) takes off from Waikoloa Heliport on the Kohala Coast. **Kenai** (329–7424 or (800) 622–3144) departs from the Royal Waikoloan Airstrip on the Kohala Coast.

BY PLANE: For a flightseeing trip by plane, try **Big Island Air** (329–4868; (800) 533–3417 within Hawaii; or (800) 367–8047, ext. 207 from the mainland). Some tours concentrate on the Big Island, while others give bird's eye views of the rest of the chain. Sightseeing flights can also be arranged through **IO Aviation** (935–3031), based at General Lyman Field in Hilo.

TO WAIPIO VALLEY: Rental cars or private vehicles are not allowed beyond Waipio Lookout. Therefore, unless you head into the deep valley on foot, you'll have to pay someone to take you there. Jeeps are the most popular mode of transport. Contact the **Waipio Valley Shuttle** (775–7121). Your driver will tell you all about the passing sights, including old legends and ancient uses for plants and flowers. You'll spend some time relaxing on the black sand beach as well. Other enjoyable ways to see the valley is on a **Mule Wagon Tour** (775–9518) or on horseback (885–7484). (Also see By Bus.)

OF PARKER RANCH: Here in Kamuela/Waimea's cowboy country, see how roping, feeding, round-ups, and branding are done. Learn all about the birth of Parker Ranch at the visitor center museum. Visit the two very different homes of the family that owns the ranch. Minivans pick up sightseers at the visitor center for full and half-day tours of the grounds. The longer tour includes visits to the museum, historic homes, the original site of the family's first home, and lunch ($40 for adults, $20 for children aged 4–12). The half day tour includes everything except lunch and the long drive to the original homestead ($16 for adults, $8 for children aged 4–12).

BY FOOT: Leaving stories about their lives for posterity, ancient Hawaiians drew stick figures in the lava flows throughout the islands. Hawaii's most extensive **petroglyph fields** are found in South Kohala and North Kona, some on the grounds of resorts. Tours can be arranged through Kona Village Resort (325–5555), Mauna Lani Resort (885–6677), or the Royal Waikoloan Hotel (885–6789). To get to know downtown **Hilo,** purchase a walking tour map (about $1.50) from the **Lyman House Memorial Museum** (935–5021).

BEACHES

From the black sand beaches of the southeast coast to the green sand of Ka Lae (South Point), the shores of the Big Island are true wonders of nature. These coasts also have their share of white sand beaches. Hapuna, on the Kohala Coast, is one of the most attractive on the island, perhaps even in the whole state. While Hawaii has many beaches, not all of them are easy to get to, and some are not calm enough for swimming. To step on Papakolea (or Green Sand Beach), for instance, you'll need a four-wheel-drive and some sturdy shoes for a three-mile hike. The water here is better for fishing than for cooling off. However, there are more than enough accessible (and swimmable) sandy stretches for any vacationer. Although many hotels and condominiums are clustered in Kailua-Kona and Keauhou, most beaches are along the Kohala Coast, where resorts are plusher and far more spread out. In geographical order (starting in the north and moving counterclockwise), here are the island's nicest beaches:

*__Waipio Valley Black Sand Beach__ • _Hamakua Coast_ • Bisected by a stream, this beach is one of Hawaii's ebony strips that were created when hot lava hit the cold Pacific. Because the waves can be strong here, the safest swimming is in the pond where the stream joins the sea. Small, smooth rocks are scattered near the water's edge and driftwood lies bleaching on the black sand. A waterfall pours down a steep oceanfront cliff. You are likely to have this spot to yourself. The few people who do come here are mainly locals and, early in the morning, surfers. You can hike the nearly vertical road into the lush valley, take the Waipio Shuttle, which departs not far from the Waipio Valley Overlook, or arrange to visit through a tour company.

*__Keokea Beach Park__ • _North Kohala_ • The pleasant drive along a winding road takes you past private homes, a graveyard, and a bright green pasture. When you reach the park, you'll see red cliffs set off by verdant vegetation and electric blue water with frothy white surf. One covered picnic area is elevated, affording a panoramic view of the rocky cove. During the summer, the water is calm enough for snorkeling and fishing. Locals often gravitate here on weekends. In addition to a camp site, the park also has restrooms and showers.

__Mahukona__ • _Northern Kohala Coast_ • Don't look for sand here. Instead, you'll have a grassy expanse that is great for picnics and a good view of the island of Maui from the rocky shore. I met a man here who had been camping his way around the Big Island and said that this was one of his favorite spots. (Restrooms and fresh water are provided.) Scramble over the rocks and you'll find some good swimming, snorkeling, and scuba diving in these waters (during the summer only, though.)

Lapakahi Park • *Northern Kohala Coast* • After wandering around the partially restored remains of an ancient fishing village, strong swimmers, snorkelers, and scuba divers will enjoy cooling off in the often rough water here. The shore is rocky. Restrooms and fresh water are on the premises.

Spencer Beach Park • *Kohala Coast* • Overlooked by Puukohola and Mailekini, the remains of two of the island's most important heiaus, this white sand beach is just north of the Mauna Kea Beach Hotel. Since it is protected by reefs, its waters are good for swimming. Camping is permitted and there are restrooms, fresh water, a paved volleyball court, tennis courts, and a red-roofed pavilion for parties and picnics.

Kauanoa Beach • *Kohala Coast* • The presence of the Mauna Kea Beach Hotel does not detract from the beauty of this ivory curve. Like all of Hawaii's beaches, this one is open to the public. However, the hotel has its own beach facilities. During the winter when the surf is high, stick to the sand for sunbathing and other dry pursuits.

Hapuna Beach State Park • *Kohala Coast* • Some people consider this Hawaii's most gorgeous beach. Although its white sands certainly draw a fair number of swimmers, snorkelers, scuba divers, and sun worshippers, it never feels crowded. The water is calmest during the summer. Rocky outcroppings enclose the half-mile stretch. At the northern end, where it looks as if the beach stops, find the shallow hidden cove. Children enjoy splashing in the tidal pools here.

Puako • *Kohala Coast* • Take a dirt road down to this white sand beach where kiawe trees provide shade. In the northern section, you'll find rewarding snorkeling around the tidal pools. A 20-minute walk leads to the petroglyphs off Puako Road.

Anaehoomalu • *Kohala Coast* • The nearby Hyatt Regency Waikoloa may have all the glitz, but the older, more sedate Royal Waikoloan hotel has the best beach. Picturesque Anaehoomalu is bordered by ancient fishponds that were reserved for the alii. Commoners had to fish in the ocean. Bathers are welcome to rent equipment here for windsurfing, sailing, scuba diving, snorkeling, and surfing.

*Honokohau • *just north of Kailua-Kona* • Adventurers will enjoy following the dirt path north of the harbor and beyond the dock that leads to this secluded beach. Lava rock covers much of the shore, but there are sandy patches here and there. Wander around the crumbling remains of ancient fishponds. You'll find an inland freshwater pool at the end of a trail that begins in the northern part of the beach.

*Alula • *just north of Kailua-Kona* • This tiny sandy cove, enclosed by ebony lava, is shaded by kiawe trees. At the southern end of Honokohau Harbor, it is popular among locals. You'll have a good view of fishing boats moving in and out of the harbor.

White Sands (a.k.a. **Disappearing Sands or Magic Sands**) • *Alii Drive, between Kailua-Kona and Keauhou* • Called by whatever name, the white sands of this beach come and go with the tides, often vanishing completely in the winter. Near petite St. Peter's Catholic Church, this is one of the island's best offshore snorkeling sites. To be caught in a swarm of fish, snorkelers bring frozen peas to feed them.

Kahaluu • *Alii Drive, between Kailua-Kona and Keauhou* • These salt and pepper sands draw many locals on weekends. The swimming and snorkeling (in only three to six foot depths) are fine during the summer, but the surf is high in the winter. Rest rooms and fresh water are provided. This beach is less than a mile from the Kona Surf Hotel.

Old Kona Airport Beach • *Kailua-Kona area* • Just offshore, intriguing coral configurations can be seen at depths of 40 to 60 feet. Snorkelers and scuba divers enjoy this beach, but plain swimming is better elsewhere. There is, however, a small sandy cove with placid tidal pools that are good for entertaining children. Rest rooms and fresh water are on the premises.

Kealakekua Bay • *just south of Kailua-Kona* • This is the target for most of the Big Island's snorkeling cruises and glass-bottom boat trips. Indeed, the marine life is varied and plentiful. Bring some frozen peas or dog biscuits, and you'll have schools of fish nibbling from your hands. Scuba diving is also popular in this area. Now a marine preserve, this is the place where Captain James Cook, the first known European to arrive in Hawaii, was killed on February 14, 1779. A monument stands in his memory. There really isn't a beach here, just a rocky coast and vegetation. The best way to approach this site is from the water.

*Ke'ei • *just south of Kealakekua Bay, Kona Coast* • Beside the village of Ke'ei this salt and pepper strand gives way to shallow waters. The swimming is fine here and the snorkeling is even better. After taking the road that leads to Kealakekua Bay, turn left at the bottom of the hill. Drive another half mile, then make a right onto a road through a lava flow and continue another half mile to the shore.

Puuhonua O Honaunau • *south of Kailua-Kona, Kona Coast* • Climb into the bay at the Place of Refuge from the boat ramp near the park complex. Both the scuba diving and snorkeling are good here. Many people combine a swim with a visit to the exhibits at this fascinating historic park that once provided sanctuary for ancient Hawaiians who broke kapus.

***Honomalino** • *Milolii, South Kona* • This calm bay is bordered by black sand shaded by palm trees. The swimming and snorkeling are great. To get here, stroll about a half mile south along an old Hawaiian path that begins by the quiet fishing village of Milolii.

***Hookena** • *South Kona* • The sand is steel-colored at this beach that is good for swimming during most of the year. The two-mile road to the shore is steep and slim, so drive with caution. Near the end of this street, the gas lampposts have been standing since the early 1900s. When Mark Twain visited the island during the 1860s, more than 2,000 people lived in the settlement here. Today the village could hardly be more quiet. Rest rooms and fresh water are provided at the beach.

***Papakolea** (or **Green Sand Beach**) • *Ka Lae (South Point)* • The unusual color of the sand comes from the olivine crystals created in volcanic eruptions. This beach is one of the most difficult to get to on the island. First you'll need to rent a four-wheel-drive for the 12 jostling miles to Ka Lae. Then you'll have to hike about three miles to the beach, where there is no shade and the water is generally much too rough for swimming. You might see some fishermen there, though. When the tides are especially strong, some of them cast their lines or nets from boats secured to the shore by rope.

Punaluu Black Sand Beach • *Ka'u, southeast coast* • These picturesque pitch-black shores are overlooked by the Sea Mountain condominiums, which have tennis courts and a golf course. In the adjacent beach park, you'll find picnic and camping facilities. Turtles, which you'll see swimming offshore, lay their eggs in the dark sand. The currents are often too strong for swimming. Walk *mauka* (inland) and you'll come to fish ponds and remnants of a heiau.

Kamoamoa Black Sand Beach • *southeast coast* • One of the world's newest beaches, this half-mile black beauty was born during volcanic eruptions that took place between January and April of 1988.

Here you'll see a recent example of how flaming lava explodes into tiny fragments when it meets the cold water.

Kalapana Black Sand Beach • *Kalapana, Puna area, southeast coat* • Just across the road from **Harry K. Brown Beach Park,** this beach has been popular among locals for fishing and surfing. Winter waves can be dangerous, but a section in the southwest usually remains calm. However, at press time a lava flow threatens to cover this shore. If Madama Pele has been merciful, on the park grounds you'll find camp sites, picnic pavilions, rest rooms, showers, and fresh water, in addition to the remnants of a heiau.

Kaimu Black Sand Beach • *Kalapana, Puna area, southeast coast* • If you've seen a photo of a black sand beach in Hawaii, chances are it's this one. The thick wall of green palms against the glistening ebony sand provides a stunning sight. Unfortunately, the water is not conducive to swimming. More bad news is that, as we go to press, it looks as if this beach will be overrun by a lava flow that would have also caused the demise of the historic **Star of the Sea Painted Church** across the street if the famed house of worship had not been moved.

Onekahakaha Beach Park • *Hilo* • About three miles from Hilo, this calm white sand beach draws many picnicking families. Lifeguards are on duty and facilities include pavillions, showers, and rest rooms.

Reeds Bay Beach Park • *Hilo* • Lapped by tranquil waters, this beach is known for its Ice Pond, fed by chilly freshwater springs. Rest rooms and showers are on the premises.

Coconut Island • *Hilo* • Overlooking Hilo Bay, with Mauna Kea in the background, these palm-shaded shores are frequented by picnickers. A small bridge from Banyan Drive will take you to this isle.

SPORTS

Like everything else on the Big Island, sports come in a wide variety. Hawaii is renowned for its excellent deep-sea fishing, particularly for marlin and tuna, along the Kona Coast. Anglers come from all over to attend the annual Hawaiian International Billfish Tournament. Kailua-Kona is the mecca for watersports enthusiasts. Fishing charters and other aquatic pursuits can be arranged here through **Kona Coast Activities**

(329–2971). On land, hiking, camping, and biking are popular pastimes among both visitors and residents. Spectator sports are also plentiful. In October, the island plays host to the Ironman World Triathlon Championship. Periodically, rodeos take place on Parker Ranch, and polo matches draw crowds to Kohala Ranch.

BIKING: Many people who really like to keep in shape hit the roads on two wheels. *Wearing helmets is highly recommended.* Guided excursions range from a week to 10 days. Reputable tour companies specializing in bike trips include **Island Bicycle Adventures** (955–6789), based in Honolulu; **On the Loose Bicycle Vacations** ((415) 527–4005) and **Backroads Bicycle Touring** ((415) 527–1789 or (800) 533–2573), both based in Berkeley, California; and **Vermont Bicycle Touring** ((802) 453–4811), based in Bristol, Vermont. Independent pedalers can rent cycles at **Dave's Triathlon Shop** (329–4522) and **B & L Bike and Sports** (329–3309), both in Kailua-Kona.

FISHING: The Kona Coast is famous for its deep-sea fishing. While tournaments are held on the Big Island throughout the year, the August Hawaiian International Billfish Tournament, centered in Kailua-Kona, is the star attraction. For details about the Kona Village Annual Marlin Tournament, call 432–5450 or (800) 367–5290.

Some of the Big Island's best fishing spots are off the beach at Samuel M. Spencer Beach County Park; off Kailua Pier in Kailua-Kona; in Kealakekua Bay; offshore at Napoopoo Beach County Park; and at Punaluu Beach County Park. For fishing charters, try **Aloha Charter Fishing** (329–2200), **A Happy Time Fishing Charters** (325–6171 or (800) 367–8014), **Bill Collector Big Game Fishing** (329–4116), **Kona Sea Charters** (329–7676 or (800) 356–KONA), **Grand Slam Sportfishing** (329–5536), or **Cheers Sportfishing** (329–6484). Boats are available year-round for marlin fishing. Most depart from Honokohau Harbor, not far north of Kailua-Kona. Prices begin at about $325 for a full day. More luxurious craft can set you back anywhere from $500 to $750. Half-day charters are also available. For further information about half- and full-day charters, contact the **Fuel Dock Fishing Center** (Honokohau Harbor, Kailua-Kona; 329–7529 or (800) 648–7529); **Kona Coast Activities** (329–2971); or **The Charter Locker** (326–2553).

GOLF: Particularly along the Kona-Kohala Coast, where black lava flows provide a wonderful contrast with the green swards, this island has some of the state's most appealing courses. *Golf Digest* rates the **Mauna Kea Beach Golf Course** (882–7222), on the Kohala Coast, among the world's best. All with ocean or dramatic mountain views— sometimes both—the Big Island's other courses aren't far behind. The Francis I'i Brown Golf Course at the **Mauna Lani Resort** (885–6655), also in Kohala, is another award-winner. This resort has a second course as well. Waikoloa sports three beautiful courses. The first two were designed by Robert Trent Jones, Jr.: the **Waikoloa Village Golf Course** (883–9621), on the mauka (mountain) side of the road, and the **Waikoloa Beach Golf Course** (885–1234), adjoining the Hyatt Regency Waikoloa and the Royal Waikoloan hotels. The third green, the **King's Course,** is also at the Hyatt Regency Waikoloa and was finished in 1989. In the Keauhou-Kona area, there's the **Kona Country Club** (322–2595). It comes as a surprise to many visitors that there is even a course in Hawaii Volcanoes National Park: **Volcano Golf and Country Club** (967–7331). In Punaluu, known for its black sand beach, you'll find the **Sea Mountain Golf Club** (928–6222) in an isolated condominium development. Green fees are lowest at Hilo's **Naniloa Country Club Golf Course** (935–3000), **Hilo Municipal Golf Course** (959–7711), and **Hamakua Country Club** (775–7244), a nine-hole course in Honokaa.

HIKING AND CAMPING: Hiking trails lead through virgin valleys, lava fields, and dense wilderness. Routes range from the rugged to the relaxing. Many footpaths cut through **Hawaii Volcanoes National Park.** Since lava can be thin, brittle, and wickedly sharp in places, you should be sure to stick to marked trails. The four-mile hike across the floor of Kilauea Iki, a dormant crater, isn't difficult. The lava beneath your feet will feel warm, even though it's rock hard. Trail maps and other information are available at the Hawaii Volcanoes Visitor Center. Hiking in green **Waipio Valley** can be extremely rewarding. Try the six-mile trail that leads from the black sand beach to the back of the valley. If you're in really good shape, you might attempt the trail over the mountains to the next valley, where hunters kill wild boar. The trails in **Pololu Valley** should also be reserved for the extremely fit. Beginning at Pololu Valley Lookout, one walk lasts about ten hours and will take you through several neighboring valleys.

Camping is best from June to October. The state and county parks have some beautiful beachfront and mountainside campsites. People can also camp in alternately stark and lush Hawaii Volcanoes National Park. With its colorful botanical garden, **Manuka State Park,** in South Kona, is great for both hiking and camping. In remote **Mauna Kea State Park,** you can rent wooden cabins with flush toilets and showers for under $15 a night. There's an incongruous phone booth sitting in front of one of the buildings. Outside, you'll also see nene geese (Hawaii's state bird) in barbed-wire pens along with Layson ducks, one of the world's rarest ducks. Also on the slopes of Mauna Kea, **Kalopa State Park** is filled with nearly extinct koa trees, eucalyptus, and ohia. These 600 acres of camping and hiking grounds are located two miles south of Honokaa on the Hamakua Coast. Although the shore is covered with lava rocks and boulders instead of sand at **Mahukona State Park** in Kohala, this campsite makes a peaceful setting. Another good place to spend the night surrounded by nature is **Punaluu Beach Park,** known for its glistening black sand beach.

For permits and further details, contact the **State of Hawaii Division of State Parks** (75 Aupuni St., Hilo Hawaii 96720) or the **County of Hawaii Department of Parks and Recreation** (25 Aupuni St., Hilo, Hawaii 96720; 961–8311). (Also see Roughing It in The Best Places For . . . , Camping and Hiking in Nuts and Bolts, and Housekeeping Cabins in Where to Sleep on Hawaii: The Big Island.

HORSEBACK RIDING AND POLO: Arrange to horseback ride on expansive **Parker Ranch,** in Waimea/Kamuela, by contacting the ranch itself (885–7655) or Mauna Kea Beach Hotel (822–7222). You'll go through wooded trails bordered by wild flowers, pass herds of cattle in pastures, and see cinder cones that seem to have fallen out of the sky onto the flat land. Rainbows aren't uncommon in this misty region. The distant hills come in endless shades of green. About a 20-minute drive from the town of Kamuela/Waimea and about 45 minutes from Kohala Coast resorts, **Ironwood Outfitters** (885–4941) also leads scenic trail rides through a working cattle ranch—Kohala Ranch, in the Kohala Mountains. You can also watch polo matches or take polo lessons here at the **Arena Polo and Equestrian Center** (531–0505). In Waikoloa Village, on the *mauka* (mountain) side of Queen Kaahummanu Highway, you can take riding lessons or trail rides through **Waikoloa Countryside Stables** (883–9335). If you'd prefer to ride closer to Kailua-Kona, try **Waiono Meadows** (329–0888) in Holualoa or **Hokukano Ranch** (323–2299) in Kealakekua.

An unforgettable Big Island experience is seeing remote Waipio Valley with **Waipio on Horseback** (885–7484). You'll spend 2½ hours in the saddle and 1½ hours touring the rest of the valley in a van. The minimum number of people taken on each of these trips is two, while the maximum is an intimate six. Don't forget your camera. During the scenic drive and ride, your guide will tell you all about the history, legends, facts, and folklore of the Big Island in general and the valley in particular. In the van, you'll descend the steep, winding dirt road and pass through the river to reach the valley floor where your horse will be waiting for you. You'll clippity-clop through waist-deep irrigation canals and past rushing streams. Waterfalls tumble hundreds of feet from mountainsides. Since the majority of the (few) people who live in the valley are taro farmers, you'll see plenty of plots where this root (used to make poi) is grown. Your guide will point out all kinds of vegetation, including jabon trees, which bear a fruit that's a cross between an orange and a grapefruit. Be sure to have a taste. You might also spot wild horses and rare birds such as the koloa. Mid-way through the ride, you'll come to the black sand beach that gleams like satin in the sun.

PARASAILING: To float in the air while suspended from a parachute that is tied to a moving boat, contact **Kona Water Sports** (329–1593).

SAILING: Most of the time when people are on boats around the Big Island, they are there to snorkel, scuba dive, or fish. The majority of pleasure boats that depart Kailua-Kona are headed to Kealakekua Bay for snorkeling excursions. If you're interested in a half- or full-day sail/snorkel charter, contact **Kona Sea Charters** (329–7676 or (800) 356–KONA) in Kailua-Kona. Through **Discovery Charters** (326–1011), in Kailua-Kona, you'll sail on a 45-foot luxury yacht complete with snorkel equipment and even a kayak for going places the larger boat can't.
    (Also see Snorkeling, below, and Tours and Cruises)

SCUBA DIVING: Diving is most rewarding for those who are certified. Various operators offer three- to five-day PADI courses for about $110 a day. Underwater exploration is concentrated along the Kona Coast. Try **Scuba Schools of Kona** (329–2661 or (800) 445–2163); **Kona Aggressor** (329–8182, (800) 344–KONA, or FAX: (808) FAX–BOAT); **Kona Coast Divers** (329–8802, (800) KOA–DIVE, or FAX: (808) 329–5741); **Jack's Diving Locker** (329–7585 or (800) 345–4807); or **Fair Wind Sailing and Diving Adventures** (322–2788), all based in Kailua-Kona.

SNORKELING: Big Island fish are especially friendly when you come bearing gifts of bread or frozen peas. The Kona and Kohala coasts are great for snorkeling. **Kapaa Beach Park,** in northern Kohala, is one of the best places for swimming among multi-colored coral and other marine life. The waters of Kona's **White Sands** (a.k.a. **Magic Sands) Beach,** which disappears in the winter, are always teeming with many different kinds of tropical fish. Several boats, such as the fun-filled **Fair Wind catamaran** (322–2788), take snorkelers to the crystal waters near the Captain Cook Monument at **Kealakekua Bay.** If you're lucky, a playful school of porpoises will swim along as you sail. Winter vacationers are sometimes treated to the sight of whales. Other good sail/snorkel operations include **Kamanu Charters** (329–2021) and **Hawaiian Cruises** (947–9971 or 329–3811). If a bouncy ride in a rubber raft that zips in and out of sea caves is more your style, contact **Captain Zodiac Rafting Expeditions** (329–3199). In addition to snorkeling excursions, this company takes sightseers on land/sea tours. Snorkeling excursions can be arranged by contacting the companies directly or through the activities desks of most hotels.

(Also see Tours and Cruises.)

SNOW SKIING: Some winters (when there's enough snow) experienced skiers can whoosh down the slopes of Mauna Kea volcano. Although conditions are best in February and March, **Ski Guides Hawaii** (885–4188) is open from around December through April. This company provides four-wheel-drive transportation, skis, warm clothing, and other gear. The cost begins at about $130 per person, including lunch.

SPECTATOR SPORTS: One of Hawaii's biggest spectacles is the **Ironman World Triathlon Championship,** held each October. When it began in 1978, only 15 people (all men) entered the biking/swimming/running competition and only 12 of them finished. Now based in Kailua-Kona, this event draws nearly 2,000 male and female athletes each year. Thousands of people also watch the **Hawaiian Canoe Races** that take place during the spring through fall season, when various clubs compete for the championship. **Polo matches** take place at Kohala Ranch (329–9551) in the Kohala Mountains every Sun. at 2 p.m., September–November. Folks on the sidelines turn the grounds into a party, with their picnic fixin's and barbecue grills. To find out about spring and summer **rodeos,** contact Parker Ranch (885–7655).

SURFING: Mainly a local sport on the Big Island, surfing is popular off shores including **Kalapana Black Sand Beach,** where there's an area called Drainpipes that has huge waves; **Leleiwi Beach; Old Airport Beach; Punaluu Beach Park;** and **White Sands** (a.k.a. Disappearing Sands or Magic Sands). The waves at both Leleiwi Beach and **Hookena Beach Park** are great for bodysurfing.

TENNIS: Tennis buffs may choose among scores of courts, especially along the Kona and Kohala coasts. Players aren't charged a fee at **Kailua Playground,** convenient to the Kailua-Kona area. Both guests and nonguests may play at no cost on the courts of the **Kona Hilton Beach and Tennis Resort** and the **Racquet Club at the Kona Surf Hotel.** A small fee is required to play at the **Royal Waikoloan, Waikoloa Village, Hotel King Kamehameha,** and **Sea Mountain Resort.** In Hilo, there's a minimal charge to play at **Hilo Tennis Stadium** and **Waiakea Racket Club.** Free courts are found at **Lincoln Park.** Guests at Hilo's Banyan drive hotel strip play at the **Naniloa Racket Club.**

Some hotels, including the following, allow only their guests to use their courts: **Mauna Kea Beach Hotel** weighs in with 13 courts. **The Ritz Carlton** gives their guests 11 courts to choose from, while the **Mauna Lani Bay Hotel** has 10. The condominiums of the **Mauna**

Lani Resort have six hard and two grass courts. **Hyatt Regency Waikoloa** and **Kona Village** also have courts that are reserved for guests.

WINDSURFING: **Anaehoomalu Bay,** where the Royal Waikoloan and Hyatt Regency hotels are located, is loved by boardsailors for its perfect winds and waves. You can take lessons or rent equipment through **Captain Nemo's Ocean Sports** (855–5555) at the Royal Waikoloan.

WORKING OUT: All on the Kona-Kohala Coast, the Ritz Carlton, the Four Seasons, the Hyatt Regency Waikoloa, the Mauna Kea, and the Mauna Lani Bay hotels have state of the art health spas.

SHOPPING

Stores on the Big Island are concentrated along Alii Drive in Kailua–Kona and most of them are geared toward tourists. Although you won't be rubbing elbows with many locals, some poking around will introduce you to intriguing boutiques with distinctive wares. Many stores in town stay open until 7 p.m. or even 9 p.m. to catch the dinner crowd. Resorts along the Kohala Coast boast quite a few wonderful (and expensive) boutiques and art galleries. I've tried to resist, but I've ended up with some gorgeous hand-painted silk dresses and scarves, funky handmade earrings, and colorful bathing suits with matching shorts and tops from stores at the Hyatt Regency Waikoloa. The Mauna Lani Bay Hotel and the Mauna Kea Beach Hotel are also known for their tempting boutiques. More upscale shops snag passersby in Kamuela/Waimea, selling everything from gourmet cheeses to bowls and sculpture made of rare native woods. The Big Island, by the way, is one of the best places in the state to find crafts made of island wood. Here are some of the places that have made the greatest impression on me:

SHOPPING MALLS: In the paniolo town of Kamuela/Waimea, the ranch house and outbuildings of **Hale Kea** (885–6094) have been converted into boutiques, art galleries, and eateries. In the same town, the **Parker Ranch Shopping Center** (885–7178) is where you'll find the Parker Ranch Visitor Center and nearly three dozen stores (selling everything from clothing and gifts to groceries and magazines). This complex, patronized by locals, is not to be confused with the smaller, newer **Parker Square** (885–7178), which has a fine collection of boutiques. Stop in at **Waimea General Store** (885–4479), which sports an eclectic mix of Japanese *yukata* bathrobes, cookbooks, and yarn, among other items. Another good place to wander around in the neighborhood is **Opelo Plaza.**

Among the many malls in Kailua-Kona are open-air **World Square Shopping Center,** open from 9 a.m. to 9 p.m., seven days a week; **Kona Inn Shopping Village,** with its attractive waterfront Kona Inn restaurant; neighboring **Kona Marketplace** (329–3539); **Kamehameha Square Shopping Center,** where a **Western Union** office is located; **Kailua Bay Inn Shopping Plaza;** and **Kona Coast Shopping Center,** where you'll find a large supermarket. In Keauhou, just south of the center of town, is **Keauhou Shopping Village** (322–3000).

Since tourism does not have a major presence in residential Hilo, prices here are lower than in resort communities. The multi-million dollar **Prince Kuhio Shopping Plaza** (959–3555), which remains open until 9 p.m. on Thursdays and Fridays, is one of the largest malls in the state. This is where you'll find **Liberty House,** Hawaii's answer to Macy's; **Sears;** and many smaller stores. **Kaiko's Mall** (935–3233) counts J.C. Penney among its stores. **Hilo Shopping Center** (935–6499) also has a wide selection of places to spend money.

ALOHA WEAR: Skip commercial **Hilo Hattie's** (with branches in both Kailua-Kona and Hilo), and head to **Cottage Crafted in Hawaii,** at Kailua-Kona's Kona Inn Shopping Village, which sells handpainted muumuus, shorts, and shirts; the lobby of **Hotel King Kamehameha,** on the main drag in Kailua-Kona; **Liberty House** department store in Hilo's Prince Kuhio Shopping Plaza (959–3555); or **Sig Zane's** (935–7077) in Hilo, which specializes in fabrics and aloha shirts in original patterns and hula costumes for the town's annual Merrie Monarch Festival. Men should check out the **Aloha Gift Factory** (324–1112) in Kealakekua, south of Kailua-Kona.

ART GALLERIES: Some of the island's most imaginative artwork is found in the galleries in **Holualoa,** an upcountry town *mauka* (inland) of Kailua-Kona. Housed in a renovated coffee plantation, these shops feature the work of many mainland and some local artists. At the **Gallery of Great Things** (885–7706) in Kamuela/Waimea, goods come from Hawaii, Asia, and the Pacific, including baskets imported from the Philippines. The **Nikko Gallery** (885–7661), also in Kamuela/Waimea, is housed in the distinctive two-story Spencer Hotel building, where both Princess Ka'iulani and Robert Louis Stevenson stayed. This shop specializes in Japanese antiques such as silk kimonos, chests, and wooden boxes. In addition, it stocks Hawaiian woodwork made from koa, hau, and other native trees. **Maya Gallery** (885–9633), at the Hale Kea shopping complex in Kamuela/Waimea, is another good place to visit.

(Also see Crafts and Koa Wood Products.)

BEACH WEAR: Some of the most attractive sports wear can be found at shops at the **Hyatt Regency Waikoloa,** but be prepared for hefty prices. Stores in Kailua-Kona are a bit easier on the wallet.
(Also see Distinctive Clothing.)

CRAFTS: To find island-made jewelry, paintings, and knickknacks, visit **Kona Arts and Crafts** (329–5590) at the Kailua Bay Inn Shopping Plaza in Kailua-Kona. For hats, bags, beach mats, and other items woven from pandanus fronds, stop at **Kimura Lauhala Shop** (324–0053) in Holualoa, an upcountry town just *mauka* (inland) of Kailua-Kona. **Alapaki's Hawaiian Things** (322–2007), in the Keauhou Shopping Village, carries woodwork and Niihau shell necklaces, made of the tiny rare shells found mainly on the remote island of Niihau. In Hawaii Volcanoes National Park, **Volcano Art Center** (967–7511) has an extensive display of koa wood bowls and cutting boards, hand-painted cotton T-shirts, unusual hand-made jewelry, paintings, and color-splashed *pareus* (a.k.a. sarongs).
(Also see Art Galleries and Koa Wood Products.)

DISTINCTIVE CLOTHING: For everything from the latest fashions in bathing suits and sportswear to evening wear, browse through the many shops at the Hyatt Regency Waikaloa on the Kohala Coast. **Noa Noa** (329–1902 at the Kim Chong Building, Alii Dr., Kailua-Kona; 329–8167 at Kona Inn Shopping Village, Alii Dr.; and 329–8187 at Parker Square shopping complex, Kamuela/Waimea) specializes in hand-painted cotton clothing and bags for women. All imported from Bali, the dresses, pants, blouses, and satchels here come in a variety of eye-catching prints.

FLOWERS: The Hilo area is the flower capital of the island—perhaps of the state. Visitors are welcome to browse through several flower nurseries, where they can arrange to have inspected blossoms sent to the mainland. Among them are **Akatsuka Orchid Gardens** (967–7660), off Hwy. 11, 22 miles outside Hilo; **Nani Mau Gardens** (959–3541), within the town; and **Hirose Nurseries** (959–4561) on Kanoelehua Avenue in town.

HAWAIIAN QUILTS: Inspired by nineteenth century American missionaries, Hawaiian women began making distinctive quilts of their own. The contemporary versions may be expensive (anywhere from several hundred to several thousand dollars), but these time-consuming artistic bed covers and wall hangings are extremely attractive—and durable. Antique quilts, out of the price range of most tourists, are on display in the corridors of the Mauna Kea Beach Hotel on the Kohala Coast. **Top-**

stitch (885–4482), at Parker Ranch Shopping Center in Kamuela/Waimea, carries quilt pillow covers in addition to full-size comforters. At **Waimea Design Center** (885–6171) in Kamuela/Waimea, wall hangings and baby quilts run about $675 while you'll pay from about $2500 to $3500 for a queen- or king-sized quilt. Because the work is so intricate, commissioned quilts can take from six to 24 months. Based in Hilo, **Doris Nosaka** (935–5666) takes about six months to create baby quilts and wall hangings (about $250) and up to two years for queen- or king-sized quilts ($3500–$4000). With the help of her brother, **Kathy Puanani Nishida** (885–7754), in Kamuela/Waimea, incorporates many colors into her quilts instead of the usual white with one contrasting shade. Her comforters run from about $1600 to $2000 for twin size, $2000 for a double, and $2000 to $4000 for a queen or king.

JEWELRY: Many shops selling jewelry made from shells, kukui nuts, coral, silver, and gold are found along Alii Dr. in Kailua-Kona. (Also see Crafts, Art Galleries, and Pottery.)

KOA WOOD PRODUCTS: Beautifully grained koa wood was once far more prevalant throughout Hawaii. In the old days, it was turned into everything from eating plates and pots for boiling water to royal surf boards and canoes. You'll find koa carvings (bowls, platters, trays, boxes, jewelry, konane boards—a game similar to checkers) at stores including the following: **Kamaaina Woods** (775–7722 in Honokaa; 885–5521 in Opelu Plaza mall in Kamuela/Waimea), which also sells work done in other woods, such as milo; and **Hawaiian Handcraft Shop Factory** (935–5587) in Hilo, which uses monkeypod and breadfruit wood as well.

(Also see Art Galleries.)

KONA COFFEE: In Kailua-Kona, try **Kona Kai Farms** (328–9015), across the street from the World Square Shopping Center; or **Long's Drugs** in the Lanihau Center (329–9333), near Alii Drive. In Hilo, stop in at **Long's Drugs** at Prince Kuhio Shopping Plaza (959–3555).

MACADAMIA NUTS: You'll find the best prices at **Long's Drugs,** at Prince Kuhio Shopping Plaza (959–3555) in Hilo and in Lanihau Center (329–9333) in Kailua Kona; and **Pay'n Save** drug stores, around the island. If you'd like a free factory tour, a complimentary sample, and the opportunity to make a purchase, the Big Island offers several choices: the **Mauna Loa Macadamia Nut Factory** (966–8612), the most popular, just south of Hilo; **Mrs. Field's Macadamia Nut Factory** (322–9515), in Kealakekua, south of Kailua-Kona; and the **Hawaiian Holiday Macadamia Nut Factory** (775–7743) in Honokaa on the Hamakua Coast.

POTTERY: Unique Japanese *raku* ceramics are on sale at the **Potter's Gallery** (935–4069) in Hilo, which also carries locally produced jewelry, baskets, and furniture.

T-SHIRTS: You'll have endless choices at the shops on and near Alii Drive in Kailua-Kona. **Crazy Shirts,** at Kona Shopping Arcade, has a state-wide reputation for good buys. Most hotels—such as **Hotel King Kamehameha** in Kailua-Kona—also have a fare share of shirts with appealing logos.

(Also see Crafts.)

NIGHT LIFE

Days on the Big Island are far more active than nights. What little after-dark frivolity there is is concentrated in Kailua-Kona, at bars and restaurants. Some hotel lounges in Kailua-Kona, Keauhou, and Kohala have Hawaiian singers and musicians or recorded entertainment, but it is generally on the low-key side. Most visitors follow the lead of locals and either *holo-holo* (move from place to place, bar hop) or turn in early.

For details about dinner cruises, turn to Tours and Cruises in What to See and Do.

Hawaiian Style

Hula • If you're planning to vacation in early April, consider attending the **Merrie Monarch Festival** (935–9168), the state's most important hula competition, which takes place over several evenings in Hilo. Both modern and traditional hula and chanting are performed. This event is named for King David Kalakaua, called the Merrie Monarch for his efforts in resuscitating the hula and other Hawaiian traditional arts that had been prohibited by New England missionaries. You'll need to order tickets months in advance.

At **Kimo's Steak & Seafood Restaurant** (329–1393), in Uncle Billy's Kona Bay Hotel in Kailua-Kona, two free hula shows are presented each night from Monday through Saturday.

Luaus • For the island's most authentic luau, make reservations at **Kona Village Resort** (325–5555), on the Kona Coasst, just north of Keahole Airport. The plentiful food, musical show, and surroundings sweep visitors into the past. Some topped with thatched roofs, Polynesian hales (cottages housing guest rooms) stand on stilts above black lava flows or at the edges of beaches or lagoons. This special event takes place on Friday nights. The Tuesday night luau at the **Mauna Kea Beach Resort** (882–7222) is free for guests. Located on the Kohala Coast, this hotel offers a menu including a variety of goodies in addition to the usual luau fare. On Mondays, Wednesdays, and Fridays, the action is at the **Hyatt Regency Waikoloa** (885–1234), north of Kailua-Kona. More than 700 people are invited to this feast and Polynesian show. Next door, the **Royal Waikoloan** (885–6789) hosts a Sunday night meal and show featuring a local hula halau (hula group). Guests even have an opportunity to purchase local crafts from artists who demonstrate their skills. If you'd prefer a luau in Kailua-Kona, try the Monday, Wednesday, or Friday affair at the **Kona Hilton Beach and Tennis Resort** (329–3111) or the feast at **Hotel King Kamehameha** (329–2911).

Local Hangouts and Happenings

Kona Inn • *Kona Inn Shopping Village, Kailua-Kona; 329–4455* • This open-air waterfront restaurant is almost as popular for nightcaps as it is for meals. Ceiling fans, rich wood panelling, and peacock chairs enhance the pleasant atmosphere.

Huggo's • *75-5828 Kahakai St., Kailua-Kona* • Overlooking a rocky shore, this restaurant is popular for drinks, especially around sunset.

Kahilu Theater • *Kamuela/Waimea; 885–6017* • Entertainment ranges from local plays and Broadway musicals to hula groups, European classical dance troupes, performances of the Honolulu symphony, and jazz musicians and singers from Hawaii and the mainland. Check local newspapers to see what's doing when.

University of Hawaii-Hilo • *Hilo; 933–3310* • Check local newspapers for shows at the school theater, which sometimes features international performers.

Other Night Spots and Discos

Spats Disco • *Hyatt Regency Waikoloa, Kohala; 885–5737* • About a 40-minute drive north of Kailua-Kona, this flashy disco is probably the liveliest night spot on the island. The cover charge is about $10 for those who aren't hotel guests or who haven't eaten at one of the resort's restaurants.

Mitchell's • *Keauhou Shopping Village, Alii Drive, Keauhou; 322–9966* • Live bands and music videos draw a youthful crowd to this disco not far from the heart of Kailua-Kona.

Eclipse Restaurant • *Kailua-Kona; 329–4686* • Stick around after dinner and you can work off those calories on the dance floor (beginning at 10 p.m.). The tunes are big-band on Sunday evenings and disco the rest of the week.

CULINARY HAWAII: THE BIG ISLAND

The dinner hour is relished on the Big Island, not simply because there are so many good restaurants to choose from, but also because eating out is just about the only thing to do at night. The most expensive places are found in the hotels along the Kohala Coast. Top rated dining rooms in this area include the Mauna Lani Resort's **Gallery,** known for its liberal use of local ingredients, and the hotel's elegant **Third Floor;** and Sri Lankan-style **Batik Room** at the Mauna Kea Beach Hotel; and **Water's Edge,** reminiscent of the interior of a majestic ocean liner, and Japanese **Imari,** both at the Hyatt Regency Waikoloa. Several good restaurants in Kamuela/Waimea convince guests from Kohala Coast resorts to take the 35 minute drive. Among them are **Bree Garden,** which has an imaginative international menu, and **Merriman's,** where diners can watch the chef in action. In Kailua-Kona, one stand-out for steak and seafood is **The Chart House** at Waterfront Row and **Ocean View Inn,** a family-run diner, is always crowded. In Hawaii Volcanoes National Park, **Kilauea Lodge** is a small inn with a big reputation for fine food. In Hilo, **Roussel's,** a New Orleans Creole restaurant, packs them in.

Those who can't live without that first cup of coffee will want to take home a bag or two of those famous Kona beans. Some of the fancier hotels stock guest rooms with fresh Kona coffee beans, grinders, and coffee makers. Another Big Island specialty is macadamia nuts, sold all over the island. Among the many sweet treats at the **Kailua Candy Company** in Kohala are macadamia nuts in a variety of incarnations. At the roadside **Tex Drive Inn** stand in Honokaa, hot, sweet *ma-*

lasadas (Portuguese balls of fried dough) are popped into many a mouth. For a cool sweet, try the **Shave Ice Company** on Alii Drive and Palani Street in Kailua-Kona. Here are some of my favorite places to dine on the Big Island:

Kohala Coast

Batik Room • *Mauna Kea Beach Hotel; 882–7222* • With batiks and other tapestries in warm tones of pink, orange, and gold, the decor of this elegant dining room underscores the Sri Lankan items on the menu. In addition to a variety of delicious curry dishes, you might find a salad of romaine lettuce, crabmeat dressing, and macadamia nuts; seafood prepared in several distinctive manners; crispy roast duck; and tempura chicken with guava mustard sauce. Lime sorbet is served between courses and dance music accompanies the meal. *Dinner only. Jackets and ties required for men. Reservations recommended. A, M, C, D. (Very Expensive)*

Teppan Yaki • *Mauna Kea Beach Hotel, the Terrace; 882–7222* • When you're in the mood for Japanese food served under the stars, this is a good choice. In flavorful marinades, the grilled seafood, vegetables, and meats are set off by colorful, artistic garnishes. *Dinner only. A, M, V, C, D. (Moderate to Expensive)*

Harrington's at Kawaihae • *Wharf Rd. and Mahukona Hwy., Kawaihae, Kohala; 882–7997* • A branch of Harrington's in Hilo, this steak and seafood restaurant gazes down on the fishing boats pulling in and out of Kawaihae Harbor. The food is plentiful and prices are lower than many of the other dining rooms in the area. Try the chicken teriyaki or the calimari. *Dinner only. Reservations recommended. M, V. (Moderate)*

Cafe Pesto/We're Talking Pizza • *882–1071 in Kawaihae, Kohala; 326–2878 in Kona* • The gourmet pizza at this eatery may bear little resemblance to the Italian variety, but it tastes fine. Eggplant and sun dried tomatoes are favorite toppings. *M, V, D. (Inexpensive)*

The Third Floor • *Mauna Lani Bay Hotel, Kawaihae; 885–6622* • Save this one for an extra special night. High-backed wicker chairs surround tables set with candles flickering inside hurricane lamps. Soft piano music floats through the air. Warm Indian naan (a cushiony bread) and liver pate come with appetizers that include smoked salmon, blackened *ahi* (tuna) with Cajun sauce, and thinly sliced opakapaka with shitake mushrooms. For entrees, the French chef prepares roast duckling with lemon grass and honey sauce, baby abalone from Keahole, and paella with tiger prawns, clams, and spicy *chorizo* (sausage). Bon bons are served over vaporous dry ice. *Dinner only. Jackets required for men. Reservations necessary. A, M, V, D, C. (Very Expensive)*

The Canoe House • *Mauna Lani Bay Resort, Kawaihae; 885–6622* • The dining tables, bar top, and fishing canoe hanging from the ceiling are all made of lustrous native koa wood at this oceanfront, open-air restaurant. An antique canoe paddle, a bowpiece, and other nautical items that were found on the resort property are on display. The water is flood-lit at night. A dance floor is adjacent to the gazebo. Tables are set with chopsticks (as well as silverware for the uninitiated). Good choices to kick off a meal are wok-fried shrimp on crunchy noodles with an orange-ginger glaze, and Filipino spring rolls filled with curried chicken and served with green papaya salad. Entrees include kiawe-smoked five-spice duck with mango relish; bamboo-steamed mahi mahi with Chinese cabbage; and rack of lamb barbecued with poha berries and served with warm breadfruit salad. Among the lighter fare are sandwiches such as grilled Hunan beef on a Chinese bun with crisp Maui onion rings. *Reservations recommended. A, V, M, D. (Expensive)*

The Gallery • *Mauna Lani Resort, Kawaihae; 885–7777* • Started by the chef who now owns Merriman's in Kamuela/Waimea, this restaurant continues to deliver the imaginative continental cuisine that built its original fine reputation. Fresh local seafood, vegetables, and fruit are integral ingredients. The food is as artistically presented as it is delicious. This dining room is in a separate building from the Mauna Lani Bay Hotel. If you're here for lunch, you might be able to watch a tennis match on the court outside the picture window. *Reservations recommended. A, M, V, D, C. (Moderate)*

Donatello's • *Hyatt Regency Waikoloa; 885–1234* • Guests rave about the Northern Italian cuisine here. Pasta comes in not two but three sizes: as an appetizer, a side dish, or a main course. In addition to gourmet pizza, seafood and meat are on the menu. Try the chicken breast with wild mushrooms and marsala sauce or the veal topped with prosciutto and mozzarella. The cheesecake with amaretto or the fresh cannoli bring any meal to a sweet end. Reserve early if you'd like a table by the window. The sunsets are fabulous from here and you can watch the boats along the canal. If you feel like shaking a leg after dinner, Spat's Disco is just upstairs. *Dinner only. Reservations recommended. A, V, M, D, C. (Moderate)*

Water's Edge • *Hyatt Regency Waikoloa; 885–1234* • At night, the sounds of a live big band fill the dance floor of this restaurant. With art deco decor, it was designed to resemble the interior of an old ocean liner. If you arrive before the sun goes down, you'll see that the restaurant has a view of a natural lagoon churning with fish. Highlights of the dinner menu are roasted pheasant and chateaubriand. The breakfast buffet has everything from fresh fish and seafood Newburg to eggs Benedict, fresh fruit, and orange-vanilla French toast. *Jackets and ties required for men at dinner. Reservations necessary. A, V, M, C, D. (Very Expensive)*

Imari • *Hyatt Regency Waikoloa; 885–1234* • Both the food and the atmosphere are very Japanese. Ponds, filled with *koi* (Japanese ornamental fish) are bordered with bamboo. Details are clearly important here, from the lacquer serving dishes and hand-painted ceramic chopstick holders to the placement of the vegetable garnishes on the plates. Watch the master chefs at work at the sushi bar. *Dinner only. Reservations recommended. A, M, V, C, D. (Expensive)*

Kona Provision Company • *Hyatt Regency Waikoloa; 885–1234* • The emphasis is on seafood at this al fresco restaurant where diners are treated to wonderful sunsets beyond the shore. Blackened fish is a house specialty. Steak is also on the menu, and there's a filling salad bar. From the lanai, where you can enjoy cocktails before dinner, you'll see the resort's waterfall and the swinging wooden bridge that spans the swimming pool. *Reservations recommended. A, M, V, C, D. (Moderate to Expensive)*

The Tiare Room • *The Royal Waikoloan Hotel, Waikoloa; 885–6789* • Crystal, etched glass, warm wood, and accents reminiscent of the era of the Hawaiian monarchy complement the strong continental menu in this attractive dining room. The salmon baked in pastry and the roast duckling with bananas and lichee nuts are especially good. *Dinner only. Reservations recommended. Closed Wednesdays. A, V, M, C, D. (Expensive)*

Kamuela/Waimea

Merriman's • *Opelo Plaza II (Rt. 19 and Opelo Rd.); 885–6822* • Peter Merriman opened this dining spot with his wife in 1988, after drawing raves at the Mauna Lani Resort's Gallery restaurant (where he became executive chef when he was only 28). He is known for immersing himself totally in his work—even diving for some of the shellfish served. He has joined forces with farmers so that his produce can be as exotic and fresh as possible. You might dine on sea urchin consomme; a salad of fern shoots, dried shrimp, and Maui onions; papaya-glazed chicken with lime-peppercorn sauce, macadamia nut pesto; or chicken with kukui nuts, green onions, and coconut. *Reservations recommended. A, V, M. (Moderate to Expensive)*

Bree Garden • *64–5188 Kinohou St.; 885–5888* • Bernd Bree spent nearly 25 years as a chef at the Mauna Kea Beach Hotel before opening this restaurant at the beginning of 1989. The architecture and decor are striking. A root-dripping banyan tree is the centerpiece of the multilevel dining room and art pieces are strategically placed here and there. The restaurant even boasts a cactus garden. Selections to try include salmon sausages with linguine, chicken tempura with a side of guava mustard sauce, and grilled steak. French and Vietnamese entrees sometimes appear on the menu. *Dinner only. A, V, M. (Moderate)*

Edelweiss • *Hwy. 19; 885–6800* • Opened in 1983 by Hans-Peter Hager, this Bavarian-accented restaurant is the oldest of Kamuela/Waimea's upscale dining places. Before settling here, Hager made the rounds as a chef at some of the state's best hotels: the Kapalua Bay on Maui and the Mauna Kea Beach and Mauna Lani Bay, both on the Big Island. The roast duck in orange sauce and the rack of lamb with mustard and garlic are good choices. Be prepared for a long wait at dinner time. *No reservations taken. Closed Mondays. M, V. (Inexpensive to Moderate)*

Auntie Alice's Pie and Coffee • *Parker Ranch Shopping Center; 885–6880* • Next door to the Parker Ranch Visitor Center, this restaurant is a local favorite. Not only does it serve many different kinds of pie and other sweets, but cooks whip up sandwiches (some vegetarian), chili, seafood chowder, and burgers (chicken, beef, or mahi mahi). A breakfast often requested by residents consists of a hamburger, a fried egg, and rice, all smothered in gravy. *(Inexpensive)*

Paniolo Country Inn • *885–4377* • The extensive menu at this rustic spot includes everything from Italian and Mexican entrees to fried chicken. *(Inexpensive)*

The Bread Depot • *Opelu Plaza; 885–6354* • In addition to sandwiches made from breads and brioche freshly baked on the premises, you'll find all kinds of muffins, soups, curries, and pastas. The paniolo sourdough wheat bread is made with wheat germ and bran.

Parker Ranch Restaurant • *Parker Ranch Shopping Center; 885–7366* • Unfortunately this restaurant where waiters dress as paniolos (cowboys) is often crowded with tour groups. However, residents swear by the juicy steaks (the beef is local). Seafood and a salad bar are available for non-carnivores. *Closed Sundays. Reservations recommended. A, V, M, D, C. (Moderate)*

Honokaa

Hotel Honokaa Club • *Manane St.; 775–0678 or 775–0533* • The building may look run down, but the food is good and the prices are right. The filling portions are accompanied by selections from the salad bar. This makes a good stop during a tour of the Hamakua Coast or a trip to or from Waipio Walley. *(Inexpensive)*

Kailua-Kona and Keauhou Area

Poo Ping • *329–2677 in Kona Inn Village; 329–0010 in the Kamehameha Square Shopping Center, Kailua-Kona* • The spicy Thai cuisine draws a steady local crowd to both of the Kailua-Kona branches of this restaurant. Many dishes are flavored with coconut milk and peanuts. Vegetarians have a selection of entrees. *A, V, M, C. (Inexpensive)*

Kimo's Steak and Seafood Restaurant • *Uncle Billy's Kona Bay Hotel, 75–5739 Alii Drive, Kailua-Kona; 329–1393* • You can watch hula shows (two a night) while you dine al fresco by the pool. There's a large selection of fish on the menu. *A, M, V, D. (Inexpensive)*

Ocean View Inn • *Alii Drive, Kailua-Kona; 329–9998* • With the atmosphere of an old fashioned diner, this no-frills restaurant is almost always packed. People stream in for three meals a day. Owned and run by a family, it serves Hawaiian, Chinese, Japanese, and American food. If you want a plate lunch to go, this is the place. *(Inexpensive)*

Fisherman's Landing • *Kona Inn Shopping Village, Kailua-Kona; 326–2555* • Many people make a habit of dining at this al fresco, oceanfront restaurant. As patrons enter, they are greeted by rows of glistening fresh fish on ice. Live fish dart around ponds inside, where waterfalls and lush plants add to the appealing atmosphere. Paths separate the various dining areas. Steak is served along with a variety of seafood. *A, M, V, D, C. (Moderate)*

Quinn's • *75–5655A Palani Rd., Kailua-Kona; 329–3822* • This restaurant is just across the street from the Hotel King Kamehameha parking lot. After walking through the bar (where a few people will probably be watching TV), guests come to the garden lanai where they dine al fresco with greenery spilling over rough lava rock walls. The teriyaki shrimp and the seafood brochette are popular, as well as the pepper steak with brandy. Burgers and sandwiches are also served (such as the vegetarian number with avocado, sprouts, tomato, and onions). *M, V. (Moderate)*

Huggo's • *75–5828 Kakakai St., Kailua-Kona; 329–1493* • A popular local hangout for sunset watching and after dinner drinks, Huggo's looks out onto the rocky shore. The water is clear enough to see the fish that seem to beg for diners to toss them crumbs. Steak and seafood are the main attractions here. *A, V, M. (Moderate)*

Kona Inn Restaurant • *75–5744 Alii Dr., Kailua-Kona; 329–4455* • Open to the ocean breezes, this waterfront restaurant is decked out in gorgeous, carved koa wood (on the walls, partitions, tables, and ceilings). Peacock chairs, oriental rugs, and slow-moving ceiling fans further enhance the atmosphere. Small birds light on the tops of chairs and the edges of tables. The perky young waitresses are happy to make suggestions. The overstuffed avocado and shrimp salad sandwich or the tuna on a croissant are good choices for lunch. Sunset watching is a popular activity here. *A, V, M. (Inexpensive to Moderate)*

The Chart House • *Waterfront Row, 75–5770 Alii Dr., Kailua-Kona; 941–6669* • Views of the Pacific come free with meals at this steak and seafood restaurant that takes up two floors. Koa wood, fresh flowers, and a waterfall are part of the attractive decor. The Alaskan king crab and prime rib move quickly. *Reservations not accepted. A, M, V, C. (Moderate)*

The Jolly Roger • *Waterfront Row, 75–5776 Alii Dr., Kailua-Kona; 329–1344* • Called the Spindrifter in an earlier life, this restaurant gazes out onto the ocean. Some people say that breakfast is better than the other meals served here. Fresh fruit, eggs, and steak are among the offerings for the first meal of the day. *No reservations accepted. A, V, M, D. (Inexpensive)*

Stan's • *Kona Seaside Hotel, 75–5646 Palani Rd., Kailua-Kona; 329–4500* • The contemporary Hawaiian food served here includes ham steak, stir-fried shrimp, beef steak, Spam, macaroni salad, and rice. This is a popular spot among locals for breakfast. *M, V. (Inexpensive)*

Hele Mai • *Kona Hilton, 75–5852 Alii Dr., Kailua-Kona; 329–3111* • With a great view of boat-studded Kailua Bay, this restaurant serves good old American steak and seafood as well as dishes with a delicious Asian twist. The shrimp and Chinese pea pods in black bean sauce is quite memorable. Ask about weekend buffets. *Reservations required. Closed Sundays. A, V, M, D. (Moderate)*

Teshima Restaurant • *Highway 11, Honalo, Kona Coast; 322–9140* • Ask anyone along the Kona Coast to direct you to a good Japanese restaurant, and chances are you'll end up here. Nine miles south of Kailua-Kona, this unpretentious eatery serves three homestyle meals a day. *(Inexpensive)*

Hawaii Volcanoes National Park

Kilauea Lodge • *Volcano Village, Old Volcano Rd. (near the entrance to the park); 967–7366* • People who've dined at this cozy mountain lodge enclosed by trees and other greenery rave about the wonderful continental food. If it's nippy enough outside, a fire flickers in the hearth during meals. *Reservations recommended. A, V, M. (Moderate to Expensive)*

Volcano Country Club Restaurant • *at the golf course; 967–7721* • A mist usually clings to the smooth greens outside the picture windows. This restaurant makes a good stop during a day of exploring the dramatic park. Sandwiches and other standard fare are on the menu. *(Inexpensive)*

Hilo Area

Roussels • *60 Keawe St.; 935–5111* • Excellent New Orleans-style Creole and Cajun food is prepared for lunch and dinner here. The spicy blackened fish and the shrimp creole are always good. Breads come fresh from the oven and desserts are also baked on the premises. This attractive restaurant is housed in one of Hilo's stately historic buildings. Reservations recommended. *A, V, M. (Moderate)*

Queen's Court • *Hilo Hawaiian Hotel, 71 Banyan Dr.; 935–9361* • Locals pour into this restaurant, which serves standard American fare. It is most crowded on Friday nights for the seafood buffet. Perhaps the best time to dine here is at breakfast. Windows look out to Hilo Bay. *Reservations recommended. A, M, V, C, D. (Inexpensive)*

Uncle Billy's • *Hilo Bay Hotel, 87 Banyan Dr.; 935–0861* • Only breakfast and dinner are served at this popular steak and seafood restaurant. Nightly hula shows accompany the evening meal. For breakfast, try the Wiki Wiki special: ham, home fries, and scrambled eggs. *A, M, V, D. (Inexpensive to Moderate)*

Nihon Saryo • *Hawaii Naniloa Hotel, 93 Banyan Dr.; 969–3333* • When you have a taste for teppan yaki and shabu shabu style Japanese cuisine, stop by this eatery any time of day. The sushi is especially well prepared. *A, M, V, D, C. (Moderate)*

Nihon Restaurant and Cultural Center • *123 Lihiwai St., Hilo; 969–1133* • Traditional Japanese food is served here. The views of Liliuokalani Gardens and Hilo Bay add to the pleasure of the good food. *M, V. (Moderate)*

Dick's Coffee House • *Hilo Shopping Center; 935–2769* • Local families often dine at this modest restaurant that serves breakfast, lunch, and dinner. The steak and chicken are especially good. *M, V. (Inexpensive)*

WHERE TO SLEEP ON HAWAII: THE BIG ISLAND

On the sunny western shore of the Big Island, the Kona-Kohala Coast has some of the world's most sumptuous resorts. Scattered along the prime beaches, these hotels reflect the diversity of the rest of the island. Guests are accommodated in high style, whether they're in multistory complexes (such as the **Mauna Kea** or the **Mauna Lani Bay Hotel**) or thatched-roof Polynesian-style *hales* (at **Kona Village**). While there are many tennis courts, championship golf courses, and endless water sports facilities, the resorts' special touches are what really make them stand out. Some hotels are decorated with dazzling Pacific and Eastern folk art. The lush grounds of others are interlaced with fish ponds once reserved for Hawaiian royalty and fields of *petroglyphs* (ancient carvings in the lava flows). Guests can arrange to be picked up from and delivered to the airport in limousines.

More moderately priced hotels are found along the rocky shore of Kailua-Kona and Keauhou, where beaches are few. However, many travelers don't mind cooling off in swimming pools overlooking the waves thrashing the craggy lava coast. Cruises for snorkeling, diving, and sightseeing are easily arranged, and golf and tennis are also excellent in this area. Good choices include the **Kona Surf Hotel, Kona Hilton Beach and Tennis Resort,** and the more moderate **Keauhou Beach Hotel.** Most of the island's stores and restaurants are in the waterfront town of Kailua-Kona. The majority of people staying in Hilo's hotels, on the wet east coast, are either tourists visiting the volcanoes, or business travelers. Try the **Hawaii Naniloa** or the **Dolphin Bay.** If you'd like to get away from the tourist meccas, consider staying in the *paniolo* (cowboy) village of Kamuela/Waimea, with its upscale boutiques and gourmet restaurants; the macadamia-producing town of Honokaa on the northern Hamakua Coast; remote, gorgeous Waipio Valley in the northeast; isolated Kaʻu, way down in the south; or Hawaii Volcanoes National Park.

Note that even very expensive one-bedroom condominiums can be quite economical when shared with another couple (living rooms usually have sofa beds). For Bed & Breakfasts other than those described, rental cottages, and housekeeping cabins, see the appropriate entries at the end of this section.

Kamuela/Waimea

★★ **Kamuela Inn B&B** • Travelers wanting to get away from the crowds yet be within shouting distance of boutiques, gourmet restaurants, and a theater should book a room at this appealing inn. Everyone raves about the large penthouse suite, which has great views from its lanai, a microwave-equipped full kitchen, and a fireplace for warming up evenings. Guests are treated to a light breakfast on the common lanai. *(Inexpensive)*

★★ **Waimea Gardens Cottage** • At the foot of the Kohala Mountains and two miles from the center of Kamuela/Waimea town, this cozy B&B opened in 1982. A stream runs through the backyard. The entrance to the building, which houses two units, is a renovated turn-of-the-century wash house that was part of an old Hawaiian homestead. Each unit sleeps two people (or three if one uses the futon) and one has a fireplace. Ruffled, country-style pillows and floral bedspreads are part of the cheerful decor. Not only are rooms equipped with stereos, remote-control TV, and beach towels, but they also have Japanese flannel robes in the winter or cotton *yukatas* during the summer. French doors open to brick patios. While the older unit contains a small full kitchen and a bath with a stall shower, the newer studio has a microwave and a bath with double sinks and a full tub. When guests arrive, they find that their refrigerators have been stocked with breakfast goodies including island juices and whatever they requested beforehand. Local Hawaiian honey, jams, fresh fruit, and Kona coffee are also on hand. Visitors, who prepare their own breakfasts, are welcome to gather fresh eggs from the chickens on the property. The beautiful beach at the Mauna Kea hotel is eight miles away. *(Moderate)*

☆ **Parker Ranch Lodge** • The decor of this modest accommodation makes it clear that *paniolo* (cowboy) country is all around. Each unit comes with a kitchenette and some are decorated with country-style artwork. Many guests begin their days with Kona coffee served in the lounge, which has a TV. *(Inexpensive)*

Hamakua Coast

☆☆ **Log House Bed & Breakfast** • *near Honokaa* • Try this contemporary log cabin for a countrified vacation on the slopes of Mauna Kea. Built during the 1970s, it draws lovers of the outdoors. The modern rooms are spacious, with glossy hard wood floors. A filling breakfast is served in a common dining room. In the evenings, guests mingle with their hosts in front of the living room fireplace. Waimea is not far, but Hilo is about a 50 minute drive from here. *(Inexpensive)*

☆ **Hamakua Hideaway** • *near Waipio Valley* • A sole cottage in a lush setting, this B&B has a loft and a full kitchen. The sound of a nearby waterfall fills the air and views take in the ruggedly beautiful Hamakua Coast. This is only for those who *really* want to be left alone. *(Moderate)*

Waipio Valley

Tom Araki's • Staying here is the next best thing to camping out. Jokingly referred to as the "Waipio Hilton," this no-frills-whatsoever accommodation is nestled deep in one of the state's most beautiful valleys. The front porch of this wooden building overlooks Mr. Araki's taro field, grapefruit trees, and other fruit trees. Instead of electricity, guests read themselves to sleep by the light of kerosene lamps. They bring their own food, which they prepare on the kerosene stove in the communal kitchen, sans refrigerator. Cold showers are taken at the end of the hall. Two of the five rooms have single beds while the others have one double bed each (sheets and pillows are provided). Outdoorspeople love Waipio Valley, which has a glistening black sand beach (a twenty-minute walk away). Swimming holes are found about a mile and a half away. This place fills up well in advance, so be sure to make reservations at least several weeks before your arrival. *(Very Inexpensive)*

Kohala Coast

★★★★ **Mauna Kea Beach Hotel** • *Mauna Kea Resort* • Built in 1965 by Laurance Rockefeller, this is the Kohala Coast resort that started it all. Set on one of the state's most attractive white sand beaches, the Mauna Kea is famed for its fabulous Pacific and Asian art collection. Art tours are conducted twice a week for both guests and outsiders. Traditional Hawaiian quilts and other antiques decorate corridors. Palm trees tower over pools packed with carp. At night, visitors peer at graceful manta rays swimming in the floodlit edge of the bay. The large, tastefully decorated guest rooms come with lanais entered through sliding louvered doors, spacious modern baths, Japanese cotton *yukatas* for visitors to wear during their stay, and (for families with children) a gift pack of peanut butter, guava jelly, and Hilo soda crackers on a frisbee. From mid-June through Labor Day, and during Christmas and Easter vacations, a complimentary children's program is supervised by trained counselors. Parents get time off while their kids are involved in Hawaiian games and crafts, sand castle contests, boogie boarding, and nature walks. Families or groups of friends should consider staying at one of the lavish villas or rental homes on the grounds. Serving East Indian curries and continental cuisine, the Batik Room is one of the island's best restaurants. To work off any unwanted calories, head to the freshwater swimming pool overlooking the ocean, the beach for an array of water sports, one of the 13 tennis courts, the Robert Trent Jones, Sr, golf course that is considered one of the best in the U.S., or the Mauna Kea Stables in Kamuela/Waimea (transportation is provided). *(Very Expensive)*

The Ritz Carlton • *Mauna Lani Resort* • Scheduled to be completed by the time you read these words, this beach resort sprawls across 32 acres. It is next to the Mauna Lani Bay Hotel and the Mauna Lani condominiums and guests have use of the two excellent golf courses there. Facilities will include a swimming pool, tennis courts, several restaurants, a health spa, and a library where afternoon tea will be served. The decor includes 18th and 19th century original art work done by European and Hawaiian artists in the Islands. Guest rooms will be elegant but comfortable, with hardwood furniture, four-poster beds, marble baths with separate shower and tub, and lanais (most with ocean views). Extras come in the form of terry cloth robes for guests' use during their stay, a second phone in the bathroom, remote-control TV, and minibars. Those who need even more pampering should book a room on the exclusive Ritz Carlton Club floor. *(Very Expensive)*

★★★★ **Mauna Lani Bay Hotel and Bungalows** • *Mauna Lani Resort* • The personal touches make this stunning hotel so special. Arriving guests are greeted with a kiss and a lei, then seated individually at a small check-in desk before being escorted to their rooms. The airy, elegant lobby is set off with white columns and a blue-tiled staircase, bordered by waterfalls, that leads down to a palm-rimmed pool. Ivy spills over balustrades and fragrant flowers are everywhere. A Hawaiian trio performs by the gardens in the afternoon and early evening while at night a combo plays jazz by the lobby bar. Three of the Big Island's most popular restaurants are found at this resort—the Third Floor, the

Gallery, and the Canoe House. Walking tours are conducted of the historic fish ponds, some with baby sharks, that meander throughout the grounds.

Named for one of Hawaii's best known golfers, the Francis I'i Brown Golf Courses are two of the most attractive and challenging in the state. In addition to a large swimming pool, the active set is drawn to the ten tennis courts, the complete lineup of water sports at the beach, and the extensive fitness center. Couples enjoy spending evenings in the Jacuzzi. All with lanais, guest rooms sport teak furniture and louvered doors, ceiling fans as well as air conditioning, and lavish baths. For the ultimate splurge, book one of the two-bedroom oceanside bungalows, each with its own swimming pool and Jacuzzi. The $1500 to $2000 a night price tag includes a chauffeured limousine, a butler around the clock, and a maid who unpacks, irons, and repacks guests' clothes. *(Very Expensive)*

★★★★ **Mauna Lani Point** • *Mauna Lani Resort* • Located on a peaceful corner of the resort, this plush condominium is run something like a hotel. All desk clerks act as concierges. With a few day's notice, guests may arrange to be served breakfast in bed or on their lanai, with ferns and flowers part of the culinary presentation. Most meals and activities can be charged at the neighboring Mauna Lani Bay Hotel. Complimentary shuttle service is provided around the resort. Many of the individually decorated one-, two-, and three-bedroom apartments have features such as sunken living rooms; baths with sunken tubs, double sinks, and rosewood trim; kitchens with ash wood cabinets, built-in cutting boards and wine racks, and micro-wave/convection ovens. Some units and the adjacent golf course have wonderful views of whales during the winter (especially February and March). The swimming pool, Jacuzzi, and dry sauna are tranquil even when the property is full. A barbecue pit and an open-air kitchen adjoin the pool. *(Very Expensive)*

★★★ **Mauna Lani Terrace** • *Mauna Lani Resort* • Done in rattan, wicker, or contemporary styles, these bright one-, two-, and three-bedroom condominums all have lanais and laundry facilities. Even the smallest units come with two baths, and kitchens are equipped with microwaves and dishwashers. Guests take advantage of the large swimming pool, the children's pool, the Jacuzzi, the sauna, and the picnic area with gas grills. Tennis courts, an exercise room, and a lap pool are also on the premises. This complex is conveniently located next to the Mauna Lani Bay Hotel and beaches are a brief stroll away. Golf at the adjacent fairway can be arranged at a reduced rate. *(Very Expensive)*

★★★★★ **Hyatt Regency Waikoloa** • *Waikoloa Resort* • Two words that describe this spectacular playground are "tastefully overdone,'' if such a condition exists. Some areas—such as the Palace Wing, with its oversized columns, humungous chandeliers, and sky-high mirrors—look like sets for *Land of the Giants*. The trio of towers is connected by the aptly named mile-long Museum Walkway. It is decked out with everything from six-foot tall urns and antique marionettes to weathered spears from Papua New Guinea. Tropical gardens are aflutter with cockatoos, macaws, and parrots. Guests are transported to their rooms in space-age monorails or boats along the lagoons. Among the wide selection of restaurants, Donatello's, for Italian food, and Imari, for Japanese cuisine, have built excellent reputations.

There's no real beach here, just a slip of sand at the edge of a lagoon. A beautiful beach is just a brief walk or a shuttle ride away. Guests spend much of their time at the three golf courses, eight tennis courts, two racquetball/squash courts, spacious health spa, and three swimming pools. They are even invited to swim with a group of Atlantic bottlenose dolphins (but reservations for this popular activity must be made well before arrival at the hotel). Big spenders should consider one of the Fantasy Vacations: How about joining a jam session with one of your favorite musicians, taking private cooking lessons with a renowned chef, or scuba diving with a film star? With a small circular driveway and valet parking, coming and going can be a real hassle here. However, many people soon forget their complaints. *(Very Expensive)*

★★★ **Shores at Waikoloa** • *Waikoloa Resort* • Between the Hyatt Regency Waikoloa and the Royal Waikoloan, this condominium is surrounded by a golf course. It is not on a beach, but sandy shores aren't far. The decor of the one-, two-, and three-bedroom units is pleasantly upscale. Kitchens feature microwaves and dishwashers. Apartments also come with laundry facilities. Tennis courts are on the premises and there is a pool, a Jacuzzi, and a picnic area with grills and a kitchen. *(Very Expensive)*

☆☆☆ **Royal Waikoloan** • *Waikoloa Resort* • Although the Royal Waikoloan has a far nicer beach than its nearly beachless neighbor, this former Sheraton is definitely in the shadow of the newer Hyatt Regency Waikoloa next door. However, many travelers prefer this more subdued hotel. The architecture of the six-story towers may be standard, but the rooms are nicely done and perfectly comfortable. Overlooking the gorgeous bay, the open-air lobby is filled with greenery and unobtrusive boutiques. Hawaiian history lives on here. Visitors may hike along the King's Trail (a.k.a. the Ala Mamalohoa) and stumble across ancient petroglyphs carved in the lava. Guests also amuse themselves with the circular freshwater pool, all kinds of water sports, six tennis courts, and two 18-hole golf courses. *(Very Expensive)*

☆☆ **Waikoloa Villas** • *Waikoloa Resort* • On the *mauka* (mountain) side of Waikoloa Resort, these condominiums are about six miles from the beach. Horseback riding is a favorite activity here, along with tennis and golf. The golf club restaurant serves those who want a break from their kitchens. Swimming pools are also on the premises. Maid service is provided once a week. *(Moderate)*

Kailua-Kona Area and Keauhou

★★★★ **Kona Village** • *Kaʻupulehu-Kona* • Popular among families, this has to be the most unusual resort on the island. When you come to the thatched roof *hale* (cottage) that appears out of nowhere along Kaahumanu Highway (#19), you'll know you've reached the guard post of the distinctive Kona Village hotel. As you drive along the chocolate-colored lava road that twists and turns through a wasteland strewn with dark crumbly boulders, your first thought is likely to be, "What have I gotten myself into?" Then you'll see the guest hales, built in the architectural styles of a variety of Polynesian peoples, from Hawaiians and Tahitians to Samoans and Fijians. Some with thatched roofs, these cottages stand on stilts above rugged lava flows, at the edges of beaches, or overlooking a lagoon. Just as when the resort was built in the 1960s, they contain no phones, radios, TVs, or air conditioners. Tradewinds and ceiling fans keep visitors comfortable. However, fresh Kona coffee beans, a grinder, a coffee maker, and a refrigerator are provided. Colorful batiks and other textiles decorate the walls and furnishings. When guests don't want to be disturbed, they simply place the room's coconut outside the door.

Sandy shores here come in black, salt and pepper, and white. There are also two swimming pools and three night-lit tennis courts. Sunsets are especially picturesque through the floor to ceiling windows of the main dining room. Three meals a day are included in the rates. Guests who dine at the Hale Samoa, the second restaurant, pay a surcharge. Tours can be arranged of the petroglyph fields and fish ponds, near where the hotel's famed luau is held. At night you may hear the wild donkeys that sometimes visit the resort. *(Very Expensive)*

☆☆ **Holualoa Inn** • *Holualoa* • Located just *mauka* (inland) of northern Kailua-Kona, this guesthouse sits in an artists' community in coffee country. Topped by a gazebo, the building contains only four guest rooms, each decorated in a different South Pacific or Asian style. Visitors cool off in the swimming pool or cool out in the hot tub. *(Moderate)*

☆☆ **Hotel King Kamehameha** • *75–5660 Palani Rd., Kailua-Kona* • Filled with a tangle of souvenir shops, the public areas are far too cluttered and commercial for me. But if you want to be in the heart of town and in a hotel with a beach (albeit small), this is a good choice. Kailua Pier is just across the way. This is the jumping-off point for fishing boats (especially during the annual Hawaiian International Billfish Tournament in late July or early August), glass bottom boat and dinner cruises, and the boat to the *Atlantis* submarine (for which you sign up in the hotel). Free guided tours are conducted of the section of the grounds that was once the home of King Kamehameha and his court. In addition to a host of water sports, there are a pool and four tennis courts (two of them night-lit). Guest rooms, which all have lanais and refrigerators, are plain but comfortable. *(Moderate)*

☆☆ **Uncle Billy's Kona Bay Hotel** • *75–5739 Alii Dr., Kailua-Kona* • Across from sandy Kailua Bay, this is another centrally located hotel. In the shape of a half moon with an island in its center, its layout ties in perfectly with its Polynesian decor. Thatched roofs, bamboo lampshades and linoleum floors create a Robinson Crusoe–style cabin atmosphere, complete with red and white shams that trim the roof of the lobby. Vending machines and table video games in the lobby are all part of the sense of fun and humor in this very informal, homey, colorful family inn. The circular pool is only five feet deep, but all kinds of other activities can be easily arranged. The simply decorated bedrooms have lanais. If you're looking for something to do after dark, catch one of the nightly hula shows in the bar and restaurant. *(Inexpensive)*

☆ **Kona Seaside Hotel** • *75–5646 Palani Rd., Kailua-Kona* • The lava rock walls and columns darken the lobby of this modest hotel. Polynesian-style hanging lanterns and rattan chairs with floral cushions brighten the surroundings. Rooms are small, with ceiling fans, refrigerators, and miniscule baths. The well-maintained grounds are lush with greenery and there's a pool for those who forgo the walk across the road to Kailua Bay. *(Inexpensive)*

☆☆ **Kona Islander Inn** • *Alii Dr., Kailua-Kona* • Kailua Bay is across the street from this condominium that features studios with and without kitchenettes. The style of the complex is reminiscent of old Hawaiian plantations. Bordered by torches and bushy palms, paths wind through the property. The pool patio is especially attractive. *(Inexpensive to Moderate)*

★★★ **Kona Hilton Beach and Tennis Resort** • *75–5852 Alii Dr., Kailua-Kona* • Ideally located, this well-maintained hotel sits at the edge of Kailua-Kona, away from the hustle and bustle but close enough to many good restaurants and shops. While the ocean isn't safe for swimming here, there's a tiny sandy beach lagoon that is great for snorkeling when the tide is high enough. Two pools are also on the premises, along with tennis courts. The three six-story towers command 11 acres of lush coastline. The center tower is sloped to resemble a volcano. Decor is contemporary Polynesian, with lots of koa wood carvings and trimmings, attractively landscaped grounds, and fish ponds. The open-air lobby is always filled as guests shop or make plans at the activities desk. Rooms all have lanais, minibars, refrigerators, and bathrobes to wear during your stay. If you want to be in one of the largest, request a corner room. Coffee makers and complimentary Kona coffee are provided. *(Expensive)*

☆☆ **Hale Kona Kai** • *75–5870 Kahakai Rd., Kailua-Kona* • Next door to the Kona Hilton, this waterfront condominium is a brief stroll away from restaurants and shops in town. Some of the one-bedroom units are nicer than others, since they are individually decorated by their owners. A pool is on the grounds. *(Inexpensive* to *Moderate)*

☆☆ **Kona Tiki Hotel** • *75–5968 Alii Dr., Kailua-Kona* • About a mile south of Kailua-Kona village, Kona Tiki is conveniently located just out of the way of the center of a busy tourist area and yet close enough for easy access to assorted restaurants and night life activity. Boasting a high percentage of repeat business, this small, unpretentious hotel seems content to remain slightly tattered around the edges. Perhaps because of the Polynesian-style decor, it has a 1960s feel. As you relax by a swaying palm, you might expect to hear Frankie and Annette crooning a tune from *Beach Blanket Bingo.* Protected by a sea wall, the hotel overlooks a shallow cove of Kailua Bay. A sandy walkway is the entry to a small private beach. However, due to rough waters, caution is advised when swimming. The staff is extremely friendly, quickly on a first name basis with guests. The lobby is usually filled with lots of laughter, back-slapping, and talking story. Walls are plastered with aged pictures such as of a fisherman with his catch, an elderly couple in leisure suits in an anonymous city, and other nostalgia. You'll also find a dog-eared collection of reading material in the small lending library. A luau is held by the swimming pool. All of the guest rooms have lanais and some also come with kitchenettes. *(Inexpensive)*

☆☆☆ **Aston Royal Sea Cliff** • *75–6040 Alii Dr., Kailua-Kona* • The entrance to this stark white terraced condominium is on the fifth floor. Balconies outside rooms overlook the sunny lobby that is lush with greenery and scattered with wicker sitting areas. Gardens, a waterfall and fish ponds add to the tropical ambiance. The waterfront here is rocky, but there are two swimming pools to choose from (one salt, one fresh) and a tennis court. Units are available as studios and one- or two-bedrooms. *(Expensive)*

☆☆☆ **Aston Kona By the Sea** • *75–6106 Alii Dr., Kailua-Kona* • On a rocky shore, this pleasant condominium boasts spacious upscale one- and two-bedroom units. A restaurant is on the grounds for those who tire of cooking. Well-manicured vegetation thrives around the freshwater oceanfront pool and Jacuzzi. In the second pool, also overlooking the sea, guests splash around in water from the Pacific. *(Very Expensive)*

☆☆ **Kona Magic Sands** • *77–6452 Alii Dr., Kailua-Kona* • Not far from the beach whose sands vanish during the winter, this condominium offers an eclectic mix of studio apartments. Decor ranges from plain to nondescript and rooms don't have telephones. The restaurant here specializes in seafood. *(Moderate)*

☆☆ **Casa De Emdeko** • *75–6082 Alii Dr., Kailua-Kona* • Some four miles south of the heart of Kailua-Kona, these low-rise condos stand along a coast dotted with small coves that are safer for sunning than swimming. The nicely furnished units have commodious living rooms and lanais with views of the ocean, swimming pools, or thick gardens. Many travelers choose this attractive resort for its out-of-the-way location *(Expensive)*

☆☆ **Kona White Sands Apartment Hotel** • *45–5782 Kuakini Hwy., Kailua-Kona* • A home away from home for many repeat vacationers, this small condominium offers apartments with kitchenettes and lanais. A white sand beach is just across the street. No maid service is provided, so guests begin to feel like residents. In a tranquil area, the two-story building is located about four miles from town. *(Inexpensive)*

★★★ **Kona Coast Resort** • *78–6842 Alii Dr., Keauhou Gardens* • Adjacent to the Kona Golf Club and across from Keauhou Shopping Center, this condominium rents very attractive one-, two-, and three-bedroom apartments. All units have lanais and the modern kitchens come with microwaves. TVs, VCRs, and laundry facilities all contribute to the home-like surroundings of each unit. A swimming pool is set amid the 12 acres of landscaped gardens. *(Very Expensive)*

★★★ **Kanaloa at Kona** • *78–261 Manukai St., Keauhou-Kona* • If you'd like a room with your own Jacuzzi, book an oceanfront suite at this plush condo. Apartments have one, two, or three bedrooms. Special touches include koa wood cabinets and marble. The modern kitchens come with microwave ovens and there's a restaurant on the premises, along with a cocktail lounge. Guests can keep in shape at the two tennis courts and three swimming pools. *(Expensive to Very Expensive)*

★★★ **Keauhou Beach Hotel** • *78–6740 Alii Dr., Keauhou* • Kahaluu Beach, known for its excellent snorkeling, is a brief stroll from this resort that was built on royal land. The oceanfront side of the six-story building overhangs a lagoon, affording an aquarium-like view of the water below. At low tide, take a walk to see the petroglyphs. The pool patio is the first place you'll want to stop even before you check into your room. The view of the ocean, the beach, the Royal Kuakina Grove all in one sweep is nothing less than breathtaking. There's also a small pool for children. The upbeat music of live band and the convenience of a full service bar may make it difficult for you to tear yourself away. Try to stick around until Sunday. The Pool Terrace serves a Sunday Brunch buffet with free champagne. Guest rooms are pleasantly done, with rattan furnishings, lanais, and ceiling fans in addition to air conditioning. Amid the lush gardens, you'll find the reconstructed summer cottage and royal bathing pool of King Kalakaua. The beautiful Keauhou Botanical Gardens are just across the street from the hotel. Shuttle buses are provided to Keauhou Shopping Village. *(Moderate)*

★★★ **Kona Surf Resort** • *78–128 Ehukai St., Keauhou* • The Japanese ownership of this modern hotel is reflected in the handsome, spare decor. The Kona Surf is a favorite among honeymooners and other tourists from Japan. Trim, colorful gardens and bright green lawns provide a wonderful contrast with the black lava of the craggy coast that is constantly pounded by the rough surf. At night, lights reveal the manta rays that swim up to the rocks at shore. Most of the attractive guest rooms are equipped with refrigerators, coffee makers, and Kona coffee. Poke around the expensive grounds, and you'll stumble onto archeological ruins of canoe sheds, stone altars, and fishing shrines. A shuttle bus takes guests to town. Kahaluu Beach Park, the closest sandy shore, is about ¾ mile away. Ask for directions to the row of lava rock swimming holes that are about ½ mile from the hotel. *(Expensive to Very Expensive)*

Ka‘u

☆ **Shirakawa Motel** • *near Naalehu* • In an isolated part of Hawaii, this small, family-run motel is not far from the southernmost town in the United States. Also nearby are the monkeypod tree that sprouted from the roots of the one planted by Mark Twain in the 1860s, and colonial-style Kauahaao Church in Waiohinu. There are no telephones in the plain motel rooms, but cooking facilities are available. Stay here only if you really want to be alone or if you simply plan to mingle with small town folk. *(Inexpensive)*

☆☆ **Sea Mountain at Punaluʻu** • *Punaluʻu* • Far off the tourist beat, this rustic condominium complex lures guests with its golf course, black sand beach, swimming pool, and tennis courts. Part of the resort is residential. Equipped with full kitchens, the studios and one- and two-bedroom apartments are comfortable, but nothing special. Maid service is once a week. There's a restaurant on the premises and a branch of the Aspen Institute for Humanistic Studies is based here. *(Moderate)*

Hawaii Volcanoes National Park

★★ **Volcano Vacation** • *near entrance to the park* • In an un-likely locale, here is an upscale cottage complete with two bedrooms, one bath, a fireplace, sauna, and laundry facilities. Most of the people who stay here come to play golf or hike in the national park. *(Moderate)*

☆☆ **Volcano House** • *rim of Kilauea Crater* • Play a round of golf on the Volcano Golf Course, then relax in a natural volcanic sauna here at this lodge perched at the rim of Kilauea Crater, 4000 feet above sea level. The original Volcano House was a thatched-roof grass structure built during the 1840s that had room for 40 guests. In 1877, it was replaced by a Western-style inn with only four bedrooms in addition to its dining room and parlor. Queen Liliuokalani, Robert Louis Stevenson, and Mark Twain were among its guests. The rustic inn that stands here today was built in 1941, and boasts 38 guest rooms all heated by steam from the volcano. The fireplace in the main building has been burning continuously for years. Anyone so inclined may pick out a tune on the koa piano here. Hearty meals, including some vegetarian selections, are served in the dining room. Uncle George's Cocktail lounge offers a magnificent view of the crater. At night, you can see the red glow of lava flowing down the side of the mountain. Guest rooms are decorated with Hawaiian quilt designs. Some have private lanais and full baths while others have stall showers. Make reservations six months in advance if you're planning to vacation in the winter and three months ahead for other times of year. *(Inexpensive)*

☆ **Volcano Bed & Breakfast** • *a mile from park entrance* • Built during the 1930s, this refurbished three-story home offers three double rooms and a shared bath. Visitors may get to know each other by the crackling fireplace or while using the common TV and VCR. Bicycles are available for exploring the area. The owners, who live in the ground floor, are happy to provide tips on sights and activities. *(Inexpensive)*

★★ **Kilauea Lodge** • *a mile from park entrance* • Highly recommended by honeymooners, this is a good place for being alone together. Thick woods enclose the rustic mountain lodge. The five attractive rooms are accented with Hawaiian or Asian touches. Each has a fireplace. Everyone raves about the restaurant. A complete breakfast is included in the room rates. Kilauea General Store and Volcano Golf Course are both nearby. *(Moderate)*

☆ **My Island Bed & Breakfast** • You'll get a hearty breakfast when you wake up in this old missionary home that was built by the Lyman family in 1886. One of the three guest rooms in this three-story building can accommodate as many as six people. Three studio apartments are also available, two of them outside the main house. *(Inexpensive)*

Hilo

☆ **Country Club Hotel** • *121 Banyan Dr.* • Although this condominium may appear somewhat rundown from the outside, the spacious rooms are relatively well-maintained. Some rooms have views of the nine-hole Naniloa Country Club Golf Course and others overlook Hilo Bay. There's a restaurant on the premises, along with a cocktail lounge and a swimming pool. *(Inexpensive)*

★★ **Hawaii Naniloa** • *93 Banyan Dr.* • Across the street from the nine-hole Naniloa Country Club Golf Course, Hilo's largest hotel also sports tennis courts and a swimming pool. Four Mile Beach, considered to be the town's best sandy stretch, is about two miles away. The nicest rooms are those that gaze out to the harbor. Stores are found in the lobby, located between the towers. From Thursday through Sunday nights, there's dancing in the lounge. The pleasantly decorated rooms are equipped with coffee machines and complimetary coffee. Most have private lanais, and views are of the bay, gardens, tennis courts, or mountains. *(Moderate)*

☆☆ **Uncle Billy's Hilo Bay Hotel** • *87 Banyan Dr.* • Similar to its sister hotel on the Kona Coast (Kona Bay Hotel), Hilo Bay is a low rise Polynesian-style resort. Hawaiian flora, native artifacts, wood carvings, and kapa prints create a colorful, homey, informal environment. Most of the smallish guest rooms have kitchenettes and all come with private lanais and stall showers. Many locals enjoy the nightly hula show. There's a swimming pool in addition to the lounge, coffee shop, and stores. *(Inexpensive)*

☆ **Hilo Hawaiian Hotel** • *71 Banyan Dr.* • In the open-air lobby, rattan lounge chairs, sprays of anthuriums, and the koa wood reception desk are about the only touches of Polynesia. Walk out the back, however, and you'll have a wonderful view of Hilo Bay. Guest rooms look out to the water and Coconut Island or Banyan Drive. The majority of rooms have lanais, and one-bedroom units come with kitchenettes. In the evenings, a live band performs in the lounge. There's a swimming pool on the grounds. *(Moderate)*

☆ **Hilo Hukilau Hotel** • *126 Banyan Dr.* • If you can tolerate the sound of planes passing overhead periodically, this hotel is not a bad deal. This is not for travelers who mind walking up stairs, since many rooms are on the second and third floors of the low-rise buildings. Some rooms have views of the lagoon while others overlook the swimming pool. Not all have lanais, so be sure to ask if you want one. Ceiling fans cool the air. The restaurant and cocktail lounge provide guests with a bit of night life, even if it's just talking story with locals. *(Inexpensive)*

☆☆ **Dolphin Bay Hotel** • *333 Iliahi St.* • In quiet, residential Pueo, this hotel is about a five-minute walk from downtown Hilo and you'll need to drive to the closest swimming beach. Guests enjoy congregating in the hotel lobby. This comfortable and cozy little room is complete with a library of donated reading material, a basket of fruit for the taking, a pay phone (there are no phones in rooms), and a charming desk clerk who lends out coolers, umbrellas, an iron and ironing board, local and some national newspapers (which you'll be asked to return for other guests) and a lot of good advice. All 18 studios (with full kitchens) have views of the lush gardens. There is no air conditioning, but small desk fans are provided. This hotel draws quite a few repeat guests, many of them older travelers, and lots of families. *(Inexpensive)*

OTHER BED & BREAKFASTS AND PRIVATE HOMES

On Hawaii, many travelers enjoy staying at B&Bs or in private homes because they see a side of the island that most vacationers miss. B&B owners and managers are as happy to help guests plan excursions, make dinner reservations, and rent cars as they are to allow them complete privacy. Totally independent travelers thrive in private rental cottages, where they are on their own. If you'd like to explore the idea of staying in a B&B besides one of those described above, or of renting a private cottage, contact the following companies. Note that a minimum number of nights may be required and that weekly rates can be less expensive than daily rates.

Hawaii's Best Bed & Breakfasts • P.O. Box 563, Kamuela, HI 96743; (800) BNB–9912 (reservations) or (808) 885–4550 (information) • This highly selective company specializes in upscale B&Bs. Double room rates range from about $65 to $115 per night.

All Islands Bed & Breakfast • 823 Kainui Dr., Kailua, HI 96734; (800) 542–0344 or (808) 263–2342 • Handles private homes, cottages, and condominium apartments as well as B&Bs. Rates average $55 to $65 per night.

Bed & Breakfast Pacific-Hawaii • 19 Kai Nani Pl., Kailua, HI 96734; (808) 254–5030 • Also handles condo apartments, private homes, and cottages. Rates range from $40 to $130 per night.

Bed & Breakfast-Hawaii • P.O. Box 449, Kapaa, Kauai, HI 96746; (800) 657–7832 or (808) 822–7771 • Also handles private homes and cottages. Rates run from $40 to $80 per night.

Bed & Breakfast Honolulu • 3242 Kaohinani Dr., Honolulu, HI 96817; (800) 288–4666 or (808) 595–7533 • Prices range from $30 to $130. Kitchens are available in some units.

South Kohala Management • P.O. Box 3301, Waikoloa, HI 96743; (800) 822–4252 • Represents private homes and estates. Rates range from $200 to $775 per night. House/car packages are available.

HOUSEKEEPING CABINS

Hawaii's state and national parks provide shelters for travelers who feel that being able to explore the outdoors is more important than sleeping in plush quarters. Some people book these housekeeping cabins more than a year in advance, so make your reservations as early as possible. In **Hawaii Volcanoes National Park,** the small A-frame shelters are about three miles from Kilauea Caldera. Each can sleep up to four people and has both a double bed and a bunk bed. There is no stove or refrigerator, but an outdoor grill is provided along with linens, blankets, towels, and soap. Showers are in a shared bathhouse. Rustic Volcano House lodge, across from the Park Visitor Center three miles from the cabins, has a restaurant. The closest grocery store is about four miles away in the town of Volcano, along with another local eating spot. The cost per cabin per night is about $28. Two other cabins, located on Mauna Loa volcano in the park, are free. However, one is at the 10,000 foot elevation, a seven mile hike from the beginning of the trail, and the second is an additional 11 miles away, at Mauna Loa's 13,679 foot summit! You'll have to bring a sleeping bag, but beds and water are provided at these shelters. To make reservations, contact **National Park Cabins** (Volcano House, Hawaii Volcanoes National Park, HI 96768).

While you're hiking around **Pohakuloa Cabins,** 6500 feet up the grassy ranching slopes of Mauna Kea, be careful of the hunters who sometimes use these shelters. You'll find the seven state park cabins just off Saddle Road, 33 miles from Hilo. Some sleeping up to six people, these units have electricity, hot showers, cooking and eating utensils, beds, linens, and towels. Some also come with fireplaces. One person would pay around $12, while for six people the cost would be about $7 each.

If you'd prefer to be down on one of the Big Island's most beautiful white sand beaches, consider **Hapuna State Park Cabins**. Beds in these shelters are built-in wooden benches, so be sure to bring a sleeping pad to put under your sleeping bag. Facilities include shared showers and a common dining area, with a refrigerator and electric stove. Cooking and eating utensils are provided. Each cabin costs about $9 a night for up to four people. Note that Hapuna Beach can be too rough for swimming during the winter.

In a region that is far lusher than arid Hapuna, **Kalopa Cabins** are found in the northeast, two miles south of Honokaa and just inland from the scenic Hamakua Coast. The hiking trails in this flourishing state park are well-marked and some of the vegetation has been identified. Cabins sleep up to eight people each on bunk beds. Bedding is provided, along with a common dining and recreation hall with a gas stove and cooking and eating utensils. The rate would be about $8 per person for two people and less for a larger group. To arrange to stay at Pohakuloa, Hapuna, or Kalopa Cabins, contact the **Division of State Parks** (P.O. Box 336, Hilo, HI 96721).

Also see Waipio Valley, above.

HAWAII: THE BIG ISLAND DETAILS

SAVING MONEY: Tour companies and airlines offer economical package deals. Through **American Express Vacations** (800/241–1700), for example, a 7-night excursion to the Big Island would include all round trip flights, the hotel, a rental car, a lei greeting, and taxes. Travelers generally fly to Honolulu, where they change to an inter-island carrier. To take off from Los Angeles during August, the cost would be about $740 per person, double occupancy, in a standard room at the moderately priced Kona Seaside. A stay at the very expensive Hyatt Regency Waikoloa would begin at about $1375 per person. To fly from Chicago, the cost of staying at the moderate hotel would start at around $1000, while it would begin at around $1630 at the expensive resort. From New York, the moderate package would be about $1010 and the expensive excursion would run around $1650.

GETTING TO AND FROM THE AIRPORTS: Chances are you'll fly into either **Keahole Airport** on the Kona Coast or **Hilo International** (a.k.a. General Lyman Field) in the east. **Kamuela Airport,** in the north, is mainly used by commuters and only small planes fly into **Upulo Point,** at the northern tip.

By Car: You'll have the most flexibility if you pick up a rental car at the airport and keep it for the duration of your stay on the island. It's best to reserve a car as far ahead of your arrival as possible.

By Shuttle: If you're staying on the Kohala Coast at the Mauna Kea Beach Hotel, the Mauna Lani Resort, the Hyatt Regency Waikoloa, or the Royal Waikoloan, you can arrange transportation (perhaps in a limousine) between the airport and the resort for less than what you'd pay in a taxi. Look for the Kohala Coast Resort Association representatives at the Hawaiian Airlines and Aloha Airlines counters. Some hotels in the Kailua-Kona and Keauhou area also provide shuttle service.

By Taxi: From Keahole Airport, fares begin at about $18 to Kailua-Kona, $25 to Keauhou, and $35 to the Waikoloa Resort in southern Kohala. The cost to the Mauna Kea Beach Hotel, the northernmost Kohala resort, should be around $47. Taxis wait for incoming flights and your hotel will be happy to call you a cab. However, in case you'd like to make arrangements yourself, try **Kona Airport Taxi Company** (329–7779) or **Marina Taxi** (329–2481). From Hilo International to the hotels along Banyan Drive, expect to pay about $8. Good companies include **Aloha** (935–1600) and **ABC** (935–0755)

By Limousine: If your hotel doesn't provide limo service, try **Carey Limousine** (836–1422) or **Limousines by Roberts** (947–3939).

GETTING AROUND HAWAII: THE BIG ISLAND: **By Car:** You'll get the most out of the Big Island by renting a car. Wheels are an absolute necessity if you're staying anywhere other than Kailua-Kona or a Kohala resort that you don't mind not leaving. In addition to state and national rental agencies, reliable local companies include **World Rent-A-Car** (329–1006), **Dream Cars Rent-A-Car** (326–5466), and **Rent & Drive** (329–3033), all in Kailua-Kona; and **Harper Car & Truck Rental** (969–1478) and **Phillip's U-Drive** (935–1936), both in Hilo.

Driving Tips: Since the island is so expansive, Big Islanders are used to spending a great deal of time behind their wheels. However, you may not be. When you're planning excursions, make sure you have a good idea of how long it will take you to get from point A to point B, especially if you don't want to be driving after dark. Even though you can certainly drive around the island in a single day, I don't recommend this exhausting endeavor. You'll have much more fun if you explore the Big Island in chunks over the course of several days. Note that Saddle Road, which cuts through Parker Ranch and connects Hilo with the Kona Coast, is best tackled in a four-wheel-drive vehicle.

By Bus: In Hilo, a shuttle runs between Banyan Drive hotels and the downtown area for about $1. Once in the morning and once in afternoon (every day except Sunday), the **Hele-On** bus takes people between Hilo and Kailua-Kona (about $7 each way).

TOURIST INFORMATION: Detailed maps and other information are available at Big Island branches of the **Hawaii Visitors Bureau** (75–5719 West Alii Dr., Kailua-Kona, HI 96740, (808) 329–7787 or 180 Kinoole St., suite 104, Hilo, HI 96720, (808) 961–5797). For questions about the Kohala Coast area, contact the **Kohala Coast Resort Association** (P.O. Box 5000, Kohala Coast, HI 96743-5000, (808) 885–4915). In Keauhou, call the **Keauhou Visitors Association** (78–6831 Alii Dr., suite 234, Kailua-Kona, HI 96740; (808) 322–3866).

RENTING VIDEO CAMERAS: To capture your vacation in action, try **Ohana Video** (329–0045) in Kailua-Kona or **Big Island Video** (935–9181) in Hilo.

POST OFFICES: To find out the location of the branch closest to you, call 329–1927 in Kailua-Kona and 935–2821 in Hilo.

EMERGENCY CASH: If you need to have cash wired to you from the mainland, contact **American Express** (885–7958 at the Hyatt Regency Waikoloa or 885–1209 at the Royal Waikoloan); or **Western Union** (329–1255 in Kailua-Kona).

TIME: Not that you should worry about this while you're on vacation, but, just in case, call 961–0212.

WEATHER: So that you can best plan your touring and activities, call 961–5582.

VOLCANO ACTION: For the latest on eruptions, call 967–7977.

ALCOHOLICS ANONYMOUS: Call 329–1212 in Kailua-Kona about participating in Big Island meetings.

WEIGHT WATCHERS: If you're interested in attending Big Island meetings, call 521–2113 on Oahu.

EMERGENCIES: Dial 911 or call the closest police station.

MEDICAL ATTENTION: In the Kailua-Kona area, contact **Kona Hospital** (Hwy. 11, Kealekekua; 322–9311). On the east coast, call **Hilo Hospital** (1190 Waianuenue Avenue; 969–4111).

MOLOKAI

Although Molokai is the closest Neighbor Island to Oahu, it couldn't possibly be more different. Lying about 25 miles across Kaiwi Channel, it is considered by many to be the most Hawaiian member of the archipelago. In part, this is because more than half of its 6500 residents are descendants of the original inhabitants of the island chain. But this perception is also due to Molokai's sleepy pace, the friendliness of its people, and its historic sights, such as ancient fishponds, crumbling *heiau* (temples), and legend-laden valleys. Hula is said to have been born on the slopes of Maunaloa, in the west, where the goddess Laka learned to dance. Almost a third of the local population turns out for the revival of the ancient Makahiki Festival each January, when competitions are held in traditional Hawaiian games. Although Molokai has a smattering of hotels and condominiums, residents have little use for the concept of tourism. No buildings rise higher than three stories and fast food chains, traffic lights, and shopping malls are all nonexistent. Kaunakakai, the only real town, consists of one main street lined with weathered single-story shops. Instead of Molokai molding itself to suit outsiders, visitors are happily absorbed into the gentle life of the island.

Molokai draws the adventurous traveler, the person who thrives on hiking, camping, or simply relaxing. A popular activity among visitors is the mule ride along a narrow cliffside trail down to Kalaupapa Peninsula, the site of Molokai's famed ''leper colony.'' Another excursion is the safari through Molokai Ranch Wildlife Preserve, where all kinds of East African and Asian animals roam freely across terrain that resembles Kenya and Tanzania. Many people also enjoy the bouncy horse-drawn wagon ride that includes stops at the island's largest heiau, a mango grove, and a beach for demonstrations in throwing Hawaiian fishing nets, husking coconuts, and creating traditional arts and crafts. Apart from swimming at some gorgeous west coast beaches, there's not much in the way of water sports here. Most of them small and unpretentious, restaurants are few and far between. Night life on this island means talking story with locals over a few beers or taking a drive to see the lights of Honolulu or Maui.

Just eight miles across the Pacific, the highrises of Maui's Kaana-

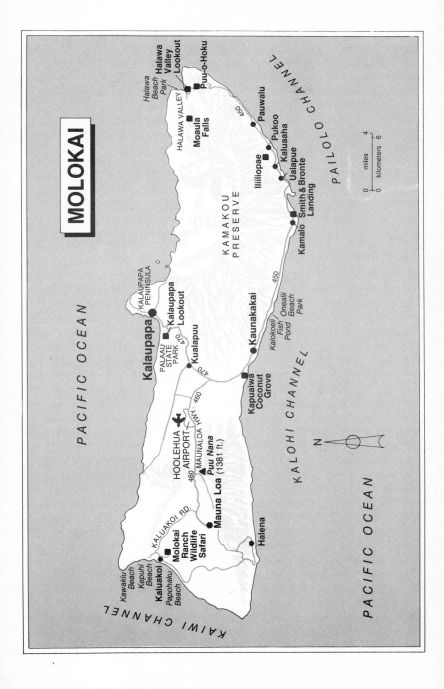

MOLOKAI

PACIFIC OCEAN

PAILOLO CHANNEL

Halawa Beach Park Halawa Valley Lookout

Puu-o-Hoku

HALAWA VALLEY

Moaula Falls

450

Pauwalu

Pukoo

Kaluaaha

Iliiliopae

Ualapue

Smith & Bronte Landing

KAMAKOU PRESERVE

Kamalo

450

KALAUPAPA PENINSULA

KALAUPAPA STATE PARK

Kalaupapa

Kalaupapa Lookout

PALAAU STATE PARK

470

Kualapuu

470

Kaunakakai

Kalokoeli Fish Pond

Onealii Beach Park

KALOHI CHANNEL

Kapuaiwa Coconut Grove

460

MAUNALOA HWY.

HOOLEHUA AIRPORT

Puu Nana (1381 ft.)

460

N

Mauna Loa

Halena

KALUAKOI RD.

Molokai Ranch Wildlife Safari

Kaluakoi

Kawakiu Beach
Kepuhi Beach
Papohaku Beach

KAIWI CHANNEL

PACIFIC OCEAN

PACIFIC OCEAN

0   miles   4
0 kilometers 6

pali Beach resort seem to be in another world. Part of Maui County, Molokai is Hawaii's fifth largest island. Lanai, eight miles to the south, is the only Hawaiian island with hotels that is less developed. A long, narrow strip of land some 261 square miles in size, Molokai was formed by two main volcanoes. Mauna Loa stands 1381 feet tall in the parched and prairie-like west while 4970 foot Kamakou soars in the jungled east. Also lush, the north shore is treated to some 245 inches of annual rainfall, which has created magnificent ravines. Clouds cling to multi-hued mountainsides. Where the elements have cracked the earth apart, gashes of red dirt peer through the green. At the bottom of a 1600-foot cliff, huge, pancake-flat Kalaupapa Peninsula seems to be a geologic afterthought. East of here, a two-mile hiking trail in flourishing Halawa Valley leads to a pool fed by towering waterfalls. While you're taking in Molokai's vivid scenery, you'll see few other cars. The fire hydrants along the country roads seem an intrusion in such pristine surroundings.

The Way It Was

Perhaps Molokai's refreshing lack of development has its roots in history. For the most part, foreign explorers left the island alone. Captain Cook, who brought Hawaii to the attention of the Western world in 1778, bypassed the island altogether. It wasn't until 1786 that a British captain (George Dixon) became the first foreigner whom island residents had ever met. After that, Molokai was again left undisturbed by outsiders, until 1832 when a group of American Protestants established a mission. Then in 1848, King Kamehameha III ordered the Great Mahele land division. In a break with tradition, land could now be owned by individuals as private property. German immigrant Rudolph Meyer got busy, buying large tracts that he turned into grazing areas for cattle and sheep. By the 1870s, King Kamehameha V had purchased much of this property, which became known as Molokai Ranch. In 1898, a group of Honolulu businessmen bought the ranch and tried to change it into a sugar plantation. They might have been successful, had it not been for the salty irrigation water.

In the early 1900s, Charles M. Cooke, a member of one of Hawaii's leading haole families, turned the land back into the cattle ranch it is today. For a time, Molokai Ranch also processed honey, and the island became one of its leading producers in the world. During the 1920s, Libby and Del Monte leased sections of the land and pineapple plantations flourished at the hands of Japanese and Filipino immigrant workers. The plantation towns of Maunaloa and Kualapuu were born. Then in the 1970s, the pineapple industry began to die on Molokai. Ironically, this was because owners had found that doing business in places such as the Philippines itself was far more profitable than having Filipinos and others work in Hawaii. Although pineapple is still the island's main agricultural product, many residents now commute by ferry to jobs in Maui's resorts.

Hawaiian Roots

There is a strong dedication to traditional Hawaiian religion on Molokai, often whether or not people also practice Western religion. Many heiau dot the landscape. Some are among the largest in the state. One of them, Iliʻiliʻopaʻe is included in the Molokai Wagon Ride tour. Toward the end of the 1500s, Lanikaula, a renowned *kahuna* (priest), was so revered that people came from all over Hawaii to ask his help in solving their problems. Kawelo, a jealous colleague from Lanai, decided to do away with Lanikaula by using sorcery. Molokai's kahuna discovered the plot, but only in time to make arrangements with his sons to hide his bones. This way, no one would be able to steal his powers. A kukui grove was planted near the place by Halawa Valley where the bones were thought to be buried. Even though the trees are now dying, the land is considered extremely sacred by contemporary Hawaiians. On several occasions during the 1980s, protests forced condominium developers who wanted to build at other sacred sites to give up their plans.

Although Polynesian settlers imported the friendly aloha spirit to Hawaii when they arrived over a millenium ago, warfare was commonplace among ancient Hawaiians. Thus every year, the four-month Makahiki festival marked a merry cease fire. This time of peace honoring the god Lono was celebrated with unbridled feasting and battles of a good natured sort. Today on Molokai, the two-day revival of this festival takes place every January in Kaunakakai Park. While the event draws a couple thousand residents, it is not well known among outsiders. The best of Hawaii's musicians and singers are brought over to perform along with top *hula halau* (hula schools). Church groups prepare kalua pig, raw and stewed fish, and all kinds of other food. Everyone is invited to help themselves. Mixed among the shorts and T-shirts in the crowd are men wearing *malo* (loincloths) and women in *paʻu* (wraparound skirts or dresses).

The celebration opens when schoolchildren march into the park displaying the traditional banners of various island districts. The star banner, draped with feather and fern leis, honors Lono, the god of fertility. As the chanting and hula begin, youngsters fidget in anticipation of the highlight of the day: competitions in Hawaiian games. Several hundred children and adults form teams to compete in *ulu maika* (lawn bowling), *ʻoʻo ihe* (spear hurling), *kukini* (foot races), *pohaku* (throwing a weighty rock), and *haka moa* (wrestling in a circle with one foot tied). From 9 to 11 a.m. of the first full day, visiting adults may sign up to participate.

Getting Around

Most visitors land at Hoolehua Airport, near the center of the island. Shuttle vans operate between the airport and hotels and condos in the Kaluakoi resort in the northwest and Kaunakakai on the southern coast. Taxis are also available. A few flights from Honolulu land at remote Kalaupapa Peninsula, which travelers are only allowed to visit through a pre-arranged tour. The *Maui Princess,* a ferry, brings people across from Maui. Ranging from seven to 10 miles wide and about 38 miles long, Molokai is best explored in a rental car, which you can pick up at the airport if you've made prior arrangements. It's difficult to get lost on this island, since main roads aren't plentiful. Just watch out for the mongooses, fond of dashing across the road in front of moving vehicles. Several van tour companies will be happy to show you the sights when you don't feel like driving.

If you'd like to see Kalaupapa Peninsula and don't want to get there on the back of a mule, you can fly in directly from Honolulu. However, you will have to make arrangements beforehand to meet one of the organized tours of the peninsula.

Kaunakakai, Central Molokai, and the North

Watched over by mountains, rustic **Kaunakakai** (pronounced *cow*-nah-cock-eye), is where you'll find what little action there is on the island. Studded with parked pick-up trucks, Ala Malama Street, the main drag, is barely two blocks long. You won't see traffic lights here or anywhere else on the island, but you will see bushy palms whose fronds rustle over telephone wires. Also bordering the street are low wooden general stores, a couple of restaurants, a post office, and a courthouse in a former Catholic church. Few people pass through town without stopping at **Kanemitsu Bakery,** a Molokai institution. Get there early, before the best goodies are snapped up. Deep-sea fishing boats leave from nearby **Kaunakakai Wharf,** which is often piled with watermelons, honey, and other goods ready for export. Just west of town along the main road, you'll come to **Kapuaiwa Grove.** These neat rows of coconut palms were planted (and nicknamed) for Prince Lot, a Molokai resident who went on to become King Kamehameha V. Planted during the mid-1800s, this is one of Hawaii's few remaining royal coconut groves. Across the street, a handful of late 19th century houses of worship stand along picturesque **Church Row.** Their simple architecture reflects the plain lifestyles of Hawaii's early missionaries.

Curving north toward central Molokai, Maunaloa Highway leads to a road that will take you to the plantation town of **Kualapuu** (''sweet potato hill''). Prosperous during the heyday of pineapple, this quiet town hit a serious slump when Del Monte pulled out in the early 1980s after nearly 50 years. The huge rubber-lined reservoir you can see from the road was built to irrigate the pineapple fields that still sprawl across the land. The nine-hole Ironwood Golf Course is nearby. North of town, the tiny A-frame shelters are used to raise fighting cocks. Although this bloody sport is illegal throughout the state, it is one of the island's most popular leisure activities.

The town of **Hoolehu** and neighboring Palaau were declared Hawaiian Homestead land in the 1920s. This means that people of Hawaiian ancestry are entitled to lease agricultural lots at little cost. However, the dry terrain and scarce water for irrigation forced farmers to lease their land to large pineapple companies, until this practice was declared illegal. After the reservoir was built during the 1960s, conditions improved. Near the airport, **Purdy's Nuts** (open 9 a.m.–1 p.m.) specializes in macadamias grown in a family-run grove. A tour of the macadamia nut farm (567–6601) includes cracking and tasting the roasted nuts, sampling fresh local fruit and honey, and stringing leis from fresh flowers. Since 1980, Tuddie Purdy has run this grove with his mother. The processing of nuts is completely natural. North of Hoolehua, near Palaau State Park, residential **Kalae** was once the homestead land of King Kamehameha V. No one could set foot on the premises without royal permission. The one-story homes are gaily painted light blue, turquoise, pale green, and yellow. You may see a striking cluster of tall trees in the area. This is the cemetery of Rudolph Meyer, the 19th-century German immigrant who bought so much Molokai Ranch land. He married a Hawaiian chieftess, Dorcas Kalama Waha, with whom he raised eleven children. Until his death in 1897, he served as manager of the ranch under the ownership of Kamehameha V, Bernice Pauahi Bishop, Charles Reed Bishop, and the Bishop Estate.

Palaau State Park is ideal for camping. Walk barefoot through the ironwood forest on a carpet of pine needles along a trail that leads to **Kauleonanahoa**. Also known as **Phallic Stone,** this huge rock points skyward. It has been shaped by the elements—with a little help from human hands, no doubt. In the old days, women who hadn't been successful in becoming pregnant would sit on the rock in an attempt to awaken their fertility. Follow the trail to **Kalaupapa Lookout,** backed by thick pines. This fabulous view takes in the ocean lapping at the huge tongue of the peninsula whose true name is Makanalua. People suffering from Hansen's Disease (leprosy) were once banished to this site cut off from the rest of the island by nearly vertical cliffs. Although they are no longer forced to live here, a few of the last members of the community have chosen to remain. Some conduct tours for visitors who come down the 1600 foot cliff on mules or swoop down in planes.

Western Molokai

West of Kaunakakai, past Kapuaiwa Grove and Church Row, the road climbs, then descends to the isolated town of **Maunaloa**. The brief main street of this former plantation settlement sports a few worthwhile artsy stores, including the amusing Big Wind Kite Factory. Past the turnoff for Kaluakoi Resort and at the end of the highway, this town was built in 1923 by the Libby corporation to house its pineapple plantation workers and management. Red dirt picks up where the paved road leaves off. The small, brown wooden pre-fab homes came all the way from the mainland. Libby pulled up stakes in 1975. Today most of the residents are the last of the Filipino and Japanese laborers, some of whom have turned to tourism for work.

In days gone by, the forests of Maunaloa volcano were filled with ohia trees. When the bright red blossoms were strung into a lei, it was believed that love was sure to follow. Kaana, on the slopes of the mountain, is where tradition says the goddess Laka learned the hula. The only reason it is performed anywhere outside of Molokai today is that Laka traveled throughout the archipelago and taught the special meaning-laden dance to as many people as she could. Perched atop a hill, **Maunaloa Piko Stone** is where the umbilical cords (piko) of babies born nearby were placed to guarantee a prosperous, happy life.

While many ancient Hawaiians saw Molokai as a religious sanctuary, others were kept away be frightening tales of island sorcery. The poisonwood gods it was known for first presented themselves at an ulu maika (stone bowling) course at Maunaloa. Among the men betting on the stone discs as they rolled them, Kaneiakama was losing badly. A god appeared to him, advising him to increase his wagers. Grateful when he won, he gave a large portion of his winnings to the god. In a flash a grove of trees appeared. Becoming their caretaker, Kaneiakama discovered that when the wood was whittled into images, it could have devastating effects on enemies. Molokai was thus able to keep hostile outsiders at bay.

Along beautiful, white **Kepuhi Beach,** the **Kaluakoi Resort** has just one hotel (the island's nicest) and a couple of condominiums. The golf course borders the stretch of sand, which is watched over by impressive Kaiaka Rock at its southern end. Just north is lovely, historic **Kawakiu Beach**. Long before the arrival of Europeans, people fished and made fishhooks and adzes in a settlement here. However, once Kamehameha V got hold of the land for ranching, commoners could no longer freely use the area. Now a beach park, the archeological sites are being preserved, including house platforms and other ruins. To the south, three-mile white sand **Papohaku Beach** is one of the most attractive in the state.

After the death of Kamehameha V in 1873, Molokai Ranch lands passed on to Princess Bernice Pauahi Bishop, whose husband built Honolulu's Bishop Museum in her honor. Today the ranch sprawls over some 50,000 acres, 1000 of which are taken up by the **Molokai Ranch Wildlife Preserve**. Photo safaris to see zebra, giraffe, and other unlikely animals can be arranged through the Kaluakoi Hotel.

Eastern Molokai

East of Kaunakakai, **Pau Hana Inn, Molokai Shores** condo, and Polynesian-style **Hotel Molokai** sit along the coast. **Kalokoeli Fishpond** is among a mere handful of ponds that remain out of more than 60 that once bordered the southern shore. Many of them were constructed during the 13th century. These rocky walls enclosed fish so that they could be fattened up while being protected from all but human predators. When they were plump enough, they were netted for the alii. Impromptu concerts, beach parties, and other frivolity often takes place at **Onealii Beach Park**. There are some beautiful wooden homes in this area. If you drive *mauka* (inland) up to arid Cavella Plantations, a residential development, you'll have a great view of the fish pond down below.

On the *makai* (ocean) side of the road at Kamalo, watch for the **Smith and Bronte Monument** that honors Ernest Smith and Emory Bronte. On their way from California to Honolulu, the pair survived the crash landing of the world's first transpacific flight in 1927. Nearby is **St. Joseph's Catholic Church,** built in 1876 by Damien Joseph De Veuster, famous for his selfless work with victims of Hansen's Disease who had been banished to Kalaupapa Peninsula. Father Damien, as he was better known, also served as pastor to the rest of the island. A few miles further down the road, he also built **Our Lady of Sorrows,** which stands behind a tall wooden cross planted in the spacious lawn. In the background looms majestic Mt. Kamakou, Molokai's tallest mountain. From the waterfront, you can gaze across to Maui and Lanai. Just east of Kamalo on the mauka side of the road, **Iliʻiliʻopaʻe Heiau** remains one of the largest and most sacred ancient temples in the state.

Between Kamalo and Pukoo, you'll pass **Wavecrest** condominium. The surrounding vegetation is extremely lush in this area, and craggy mountains soar on the left. The road narrows and the greenery becomes increasingly thick, with banana trees and palms along the coast in the Pukoo area. Run by a Filipino family, the **Neighborhood Store and Snack Bar** in Pukoo has a captive market since it's the only place to buy food or a drink from here until the end of the road at Halawa Valley Lookout. You'll pass a modern house in the shape of a geodesic dome. More trees appear, each one taller than the last, with vines clothing the entire length of their trunks. Keep an eye out for Chevy and Nova, two old cars that have become flourishing planters in the front yard of a home. Locals will tell you that the parents of the family named two of their children after the autos because that's where the youngsters got their start in life. There is good swimming as well as camping at sandy **Waialua Beach**. Nearby you might come to a self-service stand piled with fresh fruit—simply leave your money in a box. In little tent-like shelters, fighting cocks are raised in this area.

Once you see **Murphy's Beach,** you'll begin climbing uphill on a narrow, winding road through **Puʻu O Hoku**. From here you'll have spectacular views of the rocky shoreline, crashing waves, and endless greenery, including tall stands of bamboo. At **Rock Point,** a fishing and surfing area, rugged outcroppings stand like huge anthills along the coast. Soon the eye takes in rolling hills and verdant open land. Finally, you reach dramatic **Halawa Valley Overlook**. Historians believe the **Halawa Valley** is Molokai's oldest settlement, dating back to about 650 A.D. Few people have lived here since the massive tidal wave swept through in 1946, destroying both homes and crops. Just before the road begins to dip into the valley, the grove of kukui nut trees stands in memory of Lanikaula, the beloved kahuna. This is the most sacred part of the whole island. Many hikers rave about the forested coastal trek into the valley. They explore well-preserved house platforms, agricultural terraces, garden walls, and religious structures. The two-mile trail leads to twin **Moaula Falls**. Tradition demands that people determine whether it's safe to swim in the inviting pool at its base by tossing in a ti leaf. If it floats, jump on in. If it sinks to the bottom, this means that the water spirits feel like claiming a victim. The wide stream that once fed the valley's farms meanders through the lush greenery before pouring into the ocean. This shore was once a favorite surfing spot among alii.

WHAT TO SEE AND DO

PERSONAL FAVORITES

Driving east of Kaunakakai to the **Halawa Valley Overlook,** passing dramatic and ever-changing vistas along the way. (See Molokai introductory section)

Attending the very local **Makahiki Festival,** the annual recreation of the ancient Hawaiian peace-time celebration, in January. (See Molokai Introductory section)

Riding a mule along the switchback trail down the 1600 foot cliff to **Kalaupapa Peninsula**—or at least spending a few moments at **Kalaupapa Lookout**. (See Tours and Sights)

Taking a guided hike through **Kamakou Preserve** (see Hiking and Camping in Sports)

Getting close-up views of exotic East African and Asian animals during a photo safari through **Molokai Ranch Wildlife Preserve** (See Sights and Tours)

~~~~~~

SIGHTS

Iliʻiliʻopaʻe Heiau • Hwy. 450, East Molokai • Constructed during the sixteenth century, this is the largest heiau in the state. It once sprawled over more than five acres. Honoring Hawaii's highest gods, its four terraces were 150 feet wide and 50 feet tall. The rocks used to built it were lugged all the way from the Wailau Valley, separated from this shore by a mountain. Human sacrifices were performed at this heiau. An old story tells of the cruel high chief who killed nine sons of a local resident in the name of the gods. The bereft father prayed to the powerful shark god that inhabited the island's north shore waters. Suddenly, the area was hit with a terrible storm accompanied by floods. The chief and his wicked followers were washed into the Pacific, where the sharks had a feast. Today people still leave stones wrapped in ti leaves as offerings after praying here. Since this heiau is extremely sacred and on private property, you must visit it either along with other sights during the **Molokai Wagon Ride** (see Tours and Cruises) or by requesting permission from Ms. Pearl Petro (P.O. Box 125, Kaunakakai, Molokai, HI 96748; enclose a stamped, self-addressed envelope).

Kalaupapa National Historic Park • *northern coast* • Its official name is Makanalua Peninsula, but it is more commonly called Kalaupapa. The tragedy and human triumph that made this peninsula famous began after the arrival of foreigners in Hawaii. Since the indigenous population had been without contact with outsiders for so many centuries, they had no natural immunities to the communicable diseases of other peoples. When Westerners arrived, bringing their new illnesses, Hawaiians were unable to combat these alien germs. Within a century after the arrival of haoles in 1778, the population had shrunk from some 300,000 to a mere 50,000. Hawaii's first known case of Hansen's Disease (leprosy) occurred during the 1840s. The frightfully disfiguring affliction was so contagious that King Kamehamameha V, thinking first and foremost of protecting the larger general population, began banishing the victims to Molokai's isolated Makanalua Peninsula.

Like the walls of a fortress, the 2000 foot cliffs that rise up from this large flat tongue of land quashed any notion of escape. So did the rough water that hurls itself against the glossy black lava rocks on all three sides of the peninsula. At over 3000 feet, some of the sea cliffs on the north shore are the tallest in the world. Treated like criminals, the exiles were not even provided with building materials or other supplies. They were forced to live out in the blazing sun by day or in the chilly air at night. Some found shelter under trees or in caves. Others fashioned makeshift driftwood huts. These houses were always in danger of being torn apart by a stronger person who decided to steal the wood for himself—unless of course the bully simply chose to evict the occupant. The small quantities of food sent from Honolulu caused many a vicious fight between the hungry, ailing, and embittered residents.

In the beginning, there wasn't even a dock at the peninsula. As boats neared the coast, ill passengers were thrust overboard and forced to swim ashore, clutching whatever belongings they could. Many didn't make it through the treacherous water. Ancient Hawaiians had farmed taro and sweet potatoes on this fertile land. However, because of the lawlessness and physical discomfort of the angry population, these victims of Hansen's Disease were not able to make even a half-decent life for themselves here. Many Hawaiians outside the peninsula tried in vain to hide the first signs of leprosy they noticed in themselves or in loved ones. Sometimes, so that they would not be forever separated from family members, healthy people exiled themselves along with their sick relatives.

When Father Damien de Veuster, a Catholic priest from Belgium, arrived in Kalaupapa in 1873, he planned to stay only a few months. But within two days he decided to remain indefinitely. He turned St. Philomena, a chapel that had been built by a visiting priest the year before, into a hospital until a permanent one could be built. He himself slept under a tree until every other resident had shelter. This tireless, self-sacrificing man built another church and served as a doctor, farmer, and gravedigger. In 1889, Father Damien died of Hansen's Disease. In April, 1989, on the 100th anniversary of his death, a week-long tribute to this revered priest took place in Hawaii. Today, leprosy can be treated with sulfone drugs and thus the disease is far less feared. Victims of the ailment are no longer forced to live here and almost all have gone elsewhere. Those who remain do so by choice, having known no other lifestyle since they were either born here or brought as young children. Residents give tours of the settlement to visitors who take the twisting, turning mule ride down the 1600 foot cliff or who arrive by plane or hike down. (See Tours and Cruises.)

Molokai Ranch Wildlife Safari ● *Kaluakoi, West Molokai; 552–2555* ● Resembling the plains of Kenya and Tanzania, this arid, flat, red-dirt expanse is home to hundreds of animals from East Africa and Asia. They were originally imported to control (by consumption) the scrub and brushes that were interfering with the ranch's cattle pastureland. In 1978, this 1000 acre region was opened to the public as a wildlife park. Bouncing along in a 14-passenger van, travelers can come eyeball-to-eyeball with quite a few exotic beasts, including eland, greater kudu, oryx, Indian black buck, sable antelope, axis deer, Barbary sheep, ostriches, a giraffe, and zebras. Some of the animals are fed by the park's caretakers while others are left completely wild.

Cost: $13 adults; $7 children under age 12. Four tours conducted daily.

TOURS AND CRUISES

Molokai has some of Hawaii's most unusual tours, from a ride in a horse-drawn wagon to a mule-back trip along a trail that snakes down a towering cliff.

BY VAN: Half- and full-day tours are arranged through **Gray Line Molokai** (567–6177) and **Roberts Hawaii** (552–2751). On the shorter excursion, stops include Kalaupapa Lookout, the Sugar Mill at Kalae, and a macadamia nut farm. The longer trip also introduces visitors to Kaluakoi Resort; the artsy crafts shops of Maunaloa town; Kaunakakai, with a lunch stop—for an additional charge—at oceanfront Hotel Molokai; and the gorgeous east coast up to Halawa Valley Overlook. You can be picked up at your hotel, or at the airport if you're flying in for the day. **Molokai Taxi** (552–0041) takes sightseers on four-wheel-drive tours to attractions that are only accessible by dirt road, such as the Sandlewood Pit, Moomomi Beach, and Waikoulu Lookout.

Whether you ride a mule down a cliff, fly, or hike into historic **Kalaupapa Peninsula,** you are required to join an organized ground tour. Contact Gray Line Hawaii, Roberts Hawaii, or **Damien Molokai Tours** (567–6171), which fly sightseers in and out for about $70 including the ground tour. Inquire about riding a mule down and flying out. (Also see By Mule.) To visit the **Molokai Ranch Wildlife Preserve,** contact the Kaluakoi Hotel (552–2555); see Sights for further details.

BY SEA: Fishing boats and pleasure cruises take off from Kaunakakai Wharf. For day trips to the island of Lanai, sunset sails, and winter whale watching excursions, try **Molokai Charters** (553–5852). The **Maui Princess** (553–5736 in Honolulu), the ferry that transports workers between Molokai and Maui, takes passengers on whale-watching trips in season.

BY HELICOPTER: Through **Pacific Aviation International** (567–6128 or (800) 245–9696), the exciting 40-minute North Shore flight takes sightseers over cliff-edged Kalaupapa Peninsula (about $100). Helicopters lift off from Hoolehua Airport.

BY MULE: For many vacationers, the most memorable part of their stay is the **Molokai Mule Ride** along the narrow zig-zag trail down a 1600 foot cliff to Kalaupapa Peninsula. Completed in 1887 and just over three miles long, the trail begins in Palaau State Park on the north shore. The sure-footed mules get riders down in about an hour and a half. Then a van tour is conducted by one of the last remaining residents of the community where people with Hansen's Disease (leprosy) were exiled before drugs were discovered to treat the illness. Sights include St. Philomena Church, which once served as a hospital; medical facilities; houses; graveyards; and the memorial to Father Damien, the 19th century Belgian priest who made such a difference in the lives of ailing residents until he himself contracted the disease and died. Cameras are welcome, but photos of residents are not allowed. Sightseers have a picnic lunch before returning on mule-back (or leaving by plane, if they have arranged to do so). Day trips from other islands can be easily worked out. Participants must be at least sixteen years old and must weigh no more than 225 pounds. Reservations should be made at least two weeks in advance, especially during the summer. Tours begin at 9 a.m. and return by about 4 p.m. Contact **Rare Adventures** (P.O. Box 200, Kualapuu, Molokai, HI 96757; 567–6088 or 567–6515 on Molokai; 537–1845 from Oahu; or (800) 843–5978 from the mainland).

BY WAGON: During the **Molokai Wagon Ride** (daytime: 558–8380; evening: 567–6773), vacationers step into the past at sacred Iliʻiliʻopaʻe heiau (see Sights) and visit Mapulehu, site of the world's largest mango grove. Its original trees, which came from Vietnam, Laos, and Cambodia, were planted around the 1930s by the Hawaii Sugar Planters Association. The company intended to market the mangoes. Unfortunately, in those days, not enough people had a taste for the sweet, juicy fruit. Now the demand is soaring in the U.S. as well as other parts of the world, such as Japan. The 2½ hour bouncy ride through the country-side also gives travelers a chance to sample freshly picked coconut, papayas, and pineapple. At the beach barbecue, everyone feasts on treats such a kiawe-grilled white fish or chicken with Hawaiian chili peppers, octopus, taro baked in coconut milk, purple sweet potatoes, and salad.

They learn songs, the hula, how to husk a coconut, and the correct way to cast a fishing net. *Cost: $28 per person.*

ON FOOT: Filled with rare birds and other native wildlife, indigenous trees, unusual plants, and thriving ohia forests, **Kamakaou Preserve** is a must for lovers of the outdoors. Arrange an escorted day-long hike by contacting the **Nature Conservancy of Hawaii** (1116 Smith St., suite 201, Honolulu, HI 96817, 537–4508); or the Kamakou Preserve Manager (P.O. Box 40, Honolulu, Molokai, HI 96757, 576–6680). Bring your own picnic lunch and drinking water. The guide will meet your flight if you're coming for the day from Honolulu. Reservations must be made several months in advance.

(Also see Hiking and Camping in Sports)

BEACHES

Molokai's best beaches lie along the west coast, with views of Oahu in the distance. This is where you'll find Popohaku, the largest white sand beach in the state. However, during the winter, when waves grow their tallest, it's best to stick to the sand on this coast. The narrow south shore beaches that run past hotels and condos in the Kaunakakai area aren't as pretty, but their waters remain more placid year round. Here are Molokai's most appealing sandy stretches:

Po'olau Beach • *about a half mile past the Kaluakoi Resort* • Locals sometimes fish from surf boards off this inviting white shore. The waves are often good for surfing. A pleasant setting for camping out, this beach has a view that reaches all the way to Kaneohe, 35 miles away on Oahu, when the sky is clear.

Kawakiu Beach Park • *northern part of Kaluakoi Resort* • Good swimming conditions and intriguing archeological ruins make this attractive beach worth visiting. In ancient times, a Hawaiian settlement was built at this site. The hotel's outdoor showers come in handy.

Kepuhi Beach • *Kaluakoi Resort* • There's a constant breeze at this half-mile stretch of white sand that individual hotel guests often have to themselves. Be careful during the winter, when the waves are roughest.

Papohaku Beach • *two miles from the Kaluakoi Resort* • Enclosed by rugged lava flows, this broad, three-mile strip is Hawaii's most expansive white sand beach. Wells were once dug for the freshwater that gets trapped in the rocky outcroppings in back of the sand. A small fishing village once stood at this site and old stones used to grind adzes have been discovered nearby. You may not notice that anything is missing, but during the 1950s sand was taken from here and shipped to Oahu to be used in construction. Picnic facilities and a restroom are provided.

Pohakuloa Beach • *about 1½ miles past Papohaku Beach, West Molokai* • This tranquil cove is especially popular on weekends, particularly among families. However, on Molokai, there is no such thing as a crowded beach. Swimming is excellent most of the year. An outdoor shower is on the grounds.

Onealii Beach Park • *off Hwy. 450 on the south shore, near Hotel Molokai* • While cooling off in calm waters, you'll gaze across to the islands of Lanai and Maui. Although the shore is narrow here, this is the most appealing of the south shore beaches, where nature has been stingy with the sand. Tree-shaded picnic tables, outdoor showers, and rest rooms make this a good choice if you're staying in the area.

Halawa Beach Park • *at eastern end of Hwy. 450* • Way at the far eastern end of the island, a dip at this beach is a bonus after the spectacular snaking drive through this lush region. This crescent was once favored by Hawaiian royalty for surfing. Don't even go near the water during the winter, when currents are extremely dangerous. However, during the summer, swimming is usually fine. Even when you're not swimming, the setting is wonderful, so take advantage of the picnic facilities. Outdoor showers mean you don't have to feel gritty during the return drive.

SPORTS

Various activities can be arranged through the Kaluakoi Hotel & Golf Club and Hotel Molokai.

FISHING: Locals often cast lines from Kaunakakai Wharf, in the evening after the boats have stopped loading. Fall and winter are the peak fishing seasons at Halawa Beach County Park. There's some great fishing along Molokai's cliff-edged north shore. Call **Molokai Fish and Dive** (553–5926) about setting up charters for deep-sea excursions.

Sometimes visitors share trips with locals. You can also charter a boat through **Alele II Charters** (558–8266 or 558–8319) or work something out with a captain at Kaunakakai Wharf.

GOLF: The 18-hole championship **Kaluakoi Golf Course** (552–2739 or 552–2555) runs along the beach in West Molokai.

HIKING AND CAMPING: A guided hike through **Kamakou Preserve** will surround you with some of Molokai's most unhampered beauty. So as not to disturb nature at its most natural, you'll move through the rain forest along a groaning wooden boardwalk. Rare and indigenous flora and fauna thrive here. You might spot birds such as an *olomao* (Molokai thrush) or a *kakawahie* (Molokai creeper), which survives nowhere in the world except in this preserve. The topography spans the spectrum from rain forest to alpine bog. At the top of the mountain, red-blossomed ohia trees grow a mere four inches off the ground.

Before you arrive, the jeep will pass the **Sandlewood Pit,** a deep hole in the ground. It was dug to equal the size of a ship's hull. As soon as it was full, workers could lug the sweet-smelling wood down from the mountains to the next ship in line to carry this cargo to China. Unfortunately, since this business was so lucrative, Hawaii's sandlewood forests were completely denuded. In addition, this work was so arduous and laborers were forced to leave their families for such long periods that many of them tore up seedlings to diminish the growth of new trees. The entrance to Kamakou Preserve is at the **Waikolu Valley Lookout,** which opens up views of waterfalls, jungled vegetation, and the ocean in the distance. Make reservations for escorted hikes at least two months in advance by contacting the **Nature Conservancy of Hawaii** (1116 Smith St., suite 201, Honolulu, HI 96817; 537–4508); or the **Kamakou Preserve Manager** (P.O. Box 40, Kualapuu, Molokai, HI 96757, 576–6680).

Halawa Valley is another good hiking area. Be sure to take the 2-mile trail to Moaula Falls, which has a refreshing swimming hole. The trail cuts through a forest thick with guava and avocado trees and the perfume of wild ginger blossoms. Molokai's official campgrounds are at **Poʻolau Beach,** about a half mile from Kaluakoi Resort in the northwest. Camping permits must be obtained from **County Parks, Division of Parks and Recreation** (Kaunakakai, HI 96748; 553–5141).

HORSEBACK RIDING: Arrange to jump in the saddle by contacting the folks who organize the **Molokai Wagon Ride** (daytime: 558–8380; evenings: 567–6773)

MULE RIDING: See Tours and Cruises.

SAILING: For sightseeing day-sails, snorkeling or whale watching excursions, inter-island trips, and overnight cruises, contact **Whistling Swan Charters** (553–5238). Sailing lessons are also available. Inquire about other boats at Kaunakakai Wharf.

SCUBA DIVING AND SNORKELING: The **Kaluakoi Hotel** (552–2555), **Hotel Molokai** (242–8775), and **Molokai Fish and Dive** (553–5926) rent gear. (Also see Sailing.)

SPECTATOR SPORT: Join the crowd watching the commencement of the **Molokai to Oahu Canoe Race** (525–5476) on the southwest coast. Women paddle the outriggers more than 25 miles across far-from-smooth Kaiwi Channel in September, while men test their skills in October.

TENNIS: You'll find courts at the **Kaluakoi Resort** (552–2555).

SHOPPING

Although stores are certainly scarce on the island, there's a collection of imaginative shops in the small, red dirt town of Maunaloa, about seven miles from the Kaluakoi Resort in West Molokai. Here are some of my favorite places to spend money:

CRAFTS: Just next door to the famed Big Wind Kite Factory in Maunaloa, the **Plantation Gallery** stocks Bali imports, jewelry, unusual wood carvings, batiks, mobiles, and paintings by local artists. For more sculpture, bowls, and other carvings made from native wood, try **Tao Woodcarver** (552–2887) also in Maunaloa.

FRUIT AND SPICES: The **Spice Farm,** run by Grant Shule and Julie Lopez, and **Bill's Farm** are both located in Molokai Agricultural Park, in Hoolehua near the airport. These huge red dirt plantations are great places to shop for Hawaiian bananas, which are sweeter and more flavorful than the mainland variety, Hawaiian watermelon, other fruits, vegetables, and freshly prepared spices.

HAWAIIAN QUILTS: **Erline McGuire** (558–8347) charges about $2000 to $4000 for a commissioned king- or queen-sized quilt. These missionary-inspired Hawaiian bedcovers are intricately and expertly produced and will last for countless generations.

KITES: **The Big Wind Kite Factory** (552–2364) in Maunalao town is worth some time whether or not you're in the market for something to fly. Run by former comedy writer Jonathan Socher, this shop sells kites handmade on the premises, as well as Indonesian imports. Visitors are welcome to watch the craftspeople in action at the back of the store. Socher's wife, Daphne, does the graphic designs. Edges are welded so that they don't fray and all are quality controlled. There are signed and limited edition kites, mini-kites, windrocks, endangered animal species kites, hula girl kites, teddy bear kites, 2-string controllable kites, and exotic kites from Bali made with carved styrofoam. No two are exactly alike. Prices run from about $13 to $250. Custom-designed kites are also available.

MACADAMIA NUTS: For some truly fresh-roasted nuts, stop by **Purdy's Macadamia Nut Grove** (567–6601 or 567–6495), a family-run business on Hawaiian Homestead land in Hoolehua. No preservatives are used in the preparation of the nuts. Take a tour of the island's only working macadamia farm.

T-SHIRTS AND WATER SPORTS GEAR: In Maunaloa, the **Red Dirt Shirt Shop** (552–2470) is the place to go for T-shirts and beach cover-ups in winning, original designs. Another extensive T-shirt collection resides in an unlikely locale: **Molokai Fish & Dive** (553–5926) in Kaunakakai, which sells an eclectic mix of merchandise. It is owned by Jim Brocker, a bird enthusiast who boasts his own aviary of over 100 exotic birds and shares his store with more than a few of his favorites. Besides parrots and T-shirts, you'll find unusual souvenirs and water sports equipment.

NIGHT LIFE

Action after dark centers around the hotels, where dinner conversation and talking story over drinks is about all there is to do. Local newspapers will announce any community dances or church fundraisers that might be taking place. Playing mainly Top 40 tunes, live bands coax diners onto the dance floor at the Ohia Room, adjoining the main restaurant at the **Kaluakoi Resort,** from 6:30 to 9:30 every evening. Each night, free movies (no, they're not first-run) are shown to Kaluakoi guests in the rec room. You can also listen to music at **Pau Hana Inn,** in Kaunakakai, where the mellow sounds of Sunday to Thursday (6:30–9 p.m.) give way to the danceable beats of Friday and Saturday (9 p.m.–1 a.m.). Loosely translated, "pau hana" means "quittin' time," and this hotel is exactly where many locals go for happy hour when they are done with work. Informal hula shows are occasionally hosted at **Hotel Molokai,** where people sip drinks by the pool under the stars. During dinner here, guests sometimes find themselves part of the live entertainment.

CULINARY MOLOKAI

If you're into unpretentious restaurants that serve as local social centers, and enjoy homestyle food from a variety of ethnic backgrounds, then Molokai is your island. Hawaiian saimin, poi, and plate lunches, Filipino stews, Chinese chicken with cashew nuts, Korean ribs, New York strip steak—it's all here. The smallest and least expensive eateries line Ala Malama Street in Kaunakakai. The food at the Kaluakoi Hotel's **Ohia Lodge** and Hotel Molokai's **Holo Holo Kai** might not win any awards, but it's perfectly satisfying. Be sure to try some **Molokai bread,** which you can buy fresh from the oven at **Kanemitsu Bakery** in Kaunakakai. You might want to slather a slice with **Kamalo Kiawe Honey,** which gets its special flavor from bees that feed on kiawe trees.

West Molokai

JoJo's Cafe • *Maunaloa Town; 552–2803* • Known for its good home cooking and friendly atmosphere, this restaurant is run by Jojo Espaniola, with more than a little help from her family. Its Korean ribs and marlin burgers cater to the finger-licking crowd. Some folks say this is the place to try your first bowl of real saimin, the cross-cultural soup of egg noodles topped with scallions and shrimp, chicken, beef, or fish cake in a delicately seasoned broth. The homemade passionfruit sundae is a don't miss. *(Inexpensive)*

Ohia Lodge • *Kaluakoi Hotel; 552–2555* • Try to be seated by the tall, wood-framed glass doors or large windows that are open to the outdoor patio overlooking the ocean. Serving continental cuisine, this is

Molokai's most upscale restaurant—actually it's the island's *only* upscale restaurant. Don't eat too much at the salad bar, or you won't have room for the beef broccoli, seafood tempura, filet mignon, or one of the other dinner entrees. The desserts, including pies, cakes, and ice cream, are also worth a corner of your stomach. In the adjoining Ohia Room, a live band plays from 6:30 p.m. to 9:30 p.m. *Reservations recommended. A, V, M, D, C. (Moderate)*

Kaunakakai Area

Pau Hana Inn • *Kamehameha Hwy., south shore; 553–5342* • A short walk from Kaunakakai, the restaurant at the island's oldest hotel draws a very local crowd. There's a little-used fireplace in this al fresco dining room that looks out to the water. Teriyaki steak is on the menu along with such mainland favorites as barbecued ribs, broiled fish, and honey-dipped chicken. *A, V, M, D. (Inexpensive)*

Holo Holo Kai • *Hotel Molokai, south shore; 553–5347* • Order beef stew and you can try it with poi, that Hawaiian staple made from pounded, fermented taro root. This gooey, porridge-like dish eaten with the fingers is an acquired taste for many outsiders, but locals love it. You can make an entire meal out of the soup and salad bar, with some fresh Molokai bread on the side. Sauteed mahimahi, teriyaki chicken, and shrimp tempura are other good choices for dinner. Papaya pancakes move quickly at breakfast and Portuguese bean soup, made with sausage, is a hot item at lunch. In a casual beachfront setting at a Polynesian-style hotel, this open-air restaurant is not far from the center of Kaunakakai. *A, V, M, D. (Inexpensive)*

Kanemitsu Bakery • *Ala Malama St., Kaunakakai; 533–5855* • The only bakery in town, Kanemitsu is famous for its unusual breads. Choose among raisin nut, cheese, onion cheese, brown wheat, and French Molokai. Be sure to put your order in early. Two thousand loaves are baked here each day, but they are often sold out within an hour and a half of the bakery's 5:30 a.m. opening! The delicious Mexican butternut, sesame, and macadamia nut cookies are also baked fresh daily. The diner-style restaurant is open from 5:30 a.m. to 2 p.m., then again from 5 p.m. to 9:30 p.m. Try the banana hotcakes, the cheese omelette served with rice or toast, or the hamburger deluxe. *(Inexpensive)*

Oviedo's • *Ala Malama St., Kaunakakai; 553–5014* • The Filipino food served here for lunch and dinner is cooked with home-grown herbs and spices. *Adobos* (stews), the main attraction, are made with turkey tail, beef, pig's feet, or mongo beans. Order a mixed plate and your entree will come with rice and vegetables. Oviedo's has Molokai's best selection of ice cream, including butter brickle, rocky road, and mint chocolate chip. *(Inexpensive)*

Mid-Nite Inn • *Ala Malama St., Kaunakakai; 553–5302* • Easily the most popular place to eat on Molokai, this restaurant began as a saimin stand back in the 1930s. Ms. Hisae Kikukawa, who ran it then, would often keep it open late so that the men unloading steamships at Kaunakakai harbor and people waiting to leave on the midnight inter-island ferry could have a late meal. However, despite its name, the Mid-Nite Inn now closes around 9 at night, except on Sundays when it stays open only until 12:30 p.m. Three meals a day are served here. Start the morning with pancakes, French toast, or corned beef hash and eggs. Freshly caught fish is the specialty of the house. For lunch and dinner, try kiawe-grilled *ahule* (big-eyed shad), *opakapaka* (pink snapper), or *aku* (skipjack tuna), or breaded mahimahi. The teriyaki pork and breaded pork cutlet are also popular. Side dishes include *kim chee* (spicy Korean-style cabbage) and *cha wun* (a rice dish). No liquor is served, but patrons are welcome to bring their own. *(Inexpensive)*

Hop Inn • *Ala Malama St., Kaunakakai; 553–5465* • Among the items on the menu at this brightly lit Chinese-American restaurant are sweet and sour pork, squid with vegetables, chicken with cashews, tofu with vegetables, and hearty saimin. Portions are quite healthy, so bring a good appetite. Check out the merchandise at the check-out counter, which includes sandlewood-, jasmine-, and rose-scented soaps. *(Inexpensive)*

WHERE TO SLEEP ON MOLOKAI

Casual is the word that best describes both the accommodations and the friendly service at the few hotels and condominiums on Molokai. Formerly a Sheraton and spread along a beautiful beach in the west, the low-rise **Kaluakoi Hotel & Golf Club** is the only large hotel on the island. Although the beach is narrow and nothing to look at, the Polynesian architecture of **Hotel Molokai,** near town, reflects the warm aloha spirit that surrounds guests there. Crowds on Molokai just don't exist, so the whole island is a good place for escape. But if absolute seclusion is what you have in mind, eastern Molokai offers a handful of condos, bed & breakfasts, and private cottages. Note that these accommodations may require that you stay a minimum number of nights. With limited stock, grocery stores on Molokai are few and far between, so you would do well to bring at least some food with you if you plan to do any cooking. For information about B&Bs and cottages in addition to those recommended below, contact **Bed & Breakfast Hawaii** (P.O. Box 449, Kapaa, Kauai, HI 96746; (808)822–7771 or (800)657–7832).

West Molokai

☆☆☆ **Kaluakoi Hotel and Golf Club** • *Kaluakoi Resort* • Although this resort is now run by Colony Hotels, many residents (even some employees) still refer to it as the Sheraton it once was. The two-story buildings and beachfront 18-hole championship golf course are spread across 130 acres. Palm-edged Kepuhi Beach, with low lava cliffs at one end, borders the fairway. Unfortunately, the water is usually too rough for swimming, but there is a pool on the premises and calmer beaches are not far. The resort also has a Jacuzzi and four Laykold tennis courts. Wild turkeys and deer roam around the fringes of the property. Since the well-maintained grounds, sprouting palms and bougainvillea, are so wonderfully spacious, visitors sometimes get the feeling that they have the place to themselves. However, don't expect swanky decor in the guest rooms. Some with twin beds, they are modestly furnished with wood veneer dressers and tables. Lamps give off dim light. TVs are provided and rooms come with kitchenettes (guests are asked to wash dishes upon departure). Lanais are a good size for pleasant relaxation. The only problem is, some ground floor oceanfront rooms face the fairway, so passing golf carts can interfere with privacy. *(Moderate to Expensive)*

☆☆☆ **Ke Nani Kai** • *Kaluakoi Resort* • Near the Kaluakoi Hotel, this condominium offers one- and two-bedroom units, each with a full kitchen and washer/dryer. Furnished in rattan and wicker, the pleasant rooms open onto lanais. Telephones can be provided upon request. The two-story buildings overlook the golf course and colorful gardens. Tennis courts, a swimming pool, and a Jacuzzi are among the other facilities. The beach, which can be seen from some rooms, is about a five-minute walk away. *(Moderate to Expensive)*

★★★ **Paniolo Hale** • *Kaluakoi Resort* • The golf course runs between these one- and two-story condominium buildings and the beach. All of the brightly furnished studios, one-, and two-bedroom apartments have full kitchens and lanais. A couple even come with private hot tubs (guests are charged extra for heating, though). Views take in the ocean and lush gardens. In addition to a swimming pool and paddle tennis court, the gas barbecues give guests a chance to mingle. Maid service is provided once a week. The bar and restaurant of the Kaluakoi Hotel are right next door. *(Moderate* to *Expensive)*

Kaunakakai Area

☆ **Pau Hana Inn** • *south shore* • Here at Molokai's oldest hotel, the lively atmosphere almost makes up for the uninspired decor of the somewhat run-down rooms, which are found in various cottages. This is a great place to meet island residents. On weekends, the inn throbs with the sounds of a live band, and it may seem as if most of Molokai has come to party. The beach isn't attractive enough to lure people into the water. Most guests hang out at the swimming pool with its tree-shaded patio, or at the popular bar and restaurant (where many enjoy sinking their teeth into the prime rib). The sprawling banyan tree on the grounds is more than a century old. *(Inexpensive)*

★★ **Molokai Shores** • *south shore* • Skyscrapers by Molokai standards, these three-story redwood buildings house appealing one-bedroom/one-bath and two-bedroom/two bath condominium apartments. Overlooking the ocean, each unit comes with a full kitchen, lanai, TV, and ceiling fan. The beach is not good for swimming, but guests amuse themselves at the pool, nine-hole putting green, shuffle board, and picnic area with barbecue grills. The lawns are beautifully landscaped with all kinds of gardens. *(Moderate)*

★★ **Hotel Molokai** • *south shore* • Architecturally speaking, this is the hotel with the most character on Molokai. A long dug-out canoe hangs in the open-air lobby, which leads to the lush grounds. Black columns, dramatically carved like Hawaiian tikis, decorate the open-air dining room that sits at the edge of the ocean. The beach is disappointing, so guests gravitate to the small swimming pool (which is sometimes used for dips after dark). Two-story wooden cottages are topped with shingled, Polynesian-style concave roofs. The rustic guest rooms open to lanais with swinging chairs large enough for two. Inside, some have twin beds, while others sport queens or kings. Rooms vary greatly, from tiny to family-sized. Some have kitchenettes. Others make do with refrigerators only. Many units are dark and somewhat stuffy. If you want one of the few with air conditioning, be sure to ask when you make your reservation. All are equipped with fans. *(Inexpensive* to *Moderate)*

East Molokai

☆☆ **Wavecrest** • *between Kamalo and Pukoo* • On the dramatic eastern coast, these remote one- and two-bedroom condominium apartments attract travelers staying on Molokai for extended periods. Although TVs are provided, there are no phones in the neat, motel-style rooms. Shaded with tall trees, the fertile grounds burst with bird-of-paradise, both red and white ginger, hibiscus, ti plants, and croton. Lanais afford wonderful views of the landscape, the rugged, unspoiled coast, and the islands of Lanai and Maui. During the winter, guests can gaze up to Molokai's snow-capped mountains. The beach gets very muddy at times, so swimming is out, but fishing and watching the scurrying crabs is fine here. The swimming pool, night-lit tennis courts, and putting green also keep vacationers occupied. There is a small general store on the premises and the Neighborhood Store and Snack Bar is a few miles away in Pukoo. *(Inexpensive to Moderate)*

★★ **Swenson's Bed and Breakfast** • *Pukoo, south shore* • Set in a grassy coconut grove, this B&B is perfect for total tranquility. The nearby sandy beach is fine for swimming. Each home-like apartment has a large living room with a stereo and library, a separate bedroom with a king-sized bed, and a full kitchen. Fresh orange juice, coffee, and Swedish pastry are provided. When you don't feel like cooking, the Neighborhood Store and Snack Bar is close by. Make reservations to stay at Swenson's as far in advance as possible. *(Moderate)*

★★ **Honomuni House** • *Honomuni Valley* • Up to four people can stay in this valley cottage surrounded by a tropical garden. It sports a living/dining room with a convertible sofa, an enclosed sleeping area, a color TV, an outdoor shower in addition to the complete indoor bathroom, a covered lanai, and a full kitchen. Guests receive complimentary eggs as well as papayas and other fruit fresh from the garden. The beach is a brief stroll away and a rocky stream teeming with freshwater fish and prawns is also nearby. Visitors enjoy hiking to waterfalls, natural swimming pools, and the remains of ancient Hawaiian house foundations and taro terraces. Mangoes, bananas, plums, breadfruit and ginger grow wild in the forest. This historic area is important to Hawaiians since Kamehameha I set off from here to conquer Oahu. *(Inexpensive)*

☆ **Mueh Bed and Breakfast** • *18 miles from Hoolehua Airport, 10 miles from Kaunakakai* • Run by Herb and Marian Mueh (pronounced "Me"), this cottage is set in a garden with waterfall-streaked mountains towering in the background. In season, guests may have their fill of freshly-plucked fruit from the surrounding trees. The Muehs live on the five-acre grounds, but their home is far enough away for vacationers to have complete privacy. The cottage, which sleeps one or two people, has twin beds and a stall shower. Breakfast goodies are provided for guests' preparation. The lanai, visited by a variety of birds, is a pleasant place to relax. There's a game of Scrabble on hand for evenings or rainy days. Good swimming beaches are about 10 miles away. *No children. (Inexpensive)*

MOLOKAI DETAILS

SAVING MONEY: **United Airlines** (800/328–6877) offers package deals to Molokai that include round trip airfare, a double room at the Kaluakoi Hotel & Golf Club, hotel taxes, and an economy car with unlimited mileage. A 7-night excursion from San Francisco would begin at about $875 per person.

GETTING TO, FROM, AND AROUND MOLOKAI: Hoolehua Airport is located in the center of the island. It's best to arrange to rent a car before you arrive and pick it up at the airport from **Tropical, Budget, Avis,** or **Dollar.** Driving is pure pleasure in Molokai, not only because the scenery is so spectacular (particularly in the east), but because you'll run into little traffic. Just watch out for mongooses!

Some accommodations provide complimentary shuttle service from and to the airport. Otherwise, **Gray Line Molokai** (567–6177) will take you where you're going for about $7. With **Molokai Taxi** (552–0041 or 567–6527) you'll pay about $16 from Hoolehua Airport to Kaunakakai, about a 10-minute drive, and $26 to the Kaluakoi Resort, about a half hour away. This company also conducts four-wheel-drive tours to sights that can only be reached by dirt roads, such as Moomomi Beach, Waikoulu Lookout, and the Sandalwood Pit.

Carrying bikes, mopeds, scuba tanks, kayaks, canoes, and assorted other equipment at no additional cost, the *Maui Princess* (553–5736) ferries workers and tourists between Maui and Molokai.

Through various tour companies, travelers may fly from Honolulu directly to Kalaupapa Peninsula, but only to join a ground tour of the historic area.

TOURIST INFORMATION: Contact **Destination Molokai** (553–3876) or the **Maui Visitors Bureau** (111 Hana Hwy, Kahului; 871–8691).

POST OFFICES: Branches are located in Kaunakakai (553–5845), Maunaloa (552–2852), and Hoolehua (567–6144).

TIME: Although time means little on Molokai, you might need to set your watch so you don't miss your departure flight. Call 553–9211.

WEATHER: The scenic eastern region can be wet, so before you set out, call 552–2477.

ALCOHOLICS ANONYMOUS: Call 946–1438 in Oahu about participating in meetings on Molokai.

EMERGENCIES: Dial 911.

MEDICAL ATTENTION: Any time of day or night, you can receive medical assistance at **Molokai General Hospital** (553–5311) in Kaunakakai.

LANAI

"Now I guess I'll have to start locking my door," a resident of Lanai told me when we talked about the tripling of hotels on the island—from one to three. The Lodge at Koele, the second hotel, opened in the spring of 1990 and the Manele Bay is expected to welcome its first guests by early 1991. Both are Rockresorts. During a visit when rustic, 10-room Hotel Lanai was the only game in town, I got into another conversation with a man while I was wondering around the village known as Lanai City. When I told him I would be leaving the next day, he insisted on driving me to the airport. And sure enough, there he was the following afternoon, jumping out of his pick-up truck to help me with my bags. Now with far more visitors on the island, residents can't be expected to keep up this kind of hospitality towards every stranger. However, so much of the openness that has been Lanai's trademark remains.

At nearly 140 square miles, this is Hawaii's sixth largest island. Most of it belongs to Castle & Cook, the company that owns Dole Pineapple. The 2000 or so residents are of Filipino, Hawaiian, Japanese, Korean, Chinese, and European-American ancestry, as well as various mixtures of these nationalities. Almost everyone lives in Lanai City, hemmed in the center of the island by vast pineapple fields. Hardly a city, this trim plantation town of symmetrical cross-hatch streets was built to house the people who work the fields. Neat gardens ablaze with electric-green banana trees and purple, orange, and red bougainvillea adjoin the small wooden homes. A tranquil park sprawls near the collection of small shops. The town is so informal that the First Hawaiian Bank is located in a private house, where the manager lives with his wife. Since this upland village is nowhere near the beach and tall triangular Norfolk pines pierce cool, misty air, it's easy to forget that it's on a tropical island. Outside of town, only a few paved roads cut through the rich, burnt-orange earth that blankets Lanai. Although the island is a mere 13 miles wide and 18 long, it is easy to get lost driving through the endless pineapple fields and the desert-like expanses strewn with rocks and tufts of hearty brush. While searching for one sight

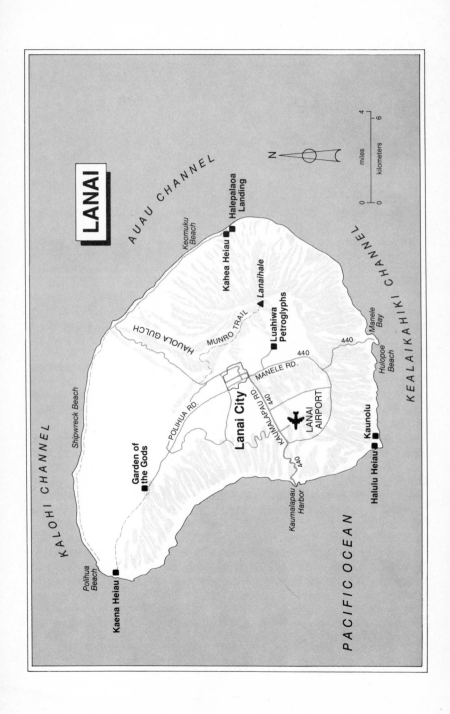

LANAI

KALOHI CHANNEL

AUAU CHANNEL

KEALAIKAHIKI CHANNEL

PACIFIC OCEAN

Polihua Beach

Kaena Heiau

Shipwreck Beach

Garden of
the Gods

Keomuku Beach

Kahea Heiau

Halepalaoa
Landing

HAUOLA GULCH

MUNRO TRAIL

Lanaihale

Luahiwa
Petroglyphs

440

POLIHUA RD.

Lanai City

MANELE RD.

440

KAUMALAPAU RD.

KAUNALAPAU RD.

440

LANAI
AIRPORT

Manele
Bay

Hulopoe
Beach

Kaunolu

Kaumalapau
Harbor

440

Halulu Heiau

N

miles

kilometers

or another, you might suddenly discover that you've been going in circles.

Before dawn, the plantation siren screams workers awake. (I guess I would have quickly lost my job, because I continually managed to sleep through it.) Amid the omnipresent rows of pineapple, pickers don floppy wide-brimmed hats above mouths and noses covered with brightly colored bandanas for protection against bugs and dust. When they remove their goggles and just their eyes are showing, they resemble surgeons or Muslim women. Even in the sweltering heat, they must also use thick gloves to prevent cuts from the serrated leaves. If you wave as you pass, they sometimes raise pineapples into the air in greeting. "Who's gonna pick pineapple now? No one," one laborer told me wistfully, commenting on the island's mini-boom in tourism. But then she went on to say how pleased she was that her children will have more than the choice of hitting the fields or leaving the island to find work.

Until the appearance of the first Rockresort, almost everyone visiting Lanai came to see friends or family, hunt deer, fish, or hike. (Camping isn't permitted.) Beautiful Hulopoe Beach, now the site of the Manele Bay Hotel, can be reached by the main road. But to see the island's other attractions—most of which are natural, ancient, or both, and all of which are outdoors—you'll need to rent a four-wheel-drive jeep. Be prepared to be covered with a gritty layer of orange dust by trip's end. There are petroglyphs, heiau, a ghost town called Keomuku, the empty sands of Shipwreck and Polihua beaches, jagged red gulches, and an eerie jumble of boulders in the middle of nowhere known as the Garden of the Gods. From Lanaihale, at the end of the Munro Trail and the highest point on the island (3370 feet), you'll be able to see almost all of the Hawaiian archipelago when the weather permits.

Since long before the Lodge at Koele made its debut next door, the nine-hole Cavendish Golf Course has satisfied those with an urge to tee off. Another challenging 18-hole oceanfront course is planned for the oceanfront Manele Bay Hotel. Swimming, snorkeling, and fishing are good off Hulopoe Beach, with its broad stretch of white sand and rugged chocolate-colored cliffs. Apart from the upscale dining rooms at Koele lodge and those coming at Manele Bay, eating out is a real low-key affair. In town, there are a couple of unassuming breakfast and lunch spots and Hotel Lanai continues to serve delicious, filling meals. For decades, this hotel's creaky front porch has been the local hangout in the afternoon and evening for drinking and talking story over snacks such as warm popcorn (jokingly referred to as "haole pupus"). Other cherished island pastimes include attending church and wagering bets on the illegal cock fights held behind the bushes at the northern edge of town, among other places.

Hawaiian Roots

Bits and pieces of old Hawaii are scattered throughout Lanai. Just south of Lanai City, a dirt road leads to Luahiwa Petroglyphs, extensive hillside rock carvings of stick figure people, animals, and boats etched during the early 1800s. Near the southern coast, temple sites and more petroglyphs can be seen at Kau No Lu, while Kaleina a Kaheekili, an awesome cliff, was once used as a testing ground of prowess among men who leaped off the edge. Crumbling fishing shrines and canoe houses remain in the Manele Bay area. Kaunolu, just west of Hulopoe Beach, is the site of Kamehameha's old fishing grounds. A little further west, part of sacred Halulu Heiau is still visible. Not far from Shipwreck Beach, in the north, among other places, red boulders are piled with towers of increasingly smaller rocks, imitating ancient shrines. These were once used as trail markers but are now built mainly for fun. Near Keomuku, an abandoned sugar plantation community on the east coast, the remants of Kahea Heiau are overgrown and an old Hawaiian village called Naha stands in ruins.

The Way It Was

Habitation came hard to Lanai. The early Polynesian settlers believed that demons lived on the island. For five centuries after they had first colonized other parts of Hawaii, they left this island alone. Imported from the Marquesas, breadfruit trees were about the only new life on Lanai then. Simply to irk his father, the prankster son of the king of Maui decided to dig up some of these prized trees. This extremely bold act earned the young man the shameful nickname Ka-ulu-laʻau ("the one who uproots breadfruit trees.") The king punished the rebellious youth by sending him to uninhabited Lanai. The evil spirits had seen to it that no one had ever survived a night there. "You think you're so clever?" the father said to his son. "Let's see if you can make it until dawn."

Ka-ulu-laʻau was told that if he could escape Lanai's wicked forces, he should let the people of Maui know by building a fire that they could see from across the water. An expert in his craft of trickery, the young man fooled the demons into thinking he was one place when he was really another, hiding from them throughout the night. To top it off, he sneaked up on a bunch of these spirits, who had had too much to drink during one of their dances on Mt. Lanaihale, and set them afire. The rest he killed by drowning. When the king and his entourage saw the fire and came to collect the son, they were amazed by what he had managed to do. They even decided to return with Ka-ulu-la‘au later to settle Lanai.

With Lanai now under his control, the king of Maui found this newest acquisition attacked by a rival Big Island chief in 1778, the same year British Captain Cook discovered that Hawaii existed. Almost everyone on Lanai, which had been a peaceful island up until then, was slaughtered. A youthful Kamehameha—who would eventually fall in love with fishing on Lanai and later rule the entire archipelago—was among the Big Island warriors. It took more than two decades after the rest of Hawaii had been introduced to foreigners for the first outsider to settle on Lanai. In 1802, Wu Tsin arrived from China with plans to grow sugarcane. But he found the island's dry climate uncooperative.

During the 1830s, New England missionaries convinced the rulers of the Hawaiian kingdom to do something about the adultery that was rampant among Hawaiians. Until these Americans arrived, having more than one spouse had been perfectly respectable. Two penal colonies were set up to keep people in line. One was on Kahoolawe, for men convicted of theft, adultery, or murder, and the other on Lanai, for women who had committed these crimes. But the men swam the six miles from Kahoolawe to Maui, stole canoes and food, and sailed to Lanai. They then took the women back to Kahoolawe with them.

In 1917, the Baldwins, a wealthy haole family from Maui, bought the island of Lanai. No one could get off the ground with sugarcane crops. Some explained that this was divine payback since Kahea Heiau had been desecrated in order to build a railroad for transporting the cane. Then, in 1922, Jim Dole had other sweet thoughts. What about a major pineapple plantation? The Baldwins sold the island to him for $1.1 million and the rest is history. Today, Castle & Cook, Dole's parent company, owns 98% of Lanai.

Getting Around

Lanai City, where the Lodge at Koele and Hotel Lanai are located, is about a 10-minute drive from Lanai Airport. Complimentary shuttles take guests to Koele lodge and will also take them to the Manele Bay Hotel. While taxis are available, there is no public transportation on the island. If you want to see anything beyond town, Hulopoe Beach, and the hotels, you'll need to rent a four-wheel-drive jeep or van. Before you set out, make sure you have *very* clear directions or are accompanied by an island resident. One way to sample the island is to sail ashore from Maui to spend the day at remote Club Lanai. Ground tours are offered as well as an opportunity to swim, snorkel, and relax at a Tahitian-style beachfront village (see Tours and Cruises).

WHAT TO SEE AND DO

PERSONAL FAVORITES

Driving to the **Garden of the Gods,** a strange rock formation, and stopping at the dramatic coastal overlooks in the area. (See Sights)

Basking on the sands of beautiful **Hulopoe Beach,** with its picturesque rocky cliffs. (See Beaches)

Searching for (and finding) the **petroglyphs** near **Shipwreck Beach** (See Sights and Beaches)

Taking the **Munro Trail** up to **Lanaihale,** the highest point on the island, for a view of most of Hawaii. (See Sights)

Visiting the abandoned town of **Keomuku.** (See Sights)

SIGHTS

You'll need to rent a four-wheel-drive vehicle to visit the following sites.

Northern Petroglyphs • *near Shipwreck Beach* • These ancient stick figures have been carved into a pile of large rocks near the beach. Be very careful when you're climbing the rocks. It's best to wear rubber-soled shoes.

When you reach the shore and come to a rock painted "Do Not Deface," head mauka (inland) toward the field of brown boulders. You'll come to the petroglyphs before you reach the boulder field.

Garden of the Gods • *northern Lanai* • Before you set out to see this attraction, ask someone who has been in the area recently if it is overgrown (and therefore invisible) as it was the last time I tried to find it. Also get *very* specific directions or go with an island resident. If you're lucky, the vegetation will have been trimmed to reveal a jumble of golden brown boulders with the ocean gleaming in the distance. As the light changes, so do the various hues of the strangely shaped rocks, which cast even stranger shadows. The most dramatic time of day to come is the early morning or late afternoon. Actually, whether or not you find the Garden of the Gods, it's fun to ride through the pumpkin colored, desert-like landscape. The red canyons that open to the Pacific are gorgeous.

Luahiwa Petroglyphs • *just south of Lanai City* • These early 19th century rock carvings aren't easy to find, so enlist the aid of a resident. They are among the best preserved of the state's petroglyphs.

The Munro Trail and Lanaihale • *near Lanai City* • Hike or take a four-wheel-drive vehicle up the 8.8 mile Munro Trail. Most of the Norfolk pines that grow here and all over Lanai were planted by George Munro, whose family was from New Zealand, around 1910. These trees help prevent soil erosion. During the course of Munro's work as manager of a ranch, he sprinkled pine seeds from his family's country everywhere, including the Lanaihale summit. From this 3370 peak, you'll have fabulous views of 2000-foot-deep Haola Gulch and, on a clear day, all the Hawaiian islands except Kauai and Niihau.

Keomuku Village • *east coast* • Now covered with scraggly vegetation, these ruins of homes and other buildings were once part of a booming sugar mill town. But in 1901, when the Maunalei Sugar Company died, so did these streets. The dilapidated church is Lanai's oldest.

Kaunolu Bay • *west of Hulopoe Beach, south shore* • During the early 1800s, Kamehameha the Great spent his summers fishing at the village that once stood here. Today all that remain are its weathered stone foundations. Adjacent to this archeological site, you'll find Kahekili's Leap, where warriors proved themselves by jumping more than 60 feet into the rough waters below.

TOURS AND CRUISES

Lanai's most worthwhile sights can be reached only by dirt roads. "Road" is actually too strong a word for some of the paths that you must blaze yourself, such as when attempting to find the Garden of the

Gods. Some people enjoy the adventure of seeking and perhaps not finding—or at least finding something other than what you originally intended. However, for those who would prefer to get where they're going with the fewest hassles, **Oshiro Tour & U-Drive** (565–6952) conducts guided tours for about $35 per hour per person.

If you're planning to be on Maui and would like to come to Lanai just for the day, consider one of the cruises from Lahaina to **Club Lanai** (871–1144 in Kahului, Maui), a beach playground on one of Lanai's remote coasts. Land tours from here to various parts of the island are available, along with snorkeling, glassbottom boat trips, and wave skiing. During the winter, vacationers often spot whales. A continental breakfast is served on board the boat and passengers are treated to a picnic lunch after they arrive. The cruise itself takes just over a half hour each way. Full day and half day trips can be arranged.

BEACHES

Although there aren't many beaches on Lanai, those that exist are extremely picturesque. The swimming is best at Hulopoe, overlooked by the Manele Bay Hotel. This is also the only beach that you can get to on a paved road. You'll need to rent a four-wheel-drive vehicle to visit the others.

Hulopoe • *south shore* • Perhaps with the opening of the Manele Bay Hotel, on a bluff overlooking the sand, schools of porpoises will no longer come as close to shore. The first time I visited, when there was only a single 10-room hotel on the island, there was one other person here. This was a weekday, and when I returned on a weekend, the beach was ''packed''—with two local families having a barbecue and playing ukuleles. However, despite the added tourism, this is still a wonderful beach, the island's most attractive. Walk or drive up a rocky road (to the left if you're facing the water), and you may see people fishing off the coffee-colored lava cliffs. Around the point, the striking monolith, Puu Pehe, just offshore, is also known as Sweetheart Rock and Kissing Rock. In front of this huge chocolate chunk, you'll see a cozy cove with even whiter sand than Hulopoe.

Shipwreck Beach • *north shore* • With its rust-colored sand and dramatic churning waves, this beach is best for very strong swimmers. When the water is at its calmest, snorkeling can be fun here. You might see some people fishing for lobster. The shore faces Molokai and Maui, whose cloud-ringed heights make for some awesome scenery. Out in the water, you'll see a large rusted ship that was salvaged, later towed, and then became mired here. This coast is very windy, resulting in some interestingly shaped boulders along the coast. You'll reach this beach after twisting and turning down a long paved road with wonderful views of pine trees against a background of the Pacific and Molokai and Maui. Then you'll turn left onto a tree-shaded dirt road, with branches forming a roof overhead. A few private houses line the road.

Polihua • *north shore* • If, and only if, two beaches aren't enough for you, attempt to find this usually empty white sand beach. It's always windy here and the water is rough, but its a peaceful setting. Molokai is the island across the water.

SPORTS

FISHING: Follow in King Kamehameha's royal footsteps and try angling from his favorite spot on Lanai: Kaunolu, on the south coast. After the barges leave, the less adventurous can try Kaumalapau Harbor, on the west coast. The fishing from Manele Bay, Hulopoe Bay, and Shipwreck Beach is o.k. for the casual sportsperson. Local fishing excursions can be set up through Lanai City Service (565–7227), the Lodge at Koele, and the upcoming Manele Bay Hotel.

GOLF: Although people have described the nine-hole Cavendish Golf Course, adjacent to the Lodge at Koele, as "very average," there's also an 18-hole Greg Norman course at the Lodge and an 18-hole oceanfront Jack Nicklaus beauty is coming at the Manele Bay Hotel on the south shore.

HIKING: Try the Norfolk pine-lined 8.8 mile Munro Trail, which winds up to Lanaihale. From this spot, you'll have a sweeping view of the island, including a dramatic canyon, as well as much of the rest of the state. This difficult hike will take a full day. Some people also enjoy hiking part of the eight miles that connect Shipwreck and Polihua beaches on the windy north shore.

SAILING: The Manele Bay Hotel plans to offer sightseeing and snorkeling cruises.

SCUBA DIVING: When it opens, the Manele Bay Hotel will be taking people down under.

SNORKELING: This sport is best right at Hulopoe Beach, where the Manele Bay Hotel is located. Along with all the colorful fish, coral, and lava formations, perhaps you'll even spot one of the dolphins that sometimes swim close to shore.

TENNIS: Check out the courts at the Lodge at Koele and the upcoming Manele Bay Hotel.

NIGHT LIFE

With some visitors sprinkled in, a local crowd is always drinking and talking story on the enclosed front porch of the Hotel Lanai. For more upscale entertainment after dark, try the Lodge at Koele and the upcoming Manele Bay Hotel. What else? Let's see . . . how about taking a drive to see the lights of Maui?

CULINARY LANAI

Beyond the few hotels, there isn't much choice of dining spots on Lanai. However, the restaurants in Lanai City are all good places to mingle with residents. In town, Hotel Lanai serves three meals a day, while the two diner-style eateries close after lunch. In addition to pineapple, Castle & Cooke plantation now sprouts all kinds of fresh fruit and vegetables—it even grows coffee beans. All these goodies are served at the Lodge at Koele and will also find their way onto the menus at the Manele Bay Hotel, as soon as it opens.

Hotel Lanai • *Lanai City; 565–7211* • Until April, 1990, when the Lodge at Koele cropped up nearby, this rustic, small hotel was the only place to go for dinner—that is, unless visitors ate with friends on the island. The wood-panelled dining room is decorated with bright, glossy photographs of island scenes. The fireplace at one end of the room takes the chill off cool winter evenings. Breakfast and dinner, with hearty portions, are served here. Try the banana pancakes. Entrees for the evening meal include well-prepared fish, chicken, and beef dishes, and good desserts. A light lunch (homemade soups and sandwiches) is available on the screened-in porch just outside the dining room. Reservations recommended. *A, V, M. (Inexpensive)*

Dahang's Bakery • *7th Ave., Lanai City; 565–6363* • The only thing missing from this ''nothing fancy'' restaurant is the greasy spoon itself. The good home cooking is all here, whether it's eggs, hash browns, and fresh pastry in the morning or a juicy burger with fries for lunch. Patrons order at the counter across from the entrance, then choose one of the rickety formica tables. Doors are open from 5:30 a.m. to 1:30 p.m. *(Inexpensive)*

S & T Property Inc. • *7th Ave., Lanai City; 565–6537* • Next door to Dahang's, this 1950s-style soda fountain, complete with worn swivel stools, is in a general store. The burgers and grilled cheese sandwiches get high marks. Only breakfast and lunch are served (closing time is 12:30 p.m.). *(Inexpensive)*

Lodge at Koele • *outskirts of town, not far from the Hotel Lanai; 565–7300* • For atmosphere, this mountain lodge is the best bet. The more formal restaurant is in an octagonal corner room with a large fireplace. The casual dining room takes up part of the large main hall, with its towering stone fireplaces. Ask to be seated on the breezy lanai, which looks out to colorful gardens. Food is basic—beef, chicken, fish, pork—but well cooked. *A, M, V. (Expensive)*

WHERE TO SLEEP ON LANAI

Two new Rockresorts will be rocking quiet Lanai, which got along fine for decades with a sole 10-room hotel. The first of these upscale accommodations, the Lodge at Koele, opened in early 1990 and the Manele Bay Hotel is scheduled to follow by early 1991. If you'd like to explore renting a private home, contact **Oshiro's Garage** (808/565–6952).

★★ **Hotel Lanai** • *Lanai City* • Built in the 1920s for guests of the Dole Company, this creaky wooden 10-room hotel has a lot of character. The small rooms are found in two wings connected by the glassed-in lanai. They have a real homey feel, with twin beds, wrought iron headboards, area rugs, and old wooden dressers. Wicker furniture decorates the front porch, where many island residents (most of them men) gather after work for drinks and conversation. From there, there's a great view of the sun setting between the pine trees. Many guests at this hotel come to hunt deer while others simply want to get away. I've met several couples from Oahu who use this as a weekend haunt. *(Inexpensive)*

★★★ **Koele Lodge** • *outskirts of Lanai City, near Hotel Lanai* • This elegantly rustic lodge was built around the sprawling banyans and tall pines that were already on the property. Eucalyptus, jacarandas, and both a Japanese hillside garden and a Hawaiian woodland garden now enhance the natural surroundings. Guests are welcome to pick fresh tropical fruit and wander along paths through macadamia groves or patches of orchids. Two huge native stone fireplaces are the focal points of the lobby. With Federal style multi-paned windows, the gray clapboard wings are trimmed in white and topped with solid copper roofs. Windows are on all walls of the octagonal public rooms. The irregular shape of some guest rooms reflects the octagonal corners of the wings. While sitting in a rocking chair on the main lanai, guests gaze across the pineapple fields and hills or watch the sun set. Afternoon tea and cocktails are served in a room next to the porch. The renovated chapel on the grounds is more than a century old. By day, guests play tennis, golf at the neighboring course, or croquet. At night, there's musical entertainment. Transportation is provided to Hulopoe Beach. *(Very Expensive)*

Manele Bay Hotel • *Hulopoe Beach, south shore* • Scheduled to open by early 1991, this will be Lanai's first full-scale luxury hotel. Despite its name, this collection of low-rise buildings is set along a grassy rise overlooking Hulopoe Beach, the island's prettiest stretch of sand. Manele Bay, the harbor where pleasure boats dock, is actually around the corner. Jack Nicklaus has designed the island's third golf course for the resort, a challenging oceanfront 18-holer. Gardens will sprinkle color throughout the manicured grounds. The main dining room will be several stories tall. Dance music after dinner on the garden terrace will encourage guests to linger. The lobby will have a panoramic view of the Pacific and the island of Maui. All of the 250 villas and suites will also face ocean. Water sports will include scuba diving, snorkeling, kayaking, and sailing. For calmer pursuits, the library, stocked with books on the Pacific, will have its own peaceful lanai. The hotel's boutiques will be some of Lanai's few places to shop. Each of the 250 villas and suites faces the water and the island of Maui. *(Very Expensive)*

LANAI DETAILS

GETTING AROUND: The Lodge at Koele provides complimentary transportation from the airport, as will the Manele Bay Hotel when it opens. The island's only national car rental agency is Dollar Rent a Car (926–4200 on Oahu or (800)342–7398), run in conjunction with Lanai City Service (565–7227). Four-wheel-drive jeeps and vans are available here as well as through Oshiro's U-Drive & Taxi (565–6952). Oshiro's and Lanai City also have taxis.

TOURIST INFORMATION: The Hawaii Visitors Bureau in Honolulu (2270 Kalakaua Avenue, Holoulu, HI 96815; 923–1811) or the Maui Visitors Bureau (111 Hana Hwy., Kahului; 871–8691) can provide you with information about Lanai.

TIME: Call 565–9211.

WEATHER: To plan ahead for touring various parts of the island, call 565–6033.

POST OFFICE: The island's Lanai City branch can be reached at 565–6517.

ALCOHOLICS ANONYMOUS: Call 946–1438 on Oahu for information about participating in local meetings.

EMERGENCIES: Dial 911.

MEDICAL ATTENTION: Contact the Lanai Community Hospital (565–6411) in Lanai City.

ACCOMMODATIONS CHARTS

The following rates are given for comparison purposes, since vacationers can usually pay less by booking a package deal or sharing a room or condo with two or three other people. Some accommodations set a portion of their rooms or apartments aside as condominiums for private use or as residential rental units. The number of units below represents the rooms or apartments available to visitors. See the end of this section for **bed & breakfast** contacts.

Page	Name, Address, Phone #	Number of Rooms, Suites, or Apartments	Approximate Daily Cost of Standard Double
	OAHU		
205	**Aston Waikiki Beach Tower** (808) 926–6400 Aston Hotels & Resorts 2255 Kuhio Ave. Honolulu, HI 96815 (808) 922–3368 (800) 922–7866	88	$200
195	**Aston Waikikian on the Beach** 1811 Ala Moana Blvd. Honolulu, HI 96815 (808) 949–5331 (800) 922–7866	132	$75–$125
203	**The Breakers Hotel** 250 Beach Walk Honolulu, HI 96815 (808) 923–3181 (800) 426–0494 FAX: (808) 923–7174	64	$80–$90
200	**Colony Surf Hotel** 2895 Kalakaua Ave. Honolulu, HI 96815 (808) 923–5751 (800) 252–7873	50	$130–200
206	**Continental Surf** 2426 Kuhio Ave. Honolulu, HI 96815 (808) 922–2755 (800) 245–7873	140	$50–$68

Page	Name, Address, Phone #	Number of Rooms, Suites, or Apartments	Approximate Daily Cost of Standard Double
200	**Diamond Head Beach Hotel** (800) 367–6046 Colony Hotels & Resorts 32 Merchant St. Honolulu, HI 96813 (808) 523–0411 FAX: (808) 924–8960	56	$110–$120
206	**Edmunds Hotel Apartments** 2411 Ala Wai Blvd. Honolulu, HI 96815 (808) 023–8381	12	$32
197	**Halekulani Hotel** 2199 Kalia Rd. Honolulu, HI 96815 (808) 923–2311 (800) 323–7500	456	$210
194	**Hawaii Prince Hotel** 100 Holomoana St. Honolulu, HI 96815 (808) 956–1111 (800) 321–6284 FAX: (808) 946–0811	521	$190
201	**Hawaiian Regent** 2552 Kalakaua Ave. Honolulu, HI 96815–3699 (808) 922–6611 (800) 367–5370 FAX: (800) 921–5255	1346	$125–$150
203	**Hawaiiana Hotel** 260 Beach Walk Honolulu, HI 96815 (808) 923–3811 (800) 367–5122 FAX: (808) 926–5723	95	$88–$95
195	**Hilton Hawaiian Village** 2005 Kalia Rd. Honolulu, HI 96815 (808) 949–4321 (800) 415–8667 FAX: (808) 947–7898	2523	$150–$245

Page	Name, Address, Phone #	Number of Rooms, Suites, or Apartments	Approximate Daily Cost of Standard Double
192	**Holiday Inn Airport** Ironwood Resorts Hawaii 3259 Koapaka St. Honolulu, HI 96819 (808) 836–0661		
201	**Holiday Inn Waikiki Beach** 2570 Kalakaua Ave. Honolulu, HI 96815 (808) 922–2511 (800) 877–7666 FAX: (808) 923–3656	716	$110–$120
204	**Hyatt Regency Waikiki** 2424 Kalakaua Ave. Honolulu, HI 96815 (808) 923–1234 (800) 233–1234 FAX: (808) 923–7839	1230	$160–$245
195	**The Ilikai** 1777 Ala Moana Honolulu, HI 96815 (808) 949–3811 (800) 367–8434 FAX: (808) 947–4523	800	$120
191	**The Kahala Hilton** 5000 Kahala Ave. Honolulu, HI 96816–5498 (808) 734–2211 (800) 367–2525 FAX: (808) 737–2478	369	$195
205	**Kaimana Villa** 2550 Kuhio Ave. Honolulu, HI 96815 (808) 922–3833 (800) 367–6060 FAX: (808) 922–8061	113	$75–$105
193	**Laniloa Lodge Hotel** 55–109 Laniloa St. Laie, Oahu, HI 96762 (808) 293–9282 (800) LANILOA FAX: (808) 293–8115	46	$80

Page	Name, Address, Phone #	Number of Rooms, Suites, or Apartments	Approximate Daily Cost of Standard Double
202	**Malihini Hotel** 217 Saratoga Rd. Honolulu, HI 96815 (808) 923–9644	29	$45–$80
192	**Manoa Valley Inn** 2001 Vancouver Dr. Honolulu, HI 96822 (808) 947–6019 (800) 634–5115 FAX: (808) 946–6168	8	$85
194	**Mokuleia Beach Colony** 69–615 Farrington Hwy. Wailua, HI 96791 (808) 637–9311	50	$70
199	**New Otani Kaimana Beach Hotel** 2863 Kalakaua Ave. Honolulu, HI 96813 (808) 923–1555 (800) 657–7949 California: (800) 252–0197 FAX: (808) 922–9404	124	$90–$105
202	**Outrigger Edgewater Hotel** 2168 Kalia Rd. Honolulu, HI 96815 (808) 922–6424 (800) 367–5170 FAX: (808) 921–6899	184	$55–$70
205	**Outrigger Prince Kuhio** 2500 Kuhio Ave. Honolulu, HI 96815 (808) 922–0811 (800) 367–5170 FAX: (808) 921–6899	626	$95–$110
196	**Outrigger Reef Hotel** 2169 Kalia Rd. Honolulu, HI 96815 (808) 924–9857 (800) 367–5170 FAX: (808) 921–6899	885	$95–$110

Page	Name, Address, Phone #	Number of Rooms, Suites, or Apartments	Approximate Daily Cost of Standard Double
203	**Outrigger Reef Lanai** 225 Saratoga Rd. Honolulu, HI 96815 (808) 923–3881 (808) 926–0679 (800) 367–5170 FAX: (808) 921–6899	110	$55–$70
203	**Outrigger Reef Towers** 227 Lewers St. Honolulu, HI 96815 (808) 926–0679 (800) 367–5170 FAX: (808) 921–6899	468	$75–$90
202	**Outrigger Royal Islander** 2164 Kalia Rd. Honolulu, HI 96815 (808) 926–0679 (800) 367–5170 FAX: (808) 921–6899	98	$60–$75
198	**Outrigger Waikiki** 2335 Kalakaua Ave. Honolulu, HI 96815 (808) 926–0679 (800) 367–5170 FAX: (808) 921–6899	530	$115–$130
202	**Outrigger Waikiki Tower** (808) 926–0679 Outrigger Hotels Hawaii P.O. Box 88559 Honolulu, HI 96830–8559 (800) 367–5170	439	$78
	Outrigger West Hotel 2330 Kuhio Ave. Honolulu, HI 96815 (808) 926–0679 (800) 367–5170 FAX: (808) 921–6899	663	$75–$90
201	**Pacific Beach Hotel** 2490 Kalakaua Ave. Honolulu, HI 96815 (808) 922–1233 (800) 367–6060 FAX: (808) 922–8061	850	$115–$125

Page	Name, Address, Phone #	Number of Rooms, Suites, or Apartments	Approximate Daily Cost of Standard Double
192	**Plantation Spa** 51–550 Kamehameha Hwy. Kaaawa, Oahu, HI 96730 (808) 237–8685 or 237–8442 (800) 422–0307	8	$435 with 3 vegetarian meals daily; massages and other treatments
192	**Ramada Renaissance-Ala Moana** 410 Atkinson Dr. Honolulu, HI 96814 (808) 955–4811 (800) 367–6025 FAX: (808) 947–7338	1171	$100–$115
206	**Royal Grove Hotel** 151 Uluniu Ave. Honolulu, HI 96815 (808) 923–7691	87	$50–$65
198	**Royal Hawaiian Hotel** 2259 Kalakaua Ave. Honolulu, HI 96815 (808) 923–7311 (800) 325–3535 FAX: 924–7098	525	$210
194	**Sheraton Makaha Resort & Country Club** P.O. Box 896 Waianae, HI 96792 (808) 695–9511 (800) 355–3535 FAX: (808) 695–5806	179	$100–$105
199	**Sheraton Moana Surfrider** 2365 Kalakaua Ave. Honolulu, HI 96815 (808) 922–3111 (800) 325–3535	793	$200
204	**Sheraton Princess Kaʻiulani** 120 Kaʻiulani Ave. Honolulu, HI 96815 (808) 922–5811 (800) 325–3535 FAX: (808) 923–9918	1150	$100–$125

Page	Name, Address, Phone #	Number of Rooms, Suites, or Apartments	Approximate Daily Cost of Standard Double
197	**Sheraton Waikiki** 2255 Kalakaua Ave. Honolulu, HI 96815 (808) 922–4422 (800) 325–3535 FAX: (808) 923–8785	1843	$155–$165
193	**Turtle Bay Hilton & Country Club** P.O. Box 187 Kahuku, Oahu, HI 96731 (808) 293–8811 (800) 445–8667 FAX: (808) 293–9147	486	$155
204	**Waikiki Beachcomber** 2300 Kalakaua Ave. Honolulu, HI 96815 (808) 922–4646 (800) 622–4646 FAX: 923–4889	498	$125
200	**Waikiki Circle Hotel** 2464 Kalakaua Ave. Honolulu, HI 96815 (808) 923–1571	100	$45–$60
205	**Waikiki Joy Hotel** 320 Lewers St. Honolulu, HI 96815 (808) 923–2300 (800) 733–5569 FAX: (808) 377–1290	99	$125–$130
206	**Waikiki Lei Apartment Hotel** 241 Kaʻiulani Ave. Honolulu, HI 96815 (808) 923–6656 or 734–8588	10	$35–$40
202	**Waikiki Parc Hotel** 2233 Helumoa Rd. Honolulu, HI 96815 (808) 921–7272 (800) 422–0450 FAX: (808) 923–1336	298	$115

Page	Name, Address, Phone #	Number of Rooms, Suites, or Apartments	Approximate Daily Cost of Standard Double
196	**Waikiki Shore Apartments** 2161 Kalia Rd. Honolulu, HI 96815 (808) 926–4733 (800) 367–2353	90	$80–$300
200	**Waikiki Surfside** 2452 Kalakaua Ave. Honolulu, HI 96815 (808) 923–0266 (800) 922–7866	80	N/A
	MAUI		
291	**Aloha Cottages** Hana, Maui, 96713 (808) 248–8420	4	N/A
280	**Aston Kaanapali Shores** 3445 Lower Honoapiilani Hwy. Lahaina, Maui, HI 96761 (808) 667–2211 (800) 922–7866	420	$135–$190
287	**Aston Kamaole Sands** 2695 S. Kihei Rd. Kihei, Maui, HI 96753 (808) 879–0666 (800) 922–7866	361	$120–$160
279	**Coconut Inn Apartment Hotel** 181 Hui Rd., F Napili, Maui, HI 96761 (808) 669–5712 (800) 367–8006 FAX: (808) 669–4485	40	$75–$90 with continental breakfast
281	**Embassy Suites Resort at Kaanapali** 104 Kaanapali Pl. Lahaina, Maui, HI 96761 (808) 661–2000 (800) 462–6284 FAX: (808) 667–5821	413	$190
289	**Four Seasons Resort Wailea** 3900 Wailea Alanui Dr. Wailea, Maui, HI 96753 (808) 874–8000 (800) 332–3442 FAX: (808) 874–6449	372	$245

Page	Name, Address, Phone #	Number of Rooms, Suites, or Apartments	Approximate Daily Cost of Standard Double
289	**Grand Hyatt Wailea Resort & Spa** (808) 921–6015 (800) 233–1234 FAX: (808) 924–8753	787	$360
287	**Hale Kamaole** 2737 S. Kihei Rd. Kihei, Maui, HI (808) 879–2698 (800) 367–2970	180	N/A
291	**Hana Kai-Maui** Box 38 Hana, Maui, HI 96713 (808) 248–8426 or 248–7742	17	N/A
291	**Heavenly Hana Inn** Box 146 Hana, Maui, HI 96713 (808) 248–8442	6	N/A
290	**Hotel Hana-Maui** P.O. Box 8 Hana, Maui, HI 96713 (808) 248–8211 (800) 321–HANA FAX: (808) 248–7202	95	$460–$560 with 3 meals daily
284	**Hyatt Regency Maui** Kaanapali Beach Resort Kaanapali, Maui, HI 96761 (808) 661–1234 (800) 233–1234 FAX: (808) 667–4499	815	$210
283	**Kaanapali Alii** 50 Nohea Kai Dr. Kaanapali, Maui, HI 96761 (808) 667–1400 (800) 642–MAUI	205	$245–$420
282	**Kaanapali Beach Hotel** 2525 Kaanapali Hwy. Lahaina, Maui, HI 96761 (808) 661–0011 (800) 657–7700	430	$140–$170

Page	Name, Address, Phone #	Number of Rooms, Suites, or Apartments	Approximate Daily Cost of Standard Double
284	**Kaanapali Plantation** 150 Puukolii Rd. Lahaina, Maui, HI 96761 (808) 661–4446		N/A
285	**Kaanapali Royal** 2560 Kekaa Dr. Lahaina, Maui, HI 96761 (808) 667–7200 (800) 367–7040	30	$140–$170
278	**Kapalua Bay Club** 1 Bay Dr. Kapalua, Maui, HI 96761 (808) 669–5656 (800) 367–8000 FAX: (808) 669–4694	194	$220–$400
278	**Kapalua Villas** 1 Bay Dr. Kapalua, Maui, HI 96761 (808) 669–5656 (800) 367–8000 FAX: (808) 669–4694	143	$155–$390
286	**Kula Lodge** RR1 Box 475 Kula, Maui, HI 96790 (808) 878–1535	5	N/A with breakfast
285	**Lahaina Shores Beach Resort** 475 Front Street Lahaina, Maui, HI 96761 (808) 661–4835 (800) 628–6699	199	$100–$110
279	**Mahina Surf** 4057 Lower Honoapiilani Rd. Honokowai, Maui, HI (808) 669–6068 (800) 367–6068		N/A
290	**Makena Surf Resort** P.O. Box 718 Kihei, Maui, HI 96753 (808) 879–5000 (800) 562–MAUI FAX: (808) 879–9936	30	$195–$300

Page	Name, Address, Phone #	Number of Rooms, Suites, or Apartments	Approximate Daily Cost of Standard Double
287	**Mana Kai-Maui** 2960 S. Kihei Rd. Kihei, Maui, HI 96753 (808) 879–1561 (800) 525–2025	134	$175–$200
284	**Maui Eldorado Resort** 2661 Kekaa Dr. Lahaina, Maui, HI 96761 (808) 661–0021 (800) 367–2167 FAX: (808) 667–7039	127	$120–$135
288	**Maui Inter-Continental Wailea** 3700 Wailea Alanui Wailea, Maui, HI 96753 (808) 879–1922 (800) 367–2960 FAX: (808) 879–7658	550	$200
284	**Maui Kaanapali Villas** 2805 Honoapiilani Lahaina, Maui, HI 96761 (808) 667–7791 (800) 922–7866	152	$125–$160
287	**Maui Lu Resort** 575 S. Kihei Rd. Kihei, Maui, HI 96753 (808) 879–5881 (800) 922–7866	170	$80–$105
283	**Maui Marriott Resort** 100 Nohea Kai Dr. Lahaina, Maui, HI 96761 (808) 667–1200 (800) 228–9290 FAX: (808) 667–2047	720	$210
289	**Maui Prince Hotel** 5400 Makena Alanui Rd. Kihei, Maui, HI 96753 (808) 874–1111 (800) 321–MAUI	300	$210
287	**Maui Sunset** 1032 S. Kihei Rd. Kihei, Maui, HI 96753 (808) 879–0674 (800) 843–5880	208	$85–$105

Page	Name, Address, Phone #	Number of Rooms, Suites, or Apartments	Approximate Daily Cost of Standard Double
280	**Napili Kai Beach Club** 5900 Honoapiilani Rd. Napili Bay, Maui, HI 96761 (808) 669–6271 (800) 367–5030	162	$155–$200
279	**Napili Point** 5295 Honoapiilani Hwy. Napili, Maui, HI 96761 (808) 669–9222 (800) 922–7866	107	$105–$200
279	**Napili Shores Resort** 5315 Honoapiilani Hwy. Lahaina, Maui, HI 96761 (808) 669–8061 (800) 367–6046	128	$70–$140
280	**Papakea Beach Resort** 3543 Honoapiilani Hwy. Lahaina, Maui, HI 96761 (808) 669–4848 (800) 367–5637	170	$70–$135
286	**Pioneer Inn** 658 Wharf St. Lahaina, Maui, HI 96761 (808) 661–3636	48	N/A
285	**Plantation Inn** 174 Lahainaluna Rd. Lahaina, Maui, HI 96761 (808) 667–9225 (800) 433–6815 FAX: (808) 667–9293	9	$105 with breakfast
286	**Puunoa Beach Estates**		N/A
281	**Royal Lahaina Resort** 2780 Kekaa Dr. Lahaina, Maui, HI 96761 (808) 661–3611 (800) 621–2151 FAX: (808) 661–6150	521	$160
281	**Sheraton Maui Hotel** 2605 Kaanapali Pkwy. Lahaina, Maui, HI 96761 (808) 661–0031 (800) 325–3535 FAX: (808) 661–0458	494	$210

Page	Name, Address, Phone #	Number of Rooms, Suites, or Apartments	Approximate Daily Cost of Standard Double
288	**Stouffer Wailea Beach** 3550 Wailea Alanui Wailea, Maui, HI 96753 (808) 879–4900 (800) 992–4532	347	$175
289	**Wailea Villas** 3750 Wailea Alanui Wailea, Maui, HI 96753 (808) 879–1595 (800) 367–5246 FAX: (808) 874–3554	155	$120–$140
282	**The Westin Maui** 2365 Kaanapali Pkwy. Lahaina, Maui, HI 96761 (808) 667–2525 (800) 228–3000 FAX: (808) 661–5764	761	$200
282	**The Whaler on Kaanapali Beach** 2481 Kaanapali Pkwy. Lahaina, Maui, HI 96761 (808) 661–4861 (800) 367–7052	170	$105–$175

KAUAI

Page	Name, Address, Phone #	Number of Rooms, Suites, or Apartments	Approximate Daily Cost of Standard Double
363	**Aston Kauai Resort** 3–5920 Kuhio Hwy. Kapaa, Kauai, HI 96746 (808) 245–3931 (800) 922–7866 FAX: (808) 822–7339	242	$110–$170
360	**Aston Pono Kai** 1250 Kuhio Hwy. Kapaa, Kauai, HI 96746 (808) 822–9831 (800) 922–7866	51	$120–$175
360	**Cliffs at Princeville** P.O. Box 1005 Hanalei, Kauai, HI 96714 (808) 826–6219 (800) 367–6046 FAX: (808) 826–2140	160	$100–$110

Page	Name, Address, Phone #	Number of Rooms, Suites, or Apartments	Approximate Daily Cost of Standard Double
362	**Coco Palms Resort** P.O. Box 631 Lihue, Kauai, HI 96766 (808) 822–4921 (800) 338–1338 FAX: (808) 822–7189	390	$105–$145
361	**Coral Reef Hotel** 1516 Kuhio Hwy. Kapaa, Kauai, HI 96746 (808) 822–4481 (800) 843–4659	26	
366	**Garden Isle Cottages** 2666 Puuholo Rd. Koloa, Kauai, HI 96756 (808) 742–6717	13	$50–$65
364	**Hale Lihue Hotel** 2931 Kalena St. Lihue, Kauai, HI 96766 (808) 245–3151	20	$22
359	**Hanalei Bay Resort** **P.O. Box 220** Hanalei, Kauai, HI 96714 (808) 826–6522 (800) 657–7922 FAX: (808) 826–6680	255	$88–$240
358	**Hanalei Colony Resort** P.O. Box 206 Hanalei, Kauai, HI 96714 (808) 826–6235 (800) 367–8047 FAX: (808) 826–9893	49	$100–$105
364	**Hyatt Regency Kauai** (808) 742–1234 (800) 233–1234	605	$230
361	**Kapaa Shore** 4–0900 Kuhio Hwy. Kapaa, Kauai, HI 96746 (808) 822–3055 (800) 922–7866	17	$85–$145

Page	Name, Address, Phone #	Number of Rooms, Suites, or Apartments	Approximate Daily Cost of Standard Double
362	**Kauai Beachboy** 484 Kuhio Hwy. Kapaa, Kauai, HI 96746 (808) 822–3441 (800) 367–6046 FAX: (808) 526–2017	243	$90–$100
363	**Kauai Hilton & Beach Villas** 4331 Kauai Beach Dr. Lihue, Kauai, HI 96766–9158 (808) 245–1955 (800) HILTONS	350	$140–$160
362	**Kauai Sands Hotel** 420 Papaloa Rd. Coconut Plantation Wailua, Kauai, HI 96746 (808) 822–4951 (800) 367–7000 FAX: (808) 922–0052	204	$70–$80
362	**Kay Barker's Bed & Breakfast** P.O. Box 740 Kapaa, Kauai, HI 96746 (808) 822–3073	4	$45 with breakfast
365	**Kiahuna Plantation** R.R. 1 P.O. Box 73 Koloa, Kauai, HI 96756 (808) 742–6411 (800) 367–7052	330	$145–$155
368	**Kokee Lodge** P.O. Box 819 Waimea, Kauai, HI 96796 (808) 335–6061	12	$38–$49
366	**Koloa Landing Cottages** 2740-B Hoonani Rd. Koloa, Kauai, HI 96756 (808) 742–1470	4	
366	**Kuhio Shores** R.R. 1 Box 70 Koloa, Kauai, HI 96756 (808) 742–6120 (800) 367–8022	75	N/A

Page	Name, Address, Phone #	Number of Rooms, Suites, or Apartments	Approximate Daily Cost of Standard Double
361	**Plantation Hale** 484 Kuhio Hwy. Kapaa, Kauai, HI 96746 (808) 822–4941 (800) 367–5170 FAX: (808) 921–6899	152	$105–$115
366	**Poipu Kapili** 2221 Kapili Rd. Koloa, Kauai, HI 96756 (808) 742–6449 (800) 443–7714 FAX: (808) 742–9162	41	$185–$235
360	**Puu Poa at Princeville** P.O. Box 1185 Princeville-Hanalei, Kauai, HI 96714 Box 38 Hana, Maui, HI 96713 (808) 826–9602 (800) 367–7042 (800) 367–8047	8	$145–$200
359	**Sandpiper Village** 4770 Pepelani Loop Princeville, Kauai, HI 96722 (808) 826–1176 (800) 367–7040	74	N/A
361	**Sheraton Coconut Beach Hotel** Coconut Plantation Kapaa, Kauai, HI 96746 (808) 822–3455 (800) 325–3535 FAX: (808) 822–1830	308	$120–$125
365	**Sheraton Kauai Hotel** 2440 Hoonani Rd. Koloa, Kauai, HI 96756 (808) 742–1661 (800) 325–3535 FAX: (808) 742–9777	460	$170
359	**Sheraton Mirage Princeville** P.O. Box 3069 Princeville, Kauai, HI 96722 (808) 826–9644 (800) 325–3535 FAX: (808) 826–1166	252	$255

Page	Name, Address, Phone #	Number of Rooms, Suites, or Apartments ·	Approximate Daily Cost of Standard Double
365	**Stouffer Poipu Beach Resort** 2251 Poipu Rd. Koloa, Kauai, HI 96756 (808) 742–1681 (800) HOTELS–1 FAX: (808) 742–7214	138	$100
364	**Stouffer Waiohai Beach Resort** 2249 Poipu Rd. Koloa, Kauai, HI 96756 (808) 742–9511 (800) HOTELS–1 FAX: (808) 742–7214	426	$165
367	**Victoria Place** P.O. Box 930 Lawai, Kauai, HI 96765 (808) 332–9300	4	$70
367	**Waimea Plantation Cottages** 9600 Kaumualii Hwy. Waimea, Kauai, HI 96796 (808) 338–1625 (800) 9–WAIMEA FAX: (808) 338–1619	28	$75–$110
363	**The Westin Kauai** Kalapaki Beach Lihue, Kauai, HI 96766 (808) 245–5050 (800) 228–3000 FAX: 245–5049		$195
367	**Whalers Cove** 2640 Puuholo Rd. Koloa, Kauai, HI 96756 (808) 742–7571 (800) 367–7040 FAX: (808) 537–3701	19	$240
435	**HAWAII: THE BIG ISLAND** **Tom Araki's** % Sueno Araki 25 Malama Pl. Hilo, HI 96720 (808) 775–0368		N/A

Page	Name, Address, Phone #	Number of Rooms, Suites, or Apartments	Approximate Daily Cost of Standard Double
441	**Aston Kona By the Sea** 75–6106 Alii Dr. Kailua-Kona, HI 96740 (808) 329–0200 (800) 922–7866	78	$150–$190
441	**Aston Royal Seacliff** 75–6040 Alii Dr. Kailua-Kona, HI 96740 (808) 329–8021 (800) 922–7866	151	$125–$150
442	**Casa de Emdeko** 75–6082 Alii Dr. Kailua-Kona, HI 96740 (808) 329–6488 or 329–7600 (800) 367–5168	106	N/A
445	**Country Club Hotel** 121 Banyan Dr. Hilo, HI 96720 (808) 935–7171	100	$38–$49
446	**Dolphin Bay Hotel** 333 Iliahi St. Hilo, HI 96720 (808) 935–1466	18	$42
441	**Hale Kona Kai** 75–5870 Kahakai Rd. Kailua-Kona, HI 96740 (808) 329–2155	27	N/A
435	**Hamakua Hideaway** P.O. Box 5104 Kukuihaele, HI 96727 (808) 775–7425	1	N/A
445	**Hawaii Naniloa Hotel** 93 Banyan Dr. Hilo, HI 96720	325	$88
446	**Hilo Hawaiian Hotel** 71 Banyan Dr. Hilo, HI 96720 (808) 935–9361 (800) 272–5275 FAX: (808) 533–0472	285	$88–$100

Page	Name, Address, Phone #	Number of Rooms, Suites, or Apartments	Approximate Daily Cost of Standard Double
446	**Hilo Hukilau** 126 Banyan Dr. Hilo, HI 96720 (808) 935–0821 (800) 367–7000	145	N/A
439	**Holualoa Inn** P.O. Box 222 Holualoa, HI 96725 (808) 324–1121	4	$80–$90 with breakfast
439	**Hotel King Kamehameha** 75–5660 Palani Rd. Kailua-Kona, HI 96740 (808) 329–2911 (800) 227–4800 FAX: (808) 329–4602	455	$95
437	**Hyatt Regency Waikoloa** 1 Waikoloa Beach Resort Waikoloa, HI 96743 (808) 885–1234 (800) 233–1234 FAX: (808) 885–5737	1241	$215–$325
434	**Kamuela Inn** P.O. Box 1994 Kamuela, HI 96743 (808) 885–4243	21	$48
442	**Kanaloa at Kona** (808) 322–2272 (800) 657–7872 Colony Hotels & Resorts 32 Merchant St. Honolulu, HI 96813 (808) 523–0411 FAX: (808) 526–2017	116	$135–$145
443	**Keauhou Beach Hotel** 78–6740 Alii Dr. Kailua-Kona, HI 96740 (808) 322–3441 (800) 367–6025 FAX: (808) 944–2974	310	$85
445	**Kilauea Lodge** P.O. Box 116 Volcano, HI 96785 (808) 967–7366	5	$80 with full breakfast

Page	Name, Address, Phone #	Number of Rooms, Suites, or Apartments	Approximate Daily Cost of Standard Double
442	**Kona Coast Resort** 78–6842 Alii Dr. Kailua-Kona, HI 96740 (808) 324–1721 (800) 367–8047	68	N/A
440	**Kona Hilton Beach & Tennis Resort** P.O. Box 1179 Kailua-Kona, HI 96745–1179 (808) 329–3111 (800) HILTONS FAX: (808) 329–9532	444	$110–$120
440	**Kona Islander Inn** P.O. Box 1239 Kailua-Kona, HI 96745 (808) 329–3181 (800) 922–7866	50	$70–$108
442	**Kona Magic Sands** 77–6452 Alii Dr. Kailua-Kona, HI 96740 (808) 329–6488	26	N/A
440	**Kona Seaside Hotel** 75–5646 Palani Rd. Kailua-Kona, HI 96740 (808) 329–2455 (800) 367–7000 FAX: 922–0052	228	$60–$70
443	**Kona Surf Resort** 78–128 Ehukai Street Kailua-Kona, HI 96740 (808) 322–3411 (800) 367–8011 FAX: 322–3245	530	$109
441	**Kona Tiki Hotel** P.O. Box 1567 Kailua-Kona, HI 96745 (808) 329–1425	15	$36–$38
439	**Kona Village Resort** P.O. Box 1299 Kaupulehu-Kona 96740 (808) 325–5555 (800) 367–5290 FAX: (808) 325–5124	125	$360 with 3 meals daily

Page	Name, Address, Phone #	Number of Rooms, Suites, or Apartments	Approximate Daily Cost of Standard Double
442	**Kona White Sands Apartment Hotel** Hawaii Resort Management 45–5782 Kuakini Hwy. Kailua-Kona, HI 96740 (808) 329–9393 (800) 553–5035 FAX: (808) 326–4137	5	$50–$55
435	**Log House Bed & Breakfast** P.O. Box 1495 Honokaa, HI 96727 (808) 775–9990	5	N/A with breakfast
435	**Mauna Kea Beach Hotel** P.O. Box 218 Kamuela, HI 96743 (808) 882–7222 (800) 228–3000 FAX: (808) 882–7593	310	$250
436	**Mauna Lani Bay Hotel & Bungalows** P.O. Box 4000 Kohala Coast, HI 96743–4000 (808) 885–6622 (800) 367–2323 FAX: (808) 885–4556	354	$275–$380
437	**Mauna Lani Point** P.O. Box 4959 Kohala Coast, HI (808) 885–5022 (800) 642–6284 (800) 221–3949	50	$190
437	**Mauna Lani Terrace** South Kohala Management P.O. Box 3301 Waikoloa, HI 96743 (800) 822–4252		$245 with compact car
445	**My Island Bed & Breakfast** P.O. Box 100 Volcano, HI 96785 (808) 967–7216	5	$50 with breakfast
434	**Parker Ranch Lodge** P.O. Box 458 Kamuela, HI 96743 (808) 885–4100	21	$75–$78

Page	Name, Address, Phone #	Number of Rooms, Suites, or Apartments	Approximate Daily Cost of Standard Double
436	**The Ritz Carlton Mauna Lani** 50 Kaniku Dr. Kohala Coast, HI 96743 (808) 885–0099 (800) 241–3333	542	$255
438	**The Royal Waikoloan** P.O. Box 5000 Waikoloa, HI 96743 (808) 885–6789 (800) 537–9800 FAX: (808) 885–7852	540	$108–$160
444	**Seamountain at Punaluʻu** **Punaluʻu Rental Management Co.** P.O. Box 70 Pahala, HI 96777 (808) 928–8301 (800) 367–8047	27	$70–$90
443	**Shirakawa Motel** P.O. Box 467 Naalehu, HI 96772 (808) 929–7462	13	$25–$30
438	**Shores at Waikoloa** South Kohala Management P.O. Box 3301 Waikoloa, HI 96743 (800) 822–4252		$195 with compact car
445	**Uncle Billy's Hilo Bay Hotel** 87 Banyan Dr. Hilo, HI 96720 (808) 935–0861 (800) 367–5102 FAX: (808) 935–7903	134	$55–$65
440	**Uncle Billy's Kona Bay Hotel** 75-5739 Alii Dr. Kailua-Kona, HI 96740 (808) 329–1393 FAX: (808) 935–7903	139	$65–$75
444	**Volcano Bed & Breakfast** P.O. Box 22 Volcano, HI 96785 (808) 967–7779 FAX: (808) 967–7619	3	$55 with breakfast

Page	Name, Address, Phone #	Number of Rooms, Suites, or Apartments	Approximate Daily Cost of Standard Double
444	**Volcano House** P.O. Box 53 Hawaii National Parks, HI 96718 (808) 967–7321	41	$63
439	**Waikoloa Villas** **Hawaiian Island Resorts, Inc.** P.O. Box 212 Honolulu, HI 96810 (808) 883–9144 or 531–7595 (800) 367–7042 FAX: (808) 961–6797	41	$80–$100
434	**Waimea Gardens Cottage** **Hawaii's Best Bed & Breakfasts** P.O. Box 563 Kamuela, HI 96743 (808) 885–4550 (800) BNB–9912	2	$90
	MOLOKAI		
474	**Hotel Molokai** **Aston Hotels & Resorts** 2255 Kuhio Ave. Honolulu, HI 96815 (808) 553–5347 (800) 423–MOLO	52	$60–$125
475	**Honomuni House** Star Route 306 Kaunakakai, Molokai, HI 96748 (808) 558–8383	1	$75
473	**Kaluakoi Hotel & Golf Club** P.O. Box 1977 Maunaloa, Molokai, HI 96770 (808) 552–2555 (800) 777–1700 Colony Hotels & Resorts (808) 523–0411 FAX: (808) 552–2821	182	$95–$120
473	**Ke Nani Kai** (808) 552–2761 Aston Hotels & Resorts 2255 Kuhio Ave. Honolulu, HI 96815 (808) 922–3368 (800) 922–7866	120	$80–$110

Page	Name, Address, Phone #	Number of Rooms, Suites, or Apartments	Approximate Daily Cost of Standard Double
474	**Molokai Shores** P.O. Box 1037 Kaunakakai, Molokai, HI 96748 (808) 553–5954 (800) 367–7042	102	N/A
475	**Mueh Bed & Breakfast** Star Route Box 128 Kaunakakai, Molokai, HI 96748 (808) 558–8236	1	$70
473	**Paniolo Hale** P.O. Box 146 Maunaloa, Molokai, HI 96770 (808) 552–2731 (800) 367–2984	42	$80–$120
474	**Pau Hana Inn** P.O. Box 860 Kaunakakai, Molokai, HI 96748 (808) 553–5342 (800) 423–MOLO	40	$55
475	**Swenson's Bed & Breakfast** Star Route 279 Kaunakakai, Molokai, HI 96748 (808) 558–8394		N/A with breakfast
474	**Wavecrest** Star Route Molokai, HI 96748 (808) 558–8101 (800) 367–2980		N/A
	LANAI		
488	**Hotel Lanai** Box A119 Lanai City, Lanai, HI 96763 (808) 565–7211 (800) 624–8849	10	$60
489	**The Lodge at Koele** (808) 565–7300 RockResorts, Inc. P.O. Box 774 Lanai City, Lanai, HI 96763 (800) 223–7637 FAX: (808) 565–4561	102	$290

Page	Name, Address, Phone #	Number of Rooms, Suites, or Apartments	Approximate Daily Cost of Standard Double
489	**Manele Bay Hotel** Rockresorts, Inc. P.O. Box 774 Lanai City, Lani, HI 96763 (800) 223–7637 FAX: (808) 565–4561	250	N/A

Companies Handling Bed & Breakfasts on All Major Islands

All Islands Bed & Breakfast
823 Kainui Dr.
Kailua, HI 96734
(808) 263–2342
(800) 542–0344

Bed & Breakfast Hawaii
P.O. Box 449
Kapaa, Kauai, HI 96746
(808) 822–7771
(808) 536–8421 (Oahu)
(800) 657–7832
FAX: (808) 822–2723

Bed & Breakfast Honolulu
3242 Kaohinani Dr.
Honolulu, HI 96817
(808) 595–7533
(800) 288–4666
FAX: (808) 595–2030

Bed & Breakfast Pacific-Hawaii
970 N. Kalaheo Ave.
Kailua, HI 96734
(808) 263–4848
(800) 999–6026
FAX: (808) 261–6573

INDEX